History of Criminology

History of Criminology

Edited by

Paul Rock

Professor of Sociology and Director of the Mannheim Centre for the Study of Criminology and Criminal Justice at the London School of Economics and Political Science

Dartmouth
Aldershot · Brookfield USA · Singapore · Sydney

Published by
Dartmouth Publishing Company Limited
Gower House
Croft Road
Aldershot
Hants GU11 3HR
England

Dartmouth Publishing Company
Old Post Road
Brookfield
Vermont 05036
USA

British Library Cataloguing in Publication Data
History of Criminology
 I. Rock, Paul
 364.09

Library of Congress Cataloging-in-Publication Data
History of criminology / edited by Paul Rock.
     p. cm.
  Includes bibliographical references and index.
  ISBN 1-85521-331-1 : $129.95 (est.)
  1. Criminology—History. I. Rock, Paul Elliott.
HV6021.H583 1994
364'.09—dc20   93–37297
                                                                          CIP

ISBN 1 85521 331 1

Printed in Great Britain at the University Press, Cambridge

Contents

PART V   THE FIFTH PHASE: THE INSTITUTIONALIZATION OF CRIMINOLOGY

Argument: Some More Big Ideas and the Young Turks
Social Reaction, Phenomenology and Symbolic Interactionism

Acknowledgements

The editor and publishers wish to thank the following for permission to use copyright material.

The American Sociological Association for the essay: Alvin W. Gouldner (1968), 'The Sociologist as Partisan: Sociology and the Welfare State', *The American Sociologist*, **3**, pp. 103–16.

Blackwell Publishers for the essay: Daniel Defoe (1927), 'The Poor Man's Plea', in *The Shortest Way with the Dissenters*, pp. 1–20. 'The Poor Man's Plea' was first published on March 31st, 1698.

Cambridge University Press for the essays: Lincoln B. Faller (1987), 'In the Absence of Adequate Causes: Efforts at an Etiology of Crime', in *Turned to Account: The Forms and Functions of Criminal Biography in Late Seventeenth and Early Eighteenth-Century England*, pp. 52–71, 225–33; V.A.C. Gatrell and T.B. Hadden (1972), 'Criminal Statistics and their Interpretation', in E.A. Wrigley (ed.) *Nineteenth-Century Society: Essays in the Use of Quantitative Methods for the Study of Social Data*, pp. 336, 338–48.

Gower Publishing Company for the essay: Trevor Jones, Brian MacLean and Jock Young (1986), 'Introduction', *The Islington Crime Survey: Crime, Victimization and Policing in Inner-city London*, pp. 1–6.

Macmillan Publishing Company, USA for the essay: Sarnoff A. Mednick (1979), 'Biosocial Factors and Primary Prevention of Antisocial Behavior', from *New Paths in Criminology: Interdisciplinary and Interculture Explorations*, Sarnoff A. Mednick and Shlomo Shoham (eds.), Lexington Books, an imprint of Macmillan Publishing Company, pp. 45–53, 219–35. Copyright © 1979 by Lexington Books.

Oxford University Press for the essays: David Garland (1985), 'The Criminal and his Science', *The British Journal of Criminology*, **25**, pp. 109–37; R.G.V. Clarke (1980), '"Situational" Crime Prevention: Theory and Practice', *The British Journal of Criminology*, **20**, pp. 136–47; Paul Rock (1990), Excerpt from *Helping Victims of Crime – The Home Office and the Rise of Victim Support in England and Wales*, Clarendon Press, pp. 317–24.

The Free Press, a Division of Macmillan Inc. for the essays: Albert K. Cohen (1955), Excerpt from 'A Delinquent Solution', *Delinquent Boys: The Culture of the Gang*, pp. 121–37. Copyright © 1955 by The Free Press. Excerpt from Howard S. Becker (1963), 'Outsiders' in *Outsiders: Studies in the Sociology of Deviance*, pp. 1–18. Copyright © 1963 by The Free Press.

Routledge for the essays: Stanley Cohen (1974), 'Criminology and the Sociology of Deviance in Britain', in Paul Rock and Mary McIntosh (eds), *Deviance and Social Control*, pp. 1–40; Frances Heidensohn (1968), 'The Deviance of Women: A Critique and an Enquiry', *British Journal of Sociology*, **XIX**, pp. 160–75; Terence Morris (1958), Excerpt from, *The Criminal Area: A Study in Social Ecology*, International Library of Sociology and Social Reconstruction, pp. 118–30; David M. Downes (1966), Excerpt from *The Delinquent Solution: A Study in Subcultural Theory*, pp. 255–62; Ian Taylor, Paul Walton and Jock Young (1975), 'Editors' Introduction', in *Critical Criminology*, International Library of Criminology, pp. 1–5.

The University of Chicago Press for the essays: M. Ignatieff (1981), 'State, Civil Society, and Total Institutions: A Critique of Recent Social Histories of Punishment', in Michael Tonry and Norval Morris (eds) *Crime and Justice, An Annual Review of Research*, **3**, pp. 153–92; Lucia Zedner (1991), 'Women, Crime and Penal Responses: A Historical Account', in Michael Tonry (ed.) *Crime and Justice: A Review of Research*, **14**, pp. 307–62; Clifford R. Shaw and Henry D. McKay (1942), Excerpt from *Juvenile Delinquency and Urban Areas: A Study of Rates of Delinquency in Relation to Differential Characteristics of Local Communities in American Cities*, pp. 3–14.

Introduction: The Emergence of Criminological Theory[1]

... the turning to activity for the sake of form is a historical event, taking place at different times for each form. The progress of a preliminary form is gradual; at some point, perhaps never precisely specifiable, the form is 'ready' to become the object, rather than the instrument, of human activity.[2]

[In 1968, Sellin argued that 'no adequate history of criminology exists and the textbooks give scanty information'.[3] What he argued then tends to hold now. There is no adequate history and there certainly never will be a *definitive* history of criminology] The discipline is an accumulation of theories, each with its own protagonists; each with its special environment of politics, methods and preoccupations; and each offering a different vantage point from which to tell a story about its evolution and the evolution of the other theories that are its complements and rivals. That, in part, is what theorists and theories are supposed to *do*: they supply a way of seeing the world and the ideas and scholarship that exist within it. Above all, they furnish the criteria by which argument should be judged.[Thus the highest form of criminology was held by the positivist, Hermann Mannheim] to be positivism;[4] by the phenomenologists, Jack Douglas (see Chapter 25) and David Matza,[5] to be existentialism;[6] by the quantitative criminologists Cohn and Farrington to be quantitative criminology;[7] by the radicals Taylor, Walton and Young (see Chapter 30)[8] to be socialist criminology (thinking having passed through 'classical' and 'positivist' phases *en route*[9]); by the feminist Carol Smart[10] to be a 'gendered theory';[11] by the post-modernist Alison Young to be post-modernist criminology;[12] and by yet other criminologists professing no theoretical allegiance to be a dogged practicality.[13] Amidst such diversity, there is unlikely to be accord about the substance, structure and significance of any imaginable intellectual history.[14]

All that discord has been magnified by the unscholarly emotions that crime and its analysis can engender. Many criminologists have seen crime as an urgent moral, political, theological or social problem that demands redress, and they have been apt to display a passion and an impatience with one another for failing to agree on what was so evidently wrong and on what must be done to put it right. Nuances and differences can become exaggerated all the while as scholars struggle to make sense of a confused world, seize on a few variables as the key to knowledge, engage in what Douglas called 'simplificationism',[15] and dismiss as knaves or fools those who do not share their appreciation of the overriding importance of race, gender, control, victims, age, space, inequality, the State or censure.

There is then a problem of multiplying stories which is compounded because theories interweave and thinkers themselves are not consistent over time. Criminologists have their own changing lives, and they can always reinterpret what they praised or neglected in the past[16] (Karl Mannheim observed that 'we become aware that we are observing the world from a moving staircase, from a dynamic platform ... ').[17] Being observed from a moving platform, being reconstructed with each telling, intellectual history changes every time it is written. There can be no timeless, neutral, atheoretical point from which criminology can be seen as it really is, once and for all, beyond contradiction. Quite the reverse.

Academic criminology will always be confused, and that is probably its greatest strength: a single, bold theory could never match the complexity, flux and ambiguity of the social world. Criminology is centred on a terrain defined *empirically* by the presence of crime and criminals; the State and the criminal law; the police, courts and prisons; victims and bystanders; reform, deterrence, treatment and punishment. Its character has been fixed chiefly by its *substance* rather than by any coherence or unity of analytic approach. It is what David Downes once called a '*rendez-vous* subject' – a subject where people from different theoretical backgrounds and with very different purposes meet and sometimes fail to understand one another.

A Pragmatic Framework

Any proposal to give order to the history of such a discipline will always be seen by some as a little arbitrary. Yet there are a number of perfectly sensible ways of representing the development of theory: one would be to focus on the political evolution of criminology (which is what Smart and Taylor, Walton and Young did); another might focus on its interaction with internal and external intellectual movements (a history of ideas). A third would attend to its response to problems and events in the world about it (and to riots, scandals and crime waves in particular); a fourth would examine the effects of changing financial and political sponsorship; a fifth could turn to the emergence of new facts and new kinds of facts (the impact of crime surveys and self-report studies has been especially momentous),[18] and a sixth would translate criminology into an artifact of institutions and controlling activities (the approach taken by those working in the tradition of Michel Foucault). I shall take yet another course and treat thought as a concomitant of practical activity.

People cannot readily develop ideas without social organization, and social organization itself flows from and refracts ideas. In this sense, criminology could be described as a form of reasoning that shapes and is shaped by the institutions in which it is set. Presenting it as the emerging outcome of social relations seems as helpful a way as any of framing a collection of papers on the history of criminology.[19]

Some time ago, Hermann Mannheim observed that:

> By and large, criminological research has hitherto usually been done in one of the following ways:
>
> (a) by private individuals working alone: for example John Howard, Jeremy Bentham, Henry Mayhew;
> (b) by public officials having access to official material, but working in a private capacity, for example A.M. Guerry, Cesare Lombroso ... ;
> (c) by public officials working in an official capacity, e.g. Charles Goring, Norwood East;
> (d) by university departments or individual teachers, which is the largest capacity;
> (e) by Government departments or special research units. ...[20]

Mannheim may not have explicitly intended it, but his apparently static classification is also a way of presenting a *history* of criminological theory. It is in effect an evolutionary morphology, a series of steps laid out in time. Defined in this manner, criminology becomes a succession of phases in which ideas, institutions and people have been clustered together in configurations that are both distinct and intertwined. Characteristically, the beginnings of each phase are attended by great intellectual activity and the energetic building of social worlds, activity that subsides only to be superseded by a comparable excitement heralding the emergence of a new phase. It is something of that pattern of succession that I shall trace in the rest of this Introduction, and I shall do so by concentrating on the emergence of criminology in one illustrative country, Britain. To attempt more would be to adopt an impossibly large canvas; however, it is reasonable to suppose that, appropriately modified, the argument should hold elsewhere.[21]

The First Phase: Ur-Criminology (1500–1750)

[Like many another social science, the study of crime and criminals[22] first appeared some 200 years ago out of a great unorganized mass of allegation, speculation and observation that may be described variously as ur-criminology, proto-criminology or shadow criminology, a mass composed of the writings of dramatists;[23] clergymen (and prison chaplains in particular); pamphleteers and essayists; journalists and doctors; lawyers[24] and magistrates;[25] reformers and would-be reformers; and anyone else who could claim an expertise on prisons and prisoners, the thieves' republics and the beggars' guilds] It was supposed to fascinate, inform, amuse, appal and instruct by turns (although its tone was sometimes little more than mock-serious). It relied on anecdote, reminiscence and the authority of social position; indeed, scholars now quarrel about the exact importance of what was said and written.[26]

[Ur-criminology was the offspring of those who professed principally to have a practical or experiential stake in the problems of crime, criminals and prisoners (there was almost no other legitimate source of expertise to be invoked); having such a stake, its public posture was principally that of the man (rarely the woman) of affairs, the administrator, the reformer and the moralizer] It came to air most of the common-sense explanations of crime available then and now, anticipating the axioms of a later academic criminology, and propounding what may be recognized as primitive versions of functionalism,[27] *anomie* theory,[28] social ecology,[29] 'labelling theory', control theory, eugenics, 'crime prevention through environmental design' and much else] But its most prevalent mode of argument, as Faller shows in this volume (see Chapter 3) was to insist on the simple depravity of the criminal.[30] Crime was a moral matter. Ur-criminology itself was characteristically idiosyncratic; it was part of no cultivated tradition and lacked obvious cumulative development.

Ur-criminologists did not profess to be academic teachers or researchers of knowledge about crime. There were no such roles for them to take. Seen retrospectively through the lens offered by academic criminology, their work often looks crude; not written in a professional language; informed by no common store of knowledge; underwritten by no sound methodology; checked by no ordered process of criticism; unorchestrated, and lacking apprentices willing to learn and transmit its ideas. It was a succession of starts that appeared to tail off into inconsequentiality. In short, it was not 'institutionalized'. It could not evolve or reproduce itself as a specific discourse (although it did persist at the margins for a very long while and was part of what Garland called 'wider cultural traditions and understandings'). It did not resemble the familiar and conventional forms of contemporary criminology and is now largely forgotten as a particular way of describing the world,[31] its achievements no longer valued and its authors omitted from the lists of criminology's 'heroic' ancestors.[32] At best, as David Garland reminded me, it represents a form of common sense about crime and morals with which academic criminology is in competition.

The Second Phase: Philanthropy and the Emergence of Criminology (1750–1830)

[It was not until the end of the 18th century that the first makings of a recognizably scientific criminology began to emerge.]These crystallized little by little out of ur-criminology, doing so as part of a larger process of institution-building.]This was, in effect, the kind of knowledge that arose when people gathered together and organized themselves to plan the construction of what would later be called the criminal justice systems[33] of Europe and North America.

A scholarly discipline requires an identity, a sense of its past and place in the world, a recognizable membership and regular meetings, orderly methods of communication, and a common language and reservoir of ideas. It requires a collective life.[34]

[Criminology was first given that life by groups promoting reform of the law, prisons, asylums and courts. Penal reform was one of the big ideas of the industrializing world, an ingredient of the political assault on what were held to be the brutalities, corruption and inefficiencies of the *ancien régime*.[In Britain, it was associated particularly with the national[35] and international[36] networks of radical Whigs, Nonconformists and Utilitarians who championed a more rational, effective and just machinery of control, surveillance and rehabilitation. Theirs was a practical, religious and philosophical inspiration that later writers would describe as 'moral'. They conceived wrong-doing to be a matter of choices badly formulated, of wills poorly disciplined, of spirituality undernourished, of populations under-controlled and of consciences underdeveloped.]Their answer was to adopt what Barnes and Teeters once called 'the civilized attitude toward crime'.[37][They planned a system of policing that was supposed to lead inexorably to the detection and capture of malefactors; a system of fair trials that did away with trading justice; and a system of correctional institutions that classified and segregated different categories of prisoners before subjecting them to carefully calibrated inducements and punishments that would be neither gratuitously lenient nor excessively severe.] The whole amounted to a machine, as Bentham put it, to 'grind rogues honest', a machine that would instil habits of sobriety, respect and discipline.[38]

The civilized attitude was espoused by reformers who banded themselves together into literary, philanthropic and scientific societies, into the Prison Discipline Society, the Society for the Suppression of Vice and the Society for Bettering the Condition of the Poor. They analysed, compared and planned. They conducted surveys, toured prisons and institutions in Europe and the US, and discovered new facts. They experimented with models of reform and with a novel social engineering whose most significant blueprints were Colquhoun's *A Treatise on the Police of the Metropolis*,[39] Bentham's *Panopticon or Inspection House* (see Chapter 5),[40] Romilly's *Observations on the Criminal Law of England* (see Chapter 4),[41] Beccaria's *On Crimes and Punishments*[42] and Howard's *The State of the Prisons in England and Wales*.[43] Although not uniform, in combination, theirs was a moral philosophy of action and a political economy of control that enjoined the State to play a greater and more effective role in the regulation of its subjects.

Some of the certainties of that new knowledge disappeared soon enough, and the reforming associations themselves were often insubstantial bases for organized enquiry (their most prominent members tended to be independent men and women of means who had no need or wish to fashion enduring careers for themselves as reformers).[44] The second phase did not last long (its very success brought about its own end), but it *had* generated the prospect of thinking about crime in a novel way:[45] theirs was a practical, enquiring, comparative methodology that rested on frequent communication between men and women embarked on the same work.

By 1830, Philips argued, the reformers' project had been largely accomplished: 'the recognizably "modern" model of administration and enforcement of the law had arrived in England – with a paid, bureaucratic police force, stipendiary magistrates, and a system of prosecution designed to encourage prosecution whenever an offence was committed'.[46] He could well have added the workhouses, the prisons, the factories and the asylums to the new model State that the reformers had constructed.[47]

The Third Phase: Criminology and the Administered State (1830–1890)

Officials of that new State had a new confidence in their ability to govern,[48] a confidence resting in part on a growing foundation of knowledge supplied by new groups of experts. The beginnings of an efficient, administered State were accompanied by the collection of reports, accounts and numerical information. The legitimating rationality of the new politics required that it should do so. The scale of the economic, political and social transformations it was undergoing (changes in what were known collectively as 'moral' conditions) was too momentous to warrant neglect. Although it would not do to exaggerate the scale of the new administration (the Home Office, for instance, was only a very small institution at first),[49] there was an appetite for, and a rhetoric about, information that was quite distinctive of early Victorian government.

The first consequence was that the State acquired its own administrative science – the tellingly-named statistics – a science that dealt with 'the collation, classification, and discussion of facts bearing on the condition of a state or community'.[50] The term 'statistics' first came into use in 1787[51] and 'statistician' in 1825. Their emergence is significant, signalling the coming of fact (and numerical facts especially) as a constitutive feature of government in Gradgrind's world. Chevalier remarked of that period in France that there was a 'determination to obtain figures for everything, to measure everything, to know everything, but to know it by numbers [it was an] encyclopedic hunger. ... '[52]

The first national census was conducted in England and Wales in 1801, and the new police, judicial and penal authorities began to produce their own annual statistical returns after the 1830s. The Metropolitan Police Criminal Returns were published first in 1831,[53] and the Prison Inspectors, established in 1835, issued annual 'published reports [that] exercised a growing influence on official and parliamentary opinion. ... '[54] Knowledge about the incidence and distribution of moral conditions became increasingly quantified in the first half of the 19th century,[55] recorded rates becoming accepted as a superior (perhaps the only really authoritative) source of evidence.[56] Rates had the appearance of being suprahuman, impersonal, reliable and *objective*.[57]

The relations between those recorded rates lent themselves to a new science of social physics that could work with all the rigour of the newly ascendant positive sciences of nature. Quetelet, Guerry and Fletcher (see Chapter 8)[58] above all represented society as a massive field of forces amenable to precise measurement and prediction. Crime itself was conceived to be marked by regularities that co-varied with other regularities in determinate fashion. The Frenchman, Guerry, could argue in 1833 that 'there are no reasonable grounds to deny that moral as well as physical events are subject to invariable laws', while the Belgian, Quetelet, claimed in 1846 that 'we can count in advance how many individuals will soil their hands with the blood of their fellows, how many will be swindlers, how many poisoners, almost as we can number in advance the births and deaths that will take place. ... '[59] Criminology (and British criminology in particular) took shape in that third phase as a distinctive, specialist study with its own subject matter. It became a handmaiden of a State that was useful to management and numerate in its methods. Garland described the tradition so formed as 'institutionally-based [and] administratively-oriented'[60]

The second consequence of the rise of the administered State was the flowering of professions whose job was to staff and legitimate the proliferating institutions of the new criminal justice system. If the reformed courts, prisons and mental hospitals were part of a new and purportedly efficient machinery of social regulation, if they were based on the application of a new rationality, their very claim to authority was grounded in the assertion of an expert *knowledge* of social problems. It was the professional, not the laity, who knew what was *really* wrong with the patient, the defendant and the inmate, and it was the professional who had the right to diagnose and cure;[61] for, as Freidson observed, 'any profession bases its claim for its position on the possession of a skill so esoteric or complex that non-members of the profession cannot perform the work safely or satisfactorily and cannot even evaluate the work properly'.[62]

The professions and quasi-professions of social control increasingly came into their own after the 1830s. Scull has written of 'the remarkable expansion and reconstitution of the traditional professions ... '[63] during that period. The British Medical Association had its origins in a professional body, the Provincial, Medical and Surgical Association, founded in 1832.[64] The Law Society had its direct antecedent in a body established in 1825. The Council of Legal Education was established in 1852,[65] and the Association of Medical Officers of Asylums and Hospitals for the Insane in 1841.[66] It was in 1848 that the word 'professional' first took its contemporary meaning of one who engages in a skilled or learned profession, and it was in 1856 that the word 'professionalism' came first to be used.

Control over problematic populations became vested more and more heavily in the professions who had charge of the legal system, the prisons and asylums. Convict management itself became a cadet science[67] – *la science pénitentiare* – canvassed energetically by prison congresses and International Commissions.[68]

In the framing of legitimacy, the moral was to be joined by the scientific,[69] and it was medicine that came to be regarded as the archetypal science of social conditions in the 19th century. What other comparable profession was on hand to apply science to wrongdoers?[70] What better metaphor could there be for the scientific rehabilitation of the criminal than the prevention of ills and the diagnosis and cure of the sick (particularly in a nation where society was still occasionally likened to a body and its limbs)? Sim claimed that 'the prison became a laboratory in which the advice and expertise of the medical profession, both physicians and psychiatrists, was geared to reintegrating the confined back to normality'.[71] Criminology became, in major measure, applied medicine. Indeed, Drapkin chose to capture the whole of what he called the 'pre-Lombrosian' phase of the criminological search for causes (all that took place before 1875) as the work of 'physiognomists, phrenologists, early psychiatrists, and prison physicians'.[72] So powerful did medicine become that even now it is still a little difficult to avoid using its terminology in talking about crime and its treatment. It was believed that criminology

> ... would replace the ineffectual niceties of legal punishment by practical technologies involving diagnostic, prevention and curative instruments and institutions. Criminality was now a knowable positive entity which, with the aid of scientific investigation and appropriate technique, could be removed from the social body.[73]

[Some of the very first men to call themselves 'criminologists' were doctors and psychiatrists. In and about the prisons, asylums and the medical schools, they classified, measured, compared, examined and treated pathological individuals and their conditions.[74] Deviance was transformed into a property of the individual, akin to physical disorder and defined, with the coming of genetics, as a transmitted pathology] Garland wrote that there

> ... existed in Britain, from the 1860s onward, a distinctive, indigenous tradition of applied medico-legal science which was sponsored by the penal and psychiatric establishments, and it was this tradition which formed the theoretical and professional space within which 'criminological science' was first developed in this country.[75]

The Fourth Phase: Criminology as an Academic Pursuit (1880–1960)

By the end of the 19th century, enough had been accomplished to persuade people to view the infant criminology as a special way of looking at the world, somewhat distinct from its parent disciplines, and amenable to detachment from the practical and immediate pursuits of the prison and asylum.[76] It could be taught and analysed as if it were an increasingly independent application of sociology, law, statistics or medicine. In this beginning of separation, it followed the more general pattern of increasing specialization of disciplines that characterized the universities of the time.[77]

[The very word 'criminology' seems to have been first used in the 1850s and come into more general use in the 1890s when the subject began to be taught in the universities of western Europe] at Marburg, Bordeaux, Lyons, Naples, Vienna and Pavia.[78] Under the spell of Cesare Lombroso,[79] in particular, criminology busied itself with measuring, comparing and classifying types of deviant.[80] Criminology was to be a positive science, wedded to the goal of changing crime and criminals, captured by David Matza's title of 'correctionalism'.[81] It was reformist, practical, interventionist and implicated in policy-making, moved, Stan Cohen remarked, 'by a sense of faith: that the business of crime and delinquency control could be made not only more efficient but also more human'.[82]

Having a foundation in moral philosophy,[83] criminology's new step-parents themselves invariably claimed a mandate to correct. Thus the new science of sociology was designed principally to put the world right.[84] One of the original and most eminent of the socio-logists of crime, Émile Durkheim, saw himself as a healer of social ills, as one who could diagnose and prescribe, incorporating and reconciling in a positive science the descriptive and the normative.[85] The early Marxist criminologists – Willem Bonger[86] and Rusche and Kirchheimer – anticipated the revolution when social pathologies would disappear. It was perhaps only in an occasional study conducted in the US that the correctionalist and political impulses of criminology were restrained,[87] and even there they were strong.[88] Cavan observed of the sociology department at the University of Chicago, the country's pre-eminent early department (indeed the country's only department of substance until the early 1930s), that 'sociology had to find its way out of the general social reform temper of the times and separate itself from the religious slant of the university itself'.[89]

According to Garland, criminology was first taught in a British university, the University of Birmingham, in the early 1920s by M. Hamblin Smith, the first man to call himself a criminologist in Britain[90] (it was perhaps unremarkable that Hamblin Smith had previously been a psychiatrically-trained prison medical officer). But it was to be some time before criminology became established in British universities, and it did so as a consequence of the flight of intellectuals from fascism in Europe in the 1930s. Three criminologists, Hermann Mannheim, Max Grünhut and Leon Radzinowicz, fled to found and then control criminology in the Universities of London, Oxford and Cambridge respectively, [91] carrying with them the emerging European criminological synthesis. Enrico Ferri's former student, Radzinowicz, established a Department of Criminal Science at Cambridge in 1941.[92] Mannheim, a Prussian judge and former student of law and political science at the Universities of Munich, Freiburg, Strasburg and Königsberg,[93] was to teach courses on crime and punishment under the aegis of the Sociology Department of the London School of Economics. In the academic session 1938–39, for instance, he delivered ten lectures on the 'Aims and History of Punishment'[94] with the professed purpose of 'giving an insight into the philosophical basis of punishment and into the historical development of the various penal methods'. He recommended the reading of English works, principally the Webbs's *English Prisons under Local Government*, John Howard's *The State of the Prisons*, Page's *Crime and the Community* and Fox's *The Modern English Prison*. His 'Principles of Criminology' course addressed the following:

> I. The meaning, methods and tasks of Criminology. The use of Criminal Statistics. History and present character of crime in England and abroad. II. The criminal types and the causes of crime: (1) Physical factors: The anthropological theory (Lombroso). The biological theory. The significance of physical defects. (2) Psychological and pathological factors: The intelligence of the criminal. Insanity and mental deficiency. The psychoanalytical explanation ... (3) Alcoholism. Climate. Race and Religion. (4) The age factor ... (5) The sex factor: Female delinquency and prostitution. (6) Social and economic factors: Family, broken homes, housing, delinquency areas ... The gang. Profession and Unemployment. Poverty. Economic and political crises.

Mannheim advised his students to read Bonger's *Introduction to Criminology*, Burt's *The Young Delinquent* (see Chapter 17), Calvert's *The Lawbreaker* and Hamblin Smith's *The Psychology of the Criminal* (see Chapter 16). It may be seen that his criminology was substantively defined, problem-driven and theoretically eclectic, a blend of the sociological, psychological, legal, historical and statistical.

British criminology in the 1940s and 1950s remained largely in that vein. It was to be fused with the activities of reforming organizations such as the Howard League, above all with the League's campaigns against corporal and capital punishment. It was periodically to import theoretical inspiration from its parent disciplines, from psychoanalysis, and from the sociology of Harvard, Columbia and Chicago Universities especially. The more adventurous criminologists toyed variously with (1) Merton's *anomie* theory[95] (Terence Morris did so in *Pentonville*[96] and, a little later, David Downes was to do so in *The Delinquent Solution*);[97] (2) with the social ecology of the 'Chicago School'[98] (it was Terence Morris who did so again in *The Criminal Area*)[99] and (3) with subcultural theory (John Mays did so in *Growing Up in the City*[100] (see Chapters 18, 21 and 22). But criminology remained the obvious progeny of medicine, psychology, the law and statistics, a progeny that served the State and the agencies and organizations of the criminal justice system. Consider the manifesto for the new *British Journal of Delinquency* that was published first in July 1950 under the editorship of Hermann Mannheim, a lawyer, Emmanuel Miller, a psychiatrist, and Edward Glover, a psychoanalyst. Its first editorial proclaimed that:

> ... the *British Journal of Delinquency* is not in the customary sense a clinical journal. Clinical contributions will of course receive special consideration, but it is hoped to publish articles, both theoretical and practical, from trained workers in the various departments of criminology; namely, medical psychology, psychiatry, psychoanalysis, organic medicine, educational psychology, sociology, economics, anthropology, psycho-biology and statistics; also from social workers, probation officers, prison and other institutional personnel, and from forensic specialists whose work brings them into intimate contact with the problem of delinquency.[101]

The Fifth Phase: The Institutionalization of Criminology

What brought an end to that phase was a triple reflex, stirred in large measure by the rise and subsequent decline in the rate of expansion of the British university. Halsey observes that 'the expansion of higher education in Britain started from a tiny base at the beginning of the century, with an accelerated growth in the 1960s and 1970s'.[102] The number of British universities grew from 30 in the early 1960s to 52 by the end of the 1980s. The number of academic staff rose from 19,000 to 46,000, and the number of full-time students in higher education from 130,000 to 600,000 (with an additional 350,000 part-time students attending higher education).

Criminology was part of that wave. A large group, 58 per cent, of a 1986 survey of criminologists teaching in universities had been appointed in the 1970s, and 30 per cent in the years between 1973 and 1976 alone.[103] The criminologists of the new wave began to write vigorously: about half the books published in the field between 1973 and 1986 appeared in the years between 1976 and 1979. Criminology became expansive, argumentative, exuberant, factious and open: in all that explosiveness, its history resembled a perfectly familiar pattern in the more general evolution of scientific knowledge.[104]

Criminology attained a critical mass of ambitious and energetic young scholars who looked to each other rather than to their elders for intellectual stimulation, formed an 'invisible college', and achieved a temporary social and intellectual independence.[105] It was what an influential criminologist working in the Home Office Research Unit was later to call 'glitzy'. For a while, indeed, criminology seemed to be free and imaginative; those visiting Britain would sometimes observe that the most promising work was being accomplished here.

In November 1968, the younger 'sociologists of deviance' broke away to found their own National Deviancy Symposium at the University of York.[106] In its first year, members heard papers by Jock Young on 'The Police as Negotiators of Reality, Translators of Phantasy and Amplifiers of Deviancy', Ian Taylor on 'Football Mad: A Speculative Sociology of Football "Hooliganism"', and Stan Cohen on 'Middle Class Violence'.[107] The Young Turks turned away from a past defined as positivistic, jostling one another to give new definition to their discipline. They flirted with the phenomenological and interactionist (largely under the influence of the Americans Edwin Lemert[108] and Howard Becker;[109] Chapters 23 and 24), with the radical (under the influence principally of the American, Alvin Gouldner)[110] and, later, with the feminist (first under the influence of Frances Heidensohn[111] – see Chapter 27 – and then, decisively, under that of Carol Smart). It was a time marked by what Gouldner once called the 'conflictual validation of the self', a validation wrought by pitting oneself against what was held to be an old and obfuscating atheoretical orthodoxy. So eager were the Young Turks to shed tradition that they eschewed the very title of criminology for a while, preferring instead to call themselves sociologists of deviance.

Stan Cohen reflected that what marked the new sociology of deviance was its insistence on a 'continuity with sociology' (the study of deviance was to move away from the statistical, the medical and the legal); its identification of 'the significance of social control' in the delineation of a field (deviance resided as much in the interaction between definers, definitions and defined as in any properties of the defined themselves); 'appreciation' (deviance was taken to be a symbolic, meaningful activity), and 'the political implications of studying deviance' (the study of deviance was itself conceived to be a politically-charged process).[112]

The new was deemed to be radical, a word which held irresoluble ambiguity. For some, radicalism signified an intellectual regeneration of criminology, a return to roots, back to Marx, to Schutz and to the Chicago School: it was a celebration of the theoretical as an independent pursuit that bowed to no questions of politics or policy. Those radicals sought to affiliate themselves intellectually with the new sociologies of North America, and with the early work and aspirations of the Society for the Study of Social Problems in particular. For others, radicalism meant a veering to the politics of the left and a realignment of criminology with the deviant, the dispossessed and the dissident (it was a time described by Haug and Sussman as the end of professional autonomy and the revolt of the client).[113] The latter sought to join with the Claimants' Union, the Mental Patients' Union and PROP (Preservation of the Rights of Prisoners), the prisoners' union.[114]

The sociology of deviance bifurcated, one part to pursue a more austerely scholarly conception of the discipline, the other to politicize scholarship (the massively influential *The New Criminology* being its fruit). Both wings sought to distance themselves from Government, one to practise a new disinterestedness and the other a partisanship.[115] Those, then, were the first two tines of the triple-pronged reflex: a rejection of criminology conceived chiefly to be a medico-legal practice and a redefinition of the relation between criminology and the State.

The third reflex came a little later, although it was presaged in the founding of the Home Office Research Unit in 1956, of the Cambridge Institute of Criminology in 1959 and the Oxford Centre for Criminological Research in 1976. Criminology was to become institutionalized. In part, the combination of a critical mass of scholars and a Government willing to fund research on social problems (Barbara Wootton once defined a social problem as something on which Governments are prepared to spend money) encouraged a growing number of criminologists to consider themselves a somewhat separate community, severing themselves from their parent departments of sociology, psychology, law and social administration.

Criminologists had become more numerous, interconnected and mature, more confident in themselves, and more professional in their work. They had settled down, no longer so quarrelsome or vexed about the collective purpose and identity of their discipline. In settling down, they allowed earlier disputes to fragment criminology into what Garland calls 'lively sub-specialisms', areas kept apart by a consensual avoidance of confrontation and an abandonment of the attempt to create one master paradigm for the entire discipline. People may not have agreed, but they agreed not to disagree too rancorously. In that, too, their history was quite characteristic of the scientific community at large.[116]

Moreover and most importantly, after the early 1980s criminologists were responding to new facts and new events, and to crime surveys in particular. Crime surveys had been initiated in the 1970s and 1980s[117] chiefly, as the phrase went, to 'improve the criminal justice data base'. Instead of relying on figures of crimes reported to the police, those conducting surveys questioned members of households directly about their experience of criminal incidents. One of the two authors of the *British Crime Survey* argued that 'the main rationale of victim surveys ... has been to get a better estimate of the number of certain crimes actually occurring than is available from offences recorded by the police'.[118] Surveys were supposed to aid computations of the extent and distribution of crime, but they did much more as well. Their main effect on criminological theory was to transform conceptions of the character, incidence and impact of crime in everyday life. Crime appeared to be more extensive, more frequent and more debilitating than had been supposed.

Theorists were obliged, as the authors of the *Islington Crime Survey* reveal in this volume (see Chapter 33), to come to terms with the implications of a new portrait of their subject. So overwhelming and indisputable did the new facts appear to many, that a change occurred in the working consensus concerning the nature of the social world and the science that should address it. It was no longer possible for radical, libertarian and phenomenological criminologists to deny the social reality of crime as a significant crisis in the lives of ordinary men and women (especially women). Perhaps, they conceded, the correctionalists had not been so wrong after all. Perhaps they *did* have some understanding of the way the world worked. Crime ceased to be treated merely as a figment of an absolutist morality or as an ideological conceit devised to distract the proletariat from real problems of oppression and exploitation. The sociology of deviance and the new criminology became solicitous, where once they had dismissed the false consciousness of the unenlightened. There was less certainty about the grand metaphysics of the 1970s, a new humility about 'who knows best',[119] and a new deference to the empirical. Radicals and non-radicals alike began to interest themselves in quite mundane questions that some of them would never have considered before. They explored the effects of police strategy, housing design, street planning and street lighting on crime prevention.

In effect, the criminology of the 1980s and 1990s was renewed by that combination of empiricism and the withering away of big theory,[120] but it was to be renewal in a cold climate. Criminology was more purposeful, but it was also necessarily more defensive. It faced the urgent problem of determining how it could compete for funds and students in a world made newly uncertain by Government policy. From about 1978 especially, it seemed as if the environment of British higher education had turned inhospitable. Universities contracted. The number of teaching staff shrank by 11 per cent between 1979–80 and 1984–85.[121] The postgraduate training budget of the Economic and Social Research Council declined, so that it was lower in real terms in 1986 than it had been in 1974. The very name of the Economic and Social Research Council was changed from the Social Science Research Council because Keith Joseph, the then Minister of Education, had declared that 'there was no social science'. Strong (although ultimately inaccurate) rumours circulated that the Home Office Research Unit was about to be disbanded. Financial cuts seemed to be ubiquitous and threatening although, in the case of criminology, the cuts were more fictitious than real, part of a prudent official rhetoric of parsimony rather than any loss of funding in real terms.[122] However, British universities and polytechnics could no longer be so sure of themselves and their place in the world. They certainly could no longer depend on stable State funding over the quinquennia. They had to *compete* for resources under a new Manchester liberalism that made market imperatives seem ever more imperious.

Towards the end of the 1980s and the beginning of the 1990s, then, criminologists took on another incarnation. They became entrepreneurs, bringing about the emergence of what one elder criminological statesman has been wont to call the 'Jock Young PLC phenomenon'. Criminologists became entrepreneurial *fauts de mieux*, founding courses for practitioners, chasing research grants and contracts, responding to what were hoped might become new student markets.[123]

What had once been distinctive of North America[124] was to be emulated in the UK.[125] Centres of criminology and criminal justice sprang up at the universities of Edinburgh in 1974, Sheffield in 1979, Bristol in 1986, Exeter in 1987, Loughborough (the Midlands Centre) in 1990, Manchester in 1988, Brunel in 1990, London in 1991, Wales in 1992–93, and elsewhere. And the consequence has been that criminological theorizing in Britain has entered a newly quiescent phase: it is less strident, less acrimonious, less argumentative, more middle-aged and more preoccupied with the empirical than the abstract, with the 'policy-relevant' than the scientifically revolutionary, directed at the practitioner as much as at the intellectual.[126] Criminologists are not all now in some simple happy state of accord with one another but, instead of entering into rank confrontation and public debate, they seem tacitly to have agreed to pull in their horns and resort to a more conventional strategy of mutual neglect. It is as if many opposing criminologists have elected not to meet each other, engage in each other's projects, criticize each other's work or, in effect, even acknowledge each other's presence. They have embarked on what Becher called 'the systematic avoidance of controversy'.[127] Theoretical debate has lapsed for want of angry champions. For a while, at least, criminology has become a 'normal science' in an institutional *laager*.

Implications

In reading what is to come, it would be best to recall how turbulent has been the making of criminology, a turbulence that has affected what people have had to say. Intellectual history is a special pursuit, exploring ideas about the history of ideas, and it can tease itself in disconcerting ways, being at once subject and object, looping back on itself as it becomes the very thing it discusses. In such a setting, commentary is often far from innocent. On the contrary, it may be motivated, designed to achieve particular ends, turning its audience towards certain conclusions. The timing of arguments and the location and relations of authors need to be heeded.

What follows is a collection of examples of argument and of argument about argument from the different phases of criminology's history. It is difficult to be comprehensive in a single volume, and readers will be able to point to other papers that could very well have been included. But the book should convey not only how criminological theory defines and arranges its themes, but also how it can change over time (and yet remain very much the same too), and that is more than valid in an introduction to a difficult field of enquiry.

The Organization of this Book

The essays reproduced in this collection illustrate the principal phases of the evolution of criminology. Part I begins with two specimen pieces of ur-criminology: a characteristic description of the cheating underworld of Elizabethan London that hints at possibilities of sub-cultural analysis, and a pamphlet from Daniel Defoe (see Chapter 2) that attempts to lodge the causes of crime and criminality in the moral workings of an hierarchical society. They are complemented by a contemporary commentary on the causal themes underpinning the writing of early criminal biography, themes that illuminate the *moral* and the individual in criminal behaviour, themes that were to be taken forward into the next phase, the phase of social engineering.

Examples of such engineering are reproduced in Part II. They include Bentham's concrete proposals for a new house of correction (that were never actually to be executed), Colquhoun's tally of the indigent and criminal classes of Great Britain, and Sir Samuel Romilly's plans to reform the penal law (see Chapter 4). Bentham and Colquhoun were concerned principally with strategies of *control* (see Chapters 5 and 6), Romilly with justice, but all three were highly influential in their day. They contributed to a new criminal justice system embedded in a new State, though contemporary historians and criminologists interpret them in a variety of ways. The construction of a new system of formal control at a time of political, economic and social change is no small matter, and commentators have read into it a great span of meanings, from the benign to the malign, from altruism to a conspiracy of class interests, from the spiritual to the material. Michael Ignatieff's 'State, Civil Society, and Total Institutions' (see Chapter 7) usefully reviews some of those debates about the motives and significance of the philanthropic reforms of the late 18th and early 19th century.

In Part III the new administered State, its statistics and its new statistical science are represented by Joseph Fletcher (see Chapter 8), a barrister, an Inspector of Schools and Honorary Secretary of the Statistical Society of London, whose *Summary of the Moral Statistics of England and Wales* represents an impressive attempt to apply Guerry's and Quetelet's methods to the moral conditions of the UK. At a greater distance, the excerpt from Gatrell's and Hadden's 'Criminal Statistics and their Interpretation' (see Chapter 9) offers an overview of the emergence and character of 19th-century criminal statistics.

The other stream of administrative criminology, the medical, is championed with fervour and some adulation by a prison chaplain of 15 years' standing in his introduction to the English edition of Lombroso's and Ferrero's *The Female Offender* (see Chapter 10). It is as fervently criticized (and for many decisively) by Charles Goring, the man who brought criminal anthropology before the bar of statistics and found it wanting. Lucia Zedner and David Garland pronounce on these and other debates in the middle and later parts of the 19th century, tracing the transition from the moral to the scientific, the rise of medicine and the lingering importance of Lombroso in the administrative response to crime.

Mayhew's observations on the pickpockets of mid-19th century London (see Chapter 14) mark the resilience of shadow criminology, a criminology that could well have prefigured the later subcultural, ecological and ethnographic work of the Chicago School and the symbolic interactionists (it was perhaps only a want of institutional continuity that prevented the earlier emergence of a social anthropology of crime). Levin and Lindesmith (himself no mean interactionist) were evidently impressed by the subterranean criminology of the 19th century, their laudatory piece on Fletcher and Mayhew being moderately successful in its attempt to sustain an otherwise neglected criminology (see Chapter 15).

Part IV on criminology as an academic pursuit records the 20th-century blossoming of the medical model of crime and criminology in the work of Hamblin Smith and Burt (see Chapters 16 and 17), but it also includes a selection of some of the significant criminological ideas that were beginning to spread from America. Subcultural analysis, social ecology and *anomie* theory were *the* paradigmatic theories of the 1930s, 1940s and 1950s. These were subject to repeated and fruitful adaptation by the 'normal' scientists of crime.

The final section narrates the rise and partial demise of theoretical criminology, a wave that began in the heady early days of the sociology of deviance (with Edwin Lemert playing John the Baptist to Howard Becker); a wave that engendered the Society for the Study of Social Problems and the National Deviancy Conference; that bifurcated into the political and the scholarly; was reproached by feminism; and finally turned against itself under the weight of a new practicality hostile to any thought seeming to lack utility. There is a new impatience with the speculative and the disinterested, and some would oblige criminology to pay every inch and centimetre of its way. No doubt the utilitarian will itself be displaced in time as a younger generation, not yet heard, takes stock and moves theory on again.

Notes

1 I am most grateful to Roger Hood and Elaine Player for their advice in the preparation of this book. I am especially grateful to David Garland, Robert Reiner and Lucia Zedner who read earlier drafts of the Introduction and made numerous perceptive and helpful comments.
2 R. Weingartner, 'Form and Content in Simmel's Philosophy of Life' in K. Wolff (ed.) (1959), *Essays on Sociology, Philosophy and Aesthetics*, New York: Harper Torchbooks, p. 48.
3 T. Sellin (1968), 'Criminology', *International Encyclopedia of the Social Sciences*, New York: Macmillan and the Free Press, Vol. 3, p. 508.
4 H. Mannheim (1960), *Pioneers in Criminology*, London: Stevens and Sons.
5 D. Matza (1969), *Becoming Deviant*, Englewood Cliffs, New Jersey: Prentice-Hall.
6 See J. Douglas (ed.) (1972), *Research on Deviance*, New York: Random House (Chapter 25).
7 See E. Cohn and D. Farrington (1990), 'Differences between British and American Criminology: An Analysis of Citations', *The British Journal of Criminology*, **30** (4), Autumn.
8 I. Taylor, P. Walton and J. Young (1973), *The New Criminology*, London: Routledge and Kegan Paul.
9 Ibid.
10 C. Smart (1977), *Women, Crime and Criminology*, London: Routledge and Kegan Paul.
11 Ibid.
12 A. Young (1991), 'Feminism and the Body of Criminology', paper delivered at the British Criminology Conference, York.
13 See J. Wilson (1975), *Thinking About Crime*, New York: Basic Books.
14 There are, to be sure, limits on the scope and character of discord. The world 'can answer back'.

As David Garland remarked, 'the historical record may not bear any and every interpretation' (personal comunication).

15 J. Douglas (1977), *The Nude Beach*, Beverly Hills: Sage, p. 51.

16 A prime example is Jock Young who was eventually to dismiss the criminology of his own *The New Criminology* as 'left idealism'. See J. Lea and J. Young (1984), *What is to be Done about Law and Order?*, Harmondsworth: Penguin.

17 From a letter to K. Wolff in K. Wolff, 'The Sociology of Knowledge and Sociological Theory' in L. Gross (ed.) (1959), *Symposium on Sociological Theory*, New York: Harper and Row, p. 571.

18 See J. Lowman and B. MacLean (1992) (eds), *Realist Criminology in the 1990s*, Toronto: University of Toronto Press.

19 Consider Geertz's observation about how the social anthropologists of knowledge conceive 'ideation'. Ideation, he says, 'subtle or otherwise, is a cultural artifact ... it is something to be characterized by construing its expressions in terms of the activities that sustain them'; C. Geertz (1983), 'The Way we Think Now' in *Local Knowledge*, New York: Basic Books, p. 152.

20 H. Mannheim (1965), *Comparative Criminology*, London: Routledge and Kegan Paul, Vol. 1, p. 79.

21 It should, of course, be remembered that the world never lays itself out very neatly, and that there are always problems of overlap and confusion at the boundaries of the phases I shall describe. Phases were never as simple or as homogeneous as a brief introduction might suggest. What I offer is simply a way of thinking about the growth of criminology, not an iron pattern into which everything *must* fit.

22 I take it that the sciences of punishment and control – penology and criminal justice – are separate, sister disciplines.

23 See, for example, the collections represented by A. Judges (1930), *The Elizabethan Underworld*, London: Routledge and Sons.

24 A prime instance of the genre is A. Knapp and W. Baldwin (1824), *The New Newgate Calendar: being Interesting Memoirs of Notorious Characters, Who have been convicted of Outrages on THE LAWS OF ENGLAND, During the Seventeenth century, brought forward to the Present Time, Chronologically Arranged ... with occasional Essays on Crimes and Punishments, Original Anecdotes, and Observations on Particular Cases: Explanations of the Criminal Laws, the Speeches, Confessions, and LAST EXCLAMATIONS OF SUFFERERS, to which is added A correct Account of the Various Modes of Punishment of Criminals in different Parts of the World*, London: J. Robins and Co., in numerous volumes.

25 See H. Fielding (1751), *An Enquiry into the Causes of the Late Increase of Robbers*, London: no named publisher; and H. Fielding (1755), *A Plan for Preventing Robberies within Twenty Miles of London*, London: A. Millar.

26 See, for instance, J. Samaha (1974), *Law and Order in Historical Perspective: The Case of Elizabethan Essex*, London: Academic Press.

27 See B. Mandeville (1714), *The Fable of the Bees*, reprinted in 1962 by Capricorn, New York.

28 See T. Nourse (1700), *Compania Foelix*, London: Bennet.

29 T. Beames (1850), *The Rookeries of London*, London: Thomas Bosworth.

30 L. Faller (1987), *Turned to Account: The Forms and Functions of Criminal Biography in Late Seventeenth- and Early Eighteenth-Century England*, Cambridge: Cambridge University Press (Chapter 3).

31 Some forms of ur-criminology persisted. Most notable was the work of Henry Mayhew in the 1860s (see Chapter 15, Levin and Lindesmith in this volume). A kind of shadow criminology still remains in popular accounts of heinous crimes and criminals (see, for instance, J. Paisnel (1972), *The Beast of Jersey*, London: New English Library; F. Schreiber (1983), *The Shoemaker*, Harmondsworth: Penguin; J. Ritchie (1988), *Myra Hindley: Inside the Mind of a Murderess*, London: Angus and Robertson; A. Rule (1980), *The Stranger Beside Me*, New York: New American Library, and D. Yallop (1981), *Deliver Us from Evil*, London: MacDonald Futura); in picture books of crime; coffee-table criminology and the like (see *The Boys' Book of Scotland Yard*, London: Burke, 1951; C. Wilson and D. Seaman (1983), *Encyclopedia of Modern Murder*, London: Pan; and H. Keating (1982), *Great Crimes* London: Artus). Shadow criminology itself is not at all uniform in its seriousness, aspirations or impact. Whilst much is knowingly sensationalist, at its best (in

the work of Roger Graeff, Norman Mailer and Tony Parker especially), it is an important and useful complement to academic criminology proper. 'They are,' observed Robert Reiner, Private Communication, 'doing outside academe what we're trying to do inside. It's only the lack of an institutional base which makes them different.'

32 See D. Crane (1972), *Invisible Colleges: Diffusion of Knowledge in Scientific Communities*, Chicago: University of Chicago Press, esp. p. 74.

33 The term would never have been in use at the time. Then and now the word 'system' conveys too great an impression of coherence, interrelatedness and formal structure. The term 'loose-coupling' captures the relations between institutions far better than 'system'. See K. Weick (1976), 'Educational Organizations as Loosely Coupled Systems', *Administrative Science Quarterly*, **21** (1), March.

34 See R. King and J. Brownell (1966), *The Curriculum and the Disciplines of Knowledge*, New York: John Wiley.

35 See J. Rose (1980), *Elizabeth Fry*, London: Macmillan, p. 111.

36 Members of the Society for the Improvement of Prison Discipline corresponded regularly with such bodies as the Boston Prison Discipline Association and the Philadelphia Association, for instance.

37 H. Barnes and N. Teeters (1943), *New Horizons in Criminology*, New York: Prentice-Hall, p. 11.

38 See, for example, M. Ignatieff (1978), *A Just Measure of Pain*, New York: Pantheon Books.

39 P. Colquhoun (1806), *A Treatise on the Police of the Metropolis*, London: C. Dilly.

40 J. Bentham (1791), *Panopticon or Inspection House*, London: T. Payne (Chapter 5).

41 Sir S. Romilly (1810), *Observations on the Criminal Law of England*, London: T. Cadell and W. Davies (Chapter 4).

42 C. Beccaria (1764), *On Crimes and Punishments*; reprinted by Bobbs-Merrill, Indianapolis, 1963.

43 J. Howard (1784), *The State of the Prisons in England and Wales*, Warrington: William Eyres, 3rd edition.

44 Frouxides described them as a 'few philanthropically-minded individuals with humane and often strong religious convictions'. He noted that members of the Society for the Improvement of Prison Discipline included two Dukes, a Marquis, ten Earls, three Lord Bishops, 11 Lords, and 19 Members of Parliament. S. Frouxides (1983), *The English Prison Inspectorate 1835–1877*, Ph.D. dissertation, London School of Economics, pp. 24–25, 97.

45 See R. Reiner, 'British Criminology and the State' in P. Rock (ed.) (1988), *A History of British Criminology*, Oxford: Clarendon Press.

46 D. Philips, 'A New Engine of Power and Authority' in V. Gatrell, B. Lenman and G. Parker (eds) (1980), *Crime and the Law: The Social History of Crime in Western Europe since 1500*, London: Europa Publications, p. 188.

47 To be sure, there was, as Lucia Zedner has reminded me, a 'marked gap between the rhetoric of reform and its achievement'. Much continued as before. It was to be some while before the prisons were uniformly brought under the State, for instance. But the emergence of a new rhetoric was to be very important for the charting of new forms of knowledge about moral conditions.

48 A confidence built, in part, on experience acquired in managing large groups of men and resources in the Napoleonic wars.

49 See R. Nelson (1969), *The Home Office, 1782–1801*, Durham NC: Duke University Press.

50 *The Shorter Oxford English Dictionary*.

51 Jeremy Bentham had been an early advocate of the orderly collection of data on convictions for crime. In *A View of the Hard-Labour Bill* published in 1778, he described statistical returns as a kind of political barometer that would assist the legislator.

52 L. Chevalier (1973), *Labouring Classes and Dangerous Classes in Paris During the First Half of the Nineteenth Century*, London: Routledge and Kegan Paul, p. 43.

53 See D. Jones (1982), *Crime, Protest, Community and Police in Nineteenth Century Britain*, London: Routledge and Kegan Paul, p. 117.

54 L. Fox (1934), *The Modern English Prison*, London: George Routledge and Sons, p. 17.

55 The establishment of an adequate system of data collection and analysis was a lengthy process that met with occasional resistance. It was perhaps not until 1857 that criminal statistics were prepared with any efficiency. See L. Radzinowicz and R. Hood, *The Emergence of Penal Policy, op. cit.*, Ch. 4.

56 Indeed, it was a long while before their authority was challenged. See, for example, J. Douglas (1967), *The Social Meanings of Suicide*, Princeton: Princeton University Press.

57 See É. Durkheim (1892), *Le Suicide*; reprinted by Routledge and Kegan Paul in 1952.

58 See J. Fletcher (1849), 'Moral and Educational Statistics of England and Wales', *Journal of the Statistical Society*, **12**, pp. 151–76 (Chapter 8).

59 In L. Radzinowicz and R. Hood (1990), *The Emergence of Penal Policy in Victorian and Edwardian England*, Oxford: Clarendon Press, p. 51.

60 D. Garland, 'British Criminology before 1935' in P. Rock (ed.), *A History of British Criminology*, *op cit.*, p. 7.

61 See T. Caplow (1964), *The Sociology of Work*, New York: McGraw-Hill, pp. 139–40.

62 E. Freidson (1970), *Profession of Medicine*, New York: Dodd, Mead, p. 45.

63 A. Scull (1991), *The Asylum as Utopia: W.A.F. Browne and the Mid-Nineteenth Century Consolidation of Psychiatry*, London: Tavistock/Routledge, p. x.

64 See P. Elliott (1972), *The Sociology of the Professions*, London: Macmillan, p. 38.

65 See A. Carr-Saunders and P. Wilson (1933), *The Professions*, London: Frank Cass, p. 8.

66 See A. Scull (1979), *Museums of Madness: The Social Organization of Insanity in Nineteenth-Century England*, Harmondsworth, Middlesex: Allen Lane, p. 164.

67 See J. Barry, 'A. Maconochie' in H. Mannheim (ed.) (1960), *Pioneers in Criminology*, London: Stevens.

68 See Sir E. Ruggles-Brise (1921), *The English Prison System*, London: Macmillan, p. XIII.

69 Vinogradoff talked about a 'craving for a scientific treatment of the problems of social life' (P. Vinogradoff (1904), *The Teaching of Sir Henry Maine*, quoted in L. Radzinowicz and R. Hood, *The Emergence of Penal Policy*, *op. cit.*, p. 30). It must however be noted that prison chaplains at first retained great power and prison chapels were the most imposing single buildings in the new penitentiaries. Perhaps the turning point was the publication of Darwin's *The Origin of Species* in 1859. See M. Wiener (1990), *Reconstructing the Criminal*, Cambridge: Cambridge University Press.

70 Eight of the 'pioneers of criminology' nominated by Hermann Mannheim were lawyers, five were members of the medical profession, two were sociologists, one was a naval officer and geographer, and one was an architect. See *Pioneers in Criminology*, *op. cit.*, p. 2.

71 J. Sim (1990), *Medical Power in Prisons: The Prison Medical Service in England 1774–1989*, Milton Keynes: Open University Press, p. 9.

72 I. Drapkin, 'Criminology: Intellectual History' in S. Kadish (ed.) (1983), *Encylopedia of Crime and Justice*, New York: The Free Press, p. 551.

73 D. Garland (1985), *Punishment and Welfare: A History of Penal Strategies*, Aldershot: Gower, p. 106.

74 See H. Ellis (1890), *The Criminal*, London: Walter Scott.

75 D. Garland, 'British Criminology before 1935' in P. Rock, *A History of British Criminology*, *op. cit.*, p. 2.

76 Garland writes of the process that 'criminology's entry into the universities and colleges has produced some small degree of independence and critical distance from the institutions of crime control ... ' (D. Garland, 'Criminological Knowledge and its Relation to Power', unpublished paper, p. 8). It was partly in that sense that it became an activity for the 'sake of form', as identified by Weingartner and Simmel.

77 See T. Caplow and R. McGee (1958), *The Academic Marketplace*, New York: Basic Books, pp. 14–15.

78 The second edition of the *Oxford English Dictionary* records the earliest reference to the word 'criminologist' in the *Saturday Review* of 1857. It took time for the new terminology to become established. The French word '*criminologie*' *was* claimed variously to have been used first in 1888 (*Lexis: Dictionnaire de la langue française*, Paris: Librairie Larousse, 1975) and 1890 (*Dictionnaire alphabétique et analogique de la langue française*, Paris: Presses Universitaires de France, 1953). Until quite a late date, some dictionaries and encyclopaedias contain no reference to criminology (see, for example, the *Dictionnaire Général de la Langue Française*, Paris: Librairie Delagrave, 1932).

79   As Garland, Zedner and others have indicated, Lombroso's influence was *relatively* weak in the
     UK despite attempts by his disciples to evangelize his work. Lombroso does nevertheless represent
     the zenith of criminal anthropology and he was much discussed (as excerpts in this volume
     illustrate).

80   A spell that was never universal in its effects and certainly weakened by the onslaught of Charles
     Goring (Chapter 11 from Goring's *The English Convict* in this volume). London: HMSO.

81   D. Matza (1969), *Becoming Deviant*, Englewood Cliffs, New Jersey: Prentice-Hall.

82   S. Cohen, 'Criminology' in A. Kuper and J. Kuper (eds) (1985), *The Social Science Encyclopedia*,
     London: Routledge, p. 174.

83   Indeed, Burton Clark called moral philosophy the 'mother subject' of political science, a science
     that in its turn gave birth to economics and then to sociology. See B. Clark (1987), *The Academic
     Life: Small Worlds, Different Worlds*, Princeton, NJ: Carnegie Foundation, p. 28.

84   See, for instance, G. Hawthorne (1976), *Enlightenment and Despair: A History of Sociology*,
     Cambridge: Cambridge University Press.

85   See É. Durkheim (1895), *The Rules of Sociological Method*; republished by the Free Press in 1958.

86   See W. Bonger (1916), *Criminology and Economic Conditions*, Boston: Little, Brown & Co.

87   See, for example, J. Landesco (1923), *Organized Crime in Chicago*, Chicago: University of
     Chicago Press, and F. Thrasher (1927), *The Gang*, Chicago: University of Chicago Press.

88   See J. Carey (1975), *Sociology and Public Affairs: The Chicago School*, Beverley Hills: Sage.

89   R. Cavan (1983), 'The Chicago School of Sociology: 1918–1933', *Urban Life*, **11** (4), January,
     p. 409.

90   D. Garland, 'British Criminology before 1935', *op cit.*, p. 8. London: Methuen & Co Ltd.,
     (Chapter 16).

91   See J.P. Martin, 'The Development of Criminology in Britain 1948–60' in P. Rock (ed.), *A
     History of British Criminology*, *op. cit.*, p. 36.

92   See L. Radzinowicz (1988), *The Cambridge Institute of Criminology: Its Background and Scope*,
     London: HMSO.

93   See L. Radzinowicz; 'Hermann Mannheim (1889–1974)' in Lord Blake and C. Nicholls (1986),
     The Dictionary of National Biography 1971–80, Oxford: Oxford University Press.

94   *The Calendar of the London School of Economics and Political Science for the Forty-Fourth Session
     1938–39*, The London School of Economics, 1938, p. 243.

95   R.K. Merton (1938), 'Social Structure and Anomie', *American Sociological Review*, **3** (Chapter 18).

96   T.P. and P. Morris (1963), *Pentonville*, London: Routledge and Kegan Paul.

97   D. Downes (1966), *The Delinquent Solution*, London: Routledge and Kegan Paul (Chapter 22).

98   See, for example, R. Park and E. Burgess (eds) (1925), *The City*, Chicago: University of Chicago
     Press.

99   T. Morris (1957), *The Criminal Area*, London: Routledge and Kegan Paul (Chapter 21).

100 J. Mays (1954), *Growing Up in the City*, Liverpool: Liverpool University Press.

101 *The British Journal of Delinquency*, 1950, **1** (1), July.

102 A. Halsey (1992), *Decline of Donnish Dominion*, Oxford: Clarendon Press, p. 4.

103 See P. Rock, 'The Present State of British Criminology' in P. Rock (ed.), *A History of British
     Criminology*, *op. cit*, p. 59.

104 See D. Crane (1972), *Invisible Colleges: Diffusion of Knowledge in Scientific Communities*,
     Chicago: University of Chicago Press, p. 2.

105 In all this, their evolution closely followed the model described by Griffith and Mullins who also
     talk about the emergence of networks out of an initial surge of interest in new ways of looking
     at the world, the growth of external boundaries and the eventual institutionalization of an approach.
     See B. Griffith and N. Mullins (1972), 'Coherent Groups in Scientific Change', *Science*, No. 177.

106 A collection of the National Deviance Conference papers published in 1971 under the editorship
     of Stan Cohen as *Images of Deviance*, Harmondsworth: Penguin Books.

107 *Register of Abstracts 1968–1972*, Sheffield: National Deviancy Conference, 1973.

108 See E.M. Lemert (1951), *Social Pathology*, New York: McGraw-Hill. (Chapter 23).

109 In particular, see H.S. Becker (1963), *Outsiders*, The Free Press, A Division of Macmillan Inc.
     (Chapter 24).

110 See A. Gouldner (1968), *The Coming Crisis of Western Sociology*, London: Heinemann.

111 See F. Heidensohn (1968), 'The Deviance of Women: A Critique and an Enquiry', *British Journal of Sociology*, **19**; London: Routledge and Kegan Paul (Chapter 27).

112 See S. Cohen, 'Criminology and the Sociology of Deviance in Britain' in P. Rock and M. McIntosh (eds) (1974), *Deviance and Social Control*, London: Tavistock Publications Limited (Chapter 26).

113 See M. Haug and M. Sussman (1969), 'Professional Autonomy and the Revolt of the Client', *Social Problems*, **17** (2), Fall.

114 See M. Fitzgerald (1971), *Prisoners in Revolt*, Harmondsworth: Penguin.

115 All that would change in time, as I narrate in 'The Present State of British Criminology', *op. cit.* There was, in any event, not much evidence that the State was very interested in the Young Turks during the late 1960s and early 1970s.

116 See D. Crane, *Invisible Colleges, op. cit.*, p. 37.

117 The large, originating survey was the American National Crime Survey, conducted first in 1966 and consolidated in 1972 (see C. Kalish *et al.* (1974), *Crimes and Victims*, Washington DC: US Department of Justice). It was followed by comparable (although smaller) surveys in England and Wales in 1982, in Canada in 1983 and elsewhere. One of the pioneering British crime surveys was R. Sparks, H. Genn and D. Dodd (1977), *Surveying Victims*, London: Wiley and Sons.

118 P. Mayhew (1984), 'The Effects of Crime: Victims and the Public', 16th Criminological Research Conference, Council of Europe, Strasbourg, p. 2.

119 For a prescient attack on the doctrine of 'we know best', see S. Cohen, 'It's All Right For You to Talk' in R. Bailey and M. Brake (eds) (1975), *Radical Social Work*, London: Edward Arnold.

120 It is probably true that, under the influence of Foucault and Habermas, penology continues to explore the influence of 'penality' on the social world, but criminology proper now tends to hover around theories of the middle range.

121 *University Statistics 1984–85, Volume One: Students and Staff*, Cheltenham: Universities Statistical Record, 1986.

122 I give precise detail in my 'Present State of British Criminology', *op. cit.*

123 The Midlands Centre for Criminology and Criminal Justice described itself as a response to 'increasing demands for courses in criminology and criminal justice. They have come from two main groups. First, and by far the largest, from professionals working in these fields. ... The second group, new graduates seeking pre-qualifying courses, are usually looking for something to give that edge in a competitive field.'

124 North American centres of criminology were created some 20 to 30 years before their British counterparts: thus the mean year in which 11 major North American centres were founded was 1968; see P. Dresser and K. Hill (eds) (1990), *Research Centers Directory*, Detroit: Gale Research, Vol. 2.

125 Thus the University of Exeter Centre for Police and Criminal Justice Studies asserts that it is intended to 'develop one of the few University postgraduate courses for policemen and people working the broad field of Criminal Justice [and] to create an interface between academics and practitioners on the US model for the study of problems in the Police and Criminal Justice Fields.'

126 In settling down in this manner, if only for a while, it seems to have followed the pattern of other disciplines whose members tend increasingly to avoid controversy. See T. Becher (1989), *Academic Tribes and Territories*, Milton Keynes: Open University Press, p. 99.

127 T. Becher (1989), *Academic Tribes and Territories*, p. 100.

Part I
The First Phase: Ur-Criminology

Argument

[1]

R. Greene

The Art of Crossbiting

The crossbiting law is a public profession of shameless cozenage, mixed with incestuous whoredoms, as ill as was practised in Gomorrah or Sodom, though not after the same unnatural manner. For the method of their mischievous art (with blushing cheeks and trembling heart let it be spoken) is, that these villainous vipers, unworthy the name of men, base rogues – yet why do I term them so well – being outcasts from God, vipers of the world and an excremental reversion of sin, doth consent, nay constrain their wives to yield the use of their bodies to other men, that, taking them together, he may crossbite the party of all the crowns he can presently make. And that the world may see their monstrous practices, I will briefly set down the manner.

They have sundry preys that they call 'simplers', which are men fondly and wantonly given, whom for a penalty of their lust, they fleece of all that ever they have; some merchants, prentices, serving-men, gentlemen, yeomen, farmers and all degrees. And this is their form: there are resident in London and the suburbs certain men attired like gentlemen, brave fellows, but basely minded, who living in want, as their last refuge, fall unto this crossbiting law, and to maintain themselves either marry with some stale whore, or else forsooth keep one as their friend; and these persons be commonly men of the eight laws before re-hearsed, either high-lawyers, versers, nips, cony-catchers, or such of the like fraternity. These, when their other trades fail – as the cheater when he has no cousin to grime with his stop dice, or the high-lawyer, when he hath no set match to ride about, and the nip when there is no Term, fair, nor time of great assembly - then, to maintain the main chance, they use the benefit of their wives or friends to the crossbiting of such as lust after their filthy enormities. Some simple men are drawn on by subtle means, which never intended such a bad matter.

In summer evenings and in the winter nights, these traffics, these common trulls I mean, walk abroad either in the fields or streets that are commonly haunted, as stales to draw men into

A NOTABLE DISCOVERY OF COZENAGE

hell, and afar off, as attending apple-squires, certain crossbiters stand aloof, as if they knew them not. Now so many men, so many affections! Some unruly mates that place their content in lust, letting slip the liberty of their eyes on their painted faces, feed upon their unchaste beauties, till their hearts be set on fire. Then come they to these minions, and court them with many sweet words. Alas, their loves needs no long suits, for they are forthwith entertained, and either they go to the tavern to seal up the match with a pottle of hippocras, or straight she carries him to some bad place, and there picks his pocket, or else the crossbiters come swearing in, and so outface the dismayed companion, that, rather than he would be brought in question, he would disburse all that he hath present. But this is but an easy cozenage.

Some other, meeting with one of that profession in the street, will question if she will drink with him a pint of wine. Their trade is never to refuse, and if for manners they do, it is but once; and then, scarce shall they be warm in the room, but in comes a terrible fellow with a side hair and a fearful beard, as though he were one of Polyphemus' cut,[6] and he comes frowning in and saith: 'What hast thou to do, base knave, to carry my sister (or my wife) to the tavern: by His 'ounds, you whore, 'tis some of your companions. I will have you both before the Justice, Deputy, or Constable, to be examined.'

The poor serving-man, apprentice, farmer, or whatsoever he is, seeing such a terrible huff-snuff, swearing with his dagger in his hand, is fearful both of him and to be brought in trouble, and therefore speaks kindly and courteously unto him, and desires him to be content, he meant no harm. The whore, that hath tears at command, falls a-weeping, and cries him mercy. At this submission of them both he triumphs like a braggard, and will take no compassion. Yet at last, through entreaty of other his companions coming in as strangers, he is pacified with some forty shillings, and the poor man goes sorrowful away, sighing out that which Solomon hath in his proverbs: *A shameless woman*

apple squires: male bawds.
hippoctas: spiced wine cordial.
by His' ounds: by (God's) wounds.

179

CONY-CATCHERS AND BAWDY BASKETS

hath honey in her lips, and her throat as sweet as honey, her throat as soft as oil: but the end of her is more bitter than aloes, and her tongue is more sharp than a two-edged sword, her feet go unto death, and her steps lead unto hell.

Again these trulls, when they have got in a novice, then straight they pick his purse, and then have they their crossbiters ready, to whom they convey the money and so offer themselves to be searched. But the poor man is so outfaced by these cross-biting ruffians that he is glad to go away content with his loss; yet are these easy practices. Oh, might the justices send out spials in the night! They should see how these streetwalkers will jet in rich guarded gowns, quaint periwigs, ruffs of the largest size, quarter- and half-deep, gloried richly with blue starch, their cheeks dyed with surfling water – thus are they tricked up, and either walk like stales up and down the streets, or stand like the devil's *Si quis* at a tavern or ale-house, as if who should say:

'If any be so minded to satisfy his filthy lust, to lend me his purse, and the devil his soul, let him come in and be welcome.'

Now, sir, comes by a country farmer, walking from his inn to perform some business and, seeing such a gorgeous damsel, he, wondering at such a brave wench, stands staring her on the face, or perhaps doth but cast a glance, and bid her good speed, as plain simple swains have their lusty humours as well as others.

The trull, straight beginning her exordium with a smile, saith: 'How now, my friend! What want you? Would you speak with anybody here?'

If the fellow have any bold spirit, perhaps he will offer the wine, and then he is caught. 'Tis enough. In he goes, and they are chambered. Then sends she for her husband, or her friend, and there either the farmer's pocket is stripped, or else the crossbiters fall upon him, and threaten him with Bridewell and the law. Then, for fear, he gives them all in his purse, and makes them some bill to pay a sum of money at a certain day.

---

jet: strut.
guarded: embroidered.
surfling water: sulphur water or similar cosmetic.
Si quis: 'If anyone'; opening words of advertisements posted at St Paul's.
exordium: introduction.

180

A NOTABLE DISCOVERY OF COZENAGE

If the poor farmer be bashful, and passeth by one of these shameless strumpets, then will she verse it with him, and claim acquaintance of him, and, by some policy or other, fall aboard on him, and carry him into some house or other. If he but enter in at the doors with her (though the poor farmer never kissed her), yet then the crossbiters, like vultures, will prey upon his purse, and rob him of every penny. If there be any young gentleman that is a novice and hath not seen their trains, to him will some common filth, that never knew love, feign an ardent and honest affection, till she and her crossbiters have versed him to the beggars' estate.

Ah, gentlemen, merchants, yeomen and farmers, let this to you all, and to every degree else, be a caveat to warn you from lust, that your inordinate desire be not a mean to impoverish your purses, discredit your good names, condemn your souls, but also that your wealth got with the sweat of your brows, or left by your parents as a patrimony, shall be a prey to those cozening crossbiters! Some fond men are so far in with these detestable trugs that they consume what they have upon them, and find nothing but a Neapolitan favour for their labour. Read the seventh of Solomon's proverbs, and there at large view the description of a shameless and impudent courtesan.

Yet is there another kind of crossbiting which is most pestilent, and that is this. There lives about this town certain householders, yet mere shifters and cozeners, who, learning some insight in the civil law, walk abroad like 'paritors, summoners and informers, being none at all, either in office or credit; and they go spying about where any merchant, or merchant's prentice, citizen, wealthy farmer, or other of credit, either accompany with any woman familiarly, or else hath gotten some maid with child (as men's natures be prone to sin); straight they come over his fallows thus: they send for him to a tavern, and there open the matter unto him, which they have cunningly learned out, telling him he must be presented to the Arches,[7] and the citation shall be peremptorily served in his parish church. The party, afraid to

Neapolitan favour: venereal disease.
'paritors: apparitors, servants or attendants of civil or ecclesiastical officers.

CONY-CATCHERS AND BAWDY BASKETS

have his credit cracked with the worshipful of the City and the rest of his neighbours, and grieving highly his wife should hear of it, straight takes composition with this cozener for some twenty marks. Nay, I heard of forty pound crossbitten at one time. And then the cozening informer, or crossbiter, promiseth to wipe him out of the book and discharge him from the matter, when it was neither known nor presented. So go they to the woman, and fetch her off if she be married, and, though they have this gross sum, yet ofttimes they crossbite her for more. Nay, thus do they *fear* citizens, prentices and farmers, that they find but anyway suspicious of the like fault. The crossbiting bawds, for no better can I term them, in that for lucre they conceal the sin and smother up lust, do not only enrich themselves mightily thereby, but also discredit, hinder and prejudice the Court of the Arches and the officers belonging to the same. There are some poor blind *patches* of that faculty, that have their tenements purchased and their plate on the board very solemnly, who only get their gains by crossbiting, as is afore rehearsed. But (leaving them to the deep insight of such as be appointed with justice to correct vice) again to the crew of my former crossbiters, whose fee-simple to live upon is nothing but the following of common, dishonest and idle trulls, and thereby maintain themselves brave, and the strumpets in handsome *furniture*. And to end this art with an English demonstration, I'll tell you a pretty tale of late performed in Bishopsgate Street:

There was there five traffics, pretty, but common *housewives*, that stood fast by a tavern door, looking if some prey would pass by for their purpose. Anon the eldest of them, and most experienced in that law, called Mall B., spied a master of a ship coming along.

'Here is a simpler,' quoth she, 'I'll verse him, or hang me. Sir,' said she, 'good even. What, are you so liberal to bestow on three good wenches that are dry, a pint of wine?'

'In faith, fair women,' quoth he, 'I was never niggard for so much': and with that he takes one of them by the hand, and

fear: make afraid.
patches: fools.
furniture: apparel and ornaments.
housewives: whores.

A NOTABLE DISCOVERY OF COZENAGE

carries them all into the tavern. There he bestowed cheer and hippocras upon them, drinking hard till the shot came to a noble, so that they three, carousing to the gentleman, made him somewhat tipsy, and then *et Venus in vinis, ignis in igne fuit!* Well, night grew on, and he would away, but this Mistress Mall B. stopped his journey thus:

'Gentleman,' quoth she, 'this undeserved favour of yours makes us so deeply beholden to you, that our ability is not able anyway to make sufficient satisfaction; yet, to show us kind in what we can, you shall not deny me this request, to see my simple house before you go.'

The gentleman, a little whittled, consented, and went with them. So the shot was paid, and away they go: without the tavern door stood two of their husbands, J.B. and J.R., and they were made privy to the practice. Home goes the gentleman with these lusty housewives, stumbling. At last he was welcome to Mistress Mall's house, and one of the three went into a chamber, and got to bed, whose name was A.B. After they had chatted a while, the gentleman would have been gone, but she told him that, before he went, he should see all the rooms of her house, and so led him up into the chamber where the party lay in bed.

'Who is here?' said the gentleman.

'Marry,' saith Mall, 'a good pretty wench, sir; and if you be not well, lie down by her; you can take no harm of her.'

Drunkenness desires lust; and so the gentleman begins to dally; and away goes she with the candle! And at last he put off his clothes and went to bed. Yet he was not so drunk, but he could after a while remember his money, and, feeling for his purse, all was gone, and three links of his whistle broken off. The sum that was in his purse was in gold and silver twenty nobles. As thus he was in a maze, though his head were well laden, in comes J.B., the goodman of the house, and two other with him, and speaking somewhat loud.

'Peace, husband,' quoth she, 'there is one in bed, speak not so loud.'

shot: bill.
et Venus . . . fuit: 'and Venus was in the wine, the heat of lust in the fire'.
whittled: drunk.

CONY-CATCHERS AND BAWDY BASKETS

'In bed?' saith he, 'Gog's Nownes! I'll go see.'

'And so will I,' saith the other.

'You shall not,' saith his wife, but strove against him; but up goes he, and his crossbiters with him, and, seeing the gentleman in bed, out with his dagger, and asked what base villain it was that there sought to dishonest his wife. Well, he sent one of them for a constable, and made the gentleman rise, who, half drunk, yet had that remembrance to speak fair and to entreat him to keep his credit. But no entreaty could serve, but to the Counter he must, and the constable must be sent for. Yet, at the last, one of them entreated that the gentleman might be honestly used, and carried to a tavern to talk of the matter till a constable come.

'Tut!' said J.B. 'I will have law upon him.'

But the base crossbiter at last stooped, and to the tavern they go, where the gentleman laid his whistle to pawn for money, and there bestowed as much of them as came to ten shillings, and sat drinking and talking until the next morrow. By that the gentleman had stolen a nap, and waking, it was daylight, and then, seeing himself compassed with these crossbiters, and remembering his night's work, soberly smiling, asked them if they knew what he was. They answered: 'Not well.'

'Why then,' quoth he, 'you base cozening rogues! You shall ere we part': and with that drawing his sword, kept them into the chamber, desiring that the constable might be sent for.

But this brave of his could not dismay Mistress Mall; for she had bidden a sharper brunt before – witness the time of her martyrdom, when upon her shoulders was engraven the history of her whorish qualities. But she replying, swore, sith he was so lusty, her husband should not put it up by no means.

'I will tell thee, thou base crossbiting bawd,' quoth he, 'and you cozening companions, I serve a nobleman, and for my credit with him, I refer me to the penalty he will impose on you; for, by God, I will make you an example to all crossbiters ere I end with you! I tell you, villains, I serve —'; and with that he named his lord.

When the guilty whores and cozeners heard of his credit and

Gog's Nownes!: God's wounds!
upon her shoulders: i.e., by whipping or branding.

A NOTABLE DISCOVERY OF COZENAGE

service, they began humbly to entreat him to be good to them.

'Then,' quoth he, 'first deliver me my money.'

They upon that gladly gave him all, and restored the links of his chain. When he had all, he smiled, and sware afresh that he would torment them for all this, that the severity of their punishment might be a caveat to others to beware of the like cozenage, and upon that knocked with his foot and said he would not let them go till he had a constable. Then in general they humbled themselves, so recompensing the party, that he agreed to pass over the matter, conditionally beside, that they would pay the sixteen shillings he had spent in charges, which they also performed. The gentleman stepped his way, and said: 'You may see the old proverb fulfilled: *Fallere fallentem non est fraus.*'

Thus have I deciphered an odious practice, not worthy to be named. And now, wishing all, of what estate soever, to beware of filthy lust and such damnable stales as draws men on to inordinate desires, and rather to spend their coin amongst honest company, than to bequeath it to such base crossbiters as prey upon men, like ravens upon dead carcases, I end with this prayer, that crossbiting and cony-catching may be as little known in England, as the eating of swines' flesh was amongst the Jews. Farewell!

Nascimur pro patria

FINIS

[2]

THE POOR MAN'S PLEA

Daniel Defoe

IN searching for a proper Cure of an Epidemick Distemper, Physicians tell us 'tis first necessary to know the Cause of that Distemper, from what Part of the Body, and from what ill Habit it proceeds; and when the Cause is discover'd, it is to be removed, that the Effect may cease of it self; but if removing the Cause will not work the Cure, then indeed they proceed to apply proper Remedies to the Disease it self, and the particular part afflicted.

Immorality is without doubt the present reigning Distemper of the Nation: And the King and Parliament, who are the proper Physicians, seem nobly inclin'd to undertake the Cure. 'Tis a great Work, well worthy their utmost Pains: The Honour of it, were it once perfected, would add more Trophies to the Crown, than all the Victories of *this Bloody War*, or the glory of *this Honourable Peace*.

But as a Person under the Violence of a Disease sends in vain for a Physician, unless he resolves to make use of his Prescription; so in vain does the King attempt to reform a Nation, unless they are willing to reform themselves, and to submit to his Prescriptions.

Wickedness is an Ancient Inhabitant in this Country, and 'tis very hard to give its Original.

But however difficult that may be, 'tis easy to look back to a Time when we were not so generally infected with Vice as we are now; and 'twill seem sufficient to enquire into the Causes of our present Defection.

The Protestant Religion seems to have an unquestion'd Title to the first introducing a strict Morality among us; and 'tis but just to give the Honour of it where 'tis so

b

eminently due. Reformation of Manners has something
of a Natural Consequence in it from Reformation in Religion: For since the Principles of the Protestant Religion disown the Indulgencies of the *Roman* Pontiff, by
which a Thousand Sins are, *as Venial Crimes,* bought off,
and the Priest, *to save God Almighty the trouble,* can blot
them out of the Account before it comes to his hand ;
common Vices lost their Charter, and men could not sin
at so cheap a Rate as before. The Protestant Religion has
in it self a natural tendency to Virtue, as a standing Testimony of its own Divine Original, and accordingly it has
suppress'd Vice and Immorality in all the Countries
where it has had a Footing: It has civiliz'd Nations, and
reform'd the very Tempers of its Professors: Christianity
and Humanity has gone Hand and Hand in the World;
and there is so visible a difference between the other Civiliz'd Governments in the World, and those who now are
under the Protestant Powers, that it carries its Evidence
in it self.

The Reformation, begun in *England* in the Days of
King *Edward* the Sixth, and afterwards gloriously finished by Queen *Elizabeth,* brought the *English* Nation to
such a degree of Humanity, and Sobriety of Conversation,
as we have reason to doubt will hardly be seen again in
our Age.

In King *James* the First's time, the Court affecting
something more of Gallantry and Gaiety, Luxury got
footing; and Twenty Years Peace, together with no extraordinary Examples from the Court, gave too great Encouragement to Licentiousness.

If it took footing in King *James* the First's time, it took a
deep Root in the Reign of his Son; and the Liberty given
the Soldiery in the Civil War, dispers'd all manner of

The P o o r M a n ' s P l e a 3

Prophaneness throughout the Kingdom. That Prince, though very Pious in his own Person and Practice, had the Misfortune to be the first King of *England*, and perhaps in the whole World, that ever establish'd Wickedness by a Law: By what unhappy Council, or secret ill Fate he was guided to it, is hard to determine; but the *Book of Sports*, as it was called, that Book to tolerate the Exercise of all Sorts of Pastimes on the Lord's Day, tended more to the vitiating the Practice of this Kingdom, *as to keeping that Day*, than all the Acts of Parliament, Proclamations, and Endeavours of future Princes have done, or perhaps ever will do, to reform it.

And yet the People of *England* express'd a general sort of an Aversion to that Liberty; *and some*, as if glutted with too much Freedom, when the Reins of Law were taken off, refused that Practice they allow'd themselves in before.

In the time of King *Charles* the Second, Lewdness and all manner of Debauchery arriv'd at its Meridian: The Encouragement it had from the Practice and Allowance of the Court, is an invincible Demonstration how far the Influence of our Governors extends in the Practice of the People.

The present King and his late Queen, whose Glorious Memory will be dear to the Nation as long as the World stands, have had all this wicked Knot to unravel. This was the first thing the Queen set upon while the King was engaged in his Wars abroad: She first gave all sorts of Vice a general Discouragement; and on the contrary, rais'd the value of Virtue and Sobriety by her Royal Example. The King having brought the War to a Glorious Conclusion, and settled an Honourable Peace, in his very first Speech in his Parliament proclaims a New War

4   *The* POOR MAN'S PLEA

against Prophaneness and Immorality, and goes on also
to discourage the Practice of it by the like Royal Example.

Thus the Work is begun nobly and regularly; and the
Parliament, the General Representative of the Nation,
readily pursues it by enacting Laws to suppress all manner of Prophaneness, &c.

These are Great Things, and well improv'd, would
give an undoubted Overthrow to the Tyranny of Vice,
and the Dominion Prophaneness has usurp'd in the
hearts of men.

But we of the *Plebeii* find our selves justly aggrieved in
all this Work of Reformation; and the Partiality of this
Reforming Rigor makes the real Work impossible:
Wherefore we find our selves forced to seek Redress of
our Grievances in the old honest way of Petitioning Hea-
ven to relieve us: And in the mean time, we solemnly
Enter our Protestation against all the Vicious Part of the
Nobility and Gentry of the Nation; as follows:

First, We Protest, That we do not find impartially enquiring into the matter, and speaking of Moral Goodness,
that you are one jot better than we are, *your Dignities,
Estates and Quality excepted.* 'Tis true, we are all bad
enough, and we are willing in good Manners to agree,
that we are as wicked as you; but we cannot find on the
exactest Scrutiny, but that in the Commonwealth of Vice,
the Devil has taken care to level Poor and Rich into one
Class, and is fairly going on to make us all Graduates in
the last degree of Immorality.

Secondly, We do not find that all the Proclamations,
Declarations, and Acts of Parliament yet made, have any
effective Power to punish *you* for your Immoralities, as
they do us. Now, while *you* make Laws to punish *us*, and
let *your selves* go free, though guilty of the same Vices and

The POOR MAN'S PLEA 5

Immoralities, those Laws are unjust and unequal in themselves.

'Tis true, the Laws do not express a Liberty to *you*, and a Punishment to *us*; and therefore the King and Parliament are free, as King and Parliament, from this our Appeal; but the Gentry and Magistrates of the Kingdom, while they execute those Laws upon us the poor Commons, and themselves practising the same Crimes, in defiance of the Laws both of God and Man, go unpunish'd; *This* is the Grievance we protest against, as unjust and unequal.

Wherefore, till the Nobility, Gentry, Justices of the Peace, and Clergy, will be pleased either to reform their own Manners, and suppress their own Immoralities, or find out some Method and Power impartially to punish themselves when guilty, we humbly crave leave to object against setting any Poor Man in the Stocks, and sending them to the House of Correction for Immoralities, as the most unequal and unjust way of proceeding in the World.

And now, Gentlemen,

That this Protestation may not seem a little too rude, and a Breach of good Manners to our Superiors, we crave Leave to subjoin our Humble Appeal to your selves; and will for once, knowing you as *English* Gentlemen, to be Men of Honour, *make you Judges in your own Case.*

First, Gentlemen, We appeal to your selves, whether ever it be likely to perfect the Reformation of Manners in this Kingdom, without you: Whether Laws to punish us, without your Example also to influence us, will ever bring the Work to pass.

The first Step from a loose vicious Practice in this Nation, was begun by King *Edward* the Sixth, back'd by a Reform'd Clergy, and a Sober Nobility: Queen *Elizabeth*

6   *The* P o o r M a n ' s P l e a

carried it on. 'Twas the Kings and the Gentry which first
again degenerated from that strict Observation of Moral
Virtues, and from thence carried Vice on to that degree
it now appears in. From the Court Vice took its *Progress*
into the Countrey; and in the Families of the Gentry and
Nobility it harbour'd, till it took heart under their Protection; and made a general Sally into the Nation; and We
the Poor Commons, who have been always easy to be
guided by the Example of our Landlords and Gentlemen,
have really been debauch'd into Vice by their Examples:
And it must be the *Example of you the Nobility and Gentry
of the Kingdom*, that must put a Stop to the Flood of Vice
and Prophaneness which is broken in upon the Countrey,
or it will never be done.

Our Laws against all manner of Vicious Practices are
already very severe: But Laws are useless insignificant
things, if the Executive Power which lies in the Magistrate be not exerted. The Justices of the Peace have the
Power to punish, but if they do not put forth that Power,
'tis all one as if they had none at all: Some have possibly
exerted this Power; but wherever it has been so put forth,
it has fallen upon us the poor Commons: These are all
Cobweb Laws, in which the small Flies are catch'd, and
great ones break through. My Lord-Mayor has whipt
about the poor Beggars, and a few scandalous Whores
have been sent to the House of Correction; some Ale-
housekeepers and Vintners have been Fin'd for drawing
Drink on the Sabbath-day; but all this falls upon us of the
Mob, the poor *Plebeii*, as if all the Vice lay among us; for
we do not find the Rich Drunkard carri'd before my
Lord Mayor, nor a Swearing Lewd Merchant Fin'd, or
Set in the Stocks. *The Man with a Gold Ring, and Gay
Cloths*, may Swear before the Justice, or at the Justice;

The POOR MAN'S PLEA 7

may reel home through the open Streets, and no man take any notice of it; but if a poor man get drunk, or swear an Oath, he muſt to the Stocks without Remedy.

In the second place, We appeal to your selves, Whether Laws or Proclamations are capable of having any Effeĉt towards a Reformation of Manners, while the very Benches of our Juſtices are infeĉted with the scandalous Vices of Swearing and Drunkenness; while our Juſtices themselves shall punish a Man for Drunkenness, with a *God damn him, set him in the Stocks*: And if Laws and Proclamations are useless in the Case, then they are good for nothing, and had as good be let alone as publish'd.

'Tis hard, Gentlemen, to be punish'd for a Crime, by a Man as guilty as our selves; and that the Figure a Man makes in the World, muſt be the reason why he shall or shall not be liable to the Law: This is really punishing men for being poor, which is no Crime at all; as a Thief may be said to be hang'd, not for the Faĉt, but for being taken.

We further Appeal to your selves, Gentlemen, to inform us, whether there be any particular reason why you should be allow'd the full Career of your corrupt Appetites, without the Reſtraint of Laws, while you your selves agree that such Offences shall be punished in us, and do really Execute the Law upon the Poor People, when brought before you for the same things.

Wherefore, That the Work of Reformation of Manners may go on, and be brought to Perfeĉtion, to the Glory of God, and the great Honour of the King and Parliament: That Debauchery and Prophaneness, Drunkenness, Whoring, and all sort of Immoralities may be suppress'd, we humbly propose the Method which may effeĉtually accomplish so great a Work.

(1.) That the Gentry and Clergy, who are the Leaders of us poor ignorant people, and our Lights erected on high places to guide and govern us, would in the first place put a voluntary force upon themselves, and effectually reform their own Lives, their way of Conversing, and their common Behaviour among their Servants and Neighbours.

1. The Gentry. They are the Original of the Modes, and Customs, and Manners of their Neighbours; and their Examples *in the Countries especially* are very moving. There are three several Vices, which have the principal Management of the greatest part of Mankind, *viz.* Drunkenness, Swearing, and Whoring; all of them very ill becoming a Gentleman, however Custom may have made them Modish: Where none of these Three are in a House, there is certainly something of a Plantation of God in the Family; for they are such Epidemick Distempers, that hardly Humane Nature is entirely free from them.

1. Drunkenness, that Brutish Vice; a Sin so sordid, and so much a Force upon Nature, that had God Almighty enjoyn'd it as a Duty, I believe many a Man would have ventur'd the Loss of Heaven, rather than have perform'd it. The Pleasure of it seems to be so secretly hid, that wild Heathen Nations know nothing of the matter; 'tis only discover'd by the wise people of these *Northern* Countries, who are grown Proficients in Vice, Philosophers in Wickedness, who can extract a Pleasure to themselves in losing their Understanding, and make themselves sick at heart for their Diversion.

If the History of this well-bred Vice was to be written, 'twould plainly appear that it begun among the Gentry, and from them was handed down to the poorer sort, who

The POOR MAN'S PLEA 9

still love to be like their Betters. After the Restitution of
King *Charles* the Second, when drinking the King's
Health became the distinction between a *Cavalier* and a
Roundhead, Drunkenness *began its Reign*, and it has
Reign'd almost Forty Years: The Gentry caress'd this
Beastly Vice at such a Rate, that no Companion, no Servant was thought proper, unless he could bear a Quantity
of Wine; And to this day 'tis added to the Character of a
Man, as an additional Title, when you speak well of him,
He is an honest drunken Fellow; as if his Drunkenness was
a Recommendation of his Honesty From the practice of
this nasty Faculty, our Gentlemen have arriv'd to the
teaching of it; and that it might be effectually preserv'd
to the next Age, have very early instructed the Youth in
it. Nay, so far has Custom prevail'd, that the Top of a
Gentleman's Entertainment has been to make his Friend
drunk; and the Friend is so much reconcil'd to it, that he
takes that for the effect of his Kindness, which he ought
as much to be affronted at, as if he had kick'd him down
Stairs: Thus 'tis become a Science; and but that the Instruction proves so easy, and the Youth too apt to learn,
possibly we might have had a Colledge erected for it before now. The further perfection of this Vice among the
Gentry, will appear in two things; that 'tis become the
Subject of their Glory, and the way of expressing their
Joy for any publick Blessing. *Jack*, said a Gentleman of
very high Quality, when after the Debate in the House
of Lords, King *William* was voted into the vacant Throne;
Jack (says he) *God damn ye* Jack, *go home to your Lady, and
tell her we have got a Protestant King and Queen; and go and
make a Bonfire as big as a House, and bid the Butler make ye
all Drunk, ye Dog*: Here was Sacrificing to the Devil, for a
Thanksgiving to God. Other Vices are committed as

Vices, and men act them in private, and are willing to
hide them; but Drunkenness they are so fond of, that
they will glory in it, boast of it, and endeavour to promote
it as much as possible in others: 'Tis a Triumph to a
Champion of the Bottle, to repeat how many Quarts of
Wine he has drank at a sitting, and how he made such and
such honest Fellows drunk. Men *Lye* and *Forswear*, and
hide it, and are *asham'd of it*, as indeed they have reason to
do: But Drunkenness and Whoring are Accomplish-
ments People value themselves upon, repeat them
with pleasure, and affect a sort of Vanity in the History;
are content all the World should be Witnesses of their Intemperance, have made the Crime a Badge of Honour to
their Breeding, and introduce the practice as a Fashion.
And whoever gives himself the trouble to reflect on the
Custom of our Gentlemen in their Families, encouraging
and promoting this Vice of Drunkenness among the poor
Commons, will not think it a Scandal upon the Gentry of
England, if we say, That the Mode of drinking, as 'tis
now practised, had its Original from the Practice of the
Country-Gentlemen, and they again from the Court.

It may be objected, and God forbid it should not, That
there are a great many of our Nobility and Gentlemen,
who are Men of Honour and Men of Morals; and therefore this Charge is not universal. To which we answer,
'Tis universal for all that, because those very Gentlemen,
though they are negatively clear as to the Commission of
the Crimes we speak of, yet are positively guilty, in not
executing that Power the Law has put into their hands,
with an Impartial Vigor. For where was that Gentleman
or Justice of the Peace ever yet found, who executed the
Terms of the Law upon a Drunken, Swearing, Lewd
Gentleman, his Neighbour, but the Quality of the Per-

son has been a License to the open Exercise of the worſt of Crimes; as if there were any Baronets, Knights, or Squires in the next World; who because of those little ſteps Cuſtom had raised them on, higher than their Neighbours, should be exempted from the Divine Judicature; or that as Captain *Vrats* said, who was Hang'd for Murth'ring Esquire *Thynn, God would show them some respect as they were Gentlemen.*

If there were any reason why a rich Man should be permitted in the publick Exercise of Open Immoralities, and not the poor Man, something might be said: But if there be any difference it lies the other way; for the Vices of a Poor Man affect only himself; but the Rich Man's Wickedness affects all the Neighbourhood, gives offence to the Sober, encourages and hardens the Lewd, and quite overthrows the weak Resolutions of such as are but indifferently fix'd in their Virtue and Morality. *If my own Watch goes false, it deceives me and none else; but if the Town-Clock goes false, it deceives the whole Parish.* The Gentry are the Leaders of the Mob; if they are Lewd and Drunken, the others ſtrive to imitate them; if they Discourage Vice and Intemperance, the other will not be so forward in it, nor so fond of it.

To think then to effect a Reformation by Punishing the Poor, while the Rich seem to Enjoy a Charter for Wickedness, is like *taking away the Effect, that the Cause may cease.*

We find some People very fond of Monopolizing a Vice, they would have all of it to themselves; they muſt, as my Lord *Rocheſter* said of himself, *Sin like a Lord*; little sneaking Sins won't serve turn; but they muſt be Lewd at a rate above the Common Size, to let the World see they are capable of it.

Our Laws seem to take no Cognizance of such, perhaps for the same reason that *Lycurgus* made no Law
against *Parricide*, because he would not have the Sin
named among his Citizens.

Now the Poor Man sees no such Dignity in Vice, as to
study Degrees; we are downright in Wickedness, as we
are in our Dealings; if we are Drunk, 'tis plain Drunkenness; Swearing and Whoring, is all Blunderbus with us;
we don't affect such Niceties in our Conversation; and
the Justices use us accordingly; nothing but the Stocks,
or the House of Correction is the Case, when we are
brought before them; but when our Masters the Gentlemen come to their Refin'd Practice, and Sin by the Rules
of Quality, we find nothing comes of it but false Herald-
ry, the Vice is punish'd by the Vice, and the Punishment
renews the Crime.

The Case in short is this; the Lewdness, Prophaneness and Immorality of the Gentry, which is the main
Cause of the General Debauchery of the Kingdom, is not
at all toucht by our Laws, as they are now Executed; and
while it remains so, the Reformation of Manners can
never be brought to pass, nor Prophaneness and Immorality Suppress'd; and therefore the punishing the Poor
distinctly, is a Mock upon the good Designs of the King
and Parliament; an Act of Injustice upon them to punish
them, and let others who are as guilty go free; and a sort
of Cruelty too, in taking the advantage of their Poverty
to make them suffer, because they want Estates to purchase their Exemption.

We have some weak Excuses for this Matter, which
must be considered: As,

(1.) The Justice of the Peace is a *Passive Magistrate*, till
an Information be brought before him, and is not to take

notice of any thing, but as it is laid in Fact, and brought
to an Affidavit. Now if an Affidavit be made before a Justice, that such or such a man Swore, or was Drunk, he
must, he cannot avoid Fining him; the Law obliges him
to it, let his Quality be what it will; so that the Defect is
not in the Law, nor in the Justice, but in the want of Information.

(2.) The Name of an Evidence or Informer is so scandalous, that to attempt to inform against a man for the
most open Breach of the Laws of Morality, is enough to
denominate a Man unfit for Society; a Rogue and an Informer are Synonimous in the Vulgar Acception; so much
is the real Detection of the openest Crimes against God,
and Civil Government, Discouraged and Avoided.

(3.) The Impossibility of the Cure is such and the
Habit has so obtain'd upon all Mankind, that it seems
twisted with Human Nature, as an Appendix to Natural
Frailty, which it is impossible to separate from it.

For Answer;

1. 'Tis 'true, the Justice of the Peace is in some respect
a *Passive Magistrate*, and does not act but by Information,
but such Information would be brought if it were encouraged; if Justices of the Peace did acquaint themselves
with their Neighbourhood, they would soon hear of the
Immoralities of the Parish; and if they did impartially
Execute the Law on such as offended, without respect of
Person, they would soon have an Account of the Persons
and Circumstances. Besides, 'tis not want of Information,
but want of punishing what they have Information of. A
Poor Man informs against a Great Man, the Witness is
discouraged, the man goes unpunish'd, and the Poor
Man gets the scandal of an Informer; and then 'tis but too
often that our Justices are not men of extraordinary Mor-

als themselves; and who shall Inform a Justice of the
Peace that such a man Swore, when he may be heard to
Swear himself as fast as another? or who shall bring a man
before a Justice for being Drunk, when the Justice is so
Drunk himself, he cannot order him to be set in the
Stocks?

(2.) Besides, the Justice has a power to punish any Fact
he himself sees committed, and to enquire into any he
hears of casually; and if he will stand still and see those
Acts of Immorality committed before his Face, who shall
bring a Poor Man before him to be punished? Thus I
have heard a Thousand horrid Oaths sworn on a Bowling-
Green, in the presence of a Justice of the Peace, and he
take no notice of it, and go home the next hour, and set a
man in the Stocks for being Drunk.

As to the Scandal of Informing, *'tis an Error in Custom*,
and a great Sin against Justice; 'tis necessary indeed that
all Judgment should be according to Evidence, and to
discourage Evidence, is to discourage Justice; but that a
man in Trial of the Morality of his Neighbour, should be
ashamed to appear, must have some particular Cause.

(1.) It proceeds from the Modishness of the Vice; it
has so obtain'd upon mens Practices, that to appear
against what almost all men approve, seems malicious,
and has a certain prospect either of Revenge, or of a Mer-
cenary Wretch, that Informs meerly to get a Reward.
'Tis true, if no Reward be plac'd upon an Information, no
man will take the trouble; and again, if too great a Reward, Men of Honour shun the thing, because they scorn
the Fee; and to Inform meerly for the Fee, has something
of a Rascal in it too; and from these Reasons arises the
backwardness of the People.

The very same Rich men we speak of are the persons

The P O O R M A N ' S P L E A 15

who discourage the Discovery of Vice, by scandalizing the Informer; a man that is any thing of a Gentleman scorns it, and the Poor ſtill Mimick the Humour of the Rich, and hate an Informer as they do the Devil. 'Tis ſtrange the Gentleman should be asham'd to deteƈt the Breach of those Laws, which they were not asham'd to make; but the very Name of an Informer has gain'd so black an Idea in the minds of People, because some who have made a Trade of Informing againſt People for Religion, have misbehaved themselves, that truly 'twill be hard to bring any man either of Credit or Quality to attempt it.

But the main thing which makes our Gentlemen backward in the prosecution of Vice, is their praƈtising the same Crimes themselves, and they have so much wicked Modeſty and Generosity in them, being really no Enemies to the thing it self, that they cannot with any sort of freedom punish in others, what they praƈtice themselves.

In the Times of Executing the Laws againſt Dissenters, we found a great many Gentlemen very Vigorous in prosecuting their Neighbours; they did not ſtick to appear in Person to diſturb Meetings, and demolish the Meeting Houses, and rather than fail, would be Informers themselves; the reason was because they had also a dislike to the thing; but we never found a Dissenting Gentleman, or Juſtice of the Peace forward to do thus, because they approved of it. Now were our Gentlemen and Magiſtrates real Enemies to the Immoralities of this Age, did they really hate Drunkenness as a Vice, they would be forward and zealous to root the praƈtice of it out of the Neighbourhood, they would not be backward or asham'd to deteƈt Vice, to diſturb Drunken Assemblies,

to disperse those Plantations of Leachery, the Publick
Bawdy-Houses, which are almost as openly allow'd as the
Burdelloes in *Italy*. They would be willing to have all sorts
of Vices Suppress'd, and glory in putting their Hands to
the Work; they would not be asham'd to appear in the
detecting Debauchery, nor afraid to embroil themselves
with their Rich Neighbours. 'Tis Guilt of the same Fact
which makes Connivance, and till that Guilt be removed,
the Gentlemen of *England* neither will, nor can indeed
with any kind of Honour put their hands to the Reforming it in their Neighbours.

But I think 'tis easy to make it appear that this difficulty of Informing may be removed, and there need not
be much occasion for that Scandalous Employment.

'Tis in the Power of the Gentry of *England* to Reform
the whole Kingdom without either Laws, Proclamations,
or Informers; and without their Concurrence, all the
Laws, Proclamations, and Declarations in the World
will have no Effect; the Vigour of the Laws consists in
their Executive Power: Ten thousand Acts of Parliament signify no more than One single Proclamation, unless the Gentlemen, in whose hands the Execution of
those Laws is placed, take care to see them duly made use
of; and how can Laws be duly Executed, but by an Impartial Distribution of equal Rewards and Punishments,
without regard to the Quality and Degree of the Persons?
The Laws push on the Justices now, and they take care to
go no faster than they are driven; but would the Justices
push on the Laws, Vice would flee before them as Dust in
the Wind, and Immoralities would be soon Suppress'd;
but it can never be expected that the Magistrates should
push on the Laws to a free Suppression of Immoralities,
till they Reform themselves, and their Great Neighbours

Reform themselves, that there may be none to punish
who are too big for the Magiſtrate to venture upon.

Would the Gentry of *England* decry the Modishness
of Vice by their own Practice; would they dash it out of
Countenance by disowning it; that Drunkenness and
Oaths might once come into *diseſteem*, and be out of
Fashion, and a man be valued the less for them; that he
that will Swear, and be Drunk, shall be counted a *Rake*,
and not fit for a Gentleman's Company: This would do
more to Reforming the reſt of Mankind, than all the Punishments the Law can inflict; the Evil encreased by Example, and muſt be suppress'd the same way. If the Gentry were thus Reform'd, their Families would be so too:
No Servant would be Entertain'd, no Workman Employ'd, no Shopkeeper would be Traded with by a Gentleman, but such as like themselves, were Sober and
Honeſt; *a Lewd, Vicious, Drunken Footman muſt Reform
or Starve*, he would get no Service; a Servant once turn'd
away for Intemperance, would be entertain'd by no body
else; *a Swearing Debauch'd Labourer or Workman muſt
Reform, or no body would Employ him*; the Drunken whoring Shop-keeper muſt grow Sober, or lose all his Cuſtom-
ers, and be Undone. *Intereſt and Good Manners would
Reform us* of the poorer sort, there would be no need of the
Stocks or Houses of Correction; *we should be sober of
course, because we should be all Beggars else*; and he that
lov'd his Vice so dearly as to purchase it with the loss of
his Trade or Employment, *would soon grow too poor for his
Vice, and be forced to leave it by his own Necessities*; there
would be no need of Informers, a Vicious Fellow would
be presently Notorious, he would be the Talk of the
Town, every one would slight and shun him for fear of
being thought like him by being seen in his Company;

c

he would expose himself, and would be punish'd [and] as
unpitied as a Thief.

So that in short, the whole Weight of this Blessed
Work of Reformation lies on the shoulders of the Gentry;
they are the Cause of our Defection, which being taken
away, the Effect would cease of course, Vice would grow
Scandalous, and all Mankind would be asham'd of it.

(2.) The Clergy also ought not to count themselves exempted in this matter, whose Lives have been, and in
some places still are so Vicious and so loose, that 'tis well
for *England* we are not subject to be much *Priest-ridden*.

'Tis a strange thing how it shou'd be otherwise than it
is with us the poor Commonalty, when the Gentry our
Patern, and the Clergy our Teachers, are as Immoral as
we. And then to consider the Coherence of the thing; *the
Parson preaches a thundering Sermon against Drunkenness,
and the Justice of Peace sets my poor Neighbour in the Stocks,
and I am like to be much the better for either, when I know
perhaps that this same Parson and this same Justice were
both Drunk together but the Night before.*

It may be true, for ought we know, that a Wicked Parson may make a good Sermon; and the *Spanish* Proverb,
may be true of the Soul as well as the Body. *If the Cure be
but wrought, let the Devil be the Doctor;* but this does not
take with the downright ignorant People in the Country;
a poor Man gets Drunk in a Country Ale-house, *Why,
are you not asham'd to be such a Beast, says a good honest
Neighbour to him the next day?* Asham'd, says the Fellow!
Why should I be asham'd? Why, there was Sir *John*——
and Sir *Robert* . . . . . and the Parson, and they were all as
Drunk as I. And why a Beast, Pray? I heard Sir *Robert*
. . . . . . say, That

The P o o r M a n ' s P l e a   19

He that Drinks leaſt,
Drinks moſt like a Beaſt.

A Vicious Parson that preaches well, but lives ill, may
be like an unskilful Horseman, who opens a Gate on the
wrong side, and lets other Folks through, but shuts himself out. This may be possible, but it seems moſt reasonable to think they are a means by that sort of living, to
hinder both themselves and others; and would the Gentry and Clergy of *England* but look back a little on the
Guilt that really lies on them, as Gentlemen by whose
Example so great a part of Mankind has been led into,
and encourag'd in the Progress of Vice, they would find
Matter of very serious reflection.

This Article of the Clergy may seem to lie in the power
of their Superiors to rectify, and therefore may be something more feasible than the other; but the Gentry who
are *Sui juris,* can no way be reduced but by their own voluntary practice. We are in *England* exceedingly govern'd
by Modes and Cuſtoms. The Gentry may effectually
Suppress Vice, would they but put it out of Fashion; but
to suppress it by Force seems impossible.

The Application of this rough Doctrine is in short both
to the Gentry and Clergy, *Physicians, Heal your selves*; if
you will leave off your Drunkenness and Lewdness firſt,
if we do not follow you, then set us in the Stocks, and send
us to the House of Correction, and punish us as you
please; if you will leave off Whoring firſt, then Brand us
in the Foreheads, or Transport or Hang us for Fornica-
tion or Adultery, and you are welcome; but to preach
againſt Drunkenness immediately after an Evening's
Debauch; to Correct a poor Fellow for Swearing with the
very Vice in your Mouths; these are the unjuſteſt ways

in the World, and have in themselves no manner of tendency towards the Reformation of Manners, which is the true Design of the Law.

'Tis acknowledg'd there are in *England* a great many Sober, Pious, Religious Persons, both among the Gentry and Clergy, and 'tis hop'd such cannot think themselves Libell'd or Injur'd in this Plea; if there were not, Laws would never have been made against those Vices, *for no men make Laws to punish themselves*; 'tis design'd to reflect upon none but such as are Guilty, and on them no farther than to put them in mind how much the Nation owes its present Degeneracy to their folly, and how much it is in their Power to Reform it again by their Example; that the King may not publish Proclamations, nor the Parliament make Laws to no purpose; but that we might live in *England* once more like Christians, and like Gentlemen, to the Glory of God, and the Honour of the present King and Parliament, who so publickly have attempted the great Work of Reformation among us, though hitherto to so little purpose.

F I N I S

Argument about Argument

[3]

Chapter 3

In the absence of adequate causes: efforts at an etiology of crime

LINCOLN B. FALLER

In the politic, as in the natural body, no disorders ever spring up without a cause . . . and such causes must be adequate to the effects which they produce.
Henry Fielding, *Providence in Murder* (1752), p. 2

It may be now expected that I should give some account what were the Reasons and Motives that instigated me to this Crime. But alas! when I consider the slender Inducements I had thereunto, I must only clap my Hand upon my Breast, and confess it was . . . my own vile and Corrupted Heart.
Edmund Kirk, *Dying Advice* (1684)

One Sin wilfully committed easily draws on another, and that more; and a Man cannot tell when or where to stop, till it end at last in a sad and shameful Death.
[N.B.], *Compleat Tryals* (1718, 1721), 3:36

The nature of Malefactors is so amply known, I need not much inlarge upon the subject; for why, they are most of them men of leud Conversations . . . who first most commonly begin with Crimes of a smaller note, and by degrees emboldened in the cursed Trade, they trample upon fear and stifle all remorse; a sympathy so frequently observed in their insolent behaviours, who often have been known, when in their Infancy, to scoff at Admonitions, and make a jest of Piety, but this is only when they are free and unrestrained, roving to and fro. . . . when they are shackled by Justice, and the ends of all their courses come before their Eyes, then they are of other minds.
Execution of 11 Prisoners (1679), pp. 3–4

If once a man indulges himself in murder, very soon he comes to think little of robbing, and from robbing he comes next to drinking and Sabbath-breaking, and from that to incivility and procrastination.
Thomas De Quincey, "On Murder Considered as
One of the Fine Arts" (1839), in *De Quincey's
Collected Writings*, ed. David Masson, 13:56

In all cultures, it seems, murder demands a response that extends beyond the workings of mere social and political institutions. Malinowski has written about the Trobriand Islanders' elaborate and ritualized reactions to cases of suspected homicide, but one can cite ex-

EFFORTS AT AN ETIOLOGY OF CRIME

amples closer to home.[1] In modern Western societies, criminals are caught, tried, and dealt with by the police, the courts, and the prisons (political institutions) under the law (a social institution). But even in cases less exacerbating than murder, this is not the full extent of the cultural response. "Somebody we know gets into trouble," writes a British criminologist, "and at once people remember that his father was once in trouble with the police when he was a boy, or that there was a cousin who went bankrupt, an aunt who was divorced, or a grandfather who got merrily drunk from time to time." Such is the effect of the common belief (in Britain at least) that "crime is 'in the blood.' " Obviously, this writer goes on to point out, such a belief is supported not by the actual evidence but by "our own emotions and needs": "it is our very similarity to the criminal we are trying to deny by portraying him as essentially someone from another world – or at least another family." This very same impulse to differentiate between ourselves and the criminal, he adds, can be expressed in other ways, for instance by blaming crime "all upon the residents of the delinquency areas, 'Them,' the disreputable slum dwellers, or the spendthrift residents of council houses."[2]

Behind both ideas, that criminal tendencies are inherited or that there is a criminal class, is the same denial mechanism, a mechanism that seems all the more obvious because both ideas are now in disfavor. Other, more respectable theories of crime, however, can seem similarly motivated – at least when they come into use on a popular level. Thus the notion that the criminal is "sick," and that this sickness is traceable to his having been "disadvantaged" socially or psychologically, is not without its comforts for the "healthy" majority. It is a notion, quite obviously, that shapes to a large extent the coverage of crime in the American press. The more heinous the criminal's act, the more fascinatingly repugnant his crime, the more doggedly journalists look into his background. Often not even waiting for the courts to find him guilty, they search out the distinctive characteristics of what criminologists call (nowadays wryly) *homo criminalis*. The fifth-grade teacher of the sex murderer or political assassin will recall that he stuttered, seemed withdrawn, had difficulty reading, perhaps even that she recommended he see the school psychologist but somehow nothing came of it. It may be found that his parents were divorced when he was very young or that his mother never married. And while the neighbors will point out that he was such a nice, quiet young man, so kind and considerate to his mother, the suspicions of those of us who live in a post-Freudian world (by now practically everyone who is literate and many who are not) will inevitably be aroused. There may be hints that his mother, a hopeless neurotic, put intolerable pressures on him all his life, that he made the mistake of marrying a woman like her, and that there were even, perhaps, grave inadequacies in the marriage bed. (This last may seem unlikely, but I seem to remember Lee Harvey Oswald's wife saying as much in *Life* magazine – or was it his mother?) And so on: He was a loner, never had a job he was good at, drifted around the country, had peculiar ideas, collected guns. We are all very familiar with the pattern.

It is not a pattern – of course – to be found in the late seventeenth and early eighteenth centuries. No surprise in that: The period was for the most part innocent of abnormal psychology. But what is surprising, at least on first encounter, is that nothing in the popular literature of crime performed an equivalent function. Whenever the question of the criminal's nature and motives arose, it was not his essential difference from the law-abiding majority that tended to be emphasized but his essential similarity. The root cause of crime, one reads again and again, is human depravity. And as all men are equally tainted from birth by original sin, criminals are not different in kind from other people, only in degree. Anyone might become a criminal. The wonder, then, was not that crime was so prevalent but that it was not universal. Given the scope of human depravity, a lot more of it ought to be happening. Only occasionally does the popular literature of crime suggest that a particular person was driven to murder or steal out of madness or necessity, and such suggestions do little to mitigate its insistence on human depravity.

The severity of this point of view might seem disingenuous on more than one account. The idea that we are all depraved makes useful social propaganda; at the very least it is a way of keeping the young and impressionable in line. In regular doses, such propaganda may also have worked prophylactically; perhaps readers of the popular literature of crime could only really feel free to enjoy themselves if, as they took their naughty pleasures, they were provided the protection of some slightly discomfiting edification. But we ought not to be too cynical, too ready to see the writers of criminal lives as serving the repressive (and prurient) interests of a society that, as it was well on its way to being middle class, must have had (shouldn't we think?) all the usual bourgeois hangups. For, whatever else their motives in arguing that the root cause of crime was the inherent depravity of human nature, such writers were trying to place the phenomenon of crime within a context where – given the limits of what they knew of human psychology and were able to see, and admit, about the nature of their society – it could be made into tolerable sense. That this context was religious was largely a matter of necessity; for all its growing obsolescence, there was simply no other scheme of looking at things with so much explanatory power.

In the late seventeenth and early eighteenth centuries the causes of crime were – or at least were made to seem – as obscure and anomalous as (how to find an appropriate analogy?) the causes of cancer now. Nowhere is the popular literature of crime able to offer more than a partial and selective account of why it was that certain men among the rest (for all men potentially were criminals) had actually broken the law and so come to forfeit their lives. This is not to say there was no inclination to search for causes; for every effect, the age was sure, there had to be a cause. The problem was that particular causes could not always be found for particular crimes – causes, that is (and this was a requirement increasingly in vogue), that declared themselves palpably to human observation and reason. It was understood that criminals differed from ordinary people in their want of feeling or understanding, or in the desperation forced on them by necessity. Curiously, however, the popular literature of crime rarely deals with extremes of either case, ignoring madmen almost entirely and regularly discounting the claims of those who said they robbed or murdered only to save their own lives. Economic necessity, or more generally poverty, did not in any case seem in itself a sufficient cause for crime. Though would-be social reformers like Fielding could argue that "an effectual provision for the poor" would "amend their morals" and so reduce crime, it was nonetheless observable that not all criminals were poor. Nor, as Fielding himself pointed out, did most poor people steal.[3] Generally, so far as published opinion was concerned, the fact that a criminal was poor was nothing more than an index to the weakness of his character. "Idleness brings a Man to Poverty," one assize sermon declares, "and Poverty maketh him to disturb the Peace by Murders and Robberies."[4]

The crucial thing about criminals, then, was not that they were driven by need or insanity, but set adrift by a want of feeling and understanding.[5] How else could they have disregarded the fearsome penalty the law so often imposed? As an anonymous writer pointed out at the turn of the century, criminals took no notice of "the great care of Magistrates of this great and Populous City, in putting the Laws in Execution against Fellons," or of "the Terrible Examples of Justice, almost every Month of the Year." Or, as another writer put it a few years later: "Notwithstanding the daily Warnings given by Persons that have come to untimely Ends, for their Cruel Murders, &c, their [sic] still remains most unaccountable Wretches among us, who act worse than the Brute Beasts."[6] Calling criminals "beasts" did not make them any the less "unaccountable," but it could serve to distract attention from the all-important and well-nigh unanswerable question: Why should some men lack the feeling and understanding that in others were sufficient, at least, to keep them from the gallows? To what could the mental and emotional incapacities of criminals be traced?[7]

In some cases, it was possible to point to heredity. Thus William Barton, a highwayman hanged in 1721, "seemed to have inherited a sort of hereditary wildness and inconstancy, his father having been always of a restless temper and addicted to every species of wickedness."[8] Occasionally, too, there is a suggestion along Lockean lines that a criminal's character may have been malformed by an especially brutal childhood or an improper education. "There cannot be a greater misfortune," begins an account of Captain John Stanley, a notorious bully who slashed his mistress to death in 1722, "than to want education, except it be the having of a bad one." Comparing "the minds of young persons" to "paper on which we may write whatever we may think fit," but which, "once blurred and blotted with improper characters" resists the inscription of "proper sentiments," this writer traces the origins of Stanley's crime back to his boyhood when he was initiated into "cruelty and blood." Stanley was only five years old when his father, a soldier, began to train him in the use of a sword, "pricking him himself and encouraging other officers to play with him in the same manner, so that his boy, as old Stanley phrased it might never be afraid of a point." By the time he was old enough to accompany his father on campaign, young Stanley had acquired "so savage a temper" that he "delighted in nothing so much as trampling on the dead carcasses in the fields after an engagement." This "wretched method of bringing up a child," the reader is assured, was "highly likely to produce the sad end he came to."[9]

Similar efforts to ground the etiology of crime on specific material conditions are rather rare. I have come across only a few instances where criminal behavior is linked to inherited characteristics, and only two or three where, in any elaborate way, it is traced to the cumulative effects of an unhappy childhood. Perhaps the most sophisticated of all such efforts is an anonymous writer's pamphlet on the "Suffolk Parricide." This is worth examining in some detail because, insofar as it defines the outer limits of rational investigation into the causes of a specific instance of criminal behavior (and I'm not speaking only of murder), it throws into sharp relief the general inability of the period to produce anything like an adequate etiology of crime.

Late one night in 1740 in a small town in Suffolk, Charles Drew knocked at the door of his father's house and then, when the old man answered, shot him point-blank in front of a witness. Given the family's local prominence, and especially Drew's persistent denials of guilt, the case attracted considerable attention. How could Drew commit so terrible a crime, insist he hadn't, and expect to go unpunished? It

seemed significant that he had been "brought up in a boorish ignorance" entirely unsuitable to his station in life. Though he gave the
appearance of a gentleman – "his Person was fine and his Parts tolerable" – he had none of a gentleman's breeding and, "for want of Culti-
vating," had in fact become "dull and senseless." So far none of this is
extraordinary. What sets it apart, however, is the writer's tendency to
probe for clues to the psychic origins of the crime. Looking further into
the evidence at hand than other writers would (or did), he is, for one
thing, not content to focus only on the criminal himself. "In order to
form a better Idea of the Son," he points out, the reader must know
something of "the Father . . . an Attorney of great Practice . . . but a
Man of an unhappy Temper, and possessed of so much Severity, that it
even amounted to Brutality." This information is given not so much to
explain the immediate motive for the crime as to illuminate the criminal's background, which is certainly peculiar.

When Charles was born, we read, the elder Drew was at first over-
joyed. Charles was the first and only son in a family of five daughters.
But then the elder Drew began to believe that Charles was not really his
son, and separated from his wife. Though he never consented to see her
again he did, however, continue to visit her house to dine with the
children, all five daughters and Charles. But then the elder Drew was
an odd sort anyway, a man who even before the breakup of his marriage would "sit whole Days" and "never converse" with his family,
"nor so much as suffer any of them to speak to him unless to answer
any Question which he should think proper to propose to them."
Given the failure of his parents' marriage, Charles received "no Education: the Father never troubled his Head about him, and his Mother was
as regardless, so that he was bred up in a rough Manner, and among
Persons in the lowest Class of Life." Not only did he not become a
gentleman, but, as he "increased in Years, the wicked Dispositions
which he had acquired increased with him." Finally

> he became of so sordid perverse a Temper that all Men conjec-
> tured Some ill End must be the Consequence of his Proceedings;
> nay, his own Father (whom he hath since so inhumanly mur-
> dered) prognosticated but a few Months ago from some Observa-
> tions which he had made in his Behaviour that his Son *Charles
> would not dye in his Bed:* The old Gentlemans Prognostication
> proved fatal to him tho' at that time he little expected that he
> himself should be the Occasion of it's [*sic*] proving true; yet could
> he have considered rightly, what else could he expect?

Denied an education, and falling in with "a Company of Smugglers
and Poachers, a Herd of mean People of little or no Understanding, but

of Resolution enough to perpetrate the most daring Villanies," Charles Drew "went on from one Degree to another till he arrived at this last fatal Pitch." The crime itself is attributed to the concurrence of two motives, one longstanding and the other a precipitant. For a long time Charles had resented the fact that his father allowed him only two hundred pounds a year, believing that he needed more to live like a proper gentleman. Rather more recently, or so he claimed, he had begun to suspect that his father was planning to divorce his mother in order to remarry and beget a new heir. As his father's divorce suit would very likely have been based on Charles's presumptive bastardy, he risked winding up with nothing at all. And so, taking heart from his friends' oft-reiterated assurances that shooting his father would be no worse than shooting "a *Cat*, or a *Dog*," he decided to do him in.[10]

I have not found a more complete account of how a given set of circumstances can combine to make a man a criminal. *The Suffolk Parricide* shows how Drew's character was shaped along special lines by experiences that few people share, and how that character, so shaped, was in more than one way the source of his crime. For as long as Drew

lived as badly as he did, his father was not likely to increase his allowance; and, too, given his character, it is possible that his fear of being
disinherited had some foundation (if only in a guilt-induced paranoia).
But, as I have said, *The Suffolk Parricide* is rare; only one or two other
biographies of actual criminals are able to go as far in developing an
etiology for the crimes they describe. It is important to specify "actual"
here, because a different situation obtains in the literature of the
period.[11] Outside the realm of the overtly fictive, however, there seems
to have been no small resistance to the idea that criminals are made, not
born.

Perhaps part of the reason was that just too many criminals appearing in the popular literature of crime came from decent and respectable
families, had been brought up as well as could be expected and given
what seemed entirely suitable educations. Thus, though the author of
Remarkable Criminals was willing to admit that the "want of education
hath brought many who might otherwise have done very well in the
world to a miserable end," still he felt obliged to point out that "the
best education and instruction are often of no effect to stubborn and
corrupt minds." Sometimes he tries to explain the existence of such
minds, but with no notable success; all he can do is point, with a good
deal of pseudoprofundity, to "the various dispositions of men." It is
these that cause the "frequent differences in their progress, either in
virtue or vice; some being disposed to cultivate this or that branch of
their duty with peculiar diligence, and others, again, plunging themselves in some immoralities they have no taste for." More typically,
however, he is content to lapse back into a general condemnation of
human nature, the task of trying to sort it out apparently beyond him.
"Such is the present depravity of human nature," he says in one of his
darker moods, "that we have sometimes instances of infant criminals
and children meriting death by their crimes before they know or can be
expected to know how to do anything to live."[12] This is the writer, we
ought to remember, who would like to think of children's minds as
blank sheets of paper on which we can write what we will. Perhaps it is
the incompatibility of this idea with the notion that human nature is
inherently depraved that makes him hedge a bit and speak of its *present*
depravity – as if the corruptions of heart and mind that concern him
were a special condition produced by circumstances operating now, and
not from the beginning of time or necessarily into the future.

The author of *Remarkable Criminals* appears to be caught in the
middle of an intellectual revolution, and that can hardly have been
comfortable. The forepart of his thinking moves with the new age of
Lockean empiricism, but the hinder part, perplexed as it is by the
difficulty of establishing a clear and coherent etiology of crime after the

new fashion of thinking, continues to drag in the past. To the question of why some people are criminals and others are not, he can finally offer no more adequate an answer than this: "such is the frailty of human nature that neither the best examples nor the most liberal education can warrant an honest life, or secure to the most careful parents the certainty of their children not becoming a disgrace to them, either in their lives or by their deaths."[13] And in this he is entirely typical of his age.

The fact was that some criminals, as some still are today, were simply inexplicable in terms of what was known or could be known of their formative years and previous behavior. But there was more to the problem than this, for despite the efforts of writers like the author of *Remarkable Criminals* the popular literature of crime was not always interested in explaining its criminals away. Christopher Slaughterford, for instance, hanged at Guildford in 1709, had been born to "very Honest and Reputable Parents." His father was "a Farmer of considerable Subsistance [sic]," and he, brought up within "the Principles of the Church of England," had been given an "Education suitable to his Birth and Qualification." "Being no way given to Swearing or Drunkeness, Vices too common to Youth in this degenerate Age," he was "look'd upon to be a hopeful and civil Young Man." Yet, pestered by a former sweetheart he'd seduced with promises of marriage and then abandoned, he lured her away and drowned her in a pond.[14] Perhaps Slaughterford's crime, which he steadfastly denied, was not so strange as it seemed. But this cannot be known from the account I've been quoting because the country churchman who wrote it, though on the spot, shows no inclination to explore his subject's background. Such an absence of effort, where the effort might so easily have been made, need not mean the parson was lazy. But it may mean that he valued Slaughterford's incomprehensibility, or was at least content to let it be. If so, he shows a tendency that often operated in the popular literature of crime, a tendency that ran contrary to explanation and often sought to magnify all that was mysterious in criminal motivation. Even *The Suffolk Parricide* shows this tendency, with all its close concern for Drew's peculiar background and its influence on his behavior. "But . . . whatever induced Mr. *Charles Drew* to perpetuate such a Scene of Inhumanity," it at one point confesses, "we cannot justly determine."[15]

This willingness to be perplexed was not unmotivated. More than simple sensationalism was involved here, however. The mysteriousness of crime suited those who held to a religious or even a political conservatism; it could be a rod with which to chastise the ungodly and/or the unruly. By insisting again and again that everyone was capable of crime, it strove to add, to the real fear that people had about being robbed or murdered, another fear: No one could know but that he or she might just come to be hanged. The perilous condition of us all is vividly described by a late seventeenth-century writer. Speaking "sadly" and out of "dayly experience," he comments on the meaning to be found in the case of the Reverend Robert Foulkes, who was hanged in 1679 for the murder of his bastard child. No sooner does God leave us "to the indirect motion of our natural courses," he warns, "but as if we were in Love with our own Ruine, we presently run headlong into the black stream of Vice and Impiety." Which means we are as good as lost: "Our Reason which should be our Pilot, then serves us in no stead; no happy birth, Litterate Education, or sacred Function is able to bribe us to study our own good; but on the contrary, our predominant corruptions overrul[e] them all."[16] Foulkes was a good example of what even the best-seeming among us have to fear from the black and errant tendencies of the human heart. As such he was remembered well into the eighteenth century. Beginning with "hypocrisy" and "uncleanness" he opened himself to the commission of far more grievous sins, says the 1734 Johnson. His "Learning and Abilities," his "sacred Eloquence," made him "exceedingly follow'd and admir'd," and, had he died "in a natural Way," he "might have been belov'd till Death . . . and then universally lamented." But then, as he himself said at the gallows, "You see in me what Sin is."[17]

The conventional wisdom could have brought little comfort even to those whose ends it served. The problems it raised for an increasingly secular, politically liberal England will be considered in the next two chapters; what I want to emphasize now is its emotional and intellectual insufficiency. Criminals supposedly were men who, more than other men, had indulged their propensity to sin. Either this caused God to withdraw His grace, leaving them to fall by the inherent weight of their wickedness – a wickedness, of course, that was not theirs alone but characteristic of every human being – or else indulgence in sin had gradually, sometimes even imperceptibly, hardened them emotionally and morally. The latter view seems to have been preferred in the eighteenth century. Thus the author of *Remarkable Criminals* declares that criminals are people who "abandon themselves to a desire of living after their own wicked inclinations, without considering the injuries they do others while they gratify their own lusts and sensual pleasures." They show how "a long and habitual course of vice so hardens the soul, that no warnings are sufficient, no dangers frightful, nor reflections so strong [to keep them from] those illegal practices which lead to a shameful death." The "common causes" of even the worst crimes, he is sure, are "vices and extravagances." This holds true even when "men of outward gravity and serious deportment" break the law, for even they will be found to have been (like Foulkes) "as wicked as those whose open licenciousness renders their . . . crimes . . . the less amazing."[18]

The limitations of any such explanation of crime are amply revealed by this last locution: At best, one could hope to make it seem "the less amazing." But that at least was something, and so, not surprisingly, the biographies of criminals took up the task of tracing those sins which, in their view, had made their subjects more than usually vulnerable to the wicked inclinations surging in us all. Their efforts, it must be noted, were directed not at developing a psychology (or even a "natural history") of crime but at finding, after the fact, appropriate events to precede it. A clear and more than usually elaborate example of just such an effort is Samuel Foote's account of Samuel Goodere, a captain in the Royal Navy who was hanged in 1740 for ordering the murder of his brother by two seamen under his command. Sir John Dinely Goodere was rich, respected, and known for "the natural Goodness of his Heart." But his brother hated him, apparently for reasons having to do with the family estates, and had him kidnapped. After holding him for a few days aboard his ship, which was anchored at Bristol, he had him killed. Foote was the victim's nephew and so would have had access to privileged information. Certainly he seems (or pretends) to know a great deal about Samuel Goodere. But with all his information he works to a curiously impoverished end. His main theme – one can guess it in advance – is that the murderer's "Inclinations, from the very Dawn of his Life to the Close of it, were very depraved."

Given the evidence he advances, Foote is hardly exaggerating. As a schoolboy, for instance, Samuel and several of his companions robbed his grandfather's house. This was rather more than the usual schoolboy prank, for during the course of the robbery Samuel (here exceeding Mary Edmondson) "clapped a Pistol to his own Mother's Breast." The poor woman's "only Fault," says Foote, was her "great Indulgence to all her children." On another occasion, demanding money from his father, he declared he'd waylay and shoot him if he didn't get it. His relations with his brother were hardly more cordial. That he frequently quarreled with him, that he threatened him with bodily harm several times before he finally had him kidnapped and killed, were all of a piece with his behavior toward the family in general.[19] All this evidence, and a good deal more which I slide over, makes it quite clear that Samuel was a moral monster long before he committed his terrible crime. But it does not do much else, and Goodere seems to have been rather more complicated.

Bad as he was, he was not beyond resenting Foote's attentions. He agreed that his crime was "as shocking as human nature could well be capable of," but thought it "hard" that it should "blacken or sully my whole past life and conversation." "I know that some *Pharisaical* censures will urge that vice is progressive, that no man is suddenly wicked," he says, "and that my crime must have been preceeded by a great many others of the like tendency." But "cruelty and ill nature," he claims, are not his "natural disposition." Appealing to "all those that ever knew me," he asks whether he "was not so well beloved in [his] neighborhood, and distinguished for strict honour as any gentleman in it." Goodere might have mentioned his military career as further evidence that he was no mere monster, but he doesn't. Even in the eighteenth century, when commissions were purchased and promotion gained by influence, one had to be more than simply maniacally wicked to get and hold command of a ship in the Royal Navy. Curiously, however, neither he nor Foote raises the matter; here even the murderer to some extent collaborates in the simplification of himself.[20]

For all his special opportunity to gather psychological detail, Foote's characterization of Goodere holds to type. It is not his motives that interest him, or how these fit into the man's larger psychology, but his moral state before the crime, and for Foote it is enough to show that this was dark "from the very Dawn of his Life." Nor does it much concern him that if indeed this were the case – and Foote, we might note, would gain some reputation as a playwright – the figure he has painted is utterly opaque. For Foote, as for his contemporaries, very little of the "why" of a crime inhered in the criminal's mind. In itself a natural event, the outcome of a long course of delinquency, the questions it prompted had to do with the consequences of that delinquency, not its psychodynamics. What had he done to have merited so hard a fate? Why had God cast him down so terribly? Such questions may seem to reflect a mentality too primitive to have existed in a so-called age of reason, but it was an age that had a taste at all levels for global explanation (but then, as anthropologists like Lévi-Strauss might ask, which age, what culture does not?). Given the notion that criminality was part of a larger pattern of behavior, and the absence of any elaborate psychology to describe that behavior, it was only by asking such questions that sense could be made of phenomena that would otherwise have had to seem senseless.

But few criminals could be made "less amazing" as easily as Foote made Goodere. Some seemed not to have been sinful men at all, even when the most careful inquiries were made. "There is scarce any thing more remarkable," comments the author of *Remarkable Criminals* at the beginning of one felon's history, "than the finding of a man who hath led an honest and reputable life, till he hath attained the summit of life, and then, without abandoning himself to any notorious vices that may be supposed to lead him into rapine and stealth . . . to take himself on a sudden to robbing on the highway, and to finish a painful and industrious life by a violent and shameful death." Here for once the awkward prose is appropriate, for the case the writer is about to discuss upsets his ease of mind. Despite the title of his work, he wants his criminals to seem as unremarkable as possible, and here is one who resists accommodation to his paradigms. The man in question is a certain John Austin, who "being under no necessities, but on the contrary, in a way very likely to do well," committed "so unaccountable an act as the knocking down a poor man and taking away his coat." Austin's description of his crime – "that though he was in a fair way of living, and had a very careful and industrious wife, yet for some time . . . had been disturbed in his mind . . . and from a sudden impulse of mind attacked the man" – could hardly do more to subvert the idea that criminals are men who grow only gradually wicked. "The son of very honest people," as the author of *Remarkable Criminals* is obliged to admit, and educated as he ought to have been, Austin worked hard, had a "fair character" from all his neighbors, displayed "no vicious principles,"

EFFORTS AT AN ETIOLOGY OF CRIME   65

and "had been guilty of very few enormous crimes, except drinking to excess sometimes, and that but seldom." "The sin which most troubled him was . . . spending the Lord's day mostly in hard work." I have been quoting in sequence, for these last few bits of comment show the writer recovering his lost equilibrium. Beginning to contradict his original view – that the case is inexplicable – he gropes for the received ideas that allow some sense, finally, to be made of the fate of this very likely lunatic man. "He was very penitent," it is in any case consoling to know, "and suffered death with much serenity and resolution."

Death and disgrace can come without warning, we are thus encouraged to infer, even from sins apparently so trivial as failing to observe the Sabbath strictly and "drinking to excess sometimes." One either accepts this inference, which sets a nearly impossible standard for safe human conduct, or else is faced with something far more disturbing: that the criminal impulse can fall more suddenly, and with far less warning, than the sudden dew from heaven. For his part the author of *Remarkable Criminals* would prefer to believe, with all that it entails, that, "generally speaking, the old saying holds true that nobody becomes superlatively wicked at once." Still he occasionally feels the need to warn that even those who never "stumble in the road of virtue" can nonetheless take, "as it were, a leap from the precipice at once."[21] Each time someone mentally deranged was hanged – for such I take Austin to have been, and probably Savage, Strodtman, and Edmondson – it may well have seemed that everybody was indeed footing it along the edge of the abyss and could, at any moment, be seized by the impulse to jump. "You are not secure of your selves, that you shall not commit the Crimes, or worse than those for which she dy'd," warns the writer of an account of a woman hanged for infanticide. "I . . . thought my self too secure and trusted to my own strengths, more than the grace and assistance of the Almighty," explains a soon-to-be-hanged murderer, nor would he have believed it, "had it been formerly told me, I should ever have come to this End." "When you read over this sad Story," declare two different pamphlets on two different murders, "we beseech you lay your hands upon your hearts, and say, 'What a mercy is it, I was neither the *Murderer* nor the *Murdered!*'"[22]

Against such pronouncements there was not much defense (which perhaps explains their becoming the central moral of so many criminals' lives; put to use, the idea behind them can seem less fearsome). There was as yet no conception of the criminal as an altogether different kind of human being. The comforts (since blasted) of Lombroso's physiognomy lay far in the future, as also the notion (not quite so far in the future) that crime was the product of a "criminal class," a particular stratum of society that was low, dangerous, and (it goes without saying) certainly not that of the reader.[23] All that writers of criminal lives could know and think was that crime was a form of indiscipline, an extreme case of the *principium laesum* unleashed. "There cannot be anything more dangerous," warns *Remarkable Criminals,* "than a too ready compliance with any [lustful or irascible] inclination of the mind," for "either transports us on the least check into wicked extravagancies, which are fatal in their consequences, and suddenly overwhelm us with both shame and ruin." All the available wisdom on the etiology of crime was summed up by one criminal who, on his way to the gallows, hoped "that all by his example would learn to stifle the first motions of wickedness and sin, since such was the depravity of human nature that no man knew how soon he might fall." No one knew, or could know, why certain men became criminals and others did not.[24]

The danger one had to live with, then, was that self-control would fail, that one would be overcome by a sudden, fatal impulse of mind. In some cases the onset of malignancy could almost be predicted, but in others its triggering factor must have seemed as mysterious and as frightening as – to us, now – a single piece of blue asbestos in the lung. Seemingly insignificant bits of moral or religious delinquency, insignificant at least on the grand scale of human reprobation, could bring on whole chains of dooming events. Or, even more sudden and starkly fatal, God might just abruptly withdraw His supporting grace, and, given the sinfulness of us all, who could blame Him? Or so the popular literature of crime encouraged its readers to believe; should we take what it says at face value? Having made no extensive search of the diaries and letters of the period, I am in no position to say whether people actually were afraid of succumbing, either gradually or suddenly, to the tendencies within them that might bring them to be hanged. The written record in any case is no sure guide; certain central anxieties may have been unspoken. Dr. Johnson, who held that man's "chief merit consists in resisting the impulses of his nature," certainly believed in human depravity. And he shared the views of those who wrote about crime for popular consumption, at least so far as to assert that "we are all thieves naturally." Yet he believed, too, that "by good instruction and good habits this is cured, till a man has not even an inclination to seize what is another's; has no struggle with himself about it."[25] Probably most people who bothered to think about these things agreed with Johnson, or so it seems reasonable to assume, if only on the grounds of the general human inclination toward psychological self-defense. I would guess, however, that it was easier to defend against the possibility that we are all potentially thieves than that we are all potentially murderers.

For murder fit the etiological paradigm in a sense too well; it could be done so suddenly, so unexpectedly, so irrationally, and so often by people who, until then, had not seemed in any way extraordinary. This would have been true especially of familiar murder, and here we have perhaps one of the most important reasons for its special treatment in the popular literature of crime. Thieves, with rare exceptions, could seem comfortably different from the general run of humanity if only for the fact that, however they started, they generally lived for some time as part of the London underworld before they were caught and hanged. The most notorious thieves, almost always professionals, were unlike other people not only in their habits and associations but even in their language.[26] Murderers, however, often showed no such distinctive features. How was a potential Savage, Strodtman, or Edmondson to be told apart from other men and women? Nor were the motives of murderers at all easy to define or comprehend. Robberies could seem at least prompted by some prior calculation, whether in fact they had been or not, and though stupid and short-sighted such calculations could at least seem comprehensible. As one highwayman about to be hanged supposedly sang out, "a merry life and a short one."[27] But rarely was there anything so lucid in the motives of familiar murderers; they killed for obscure or trivial reasons, or perhaps for no discernible reason at all.

More than any other crime, familiar murder thus confirmed not only the darkest suppositions about human nature but the moral precariousness of just about everyone. It could indeed make it seem that all of us were at risk, unless, more scrupulously than most of us would care to, we strove to keep to the strait and narrow. And even then, as the moral propaganda of the popular literature of crime reiterated again and again, we could not be sure of our safety.[28] Such propaganda may have been troubling, as much to those who agreed with its assumptions as to those who rejected it out of hand. So insistent is it, so ugly in its implications, that even those whose views it echoed must have been obliged, if only for their peace of mind, to put it at some tolerable distance. Perhaps this meant that such people reasoned, as we have just seen Dr. Johnson doing in the matter of theft, that the murderous impulse could be cured or controlled. Others, less disposed to dark thoughts on the nature of man, may have joined in with the coffee-house wits who laughed at murderers' confessions; but laughter, too, is a way of protecting oneself, especially when other means are not available. In any case, if familiar murder were to be put to use, either as an object lesson for the masses or merely as a semiobscene entertainment, means had to be found to modify its starkest implications, to counterbalance and so control all that it so unsettlingly suggested of the human condition. Any presentation of the event that lacked such means risked inattention or, worse, mocking disregard.

THE CRIMINAL AS SINNER

By now I hope to have shown the inadequacy of reason, given the state of contemporary psychology, to account for a crime so apparently without motive and so generally gruesome as familiar murder. Beyond affirming the general depravity of human nature – an affirmation which, as it happened, was increasingly out of step with a culture coming to take a more optimistic view of human capacities – the myth did not much inquire into the crime's etiology, nor could it. Instead of explaining the crime, it sought to counter its effect (or should I say affect?), making it seem, at minimum, part of a whole. At maximum, it tried to make it seem part of a reassuring whole. The reassurance came with the criminal's readiness to confess and accept responsibility for his crime, to convert and die an enthusiastic Christian, to close out his life in a peculiar mixture of self-abasement and self-glorification. Why and how this should have been reassuring is a question for the next two chapters; here we might pause to consider how far we've come toward understanding one of the central features of the myth that attached to familiar murder, the great stress put on the criminal's confession. There is something more to be said, too, about the tendency of the myth to dwell on the bloody details of the murder itself.[29]

The search for causes or, failing these, precedents adequate to the murderer's crime required information, and often that information could come only from the criminal himself. In its absence, writers dredged up what they could. Anything shady in the murderer's past was likely to be exploited if it could be made to indicate, and practically anything could, that his crime was part and parcel of an enduring and egregious wickedness. But such searches needed confirmation. Thus Catherine Hayes, who murdered her husband in a highly lurid fashion (cutting off his head, dismembering him, scattering his body parts all over London, for which she was burned at the stake) was pressured to confess she committed incest. It seems that one of her accomplices, hardly more than a boy, was not only her lover but also a foundling. This, and evidence suggesting she led a wandering and dissolute life before marrying (a good deal is made of this by itself), prompted the suspicion that her lover was her son, that she knew it and didn't care. Catherine Hayes neither denied nor confirmed this suspicion, but it was not without its logic. For had she in fact violated one of the two great taboos on which human society is built, it could hardly seem surprising that she'd gone on to violate the other, and in so atrocious a fashion. Sabbath-breaking would do when it came to finding appropriate precedents for murder, drinking and whoring were convenient, and a history of violence still better, but sometimes – and the Hayes case was not

unique – incest was best.[30] But such dark doings were more easily suspected than proved.

Nothing so remarkable is alleged of Mary Edmondson, though she
too was inconvenient in her silence. In the absence of a confession that
might have supplied precedents appropriate to her crime, writers were
encouraged to use their imaginations. Thus Mary was made to quarrel
with her aunt, to be disinherited and to resent it, even to stab her
mother. All these "facts," like her aunt's variously alleged generosity,
made Mary's crime not only the more abominable, and so the more
richly illustrative of human depravity, but as well the less amazing. No
more than Savage or Strodtman (or Stanley, Drew, Goodere, or Hayes)
did she leap from the precipice at once. Without these "facts" her case
would be bleak indeed, for Mary would otherwise appear to have committed no previous delinquencies of any real significance – unless, of
course, one were willing to attach sinister connotations to the hiding
away of some coals and a mop. Significantly, this is just what some
people did. Mary's case would have been less embellished, I suspect,
had she confessed as fulsomely as Savage or Strodtman, showing how
one sin led on to another, even from something so simple as Sabbath-

breaking. But as it was, even the Sabbath-breaking had to be supplied (or at least its equivalent), for so I take the claim in one account that she stayed out late at a Christmas party. Did she? And was so seemingly innocuous an excess significant? Mary was the best person to say so, and for other, less crucial information she was certainly the most convenient source.

Mary Edmondson's refusal to confess had one interesting effect in particular. It led one writer to describe the stabbing of her aunt with a fullness of detail that rivals the descriptions of Savage's and Strodtman's crimes, and in a language that closely parallels those descriptions. It is an interesting language, and all the more because it is so conventional, a standard fixture in countless accounts of murder. In "flat," affectless tones, it enumerates with near pedantic precision the blows and thrusts delivered, the blood spilled, and the victim's dying groans; it does not moralize or even comment on what it is describing. It might be argued that this absence of evaluative and judgmental comment served to forward vicarious involvement. But such language is lacking, too, in the sense of excitement one generally finds in prurient writing. There is a tension in it, to be sure; one feels a mounting sense of horror, but this is produced by its peculiar objectivity, its troubling lack of affect compared to the writing around it. And in those instances where writers do interpose themselves to comment evaluatively, it is to pile on all the moral disapproval they can muster. There is never the tiniest suggestion that the victim invited what he got, or deserved it, though such suggestions are rife and loom large in descriptions of violence done by highwaymen and other rogues.

Obscenities are never gratuitous, and the tendency to dwell on the bloody details of murder in the middle of most accounts of the crime ought to seem more than a means of quickening the pulse of readers clogged with moral comment. But, as I have been suggesting, it ought also to seem more than a means of gratifying unconscious hostilities characteristic of the age. Either view assumes that the violence in such accounts is an interpolation, a gratifying departure from boring business that must be done, or the real business of the piece, tolerable only because it is hemmed in by stretches of superego-sanctioned discourse. It seems to me, however, that these descriptions of violence are an integral part of the whole myth. Physically at its center, they are in every sense its starting point, the thing from which it exfoliates (and the thing the text would decently clothe within its leaves). With their strange clarity and frequent lack of emotion these descriptions seem, as much as anything else, efforts at coming to terms with an object of special dread by looking, full-face and unflinchingly, on the thing itself. Or, rather, not the thing itself but a redacted version of it. Written

EFFORTS AT AN ETIOLOGY OF CRIME   71

down and broken up into its component parts, the act of murder becomes – in the process of being preserved, in words, as it actually was –
something other than what it actually was. And in being made something other, it becomes not only more endurable but more manageable:
Surrounded by other sets of words, it becomes one moment among
many in the course of a whole life, one event in a set of other events,
one sign in a system of other signs.

Once described, the act of murder can begin to lose its dreadful and
astonishing singularity; inscribed, it can be written into larger constructs of meaning. It may have been this aim – just as much as any
wish to sensationalize the event, to titillate the audience – that caused the
murder of Edmondson's aunt to be described as fully and particularly as
if she had indeed confessed, had been as helpful and free as Strodtman
and Savage in giving all the horrid details. Still, though such cooperation as the murderer could give in the inscribing of his crime was
important, there are other reasons for the great value placed on his
confession and, more generally, for the great interest shown in his state
of consciousness not only before his crime and while he was committing it but afterward, right up to the moment he was hanged. These
reasons are more solidly inferable from contemporary concerns, and are
about to concern us.

Myths, Malinowski says, seek not to explain but to explain away.
Or so it seems from our point of view, for any effort to explain the
"peculiar" ideas of another culture asks not only what and how they
think but why (at some level or other) they do not or cannot or will not
think like us, that is, "correctly." Unable to deal as we would with the
human depravity expressed in such crimes, the myth that attached to
familiar murder strove to show how that depravity, inevitably, had
been checked and overbalanced. At its simplest, as we are about to see,
it counterposed God's providence, His justice and mercy, against one of
the most vicious – and vividest – expressions of human evil. At a more
complicated level, it was concerned to show that even the worst of men
could know, want, and achieve goodness. The myth thus had a double
aim: to justify the ways of God to man, and to justify man to himself.
And as the latter had considerable implications for the justice, health,
and prospects of English society, the myth contributed to social solidarity as well. Whatever our prejudice in like matters, then, it was not this
myth's efforts at an etiology of crime, psychological or moral, that
allowed it finally to achieve coherence, to close its structure over one of
the most disturbing things men might do. It would be some time yet
before the reading public could seize onto the comfortable conviction
that the "criminal intellect" was nothing like "the average intellect of
average men" – to quote Dickens – but "a horrible wonder apart."[31]

CHAPTER 3

1 Bronislaw Malinowski, *Crime and Custom in Savage Society* (1967), pp.87–91.
2 Howard Jones, *Crime in a Changing Society* (1967), p. 38.
3 "The Wonder in fact is," says Fielding, "that we have not a thousand more Robbers than we have; indeed, that all these Wretches are not Thieves, must give us either a very high Idea of their Honesty, or a very mean one of their Capacity and Courage" (*Late Increase of Robbers* [1751], p. 143). See also his *Proposal for Making an Effectual Provision for the Poor* (1753), where he says "the sufferings of the Poor are indeed less observed than their Misdeeds" (p. 9) but points out the two are directly connected. Fielding proposes to diminish both by forcing the poor into workhouses, an idea by no means original to him (thus see also, for example, *An Account of the Corporation for the Poor of London* [1713], pp. 17–18, and *An Account of Several Work-Houses for Employing and Maintaining the Poor,* 2nd ed. [1732], p. xii).
4 John Haslewood, Assize Sermon, 24 July 1707, p. 8. The 1734 Johnson echoes this point, saying that "a Man who has given a Loose to his Inclinations, and always placed his Happiness in the pursuit of irregular pleasures, will, when Necessity stares him in the Face, do any thing in the World, rather than quit the Chace and make Virtue the Object of his Wishes and Pains" (*Highwaymen* [1734], p. 370). The author of *Remarkable Criminals* (1735a) takes an even harder line. Noting that necessity is often "urged" by thieves because "nothing could be a greater alleviation of [their] crime," he

finds it "hard to judge the reasonableness of such an excuse" because the
meaning of the word is "so equivocal" (p. 437). Elsewhere he goes so far
as to say that "in all the loads of papers I have turned over to this purpose"
he has never found, "in strictness," a true case of necessity prompting
crime, "though as the best motive to excite compassion, and consequently
to obtain mercy, it is made very often a pretence" (p. 228). "Our Laws
[make] such provision for the poor," wrote Jeremy Collier, that it is rare
indeed that anyone should have "neither Friends nor Strength to support
him," and so be obliged to steal "to keep Life and Soul together" (*Essays
upon Several Moral Subjects. Part IV* [1709], p. 30; see also Gabriel Tower-
son, *An Exposition of the Catechism of the Church of England. Part II* [1681],
p. 425, and *The Explanation of the Ten Commandments* [1796?], part 3, pp.
3–4). Though Defoe would not have agreed with these last opinions, he,
too, thought little of necessity as a reason or justification for criminal
behavior. "When Men are poor, and are found guilty of little Prevarica-
tions and Infractions of Principle, Necessity and Poverty is the Plea, and
passes with some People for an Excuse; though, by the Way," he wrote,
"it is no more so, than Poverty is a Plea at the *Old baily*, for committing a
Robbery or a Burglary" (*Complete English Tradesman*, 2nd. ed. [1727], vol.
2, part. 1, p. 20). Though he believed that "Necessity will make us all
Thieves," he did not believe people became necessitous innocently: "*the
Crime,*" he insisted, "*is in the Cause of that Necessity*" (the *Review*, 3:113a [7
March 1706], ed. Arthur Wellesley Secord [1938]; see Maximillian E. No-
vak, *Defoe and the Nature of Man* [1963], pp. 65–88, for a thorough discussion of Defoe's views on necessity). Despite the severity of all this discourse, pleas of necessity could apparently mitigate the decisions of the
courts on degrees of guilt and punishment. Thus Douglas Hay notes that
during periods of high food prices juries tended more often to convict on
reduced and so noncapital charges than when prices were low ("War,
Dearth and Theft in the Eighteenth Century: The Record of the English
Courts," *Past and Present* 95 [1982]: 154–55). On this same subject, see also
John Langbein's anecdotal evidence on recommendations for pardon ("Albion's Fatal Flaws," *Past and Present* 98 [1983]: 111–12, 113) and Peter
King's interpretation of sentencing statistics as indicating "general sympathies for destitute convicts and their innocent families" ("Decision-
Makers and Decision-Making in the English Criminal Law, 1750–1800,"
The Historical Journal 27 [1984]: 41–42). Whatever people may have *said*,
they seem nonetheless to have been able to entertain, at least at some level,
the possibility that individual criminals were not entirely at fault for their
crimes. For more on the possible disparity between public talk and private
feeling, see Chapter 7. For the social and economic factors that actually
influenced eighteenth-century crime rates, often unbeknownst to contemporaries, see Hay, "War, Dearth and Theft," pp. 122–46, and J. M. Beattie, "The Pattern of Crime in England," *Past and Present* 62 (1974): 84–95.

5   Lunacy gets even shorter shrift as a motive in the popular literature of
    crime, there being more than a few cases of its reporting criminals found

compos mentis despite extraordinary evidence to the contrary. One of the most lurid of these to my knowledge is the case of Edmund Audley, hanged in 1698 for the murder of Hannah Bullevant. Audley had a history of threatening people on the grounds they were conspiring against the Protestant Succession in the interests of the exiled King James. Fixing on Mrs. Bullevant, whom he saw at a meeting house, he bought pistols, stalked her through the streets, and shot her dead in the glover's shop where she had taken refuge when his first shot missed. His victim, he claimed, was Queen Mary, James's consort, and this was not the first time he had seen her in a London meeting house. He had also seen the Prince of Wales, James's son and heir, at the House of Commons. Convinced that his trial was part of the plot, he demanded to see King William to give him his information. Audley persisted in his "Whimsical Stories" even after he was found guilty, but the notion that he was "a Lunatick, or distracted Person," was utterly dismissed. The divines who gathered around him, hoping to bring him to a condign repentance, found only that he "much [depended] on his own conceited knowledge, and continued sullen and obstinate" (*Account of Audley* [1698], p. 8). Less spectacular instances of obvious insanity show the same tendency to discount madness as a source of crime. In 1712 Joseph Philips slit the throat of a six-year-old child because, he said, "he had a mind to die." "Several Witnesses endeavour'd to prove him lunatick, but by a great many others it appeared to be quite otherwise, and that he was rather sullen than mad" (*Compleat Tryals* [1718, 1721], 3:109). Philips was hanged in due course, as was the murderer of a five-year-old child in 1751, who "said, that about six Weeks before this Violence offered to the poor Infant, she had laboured under a severe Fever, which held her for three Weeks, which Nature at length got the better of, very little assisted by Physick. And she constantly affirmed, that from that Time she was always in a Hurry and Confusion of Spirits, and could have no Rest Day or Night, seldom shut her Eyes to sleep, or if she did, she was disturbed with Starts and Fears. She was continually running up and down Stairs, and could never sit down long to Business, her Spirits being continually agitated and flurried, but by what Means she could give no Account: She said, she had been several Times tempted to lay violent Hands on herself, at other Times on her own Children, of which she acquainted her husband, who only said she was whimsical or maggotty; but never took any Pains to find out the Cause of this Disorder in her Senses." "After the Warrant for Execution came down," the text adds, "she seemed much better . . . but could give no farther or better Account than as above" (*Select Trials* [1764] 2:126–27, 128). Such evidence must be treated carefully, for of course it deals only with criminals found guilty and punished. Lunacy was an allowable plea before the law in seventeenth- and eighteenth-century England, and it was not infrequently a successful defense (thus see Applebee's *Original Weekly Journal*, 25 July 1719 and 6 May 1721, for cases where criminals were judged lunatic, and also the standard history of the treatment of mental disorder in criminal law, Nigel Walker,

Crime and Insanity in England, vol. 1: *The Historical Perspective* [1968], esp. chaps. 2 and 3). My main point, however, is that the popular literature of crime was in no position to reopen the cases of criminals already hanged; in fact, it wanted to keep them closed. People were "executed for Murder . . . that others may fear to offend," writes J. Brydall, "and therefore a Man that is *non compos mentis* . . . is not . . . within the statute . . . for the end of punishment is that others may be deterred. . . . but such punishment can be no example to mad Men" (J[ohn] B[rydall], *A Compendious Collection of the Laws of England, Touching Matters Criminal* [1675], pp. 14, 114). We need only to consider the logic of this to see why, once they were executed, the insanity of lunatic criminals had to be disregarded.

6 *An Account of a Bold Desperate and Notorious Robbery* (1700), and *A Full and True Account of a Most Horrid and Barbarous Murder Committed Yesterday, April 24th* (1711). For similar sentiments, see *A True Account of a Bloody Murther Committed by Three Foot-Padders in Fig-Lane* (1685/6), p. 1; *An Account of the Malefactors That Received Their Majesties Most Gracious Pardon* (1693); and *The Life of Mr. Charles Drew* (1740), p. 3.

7 An earlier, more credulous age had been content to blame the Devil, and the law, always conservative, retained a trace of this belief. "Not having the fear of God before his/her eyes," bills of indictment typically ran, "but being moved by the instigation of the Devil," the prisoner before the bar had committed such-and-such a crime. How much this was only a figure of speech by the late seventeenth century is difficult to know; certainly it could not have had much explanatory power. "It is the Devil that animates men on to murther," declared one mid-seventeenth-century writer in no uncertain terms, but his description of the process leaves much to be desired: "when men, for want of Grace, do forsake God, God doth justly forsake them; and then the Devil enters into them, and carrieth them forth into all manner of wickedness." He is better when less prolix: "men kill and slay," he rhymes, "Their dearest Friends, the Devil to obey" (*The Devils Reign upon Earth, Being a Relation of Several Sad and Bloudy Murthers Lately Committed* [1655], pp. 10, [14]). It is a fact that certain murderers did lay their crimes to the Devil's power over them, even so late as the eighteenth century, and some claimed to have felt this power firsthand. "The Devil being strong with me, persuaded me to be revenged of her," explained John Marketman in 1680 after killing his wife (*A Full and True Account of the Penitence of John Marketman* [1680], pp. 4–50). When Paul Lorrain asked Mary Ellenor in 1708 how she could be "so cruel and hardhearted" as to suffocate her infant in a jakes, pushing him down with a broomstick when he continued to cry, she said "the Devil had too much power over her" (Lorrain, Ordinary Account, 27 October 1708). Such confessions were conventional enough, but sometimes the Devil could be reported to have taken on tangible form. In 1655 Theophilus Higgons sought to dispel a number of rumors about a murder committed in his neighborhood, one of them being that the Devil had appeared to the murderer "in a visible shape and that he had a conference with him"

(R[obert] Boreman, *A Mirrour of Mercy and Iudgement. Or, an Exact True Narrative of the Life and Death of Freeman Sonds Esquier* [1655], p. 20). In 1690 Edward Mangall claimed that he murdered Elizabeth Johnson because "the Devil put him upon it; appearing to him in a *Flash of Lightening*, and directing him where to find the *Club*, wherewith he committed the *Murder*" (*A Full and True Relation of the Examination and Confession of W. Barwick and E. Mangall, of Two Horrid Murders* [1690], p. 4). An even more bizarre story was told by Charity Philpot in 1681. "Being certainly Instigated by the Devil, and not having the fear of God before her eyes," she "on a sudden without cause given [had] rushed in upon her Mistress, who was in a Room with her Child . . . and told her Mistress, that she came to kill her, and then she would fire her House." Her mistress fled in fright but unfortunately left her child behind, and Charity slit its throat. Though she had nothing specific to say about the Devil, she did tell the people who seized her that "a Man in a High-crown'd Hat bid her to do it, and he had whetted the knife and put it into her hand, and also told her she should fire the House." How much her neighbors and friends were satisfied by such an explanation we have no way of telling, for Charity was found dead the next morning by her own hand and the case never came to trial (*Murther by a Maid Who Poysoned Her Self* [1681], pp. 1–2). Whether the Devil was accepted as a real force in human motivation or not, the mere concept of him could make for interesting stories. I particularly like the following example: "The Devil tempting a young man to one of these three sins, either to kill his Father, or else to lie with his mother, or else to be drunk; he thinking to yeeld to the lesser, namely to be drunk, that thereby he might (as he conceived) be freed from the other, which no doubt were then odious in his eyes, he yeelded to the Devil to be drunk, and then being drunk, he first killed his father, and after committed abomination with his mother" (*The Devils Reign* [1655], pp. 12–13). A version of this story appears in Defoe's *Colonel Jack* (1965; 1st pub. 1722), p. 241.

8 *Remarkable Criminals* (1735a), p. 20.

9 Ibid., pp. 136–37; see also *The Life of Mr. John Stanley* (1723), which serves as the source of the account quoted here and makes the same points at greater length and more vividly.

10 *The Suffolk Parricide, Being, the Trial, Life, Transactions, and Last Dying Words, of Charles Drew, of Long-Melford. . . . By a Gentleman of Long-Melford* (1740), pp. 3–6, 32–33. For other accounts of Drew, see *The Genuine Trial of Charles Drew. . . . By a Gentleman of Bury* (1740), and *The Life of Mr. Charles Drew* (1740). Consider also the account of Drew in *The Newgate Calendar* (1773), 3:3–9, which greatly simplifies Drew's motives, blaming the crime wholly on the instigations of his mistress, a greedy, sex-crazed widow.

11 Cf. not only Defoe's *Moll Flanders* (1722), *Colonel Jack* (1722), and *Roxana* (1724) but also plays like Edward Young's *The Revenge* (1721), Aaron Hill's *Fatal Extravagance* (1721, 1726), George Lillo's *The London Merchant* (1731), and Edward Moore's *The Gamester* (1753), each of which takes

pains to endow its leading wrongdoers with psychological case histories that, though often crude by modern standards, are more or less sufficient to explain their crimes; see, for example, Millwood's self-justifying speech in 4:2 of *The London Merchant*, which explains both her own corruption and her power over Barnwell.

12 *Remarkable Criminals* (1735a), p.324 (see also, e.g., pp. 54, 62, 114); pp. 83, 80.

13 Ibid., p. 156.

14 William Price, *The Birth, Parentage, and Education, Life and Conversation of Mr. Christopher Slaughterford* (1709), p. 2.

15 *The Suffolk Parricide* (1740), p. 7.

16 *A True and Perfect Relation of the Tryal and Condemnation, Execution and Last Speech of That Unfortunate Gentleman Mr. Robert Foulks* (1678/[9]), p. 4.

17 Johnson, *Highwaymen* (1734), pp. 316–17.

18 *Remarkable Criminals* (1735a), pp. 128, 451, 118.

19 S[amuel] Foote, *The Genuine Memoirs of the Life of Sir John Dinely Goodere, Bart. Who was Murder'd by the Contrivance of His Own Brother* (1741), pp. 7, 9, 9–10. The title page identifies Foote as "of Worcester-College, Oxford, and a Nephew to the late Sir John." For a fascinating account of the erratic (but in some ways typical) life of Sir John Dinely Goodere, and the complicated background to his murder, see Lawrence Stone, "Money, Sex and Murder in Eighteenth-Century England," in *Women and Society in the Eighteenth Century*, ed. Ian P. H. Duffy (1983), pp. 15–28.

20 [J. Penrose], *The Reverend Mr. Penrose's Account of the Behaviour, Confession, and Last Dying Words, of the Four Malefactors Executed at Bristol* (Bristol and London, 1741), pp. 11–12. Penrose prints Goodere's account of his part in Admiral Byng's expedition to Spain in 1719 and says that as a naval officer he "behaved with great gallantry and bravery." Penrose points out that he got his command by "merit and interest," and Goodere's own men had also a high opinion of him. At the trial an "abundance" of sailors appeared in his behalf, some testifying "in the most moving manner, that he was as gallant and brave a sailor as ever step [sic] between stem and stern of a ship, and he was so belov'd of them, that they would go to the mouth of a cannon to serve him" (pp. 6–7; *Trial of Goodere* [1741], p. 24).

21 *Remarkable Criminals* (1735a), pp. 292–93, 451, 241.

22 *Fair Warning to Murderers of Infants* (1692), p. [iii]; Edmund Kirk, *The Sufferers Legacy to Surviving Sinners: or Edmund Kirk's Dying Advice* (1684); *A Serious Advice to the Citizens of London* ([1657]; t.p. missing in Brit. Lib. copy), pp. [5–6], and also *The Unhappy Citizen* (1691), p. 9.

23 The "concept" of a separate criminal class, John J. Tobias suggests, "developed gradually after 1815" (*Crime and Industrial Society in the Nineteenth Century* [1972], pp. 59 ff.). If true, and the eighteenth century does seem to have lacked this concept, it is curious indeed that a class of professional criminals should have existed relatively unnoticed some 250 years before it was finally recognized as a social category in its own right; see also n. 26 to this chapter.

24 *Remarkable Criminals* (1735a), pp. 279, 150. "Let us labour to keep our selves from envie and hatred, and take heede of revenge," advise John Dod and Robert Cleaver, "and God will keepe us from committing murder. He that makes conscience and prayeth against the least, shall keepe himselfe safe from falling into the greatest" (*A Plain and Familiar Exposition of the Ten Commandments* [1635], p. 243). Cynthia Herrup has appropriately called such doctrine "a 'domino theory' of human character"; for its possible effect on the actual treatment of criminals within the legal process, see her article, "Law and Morality in Seventeenth-Century England," *Past and Present* 106 (1985): 102–23.

25 George Birkbeck Hill, ed., *Johnsonian Miscellanies* (1897), 2:285, and Boswell's *Life of Johnson*, ed. George Birkbeck Hill and L. F. Powell (1934), 3:271.

26 Smith includes "The Thieves' New Canting Dictionary" in the fifth edition of the *Highwaymen* (1719). Richard Head gives a word list of thieves' slang in part 1 of *The English Rogue* and claims "the first inventor of canting . . . was hanged about four-score years [ago]" (Richard Head and Francis Kirkman, *The English Rogue* [1928; 1st pub. 1665], pp. 29–34). Actually, Thomas Harman published a commentary on thieves' slang in 1566; see *A Caueat for Common Cvrsetors*, most recently rptd. by Gāmini Salgādo, ed., *Cony-Catchers and Bawdy Baskets* (1972). The existence of a criminal underworld – "these Rogues have a Society among themselves, over which they have a Principal, or President" – is indicated by *The Catterpillers of This Nation* (1659), p. 3, and also by *The Devils Cabinet Broke Open: Or a New Discovery of the High-Way Thieves* (1658), pp. 38–39; *The Life and Death of Mary Frith* (1662), p. 25; [Charles Hitchin?], *The Regulator: Or, a Discovery of the Thieves, Thief-Takers, and Locks, Alias Receivers of Stolen Goods* (1718); and of course all the accounts of Jonathan Wild stimulated by his arrest and execution in 1725.

27 Smith, *Highwaymen* (1719a), p. 304. It is typical, in fact, for thieves' lives to stress the rational calculation behind their actions. Unable to "confine himself in his Expences and Attendance, within the narrow bounds and limits of a Servant," and realizing "he must have some new way to get money," Duval is "not long unresolved what course to take, for being brought acquainted with a Knot of High-way-men, (having before observed their way of living) a little perswasion now serves his turn; he resolves to make one with Them" (*Life of Deval* [1669/70], p. 3). William Page shows even more deliberation. Before deciding to take to the highway, he "seriously consider'd the Hazards he must necessarily encounter" and his own fitness to deal with them: " 'Tis true, he was conscious that he had Courage enough. . . . But then, on the other Hand, he was equally sensible, that Courage was no Defence against the Chance Stroke of a Bullet." He is aware that highwaymen "seldom" escape hanging, but he sees "no other Way to extricate himself from [his present Distress]," and so, "being thus resolv'd, his first Care was to provide himself with a Brace of Pistols" (*Genuine Life of Page* [1758], pp. 4–5). For similar uses of the

word "resolved," see, for example, Smith, *Highwaymen* (1719a), pp. 26, 68, 223; James Guthrie, Ordinary Accounts, 13 February 1739, 16 September 1741; *Select Trials* (1742), 1:210.

28   As it happened, two of Dr. Johnson's closest friends, Savage and Baretti, came close to proving his point. Some years before Johnson met him, Savage killed a man during the course of a fight in a tavern. Found guilty of manslaughter, he was allowed to plead benefit of clergy and so escaped hanging (see *The Life of Mr. Richard Savage, Condemned for the Murder of Mr J. Sinclair* [1727], and also *Select Trials* [1742], 3:77–89). Baretti would seem a man far less likely to get in trouble with the law, but in eighteenth-century London even an Italian musicologist could find himself involved in a brawl, kill a man, be arrested, imprisoned, and tried for his life. Walking through the Haymarket, Baretti was accosted by a prostitute who squeezed his groin. He struck her, almost by reflex, and her bully, who was standing nearby, became threatening. Baretti tried to flee but was mobbed. His glasses broken, he slashed out desperately with a knife he normally carried to peel fruit, cut a man who bled to death, and was committed to Newgate. There Johnson visited him and, typically, advised him to anticipate the worst. At his trial Baretti was acquitted on grounds of self-defense, Johnson, Goldsmith, Burke, Reynolds, and Garrick all testifying to his good character and the court deciding there was nothing suspicious in an Italian carrying a knife to peel fruit (see Old Bailey Sessions Paper, 18–21, 23 October 1769).

29   In France, for instance, such descriptions are notably absent. Thus, despite a taste for "the horrible details" in sixteenth- and seventeenth-century accounts of various accidents and catastrophes, Jean-Pierre Seguin points out, the popular literature of crime "remain[s] fairly discreet about the circumstances of murders, often recounting them in a few lines" ("L'Information en France avant le périodique: 500 canards imprimés entre 1529 et 1631," *Arts et traditions populaires* 11 [1963]: 126). In my experience the point holds true for eighteenth-century French texts as well (for sample titles, see Chapter 5, n. 17).

30   For allegations of incest in the Hayes case, see *A Narrative of the Barbarous and Unheard of Murder of Mr. John Hayes, by Catherine His Wife* (1726), pp. 24, 27, 28. In their accounts of the Hayes case, *Remarkable Criminals* (1735a), pp. 327–50, and *The Newgate Calendar* (1773), 2:185–211, simply assert the filial connection between Catherine and her accomplice, claiming (incorrectly) that she acknowledged it but omitting all mention of incest. In 1722 Mathias Brinsden, who had murdered his wife, was "prest so much [by the Newgate ordinary] to own . . . Incest with his Daughter" that he and the other condemned prisoners complained they were being hindered in their efforts to come to terms with God (See R. Manson, *The Case of Mathias Brinsden*, rptd. in *Select Trials* [1742], 1:254). Eugene Aram was also accused of incest with his daughter, and credited as well with atheism: "Nor is it to be wondered at . . . that he . . . shou'd make no scruple of acting contrary to, and infringing on every law both human and divine"

(*The Genuine and Authentic Account of the Murder of Daniel Clarke* [1759], pp.
11–12). In 1708 a certain R.W. was accused of having committed incest
with his mother merely because he gathered and published the letters of
another man, who was about to be hanged for matricide (see R.W., *The
Case of John Palmer and Thomas Symonds* [1708], and *The Truth of the Case.
Or, a Full and True Account of the Horrid Murders, Robberies and Burnings,
Committed [by] John Palmer, and Tho. Symonds, Gent[s]., William Hobbins,
and John Allen, Labourers* [1708], p. 3).

31 Dickens, *The Mystery of Edwin Drood* (1956; 1st. pub. 1870), p. 225.

Part II
The Second Phase: Philanthropy and the Emergence of Criminology

Argument

OBSERVATIONS, &c.

S. ROMILLY

THERE is probably no other country in the world in which so many and so great a variety of human actions are punishable with loss of life as in England. These sanguinary statutes, however, are not carried into execution. For some time past the sentence of death has not been executed on more than a sixth part of all the persons on whom it has been pronounced, even taking into the calculation crimes the most atrocious and the most dangerous to society, murders, rapes, burning of houses, coining, forgeries, and attempts to commit murder. If we exclude these from our consideration, we shall find that the proportion which the number executed bears to those convicted is, per

4

haps, as one to twenty : and if we proceed still
further, and, laying out of the account burglaries, highway robberies, horse-stealing, sheep-
stealing, and returning from transportation,
confine our observations to those larcenies, un-
accompanied with any circumstance of aggravation, for which a capital punishment is appointed by law, such as stealing privately in
shops, and stealing in dwelling-houses and on
board ships, property of the value mentioned
in the statutes, we shall find the proportion of
those executed reduced very far indeed below
that even of one to twenty.

This mode of administering justice is supposed by some persons to be a regular, matured,
and well-digested system. They imagine, that
the state of things which we see existing, is exactly that which was originally intended; that
laws have been enacted which were never meant
to be regularly enforced, but were to stand as
objects of terror in our statute-book, and to be
called into action only occasionally, and under
extraordinary circumstances, at the discretion
of the judges. Such being supposed to be our
criminal system, it is not surprising that there
should have been found ingenious men to defend

5

and to applaud it. Nothing, however, can be more erroneous than this notion. Whether the practice which now prevails be right or wrong, whether beneficial or injurious to the community, it is certain that it is the effect not of design, but of that change which has slowly taken place in the manners and character of the nation, which are now so repugnant to the spirit of these laws, that it has become impossible to carry them into execution.

There probably never was a law made in this country which the legislature that passed it did not intend should be strictly enforced. Even the Act of Queen Elizabeth, which made it a capital offence for any person above the age of fourteen to be found associating for a month with persons calling themselves Egyptians, the most barbarous statute, perhaps, that ever disgraced our criminal code, was executed down to the reign of King Charles the first, and Lord Hale mentions 13 persons having in his time been executed upon it at one assizes. It is only in modern times that this relaxation of the law has taken place, and only in the course of the present reign that it has taken place to a considerable degree. If we look back to remote

6

times, there is reason to believe that the laws were very rigidly executed. The materials, indeed, from which we can form any judgment on this subject, are extremely scanty; for in this, as in other countries, historians, occupied with recording the actions of princes, the events of wars, and the negotiations of treaties, have seldom deigned to notice those facts from which can be best collected the state of morals of the people, and the degree of happiness which a nation has at any particular period enjoyed. Sir John Fortescue, the chief justice, and afterwards the chancellor of Henry VI., in a very curious tract on absolute and limited monarchy, in which he draws a comparison between England and France, says, that at that time more persons were executed in England for robberies in one year than in all France in seven. In the long and sanguinary reign of Henry VIII. it is stated by Hollinshed that 72,000 persons died by the hands of the executioner, which is at the rate of 2,000 in every year. In the time of Queen Elizabeth, there appears to have been a great relaxation of the penal laws, but not on the part of the crown; and Sir Nicholas Bacon, the lord keeper, in an earnest complaint which he makes to parliament on the subject, says,

7

" it remains to see in whose default this is;"
and he adds, " certain it is, that her Majesty
" leaveth nothing undone meet for her to do for
" the execution of laws;"* and it is related, that
in the course of her reign 400 persons were
upon an average executed in a year.

These statements, however, it must be admitted, are extremely vague and uncertain, and
it is not till about the middle of the last century
that we have any accurate information which
can enable us to compare the number capitally
convicted with the number executed. Sir Stephen Janssen, who was chamberlain of London,
preserved tables of the convicts at the Old
Bailey and of the executions. These tables
have been published by Mr. Howard, and they
extend from 1749 to 1772. From them it appears, that in 1749 the whole number convicted
capitally in London and Middlesex was 61, and
the number executed 44, being above two-thirds.
In 1750 there were convicted 84, and executed
56; exactly two-thirds. In 1751, convicted 85,
executed 63; about three-fourths. In the seven
years which elapsed, from 1749 to 1756 inclu-

* D'Ewes's Journ. 234.

8

sive, there were convicted 428, executed 306:
rather less than three-fourths. From 1756 to
1764, of 236 convicted, 139 were executed,
being much more than half. From 1764 to
1772, 457 were convicted, and of these 233
were executed; a little more than half. From
this period to 1802 there has not been published
any accurate statement on this subject. But
from 1802 to 1808 inclusive, there have been
printed, under the direction of the Secretary
of State for the Home Department, regular
tables of the number of persons convicted capitally; and of those on whom the law has
been executed; and from these we find, that
in London and Middlesex, the numbers are as
follows:

	Convicted.	Executed.		
In 1802	- - 97	- - 10	about	1-10th
1803	- - 81	- - 9	——	1-9th
1804	- - 66	- - 8	about	1-9th
1805	- - 63	- - 10	about	1-6th
1806	- - 60	- - 13	about	1-5th
1807	- - 74	- - 14	about	1-5th
1808	- - 87	- - 3	——	1-29th

Total - 528   67 rather more than 1-8th

9

It appears, therefore, that at the commencement of the present reign, the number of convicts executed exceeded the number of those
who were pardoned; but that at the present
time, the number pardoned very far exceeds the
number of those who are executed. This lenity I am very far from censuring; on the con-
traty, I applaud the wisdom as well as the humanity of it. If the law were unremittingly
executed, the evil would be still greater, and
many more offenders would escape with full
impunity: much fewer persons would be found
to prosecute, witnesses would more frequently
withhold the truth which they are sworn to
speak, and juries would oftener in violation of
their oaths acquit those who were manifestly
guilty. But a stronger proof can hardly be required than this comparison affords, that the
present method of administering the law is not,
as has been by some imagined, a system mature-
ly formed and regularly established, but that it
is a practice which has gradually prevailed, as
the laws have become less adapted to the state
of society in which we live.

There is no instance in which this alteration
in the mode of administering the law has been

10

more remarkable, than in those of privately
stealing in a shop or stable, goods of the value
of five shillings, which is made punishable with
death by the statute of 10 and 11 William III.,
and of stealing in a dwelling-house property of
the value of forty shillings, for which the same
punishment is appointed by the statute of 12
Ann, and which statutes it is now proposed to
repeal. The exact numbers cannot, from any
thing that has hitherto been published, be
correctly ascertained; but from Sir Stephen
Janssen's tables it appears, that after laying out
of the calculation the numbers convicted of
murder, burglary, highway robbery, forgery,
coining, returning from transportation, and
fraudulent bankruptcies, there remains convicted at the Old Bailey of shop-lifting and other
offences of the same nature, in the period from
1749 to 1771, 240 persons, and of those no less
than 109 were executed.

What has been the number of persons convicted of those offences within the last seven
years does not appear; but from the tables published under the authority of the Secretary of
State, we find that within that period there
were committed to Newgate for trial, charged

11

with the crime of stealing in dwelling-houses,
599 men and 414 women ; and charged with the
crime of shop-lifting, 506 men and 353 women;
in all 1,872 persons, and of these only one was
executed.

In how many instances such crimes have been
committed, and the persons robbed have not
proceeded so far against the offenders as even
to have them committed to prison: how many
of the 1,872 thus committed were discharged,
because those who had suffered by their crimes
would not appear to give evidence upon their
trial: in how many cases the witnesses who
did appear withheld the evidence that they
could have given: and how numerous were the
instances in which juries found a compassionate
verdict, in direct contradiction to the plain facts
clearly established before them, we do not know;
but that these evils must all have existed to a
considerable degree, no man can doubt.

Notwithstanding these facts, however, and
whether this mode of administering justice be
the result of design or of accident, there are
many persons who conceive that it is upon the
whole wise and beneficial to the community.

12

It cannot, therefore, but be useful to examine
the arguments by which it is defended. Discussions on such subjects are always productive
of good. They either lead to important improvements of the law, or they afford additional
reasons for being satisfied with what is already
established.

It is alleged by those who approve of the
present practice, that the actions which fall
under the cognizance of human laws are so varied by the circumstances which attend them,
that if the punishment appointed by the law
were invariably inflicted for the same species of
crime, it must be too severe for the offence,
with the extenuating circumstances which
in some instances attend it, and it must in
others fall far short of the moral guilt of the
crime, with its accompanying aggravations:
that the only remedy for this, the only way in
which it can be provided that the guilt and the
punishment shall in all cases be commensurate,
is to announce death as the appointed punishment, and to leave a wide discretion in the
judge of relaxing that severity, and substituting
a milder sentence in its place.

13

If this be a just view of the subject, it would render the system more perfect, if in no case specific punishments were enacted, but it were always left to the judge, after the guilt of the criminal had been ascertained, to fix the punishment which he should suffer, from the severest allowed by our law to the slightest penalty which it knows: and yet what Englishman would not be alarmed at the idea of living under a law which was thus uncertain and unknown, and of being continually exposed to the arbitrary severity of a magistrate? All men would be shocked at a law which should declare that the offences of stealing in shops or dwelling-houses, or on board ships, property of the different values mentioned in the several statutes, should in general be punished with transportation, but that the King and his judges should have the power, under circumstances of great aggravation, respecting which they should be the sole arbiters, to order that the offender should suffer death; yet such is in practice the law of England.

In some respects, however, it would be far better that this ample and awful discretion should be formally vested in the judges, than

14

that the present practice should obtain; for it would then be executed under a degree of responsibility which does not now belong to it. If a man were found guilty of having pilfered in a dwelling-house, property worth forty shillings, or in a shop that which was of the value only of five shillings, with no one circumstance whatever of aggravation, what judge whom the constitution had intrusted with an absolute discretion, and had left answerable only to public opinion for the exercise of it, would venture for such a transgression to inflict the punishment of death : but if in such a case, the law having fixed the punishment, the judge merely suffers that law to take its course, and does not interpose to snatch the miserable victim from his fate, who has a right to complain? A discretion to fix the doom of every convict, expressly given to the judges, would in all cases be most anxiously and scrupulously exercised; but appoint the punishment by law, and give the judge the power of remitting it, the case immediately assumes a very different complexion. A man is convicted of one of those larcenies made capital by law, and is besides a person of very bad character. It is not to such a man that mercy is to be extended; and, the sentence

15

of the law denouncing death, a remission of it must be called by the name of mercy ; the man, therefore, is hanged; but in truth it is not for his crime that he suffers death, but for the badness of his reputation. Another man is suspected of a murder, of which there is not legal evidence to convict him; there is proof, however, of his having committed a larceny to the amount of forty shillings in a dwelling-house, and of that he is convicted. He, too, is not thought a fit object of clemency, and he is hanged, not for the crime of which he has been convicted, but for that of which he is only suspected. A third upon his trial for a capital larceny attempts to establish his innocence by witnesses whom the jury disbelieve, and he is left for execution, because he has greatly enhanced his guilt by the subornation of perjured witnesses. In truth, he suffers death, not for felony, but for subornation of perjury, although that be not the legal punishment of this offence.

If so large a discretion as this can safely be intrusted to any magistrates, the legislature ought at least to lay down some general rules to direct or assist them in the exercise of it, that

16

there might be, if not a perfect uniformity in
the administration of justice, yet the same spirit
always prevailing, and the same maxims always
kept in view; and that the law, as it is executed,
not being to be found in any written code,
might at least be collected with some degree of
certainty from an attentive observation of the
actual execution of it. If this be not done, if
every judge be left to follow the light of his
own understanding, and to act upon the principles and the system which he has derived partly
from his own observation, and his reading,
and partly from his natural temper and his
early impressions, the law, invariable only in
theory, must in practice be continually shifting
with the temper, and habits, and opinions of
those by whom it is administered.   No man can
have frequently attended our criminal courts,
and have been an attentive observer of what
was passing there, without having been deeply
impressed with the great anxiety which the
judges feel to discharge most faithfully their
important duties to the public. Their perfect
impartiality, their earnest desire in every case
to prevent a failure of justice, to punish guilt,
and to protect innocence, and the total absence

17

with them of all distinctions between the rich
and the poor, the powerful and the unprotected,
are matters upon which all men are agreed. In
these particulars the judges are all actuated by
one spirit, and the practice of all of them is
uniform. But in seeking to attain the same object, they frequently do, and of necessity must,
from the variety of opinions which must be
found in different men, pursue very different
courses. The same benevolence and humanity,
understood in a more confined or a more enlarged sense, will determine one judge to pardon and another to punish. It has often happened, it necessarily must have happened, that
the very same circumstance which is considered
by one judge as matter of extenuation, is deemed by another a high aggravation of the crime.
The former good character of the delinquent,
his having come into a country in which he was
a stranger to commit the offence, the frequency
or the novelty of the crime, are all circumstances
which have been upon some occasions considered by different judges in those opposite lights:
and it is not merely the particular circumstances
attending the crime, it is the crime itself, which
different judges sometimes consider in quite different points of view.

C

18

Not a great many years ago, upon the Norfolk circuit, a larceny was committed by two men in a poultry yard, but only one of them was apprehended; the other having escaped into a distant part of the country, had eluded all pursuit. At the next assizes the apprehended thief was tried and convicted; but Lord Loughborough, before whom he was tried, thinking the offence a very slight one, sentenced him only to a few months imprisonment. The news of this sentence having reached the accomplice in his retreat, he immediately returned, and surrendered himself to take his trial at the next assizes. The next assizes came; but, unfortunately for the prisoner, it was a different judge who presided; and still more unfortunately, Mr. Justice Gould, who happened to be the judge, though of a very mild and indulgent disposition, had observed, or thought he had observed, that men who set out with stealing fowls, generally end by committing the most atrocious crimes; and building a sort of system upon this observation, had made it a rule to punish this offence with very great severity, and he accordingly, to the great astonishment of this unhappy man, sentenced him to be transported. While one was taking his departure for Botany Bay, the term of the other's impri-

19

sonment had expired; and what must have been the notions which that little public, who witnessed and compared these two examples, formed of our system of criminal jurisprudence?

In this uncertain administration of justice, not only different judges act upon different principles, but the same judge, under the same circumstances, acts differently at different times. It has been observed, that in the exercise of this judicial discretion, judges, soon after their promotion, are generally inclined to great lenity; and that their practical principles alter, or, as it is commonly expressed, they become more severe as they become more habituated to investigate the details of human misery and human depravity.

Let us only reflect how all these fluctuations of opinion and variations in practice must operate upon that portion of mankind, who are rendered obedient to the law only by the terror of punishment. After giving full weight to all the chances of complete impunity which they can suggest to their minds, they have besides to calculate upon the probabilities which there are, after conviction, of their escaping a

20

severe punishment; to speculate upon what
judge will go the circuit, and upon the prospect
of its being one of those who have been recently elevated to the bench. As it has been truly
observed, that most men are apt to confide in
their supposed good fortune, and to miscalcu-
late as to the number of prizes which there
are in the lottery of life, so are those dissolute
and thoughtless men, whose evil dispositions
penal laws are most necessary to repress, much
too prone to deceive themselves in their speculations upon what I am afraid they accustom
themselves to consider as the lottery of justice.

Let it at the same time be remembered, that it
is universally agreed, that the certainty of punishment is much more efficacious than any severity of example for the prevention of crimes.
Indeed this is so evident, that if it were possible
that punishment, as the consequence of guilt,
could be reduced to an absolute certainty, a
very slight penalty would be sufficient to prevent almost every species of crime, except those
which arise from sudden gusts of ungovernable
passion. If the restoration of the property stolen,
and only a few weeks, or even a few days
imprisonment, were the unavoidable conse-

21

quence of theft, no theft would ever be committed. No man would steal what he was sure that he could not keep; no man would, by a voluntary act, deprive himself of his liberty, though but for a few days. It is the desire of a supposed good which is the incentive to every crime: no crime, therefore, could exist, if it were infallibly certain that not good, but evil must follow, as an unavoidable consequence to the person who committed it. This absolute certainty, however, is unattainable, where facts are to be ascertained by human testimony, and questions are to be decided by human judgments. All that can be done is, by a vigilant police, by rational rules of evidence, by clear laws, and by punishments proportioned to the guilt of the offender, to approach as nearly to that certainty as human imperfection will admit.

There is another point of view in which this matter may be considered; and which will make it evident that it would be more expedient that the judges should have the power vested in them by law, of appointing the punishment of every offence after it had been established with all its circumstances in proof, and of proportion-

22

ing the particular nature and degree of the punishment to those circumstances, than that, for
such offences as I am speaking of, so severe a
punishment should be fixed by law, with a
power left in the judges according to circumstances, to relax it.   In the former case it is
highly probable that the discretion would in
practice be exercised by none but the judges,
that is, by magistrates accustomed to judicial
investigations, fully aware of the importance
of the duties which they are called on to discharge, and who from the eminence of their
stations, are, and cannot but be sensible, that
they are under a very great degree of responsibility to the public.   According to the practice which now prevails, this most important
discretion is constantly assumed by persons to
whom the constitution has not intrusted it, and
to whom it certainly cannot with the same
safety be intrusted; by prosecutors, by juries,
and by witnesses.   Though for those thefts
which are made capital by law, death is seldom
in practice inflicted; yet as it is the legal appointed punishment, prosecutors, witnesses, and
juries, consider death as that which, if it will not
with certainty, yet possibly may be the consequence, of the several parts which they have to

23

act in the judicial proceeding: and they act their parts accordingly, though they never can, in this indirect way, take upon themselves to prevent the execution of the law, without abandoning their duty; and in the case of jurymen and witnesses, without a violation of their oaths.

There is still another view which may be taken of this subject, and which is perhaps more important than those which have been already considered. The sole object of human punishments, it is admitted, is the prevention of crimes; and to this end, they operate principally by the terror of example. In the present system, however, the benefit of example is entirely lost, for the real cause of the convict's execution is not declared in his sentence, nor is it in any other mode published to the world. A man is publickly put to death. All that is told to the spectators of this tragedy, and to that part of the public who hear or who read of it, is, that he stole a sheep, or five shillings worth of goods privately in a shop, or that he pilfered to the value of forty shillings from his employer in a dwelling-house, and they are left in total ignorance that

24

the criminal produced upon his trial perjured witnesses to prove an alibi, or some other defence, and that it is for that aggravation of his crime that he suffers death. The example cannot operate to prevent subornation of witnesses to establish a false defence, for it is not known to any but those who were present at the trial, that such was the offender's crime ; neither can it operate to prevent sheep-stealing, or privately stealing in a shop, or larceny in a dwelling-house, because it is notorious that these are offences for which, if attended with no aggravating circumstances, death is not in practice inflicted. Nothing more is learned from the execution of the sentence, than that a man has lost his life because he has done that which by a law not generally executed, is made capital, and because some unknown circumstance or other existed either in the crime itself, or in the past life of the criminal, which in the opinion of the judge who tried him, rendered him a fit subject to be singled out for punishment. Surely if this system is to be persevered in, the judge should be required in a formal sentence to declare why death is inflicted, that the sufferings and the privations of the individual might be rendered useful to society in deterring others

25

from acting as he has done, and drawing on themselves a similar doom. The judge would undoubtedly be required to do this if the discretion which he exercises in point of fact, were expressly confided to him by law. But unfortunately, as the law stands, he is supposed not to select for capital punishment, but to determine to whom mercy shall be extended; although these objects of mercy, as compared with those who suffer, are in the proportion of six to one. Were recorded reasons to be required of the judge, it will be said, they must be his reasons for extending mercy, which is his act, not his reasons for inflicting punishment, which is the act of the law: an additional proof of the mischief which results from leaving the theory and the practice of the law so much at variance.

In truth, where the law which is executed is different from that which is to be found in the written statutes, great care should be taken to make the law which is executed known, because it is that law alone which can operate to the prevention of crimes. An unexecuted law can no more have that effect, than the law of a foreign country; and the only mode that can be

26

adopted for making known the law which is
executed, is that of stating in a written sentence
the circumstances which have rendered the
crime capital. Such written sentences, like the
reported decisions upon the common law, would
stand in the place of statutes. It must, however,
be admitted, that it would be still more desirable,
that instead of having recourse to such substitutes, the law should be embodied in written
statutes.

58

Of all the duties, indeed, which a judge has to
discharge, the exercise of this discretion must
be the most painful. It is true that there are
no duties, however awful, no situation, however difficult, with which long habit will not render the best of men familiar; but if we represent to
ourselves a judge newly raised to that eminence,
just entering upon the circuit, and become for
the first time the arbiter of the lives of his fel-
low-creatures, we shall be able to form to our-

59

selves some idea of the difficulties he has o encounter, and of the anxiety which he must necessarily feel.   Sworn to administer the law, he
is at the same time the depositary of that royal
clemency which is to interrupt its execution.
In danger of obstructing the due course of justice on the one hand, or of refusing mercy to
those who have a fair claim to it on the other,
he finds no rules laid down, or principles established by the legislature, to guide his judgment.
He must fix for himself the principles and the
rules by which he is to act, at the same time that
he is to apply them and bring them into action,
and yet he cannot but be aware, that the principles which he shall adopt will probably not be
those of his successor, who will have maxims
of justice and of mercy of his own, but which
cannot possibly be foreseen; and at the same
time he must know that it is nothing but a uniformity of practice which can make the exercise either of severity or of lenity useful to
the public.   In such a state of embarrassment, it
is, that he is called upon to decide, and upon his
decision the life of an individual depends; nay,
upon the decision of a single case may depend
the lives of many individuals.   The clemency
he shews, though it spares the life of a single

60

convict, may be the means of alluring others to the commission of the same crime, who from other judges will not meet with the same lenity. The execution of a severe judgment may be the means of procuring impunity to many other criminals by inducing prosecutors to shrink from their duty, and jurymen to violate their oaths.

From the foregoing observations it should seem, that the laws, which it is proposed to repeal, cannot well be defended as part of a general system of criminal jurisprudence. Taken by themselves, it seems still more difficult to justify them. They are of such inordinate severity, that, as laws now to be executed, no person would speak in their defence. They have, indeed, by a change of circumstances, become far more severe than they were when originally passed. Not to dwell on the circumstance of their severity having increased just in the proportion that the value of money has diminished, the state of the criminal law in other respects, at the time when these laws were enacted, afforded an excuse for passing them which has long ceased to exist,

When, in the reign of King William, the be-

61

nefit of clergy was taken away from the crime of privately stealing, in a shop, goods of the value of five shillings, that offence was already punishable capitally on all but those who could read. The statute had no other effect, therefore, than to place men, whose crime was aggravated by the education which they had received, upon a level with those who had to urge, in extenuation of their guilt, the deplorable ignorance in which they had been left by their parents and by the state.

The same observation cannot, indeed, be made on the Act of the 12th Anne, which relates to stealing money or goods in a dwelling-house: but when it passed, only seven years had elapsed since the adoption of the law, which extended the benefit of clergy to the illiterate, as well as to those who could read: and men who had been accustomed to see ignorant persons convicted capitally, for stealing what was of the value only of thirteen-pence, in any place, or under any circumstances, could not have thought it an act of great severity, to appoint death as a punishment for stealing in a dwelling-house property of the value of forty shillings.

62

It is sufficient, however, to say of those laws, that they are not, and that it is impossible that they should, be executed; and that instead of preventing, they have multiplied crimes, the very crimes they were intended to repress, and others no less alarming to society, perjury, and the obstructing the administration of justice.

But although these laws are not executed, and may be said, therefore, to exist only in theory, they are attended with many most serious practical consequences. Amongst these, it is not the least important, that they form a kind of standard of cruelty, to justify every harsh and excessive exercise of authority. Upon all such occasions these unexecuted laws are appealed to as if they were in daily execution. Complain of the very severe punishments which prevail in the army and the navy, and you are told that the offences, which are so chastised, would by the municipal law be punished with death. When not long since a governor of one of the West India islands was accused of having ordered that a young woman should be tortured, his counsel said in his defence, that the

63

woman had been guilty of a theft, and that by
the laws of this country her life would have
been forfeited.   When, in the framing new laws,
it is proposed to appoint for a very slight transgression a very severe punishment, the argument always urged in support of it is, that actions, not much more criminal, are by the
already existing law punished with death.   So
in the exercise of that large discretion which is
left to the judges, the state of the law affords a
justification for severities, which could not
otherwise be justified.   When for an offence,
which is very low in the scale of moral turpitude, the punishment of transportation for life
is inflicted, a man who only compared the crime
with the punishment, would be struck with its
extraordinary severity; but he finds, upon inquiry, that all that mass of human suffering
which is comprised in the sentence, passes by
the names of tenderness and mercy, because
death is affixed to the crime by a law scarcely
ever executed, and, as some persons imagine,
never intended to be executed.

For the honour of our national character—
for the prevention of crimes—for the mainte-

64

nance of that respect which is due to the laws, and to the administration of justice—and for the sake of preserving the sanctity of oaths— it is highly expedient that these statutes should be repealed.

§ 2. THE INDIGENT AND CRIMINAL CLASSES OF GREAT BRITAIN.

1. Indigent persons already stated to be objects of parochial relief   1,040,716

2. Mendicants, comprising *indigent and distressed beggars, sturdy beggars, trampers, persons* pretending to have been in the *army and navy,* lame and maimed, travelling all over the country, and using many devices to excite compassion, estimated, including their children, at about   50,000

3. *Vagrants,* under which description are to be included gypsies, and another race of vagabonds who imitate their manners, although not of that community, now become pretty numerous, wandering about the country with jack-asses, sleeping in the open air under hedges, and in huts and tents, loving idleness better than work, and stealing wherever opportunities offer; including wives and children, this class cannot amount to less, in every part of the country, than   20,000

4. *Idle and immoral persons,* who are able to work, but who work only occasionally, who neglect their families, and either desert them totally, or loiter away their time idly in alehouses, and half support them, leaving the deficiency to be scantily made up by the parishes — this class of depraved characters are pretty numerous, and in the whole country must exceed   10,000

5. *Lewd and immoral women,* who live wholly or partly by prostitution. It is impossible to ascertain their number in every part of the kingdom; but when it is considered how much female prostitution has increased in all the provincial towns of late years, particularly at the sea-ports and the large manufacturing towns (which, including the metropolis, comprise about one third of the population), and taking into account the prodigious number among the lower classes who cohabit together without marriage, and again separate when a difference ensues, it is perhaps not too much to say, that upon the whole there must be of both these classes of unfortunate females at least   100,000

6. *Persons described in the statute of 17 Geo. 2, as rogues and vagabonds,* comprising *wandering players of interludes at fairs, mountebanks, stage-dancers and tumblers, exhibiting in the open air, showmen, ballad-singers, minstrels with hurdy-gurdies and hand-organs,* etc. *vagabonds with dancing bears and monkies, low gamblers with E O tables, wheels of fortune,* and other seductive implements of gaming; *duffers with waistcoat pieces and other smuggled goods, and petty chapmen and low Jews,* with trinkets without licenses, alluring ignorant purchasers by apparent good bargains, and securing, notwithstanding, a large profit by giving change in bad money; *pretended horse-dealers* without licenses, exposing stolen horses for sale. All these different classes of vagabonds visit almost every fair and horse-race in the country, and live generally by fraud and deception. Foreign vagabonds, who also wander about the country, pretending to sell pictures, but who are also dealers in obscene books and prints, which they introduce into boarding-schools, on pretence of selling prints of flowers, whereby the youth of both sexes are corrupted, while at the same time some of these wanderers are suspected of being employed by the enemy as spies. The number of these different classes fluctuate, and cannot be easily ascertained, but it is probable they may amount upon the whole to   10,000

7. Lottery vagrants, or persons employed in procuring insurances during the drawing of the lotteries, or as proprietors of Little Go lotteries, confined chiefly to the metropolis. This class have fluctuated of late years; but they are still numerous, and perhaps may be fairly estimated, including male and female, at   10,000

8. *Criminal offenders,* comprising *highway robbers, footpad robbers, burglars, housebreakers, pick-pockets, horse-stealers, sheep-stealers, stealers of hogs and cattle, deer-stealers, common thieves, petty thieves, occasional thieves who cannot resist temptations, receivers of stolen goods, coiners of base money, venders and utterers of counterfeit bank notes, cheats, swindlers, embezzlers of goods and money, return transports,* and other offenders. When it is considered what a multitude of the offences above enumerated never come under the review of magistrates — the great number of larcenies which are never discovered, or concealed if found out, to avoid the trouble and expense of prosecution — it is more than probable, that upon the whole the number of persons who chiefly support themselves by criminal offences, must exceed, with their families ...   80,000

Total number presumed to live chiefly or wholly upon the labours of others   1,820,716

An extract from Patrick Colquhoun's *Treatise on Indigence,* 1806

[5]

PANOPTICON;

OR,

THE INSPECTION-HOUSE
JEREMY BENTHAM

LETTER I.
IDEA OF THE INSPECTION PRINCIPLE.

Crecheff in White Russia,
—— 1787.

Dear * * * *, — I observed t'other day in one of your English papers, an advertisement relative to a House of Correction therein spoken of, as intended for * * * * * * *. It occurred to me, that the plan of a building, lately contrived by my brother, for purposes in some respects similar, and which, under the name of the *Inspection House*, or the *Elaboratory*, he is about erecting here, might afford some hints for the above establishment.* I have accordingly obtained some drawings relative to it, which I here inclose. Indeed I look upon it as capable of applications of the most extensive nature ; and that for reasons which you will soon perceive.

To say all in one word, it will be found applicable, I think, without exception, to all establishments whatsoever, in which, within a space not too large to be covered or commanded by buildings, a number of persons are meant to be kept under inspection. No matter how different, or even opposite the purpose: whether it be that of *punishing the incorrigible, guarding the insane, reforming the vicious, confining the suspected, employing the idle, maintaining the helpless, curing the sick, instructing the willing* in any branch of industry, or *training the rising race* in the path of *education*: in a word, whether it be applied to the purposes of *perpetual prisons* in the room of death, or *prisons for confinement* before trial, or *penitentiary-houses*, or *houses of correction*, or *work-houses*, or *manufactories*, or *mad-houses*, or *hospitals*, or *schools*.

It is obvious that, in all these instances,

* The sudden breaking out of the war between the Turks and Russians, in consequence of an unexpected attack made by the former on the latter, concurred with some other incidents in putting a stop to the design. The person here spoken of, at that time Lieutenant-Colonel Commandant of a battalion in the Empress's service, having obtained a regiment and other honours for his services in the course of the war, is now stationed with his regiment in a distant part of the country.

the more constantly the persons to be inspected are under the eyes of the persons who should inspect them, the more perfectly will the purpose of the establishment have been attained. Ideal perfection, if that were the object, would require that each person should actually be in that predicament, during every instant of time. This being impossible, the next thing to be wished for is, that, at every instant, seeing reason to believe as much, and not being able to satisfy himself to the contrary, he should *conceive* himself to be so. This point, you will immediately see, is most completely secured by my brother's plan; and, I think, it will appear equally manifest, that it cannot be compassed by any other, or to speak more properly, that if it be compassed by any other, it can only be in proportion as such other may approach to this.

To cut the matter as short as possible, I will consider it at once in its application to such purposes as, being most complicated, will serve to exemplify the greatest force and variety of precautionary contrivance. Such are those which have suggested the idea of *penitentiary-houses:* in which the objects of *safe custody, confinement, solitude, forced labour*, and *instruction*, were all of them to be kept in view. If all these objects can be accomplished together, of course with at least equal certainty and facility may any lesser number of them.

LETTER II.
PLAN FOR A PENITENTIARY INSPECTION-HOUSE.

Before you look at the plan, take in words the general idea of it.

The building is circular.

The apartments of the prisoners occupy the circumference. You may call them, if you please, the *cells*.

These *cells* are divided from one another, and the prisoners by that means secluded from all communication with each other, by *partitions* in the form of *radii* issuing from the circumference towards the centre, and extending as many feet as shall be thought necessary to form the largest dimension of the cell.

The apartment of the inspector occupies the centre; you may call it if you please the *inspector's lodge*.

It will be convenient in most, if not in all cases, to have a vacant space or *area* all round, between such centre and such circumference. You may call it if you please the *intermediate* or *annular area*.

About the width of a cell may be sufficient for a *passage* from the outside of the building to the lodge.

Each cell has in the outward circumference,

a *window*, large enough, not only to light the cell, but, through the cell, to afford light enough to the correspondent part of the lodge.

The inner circumference of the cell is formed by an iron *grating*, so light as not to screen any part of the cell from the inspector's view.

Of this grating, a part sufficiently large opens, in form of a *door*, to admit the prisoner at his first entrance; and to give admission at any time to the inspector or any of his attendants.

To cut off from each prisoner the view of every other, the partitions are carried on a few feet beyond the grating into the intermediate area: such projecting parts I call the *protracted partitions*.

It is conceived, that the light, coming in in this manner through the cells, and so across the intermediate area, will be sufficient for the inspector's lodge. But, for this purpose, both the windows in the cells, and those corresponding to them in the lodge, should be as large as the strength of the building, and what shall be deemed a necessary attention to economy, will permit.

To the windows of the lodge there are *blinds*, as high up as the eyes of the prisoners in their cells can, by any means they can employ, be made to reach.

To prevent *thorough light*, whereby, notwithstanding the blinds, the prisoners would see from the cells whether or no any person was in the lodge, that apartment is divided into quarters, by *partitions* formed by two diameters to the circle, crossing each other at right angles. For these partitions the thinnest materials might serve; and they might be made removeable at pleasure; their height, sufficient to prevent the prisoners seeing over them from the cells. Doors to these partitions, if left open at any time, might produce the thorough light. To prevent this, divide each partition into two, at any part required, setting down the one-half at such distance from the other as shall be equal to the aperture of a door.

These windows of the inspector's lodge open into the intermediate area, in the form of *doors*, in as many places as shall be deemed necessary to admit of his communicating readily with any of the cells.

Small *lamps*, in the outside of each window of the lodge, backed by a reflector, to throw the light into the corresponding cells, would extend to the night the security of the day.

To save the troublesome exertion of voice that might otherwise be necessary, and to prevent one prisoner from knowing that the inspector was occupied by another prisoner at a distance, a small *tin tube* might reach from each cell to the inspector's lodge, passing across the area, and so in at the side of the correspondent window of the lodge. By means of this implement, the slightest whis-

per of the one might be heard by the other, especially if he had proper notice to apply his ear to the tube.

With regard to *instruction*, in cases where it cannot be duly given without the instructor's being close to the work, or without setting his hand to it by way of example before the learner's face, the instructor must indeed here as elsewhere, shift his station as often as there is occasion to visit different workmen; unless he calls the workmen to him, which in some of the instances to which this sort of building is applicable, such as that of imprisoned felons, could not so well be. But in all cases where directions, given verbally and at a distance, are sufficient, these tubes will be found of use. They will save, on the one hand, the exertion of voice it would require, on the part of the instructor, to communicate instruction to the workmen without quitting his central station in the lodge; and, on the other, the confusion which would ensue if different instructors or persons in the lodge were calling to the cells at the same time. And, in the case of hospitals, the quiet that may be insured by this little contrivance, trifling as it may seem at first sight, affords an additional advantage.

A *bell*, appropriated exclusively to the purposes of *alarm*, hangs in a *belfry* with which the building is crowned, communicating by a rope with the inspector's lodge.

The most economical, and perhaps the most convenient, way of *warming* the cells and area, would be by flues surrounding it, upon the principle of those in hot-houses. A total want of every means of producing artificial heat might, in such weather as we sometimes have in England, be fatal to the lives of the prisoners; at any rate, it would often times be altogether incompatible with their working at any sedentary employment. The flues, however, and the fire-places belonging to them, instead of being on the outside, as in hot-houses, should be in the inside. By this means, there would be less waste of heat, and the current of air that would rush in on all sides through the cells, to supply the draught made by the fires, would answer so far the purpose of ventilation. But of this more under the head of Hospitals.*

---

* There is one subject, which, though not of the most dignified kind, nor of the most pleasant kind to expatiate upon, is of too great importance to health and safe custody to be passed over unconsidered: I mean the provision to be made for carrying off the result of necessary evacuations. A common necessary might be dangerous to security, and would be altogether incompatible with the plan of solitude. To have the filth carried off by the attendants, would be altogether as incompatible with cleanliness; since without such a degree of regularity as it would be difficult, if not ridiculous, to attempt to enforce in case of health, and altogether impossible in case of sickness, the air of each cell, and by that means the

LETTER III.

EXTENT FOR A SINGLE BUILDING.

So far as to the characteristic parts of the principle of construction. You may now,

lodge itself would be liable to be kept in a state of constant contamination, in the intervals betwixt one visit and another. This being the case, I can see no other eligible means, than that of having in each cell a fixed provision made for this purpose in the construction of the building.

Betwixt every other two cells, at the end of the partition which divides them, a hollow shaft or tunnel is left in the brick-work of the exterior wall; which tunnel, if there be several stories to the building, is carried up through all of them.

Into this tunnel is inserted, under each cell, the bottom of an EARTHEN PIPE (like those applied in England to the tops of chimneys) glazed in the inside. The upper end, opening into the cell, is covered by a seat of cast-iron, bedded into the brick-work; with an aperture, which neither by its size nor shape shall be capable of admitting the body of a man. To gain the tunnel from the inside of the cell, the position of this pipe will of course be slanting. At the bottom of the tunnel, on the outside of the building, an arched opening, so low as scarcely to be discernible, admits of the filth being carried away. No one, who has been at all attentive to the history of prisons, but must have observed how often escapes have been effected or attempted through this channel.

A slight screen, which the prisoner might occasionally interpose, may perhaps not be thought superfluous. This, while it answers the purpose of decency, might be so adjusted as to prevent his concealing from the eye of the inspector any forbidden enterprise.

For each cell, the whole apparatus would not come to many shillings: a small consideration for a great degree of security. In this manner, without any relaxation of the discipline, the advantages of cleanliness, and its concomitant health, may be attained to as great a degree as in most private houses.

It would be regarded, perhaps, as a luxury too great for an establishment of this kind, were I to venture to propose the addition of a WATER-PIPE all around, with a cock to it in each cell. The clear expense would, however, not be quite so great as it might seem: since by this means a considerable quantity of attendance would be saved. To each prisoner, some allowance of water must necessarily be afforded, if it were only for drink, without regard to cleanliness. To forward that allowance by hand to two or three hundred prisoners in so many different apartments, might perhaps be as much as one man could do, if constantly employed. For the raising the water by pumps to necessary elevation, the labour of the prisoners would suffice.

As to the MATERIALS, brick, as every body knows, would be the cheapest in ***, and either brick or stone, in every other part of England. Thus much as to the shell. But in a building calculated for duration, as this would be, the expense of allowing the same materials to the FLOORS, and laying them upon ARCHES, would, I imagine, not be deemed an unsuitable one; especially when the advantage of a perfect security from fire is taken into the account.

perhaps, be curious to know to what extent a building upon this principle is capable of being carried, consistently with the various purposes to which it may come to be applied. Upon this subject, to speak with confidence belongs only to architects by profession. Indulge me, however, with a few words at a venture.

As to the *cells*, they will of course be more or less spacious, according to the employment which it is designed should be carried on in them.

As to the *whole building*, if it be too small, the circumference will not be large enough to afford a sufficient number of cells: if too large, the depth from the exterior windows will be too great; and there will not be light enough in the lodge.

As to this individual building of my brother's, the dimensions of it were determined by the consideration of the most convenient scantlings of the timbers, (that being in his situation the cheapest material,) and by other local considerations. It is to have two stories, and the diameter of the whole building is to be 100 feet out and out.

Merely to help conception, I will take this size for an example of such a building as he would propose for England.

Taking the diameter 100 feet, this admits of 48 *cells*, 6 feet wide each at the outside, walls included; with a *passage* through the building, of 8 or 9 feet.

I begin with supposing two stories of cells.

In the *under* story, thickness of the walls 2½ feet.

From thence, clear *depth* of each cell from the window to the grating, 13 feet.

From thence to the ends of the *partition walls*, 3 feet more; which gives the length of the *protracted partitions*.

Breadth of the *intermediate area*, 14.

Total from the outside of the building to the *lodge*, 32½ feet.

The double of this, 65 feet, leaves for the *diameter of the lodge*, 35 feet; including the thickness of its walls.

In the *upper* story, the *cells* will be but 9 feet deep; the difference between that and the 13 feet, which is their depth in the under story, being taken up by a *gallery* which surrounds the protracted partitions.

This gallery supplies, in the upper story, the place of an intermediate area on that floor; and by means of *steps*, which I shall come to presently, forms the communication between the upper story of cells to which it is attached, and the lower story of the cells, together with the intermediate area and the lodge.

The spot most remote from the place where the light comes in from, I mean the centrical spot of the building and of the lodge, will not be more than 50 feet distant from that place; a distance not greater, I imagine, than what is often times exemplified in churches; even in such as are not furnished in the manner of this building, with windows in every part of the exterior boundary. But the inspector's *windows* will not be more than about 32½ feet from the open light.

It would be found convenient, I believe, on many accounts, and in most instances, to make *one story* of the *lodge* serve for *two stories* of the *cells;* especially in any situation where ground is valuable, the number of persons to be inspected large, the room necessary for each person not very considerable, and frugality and necessity more attended to than appearance.

For this purpose, the *floor* of the *ground story of the lodge* is elevated to within about 4½ feet of the floor of the *first story* of the *cells.* By this means, the inspector's eye, when he stands up, will be on. or a little above, the level of the floor of the above mentioned upper story of the cells; and, at any rate, he will command both that and the ground story of the cells without difficulty, and without change of posture.

As to the *intermediate area*, the *floor* of it is upon a level, not with the *floor* of the *lodge*, but with that of the *lower story* of the cells. But at the *upper* story of the cells, its place, as I have already mentioned, is supplied by the above-mentioned *gallery;* so that the altitude of this area from the floor to the ceiling is equal to that of both stories of the cells put together.

The floor of the lodge not being on a level with either story of the cells, but between both, it must at convenient intervals be provided with flights of *steps*, to go *down* to the ground story of the cells by the intermediate area, and *up* to the first floor of the cells by the gallery. The ascending flights, joined to the *descending*, enable the servants of the house to go to the upper story of the cells, without passing through the apartment of the inspector.

As to the *height* of the whole, and of the several parts, it is supposed that 18 feet might serve for *the two stories of cells*, to be inspected, as above, by *one story* of the *lodge.* This would hold 96 persons.

36 feet for four stories of *cells*, and two of the lodge: this would hold 192 persons.

54 feet for six stories of the cells, and three of the lodge : this would hold 288 persons.

And 54 feet, it is conceived, would not be an immoderate elevation.

The drawings which, I believe, will accompany this, suppose *four* for the number of stories of the cells.

You will see, under the head of hospitals, the reasons why I conceive that even a less height than 9 feet, deducting the thickness of a floor supported by arches, might be sufficient for the cells.

The *passage* might have, for its *height*, either the height of one story, or of two stories of the cells, according as the number of those cells was two or four. The part over the passage might, in either case, be added to the lodge, to which it would thereby give a communication, at each end, with the world without doors, and ensure a keeper against the danger of finding himself a prisoner among his prisoners.

Should it be thought, that, in this way, the lodge would not have light enough, for the convenience of a man of a station competent to the office, the deficiency might be supplied by a void space left in that part, all the way up. You may call it if you please the *central area.* Into this space windows may open where they are wanted, from the apartments of the lodge. It may be either left *open* at the top, or covered with a *sky-light.* But this expedient, though it might add, in some respects, to the convenience of the lodge, could not but add considerably to the quantity and expense of the building.

On the other hand, it would be assistant to ventilation. Here, too, would be a proper place for the *chapel :* the prisoners remaining in their cells, and the windows of the lodge, which is almost all window, being thrown open. The advantages derivable from it in point of light and ventilation depending upon its being kept vacant, it can never be wanted for any profane use. It may therefore, with the greater propriety, be allotted to divine service, and receive a regular consecration. The *pulpit* and *sounding-board* may be moveable. During the term of service, the sky-light, at all other times kept as open as possible, might be shut.

LETTER IV.

THE PRINCIPLE EXTENDED TO UNCOVERED AREAS.

IN my two last letters, I gave you such idea as it was in my power to give you by words, of this new plan of construction, considered in its most *simple* form. A few more with regard to what further *extensions* it may admit of.

The utmost number of persons that could be stowed in a single building of this sort, consistently with the purposes of each several institution, being ascertained, to increase the number, that of the buildings must of course be increased. Suppose *two* of these *rotundas* requisite: these two might, *by a covered gallery* constructed upon the same principles, be consolidated into one inspection-house. And by the help of such a covered gallery, *the field of inspection* might be dilated to any extent.

If the number of rotundas were extended to *four*, a regular uncovered area might in that way be inclosed; and being surrounded by covered galleries, would be commanded in this manner from all sides, instead of being commanded only from one.

The area thus inclosed might be either *circular* like the buildings, or *square*, or *oblong*, as one or other of those forms were best adapted to the prevailing ideas of beauty or local convenience. A chain of any length, composed of inspection-houses adapted to the same or different purposes, might in this way be carried round an area of any extent.

On such a plan, either one inspector might serve for two or more rotundas, or if there were one to each, *the inspective force*, if I may use the expression, would be greater in such a compound building, than in any of the number singly taken, of which it was composed; since each inspector might be relieved occasionally by every other.

In the uncovered area thus brought within the field of inspection, out-door employments, or any employments requiring a greater covered space than the general form of construction will allow, might be carried on upon the same principle. A kitchen-garden might then be cultivated for the use of the whole society, by a few members of it at a time, to whom such an opportunity of airing and exercising themselves would be a refreshment and indulgence.

Many writers have expatiated with great force and justice, on the unpopular and unedifying cast of that undistinguishing discipline, which, in situation and treatment, confounds the lot of those who *may* prove innocent, with the lot of those who *have been* proved to be guilty. The same roof, it has been said, ought not to inclose persons who stand in predicaments so dissimilar. In a combination of inspection-houses, this delicacy might be observed without any abatement of that vigilance with regard to safe custody, which in both cases is equally indispensable.

LETTER V.

ESSENTIAL POINTS OF THE PLAN.

It may be of use, that among all the particulars you have seen, it should be clearly understood what circumstances are, and what are not, essential to the plan. The essence of it consists, then, in the *centrality* of the inspector's situation, combined with the well-known and most effectual contrivances for *seeing without being seen*. As to the *general form* of the building, the most commodious for most purposes seems to be the circular: but this is not an absolutely essential circumstance. Of all figures, however, this, you will observe, is the only one that affords a perfect view, and the same view, of an indefinite number of apartments of the same

dimensions: that affords a spot from which, without any change of situation, a man may survey, in the same perfection, the whole number, and without so much as a change of posture, the half of the whole number, at the same time: that, within a boundary of a given extent, contains the greatest quantity of room:—that places the centre at the least distance from the light:—that gives the cells most width, at the part where, on account of the light, most light may, for the purposes of work, be wanted:—and that reduces to the greatest possible shortness the path taken by the inspector, in passing from each part of the field of inspection to every other.

You will please to observe, that though perhaps it is the most important point, that *the persons to be inspected should always feel themselves as if under inspection*, at least as standing a great chance of being so, yet it is not by any means the *only* one. If it were, the same advantage might be given to buildings of almost any form. What is also of importance is, that for the greatest proportion of time possible, each man should actually *be* under inspection. This is material in *all* cases, that the inspector may have the satisfaction of knowing, that the discipline actually has the effect which it is designed to have: and it is more particularly material in such cases where the inspector, besides seeing that they conform to such standing rules as are prescribed, has more or less frequent occasion to give them such transient and incidental directions as will require to be given and enforced, at the commencement at least of every course of industry. And I think, it needs not much argument to prove, that the business of inspection, like every other, will be performed to a greater degree of perfection, the less trouble the performance of it requires.

Not only so, but the greater chance there is, of a given person's being at a given time actually under inspection, the more strong will be the persuasion—the more *intense*, if I may say so, the *feeling*, he has of his being so. How little turn soever the greater number of persons so circumstanced may be supposed to have for calculation, some rough sort of calculation can scarcely, under such circumstances, avoid forcing itself upon the rudest mind. Experiment, venturing first upon slight transgressions, and so on, in proportion to success, upon more and more considerable ones, will not fail to teach him the difference between a loose inspection and a strict one.

It is for these reasons, that I cannot help looking upon every form as less and less eligible, in proportion as it deviates from the *circular*.

A very material point is, that room be

allotted to the lodge, sufficient to adapt it to the purpose of a complete and constant habitation for the principal inspector or head-keeper, and his family. The more numerous also the family, the better; since, by this means, there will in fact be as many inspectors, as the family consists of persons, though only one be paid for it. Neither the orders of the inspector himself, nor any interest which they may feel, or not feel, in the regular performance of his duty, would be requisite to find them motives adequate to the purpose. Secluded oftentimes, by their situation, from every other object, they will naturally, and in a manner unavoidably, give their eyes a direction conformable to that purpose, in every momentary interval of their ordinary occupations. It will supply in their instance the place of that great and constant fund of entertainment to the sedentary and vacant in towns—the looking out of the window. The scene, though a confined, would be a very various, and therefore, perhaps, not altogether an unamusing one.

LETTER VI.

ADVANTAGES OF THE PLAN.

I FLATTER myself there can now be little doubt of the plan's possessing the fundamental advantages I have been attributing to it: I mean, the *apparent omnipresence* of the inspector (if divines will allow me the expression,) combined with the extreme facility of his *real presence.*

A collateral advantage it possesses, and on the score of frugality a very material one, is that which respects the *number* of the inspectors requisite. If this plan required more than another, the additional number would form an objection, which, were the difference to a certain degree considerable, might rise so high as to be conclusive: so far from it, that a greater multitude than ever were yet lodged in one house might be inspected by a single person; for the trouble of inspection is diminished in no less proportion than the strictness of inspection is increased.

Another very important advantage, whatever purposes the plan may be applied to, particularly where it is applied to the severest and most coercive purposes, is, that the *under* keepers or inspectors, the servants and subordinates of every kind, will be under the same irresistible controul with respect to the *head* keeper or inspector, as the prisoners or other persons to be governed are with respect to *them.* On the common plans, what means, what possibility, has the prisoner, of appealing to the humanity of the principal for redress against the neglect or oppression of subordinates in that rigid sphere, but the *few* opportunities which, in a crowded pri-

son, the most conscientious keeper *can* afford — but the none at all which many a keeper *thinks* fit to give them? How different would their lot be upon this plan!

In no instance could his subordinates either perform or depart from their duty, but he must know the time and degree and manner of their doing so. It presents an answer, and that a satisfactory one, to one of the most puzzling of political questions—*quis custodiet ipsos custodes?* And, as the fulfilling of his, as well as their, duty would be rendered so much easier, than it can ever have been hitherto, so might, and so should, any departure from it be punished with the more inflexible severity. It is this circumstance that renders the influence of this plan not less beneficial to what is called *liberty*, than to necessary coercion: not less powerful as a controul upon subordinate power, than as a curb to delinquency; as a shield to innocence, than as a scourge to guilt.

Another advantage, still operating to the same ends, is the great load of trouble and disgust which it takes off the shoulders of those occasional inspectors of a higher order, such as *judges* and other *magistrates*, who, called down to this irksome task from the superior ranks of life, cannot but feel a proportionable repugnance to the discharge of it. Think how it is with them upon the present plans, and how it still must be upon the best plans that have been hitherto devised! The cells or apartments, however constructed, must, if there be nine hundred of them (as there were to have been upon the penitentiary-house plan,) be opened to the visitors, one by one. To do their business to any purpose, they must approach near to, and come almost in contact with each inhabitant; whose situation being watched over according to no other than the loose methods of inspection at present practicable, will on that account require the more minute and troublesome investigation on the part of these occasional superintendents. By this new plan, the disgust is entirely removed, and the trouble of going into such a room as the lodge, is no more than the trouble of going into any other.

Were *Newgate* upon this plan, all Newgate might be inspected by a quarter of an hour's visit to Mr. Akerman.

Among the other causes of that reluctance, none at present so forcible, none so unhappily well grounded, none which affords so natural an excuse, nor so strong a reason against accepting of any excuse, as the danger of *infection*—a circumstance which carries death, in one of its most tremendous forms, from the seat of guilt to the seat of justice, involving in one common catastrophe the violator and the upholder of the laws. But in a spot so constructed, and under a

46   PANOPTICON; OR, THE INSPECTION-HOUSE.   [LETTER VII.

course of discipline so insured, how should infection ever arise? or how should it continue? Against every danger of this kind, what private house of the poor, one might almost say, or even of the most opulent, can be equally secure?

Nor is the disagreeableness of the task of superintendence diminished by this plan, in a much greater degree than the efficacy of it is increased. On all others, be the superintendent's visit ever so unexpected, and his motions ever so quick, time there must always be for preparations blinding the real state of things. Out of nine hundred cells, he can visit but one at a time, and, in the meanwhile, the worst of the others may be arranged, and the inhabitants threatened, and tutored how to receive him. On this plan, no sooner is the superintendent announced, than the whole scene opens instantaneously to his view.

In mentioning inspectors and superintendents who are such by office, I must not overlook that system of inspection, which, however little heeded, will not be the less useful and efficacious: I mean, the part which individuals may be disposed to take in the business, without intending, perhaps, or even without thinking of, any other effects of their visits, than the gratification of their own particular curiosity. What the inspector's or keeper's family are with respect to *him*, that, and more, will these spontaneous visitors be to the superintendent, — assistants, deputies, in so far as he is faithful, witnesses and judges, should he ever be unfaithful, to his trust. So as they are but there, what the motives were that drew them thither is perfectly immaterial; whether the relieving of their anxieties by the affecting prospect of their respective friends and relatives thus detained in durance, or merely the satisfying that general curiosity, which an establishment, on various accounts so interesting to human feelings, may naturally be expected to excite.

You see, I take for granted as a matter of course, that under the necessary regulations for preventing interruption and disturbance, the doors of these establishments will be, as, without very special reasons to the contrary, the doors of all public establishments ought to be, thrown wide open to the body of the curious at large — the great *open committee* of the tribunal of the world. And who ever objects to such publicity, where it is practicable, but those whose motives for objection afford the strongest reasons for it?

LETTER VII.

PENITENTIARY-HOUSES—SAFE CUSTODY.

DECOMPOSING the plan, I will now take the liberty of offering a few separate considera-

tions, applicable to the different purposes to which it appears capable of being applied.

A *Penitentiary-house*, more particularly is (I am sorry I must correct myself, and say, was to have been) what every prison might, and in some degree at least ought to be, designed at once as a place of *safe custody*, and a place of *labour*. Every such place must necessarily be, whether designed or not, an *hospital*—a place where sickness will be found at least, whether provision be or be not made for its relief. I will consider this plan in its application to these three distinguishable purposes.

Against *escapes*, and in particular on the part of felons of every description, as well before as after conviction, persons from the desperateness of whose situation attempts to escape are more particularly to be apprehended, it would afford, as I dare say you see already, a degree of security, which, perhaps, has been scarce hitherto reached by conception, much less by practice. Overpowering the guard requires an union of hands, and a concert among minds. But what union, or what concert, can there be among persons, no one of whom will have set eyes on any other from the first moment of his entrance? Undermining walls, forcing iron bars, requires commonly a concert, always a length of time exempt from interruption. But who would think of beginning a work of hours and days, without any tolerable prospect of making so much as the first motion towards it unobserved? Such attempts have been seldom made without the assistance of implements introduced by accomplices from without. But who would expose themselves even to the slightest punishment, or even to the mortification of the disappointment, without so much as a tolerable chance of escaping instantaneous detection?—Who would think of bringing in before the keeper's face, so much as a small file, or a phial of *aqua fortis*, to a person not prepared to receive any such thing, nor in a condition to make use of it?* Upon all plans hitherto pursued, the thickest walls have been found occasionally unavailing: upon this plan, the thinnest would be sufficient — a circumstance which must operate, in a striking degree, towards a diminution of the expense.

In this, as in every other application of the

---

* Should such strictness be thought requisite, visitors, if admitted into the intermediate area, might be precluded by a rail, from approaching nearer than to a certain distance from the cells; and, in some cases, all conversation between them and the prisoners might be interdicted altogether. The propriety of such a regulation may be thought to stand upon a different footing, according as the confinement were previous or subsequent to conviction, and according to the nature of the offence, and the intended severity of the punishment.

plan, you will find its lenient, not less conspicuous than its coercive, tendency; insomuch that, if you were to be asked who had most cause to wish for its adoption, you might find yourself at some loss to determine between the malefactors themselves, and those for whose sake they are consigned to punishment.

In this view I am sure you cannot overlook the effect which it would have in rendering unnecessary that inexhaustible fund of disproportionate, too often needless, and always unpopular severity, not to say torture—the use of *irons*. Confined in one of these cells, every motion of the limbs, and every muscle of the face exposed to view, what pretence could there be for exposing to this hardship the most boisterous malefactor? Indulged with perfect liberty within the space allotted to him, in what worse way could he vent his rage, than by beating his head against the walls? and who but himself would be a sufferer by such folly? Noise, the only offence by which a man thus engaged could render himself troublesome (an offence, by the bye, against which irons themselves afford no security,) might, if found otherwise incorrigible, be subdued by *gagging*—a most natural and efficacious mode of prevention, as well as punishment, the prospect of which would probably be for ever sufficient to render the infliction of it unnecessary. Punishment, even in its most hideous forms, loses its odious character, when bereft of that *uncertainty*, without which the rashest desperado would not expose himself to its stroke. If an instance be wanted, think what the means are, which the so much admired law of England makes use of, and that in one of its most admired branches, to work, not upon criminals, but upon its favourite class of judges? what but death? and that no common death, but death the slow but necessary result of lingering torture. And yet, whatever other reproach the law may be thought to merit, in what instance was it ever seen to expose itself in this way to the reproach of cruelty?

LETTER VIII.

USES — PENITENTIARY-HOUSES — REFORMATION.

IN my last, I endeavoured to state to you the advantages which a receptacle, upon the plan of the proposed building, seemed to promise in its application to places of *confinement*, considered merely in that view. Give me leave now to consider it as applicable to the joint purposes of *punishment, reformation,* and *pecuniary economy.*

That in regard to persons of the description of those to whom punishments of the nature in question are destined, solitude is in its nature subservient to the purpose of reformation, seems to be as little disputed, as its tendency to operate in addition to the mass of sufferance. But that upon this plan that purpose would be effected, at least as completely as it could be on any other, you cannot but see at the first glance, or rather you must have observed already. In the condition of *our* prisoners (for so I will call them for shortness sake) you may see the student's paradox, *nunquam minus solus quam cum solus,* realized in a new way: to the keeper, a *multitude,* though not a *crowd;* to themselves, they are *solitary* and *sequestered* individuals.

What is more, you will see this purpose answered more completely by this plan, than it could possibly be on any other. What degree of solitude it was proposed to reduce them to in the once-intended penitentiary-houses, need not be considered. But for one purpose, in buildings of any mode of construction that could then and there have been in view, it would have been necessary, according to the express regulations of that plan, that the law of solitude should be dispensed with; I mean, so often as the prisoners were to receive the benefits of attendance on Divine service. But in my brother's circular penitentiary-houses, they might receive these benefits, in every circumstance, without stirring from their cells. No thronging nor jostling in the way between the scene of work and the scene destined to devotion; no quarrellings, nor confederatings, nor plottings to escape; nor yet any whips or fetters to prevent it.

LETTER IX.

PENITENTIARY-HOUSES — ECONOMY — CONTRACT — PLAN.

I AM come now to the article of *pecuniary economy;* and as this is the great rock upon which the original penitentiary-plan I understand has split, I cannot resist the temptation of throwing out a few hints relative to the mode of management, which I look upon as the most eligible in this view; but which could not, as you will see, have been established with anything like the advantage, upon any other ground than that of my brother's inspection principle.

To come to the point at once, I would do the whole by *contract.* I would farm out the profits, the no-profits, or if you please the losses, to him who, being in other respects unexceptionable, offered the best terms. Undertaking an enterprise new in its extent, in the description of the persons to be subjected to his management, and in many other circumstances, his success in it, if he does succeed, may be regarded in the light of an invention, and rewarded accordingly, just as success in other inventions is rewarded, by the profit which a monopoly secured by patent enables a man to make; and that in proportion to the success which constitutes their merit. He should have it during *good behaviour;* which you know is as much as to say, unless specific instances of misbehaviour, flagrant enough to render his removal expedient, be proved on him in a legal way, he shall have it for his *life.* Besides that when thus secured he can afford to give the better price for his bargain, you will presently see more material reasons to counterbalance the seeming unthriftiness of granting him a term, which may prove so long a one. In other respects, the terms of the contract must, of course, depend upon the proportion of capital, of which the contract gave him the use. Supposing the advance to amount to the whole manufacturing stock, he must of course either pay something for his contract, or be contented with a *share* of the gross profits, instead of the whole, unless that from such profits an interest upon the capital so advanced to him should be deducted: in which case, nobody, I suppose, would grudge him the whole net profit after such deduction, even though the rate of interest were much below the ordinary one: the difference between such reduced rate of interest and the ordinary one, would constitute the whole of the expense which the public would be at. Suppose, to speak at random, this expense were to amount to £6000, £8000, or £10,000 a-year, for the 3000 convicts which, it was computed, would be the standing number to be maintained in England,* I should not imagine that such a sum as even this latter would be much grudged. I fancy the intended expedition to Botany Bay, of which I am just apprized, will be rather more expensive. Not that it appears to me that the nation would remain saddled with any such expense as this at the long run, or indeed with any part of it. But of this hereafter.

In the next place, I would give my contractor all the *powers* that his interest could prompt him to wish for, in order to enable him to make the most of his bargain, with only some slight reservations, which I will mention afterwards; for very slight ones you will find they will be, that can be needful or even serviceable in the view of preventing abuse.

But the greater latitude he has in taking such measures, the less will he grudge the letting it be known what the measures are which he *does* take, knowing, at the same time, that no advantage can be taken of such knowledge, by turning him out in case of his

* According to the hard-labour bill, 2865. See the table to my View of that bill: since then, I fear, the number has rather increased than diminished.

success, and putting in another to reap the fruits of his contrivance. I will then require him to *disclose,* and even to print and *publish* his accounts — the whole process and detail of his management — the whole history of the prison. I will require him, I say, on pain of forfeiture or other adequate punishment, to publish these accounts, and that upon oath. I have no fear of his not publishing *some* accounts, because, if the time is elapsed and some accounts not published—a fact not liable to dispute — the punishment takes place of course: and I have not much fear that the accounts, when published, will not be *true;* because, having power to do every thing that is for his advantage, there is nothing which it is his interest to conceal; and the interest which the punishment for perjury gives him not to conceal, is manifest, more especially as I make him examinable and cross-examinable *viva voce* upon oath at any time.

It is for clearing away as much as possible every motive of pecuniary interest that could prompt him to throw any kind of cloak or reserve upon any of his expedients for increasing his profits, that I would insure them to him for *life.*

From the information thus got from him, I derive this advantage. In the case of his *ill* success, I see the causes of it, and not only I, but every body else that pleases, may see the causes of it; and amongst the rest, those who, in case of their taking the management out of his hands, would have an interest in being acquainted with such causes, in order to obviate or avoid them. More than that, if his ill success is owing to incapacity, and that incapacity such as, if continued, might raise my expense above the calculation, I can make him stop in time—a measure to which he can have as little objection as myself; for it is one advantage of this plan, that whatever mischief happens must have more than eaten out all *his* profits before it reaches *me.*

In the case of his good success, I see the causes of that too; and every body sees them, as before; and, amongst others, all persons who could propose to themselves to get into a situation similar to his, and who in such case would naturally promise themselves, in the event of their getting into his situation, a success equal to his — or rather superior; for such is the presumption and vanity natural to man.

Without such publication, whom should I have to deal with, besides him? certainly, in comparison, but a very few; not many more than I may have had at first: the terms, of course, disadvantageous as at first; for disadvantageous terms at first, while all is yet in darkness, they certainly must be.

After such publication, whom should I have then? I should have every body; every body who, by fortune, experience, judgment, disposition, should conceive himself able, and find himself inclined, to engage in such a business : and each person seeing what advantage had been made, and how, would be willing to make his offer in proportion. What situation more favourable for making the best terms ?

These best terms, then, I should make at his death, even for his establishment ; but long before that, had I others upon the carpet, I should make similar good terms for all those others. Thus I make his advantage mine, not only after it has ceased to be his, but almost as soon as it commences so to be : I thus get his success in all the rest, by paying for it only in the one ; and in that not more than it was necessary to pay for it.

But *contractors*, you will say perhaps, or at least if you don't, there are enough that will, " *are a good-for-nothing set of people ; and why should we be fleeced by them ? One of them perjured himself not long ago, and we put him into the pillory. They are the same sort of gentry that are called farmers-general in France, and publicans in the Gospel, where they are ranked with sinners ; and nobody likes them anywhere.*" All this, to be sure, is very true : but if you put one of them into the *pillory*, you put another of them into the *post-office* ; and if in the devoted city five righteous would have screened the whole gang from the perdition called for by the enormities of ninety-five unrighteous, why should not the merits of one Palmer be enough to make it up for the demerits of twenty Atkinsons ? Gentlemen in general, as I have had manifold occasion to observe, love close reasoning, and here they have it. It might be thought straying from the point, if I ventured to add, that gentlemen in the corn trade, or in any other trade, have not commonly quite so many witnesses to *their bargains*, as my contractor would have to the management of his house.

[6]

A

TREATISE ON INDIGENCE

P. COLQUHOUN, Esq. L.L.D.

It is probable that the indigent of the present period (including all descriptions) are not only upon the whole less moral; but also, from more dissolute habits, less frugal, than a century ago: and there is no doubt also, that they experience more attention, and much greater assistance than was afforded to the same class at that period; yet, notwithstanding the

33   * See page 36.

34   PRELIMINARY ELUCIDATIONS.

enormous sums expended, it has been already seen, and will be further disclosed in the progress of this work, how much the evil has increased, and also the mass of turpitude which envelopes the chief part of the indigent who are assisted or supported by parochial assessments and private benevolence.

It is a generally received observation, that where-ever riches are placed in one scale, the apparent good is counterbalanced by an increased quantum of profligacy and crimes in the other : excessive luxury and dissipation—an indulgence in all those gratifications which too often afford a momentary pleasure followed up by permanent pain ; holding out examples to the thoughtless and inconsiderate to follow courses of extravagance which they can-not support, and producing ultimately the miseries of a prison, the pursuits of a gaming-table, or cri-minal delinquency, as a resource for subsistence.

The force of example works its way through all ranks of society, while in the superabundant circu-lation of riches, the gains of the low gambler, the swindler, the common prostitute, and the criminal offender, increase as the wealth of the nation is augmenting. It descends even to the lowest classes of society, who indulge in luxuries little known a century ago *.   Those who have been carelessly or viciously educated, or who, from habits of idle-

---

* *Tea, sugar, tobacco, malt liquor,* and *corn spirits,* are now immense articles of consumption among the inferior classes of society : taking quantity and value together, they have perhaps increased twenty fold in the course of a century.

PRELIMINARY ELUCIDATIONS.   35

ness, are indisposed to labour, find by various means a source of subsistence produced by an extensive circulation of property, diverted into numerous channels, where even the highway robber and the burglar are enabled to live, by various devices, which did not heretofore exist, and which they naturally prefer to the risks attending the extortion of money by acts of violence constituting capital offences; and hence it is that such offences have been gradually diminishing within the last fifty years; while the general turpitude of the idle and dissolute is increasing every day in other channels, equally injurious to the privileges of innocence, although in its aspect less terrific.

In contemplating the state of the indigent, there is perhaps more to be dreaded from the increasing depravity of manners than from the great expense incurred in supporting them, enormous as it certainly is,—and rapid as its growth has been within the last fourteen years.

Like the progress of vice and dissipation, it seems to have kept pace with the increase of the wealth and commerce of the country, as will be seen from the following table.

c

TABLE, *shewing the progressive Rise of the Poor's Rate, Revenue, national Debt, and Commerce, from 1673 to 1803—being 130 Years.*

Years.	Poor's Rate. £.	Years.	Revenue. £.	Years.	National Debt. £.	Years.	Custom-house Value of Cargoes exported. £.	Population.
1673	840,000	Average in Charles ii.'s Reign.	1,800,000	—	—	1663 } 1669	2,043,043	5,000,000
1677	608,333					1688	4,086,087	5,000,000
1677	700,000	1689	2,001,855	—	—	1697	3,525,907	5,400,000
1685	665,362		—	1689	664,263	1700	6,045,432	5,475,000
1698	819,000	1701	3,895,285	1701	16,394,702			
1700	1,000,000	1710	5,691,803	1714	54,145,363	1709	5,913,357	5,240,000
Queen Anne's Reign	1,000,000	1759	8,523,540	1748 } 1775	78,293,313 } 135,943,051	1749 } 1751	12,599,112	6,467,000
1751	3,000,000	1776	10,265,405			1776	14,755,699	7,600,000
1776	1,720,316	1786	15,096,112 Gross	1784	257,213,043	1786	16,300,725	8,016,000
1783	2,167,749	1783	37,996,088	1803	567,050,606	1783	34,953,000	9,000,000
1784								
1785								
1803	5,348,205							

* The first seven sums under the column Poor Rates, are given on the authority of different writers, and can be considered as nothing more than *estimates*, although from the accuracy of many of the authors they are supposed to be pretty near the truth.

† The price of grain was very high in the year 1751. Mr. Alcock, a respectable writer of that period, states, that the whole sum laid out on the poor for four years preceding 1752, amounted at a medium to £3,000,000 a year.

‡ The last three sums are taken from the Parliamentary Returns.

Thus it appears that the revenue, the national debt, and the commerce of the country, have nearly kept pace with the advance in the rates for the support of the indigent; but these rates have of late years far outstretched the increase of the population; and, indeed, it must be a matter of astonishment to all Europe, how such a population, which (including the increase from 1801 to 1803) can scarcely be supposed to exceed nine millions of people, constantly resident in England and Wales, can support such an establishment.

While so large a proportion of the people * are wholly or partly fed and clothed at the expense of the public, whose labour is totally unproductive to the state, the industry and enterprise of those who support them are certainly beyond all ex-

---

* *The following results are extracted from the Parliamentary Abstracts in* 1803 :

Paupers relieved out of work-houses, not including children — —		336,199
Pauper children under 5 years relieved	120,236	
Pauper children from 5 to 14 years relieved — — —	194,914	
		315,150
Paupers relieved in work-houses, including children — — — —		83,468
		734;817
Paupers, supposed chiefly to be mendicants, occasionally relieved — — —		305,899
Total		1,040,716

c 2

38   PRELIMINARY ELUCIDATIONS.

ample in the history of the world. With what astonishment would the writers of the 17th and the early part of the 18th centuries, who exclaimed so vehemently against the excessive burdens of the poor, behold the present state of things! The evil is, notwithstanding, as excessive as the means of finding an effectual remedy are difficult.

The calamity is also greatly heightened, not so much by the contemplation of the casualties and misfortunes, and, in many instances, the corruption of morals which have produced this mass of *indigence*, as by the numerous ramifications of moral depravity, which are disclosed in the following collected view of the different classes whose vices and criminal pursuits also render them a burden on the innocent and industrious part of the community.

1. *Indigent persons* already stated to be objects of parochial relief   —   —   1,040,716
2. *Mendicants*, comprising *indigent and distressed beggars, sturdy beggars, trampers,* persons pretending to have been *in the army and navy*, lame and maimed, travelling all over the country, and using many devices to excite compassion, estimated, including their children, at about   *50,000

Carried over   1,090,716

* His Majesty's Principal Secretary of State for the Home Department having authorized Matthew Martin, Esq. of Westminster, to ascertain the state of mendicity in the metropolis, he

Brought over   1,090,716

3. *Vagrants,* under which description are to be included gypsies, and another race of vagabonds who imitate their manners, although not of that community, now become pretty numerous, wandering about the country with jack-asses, sleeping in the open air under hedges, and in huts

Carried over   1,090,716

followed up his inquiries for several years with the most meritorious zeal and perseverance, until the end of the year 1802, when his report, which was published in March 1803, disclosed the following interesting facts :

	Adults.	Children.	Total.
1. That the mendicants belonging to parishes in the metropolis and its vicinity who solicited alms in the streets, amounted to	2541	4152	6693
2. Vagrants belonging to distant parishes having settlements	1137	1467	2604
3. Irish vagrants having no settlements	2037	3273	5310
4. Scotch vagrants, idem	195	309	504
5. Foreign vagrants, idem	90	87	177
	6000	9288	15,288

Mr. Martin estimates the sums extorted from the public by the above mendicants at £97,126 a year—thus:

	£.	s.	d.
6000 adults at 6*d.* a day each, lodging and clothes inclusive	54,750	0	0
9288 children at 3*d.* a day, idem	42,376	0	0
	97,126	0	0

He supposes however that the professed and systematic beggars seldom obtained less than 3*s.* to 3*s.* 6*d.* a day on an average, and he estimates the number of this class at 2000 at all times, who lay the public under contribution to the extent £300 per diem, or about £90,000 a year!

c 3

Brought over	1,090,716

and tents, loving idleness better than work, and stealing wherever opportunities offer :—including wives and children, this class cannot amount to less, in every part of the country, than   —   —   **20,000**

4. *Idle and immoral persons*, who are able to work, but who work only occasionally, who neglect their families, and either desert them totally, or loiter away their time idly in alehouses, and half support them, leaving the deficiency to be scantily made up by the parishes—this class of depraved characters are pretty numerous, and in the whole country must exceed   —   **10,000**

5. *Lewd and immoral women*, who live wholly or partly by prostitution. It is impossible to ascertain their number in every part of the kingdom : but when it is considered how much female prostitution has increased in all the provincial towns of late years, particularly at the sea-ports and the large manufacturing towns (which, including the metropolis, comprise about one third of the population), and taking into the account the prodigious number among the lower classes who cohabit together without marriage, and again separate when a difference ensues, it is perhaps not too much to say, that upon the whole there must be of both these classes of unfortunate females at least   —   —   —   —   **100,000**

Carried over	1,220,716

PRELIMINARY ELUCIDATIONS. 41

Brought over   1,220,716

6. *Persons described in the statute of 17 Geo. II. as rogues and vagabonds,* comprising wandering players of interludes at fairs, *mountebanks, stage-dancers and tumblers exhibiting in the open air, showmen, ballad-singers, minstrels with hurdy-gurdies and hand-organs, &c. vagabonds with dancing bears and monkies, low gamblers with E O tables,* wheels of fortune, and other seductive implements of gaming; *duffers* with waistcoat pieces and *other smuggled goods, and petty chapmen and low Jews,* with trinkets without licenses, alluring ignorant purchasers by apparent good bargains, and securing, notwithstanding, a large profit by giving change in bad money; *pretended horse-dealers* without licenses, exposing stolen horses for sale. All these different classes of vagabonds visit almost every fair and horse-race in the country, and live generally by fraud and deception. Foreign vagabonds, who also wander about the country, pretending to sell pictures, but who are also dealers in obscene books and prints, which they introduce into boarding-schools, on pretence of selling prints of flowers, whereby the youth of both sexes are corrupted, while at the same time some of these wanderers are suspected of being employed by the enemy

Carried over   1,220,716

42   PRELIMINARY ELUCIDATIONS.

Brought over	1,220,716

as spies. The number of these different
classes fluctuate, and cannot be easily ascertained, but it is probable they may
amount upon the whole to   —   —   10,000

7. *Lottery vagrants,* or persons employed
in procuring insurances during the drawing of the lotteries, or as proprietors of
Little Go lotteries, confined chiefly to the
metropolis. This class have fluctuated of
late years ; but they are still numerous,
and perhaps may be fairly estimated, including male and female, at   —   10,000

8. *Criminal offenders,* comprising *highway
robbers, footpad robbers, burglars, housebreakers, pickpockets, horse-stealers, sheep-
stealers, stealers of hogs and cattle, deer-
stealers, common thieves, petty thieves,
occasional thieves who cannot resist temptations, receivers of stolen goods, coiners
of base money, venders and utterers of
base coin, forgers of all descriptions,
utterers of counterfeit bank notes, cheats,
swindlers, embezzlers of goods and
money, return transports,* and other offenders. When it is considered what a
multitude of the offences above enumerated never come under the review of magistrates—the great number of larcenies
which are never discovered, or concealed
if found out, to avoid the trouble and expense of prosecution—-it is more than

Carried over	1,240,716

PRELIMINARY ELUCIDATIONS. 43

Brought over	1,240,716
probable, that upon the whole the number of persons who chiefly support themselves by criminal offences, must exceed, with their families — — —	*80,000
Total number presumed to live chiefly or wholly upon the labour of others —	1,320,716

In order still further to elucidate in some degree this general view of the immoral and criminal pursuits of, alas! too many individuals who compose the body politic, it may not be inapplicable to the object in contemplation, of investigating the means of providing a remedy, to insert the following authentic statement of the number of criminal offenders who were committed to the several gaols of England and Wales for trial in the year 1805,

---

* It is not however to be inferred from this aggregate view of indigence, idleness, and turpitude, notwithstanding the shocking deformity which it exhibits, that the morals of the nation at large are worse than those of many of the countries in Europe. Were it possible to take a similar view of the state of society in France and other countries depending on it, the result would undoubtedly be more shocking, and the turpitude even more extensive in proportion to the population. The evils as they relate to England are chiefly to be attributed to the great deficiency of the laws, which have done enough to punish, but little to prevent criminal offences. A remedy may be found in the improvement of the police system, while in the mean time the evil is in some degree counterbalanced by a greater portion of active benevolence, humanity, charity, and other virtues among the innocent part of the community than are to be found in any other country in the world.

44   PRELIMINARY ELUCIDATIONS.

at the Old Bailey and the assizes ; but as it does
not include those committed during the same period for minor criminal offences cognizable by the
justices, assembled in their general and quarter
sessions, which are upon the whole nearly as numerous as those tried at the superior courts, an
estimate is attempted in round numbers of these
also, and likewise of the commitments and discharges by justices out of sessions of numerous
persons accused of criminal offences, and not ultimately sent for trial for want of legal evidence,
including those culprits who are convicted of misdemeanors or lesser crimes by summary process.

PRELIMINARY ELUCIDATIONS. **45**

Number of Persons committed in each County in England and Wales for Trial at the Old Bailey and the Assizes, in the Year 1805.

Counties. England.	Males.	Females.	Total of Males and Females.	Population of each County.
Middlesex —	732	485	1217	818,129
Lancaster —	206	165	371	672,731
York — —	181	64	245	858,892
Kent — —	169	41	210	307,624
Surrey — —	147	52	199	269,043
Norfolk —	114	49	163	273,371
Warwick —	120	40	160	208,190
Hants — —	105	42	147	219,656
Essex — —	127	17	144	226,437
Gloucester, including Bristol —}	108	33	141	250,809
Suffolk — —	96	13	109	210,431
Somerset —	79	27	106	273,750
Sussex — —	93	12	105	159,311
Devon — —	69	27	96	343,001
Stafford — —	67	24	91	239,153
Chester — —	56	24	80	191,751
Salop — —	59	20	79	167,639
Wilts — —	61	14	75	185,107
Nottingham —	60	14	74	140,350
Berks — —	50	12	62	109,215
Lincoln —	44	14	58	208,557
Worcester —	44	7	51	139,333
Leicester —	33	14	47	130,081
Cornwall —	35	10	45	188,269
Herts — —	36	7	43	97,577
Northampton —	35	7	42	131,757
Cambridge —	36	4	40	89,346
Derby — —	34	5	39	161,142
Oxford — —	34	4	38	109,620
Dorset — —	28	10	38	115,319
Northumberland —	18	20	38	157,101
Bucks — —	29	4	33	107,444
Hereford — —	29	2	31	89,191
Durham — —	27	5	27	160,361
Bedford — —	17	3	20	63,393
Monmouth —	14	6	20	45,582
Cumberland —	9	9	18	117,230
Huntingdon —	13	2	15	37,568
Westmoreland —	4	2	6	41,617
Rutland — —	4	0	4	16,356
	3217	1310	4527	8,331,434

46   PRELIMINARY ELUCIDATIONS.

*Number of Persons committed in each County in England
and Wales for Trial—continued.*

Counties. *Wales.*	Males.	Females.	Total of Males and Females.	Population of each County.
Glamorgan —	10	5	15	71,525
Montgomery —	10	5	15	47,978
Pembroke —	7	5	12	56,280
Carmarthen —	5	3	8	67,317
Brecon — —	3	4	7	31,633
Carnarvon —	4	2	6	41,521
Radnor — —	3	3	6	19,050
Flint — —	3	1	4	39,622
Denbigh — —	2	0	2	60,352
Cardigan — —	2	0	2	42,956
Anglesey — —	1	0	1	33,806
Merioneth —	0	0	0	29,506
Total Wales	50	28	78	541,546
Total England	3217	1310	4527	8,331,434
Total for England and Wales — }	3267	1338	4605	8,872,980
To which add the offenders committed for trial at 220 general and quarter sessions held in England and Wales, estimated at			4395	Of which population about six millions are above fifteen years of age.
Add also commitments by magistrates out of sessions not sent to superior courts, estimated at			3000	
Total			12,000	

For the purpose of giving the reader a view of
the particular offences, and the different shades of
criminality applicable to the 3267 males and the
1338 female offenders, who were thus committed
to the several gaols of England and Wales for trial
in the year 1805, with the particular punishments
inflicted by the superior judges, the following abstract has been framed.

PRELIMINARY ELUCIDATIONS. 47

Crimes charged.	Persons.
Larceny, or stealing from houses, persons, &c.	3555
Receivers of stolen goods	137
Burglars and house-breakers	136
Uttering base money	108
Fraud and conspiracy	94
Sheep-stealers	71
Horse-stealers	65
Highway robbery	63
Manslaughter	56
Murder, in which are included twenty-seven females for the murder of their infants	53
Rapes, including attempts to violate female chastity	38
Stealing cows and pigs	38
Forgery	36
Ditto of Bank notes, and uttering ditto	28
Bigamy	23
Cutting and maiming	21
Shooting at others	14
Sodomy and bestiality, including attempts	15
Coining base money	15
Returning from transportation	15
Arson, or house-burning, &c.	13
Piracy	7
Sedition	4
Total	4605

Sentences pronounced, &c.		Persons.
Death		350
Transported { 14 years		34
7 years		561
Imprisoned { 3 years — 5; 1 to 2 years — 123; ½ year to 1 year — 333; 6 months & under — 1219		1680
Whipped and fined		105
Sent to the army and navy		53
Tried and acquitted		1092
Discharged by proclamation, no bill being found		730
Total		4605

Punishment of Death. Executed.	Persons.
For burglary	15
murder	10
horse-stealing	7
forging and uttering Bank notes	7
forgery	6
sheep-stealing	5
rapes	5
highway robbery	4
coining	3
arson	2
larceny in a dwelling-house	2
cutting and maiming	1
shooting at	1
Total executed	68

Recapitulation.

Executed	68
Sent out of the country	877
	945
Imprisoned to return on society	1680
Whipped ditto	105
Discharged ditto	1822
	3607
Sent to the army and navy	53
Total	4605

A similar abstract of offences tried by the justices in their sessions (were it practicable to frame it from accurate returns) would disclose a catalogue of human depravity nearly of equal extent, with the same results (the punishment of death only excepted) as to *transportation, whipping, imprisonment,* and the *pillory,* with numerous discharges of criminal and depraved characters every year, in consequence of acquittals arising from evidence different from what was exhibited before the committing magistrate, and by various other devices to elude justice. The discharges also, by proclamation, of persons committed for want of bail, who, although the offences cannot, according to the general acceptation of the word, be denominated *criminal,* are extremely numerous, and send back upon society a vast number of depraved characters, rendered worse by having become the inhabitants of gaols, and from associating with the most abandoned classes of the community.

It is scarcely possible to have a just conception of the various remedies which it may be necessary to apply with respect to the system of the poor and the more effectual relief of *indigence,* without thus taking a general view of the turpitude and criminality of the nation at large; since it is a state of *indigence,* fostered by idleness, which produces a disposition to moral and criminal offences, and they are so linked together, that it will be found impracticable to ameliorate the condition of the poor without taking more effectual measures at the same time for the prevention of criminal offences.

Suggestions for this purpose have long since been disclosed to the public, which have not only been generally admitted to be practicable, but after the fullest consideration have received the sanction, and obtained, above six years ago, the recommendation of the Select Committee of the House of Commons, on finance.

It is better, to use the words of an elegant writer, to prevent moral and criminal offences than to punish them. This is the fundamental principle of good legislation. It is the art of conducting a nation to the maximum of happiness and the minimum of misery. To prevent the evils which are disclosed in this work, the laws should be clear and simple ; they should be adapted to the existing state of society and manners, and the whole force of the nation should be united in their due execution and defence.

Argument about Argument

[7]

Michael Ignatieff

State, Civil Society, and Total Institutions: A Critique of Recent Social Histories of Punishment

ABSTRACT

Three books published during the seventies, by Michel Foucault, Michael Ignatieff, and David Rothman, greatly revised the history of the penitentiary. Contrary to the received wisdom which located the penitentiary's origin in the altruism of Quakers and other humanitarian reformers, and portrayed it as a humane advance from the squalid jails and workhouses, corporal and capital punishment, and transportation that preceded it, the revisionist accounts characterized the penitentiary, and other nineteenth-century "asylums" as weapons of class conflict or instruments of "social control." Social theories on a grand scale, such as Marxism or structural-functionalism, however, claim too much. The revisionist historiography of the prison followed these theories into three major misconceptions: that the state controls a monopoly over punitive regulation of behavior, that the state's moral authority and practical power are the major sources of social order, and that all social relations can be described in terms of power and subordination. The next generation of historical writing on crime and punishment must subject these distorting misconceptions to empirical examination.

Until recently, the history of prisons in most countries was written as a narrative of reform. According to this story, a band of philanthropic reformers in the second half of the eighteenth century, secular Enlightenment theorists like Beccaria and Bentham and religious men and women of conscience like the Evangelicals and the Quakers, set out to convince the political

Michael Ignatieff is a Fellow of King's College, Cambridge.

leadership of their societies that public punishments of the body like hanging, branding, whipping, and even, in some European countries, torture were arbitrary, cruel, and illegitimate and that a new range of penalties, chiefly imprisonment at hard labor, could be at once humane, reformative, and punitive. This campaign in Europe and America was powered by revulsion at physical cruelty, by a new conception of social obligation to the confined, and by impatience with the administrative inefficiency manifested in the squalid neglect of prisoners. The Enlightenment critique of legal arbitrariness and the vernacular of religious humanitarianism gradually created a moral consensus for reform which, after many delays and reversals, culminated by 1850 in the curtailment of hanging, the abolition of branding and the stocks, and the widespread adoption of the penitentiary as the punishment of first resort for major crime (Whiting 1975; Cooper 1976; Condon 1962; Stockdale 1977; O. Lewis 1967; Teeters 1935; D. Lewis 1965).

All of these accounts emphasized conscience as the motor of institutional change and assumed that the reformative practice of punishment proposed by the reformers was both in intention and in result more humane than the retributive practices of the eighteenth century. A third common feature of these accounts was their administrative and institutional focus on change within the walls and within the political system which ratified or resisted these changes. With the exception of Rusche and Kirchheimer's work (1939) on the relation between prison routines and emerging patterns of labor market discipline after 1550, few studies of imprisonment ventured beyond the walls of the prison itself.

The history of prisons therefore was written as a sub-branch of the institutional history of the modern welfare state. As such it has had an implicitly teleological bias, treating the history as a progress from cruelty to enlightenment. In the early sixties, historians in a number of fields, not just in the history of prisons but also in the history of mental health, public welfare, juvenile care, hospitals, and medicine, began to point up the political implications of this history of reform. To interpret contemporary

155   State, Civil Society, and Total Institutions

institutions as the culmination of a story of progress was to justify them at least in relation to the past and to suggest that they
could be improved by the same incremental process of philanthropic activism in the future. A reformist historiography thus
served a liberalism of good intentions, which in turn seemed
to legitimize dubious new initiatives—psychosurgery, chemo-
therapy, and behavior modification—as legitimate descen-
dants of the reforming tradition. It was in part to question
the legitimacy of these "reforms" in the present that a new group
of revisionist historians set out to study the reforms of the past.
Another broader motive was perhaps at work too—the libertarian, populist politics of the 1960s revised historians' attitudes
toward the size and intrusiveness of the modern state; the history
of the prison, the school, the hospital, the asylum seemed more
easily understood as a history of Leviathan than as a history of
reform.

Some, if not all, of the new historiography was avowedly
political. Moreover, it saw itself offering intellectual support for
the welfare rights, mental patients' rights, and prisoners' rights
campaigns of the time. These motives inspired an outpouring of
new revisionist history on the modern urban school (Katz 1968;
Lazerson 1971), the welfare system (Piven and Cloward 1971),
the asylum (Scull 1979), the juvenile court (Platt 1969), and the
prison. Three works best embody the revisionist current as far as
prisons were concerned. The first was David Rothman's *The
Discovery of the Asylum* (1971), an ambitious and justly well-
received attempt to relate the emergence of the penitentiary,
the mental institution, juvenile reformatory, and the urban
school to the transformation of American society from the late
colonial to the Jacksonian period. The second major work, dealing with France, was Michel Foucault's *Discipline and Punish*
(1978), which followed his studies of the origins of the mental
institution (*Madness and Civilization* 1967) and the origins of the
hospital (*Birth of the Clinic* 1973) and his work on the evolution of
the social and natural sciences in the eighteenth and nineteenth
centuries (*The Order of Things* 1970). *Discipline and Punish* was not
only about imprisonment but about the disciplinary ideology at

156   Michael Ignatieff

work in education and in the army, and in the new psychology and criminology which claimed to offer a scientific analysis of criminal behavior and intention. The third major work of the revisionist current was my own *A Just Measure of Pain: The Penitentiary in the Industrial Revolution* (1978). Narrower in scope than the others, it concentrates only on the penitentiary's emergence in England in the period from 1770 to 1840.

Despite these differences of scope and intention, all three agreed that the motives and program of reform were more complicated than a simple revulsion at cruelty or impatience with administrative   incompetence—the   reformer's   critique   of eighteenth-century punishment flowed from a more not less ambitious conception of power, aiming for the first time at altering the criminal personality. This strategy of power could not be understood unless the history of the prison was incorporated into a history of the philosophy of authority and the exercise of class power in general. The prison was thus studied not for itself but for what its rituals of humiliation could reveal about a society's ruling conceptions of power, social obligation, and human malleability.

Within the last two or three years, however, as the wider political climate has changed, these revisionist accounts have come under increasing attack for overschematizing a complex story, and for reducing the intentions behind the new institution to conspiratorial class strategies of divide and rule. The critique has put into question the viability of both Marxist and structural-functionalist social theory and historical explanation, not only in the area of prisons, but by extension in other areas of historical research. These larger implications make the revisionist anti-revisionist debate of interest to readers beyond the historians' parish.

What this review of the debate hopes to show is that revisionist arguments, my own included, contained three basic misconceptions: that the state enjoys a monopoly over punitive regulation of behavior in society, that its moral authority and practical power are the binding sources of social order, and that all social relations can be described in the language of subordina-

157   State, Civil Society, and Total Institutions

tion. This does not, by implication, make the counter-revisionist position correct. Insofar as it is a position at all, it merely maintains that historical reality is more complex than the revisionists assumed, that reformers were more humanitarian than revisionsits have made them out to be, and that there are no such things as classes. This position abdicates from the task of historical explanation altogether. The real challenge is to find a model of historical explanation which accounts for institutional change without imputing conspiratorial rationality to a ruling class, without reducing institutional development to a formless ad hoc adjustment to contingent crisis, and without assuming a hyper-idealist, all triumphant humanitarian crusade. These are the pitfalls; the problem is to develop a model that avoids these while actually providing explanation. This paper is a step toward such a model, but only a step. Since I am a former, though unrepentant, member of the revisionist school, this exercise is necessarily an exercise in self-criticism.

The focus on three books, and on a narrow if crucial period, is necessary because this is where debate has been most pointed and most useful. With the exception of David Rothman's *Conscience and Convenience* (1980a), Steven Schlossman's *Love and the American Delinquent* (1977), James Jacobs's *Stateville* (1977), and Anthony Platt's *The Child Savers* (1969), the revisionist and counter-revisionist debate has not extended itself into the terrain of the twentieth century. We are still awaiting a new historiography on the disintegration of the nineteenth-century penitentiary routines of lockstep and silence; the rise of probation, parole, and juvenile court; the ascendancy of the psychiatrist, social worker, doctor, and the decline of the chaplain within the penal system; the history of drug use as therapeutic and control devices; the impact of electric and TV surveillance systems on the nineteenth-century institutional inheritance; the unionization of custodial personnel; the impact of rising standards of living upon levels of institutional amenity and inmate expectation; the long-term pattern of sentencing and the changing styles of judicial and administrative discretion; the history of ethnic and race relations within the walls; the social and institutional origins of

the waves of prison rioting in the 1950s and late 1960s. This is
the work that needs to be done if historians are to explain the
contemporary crisis in prison order epitomized at Attica and
more recently at Santa Fe (Wicker 1975; Silberman 1978; for
England, see Fitzgerald 1977). The classics of prison sociology in
the forties and fifties described prisons as communities, guaranteeing a measure of order and security through a division of
power between captors and captives (Sykes 1958; Clemmer
1940). Why has this division of power broken down so often in
the sixties and seventies? Thus far, only Jacobs's exemplary
study of Stateville penitentiary in Illinois has offered a truly
historical answer integrating changes in institutional governance,
inmate composition and expectation, and the racial politics of the
outside world into a working explanation. His conclusions, that
prisoners were often surer of their physical safety under the
tighter and more self-confident authoritarian regimes of the forties than they were under the well-meaning but confused reformist regimes of the sixties, might appear to suggest that a
return to authoritarianism is the best way to guarantee prisoners'
and guards' physical security, if nothing else. Unionized guards
and the militant prisoners of today will not permit a return to the
prisons of the forties. But if we cannot and ought not repeat
history, we can at least learn from history where we went wrong.
In the market place of good ideas—decarceration, inmate self-
management, due process grievance procedures, institutional re-
design, token economies, behavior modification—history offers a
reliable guide to consumer choice and its invariable lesson in
caveat emptor. Criminal justice activists may be disappointed by
the literature I will review here because no answers are offered to
the question, What is to be done? I do hope there is use, however, in learning some of the subtler errors which good intentions
can entrain.

I. What Happened: the Revisionist Account

Let me begin by describing the revolution in punishment between 1780 and 1850. Rothman, Foucault, and my own work
may differ about explanation but we do agree about what happened. In each society the key developments seem to have been:

159   State, Civil Society, and Total Institutions

The decline of punishments involving the public infliction of physical pain to the body. Beccaria's campaign against the death penalty in the 1760s, the Pennsylvania statute of 1786, the reformed codes of the "enlightened despots," the French revolutionary decrees against the capital penalty, and Romilly and MacIntosh's capital statutes campaign in England culminated by the 1850s in the restriction of the death penalty to first degree murder and treason. The form of execution was also changed—in France the guillotine was adopted in 1792 as a scientific instrument of death sparing the victim the possible incompetence of the hangman; the traditional Tyburn processional of the condemned through the streets of London was abolished in 1783 in order to curtail the public symbolism of the death spectacle (Foucault 1978; Linebaugh 1975, pp. 65–119; Linebaugh 1977, pp. 246–70); public executions in England ended in the 1860s, and hanging henceforth took place behind prison walls (D. Cooper 1974). The lesser physical penalties were also curtailed or abolished (abolition of branding in England, 1779; pillory, 1837; whipping of women, 1819; see also Perrot 1980, pp. 59–60, for France). By 1860 the public ritual of physical punishment had been successfully redefined as a cruel and politically illegitimate means of inflicting pain.

The emergence of imprisonment as the preeminent penalty for most serious offenses. Imprisonment had been used as punishment on a selective but insubstantial scale prior to 1770. Places of confinement were generally used as waystations for persons awaiting trial, for convicted felons awaiting execution or transportation, and crucially for debtors. Nearly 60 percent of the institutional population in Howard's census of 1777 were debtors (Ignatieff 1978, p. 28; Pugh 1968; Sheehan 1977). Vagrants and disobedient servants convicted for a range of minor, work-related property offenses punishable at summary jurisdiction were confined at hard labor in houses of correction (Innes 1980b; DeLacy 1980, chap. 1; Beattie 1974, 1977). This use of imprisonment increased in the eighteenth century, for reasons we do not yet understand. In England it was not until the suspension of transportation in 1776 that English JP's and assize judges began to substitute sentences of imprisonment for sentences of transportation (Webb

160   Michael Ignatieff

and Webb 1963; Ignatieff 1978, chap. 4). At first criminal law reformers like Beccaria showed no particular enthusiasm for imprisonment itself, preferring to replace hanging with penalities ranging from hard labor in public to fines. It was only after 1776 in America and after 1789 in France that imprisonment began to replace hanging as *the* penalty appropriate to modern, enlightened republics (Foucault 1978, p. 115; Rothman 1971, p. 59).

The penitentiary came to be the bearer of reformers' hopes for a punishment capable of reconciling deterrence and reform, terror and humanity. In England between 1780 and 1812, half a dozen counties built small penitentiaries mostly for the control of minor delinquency. The first national penitentiary, Millbank, was opened in 1816. An enormous warren of passages and cells built in the style of a turreted medieval fortress near the Houses of Parliament, it soon was condemned as a costly failure—the prisoners were in revolt against the discipline more or less continuously in the 1820s; a violent outbreak of scurvy closed the prison for a year in 1824; but the lessons of failure were learned at Pentonville, opened in 1842. Its penitential regime of solitude, hard labor, and religious indoctrination became the model for all national penal servitude prisons and most county prisons besides. In America the key developments of the penitentiary regime occurred between 1820 and 1830—Auburn, 1819–23; Ossining, 1825; Pittsburgh, 1826; Philadelphia, 1829 (Rothman 1971, pp. 80–81), and in France, La Petite Rocquette, 1836, and the juvenile reformatory at Mettray, 1844 (Perrot 1980, pp. 60–1).

As systems of authority, the new prisons substituted the pains of intention for the pains of neglect (Ignatieff 1978, p. 113). Reformers like Howard were appalled that the squalor in neglected institutions was justified for its deterrent value. Accordingly, regular diets replaced the fitful provision of food in eighteenth-century institutions; uniforms replaced rags and personal clothing; prisoners received regular medical attention, and new hygienic rituals (head shaving, entrance examination, and bath) did away with the typhus epidemics which were an intermittent feature of eighteenth-century European prison life.

161   State, Civil Society, and Total Institutions

These hygienic rituals in turn became a means of stripping inmates of their personal identity. This indicates the ambivalence of "humanitarian" reform: the same measures that protected prisoners' health were explicitly justified as a salutary mortification of the spirit (Ignatieff 1978, p. 100).

The new prisons substituted the rule of rules for the rule of custom and put an end to the old division of power between the inmate community and the keepers. All accounts of eighteenth-century prisons stress the autonomy and self-government of prisoner communities. Since common law forbade the imposition of coercive routines on prisoners awaiting trial and debtors, they were able to take over the internal government of their wards, allocating cells, establishing their own rules, grievance procedures, and punishments (Innes 1980a, 1980b; Sheehan 1977, p. 233; De-Lacy 1980, chap. 2). The implied authority model of the colonial American and British prison was the household. The keeper and his family often resided in the institution and the prisoners were called "a family." They did not wear uniforms, they were not kept to routines, and they defended an oral and common law tradition of rights, privileges, and immunities (Rothman 1971, p. 55). By the 1840s in all three societies, a silent routine had been imposed to stamp out the association of the confined and to wipe out a subculture which was held to corrupt the novice and foster criminal behavior. Under the silent associated system of discipline, prisoners were allowed to congregate in workshops but were strictly forbidden to communicate. In the separate system at Pentonville and Philadelphia, prisoners were kept in complete cellular isolation and were forbidden any form of communication or association (Rothman 1971, p. 81; Ignatieff 1978, chap. 1; Henriques 1972). While advocates of both systems argued fiercely over their respective merits, they both agreed in principle on the necessity of suppressing the prison subculture and ending the tacit division of authority between captors and captives which had prevailed in the *ancien régime*. From a positive point of view, solitude exposed the individual prisoner to the obedience training of routine and the religious exhortation of the chaplain.

162   Michael Ignatieff

The chaplain, not the doctor or the governor, became the chief ideologist of the penitentiary, justifying its deprivations in the language of belief.

The new institutions enforced a markedly greater social distance between the confined and the outside world. High walls, sharply restricted visiting privileges, constant searches and patrols ended the mingling of outside and inside in the unreformed prison. Before reform, visitors enjoyed the run of the yards, women commonly brought their husbands meals, and debtors and outsiders drank together in the prison taproom. The aim of reform was to withdraw the prisoner from the corrupting influence of his former milieu and, at the same time, to inflict the pains of emotional and sexual isolation. Once again the mixture of humane and coercive motivations becomes apparent. As an unintended consequence, however, the check to the power of institutional personnel offered by constant visitors was reduced. The new institutions, therefore, did not resolve the old question, Who guards the guards? Instead they posed the question in a new and thus far more intractable way (Ignatieff 1978, conclusion; DeLacy 1980, conclusion).

All three versions agree that the emergence of the modern prison cannot be understood apart from the parallel history of the other total institutions created in this period—the lunatic asylum, the union workhouse, the juvenile reformatory and industrial school, and the monitorial school. Besides being the work of the same constituency of philanthropic and administrative reformers, these institutions enforced a similar economy of time and the same order of surveillance and control. They also expressed a common belief in the reformative powers of enforced asceticism, hard labor, religious instruction and routine.

The preceding paragraphs provide a schematic summary of the revolution in discipline as the revisionist account would have it. Before considering the explanations offered for this revolution, we ought to pause to consider the objections that have been raised to the revisionist account as valid description. A

163   State, Civil Society, and Total Institutions

number of theses and monographs completed within the last couple of years have insisted that the descriptive picture is more complex, contradictory, and inchoate than Foucault, Rothman, or I have suggested.

Margaret DeLacy's excellent Princeton dissertation on county prison administration in Lancashire, 1690–1850, argues that even a relatively dynamic county administration like Lancashire lacked the resources to impose the highly rationalized Pentonville model on all the county institutions (1980). Many of these remained much the same as they had been in the eighteenth century. Eighteenth-century historians, particularly Joanna Innes, have argued that the prereform prison was neither as squalid nor as incompetently administered as the reformers made it out to be (Innes 1980b). By implication, therefore, the revisionist account may have been taken in by the reformers' sources. It is less clear, therefore, that the history of the institution between 1780 and 1840 can be described as a passage from squalid neglect to hygienic order.

Michelle Perrot and Jacques Leonard have made the same case for France, arguing that the highly rationalized institutions like La Rocquette and La Mettray cannot be taken as typical of the mass of local lockups, jails and hulks in mid-nineteenth-century France. In these institutions, the persistence of disease and the continued use of whipping and chains would appear to suggest a melancholy continuity with the worst features of the *ancien régime* (Perrot 1980).

It appears then that the revolution in punishment was not the generalized triumph of Weberian rationalization which the revisionist account suggested. Foucault's work (and my own as well) remained captive of that Weberian equation of the *ancien régime* with the customary, the traditional, and the particularistic, and of the modern with the rational, the disciplined, the impersonal, and the bureaucratic. The gulf between the reformers' rationalizing intentions and the institutionalized results of their work ought to make us rethink this equation of modernity and rationalization, or at least to give greater room for the idea that modernity is the site of a recurring battle between rationalizing intention and institutions, interests and communities which resist, often with persistent success.

Yet even if we admit that Pentonville and the Panopticon (Bentham 1791), Auburn and La Rocquette were "ideal types" rather than exemplary realities of their time, we still have to explain why it became possible between 1780 and 1840 and not before to conceive and construct them. However much else remained unchanged in the passage from the *ancien régime* to the industrial world of the nineteenth century, the penitentiary was something new and unprecedented and was understood as such by the great observers of the age, Alexis de Tocqueville, Charles Dickens, and Thomas Carlyle. A counter-revisionist account that considers only the local institutions, which went on much the same as before, will miss what contemporaries knew had to be explained about their own age.

II. Jacksonian America: The Emergence of the Asylum

Let us turn to this business of explanation and let us begin with the American case, with the work of David Rothman. In Rothman's account, the new total institutions of the Jacksonian period emerged in an overwhelmingly rural and agricultural society, growing beyond the boundaries of the colonial past yet still a generation away from the factory system, industrialism, European immigration, and the big city. It is a fundamental mistake, he argues, to interpret the total institution as an "automatic and inevitable response of an industrial and urban society to crime and poverty" (Rothman 1971, p. xvi). Americans were anxious about the passage of colonial society and the emergence of a restless, socially mobile population moving beyond the controls of family, farm, and town meeting, but there was nothing in this process which itself required the emergence of the new asylums and prisons. The catalyst for institutionalized instruction was not social change itself but the way it was organized into an alarmist interpretation of disorder and dislocation by philanthropic reformers. Crime was read for

165   State, Civil Society, and Total Institutions

the first time not as the wickedness of individuals but as an indictment of a disordered society. This explains the emergence of new institutions aiming at the reformation and discipline of the deviant, disorderly, and deranged.

For a society which interpreted crime as the sign of the passing of the colonial order, the penitentiary symbolized an attempt to re-create the godly superintendence and moral discipline of the past within a modern setting. Rothman demonstrates brilliantly that the language developed in a society to explain disorder and deviance also defines the solutions it develops for these problems. An environmentalist theory of crime and faith in the reformative effects of isolation from the environment were linked together in a system of ideas, each legitimizing the other.

Rothman is better at re-creating the reformers' systems of belief than in locating these beliefs in a believable social and economic context. We need to know something about actual trends in crime during 1780–1820 if we are to understand the changing fit between reform and rhetoric and their social context. In the absence of such data, crime becomes a static and empty category in Rothman's analysis, and the reformers' alarmist discourse drifts away from any point of reference.

Why, we need to know, were the Jacksonians so specially anxious about change and disorder, and why did they look back with such nostalgia to colonial society? Rothman simply accepts the Jacksonian reformers' picture of the stable pre-revolutionary society they were leaving behind, but surely this was a questionable historical fable. Many eighteenth-century Europeans regarded colonial America as a restless, rootless, dynamic, and explosive society. Tom Paine's Philadelphia was no deferential idyll (Foner 1976). Yet Rothman never questions the Jacksonian's rosy image of their own past, never asks how their account of it should have been so out of joint with what we know of colonial society.

One would also have liked Rothman to explore the relationship between the rise of the total institution and the theory and practice of Jacksonian democracy. This was after all

166   Michael Ignatieff

the period of the extension of universal manhood suffrage in the
United States. Tocqueville himself thought the relation was one
of contradiction: "While society in the United States gives the
example of the most extended liberty, the prisons of the same
country offer the spectacle of the most complete despotism"
(Beaumont and Tocqueville 1964, p. 79). As Tocqueville
suggested in the "tyranny of the majority" sections of *Democracy
in America*, democratic republics which represent law and order
as the embodied will of all the people treat disobedient
minorities more severely than monarchical societies which have
no ideological commitment to the consensual attachment of
their citizens. Rothman suggests but leaves unexplored the possibility of a connection between Jacksonian popular
sovereignty, an environmentalist theory of crime as being the
responsibility of society, and an interventionist social therapy
taking the form of the "total institution."

III. Sovereignty and the Margin of Illegality

If we turn to Foucault, we find that the relation between forms
of sovereignty outside the walls and carceral regimes inside constitutes the main axis of his interpretation. Public executions,
which the reformers of the Enlightenment condemned as a car-
nal and irrational indulgence, can be read, Foucault argues, as
symbolic displays of the highly personalized sovereignty of the
king and of his alternatively vengeful, merciful relation toward
his wicked subjects.

The execution suited a philosophy of order that ignored
minor delinquency to concentrate instead on the ritualized dis-
patch of selected miscreants. This exercise of sovereignty in
turn implied a loosely articulated political nation in which

> each of the different social strata had its margin of tolerated
> illegality; the non-application of the rule, the non-observance
> of the innumerable edicts or ordinances were a condition of
> the political and economic functioning of society. . . . the least
> favoured strata of the population did not have in principle
> any privileges, but they benefited within the margins of what

167   State, Civil Society, and Total Institutions

was imposed on them by law or custom, from a space of
tolerance, gained by force or obstinacy. (Foucault 1978, pp.
84–5)

The illegalities of the poor, like the tax exemptions of the
rich, were tolerated because of the persistent weakness of an
underfinanced, chronically indebted state, the tenacious survival of regional and local immunities, and the persistent countervailing power of the *parlements* (see Montesquieu, *The Spirit of
the Laws*, 1748), the judiciary, and the nobility. Above all, the
margin of illegality enjoyed by the poor reflected a ruling conception of national power as the sovereign's will rather than the
operation of a bureaucratic machine. The state, moreover,
shared the punitive function with civil society, in the double
sense that its public rituals (execution, pillory, whipping, and
branding) required completion by the opprobrium of the crowd
if they were to have full symbolic effect, and in the sense that
household heads, masters, and employers punished directly
without invoking the state's power.

Independently of Foucault, Edward Thompson and Douglas
Hay seem to have reached a similar description of the exercise
of sovereign power in eighteenth-century England. They put
the same emphasis on the symbolic centrality of the public
hanging in reproducing awe and deference before the
sovereign's mighty but merciful power, and they describe a
philosophy of order essentially similar in its permissive approach to the small fish.

Permissive, however, is too nostalgic or sentimental a word
for a tactics of order uneasily poised between an obvious and
sometimes brutal concern to defend property rights and an
equal distaste, moral, libertarian and economic, for the apparatus of state police (Hay 1975, pp. 17–65; Thompson 1975,
conclusion). The Revolution Settlement and the common law
tradition imposed limits on the discretionary power of
eighteenth-century magistrates, and the common people themselves were quite capable of forcibly reminding magistrates of
"the rights of free born Englishmen" and of the protocol of

customs guaranteeing free assembly (Thompson 1971). It is possible that there was no corresponding corpus of rights in common law available to the French poor, but is is hard to believe that they did not hold to some customary beliefs and traditions about the proper bounds of monarchical "police."

Hay's and Thompson's works show up Foucault's tacit assumption that the only limits on public order policy were the mental assumptions of the authorities themselves and the structural weaknesses of the state apparatus. What is missing in his work is the idea that public order strategies were defined within limits marked out not only by the holders of power but also by those they were trying, often vainly, to persuade, subdue, cajole, or repress. Foucault's account consistently portrays authority as having a clear field, able to carry out its strategies without let or hindrance from its own legal principles or from popular opposition. Power is always seen as a strategy, as an instrumentality, never as a social relation between contending social forces. We need to know much more about the social process by which the margin of illegality enjoyed by the poor in the *ancien régime* was established before we conclude with Foucault that it owed its existence to the toleration of the authorities.

IV. Class Conflict and the Prison

However we interpret the margin of popular illegality under the *ancien régime*, Foucault and I agree that the penitentiary formed part of a new strategy of power aiming at its circumscription between 1780 and 1850. This new strategy was the work of Burke's "sophisters, economists, and calculators"—the monarchical administrators like Turgot and Le Trosne, and gentry men of letters like Beccaria. In England, the new ideology found expression in Henry Fielding's proposals for reform of London police in the 1760s, in Howard's penitentiary scheme of the 1770s, and in the hospital and asylum reforms led by the provincial Nonconformist professional classes in the 1790s (Ignatieff 1978, chap. 3). In the

169   State, Civil Society, and Total Institutions

1780s, too, Bentham and Romilly began their campaigns for the codification of law and for the curtailment of public executions.

The ideal of reforming through punishment and of apportioning just measures of pain to crimes previously tolerated or ignored was compatible with the democratic ideals of the French Revolution—equal rights, equal citizenship, equal punishment—but it proved no less compatible with Napoleonic centralism and the Bourbon Restoration. Beneath the whole surface play of debate about political rights and regimes between the 1770s and 1840s, Foucault argues, a new "carceral archipelago" of asylums, prisons, workhouses, and reformatories slipped into place. The political divisions over regimes and rights hid a deeper, unstated consensus among the ruling orders on the exercise of power over the criminal, the insane, and the pauper. This ideology forged in the 1760s by the Enlightenment reformers and opponents of the *ancien régime* was transmitted and reproduced by social interests in the Restoration and the July Monarchy often deeply hostile to the rationalist or egalitarian spirit of the philosophers themselves.

In England, the first bearers of the new disciplinary ideology were the reforming county magistrates and the Dissenting professional classes of the provinces—reformist in politics, scientific in mental outlook, rational and improving in their management of labor, county finance, and personal estates. The new asylums, prisons, workhouses, and schools which they built appealed to their residual religious asceticism, to their scientific and rationalist outlook, and to their impatience with the administrative incompetence and political corruption of the *ancien régime*. In the crisis years of early industrialization after 1815, the disciplinary ideology was taken up by the evangelized professional, mercantile, and industrial classes seeking to cope with the dissolution of a society of ranks and orders and the emergence of a society of strangers. The philanthropic campaigns to reform old institutions and to build new asylums, workhouses, prisons, and hospitals gave expression to a new strategy of class relations. In return for the humanity of minimal institutional provision, the disobedient poor were drawn into a circle of asceticism, industriousness, and obedience. They would return to society convinced of the moral legitimacy of their rulers. The persistent ideal of prison reform was a kind of punishment at once so humane and so just that it would convince the offender of the moral legitimacy of the law and its custodians. The penitentiary was designed to embody this reconciliation of the imperatives of discipline with the imperatives of humanity.

My own account places more stress than Foucault's on the religious and philanthropic impulses behind institutional reform. His version of the disciplinary ideology retains the secular rationalist tone of its initial Enlightenment formulation, while mine stresses the fusion of the secular rationalism embodied in Benthamism with the Quaker and Evangelical language of conscience epitomized by Elizabeth Fry. The penitentiary in England had at its core the religious discourse of the chaplain, just as the new Evangelical language of class relations had at its core the idea of rich and poor bound together in the common experience of sin and the common salvation of faith and industry.

My own account also places more stress than Foucault's upon the reformers' concern to defend and explain institutional routines to the confined. As a consequence I have put more emphasis on the humanitarian intentions of the reformers. They were genuinely repelled by the chains, squalor, and neglect they discovered in existing institutions, especially because these compromised the moral legitimacy of the social system in the eyes of the confined. In their theory of the reform of character, the crucial task was to persuade the poor to accept the benevolent intention behind institutional deprivations. Once convinced of the benevolence of the system, reformers argued, prisoners would be unable to take refuge from their own guilt in attacking their confiners. Personal reformation thus meant succumbing to the benevolent logic of their captors. In Foucault's account on the other hand, reformers were not centrally concerned to legitimize new penal measures as humane.

171   State, Civil Society, and Total Institutions

Reformers in his account simply took the humanity of their measures for granted and looked to the discipline to routinize the habits of the poor. My model of the reform of character is one of symbolic persuasion; Foucault's is of disciplinary routinization.

We both agree, however, on the relation between this new strategy of power and the social crisis of the post-1815 period, exemplified in recurrent surges of distress-related crime, pauperism, and collective pauper unrest. Foucault is sketchy in the extreme about the causation of this social crisis, but it is clearly implied as the backdrop of the institutional revolution in France. My account likewise does not purport to be a social history of crime and pauperism in the 1815–48 period, but it does locate three major sites of crisis. The first was the breakdown of social relations in the agricultural counties of the southeast between 1815 and 1831 as a result of the casualization of the agricultural proletariat. Rising rates of vagrancy, pauperism, and petty crime through the 1820s and the explosion of the Swing Riots in 1831 are the symptoms of this crisis in rural social relations. The second site of crisis was in London, where the Anti–Corn Law Riots of 1815, the Spa Field disturbances of 1816, and the riots attendant upon Queen Caroline's trial proved that the existing parish constabulary was hopelessly outdated in coping with urban crowd control while the soldiery brought in upon these occasions was a clumsy, brutal, and therefore alienating instrument of order (Silver 1967). In addition there was growing anxiety among magistrates and philanthropists about the rising incidence of juvenile crime in the metropolis after 1815. Masterless apprentices, orphans, underemployed youths, child prostitutes, all seemed to symbolize a breakdown in the order of the family, the parish, and the workshop. The third site of crisis lay in the new northern industrial towns where regional labor markets tied to single industries like cotton proved extremely vulnerable to cycles of demand in the international economy. Mass unemployment in "bad years" like 1826 threw up the specter of recurrent breakdown in labor market disciplines (Ignatieff 1978, chap. 6).

172   Michael Ignatieff

There cannot be much doubt that the new strategy of mass imprisonment, the creation of the Metropolitan Police in 1829, and the diffusion of paid constabularies through the agricultural counties and the industrial towns in the 1830s, 40s, and 50s must be seen as a "response" to this crisis of public order (Storch 1975). The creation of permanent police courts, the expansion of the scope of the vagrancy and trespass statutes, and the formation of the union workhouse system in 1834 represented additional attempts to "grapple for control," to cope with a social order problem the size and magnitude of which clearly grew faster than any of the authorities anticipated (Silver 1967; Hart 1955, 1965; Radzinowicz 1968, vol. 5; DeLacy 1980; Philips 1977).

Yet there are dangers of social reductionism in this explanation. Institutional reformers did not justify their program as a response to the labor discipline needs of employers. Indeed the reform discourse antedates the labor discipline crisis. Howard's penitentiary schemes, the police theory of the late Enlightenment, the hospital and asylum campaigns of the 1790s, all anticipated the post-1815 crisis. Moreover, as Rothman pointed out in the American case, the fact of crisis itself would not explain why authorities chose the particular remedies they did, why they put such faith in institutional confinement when greater resort to hanging or to convict gang labor in public might have been equally eligible responses to the perceived breakdown of social controls.

A. Divide and Rule

Foucault's argument and mine nonetheless is that the massive investment in institutional solutions would have been inconceivable unless the authorities had believed that they were faced with the breakdown of a society of stable ranks and the emergence of a society of hostile classes. This diagnosis of the malaise of their times in turn suggested an institutional solution. Mass imprisonment offered a new strategic possibility—isolating a criminal class from the working class, incarcerating the one so that it would not corrupt the industriousness of the

173   State, Civil Society, and Total Institutions

other. The workhouse likewise would quarantine pauperism
from honest poverty (Foucault 1978, pp. 276–78). Beneath the
surface debate over whether these institutions were capable of
reforming or deterring their target populations, Foucault argues, lay a deeper consensus among the ruling orders about
using institutionalization to manufacture and reproduce social
divisions within the working classes between working and
criminal, rough and respectable, poor and pauperized. Foucault
claims that this strategy of division actually worked—that the
institutional quarantine of the criminal did create a criminal
class separate from the working-class community. In this lay
the secret "success" of prison, beneath all its apparent failures
as an institution of reform and deterrence.

The divide and rule argument works best in respect to the
workhouse, where the creation of the Bastilles of 1834 (see
Babington 1972) does appear to have succeeded in making
pauperism disgraceful to the poor. Before the Bastilles, the poor
conceived of relief as a right and did not look upon it as a disgrace; afterwards while many continued to insist on their
rights, working-class respectability came to insist on avoiding
the degradation of appealing for relief and ending one's days in
the public ward. The Bastilles do seem to have dug the gulf
deeper between pauperism and poverty within the value system
and the social behavior of the poor themselves.

As regards imprisonment, however, the divide and rule argument seems to me now to have fallen prey unwittingly to the
problem inherent in what criminologists call "labeling theory."
The notorious difficulty with this approach is that it makes the
state's sanctions the exclusive source of the boundary between
the deviant and the respectable. This would seem to ignore the
degree to which, in the nineteenth as in the twentieth century,
the moral sanctions condemning murder, rape, and sexual and
personal assault were prior to and independent of the punitive
sanction, commanding assent across class lines. In punishing
these offenses, the state simply ratified a line of demarcation
already indigenous to the poor. Even in the case of petty property crime, it is not clear that the criminal sanction was labeling

174   Michael Ignatieff

acts which the poor excused as an inevitable response to distress
or which they justified in the vernacular of natural justice. The
poor, no less than the rich, were victims of property crime, and
any study of London police courts in the nineteenth century
shows they were prepared to go to law to punish members of
their own class (Davis 1980; Philips 1977). If a constant process
of demarcation was underway between criminals and the
working classes, it was a process in which the working classes
themselves played a prominent part, both in their resort to law
and in the informal sanctioning behavior which enforced their
own codes of respectability. Doubtless there was sympathy for
the first-time offenders and juveniles convicted for minor property offenses during hard times; doubtless there were offenders
whom working people felt were unjustly convicted. Certainly
repeated imprisonment did isolate the criminal from his own
class. But it is a serious overestimation of the role of the state to
assume that its sanctioning powers were the exclusive source of
the social division between criminal and respectable. The strategy of mass imprisonment is better understood in class terms as
an attempt by the authorities to lend symbolic reinforcement to
values of personal honor which they themselves knew were indigenous to the poor.

The behavior of the politicized sections of the working classes
leaves no doubt that they drew a very strict demarcation between
themselves and the criminal. Michelle Perrot's study of French
prisons in 1848 shows that the revolutionary crowds who
stormed the prisons reserved liberation for prostitutes, political
offenders, and conscripts, not for ordinary criminal offenders
(Perrot 1980, p. 241). In England, while political radicals often
cited the criminal statistics as proof of the grinding pressure of
distress on the poor, they never questioned the ultimate legitimacy of their convictions (Ignatieff 1978, chap. 4; DeLacy
1980).

B. Class Fear

Thus if fears by the ruling orders of a potential union of
interest and action between the criminal and working classes are

175   State, Civil Society, and Total Institutions

to be regarded as having had some influence in generating public support for mass imprisonment, it must be recognized that
these fears were without actual sociological foundation. We are
dealing with a form of social fantasy detached from observable
reality. Moreover, it is not clear how general these fantasies of
revolution were or even how influential they were in galvaniz-
ing public opinion in support of the total institution. The difficulty with arguments from class fear is that they are simply too
vague, too global, to account for the specific timing of institutional or legislative change. Class fear among educated
public opinion in the 1820s and 1830s may have contributed
something to the consensus that public order was too parlous
and insecure to go on with the haphazard punishment and
police strategies of the eighteenth century. But class fear cannot
account for the specific idiosyncrasies of the institutional solution—the faith in silence, solitude, religious indoctrination,
and hard labor.

   If we return to what reformers said they were doing, it becomes clearer to me now than it was when I wrote *A Just Measure of Pain* that the adoption of the penitentiary in particular
and the institutional solution in general cannot be explained in
terms of their supposed utility in manufacturing social divisions
within the working class. This is because at bottom reformers
like most of their own class understood deviance in irreducibly
individual rather than collective terms, not ultimately as collective social disobedience, however much distress and collective
alienation influenced individuals, but as a highly personal descent into sin and error. Given this individualist reading of deviance, the appeal of institutional solutions lay in the drama of
guilt which they forced each offender to play out—the drama of
suffering, repentance, reflection, and amendment, watched over
by the tutelary eye of the chaplain. Foucault's neglect of the
religious vernacular of reform argument obscures the deep hold
which this symbolic drama of guilt and repentance held for the
Victorian imagination. To be sure, this hypothetical drama
bore little if any relation to what actually happened in prisons,
asylums, and workhouses, and many Victorians, Charles Dick-

ens among them, knew this full well. But nevertheless, even skeptics like Dickens and Mayhew were not immune to the appeal of a symbolic system of associations in which the reform of the guilty criminal was held to reveal the triumph of good over evil, conscience over desire, in all men and women. If there was a social message in the ideal of reform through institutional discipline it was that the institutional salvation of the deviant acted out the salvation of all men and women, rich and poor alike.

V. Who Directed the Carceral Archipelago?

Where does all this leave the problem of agency? Whose interests did the new institutions serve? In whose name were the reformers speaking?

A. Foucault and the Disciplinary "Savoir"

On these questions of agency, Foucault's answers are notoriously cloudy. At some points, he refers to the "bourgeoisie" though this is hardly an adequate categorization of the shifting alignment of class fragments, aristocrats, financiers, professionals, industrialists, who competed for power in France between 1815 and 1848. At other points, Foucault slips into a use of the passive voice which makes it impossible to identify who, if anyone, was the historical agent of the tactics and strategies he describes. Yet before we condemn them out of hand it is worth noting that Foucault is trying to work free of what he regards as the vulgar Marxist conception of agency according to which the prison is a tool of a definable class with a clear-sighted conception of its strategic requirements. He also rejects the functionalist model according to which the prison is the designated punitive instrument within a social division of labor. In place of these accounts, he argues that punitive power is dispersed throughout the social system: it is literally everywhere, in the sense that the disciplinary ideology, the *savoir* which directs and legitimizes power, permeates all social groups (with the exception of the marginal and deviant), ordering the self-repression of the repressors themselves. The prison is only the most extreme site for an exercise of power which extends

177   State, Civil Society, and Total Institutions

along the whole continuum of social relations from the family, to the market, to the workplace, and to citizenship. If prisons and factories came to resemble each other in their rituals of time and discipline, therefore, it was not because the state acted in response to the labor discipline strategies initiated by employers but because both public order authorities and employers shared the same universe of assumptions about the regulation of the body and the ordering of institutional time.

Given that all social relations were inscribed within relations of domination and subordination, ordered, so he says, by a continuous disciplinary discourse, it is impossible to identify the privileged sites or actors that controlled all the others. The disciplinary ideology of modern society *can* be identified as the work of specific social actors but once such an ideology was institutionalized, once its rationality came to be taken for granted, a fully exterior challenge to its logic became impossible. The institutional system took on a life of its own. One cannot say, Foucault argues, that the political apparatus of modern states actually controls the prison system. There is a formal chain of delegation and responsibility from the legislature to the bureaucracy, from the bureaucracy to the warden, and from the warden to guards and prisoners, but this does not take into account the way institutional systems develop their own inertial logic which each "actor" feels powerless to change (even those at its very summit).

Since the appearance of *Discipline and Punish*, Foucault has reformulated this problem of agency as one of historical causation, putting a new stress on the way in which the new institutions emerged as the unintended consequence of levels of change, which in themselves were independent of each other—the new discourse on discipline in the Enlightenment, the search by the propertied for stricter legal and social protection, and the crisis in public order. The new discourse emerged prior to the social revolution of the nineteenth century and prior to the labor discipline needs of employers, but once in play ideologically, it provided the program around which constituencies assembled their response to social turbulence and

178   Michael Ignatieff

labor indiscipline. Once the disciplinary discourse's independence of its social grounding is granted, it becomes possible to work free of the various traps which the problem of
agency has caused for historians—the conspiratorial all-seeing
ruling classes of the Marxist account; the low rationality model
of ad hoc responses to social crisis, and the hyperidealist version
of reform as a humanitarian crusade (see Foucault's interview in
Perrot 1980).

B. *The Middle Class as a Ruling Class*

But where does this leave the concept of a ruling class as the
historical actor behind the making of the penitentiary? My own
work has been criticized for using middle class as a synonym
for ruling class in a period in which it would be more accurate
to speak of a bewilderingly complex competition for political
power and social influence by different class fractions, professionals, industrialists, and merchants, aristocratic magnates,
and small gentry farmers. While it is a convention of Marxist
argument that such division of interest and jockeying for power
were stilled whenever "the class as a whole" felt threatened
from below, my own work on the intense debates about social
order policy suggests that choral unanimity was rare even in
moments of universally recognized crisis. Unquestionably justices, members of Parliament, and philanthropists recognized
each other as the rich and regarded vagrants, pickpockets, and
the clamoring political mob as the lower orders, but their sense
of "we" versus "they" was not enough to make the ruling class
into a collective social actor. One can speak of a ruling class in
the sense that access to strategic levers of power was systematically restricted according to wealth and inheritance, but one
cannot speak of its acting or thinking as a collective historical
subject. One can only ascribe historical effectivity to identifiable social constituencies of individuals who managed to secure
political approval for penal change through a process of debate
and argument in the society's sites of power. It would be wrong
to think of these constituencies of institutional reformers as
acting for their class or expressing the logic of its strategic im-

179   State, Civil Society, and Total Institutions

peratives. This would make them into ventriloquists for a clair-
voyant and unanimous social consensus. In fact they managed
to secure only the most grudging and limited kind of approval
for their program. The penitentiary continued to be criticized
from multiple and contradictory points of view: it was in-
humanly severe; it was too lenient; it was too expensive; it
could not reconcile deterrence and reform; the reformation of
criminals was a sentimental delusion; and so on.

In his most recent reflections, Foucault himself admits that
the new carceral system was not the work of an overarching
strategic consensus by a ruling class, but instead fell into place
as a result of a conjuncture between transformations in the
phenomena of social order, new policing needs by the propertied, and a new discourse on the exercise of power.

Yet for all his disclaimers, Foucault's conception of the disciplinary world view, the *savoir* as he calls it, effectively fore-
closes on the possibility that the *savoir* itself was a site of contradiction, argument, and conflict. In England at least, for
example, a preexisting legal tradition of rights imposed specific
limits to the elaboration of new powers of arrest, new summary
jurisdiction procedures, just as habeas corpus limited carceral
practice toward the unconvicted. At every point, new proposals
for police, prisons, and new statutory powers raised the question of how to balance the changing conceptions of security
against preexisting conceptions of the liberty of the subject.
Foucault makes no mention of these legal limits.

There is more than a touch of Marxist reductionism in Foucault's treatment of law as a pliable instrument of the ruling
class. Recent Marxist legal theory describes the autonomy of
law as a historical sedimentation of the outcome of earlier
struggles over the competing rights of subjects which as such
imposes rules not only on subjects but on rulers themselves.
The jury system, the legal criteria of evidence and proof, and
the legal ideology of the "rights of free-born Englishmen" constituted a court of appeal in England against plans or projects
for tightening the law's grip (Pashukanis 1978; Renner 1949;
Fine et al. 1979, pp. 22–24; Thompson 1975, conclusion). Penal

180   Michael Ignatieff

practice, far from representing the unfolding of an all-
embracing disciplinary *savoir*, should be seen as embodying the
compromise outcomes of often heated political and legal debates.
Foucault seems to ignore the possibility of conflict between the
claims of private wealth and the requirements of public order.
Compromise was also required between the desire to punish
minor delinquency more strictly and the desire to avoid crimi-
nalizing normally law-abiding members of the popular classes
through mass imprisonment. The conflict between these two
imperatives frequently pitted policemen against magistrates,
and magistrates against employers (Ignatieff 1978, pp. 186–87).
The erratic line of policy traced out by these conflicts could be
said to have been functional to the reproduction of a ruling class
only in the relatively trivial sense that the existing distribution
of social relations was not overthrown by revolution; but once
the elaboration of carceral policy is seen as the unplanned
outcome of compromise and conflict, it seems rationalist and
conspiratorial to call it an unfolding strategy of a carceral
savoir.

VI. "Social Control" as Historical Explanation

These questions about the ruling class as a historical actor
ought to be connected to earlier questions raised about the role
of prisons in disciplining the working class. Given the frequency with which the popular classes themselves sought to
invoke the penal sanction against members of their own social
group, it would be difficult to maintain that they were simple
objects of the punitive sanction. While the majority of punished
offenders undoubtedly came from the popular classes, it would
not follow from this that the function of imprisonment was to
control those classes as such. Foucault's and my own work, I
think, confused statements about the social fears motivating the
construction of institutions with statements about their actual
function.

The "social control" model of the prison's function which
informed my own work assumed that capitalist society was systematically incapable of reproducing itself without the constant

181   State, Civil Society, and Total Institutions

interposition of state agencies of control and repression. This model essentially appropriated the social control models of American Progressivist sociology according to which society was a functional equilibrium of institutional mechanisms in the family, the workplace, and marketplace working together to ensure the cooperation of individuals in the interests of social order (Stedman Jones 1977; Rothman 1980b; Muraskin 1976). As Stedman Jones has pointed out, the Marxist version of this idea, and the structuralist version of it reproduced in Foucault, carries on the assumption of society as a functionally efficient totality of institutions. When applied to prison history, this model implies that institutions "work," whereas the prison is perhaps *the* classic example of an institution which works badly and which nonetheless survives in the face of recurrent skepticism as to its deterrent or reformative capacity. Instead of looking for some hidden function which prisons actually succeed in discharging, we ought to work free of such functionalist assumptions altogether and begin to think of society in much more dynamic and historical terms, as being ordered by institutions like the prisons which fail their constituencies and which limp along because no alternative can be found or because conflict over alternatives is too great to be mediated into compromise.

The second assumption in Marxist social control theory is that the use of the state penal sanction is essential to the reproduction of the unequal and exploitative social relations of the capitalist system. Marx himself qualified the centrality of state coercion, arguing that while the hangman and the house of correction were central in the "primitive accumulation" process, that is, in the forcible establishment of wage relations, once such wage relations were in place, "the silent compulsions of economic relations" "set the seal on the domination of the capitalist over the worker." The extra-economic coercion of the state penal sanction was then invoked only in "exceptional" cases (Marx 1976, p. 899). My own work on the expansion of vagrancy, trespass, and petty larceny statutes in the 1820s and 1830s suggested that state penal sanctions were required by employers, especially in the agricultural counties, to prevent their chronically underemployed casual labor force from passing out of the wage system into theft and vagrancy (Ignatieff 1978, pp. 180–83; also Linebaugh, forthcoming).

Important as the penal sanction may have been in sustaining discipline in pauperized labor markets, or in constituting wage discipline itself in the face of worker resistance, we ought not to take these instances as typical of the role of state force once the wage bargain has been broadly accepted. We ought not to assume that exploitative social relations are impossible to reproduce without threat of force. Even in objectively exploitative, underpaid, and unhealthy conditions of labor, one can conceive of men and women voluntarily coming to work not in the sense that they are free to choose wage labor but in the specific sense that they derive intrinsic satisfaction from the sociability of labor, from the activity itself, from the skill they manage to acquire, and from the pride they take in their work. Marxist theories of labor discipline consistently ignore these aspects of submission to the wage bargain and consequently overstate the centrality of penal force in reproducing those relations. The fact that workers do submit to the wage bargain need not imply that they accept the terms of their subordination as legitimate; it is a cliché of labor history that those whose wage levels, skill, and pride in craftsmanship gave them the most reasons for satisfaction with industrial labor were often the most militant in their political and moral challenge to it as a system. The point is simply that the punitive sanction of the state need not be regarded as decisive in the reproduction of exploitative and unequal social relations.

Going still further, it could be asked whether force itself, apart from its specific embodiment in state apparatuses of coercion, is decisive to the maintenance of social order. The tacit social theory of Foucault's *Discipline and Punish* describes all social relations in the language of power, domination, and subordination. This would imply that individuals are naturally unsocial or asocial, requiring discipline and domination before they will submit to social rules. Not surprisingly, therefore,

183   State, Civil Society, and Total Institutions

Foucault sees tne family as an authority system, linked to the carceral system of the state outside:

> We should show how intra-familial relations, essentially in the parent-children cell, have become "disciplined," absorbing since the classical age external schemata first educational and military, then medical, psychiatric, psychological, which have made the family the privileged locus of emergence for the disciplinary question of the normal and the abnormal. (Foucault 1978, p. 215)

Can fathers' or mothers' social relations toward their children really be defined only in terms of Foucault's disciplinary question? Foucault would seem to be taking to the limits of parody a fashionable current of thought, nourishing itself in the Freudian analysis of Oedipal conflict and in the feminist critique of patriarchal domination, which has, to my way of thinking, "over-politicized" family social relations, neglecting the collaborative and sacrificial elements of family attachment and over-emphasizing the power aspects of family interaction. This makes it easy to locate the family as an institution of domination on a continuum with the prison, enforcing the same over-arching disciplinary rationality, but it does so by ignoring obvious distinctions between the basis of our obligations as family members and our obligations as citizens to the law. It also neglects the extent to which loyalty to one's family or the desire to maintain one's authority as a family head can constitute the basis for rejection of state authority, for example, in resistance by families to the introduction of compulsory school attendance.

By describing all social relations as relations of domination, Foucault neglects the large aspects of human sociability, in the family and in civil society generally, which are conducted by the norms of cooperation, reciprocity, and the "gift relationship." He neglects that human capacity which Adam Smith called "sympathy," by which we voluntarily adjust our behavior to norms of propriety in order to stand well in the eyes of our fellows (Smith 1759). In Smith's social theory the order of civil society was reproduced, without state direction or class design, by an uncoordinated molecular process of individual self-regulation. Our obedience to legal norms could be understood both in terms of this largely subconscious order-seeking behavior and as an expression of conscious belief in the utility and the justice of such rules in themselves. In Smith's theory threat of penal sanction was not necessary to the reproduction of normal patterns of obedience. Punishment did not constitute the order of civil society; rather, it gave ritual and symbolic expression, in retributive form, to the moral value attached by individuals to rule-obedient behavior (Smith 1763).

Smith's theory of social order may underestimate human beings' mutual malignity, and it is justly criticized by Marxists for writing the facts of power, domination, and subordination out of its account of the social process. But precisely because it tried to think of social order in terms that go beyond the language of power, it offers a more persuasive account of those social activities which we do experience as uncoerced subjects than one which conceives of order as the grid imposed by a carceral archipelago.

My point here is not to argue the virtues of Smithian social theory as against Foucault's structural functionalism or Marxist social control, but rather to use Smith to point to hidden features of both: their state-centered conception of social order and their tendency to reduce all social relations to relations of domination.

How then are we to think through a theory of the reproduction of social life which would give relative weights to the compelled and the consensual, the bound and the free, the chosen and the determined dimensions of human action in given historical societies? Contemporary social theory is increasingly aware that it has been ill-served by the grand theoretical tradition in its approach to these questions—a Parsonian functionalism which restricts human action to the discharge of prescribed roles and the internalization of values; a Marxism which in its hostility to the idealist account of human subjectivity went a long way toward making the active human

185   State, Civil Society, and Total Institutions

subject the determined object of ideological system and social formation; and a structuralism which likewise seems to make individual intellectual creativity and moral choice the determined result of cultural and discursive structure (Giddens 1976). Work-a-day historians and sociologists of criminal justice may well ask at this point what this high-flown theoretical debate has to do with them, or what they could possibly contribute to it. Its relevance is that any theory or history of punishment must make some ultimate judgment about what weight to attach to the state's penal sanction in the reproduction of obedient behavior. What weight you give depends ultimately on how much importance you attach to the consensual and voluntary aspects of human behavior. The social control theory of the 1920s, as Rothman points out in an excellent review of that literature, placed so much stress on the consensual that it neglected the coercive; the social control literature of the seventies exaggerated the coercive at the expense of the consensual (Rothman 1980b). The first step back to a balance between these perspectives will require us to ask how crucial the state has been historically in the reproduction of the order of civil society. My suspicion is that the new social history of law and punishment in the seventies exaggerated the centrality of the state, the police, the prison, the workhouse, and the asylum.

If we are going to get beyond our present almost exclusive focus on the state as the constitutive element of order, we will have to begin to reconstitute the whole complex of informal rituals and processes within civil society for the adjudication of grievances, the settling of disputes, and the compensation of injury. Historians have only just begun to study dispute and grievance procedures within civil society in the same way as these are studied in the anthropology of law (Diamond 1974; Roberts 1980). Among such studies are Edward Thompson's discussion of the "rough justice" rituals of sixteenth- and seventeenth-century English villages, by means of which wife-beaters, scolds, and couples who married out of their age cohort were subjected to public scorn and humiliation by their neigh-

186   Michael Ignatieff

bors (see also Davis 1975; Thompson 1972; Thomas 1971). Because studies of such grievance procedures exist only for the
early modern period, it would be easy to conclude that the state
expropriated such functions in its courts and prisons in the
course of consolidating its monopoly over the means of legitimate violence (Weber 1947, pp. 324–37).

But the idea that the state enjoys a monopoly over legitimate
means of violence is long overdue for challenge. The crimes
which it visits with punishment ought to be interpreted as the
tip of an iceberg, as a small part of those disputes, conflicts,
thefts, assaults too damaging, too threatening, too morally outrageous to be handled within the family, the work unit, the
neighborhood, the street. It would be wrong, I think, to conclude that early modern English villages were the only communities capable of exercising these de facto judicial powers.
Until recently, social histories of the working-class family and
the working-class neighborhood were too confined within their
subdisciplines to include discussion of the anthropology of dispute settlement and the social history of relations with the
police, the courts, and the prisons. But what is now opening up
as an area of study is the social process by which crime was
identified within these units of civil society, and how decisions
were taken to channel certain acts or disputes for adjudication
or punishment by the state. The correlative process, from the
state side, is how agents like the police worked out a tacit
agreement with the local enforcers of norms, determining
which offenses were theirs to control, and which were to be left
to the family, the employer, or the neighborhood (Fine et al.
1979, pp. 118–37). Such research would indicate, I think, that
powers of moral and punitive enforcement are distributed
throughout civil society, and that the function of prison can
only be understood once its position within a whole invisible
framework of sanctioning and dispute regulation procedure in
civil society has been determined. We have always known that
prisons and the courts handled only a tiny fraction of delinquency known to the police. Now we must begin, if we can,
to uncover the network which handled the "dark figure," which

187   State, Civil Society, and Total Institutions

recovered stolen goods, visited retribution on known villains, demarcated the respectable, hid the innocent, and delivered up the guilty. This new area of research will not open up by itself. Empirical fields of this sort become visible only if theory guides historians to new questions. This essay amounts to a plea to historians, criminologists, and sociologists to involve themselves seriously with texts they have been apt to dismiss as abstract and ahistorical—the classical social theory tradition of Smith, Marx, Durkheim, and Weber. The involvement ought to take the form of self-criticism, for if I have argued correctly, these texts are the hidden source of some basic misconceptions—that the state enjoys a monopoly of the punitive sanction, that its moral authority and practical power are *the* binding sources of social order, and that all social relations can be described in the language of power and domination. If we could at least subject these ideas to practical empirical examination, a new social history of order, authority, law, and punishment would begin to emerge.

REFERENCES AND SELECTED BIBLIOGRAPHY

Babington, Anthony. 1971. *The English Bastille*. New York: St. Martin's Press.
Bailey, Victor. 1975. "The Dangerous Classes in Late Victorian England." Ph.D. dissertation, Warwick University.
Beattie, J. M. 1974. "The Pattern of Crime in England, 1660–1800," *Past and Present* 62:47–95.
———. 1977. "Crime and the Courts in Surrey, 1736–53." In *Crime in England, 1550–1800*, ed. J. S. Cockburn. London: Methuen.
Beaumont, Gustave de, and de Tocqueville, Alexis. 1964. *On the Penitentiary System of the United States*. Reprint. Carbondale: Southern Illinois University Press. Originally published 1835.
Bellamy, John. 1973. *Crime and Public Order in England in the Later Middle Ages*. London: Routledge and Kegan Paul.
Bentham, Jeremy. 1791. *Panopticon; or the Inspection House*. London: T. Payne.

188   Michael Ignatieff

Branch, Johnson W. 1970. *The English Prison Hulks*. Chichester: Phillimore.

Chill, Emmanuel. 1962. "Religion and Mendicity in Seventeenth Century France," *International Review of Social History* 7:400–25.

Clemmer, Donald. 1940. *The Prison Community*. New York: Holt, Rinehart and Winston.

Cockburn, J. S., ed. 1977. *Crime in England, 1550–1800*. London: Methuen.

Condon, R. 1962. "The Reform of English Prisons, 1773–1816." Ph.D. dissertation, Brown University.

Cooper, David D. 1976. *The Lesson of the Scaffold: The Public Execution Controversy in Victorian England*. London: Allen Lane.

Cooper, Robert Alan. 1976. "Ideas and Their Execution: English Prison Reform," *Eighteenth Century Studies* 10:73–93.

Davis, Jennifer. 1980. "The London Garroting Panic of 1862: A Moral Panic and the Creation of a Criminal Class in Mid-Victorian England." In *Crime and Law in Western Societies: Historical Essays*, ed. V. A. C. Gatrell, B. Lenman, G. Parker. London: Europa.

Davis, Natalie. 1975. "The Reasons of Misrule." In her *Society and Culture in Early Modern France*. Stanford, Calif.: Stanford University Press.

DeLacy, Margaret Eisenstein. 1980. "County Prison Administration in Lancashire, 1690–1850." Ph.D. dissertation, Princeton University.

Diamond, Stanley. 1974. "The Rule of Law versus the Order of Custom." In his *In Search of the Primitive: A Critique of Civilization*. New Brunswick, N.J.: Transaction Books.

Donajgrodzki, A. P., ed. 1977. *Social Control in Nineteenth Century Britain*. London: Croom Helm.

Evans, Robin. 1975. "A Rational Plan for Softening the Mind: Prison Design, 1750–1842." Ph.D. dissertation, University of Essex.

Fine, Bob, R. Lea J. Kinsey, S. Picciotto, and J. Young, eds. 1979. *Capitalism and the Rule of Law: From Deviancy Theory to Marxism*. Harmondsworth: Penguin.

Fitzgerald, Mike. 1977. *Prisoners in Revolt*. London: Penguin.

Fitzgerald, Mike, and Joe Sim. 1979. *British Prisons*. Oxford: Basil Blackwell.

Foner, Eric. 1976. *Tom Paine and Revolutionary America*. London: Oxford University Press.

Foucault, Michel. 1967. *Madness and Civilization*. Translated by Richard Howard. London: Tavistock.

———, ed. 1973. *Moi, Pierre Rivière . . . un cas de parricide au XIXe siècle*. Paris: Gallimard Julliard.

189   State, Civil Society, and Total Institutions

————. 1976. *La volonté de savoir: histoire de la sexualité.* Paris: Gallimard.

————. 1978. *Discipline and Punish.* Translated by Alan Sheridan. New York: Pantheon.

Giddens, Anthony. 1976. *New Rules of Sociological Method.* New York: Basic Books.

Goffman, Erving. 1961. *Asylums.* Garden City: Doubleday/Anchor.

Gramsci, Antonio. 1971. *Prison Notebooks.* London: Lawrence and Wishart.

Hart, Jennifer. 1955. "Reform of the Borough Police, 1835–1856," *English Historical Review* 70:411–27.

————. 1965. "Nineteenth Century Social Reform: A Tory Interpretation of History," *Past and Present* 31:39–61.

Hay, Douglas. 1975. "Property, Authority and Criminal Law." In *Albion's Fatal Tree*, ed. D. Hay, P. Linebaugh, J. Rule, E. P. Thompson, and C. Winslow. London: Allen Lane.

Henriques, Ursula. 1972. "The Rise and Decline of the Separate System of Prison Discipline," *Past and Present* 54:61–93.

Himmelfarb, Gertrude. 1968. *Victorian Minds.* New York: Harper.

Ignatieff, Michael. 1978. *A Just Measure of Pain: The Penitentiary in the Industrial Revolution, 1750–1850.* New York: Pantheon.

Innes, Joanna. 1980a. "The King's Bench Prison in the Later Eighteenth Century: Law, Authority and Order in a London Debtor's Prison." In *An Ungovernable People: Englishmen and the Law in the 17th and 18th Centuries*, John Brewer and John Styles. London: Hutchinson.

————. 1980b. "English Prisons in the Eighteenth Century." Ph.D. dissertation, Cambridge University.

Jacobs, James. 1977. *Stateville: The Penitentiary in Mass Society.* Chicago: University of Chicago Press.

Katz, Michael. 1968. *The Ironies of Early School Reform.* Cambridge, Mass.: Harvard University Press.

Labour History Society, Great Britain. 1972. *Bulletin: Crime and Industrial Society Conference Report.*

Lasch, Christopher. 1973. "The Discovery of the Asylum." In his *The World of Nations.* New York: Vintage.

Lazerson, Marvin. 1971. *The Origins of the Urban School.* Cambridge, Mass.: Harvard University Press.

Leroy, Ladurie E. 1973. "La décroissance de crime au XVIIIe siècle: bilan d'historiens," *Contrepoint* 9:227–33.

Lewis, W. David. 1965. *From Newgate to Dannemora: The Rise of the Penitentiary in New York, 1796–1848.* Ithaca, N.Y.: Cornell University Press.

Lewis, Orlando F. 1967. *The Development of American Prisons and Prison Customs, 1776–1845.* Reprint. Montclair, N.J.: Patterson Smith. Originally published 1922.

Linebaugh, Peter. 1975. "The Tyburn Riot against the Surgeons." In *Albion's Fatal Tree,* ed. D. Hay, P. Linebaugh, J. Rule, E. P. Thompson, and C. Winslow. London: Allen Lane.

———. 1976. "Karl Marx, the Theft of Wood and Working Class Composition: A Contribution to the Current Debate," *Crime and Social Justice* 6:5–16.

———. 1977. "The Ordinary of Newgate and His Account." In *Crime in England, 1550–1800,* ed. J. S. Cockburn. London: Methuen.

———. Forthcoming. *Crime and the Wage in the Eighteenth Century.*

McConville, Sean. 1977. "Penal Ideas and Prison Management in England, 1700–1850." Ph.D. dissertation, Cambridge University.

McKelvey, Blake. 1977. *American Prisons.* Montclair, N.J.: Patterson Smith.

Marx, K. 1976. *Capital,* I. Harmondsworth: Penguin.

Muraskin, W. A. 1976. "The Social Control Theory in American History: A Critique," *Journal of Social History* 11:559–68.

Pashukanis, B. 1978. *Law and Marxism: A General Theory,* 3d ed. London: Ink Links.

Perrot, Michelle. 1975. "Delinquance et systèmes penitentiaire en France au XIXe siècle," *Annales: économies, sociétés, civilizations* 30:67–91.

———, ed. 1980. *L'impossible prison: recherches sur le système penitentiaire au XIXe siècle.* Paris: Seuil.

Philips, David. 1977. *Crime and Authority in Victorian England: The Black Country, 1835–60.* London: Croom Helm.

Piven, Francis F., and Richard Cloward. 1971. *Regulating the Poor.* New York: Vintage.

Platt, Anthony M. 1969. *The Child Savers: The Invention of Delinquency.* Chicago: University of Chicago Press.

Playfair, Giles. 1971. *The Punitive Obsession.* London: Victor Gollancz.

Pugh, R. B. 1968. *Imprisonment in Medieval England.* Cambridge: Cambridge University Press.

Radzinowicz, Sir Leon. 1948–68. *A History of English Criminal Law.* Vols. 1–6. London: Stevens.

Renner, Karl. 1949. *The Institutions of Private Law and Their Social Functions.* London: Routledge and Kegan Paul.

Roberts, Simon. 1980. "Changing Modes of Dispute Settlement: An Anthropological Perspective." Paper presented at the Past and Present Society Conference on Law and Human Relations, London, 2 July 1980.

191   State, Civil Society, and Total Institutions

Rothman, David J. 1971. *The Discovery of the Asylum*. Boston: Little, Brown.

———. 1980a. *Conscience and Convenience: The Asylum and Its Alternatives in Progressive America*. Boston: Little, Brown.

———. 1980b. "Social Control: The Uses and Abuses of the Concept in the History of Incarceration." Department of History, Columbia University. Unpublished paper.

Rusche, George, and Otto Kirchheimer. 1939. *Punishment and Social Structure*. New York: Columbia University Press.

Schlossman, Steven L. 1977. *Love and the American Delinquent: The Theory and Practice of "Progressive" Juvenile Justice, 1825–1920*. Chicago: University of Chicago Press.

Scull, Andrew T. 1977. *Decarceration: Community Treatment and the Deviant—a Radical View*. Englewood Cliffs, N.J.: Prentice-Hall.

———. 1979. *Museums of Madness*. London: Allen Lane.

Shaw, A. G. L. 1971. *Convicts and the Colonies*. London: Faber.

Sheehan, W. J. 1977. "Finding Solace in 18th Century Newgate." In *Crime in England, 1550–1800*, ed. J. S. Cockburn. London: Methuen.

Silberman, Charles E. 1978. *Criminal Violence, Criminal Justice*. New York: Random House.

Silver, Alan. 1967. "The Demand for Order in Civil Society: A Review of Some Themes in the History of Urban Crime, Police and Riot." In *The Police: Six Sociological Essays*, ed. D. Bordua. New York: Wiley.

Smith, Adam. 1976. *The Theory of Moral Sentiments*. Edited by D. D. Raphael. Oxford: Clarendon Press. Originally published 1759.

———. 1978. *Lectures on Jurisprudence*. Edited by R. L. Meek, D. D. Raphael, and P. G. Stein. Oxford: Clarendon Press. Originally delivered 1763.

Stedman Jones, Gareth. 1971. *Outcast London*. London: Penguin.

———. 1977. "Class Expression versus Social Control?" *History Workshop Journal* 4:163–71.

Stockdale, Eric. 1977. *A Study of Bedford Prison, 1660–1877*. London: Phillimore.

Storch, Robert D. 1975. "The Plague of the Blue Locusts: Police Reform and Popular Resistance in Northern England, 1840–1857," *International Review of Social History* 20:61–90.

Stone, Lawrence. 1979. *Family, Sex and Marriage in England, 1500–1800*. Harmondsworth: Penguin.

Sykes, Gresham. 1958. *The Society of Captives*. Princeton: Princeton University Press.

Teeters, Negley D. 1935. *The Cradle of the Penitentiary: The Walnut Street Jail at Philadelphia, 1773–1835*. Philadelphia: Lippincott.

192   Michael Ignatieff

Thompson, E. P. 1963. *The Making of the English Working Class*. New York: Pantheon.
———. 1971. "The Moral Economy of the English Crowd," *Past and Present* 50:76–136.
———. 1972. "Rough Music! le charivari anglais," *Annales: économies, sociétés, civilisations* 27:285–312.
———. 1975. *Whigs and Hunters*. London: Allen Lane.
———. 1980. *Writing by Candlelight*. London: Merlin.
Tobias, J. J. 1972. *Crime and Industrial Society in the Nineteenth Century*. New York: Schocken.
Tocqueville, Alexis de. 1969. *Democracy in America*. Edited by J. P. Mayer. New York: Doubleday/Anchor.
Tomlinson, Margaret Heather. 1975. "Victorian Prisons: Administration and Architecture." Ph.D. dissertation, Bedford College, London University.
Trumbach, Randolph. 1978. *The Rise of the Egalitarian Family: Aristocratic Kinship and Domestic Relations in 18th Century England*. London: Academic Press.
Webb, Beatrice and Sidney. 1963. *English Prisons under Local Government*. London: Frank Cass. Originally published 1922.
Weber, Marx. 1947. *The Theory of Social and Economic Organization*. Edited by Talcott Parsons. Glencoe: Free Press.
Whiting, J. R. S. 1975. *Prison Reform in Gloucestershire, 1775–1820*. London: Phillimore.
Wicker, Tom. 1975. *A Time to Die*. New York: Quadrangle.

Part III
The Third Phase: Criminology and the Administered State

Argument: The Statistical

[8]

JOSEPH FLETCHER

MORAL AND EDUCATIONAL STATISTICS

OF

ENGLAND AND WALES.

I WISH to submit to the Section a few facts illustrative of the moral and intellectual condition of the English people. These facts form a very imperfect body of evidence; but gentlemen who are acquainted with the true nature of Statistics, or of science in general, will not therefore reject it, if it be the result of continuous and conscientious labour, applied to remove the frontier of the doubt and ignorance which surround us but one step further back. Those who have expected our science to spring into existence ready armed like another Minerva, and complain that Statists can know nothing because they do not know everything in the field of investigation which they propose to themselves, ask of us what they ask of the labourers in no other department of inquiry, and might as well refuse to Newton his immortal name, because he did not discover the uttermost planet recently detected by Adams and Leverrier. It might rather be rejoined, that the more neglected are Statistics, the greater the reproach upon the age and country in which their consequent imperfection is witnessed. They can have no existence in a state of barbarism; for rude despotism acts without asking many questions. In a state of society somewhat advanced, they enter imperfectly into the arts of government, in the shape of hasty inductions from narrow experience, applied as general truths in the exigency of the moment. It is only in the highest state of modern civilization that we see governments keeping up some acquaintance, by extended and refined observation, with the real condition of the masses of their people; for in social as in individual history, it is by no means the earliest stage of progress in which we ask ourselves what is really our own moral constitution, what is the practical course of our own conduct, and what are the real springs of our own actions. Yet, to society at large, such questions are as essential as to the individual; for not a single prevailing defect will remain without its reflected and reproducing evil in our united conduct, whenever it shall please God that we be tried in a manner to test its existence or its dominance. Most of our societies of philanthropy and of missionary labour assume this truth as their basis; and it is not less felt in legislation for the reformatory discipline of gaols and workhouses, and for the advancement of public

A

2   *Moral and Educational Statistics*

education.   The necessities of art even in this case have had to awaken science to her aid, as in so many and such various other fields.   We have more reason, therefore, to be thankful for the existence of a science demanded chiefly by the arts of philanthropy, than discouraged by its imperfections.

All that we practically know of men individually is defective enough; and yet more defective is our personal knowledge of the extent to which the qualities which we do perceive and appreciate in others, prevail in the great mass of society, in places, and among classes, and under circumstances, entirely beyond the reach of any one person's observation; the fruits of which, however extensive it may be, will not have the exactitude of an exhaustive enumeration of well-defined facts.   It is to such an enumeration of facts, therefore, that the Statist looks with intense interest, whether of those relating to whole states, which can be collected only by governments and on a limited scale, or those which are elaborated in much greater detail and applied to proportionally limited parts of the population, at the expense of individuals or of societies, such as the Statistical Societies of London and Manchester.   That these censuses of facts are not inquisitorial, in the injurious sense of that term, is proved by their being more extensive and varied, and more easily made, just in proportion to the freedom of each country's spirit and institutions.

As it is of the whole kingdom that I purpose to speak, it is of the *public* enumerations that I must now chiefly make use; and by the nature of the subject I am required to use principally the last Census of the Population; the Income Tax Returns; the Reports of the Registrar-General of Births, Deaths, and Marriages; the Home Office Tables of Criminal Offenders; the latest Reports of the Poor Law Commissioners; and a Summary of Savings Banks, published by the Barrister appointed to certify their rules.   It is by the agency of such departments as produce these documents that the State takes cognizance of all or of certain classes of its subjects, at various periods, and under the occurrence of very dissimilar events; and from the records of this momentary cognizance the following results are derived; while many more of equal interest may be obtained by those who have the desire and the opportunity to elaborate them.   I contribute on the present occasion only the results of some first efforts, which, if they serve to indicate the direction in which another may profitably proceed, will not have been made in vain.

All the first figures of such records as are now adduced, profess to register, exhaustively, certain definitely described circumstances, as those attaching to a stated number or class of individuals, at a specified time, in a place with limits accurately described; and all the value of the results is involved in the character of the first observation never being obscured by any subsequent operations, as, by averages so crude as to conceal all distinctiveness of character; or by applying an ascertained rate of progress in one set of elements to another set, as that of population to crime, for instance; or by the comparison of results between which no parity really exists.   Rather than rush to one generalization upon aggregate results, it is better to retain the facts in manageable groups, by means of which to compare one class with another, one district with another, and one period with another; and by the alternate use of analytical and synthetical methods, to bring the several elements into every possible combination, and detect the laws of their coincidence and relationship, or obtain new views as to the direction which should be given to more refined observation.

The man who studies society, however, labours under a great difficulty in being entirely denied the use of experiment, and limited most rigidly to observation; the observation of elements most subtilly combined, in a state of unceasing change, and wholly beyond his control. Analysis, therefore, in the sense of the chemist, is absolutely impossible; but by exhaustive enumerations of facts which are strongly indicative of the existence of many others, or are their invariable concomitants, we get a means of detecting the excess or deficiency of certain social elements in definite classes or localities; and by multiplying these lines of observation, and the combinations in which they are arranged for purposes of comparison, we gradually arrive at higher and safer inductions, which will sometimes corroborate principles which we have reached by deductive reasoning from the moral elements of individual character, and by observations on society in the limited field of our personal experience, and at others will present irreconcileable results, which the bigot of theory will despise, but which the man of science knows how to prize as uncut gems. He who seeks facts merely to illustrate a hypothesis in which he believes with a blind faith, will throw them away in disgust; but he who uses a hypothesis merely to discover truth, will, on the contrary, abandon its use in the moment that he arrives at facts which resist all efforts to reduce them into accordance with it.

Neither, in the present state of statistical knowledge, when a practical acquaintance with the value of its figures is limited to a few, is it beneath our endeavours to arrange the results to which we attain under the true names of the original data, in an order which can readily be understood; and they will then have a useful practical influence, while yet, in the eyes of the man of science, they offer but imperfect indications towards the ultimate discovery of higher truths. For notwithstanding that Statistics are often despised for the uncertainty which attaches to their use in the hands of the unpractised, the uncandid, or the prejudiced, they exercise, even in their imperfect state, an important sway over all inductive reasoning from social experience; and since we cannot live a single day without acting on the dictates of such reasoning, however imperfect it may be, there is no field in which a new truth so rapidly forces upon the world a practical recognition as in that of Statistics.

In so
far as the laws of these influences the best summary of the continental experience is that supplied by the Statistique Morale of M.
Quetelet, published in 1846 *, though the Statistique Morale de la
France of M. Guerry, published in 1833, will always challenge our
regard as the greatest work of the kind for its time.   But to demonstrate or correct these laws has not been the object of the present
investigation.   They have been not only presupposed but *used* in the
course of it, with the hope of making that further step at which
M. Quetelet, as well as M. Guerry and my coadjutor, have stopped
short; viz., to detect, by statistical analysis, some of the causes of that
difference in the relative amount of crime, or other moral failure,
which characterises different regions; in fact, to discover, as M.
Quetelet expresses it, ere we can "modify, the causes which rule our
social system, and thereby modify also the deplorable results which
are annually read in the annals of crime and suicide."   Limited and
imperfect as the progress made in this labour necessarily is, those who
best know the difficulty of demonstrating a new truth in social science,
or its value as a barrier against a host of errors when once proved, will
not regard as valueless either the faithful co-ordination of new facts
which forms the body of the present paper, or the following results of
their various comparison.

Conclusions.

1. In comparing the gross commitments for criminal offences with
the proportion of instruction in each district, there is found to be a
small balance *in favour* of the most instructed districts in the years of
most industrial depression (1842-3-4), but a greater one *against* them
in the years of less industrial depression (1845-6-7); while in comparing the more with the less instructed portions of each district, the
final result is against the former at both periods, though four-fold
at the latter what it is at the former.

2. No correction for the ages of the population in different districts,
to meet the excess of criminals at certain younger periods of life, will
change the character of this superficial evidence against instruction;

* Mémoires de l'Académie Royale de la Belgique, tome xxi.

every legitimate allowance of the kind having already been made in arriving at these results.

3. Down to this period, therefore, the comparison of the criminal and educational returns of this, any more than of any other, country of Europe. has afforded no sound statistical evidence in favour, and as little against, the moral effects associated with instruction, as actually disseminated among the people.

4. The intractable mass of gross commitments requiring, therefore, some further correction, to make them declare decisively either in favour of or against popular instruction, as actually conveyed, it has been endeavoured to apply one for the *migration* of the dishonest into the more wealthy, populous, and instructed localities, by drawing a distinction between those classes of offences which arise from general depravity, and those which will obviously be in excess in certain localities, because generally associated with the professional vice or vagabondage which seeks its home in them; and, by proving statistically the existence of such a distinction, likewise the influence of the denser populations rather to *assemble* the demoralized than to *breed* an excess of demoralization.

5. The great class of the more serious offences against the person and malicious offences against property is obviously that least affected by migrations of the depraved, and affords strong testimony, by *its universal excess wherever ignorance is in excess*, that many of the offences against *property* which are in such excess in the more instructed and populous localities, are committed by delinquents bred in the places indicated by the excess of the former offences.

6. It is this great class of offences, therefore, and not the gross commitments, which should be regarded as the *index crime* to the relative moral character of each district, not as a perfect test, but as one approximating to the truth much nearer than the latter; being affected in a smaller degree by the migration of the depraved towards the more instructed centres of resort; a further correction for which, in the case of the index crime itself, were it attainable, would render its universal testimony in favour of the good influences associated with instruction in England yet stronger.

7. The whole excess above the average of such crime is found in the South Midland and Eastern Agricultural Counties, especially those with dispersed domestic manufactures, and in the manufacturing counties of dispersed trades, and arises in some part from the excess of malicious offences against property, in the counties of dispersed trades, and those of greatest industrial demoralization under the old systems of poor law mismanagement, in the spirit of which they are still bound up.

8. In like manner, the whole excess of offences against property is found in the South Midland and Eastern Agricultural Counties, especially those with domestic manufactures, with the addition of the Metropolis, which here takes the place held by the manufacturing counties of dispersed trades in the former category.

9. The excess of offences against property, with violence, is always in the more ignorant districts, and this class, with malicious offences against property, and offences against the currency, is the most affected by fluctuations in employment, while a progressive wave of larceny flows forward from times of depression, unheeding of revived

M

industry, especially in the Metropolis and the South Midland and Eastern Agricultural Counties, in which the offences against the currency are peculiarly in excess.

10. A great excess of crime is observed to follow every considerable access to the price of food, and consequent disturbance of credit and industry, without any commensurate recoil when prices are lowered and manufacturing prosperity restored; while, on the other hand, a steady decline of assaults shows a favourable progress in manners in the more policed districts.

11. The six-fold increase in crime in the 30 years from 1811 to 1841, has been by far the least in the Metropolitan, or best educated and policed counties, and most in the Mining and Manufacturing, or those worst educated and policed; reference being had to the density of the population.

12. There is in England an apparent fostering of crime by bad judicial and correctional arrangements, coincident with a too ready use of the arm of the magistrate in the correction of the very young.

13. There has been, however, an analogous augmentation in the criminal calendars of other countries, as of France, which exhibit the like excessive proportion of petty offenders as our own.

14. The greatest proportionate excess of the *gross* commitments is found in the Metropolis, and some of the Western Counties of England, and the remainder of the excess in the Southern and Eastern Agricultural Counties, especially those with domestic manufactures.

15. The adoption of the class of serious offences against the person and malicious offences against property, as the *index class of crime*, is justified by the results of an entirely different set of observations, agreeing with these only in their comparative absence of influence from migration, viz., the returns of *improvident marriages* (designating as such all those of males under 21 years of age), which are likewise universally in excess only where ignorance is in excess, except amongst the rude populations of the North and West of Yorkshire.

16. Its adoption is equally supported by the returns of *bastardy*, which afford the same general testimony in favour of the influences associated with instruction, except in the cases of two other of the Northern Counties (Cumberland and Westmorland), characterised by the same rudeness of manners.

17. The amalgamation of the two latter bodies of facts, were it possible, would afford a yet more accurate coincidence with the class adopted as that of index crime (since they represent, to a great extent, alternative forms of improvidence); and an equal support to it, in regard to the south and east of England, is supplied by the returns of *paupers* relieved, and of *deposits* accumulated in savings' banks.

18. The excessive influence of fluctuations in the national industry upon the condition of the mining and manufacturing districts is shown, not only in the peculiar excess of commitments observed in them in "bad times" (the result, as appears by their very character, rather of the idleness than the distress of such times), but also in the excess of improvident marriages and of bastardy which characterise them in the "good times;" the Metropolis also sharing in the latter excess, especially under a gambling excitement, like that of the railway mania.

19. These various data afford a testimony in favour of the educational influences generally associated with instruction far more powerful than any that has yet been supplied; and yet these influences are by no means unmixed with others, of which it is impossible to estimate the exact force, but every reasonable allowance for which will still leave a large balance to the credit of the school, so long as a deficiency of instruction among the population at large is accompanied by a proportionate excess of criminal commitments of the kinds least influenced by migration, and by every other indication of relative weakness and corruption.

20. Wherever there is a less amount of instruction, that which is being conveyed is also inferior in quality as a detergent from moral failure, insomuch that a number possessed of this inferior instruction, more than proportionate to those who receive it among the population at large, are brought to the bar of justice.

21. The progress of such education among the body of the people as supplies this detergent influence, shows itself in the criminal calendars by a *general* decrease in the commitments, and, above all, in the proportion of those who can "read and write well," rather than of those who are of an inferior grade of instruction, whose numbers necessarily *increase* with the *extension* of instruction, the good effects of which must be sought, therefore, in the higher tests pointing to its *quality.*

22. The decline of absolute inability to read and write at double the rate among those brought up to the bar of justice that is observed among those who come to be married, is a decisive evidence *against* the influences associated with *some* of the instruction now conveyed in the remoter agricultural and manufacturing districts, where this effect is most obvious, by the weakest of the day and the most over-tasked of the Sunday schools; though none against those associated with the greater and better part of it, or against the conviction that without these influences a far worse state of society would have supervened; as appears by the augmentation of crime as the concomitant of *every* relative increase of ignorance in several of the counties.

23. The conclusion is therefore irresistible that *education* is not only essential to the security of modern society, but that such education should be solid, useful, and above all, Christian, in supersedence of much that is given by the weakest of the day schools and attempted by the most secular of the Sunday schools.

24. The *Christian School*, therefore, is one great instrument for the moral elevation of society, which even the unchristian should support, on considerations of the most selfish interest.

25. Next to education, the organization of industry appears to have the most powerful influence on the moral aspects of society, and is therefore a feature which has been kept in view in the present investigation with almost equal constancy; an aggravation of every evil appearing, *cæteris paribus,* wherever light domestic industry, furnishing a produce for sale and not for home use, is found for the women and children; with the effect of relieving the labour of the male head of the family from much of its support, and thereby encouraging both bastardy and early marriages, with their attendant train of excessive numbers, depending on a fluctuating trade and a half-employed man-

hood; such being especially the case in the South Midland Agricultural Counties with domestic manufactures, and the Manufacturing Counties with dispersed trades; the worst combination of all being that of domestic manufactures, agricultural labour, and old poor-law habits, as in Buckinghamshire and Bedfordshire.

26. The "small husbandry," on the other hand, appears to be at the end of the scale the very opposite to the "small manufactures;" being accompanied, whether in the Celtic regions of the west, where it prevails universally, or in the Scandinavian regions of the north, where it prevails extensively, by a great deficiency of every feature of evil, except bastardy, which is in partial excess, but much *less* in the west than in the north*.

27. The large-capital systems of industry, whether agricultural or manufacturing, hold a varying moral position between the small husbandry and the small manufactures, in general accordance with their degree of ignorance, whether in respect of crime, incontinence, pauperism, or want of providence; *the agricultural being, on the whole, the most ignorant and therefore the most depraved;* though shades of both crime and ignorance darker than those of the agricultural regions *in the same latitude,* characterise the manufacturing districts in their extension northward, while, on the other hand, they have greatly the advantage of the agricultural districts in regard to pauperism; the deficiency of bastardy in some of the coal and iron districts being likewise very remarkable.

28. The excess of *real property* in proportion to the population is assumed to afford some rude index to the extent of the culture by larger farms, which has been considered with reference to the organization of industry; and the result derivable from the generally unfavourable aspect of the districts where real property is in the greatest relative excess, is obviously that a higher development of industry demands a higher development of moral character among the population to work it with social safety.

29. The excess of *persons of independent means* is seen generally to coincide with the excess of instruction, and their direct influence cannot, therefore, be wholly distinguished from that portion of it which is exercised through the agency of the schools.

30. The *concentration of the population* into masses appears to have the effect of augmenting the gross commitments, and especially those for offences against property without violence, but, for the reasons already stated, may be concluded to have little or no effect in augmenting the proportion of delinquents, but only in aggregating the ill-disposed in peculiar excess.

31. *Eleemosynary relief* has undoubtedly an influence to the same result, in the places of more genteel residence; and the most pauperised districts are those in which the farmers, in the boards of guardians, and in the administration of the highway rates, still, in a sordid misconception of their own interests, use the public funds, to the full extent of their ability, to keep up that excess of labour in the market,

* The moral effect of small properties and holdings has been elaborated with great care in a paper by John Barton, Esq., of Elmsleigh, read before the Statistical Society, in May, 1849, and which will appear in a subsequent number of this Society's Journal.

and therefore, as they vainly imagine, that cheapness of it, which the farmers of Buckinghamshire and Bedfordshire find, without any such contrivance, among the poor peasantry of those counties, half dependent on their petty domestic manufactures of straw and lace.

32. The moral influences of improved *police*, too, are obviously greater than has generally been supposed, in its repression of the small pot-house crime which the present data prove to have an immediate sympathy with the violent and malicious offences against property, and offences against the currency, and to be, in all probability, a sort of nursing crime, through which (in times of disordered industry more especially) the hardier of the young and unprincipled graduate into professional crime; influences which are obvious in the comparative *deficiency* of these minor commitments in proportion to the more serious in the best policed counties.

33. The influence of *race*, too, can scarcely be doubted, in contemplating many of the facts here brought to account, such as those which give a peculiar aspect, throughout, to the Celtic populations of the west; whose ignorance, poverty, and excess of numbers in proportion to the produce of the soil, are as obvious as their relative deficiency of crime and improvident marriages, with only the average of incontinence in other respects, and a deficiency of savings in banks, which, however indicative of their genuine poverty, in no respect impugns the exceeding parsimony which characterises the daily life of their peasantry; features which all indicate considerable popular misapprehensions as to the Celtic character, and the structure of society which it is calculated to produce.

34. There is likewise a very remarkable general resemblance in moral features between the Celtic regions of the west and the Scandinavian districts of the north, except in the greater amount of energy, instruction, and means possessed by the latter; the second as well as the third, being probably a result of the first; a characteristic of race associated with higher habits of co-operation.

35. The Celtic districts, considered *apart*, always give the same results as those supplied by the rest of the kingdom, with reference to the predominantly beneficial influences associated with instruction, although they often appear, in the more general comparison with the kingdom at large, to give opposite testimony.

36. For the many minor inductions which have been adventured, I would refer to the preceding pages*; and they will be found the more trustworthy because exempt from the common fallacy which would regard every moral phenomenon as the result of *one cause* only, if it do but exhibit some numerical accordance with any *one concomitant* placed in such a light by the imagination of the inquirer. I am well aware of the various objections which may be brought against some of them; but they involve what appeared to me to be the most probable hypotheses for the reconciliation of the facts; and to anticipate objections would be a very unprofitable labour, especially to one who trusts to find in the reader as much candour as may have been permitted to his own mind, in the course of his present endeavour to distinguish the predominant from the subordinate influences, and their various effect under different combinations.

M 3

Argument about Argument: The Statistical

8. Criminal statistics and their interpretation

V. A. C. Gatrell and T. B. Hadden

Annual statistical returns relating to criminal behaviour in England and Wales have been published in the parliamentary papers since 1805. In the early decades of the century they were limited in scope, but from 1857 onwards they contained the several distinct types of information which form the basis of criminal statistics even today: the numbers of indictable offences known to the police, the numbers of people committed to trial for indictable and summary offences respectively, and the numbers and personal characteristics of the people imprisoned upon conviction. These returns enable us to plot across a period of years the long-term trends and the short-term fluctuations in the incidence of criminal activity of different kinds, in England and Wales as a whole and in different parts of the country, and to say something also, with a fair degree of certainty, about the kinds of people who came before the courts.[1]

Of the several kinds of numerical data on nineteenth-century social behaviour at our disposal, the criminal statistics are among the most comprehensive and copious. Since the incidence of criminal activity in certain forms, at different periods, and in different parts of the country can sometimes be explained in terms of the impact of social and economic conditions on the population at large, the records of crime may reflect directly on the degree of security which the English social and economic system assured or failed to assure to the mass of its people at a time of rapid urban and industrial growth.

338   V. A. C. GATRELL AND T. B. HADDEN

Many commentators in the 1830s and 1840s were more consistently aware of the potential importance of analyses of this kind than recent historians have shown themselves to be.[3] A new statistical consciousness in those years, and a widespread alarm at the apparent increase in crime over the previous quarter century, generated a sizeable criminological literature in which a direct relationship between crime and the impact upon the population of economic and social conditions was largely taken for granted. Indeed, the varying incidence of crime, from year to year and from county to county, was frequently regarded as a legitimate index of a pattern of social dislocation in the country at large. But if these writers anticipated our hypotheses, they did not develop them fully, and tended to be unsatisfactory in their statistical methods. And by the late 1850s, as police control grew more effective and the political climate changed, the focus of attention turned from general questions about the total incidence of various types of crime to the consideration of particular problems such as juvenile delinquency or drunkenness.

8. *Criminal statistics and their interpretation* 339

The real difficulty, however, arises from the fact that few contemporaries were either in a position or had the inclination to attempt an extended survey of the records over a period of several decades; nor were they always critically aware of the dangers inherent in the figures which all modern commentators must recognise. Thus even when they did use the official statistics their conclusions were often based upon incomplete and ill-assimilated evidence. More than this, the discussion of crime was fraught with presupposition and prejudice then as it is now. It was commonly loaded with moral judgement, and no less frequently biased in favour of certain prior assumptions. By judicious selection of data it was as possible for one writer to demonstrate the 'criminality' of rural counties as it was for another to demonstrate the depravity of industrial counties. And from the 1850s onwards the growing preoccupation with the problems of drunkenness and juvenile delinquency tended to preclude a balanced assessment of criminal activity as a whole.

340   V. A. C. GATRELL AND T. B. HADDEN

1. THE AVAILABLE MATERIAL

At their most comprehensive, English criminal statistics contain four kinds of
information upon which any detailed examination of criminal behaviour will
have to be based. They may be listed as follows.

(a) The numbers of males and females, in each county and in England and
    Wales as a whole, committed to trial for an indictable offence (that is an
    offence tried before a jury in the superior courts of assize or quarter
    sessions). These are referred to as *indictable committals*, and in the nine-
    teenth century they were published in the set of returns headed Judicial
    Proceedings or Criminal Offenders from 1805 onwards.

(b) The numbers of males and females in each county and in England and
    Wales, *committed to prison* after conviction, either on an indictable
    or on a summarily tried offence, together with their ages, degrees of

8. Criminal statistics and their interpretation 341

instruction, previous records, etc. These were published in the set of returns headed Gaols and Prisons, from 1836 onwards.

(c) The numbers of males and females, in each police district and county, and in England and Wales as a whole, brought before a magistrate on summary jurisdiction for less serious offences. These are referred to as *summary committals*, and they were published in the set of returns which appeared from 1857 onwards headed Police Returns.

(d) The numbers of *indictable offences known to the police* to have been committed in each police district or county and in England and Wales as a whole, whether or not the offender was actually traced and brought to trial. These were also published in the Police Returns from 1857 onwards.

The continuity of these series was affected by two major reorganisations in 1833–4 and in 1856–7 and to a lesser extent by a third in 1893. To describe the contents of the criminal statistics in more detail, therefore, it is convenient to isolate the three periods marked off by these dates (1805–33, 1834–56, and 1857–92) and to treat them separately.

FIRST PERIOD 1805–33: *indictable committals*

The stimulus for the collection of the first committal returns was the contemporary debate on the death penalty, which caused the Home Secretary in 1805 to direct the clerks of each court or circuit to make an annual return of the numbers of indictable committals for trial, of capital convictions, and of executions.[7] In 1810 the House of Commons passed a motion proposed by Romilly for the collection of much fuller returns covering both indictable and summary offences, but though no summary returns were collected in this period, the motion did secure the publication of the figures collected for 1805–9, and thereby established the standard format of the committals statistics up to 1834.[8] For this period, then, figures are available for the number of persons in England and Wales as a whole, and in each county respectively, (i) committed for trial on an indictable offence, (ii) discharged on 'no true bill' being found, (iii) acquitted and (iv) convicted. This information was given for each of an alphabetical list of some fifty major offences, covering most forms of homicide, robbery, housebreaking, larceny, and the more serious political offences such as riot and machine-breaking.

These first statistics were thus no more than court records of all those dealt with for a restricted group of offences defined as 'serious' only in terms of legal history. But they can be used for the study of long-term trends in certain forms of criminal behaviour from the start of the century.

SECOND PERIOD 1834–56: (a) *Indictable committals and* (b) *Commitments to prison*

(a) *Indictable committals*

In 1833 Samuel Redgrave, the Criminal Registrar, reorganised the presentation

342   V. A. C. GATRELL AND T. B. HADDEN

of the returns for indictable committals by replacing the old alphabetical list of fifty or so indictable offences with a new and expanded classification. Seventy-five offences were now rearranged under the following six main headings which have survived with minor variations in their content until the present day:

(i) offences against the person (homicide, wounding etc., including for the first time simple assaults and assaults on police officers);
(ii) offences against property involving violence (robbery, burglary, house-breaking etc.);
(iii) offences against property not involving violence (larceny etc.);
(iv) malicious offences against property (arson, machine-breaking, rick-burning etc.);
(v) offences against the currency (forgery, coining etc.);
(vi) miscellaneous offences (including notably treason, sedition, riot etc.)

Apart from this rearrangement, the returns of persons in each county com-mitted to trial, acquitted, and convicted, for each of the seventy-five offences thus categorised, were continued much as before, together with a statement of the sentences imposed. Thus by linking these returns with those for 1805–34, it is relatively easy to construct a general table for the incidence of indictable com-mitals in the first half of the century, both regionally and nationally.

For the brief period 1834–49 there was one exceptional addition to the con-tents of the committal returns – probably in response to the growing interest in the characteristics of offenders fostered by the statistical societies established in the 1830s. This was the provision of data on the 'character' of those committed for indictable offences: their ages, sex, and degree of instruction. This series was discontinued in 1849 since it more or less duplicated the comparable information given for prisoners in the Prison Returns; and it was in any case reasonably argued that prison officials were better placed to compile reliable returns of character than the officials of the courts.

(b) *Commitments to prison*

An unsatisfactory series of Prison Returns had been published since 1820, for the most part containing only written reports from each county on the con-ditions of individual gaols. From 1836, the information relating to gaols and prisoners was systematised in tabular form in an annual digest. Until 1856 this was published as an appendix to the report of the inspector of prisons for the Home Counties, and thereafter it was brought within the composite volume of Statistics to which we have already referred.

The importance of these new returns is twofold. First, they contain compre-hensive information on the character of offenders, and this was published in a similar form throughout the century. From the start the Prison Returns gave the age, sex, degree of instruction, and number of previous commitments to gaol of all prisoners, distinguishing between those imprisoned for indictable and for

8. *Criminal statistics and their interpretation* 343

summary offences respectively. Secondly, the distinction drawn between committals to prison for indictable and for summary offences respectively makes the Prison Returns our only source for the number of summary offences committed in the period before 1857. It is, however, an indirect and necessarily inaccurate one: the different kinds of summary offences for which the prisoners were gaoled were not fully specified; and in any case many offences tried summarily would not be included in the total because many petty offenders might merely be discharged with a caution or fined.

THIRD PERIOD 1857–1892: (a) *Indictable committals*, (b) *Commitments to prison*, (c) *Summary committals* and (d) *Indictable offences known to the police*

In 1856–7 Redgrave undertook a thoroughgoing reorganisation of the official returns following on the Police Act passed in 1856 'to render more effectual the police in the counties and boroughs of England and Wales'.[9] This marks the main turning point in the structure of the statistics for three reasons.

First, the existing returns from the courts and from the prisons were supplemented by a new set of Police Returns from the newly-constituted police districts, now based on boroughs as well as on counties. For each district the Police Returns now provided two kinds of information hitherto lacking: the number of offenders tried summarily for each offence and the number of indictable offences in the existing classification known to the police to have been committed. Secondly, all this information, relating to indictable committals, to prisons and prisoners, to summary committals, and to indictable offences known to the police, was henceforth brought together in one annual volume. Thirdly, each volume from 1859 onwards was prefaced by a full review written by the Criminal Registrar. This contained a number of useful summaries and analyses of the information in the subsequent tables, as well as occasional further information not otherwise published. In these prefaces, moreover, Redgrave and his successors maintained a running commentary on the effects of legal changes on the statistics, and speculated with varying degrees of perceptivity on the causes of the changes in the patterns of criminal behaviour observed from year to year and decade to decade. The prefaces written towards the end of the century naturally tended to be more sophisticated than those written earlier; but in all cases they are worth consulting, not merely for their useful synopses, but also in their own right, in so far as they exemplify the thinking of perhaps the most professional of all nineteenth-century criminologists.

Redgrave himself described the new structure of the returns as follows:

The principle of arrangement adopted has been that the three separate heads shall form one document, and that under each such facts shall be included, among others, as more peculiarly appertain to it. Thus under the head *Police* will be found such

344   V. A. C. GATRELL AND T. B. HADDEN

particulars as can be obtained relative to the crimes committed, the numerous petty offences punished summarily, and the antecedents and previous habits and character of the offenders. The head *Criminal Proceedings* will be chiefly confined to an accurate definition of the offences, result of trial, and punishments of those charged with indict-able crimes; and the *Prisons* portion will contain more full information as to the ages of prisoners, their state of instruction, number of previous convictions, and such other particulars as the gaol officers have the best means of ascertaining, but in no case has an attempt been made to obtain information not properly within the knowledge of the officers making the returns, and upon which reliance may not be placed.[10]

The contents and significance of the new series may be summarised as follows.

(a) *Indictable committals*

These were continued without alteration under the classification introduced in 1834. Thus the analyses which are possible on the earlier returns can be carried through to the end of the century without difficulty. One interesting addition to the tables published under this heading related to the number of juvenile offenders committed to the reformatories and industrial schools established from the 1850s onwards. The number of these juveniles, however, was always included in the returns for indictable or summary committals as the case might be; and since every juvenile sent to one of these institutions had to serve a brief time in prison beforehand, they are included in the Prison Returns as well. Thus the development of differential treatment for juveniles involved no dis-tortion of the main statistical records.

(b) *Commitments to prison*

The Prison Returns were also continued without major alteration, although information on the occupations and birthplaces of prisoners was added to that given in the earlier period on their ages, sex, literacy, and previous records.

(c) *Summary committals*

The importance of the new information given in the Police Returns should not be underestimated. That relating to summary offences enables us to allow for the appreciable extension from the 1820s onwards in the summary jurisdiction of magistrates' courts over offences which had previously been considered indictable and reserved for the superior courts.[11] Naturally this process seriously affected the long-term comparability of the records both of indictable committals and of indictable offences known to the police, since indictable offences which were in fact tried summarily were normally deducted from the total of indictable offences. More direct and comprehensive information than that previously obtainable from the Prison Returns about each type of offence dealt with sum-marily is thus essential if these distortions are to be corrected. In any case it is

8. *Criminal statistics and their interpretation* 345

obviously advisable to include in any index of 'serious' crime the incidence of the more important larcenies and assaults which were in the event tried summarily. Even some of those offences which were not 'serious', such as drunkenness and disorderliness, are clearly of interest in their own right.

(d) *Indictable offences known to the police*

The publication of these figures in the Police Returns after 1857 is perhaps of even greater importance than the publication of the figures for summary committals. They constitute what is generally recognised as the best available indication of the 'actual' incidence of various kinds of criminal activity in the society at large, since they are less subject than all other figures to the distorting effects of local differences in police practice or of national developments in police efficiency, prosecution practice, and court procedure. On the basis of these figures, moreover it is possible to attempt a very approximate estimate of police efficiency in tracing offenders, by comparing the numbers of offences known with the numbers of people committed to trial for those offences.

Apart from the information on (c) and (d) above, the Police Returns contain two further kinds of data of rather less importance. First, tables are given on the size, expense, and ratio of individual police forces to the populations of their districts. This enables us to estimate the differing strength of police forces across the country, a process which for the period before 1857 could be attempted only from local sources and occasional parliamentary papers.[12] Secondly, tables were provided on the size in each district of the 'criminal class', defined as known thieves and depradators, receivers of stolen goods, suspicious characters, etc.

1893 AND AFTER

Although this chapter is primarily concerned with the nineteenth-century returns, it may be helpful to give a brief description of the changes which took place in 1893 following the recommendations of the Select Committee to Revise the Criminal Portion of the Judicial Statistics.[13] They were quite straightforward and can be simply listed. Whereas hitherto annual police and prison returns had been based on the year ending 30 September and 31 March respectively, all returns from 1893 onwards were standardised on the calendar year. All figures were given as ratios per 100,000 of the population, whether male or female, in order to allow easier comparison with rates in earlier years. Certain elementary illogicalities in the previous returns were rectified: thus the practice of excluding from the returns all reported cases of simple larceny involving less than five shillings, except where an arrest took place, was discontinued;[14] and the figures for indictable offences which were in the event tried summarily were no longer deducted from those for indictable offences known to the police. The enumera-

M

346   V. A. C. GATRELL AND T. B. HADDEN

tion of offences was slightly altered, but the basic categories introduced in 1834 were retained. The returns for summary committals were transferred from the Police to the Judicial Returns. Finally, the Criminal Registrar's introductory reports were considerably expanded and simplified. Henceforth they contained clearer and more detailed analyses of the incidence of various types of crime over periods of twenty years, maps showing the geographical distribution of certain offences, and precise accounts of the effects of legal reforms on the continuity of the statistical records.

Though the organisation of the returns was rationalised and their use made correspondingly less time-consuming, the information they contained was not seriously altered, and the possibility of carrying analyses and comparisons into the twentieth century is not, therefore, unduly affected.

It will be clear from this discussion that to exploit fully the information contained in the official returns across the whole century is no simple task. To collate and tabulate even a simple series of figures over an appreciable period may involve a considerable amount of cross-reference from one set of returns to another, the format of which in various periods may well be quite different. If only on this account, it is important to be quite clear before beginning to collect figures what combinations of data will provide the best answer to the questions asked of them. One must always bear in mind for instance the advisability of combining figures for summary committals with those for indictable offences, whether these last relate to indictable committals or to indictable offences known to the police.

The simplest of the tables and graphs presented in the later sections of this chapter illustrates the relationship between the incidence of assaults and of drunkenness respectively, and it may serve as an example of several of the processes involved in the use of the returns.[15] For each year covered it was necessary to locate in separate tables in the Police Returns and then to tabulate the numbers of summarily tried assaults and summarily tried offences of drunkenness and disorderliness; a further table in the Police Returns had to be consulted for the number of indictable assaults known to the police; the two figures for assaults had to be added; and both this composite figure, and the figure for drunkenness, had to be reduced to rates per 100,000 of the relevant population. The compilation of other tabulations may be even more complex. If, as is sometimes the case, the difference between male and female behaviour is of importance, the process must be carried out twice. And if regional variations are required it must be repeated for each area, usually from data published in different tables on different pages, and occasionally in a different form, from those containing the national figures. In some cases, moreover, the straight tabulations of the rates thus compiled have to be corrected either numerically or graphically in order to allow for the many distortions in the original figures which derive from the administrative and procedural changes with which we shall be concerned in the next section.

8. *Criminal statistics and their interpretation*   347

The basic information included in the foregoing general description can be summarised, and in some respects supplemented, in a tabular form, showing for the several different periods the availability and location of the most important material in the returns: table 1 indicates the location and the completeness of the information at various times on the incidence of *offences*, as these are reflected in data on (i) indictable offences known to the police; (ii) committals for trial for indictable offences; and (iii) committals for trial for summary offences; table 2 summarises in a different form the location and extent of the material which is available at various times on *offenders'* characteristics.

Table 1   *The availability of published figures relating to offences: 1805–92**

	Offences known to the police	Committals for indictable offences	Offences tried summarily
1805–08	—	National figures and sex of offenders for each offence (CO)	—
1809	—	National figures and sex of offenders for block totals only (CO)	—
1810–23	—	National figures for each offence; sex of offenders for block total only (CO)	—
1824–34	—	As above (CO)	Some unsystematic county figures for summary offenders imprisoned (PR)
1834–35	—	National and county figures and sex of offenders for each offence under new classification (CP)	As above
1836–51	—	As above	National and county figures for committals to gaol for each main summary offence; sex of offenders for each (PR)
1852–54	—	National and county figures, but not sex of offenders, for each main offence (CP)	As above but sex of offenders for block totals only (PR)
1855–56	—	As above	Block totals only for national and county returns and for sex of offenders (PR)
1857–92	National and police district figures for each main indictable offence (PolR)	National and county figures and sex of offenders for each main offence (CP)	National and (from 1858) county figures for each main offence summarily tried; sex of offenders for national figures, but for block total only for county (PolR)

* Location indicated in brackets: CO = Criminal Offenders; PR = Prison Returns; CP = Criminal Proceedings; PolR = Police Returns.

348   V. A. C. GATRELL AND T. B. HADDEN

Table 2 *The availability of published figures on the characteristics of offenders: 1805–92*

	Prison Returns (all prisoners)	Police Returns (summary and indictable)	Criminal Proceedings (indictable committals)
Sex	1836–92*	1857–92	1805–92
Age	1836–92*	—	1834–49
Degree of instruction	1836–92*	—	1834–49
Place of birth	1857–92	—	—
Occupation	1857–92	—	—
Recommittals	1836–92*	—	—
Criminality of offenders	—	1857–92†	—
Known thieves at large	—	1857–92‡	—

* Listed by offence and county from 1834 to 1839, by county only from 1840 to 1856, and by county and police district from 1857; data given separately for prisoners for indictable and summary offenders until 1856, thereafter for all offenders without discrimination.

† Classified as: prostitutes; known thieves; vagrants, tramps and others without visible means of subsistence; suspicious characters; habitual drunkards.

‡ Classified as: known thieves and depredators; receivers of stolen goods; suspected persons. Each group is divided into those above and below the age of 16.

Argument: The Lombrosian Paradigm

[10]

INTRODUCTION.

W. DOUGLAS MORRISON

If the criminal population was composed of ordinary men it is possible that the purely punitive principles on which the penal code reposes would constitute an efficient check on the tendency to crime. But is it a fact that the criminal population is composed of ordinary men? Is there any evidence to show that the great army of offenders who are passing through our prisons, penitentiaries, and penal servitude establishments in a ceaseless stream is made up of the same elements as the law-abiding sections of the community? On the contrary, there is every reason to believe that vast numbers of the criminal

viii

population do not live under ordinary social and biological conditions. It is indeed a certainty that a high percentage of them live under anomalous biological and social conditions. And it is these anomalous conditions acting upon the offender either independently or, as is more often the case, in combination which make him what he is.

Penal laws pay exceedingly little attention to this cardinal and dominating fact. These laws assume that the criminal is existing under the same set of conditions as an ordinary man. They are framed and administered on this hypothesis ; and they fail in their operation because this hypothesis is fundamentally false. It is perfectly evident that a legislative and administrative system which is drawn up to meet one set of conditions will not be successful if in practice it is called upon to cope with a totally different set. A patient suffering from an attack of typhoid fever cannot be subjected to the same regimen, to the same dietary, to the same exercise as another person in the enjoyment of ordinary health. The regimen to which the patient is subjected must be suited to the anomalous condition in which he happens to be placed. Criminal codes to be effective must act upon precisely the same principle. They must be constructed so as to cope with the social and individual conditions which distinguish the bulk of the criminal population, and it is because they are not constituted upon this principle that these enactments are so helpless in the contest with crime.

The impotence of criminal legislation is also due to another circumstance. It follows from the fallax INTRODUCTION.

cious principle that the offender is an ordinary man, that each offender must be dealt with on exactly the same footing if he has committed the same offence. On this principle all offenders convicted of the same offences must be subjected to the same length of sentence, the same penal treatment, the same punitive regulations in every shape and form. This idea finds expression from time to time in popular outcries against the inequality of sentences. It is seen in the newspapers that one person is sentenced to six months' imprisonment for an offence of the same nature and gravity as another person who is only sentenced to six days. The offences are in all essential respects the same, but the sentences are absurdly different. It is immediately assumed that there has been some miscarriage of justice, and a great deal of popular indignation is the result. In many cases there can be no doubt that the popular instinct is right. Existing methods of penal treatment do not admit of the application to any great extent of sentences of unequal length for offences of a similar character. Our penitentiary systems are based upon the principle of uniformity of treatment for all offenders. In this respect they resemble our penal laws and are like them equally barren of good results. As long, therefore, as we have almost exactly the same kind of prison treatment for all sorts and conditions of offenders, so long will public opinion be to a large extent justified in protesting against the unequal duration of sentences for offences of a similar nature and gravity.

But, apart from the considerations which have just

been mentioned, the principle of equality of sentences, as far as their mere duration is concerned, is fundamentally erroneous. The duration and nature of sentences, as well as the duration and nature of prison treatment, must be adjusted to the character of the offender as well as to the character of the offence. In other words, judicial sentences and disciplinary treatment must be determined by the social and biological conditions of the offender quite as much as by the offence he has committed. In certain cases this principle is acted upon now, but if penal methods are to be made of greater social utility, it is a principle which must be much more extensively applied.

The principle of adjusting penal treatment to the social and biological condition of the offender is acted on, for instance, in the case of children. A theft committed by a child of twelve is not dealt with by our judges and magistrates in the same manner as a theft of precisely the same kind by a person of mature years. In the one case the juvenile is perhaps dismissed with an admonition, or if his parental conditions are defective, he is ordered to be detained in an industrial or reformatory school. In the other case the offender of mature years is usually committed to prison. But according to the maxim that the punishment should be adjusted to the crime, both these offenders should be sentenced to exactly the same form of penal treatment. Again, in the case of offences committed by adults, if the one offender is a man and the other a woman the sentences are not the same, although the offence may be precisely the same. Or again, in the case of offences committed by men the sentences are not the same if the one is discovered to be feeble-minded and the other is in possession of his senses. In all these instances justice works upon the maxim : *Si duo faciunt idem, non est idem.* It sets aside the notion that two offences of equal gravity are to be dealt with by awarding the same amount of punishment to both. In such circumstances equality would be gained at the expense of justice.

The principle that punishment should be adjusted to the condition of the offender as well as to the nature of the offence is distinctly laid down by Bentham. " It is further to be observed," he says, " that owing to the different manners and degrees in which persons under different circumstances are affected by the same exciting cause, a punishment which is the same in name will not always either really produce, or even so much as appear to others to produce, in two different persons the same degree of pain. Therefore, that the quantity actually inflicted on each individual offender may correspond to the quantity intended for similar offenders in general, the several circumstances influencing sensibility ought always to be taken into account." As he says elsewhere, " These circumstances cannot be fully provided for by the legislator ; but as the existence of them in every sort of case is capable of being ascertained, and the degree in which they take place is capable of being measured, provision may be made for them by the judge or other executive magistrate to whom the several individuals that happen to be concerned may be made known." In both these passages Bentham

History of Criminology

makes it perfectly plain that in penal legislation and administration other circumstances must be taken into account besides the actual offence ; and the circumstances to which he alludes are what we have already described as the social and biological conditions of the offender.

The question therefore arises, What are these conditions, and how are they to be ascertained ? What these conditions are and how they can be ascertained can easily be got at by an examination of the delinquent population in our penitentiary establishments of various kinds. Let us look first at social conditions. In the sixteenth Year Book of the New York State Reformatory a very excellent account is given of the social antecedents of the inmates. According to the returns 2,550, or 52·6 per cent., of the inmates came from homes which were positively bad, and only 373, or 7·6 per cent., came from homes which were positively good. It is also stated that 1,998, or 41·1 per cent., of the population left home before or soon after reaching the age of fourteen, and in a total population of 4,859 it is recorded that only 69, or 1 and a fraction per cent., were surrounded by wholesome influences at the time of their lapse into crime. When we come to look at the social condition of juveniles committed to Reformatory Schools in England we are confronted with a very similar set of results. According to the returns for 1892, in a total of 1,085 juveniles committed to these institutions, only 425 were living under the control of both parents. All the others had only one parent, or had one or both parents in

prison, or had been deserted by their parents altogether. The social condition of the juvenile population in the prisons of our large cities is equally as bad.
In a high percentage of cases they have either no
homes or no parents, and are without skilled occupation in any shape.

Instances such as these—and they might be multiplied a hundredfold—make it quite plain that it is
useless attempting to deal with the offence without
looking at the same time at the social conditions
of the offender. In the majority of cases the offence
is the natural and almost inevitable product of these
social conditions. Up to the age of sixteen the
magistrates and judges in England are empowered
by law to take these adverse circumstances into
account, and to send the offender to a school instead
of committing him to prison. But after the age of
sixteen has been passed our penal legislation makes
absolutely no provision for the unhappy juvenile
bereft of paternal support and paternal counsel at the
most critical period of his existence. Imprisonment
is its only remedy. But as imprisonment does nothing to remove the adverse social circumstances
which have turned the juvenile into a criminal, it has
absolutely no effect in preventing him from continuing
to pursue a career of crime. As long as the conditions which produce the offender remain he will
continue to offend, and as long as Penal law shuts its
eyes to this transparent fact it is doomed to impotence as a weapon against crime.

The criminal, as we have said, is a product of
anomalous biological conditions as well as adverse

INTRODUCTION.   XV

social circumstances. Dr. Lombroso's distinctive merit
consists in the fact that he has devoted a laborious
life to the examination of these biological or, as he
prefers to call them, anthropological anomalies.
Criminal anthropology, as he has termed his investigations, is really an inquiry on scientific principles
into the physical, mental, and pathological characteristics of the criminal population.   The present
volume is an example of the method in which these
inquiries are conducted.   It is a translation of that
portion of Dr. Lombroso's *La Donna Delinquentz* which
deals with the female criminal.   Dr. Lombroso had
predecessors in France in such men as Morel, Legrand
du Saulle, Brierre de Boismont, and Prosper Despine ;
and in England in Pritchard, Thomson and Dr. Nicolson. But he has surpassed all these writers in covering
a wider field of investigation, in imparting a more
systematic character to his inquiries, and in the practical conclusions which he draws from them.   Dr.
Lombroso proceeds from the principle that there is
an intimate co-relation between bodily and mental
conditions and processes. In accordance with this
principle he commences with an examination of the
physical characteristics and peculiarities of the criminal
offender.   As a result of this examination he finds
that the criminal population as a whole, but the
habitual criminal in particular, is to be distinguished
from the average member of the community by a
much higher percentage of physical anomalies. These
anomalies consist of malformations in the skull and
brain and face.   The organs of sense are also the
seat of many anomalies, such as abnormal develop-

I A

xvi INTRODUCTION.

ment of the ear, abnormalities of the eye and its protecting organs, abnormalities of the nose, such as a total absence or defective development of the bony skeleton ; abnormalities of the mouth, such as hare-lip, high palate, and malformations of the teeth and tongue. The criminal population also exhibits a considerable percentage of anomalies connected with the limbs, such as excessive development of the arms or defective development of the legs. We have also sexual peculiarities, such as femininism in men, masculism in women, and infantilism in both. Where a considerable number of deep-seated physical anomalies are found in combination in the same individual, we usually see that they are accompanied by nervous and mental anomalies of a more or less morbid character. These mental anomalies are visible among the criminal population in an absence of moral sensibility, in general instability of character, in excessive vanity, excessive irritability, a love of revenge, and, as far as habits are concerned, a descent to customs and pleasures akin in their nature to the orgies of uncivilised tribes. In short, the habitual criminal is a product, according to Dr. Lombroso, of pathological and atavistic anomalies ; he stands midway between the lunatic and the savage ; and he represents a special type of the human race.

It is almost needless to remark that Dr. Lombroso's doctrine of criminal atavism and the criminal type has provoked a considerable amount of opposition and controversy. It is impossible in the space at our command to examine the question in detail. The most weighty objection to the doctrine of a distinctively

INTRODUCTION.   xvii

criminal type is to be found in the circumstance that
the mental and physical peculiarities which are said to
be characteristic of the criminal are in reality common
to him with the lunatic, the epileptic, the alcoholic,
the prostitute, the habitual pauper. The criminal is
only one branch of a decadent stem ; he is only one
member of a family group ; his abnormalities are not
peculiar to himself; they have a common origin, and
he shares them in common with the degenerate type
of which he furnishes an example.

Let us give a few instances of the ratio of degeneracy among the criminal population of Great
Britain and the United States. Among the inmates
of the New York State Reformatory 12 per cent.
were descended from insane or epileptic parents, 38
per cent. were the children of drunken parents, and
4 per cent. were the children of pauper parents. In
England suicide is five times more prevalent among
the prison population than among the general community, insanity is twenty-eight times more prevalent.
According to a census taken of the English convict
establishments in 1873 it was found that 30 male
convicts per thousand were suffering from weak mind,
insanity, or epilepsy. It was also found that 109 per
thousand were suffering from scrofula and chronic
diseases of the lungs and heart, and that 231 per
thousand were afflicted with congenital or acquired
deformities and defects. In Scotland 33 per cent. of
the cases of insanity occur among offenders who have
been in prison before, and in England 41 per cent. of
the cases of suicide occur among offenders who have
been in prison before. More minute investigation

xviii   *INTRODUCTION.*

into each individual case would undoubtedly heighten
all these percentages. But as they stand they are
sufficiently striking, and they establish beyond the
possibility of a doubt that the criminal population
exhibits a high percentage of defective biological
conditions.

In what way do our existing methods of penal law
and administration attempt to deal with the offender
exhibiting these anomalous conditions? Do we
act upon the principle so clearly enunciated by
Bentham of adjusting our methods of penal treatment to the nature of the offender as well as to the
nature of the offence? On the contrary, as far as
adults are concerned, the existence of this principle is
practically ignored. It is assumed that all offenders
are the same, and are therefore affected in exactly
the same way and to the same extent by penal
discipline. And what is the result? A steady and
uninterrupted increase of recidivism; a failure of
penal law and penal administration as instruments of
social defence, a constant augmentation of expenditure in connexion with the repression of crime.

What are the best means of mitigating this
unsatisfactory state of affairs? In the first place
penal law must be constructed with a view to cope
with the conditions which produce the criminal
population. At present the principal office of a
criminal court is to ascertain whether a person under
trial for a criminal offence is innocent or guilty; if
he is found to be guilty the sentence is almost
entirely determined by the character of the offence.
Except in glaring cases of lunacy the court takes

little or no cognisance of the individual and social conditions of the offender. The sentence is not adjusted to contend with these conditions. In fact it is often calculated to aggravate them, and in such instances is worse than useless as a weapon against the tendency to crime. It should be made the business of a criminal court to inquire not merely into the alleged offence, but in cases of conviction into the conditions of the offender who committed it ; and the duration and nature of the sentence must be determined by the results of this inquiry quite as much as by the nature of the offence. It may be said that this proposal is throwing new and unaccustomed functions upon courts of justice, and to a certain extent this is no doubt the fact. But it is also to be remembered that as social organisation increases in complexity, the machinery of government must be adapted to these new conditions. The judicial machine is at present of too primitive a character : in order to do its work efficiently it must be reconstructed, its functions must be enlarged.

In the next place penal establishments must be placed upon the same basis as penal law. In other words, they, too, must be classified and administered with a view to deal with the conditions which produce the offender. At present these establishments are all of practically the same type ; they are all administered on the same lines. Except in extreme cases the same kind of penal treatment is meted out to all classes of offenders. Uniformity of penal establishments and uniformity of penal discipline rest upon the assumption that all offenders are of the same type

XX *INTRODUCTION.*

and are produced by exactly the same conditions. A practical acquaintance with the criminal population shows that this is not the fact. The criminal population is composed of many types. It is composed of casual offenders who do not differ to any great extent from the ordinary man ; it is composed of juvenile offenders ; it is composed of insane, weak-minded, and epileptic offenders ; it is composed of habitual drunkards, beggars, and vagrants ; and finally there is a distinct class consisting of habitual offenders against property. It is useless applying the same method of penal treatment to each and all of these classes of offenders. The treatment must be differentiated, and determined as far as practicable by the kind of criminal type to which the offender belongs. In order to effect this object, penal establishments must as far as possible be classified. Where classification of penal establishments is impossible, and where, in consequence, offenders of various types have to be incarcerated in the same establishment, these offenders should be classified in accordance with the type to which they belong, and subjected to a regimen adapted to their class. If these principles of penal treatment were applied to the criminal population it is certain that recidivism would diminish; it is certain that the habitual criminal would become a greater rarity, and, most important of all, it is certain that society would enjoy a greater immunity from crime.

W. D. M.

Argument about Argument:
The Lombrosian Paradigm

[11]

CHARLES GORING

9

THE CRIMINAL OF ENGLISH PRISONS.

A STATISTICAL STUDY.

INTRODUCTION.

I.—THE SUPERSTITION OF CRIMINOLOGY.

The recent application of exact and standardised methods to the study of anthropology has revealed the extent to which this science has been dominated and confused by conventional prejudices and unfounded beliefs. And of these beliefs there seems to be none more deeply rooted, more widely spread, than the conviction that the inward disposition of man is reflected and revealed by the configuration of his body. It would be a lengthy, though not a difficult task, to account for the tenacity of this conviction. Let us content ourselves, for the present, with the statement that the belief does exist, and that it is eagerly supported by the imagination. It is a survival, no doubt, from a multitude of similar *a priori* credulities. It is kith and kin with the misnamed "sciences" of phrenology, chiromancy and physiognomy. Such systems of belief have, for the most part, disappeared; a few of the more cherished alone remaining to defy criticism. Thus, time has shown sane minds that the once popular dislike of red hair had no occult justification; had no justification of any kind except as a whim of æsthetics. To distrust a woman with a man's voice, or to avoid a pale face and green eyes as synonymous with evil and Becky Sharp—time has shown us that to shape one's action from such antipathies would entail inconvenient practical consequences, quite disproportionate in value to the worth of these beliefs as an imaginative luxury. On the other hand, parallel notions, more polite in their implications, and especially those beliefs which, based upon quantitative rather than qualitative estimates, are infinitely adaptable to circumstances—such parallel, plastic beliefs still remain with us. A case in point is the common contention that the size of head and the frontal development are reliable indices of character and intellectual worth. How baffling to criticism! For, whereas red hair and green eyes are always red and green, a forehead which to-day will seem low and receding may to-morrow, when more genially viewed, appear quite inoffensively normal.

The belief we have just referred to, that size of head is an index to ability, has been selected for survival; and so loyally is the conviction upheld to-day that its recent scrutiny by Science created genuine and wide-spread resentment. One is familiar with the objection usually put forward, in the circumstances, to face criticism. Can a doctrine which has obtained universal credit and currency possibly be without any basis in fact? is the typical question. In the absence of the facts, however, this plausible

10

argument is merely a plea for the general validity of tradition. And that is why one calls a belief in this doctrine a *superstitious* belief. It may be true; but, if so, it is true in spite of, and not because of, the spurious evidence of its supporters. A strictly *scientific* belief—a belief, that is to say, which has been arrived at by disinterested and exact methods—may be entirely erroneous. Yet, the old superstition of the alchemists is none the less a superstition because Sir William Ramsay has scientifically shown that the transmutation of elements is possibly a fact. Cranial development may be an index of ability: but since the only evidence in favour of this belief, whether true or false, is the evidence, not of disinterested and exact investigation, but of imagination and tradition, we are justified in asserting that it originates in, and is entirely based upon, a superstition.

Now, the so-called science of criminology, which is our immediate concern, and some of whose salient features we would portray in this introductory note—the science of criminology, we contend, has been, up to the present, warped by its subjection to all kinds of superstitious and conventional dogmas.

What, in the first place, is commonly meant by "criminology"? In its most legitimate significance, the term should denote the scientific study of crime and the criminal: that is to say, any examination of the subject conducted upon standardised scientific methods, and in pursuance of the scientific aim. Thus understood, however, the name covers much that we are not here considering. Of late years, the criminal has been studied scientifically by many independent workers, whose sporadic contributions to books, journals, and Proceedings of Societies, will, when collected, form an invaluable asset in our knowledge of the criminal. For the present, however, we are limiting our attention exclusively to criminology in the narrower and more conventional sense of the term, which excludes all work of the above order.

In its narrower meaning, criminology denotes the criticism of crime and criminals as it has been carried out by certain conventional cliques of investigators; and, thus understood, it consists of the doctrines, dogmas, and propaganda of what are improperly known as three Schools of Criminology: the Classical School, the Correctionist School, and the Positive or Continental School of Criminology.

The Classical School arose about the middle of the eighteenth century, and represented a spirit of reaction against the neglect and brutality of which criminals were the victims at that time. It drew its inspiration from Beccaria, the Italian philanthropist and reformer, who, as early as 1764, published a famous work on " Crimes and Punishments," which led to subsequent reform in the penal code of all European nations. The fundamental doctrine of this school was that the criminal has a " natural right" to be humanely treated, in spite of his own wrong-doing, and in spite of the fact that he is a normal being, responsible for his actions. The Correctionist School was a later development of the Classical School. Influenced by the same humanitarian spirit, its efforts were directed towards the further amendment of the criminal law. But the Correctionist School, in direct oppo-

11

sition to its predecessor, which held that punishment should be graduated to fit the offence committed, without regard to the personality of the offender—the second school recognised the fact that the character of the criminal cannot be completely dissociated from his crime; and maintained that age and mental alienation, at any rate, must be taken into account in our estimation of personal responsibility. Our present modification of the law, with regard to criminal lunatics and juvenile offenders, and our modern reformatory system, derive their origin from the work and efforts of the Correctionists. Both schools,* it will be seen, concern themselves more with penology than with criminology; nor can they, in the strict sense of the word, be described as scientific. The pretensions of criminology to rank as a science were not recognised until the inauguration, about 40 years ago, of the world-famous school, known as the Positive School of Criminology because, for the first time, methods and aim claimed to be those of the positive sciences.

The founder of the Positive School, the creator, and most famous exponent of its doctrine, was the late Professor Cesare Lombroso: an Italian of genius, an indefatigable worker, and a man of strong personality, attracting to himself many disciples and co-workers from all countries of Europe. Lombroso's distinctive merit lay, not in his scientific study of the criminal, but in his humanitarianism: in the influence he exerted towards ameliorating the lot of the criminal. All thinking people to-day, legislators and judges, as well as the general public, the morality of the age, as well as the voice of science, attest the truth which Lombroso was the first to enunciate as the fundamental principle of criminology and penology: the principle that it is the criminal and not the crime we should study and consider; that it is the criminal and not the crime we ought to penalise. " The father of criminal anthropology " he has been called, with some appropriateness: but, if the title survives, it will, in the future, be associated, not with Lombroso the anthropologist, but with Lombroso, enunciator of the humane truth that iniquity and righteousness depend upon what an individual is, and not upon what he does; the practical corollary of this truth being that, in dealing justice to him, we must understand the criminal both as he is in himself, and as he becomes through the influence of environment.

Let us, at this point, briefly resume our position. Criminology, as it is understood to-day, consists of the doctrines of the three Schools of criminology just referred to. The Classical School, after Beccaria, taught that all criminals were equally responsible in the eyes of the law; that they should be punished according to the crimes they had committed; but that, despite their wrongdoing, they retained a natural right, common to all men, to be humanely treated. The Correctionist School, improving upon its predecessor, established the relative responsibility of lunatics and juvenile offenders, and led the way to our modern reformatory system. Finally the School of Lombroso, more humane still,

---

* For a complete account of these schools see *the principles of Anthropology and Sociology in their Relations to Criminal Procedure* by Maurice Parmelee.

12

declared it was the criminal and not the crime who ought to be studied and punished, and expounded a doctrine known as the new science of criminal anthropology.

We fully admit the value of this progressive humanitarianism, and the particular merit of Lombroso's own standpoint and aims, while pointing out the absence of any virtue of Science in the doctrines of all three schools, and insisting upon the total lack of the scientific spirit in the mind and methods of Lombroso himself. Nothing is more remarkable than the array of incompatibles, of false and true notions, cheek by jowl, what there is of truth dangerously marred by exaggeration and fallacy—nothing is more startling than the organised confusion masquerading to-day under the scientific name of criminology. There is a certain naïve confession of Lombroso's which reveals the character of his mind, and, consequently, the nature of his work. He tells how he first came by his doctrine, in these words*: —" In 1870 I was carrying on for several months researches in the prisons and asylums of Pavia upon cadavers and living persons, in order to determine upon substantial differences between the insane and criminals without succeeding very well. Suddenly the morning of a gloomy day in December, I found in the skull of a brigand a very long series of atavistic anomalies, above all an enormous middle occipital fossa and a hypertrophy of the vermis, analogous to those that are found in inferior invertebrates. At the sight of these strange anomalies, as a large plain appears under an inflamed horizon, the problem of the nature and of the origin of the criminal seemed to me resolved; the characters of primitive men and of inferior animals must be reproduced in our time."†

We will limit ourselves to an outline of Lombroso's doctrine, which is becoming more and more popularly accepted; which has already influenced legislation in America; and which is to the effect that the criminal, as found in prison, is a definite, anomalous, human type: that is to say, he is a specific product of anomalous biological conditions. As evidence of this doctrine, it is supposed to have been proved that the criminal is distinguished from the law-abiding community by marked differences in physique, revealed by measurements, and by the presence of conspicuous physical anomalies, or stigmata. And, based upon what we call a superstitious belief that there is an intimate relation between the spiritual and physical conditions of man, it has been deduced, from the supposed presence of these anomalies, that the moral condition of the criminal is akin to the mental

---

* From a speech made by Lombroso at the Congress of Criminal Anthropology, held at Turin in 1906.

† Note how, following the custom of ancient astrologers, the time of day, the month, and state of weather are recorded. That "morning of the gloomy day in December"! That "large plain" and its "inflamed horizon"!—Science knows nothing of them. Newton must work by other laws than Victor Hugo's. At the risk of appearing trivial, we confess it seems to us that the race of brigands might quite properly resent the implication of the father of criminal anthropology; and, we have no doubt whatever, that the skull of that particular brigand, in the hands of Lombroso, has ever since been a menace to the spirit of sane criticism

13

condition of the insane, and that, consequently, he should not be held responsible for the crimes he commits. According to Lombroso's original doctrine, the criminal, thus stigmatised, is an atavistic anomaly. According to others, he is morally insane. A third group would not place him in either of these categories, but somewhere between the two: he is not strictly atavistic nor insane; he is, rather, a healthy-minded savage who, having wandered into a strange environment, becomes relatively insane. A fourth group of criminologists find the anomalies of the criminal not peculiar to him, but common to other varieties of decadent stock: so they proclaim him a typical example of the generally degenerate. Atavistic, insane, savage, degenerate, all or any of these things, whatever they may mean, the criminal may be; one thing the criminologists will not let him be: he is not, he never is, say the Lombrosians, a perfectly normal human being, responsible for his own actions. No matter what is the nature of the defect—and even amongst Lombroso's immediate disciples there has been much divergence of opinion in this respect—the essential fact upon which all are agreed is that the mind of the criminal is defective in some way; that the criminal is either mentally diseased, or so mentally anomalous that he ought not to be judged by the ordinary standards of morality. And this doctrine, they declare, flows naturally from the facts of criminal anthropology, *i.e.*, from the facts which have been elicited by direct observation of criminals as found in prisons.

Now, we have seen, upon Lombroso's own confession, how the inception of his criminological doctrine lay in the discovery—on that gloomy morning of December!—of certain anomalous structures in the skull of a brigand. Starting, then, with a working hypothesis as to the eccentric mental condition of the criminal, and proceeding upon the supposition that this condition, if existent, would be physically demonstrable,* Lombroso proceeded to search for evidence of physical peculiarities among imprisoned criminals. Naturally, and almost inevitably, considering the crudity of his methods of investigation, he soon found the evidence he sought. As a result of the examinations made by Lombroso and his followers, the theory was by them established that, literally, from top to toe, in every organ and structure of his body, from the quality of his hair at one extreme to the deformity of his feet at the other, the criminal is beset with definite, morbid, physical stigmata.

We will now describe in detail some of the salient "criminal characteristics," according to the teaching of Lombroso's school. The *hair* of the criminal has been found by observers of this school (Marro, Salsotto, Ottolenghi, Boer) to be anomalous in many ways. Typical hair is dark and thick, they tell us; another common type is woolly in texture; whereas red and grey hair, and baldness, are relatively rare amongst criminals.†　The

---

* In accordance with the assumed but unproven principle that the mental and physical conditions of man are closely co-related.

† The so-called "characteristics" herein described have, of course, in every case received their definition from the comparison of criminals with the law-abiding community. Thus, thick and dark hair, defined as a criminal characteristic, does not mean that all criminals have hair of this shade and quality: it

14

head is alleged to be anomalous (Corre, Laurent, Lydston, Talbot, Benedikt, Lauvergne, Debierre, Pitard, Bordier, Héger, Dallemagne, Ferri, Winkler, Van der Plaats, Berends, Tenchini, Pellacani, Marimo, Gambara, Mingazzini, Vans Clarke) in shape, and in its dimensions. Dimensionally, there are two types of criminal heads : the one larger, the other smaller than the normal type. In shape, five types are described :—the head of the criminal may rise, rounded like a dome; or it may be depressed, like a roof that is flat and low; or its vault may be keel-shaped, from premature union of the median suture; or it may be a bulging type of head, with the protuberance on one side, or on both sides, or in front, or behind; or it may have a sugar-loaf appearance—the true Satanic type. In other words—to quote Lombroso—the head of the criminal is oxy-cephalic, trigono-cephalic, scapho-cephalic, plagio-cephalic, hydro-cephalic and sub-micro-cephalic. The *organs of sense*, criminologists affirm, are the seat of erratic conditions (Beddoe, Vans Clarke, Knult, Ottolenghi, Grohmann, Morel, Frigerio, Marro, Gradenigo, Talbot). Typical criminal *eyes* are anomalous in colour, position and shape, with *eyebrows* characteristically bushy, or characteristically scanty; the typical *nose* is defective in shape and is frequently without a bony skeleton ; the typical *ears* project, are long, voluminous, and are often prehensile. Then, say the anthropologists (Corre, Debierre, Francotti, Ferri, Talbot, Manouvrier, Näcke, Pali, Carrara, Tarnowskaia, V. Clarke, Marro, Knecht, Ottolenghi), there is the pale and wrinkled *skin;* there are the *lips* that are cleft; there are the absent wisdom *teeth*, the undeveloped molars, the over-developed canine teeth; there are the *palates* that are Λ-shaped, saddle-shaped, unduly high, round, and narrow; there is the receding *chin*, or there is the chin that projects; there are the two types of upper *jaw*, the one depressed and the other protruding, the latter approximating to types of jaw found in savages, anthropoid apes and prehistoric man. Finally, there are two characteristic *physiognomies* by which the criminal can be detected. In one the expression is cringing, timid, humble, suppliant; in the other it is brazen, shameless, ferocious, brutal. " The criminal has often the face of an angel," declares Lombroso: then, with picturesque im-

---

means that, on the whole, the hair of the criminal is darker and thicker than the hair of people who are morally well conditioned. To quote a specific example, Ottolenghi found that 60 per cent. of law-abiding peasants had grey hair, whereas, amongst a sample of criminals, only 12 per cent. showed this quality. The assumption in this case, that absence of grey hair is a criminal characteristic, is based solely on the difference of percentages found for the two contrasted sections of the population. At the same time, it must be insisted upon that the only logical interpretation of a veritable criminal characteristic is that the degree or quality of a character so designated is modified by the criminal tendencies of its possessor. If thick and dark hair be defined as a criminal characteristic, the implication cannot be evaded that, whatever be the actual colour and quality of individual criminal's hair, the colour is darker, its quantity is greater, than it would have been were he mentally constituted a law abiding citizen. Lombroso verbally avoided, but does not evade, this implication, by describing his criminal characteristics as " anomalies " or " stigmata," *i.e.*, as conditions which should not be present in the normal body. Low foreheads, high palates, outstanding ears, all marked deviations from the mean value of any character, are, according to Lombroso's diction, " anomalies," despite the fact that these characters, in some degree, are possessed by the whole human race.

15

partiality: " The criminal has a face like a bird of prey "! The *limbs, trunk, viscera*, and other structures of his body are also affirmed to be morbidly constituted; certain observers maintain that the criminal is shorter in stature, and lighter in weight, than are law-abiding people (Lombroso, however, found him to be taller and heavier); and that his *muscular condition* is more feeble and flabby; that his *arms* are longer and more developed, his *legs* are shorter and less developed, his *spine* is more curved, his *shoulders* are more sloping; and that he is afflicted unduly with all diseases, and suffers more frequently from flat feet. Finally, to select from a host of remaining characteristics, we must add that, according to various authorities, the male criminal has often the bust of a female and the female criminal the beard of a man, and that both male and female suffer from infantilism; that the criminal has an ape-like agility and a prehensile foot; that he is left-handed and ambidextrous, with his right hand smaller than his left and his left foot smaller than his right; that he stammers and squints; that he sleeps soundly, tattoos his body, is given to the early use of tobacco, is sensitive to the weather, and is seldom seen to blush!

Lombroso's science has advanced to an even finer perception of criminal proclivities. Murderers, we are told, can be detected by a deficiency in their frontal curve, combined with a projecting occiput and receding forehead. Thieves are revealed by their enlarged orbital capacity and bulging forehead; sexual offenders by their bright eyes, rough voices, over-developed jaw, swollen eyelids and lips, and by the fact that, occasionally, they are hump-backed. The nose of the thief is rectilinear, short and large; the eye of the homicide is " glassy, cold and fixed "; while the forger has generally a " clerical appearance," a " singular air of bonhomie." Nor were the adventures of Lombroso confined within prison walls. On one occasion, he pointed out, as an example of the criminal type, a youth who had never appeared in a court of justice: " he may not be a legal criminal," was the airy utterance, " but he is a criminal anthropologically." At pause before the skull of Gasparonne, a famous nineteenth century brigand, the seeker found many of the stigmata common to the skulls of ordinary prison inmates. Thus, he tells us, there was, in the unfortunate Gasparonne, a wormian bone: micro-cephaly of the frontal region, erignathism, oxycephaly, dolico-cephaly, and enlarged orbital capacity, were also implacably present. Charlotte Corday's skull inspires this eloquence: " Not even the purest political crime, that which springs from passion, is exempt from the law which we have laid down!"* And, borne onward by the flood of enthusiasm, our intrepid explorer sets foot at last upon the shores of antiquity. Confronting the effigy of Messalina, he sees in triumph the unmistakable criminal stamp—the heavy jaw, the low forehead, the wavy hair: he recognises them all! . . . Perhaps, however, he is at his best, his happiest, in contemplation before the old woman of Palermo, who poisoned so many people with arseniated vinegar.

---

* He adds " In the skull of Charlotte Corday, after a rapid inspection, I affirmed the presence of an extraordinary number of anomalies."

16

" The bust," writes Lombroso, " which we possess of this criminal, so full of virile angularity, and above all, so deeply wrinkled, with its Satanic leer, suffices of itself to prove that the woman in question was born to do evil, and that, if one occasion to commit it had failed, she would have found others."

As a result of this attitude of mind, of its haphazard methods of investigation, of its desire to adjust fact to theory, rather than to formulate a theory by observation of fact—as a result of all this, we have that modern criminology we have described: an organised system of self-evident confusion whose parallel is only to be found in the astrology, alchemy, and other credulities of the Middle Ages. And, just as alchemy was a superstitious study, based upon a preconceived belief in the philosopher's stone; just as astrology was a superstitious study, based upon a preconceived belief in the influence of the heavenly bodies on terrestrial affairs: so has criminology been a superstitious study, based upon a preconceived notion of the criminality of criminals as found in prison.

The preconceived, and, in our opinion, totally unfounded, Lombrosian notion, was that criminality is a specific condition of mind or soul: is a definite state of psychical instability. And this psychical state, with its outward and physical signs of an inward and spiritual darkness, this mental and moral instability, underlay, according to the above supposition, any and every form of lawlessness, and potentiality for crime;* and was its only explanation, and its sole promoter. Murder, larceny, fraud, every kind of law-breaking, from the most elaborate to the simplest instances, were all, in varying degrees, expressions, or revelations, of an identical abnormal state of being. Not the petty thief in prison to-day, nor the supreme criminals of history; neither Gasparonne the brigand, nor Charlotte Corday the patriot, were exempt from the law Lombroso had laid down. There is, in short, according to Lombroso, a definite line of demarcation, an absolute difference in nature, as opposed to degree, between those human beings who are, and those who are not, criminal. But, since this belief of Lombroso's was arrived at, not by methods of disinterested investigation, but, rather, by a leap of the imagination, the notion thus reached then forming the basis upon which he conducted his researches, and constructed his theory— the whole fabric of the Lombrosian doctrine, judged by the standards of science, is fundamentally unsound.

It must not be understood that we are here condemning the Lombrosian investigation merely on the ground that it was directed by a working hypothesis. As Darwin said: " Without hypothesis and speculation, good and sound investigation is impossible." But, unless employed in conditions where the rigour of the scientific method is scrupulously respected, the working hypothesis is a dangerous thing. And it is particularly dangerous unless the notion of it resumes in its formula a certain number of unquestionable facts. Now, behind Lombroso's notion

* The designation " criminal" with Lombroso includes not only the criminal who is a legal fact, but also that vague, nightmare abstraction, " the anthropological criminal."

17

there were positively no facts at all. He had been studying the cadavers and living persons of criminals for months, when, suddenly, at the sight of certain anomalies in the skull of one particular brigand,* revelation flashed through the surrounding gloom: the hypothesis was framed. We contend that a notion arrived at in these romantic and emotional conditions could not legitimately be employed as a working hypothesis for directing a disinterested investigation; we maintain that the whole of Lombroso's enterprise was conducted, we do not say with the express purpose, but with the unconscious intention, of stamping a preconceived idea with the hall mark of science. As evidence for this contention we need not probe further than the facts of criminal anthropology we have described, and the particular method, invented by Lombroso, by which these facts were elicited.

In the opening paragraph of his book, "The Female Offender," Professor Lombroso refers to his special method of investigation, which he calls the " anatomico-pathological method." We quote the passages verbatim, ·because they contain a frank and unequivocal statement of the reasons why Lombroso adopted this method, and recommended it to the notice of other investigators.

" When the present writer began his observations on delinquents some thirty years ago, he professed a firm faith in anthropometry,† which he regarded as the backbone of the new human statue of which he was at the time attempting the creation, and only learnt the vanity of such hopes when use, as is usual, had degenerated into abuse.

" For all the differences between criminologists and the most authoritative modern anthropologists arise precisely from the fact that the variation in measurement between the normal and the abnormal subject are so small as to defy all but the most minute research.

" The writer only became convinced of this fact when Zampa's observations upon the crania of four assassins in Ravenna disclosed an exact correspondence between their measurements and those found in an average taken upon ten normal Ravennese. And while the anthropometrical system failed thus to reveal any salient differences whatever, anatomico-pathological investigation, on being applied to the same crania, proved the existence in them of no less than thirty-three anomalies.

" But, unfortunately, the attention of inquirers had been diverted from the anatomico-pathological method to anthropometry, with the consequence that the former came to be rashly abandoned. And as one result of this we may mention that Topinard and Manouvrier, being deficient in anatomico-pathological knowledge, failed to detect the immense anomalies existent in certain crania of assassins; and because there were no salient anthropometrical differences in those skulls and the skull of Charlotte Corday, they rejected the theory of anomaly altogether.

" We must not, however, be understood to advocate the total

---

* We assume that in the skulls examined during the previous months, no similar anomalies had been noted.

† *I.e.*, the knowledge of man to be obtained by measurement.

18

abandonment of measurements. On the contrary, we would retain them as the frame, so to speak, of the picture; and we would recommend such retention the more, that whenever a difference does result on measurement, the importance of the anomaly is doubled.''

Lombroso clearly had no liking for the exact scientific method of precise measurement. The differences between normal and abnormal subjects, revealed by measurement, were too small for the purpose of criminological investigation. This method might be retained, however, on one condition. If any differences between the normal and abnormal subject could be made to emerge by measurement, such differences should appear in the foreground of the " picture ": they were " doubly " significant. But if measurements failed in this respect—no, the negative results must not be discarded; they must be relegated to the picture's " frame ": the picture itself must be filled in only with positive results, which the anatomico-pathological method might always be relied upon to supply.* Could anything be more *naïvely* satisfactory?

Now, we divine that the method dignified by the name anato-mico-pathological is simply direct observation by the senses, and without the aid of instruments, of abnormal anatomical characters in man, *i.e.*, structures which, differentiated by their quality, as opposed to their degree, cannot be measured—cannot be investi-gated anthropometrically. For instance, when observing the physical signs of disease—symptoms of insanity, let us say, or congenital malformations in man—the so-called anatomico-patho-logical method is the first, and, in the present state of our know-ledge, is generally the most fruitful method to employ; but if the subject of inquiry be a comparative study of the physical and mental characters of normal man, then, callipers, tape, and other instruments for refined measurement are undoubtedly the appropriate tools.† And this was also Lombroso's standpoint. Preconceiving criminality to be a diseased or anomalous mental condition, he realised—although, not, be it noted, until measure-ments had failed him—that this conception could only become universally acceptable by demonstration of the presence in the criminal of physical and mental abnormalities, *i.e.*, of structures and conditions in him by which the criminal could be qualita-tively differentiated from the law-abiding community. But, unfortunately, there are no signs peculiar to the criminal by which he can be inevitably detected. And so, to circumvent this

---

* Lombroso's ingenuity in abstracting positive results even from recalcitrant measurements is illustrated by the following passage, which we cannot refrain from quoting, so typical is it, in a flagrant way, of the man's temper as an observer, and of the combination in him of inherent honesty and fanatical casuistry. Seeking to establish the inferior cranial capacity of criminals, he has to record that "arithmetically speaking the average capacity of criminals (1322 cc) is higher than the average shown by normals (1310 cc)"; but, the author adds, "in only 14 per cent. of normals was the capacity below 1200 cc, whereas, among criminals, 20 per cent. fell below this figure : a result which establishes the inferiority of criminals."

† The methods we have been discussing differentiate the descriptive, a priori systems of knowledge, from exact science The modern contention is that all scientific knowledge should be exact : that "science is measurement."

19

rather formidable obstacle to the development of his plan, Lombroso availed himself of a series of subterfuges, among which figured conspicuously his invention of a " theory of anomaly."

The theory of anomaly, so ruthlessly rejected by **Topinard and Manouvrier,** pre-supposed that all marked deviations from the mean value of any character in man were " anomalies "; and that a definite line of demarcation existed between characters which were, and were not, thus designated anomalous; and that, according to the anomalies stigmatising them, **the degree of moral alienation** in individuals could be diagnosed.* The following is a list of some of the principal characters that have been enrolled as " human anomalies."†

The various forms of cranial asymmetry : —

> Oxycephaly, scapho-cephaly, platy-cephaly, plagio-cephaly, trigono-cephaly.

Size of head : —Very large heads, very small heads :
Low, narrow and receding foreheads :
Facial asymmetry :
Great development of lower jaw :
Projecting cheekbones :
Projecting ears :
Prognathism :
Virile, ferocious, idiotic physiognomies :
Defective teeth :
Shape and deflection of nose :
Thin lips :
Hairiness :
Wrinkles :
Tattooing :
High, narrow, Λ-shaped, saddle-shaped palates.

It is unnecessary to point out that although some of the characters just enumerated may, in special cases, be abnormal, none of them are, in any intelligent meaning of the word, inevitably so. A high palate may sometimes result from congenital malformation; voluminous ears may, on rare occasions, be an expression of acromegaly; mis-shapen heads may frequently be the result of rachitis; hydrocephaly may be the result of ventricular disease, &c. In such conditions, these characters are rightly called " anomalies." But to assume that every high palate, that every very large or very small head, that all deviations from an artistic ideal of beauty and symmetry, are human abnormalities, is obviously absurd. Moreover, despite their polysyllabic terminology, all the characters we have enumerated, are measurable characters. They are more or less *extreme* degrees of characters which in *some* degree are present in all men : and which differ in degree only, never in quality, as possessed by different members of the human race. To the scientific imagination, all foreheads

---

* A corollary to this theory is that all people are more or less morally insane. The objection, however, was met by the limiting of criminality to individuals stigmatised by a certain number of anomalous characters. It was decided that the normal individual might be allowed three cranial anomalies, and that more than three should indicate an incomplete criminal type, the complete type including only those individuals with more than five anomalies.

† See list of anomalies in criminal women, Table V.—The Female Offender.

20

have some degree of lowness; all ears outstand to some negative or positive extent. Individuals are not distinguished by the possession of low foreheads, high palates, small heads: the terms high, low, and small are only convenient descriptions of extreme degrees of characters common to the whole human race, which, by insensible gradations, do all merge into their opposite extremes. Low foreheads, high palates, outstanding ears, oxycephaly, hydrocephaly, sub-microcephaly, &c. are only colloquial descriptions of rough measurements on a coarsely divided scale of characters which, precisely described, must be exactly measured upon a scale finely and accurately divided.

It will be seen that the advocacy, by Lombroso, of the anatomico-pathological, in lieu of the anthropometric, method, is merely a plea for the superior virtue of rough anthropometrics over precise anthropometry—a virtue, which, from the Lombrosian standpoint, is particularly valuable. Roughness of method condones a wide range of error due to personal equation; and almost any degree of error when, anticipating certain looked-for results, the mind of the observer is sufficiently biassed. While the one (*i.e.*, the precise) method, to quote Lombroso's own statement, fails to reveal any salient differences whatever between normal and abnormal subjects, the other (*i.e.*, the rough) method of investigation proves the existence, in the abnormal subjects, of any number of anomalies. A forehead which, noted to-day by a biassed observer, may seem low and receding, may to-morrow, when viewed with an open mind, appear quite inoffensively normal. In short, the range of error possible to this order of observation may be so great as to render the results of the investigation entirely nugatory.

And so our knowledge of the criminal to-day is where it was forty years ago, when Lombroso, remarking certain abnormal structures in the skull of a brigand, formulated his theory of a criminal type. The " facts " of criminal anthropology, gathered by prejudiced observers employing unscientific methods, are inadmissible as evidence either for, or against, the existence of this type. The criminal type may be a real thing: but if so, it is real despite of, and not because of, the spurious evidence of its supporters; its existence may be scientifically proved by future investigation: yet Lombroso's doctrine will never, by the scientific critic, be otherwise regarded than as the superstition of criminology.

II.—THE SCIENTIFIC STUDY OF THE CRIMINAL.

Now, although it is true, that Lombroso's criminology is dead as a science, it is equally true that, as a superstition, it is not dead. As a superstition, in the mind of the general public, it is still dangerously alive. There is some quality in it which has appealed to those imaginations whose impressions of the criminal have been gained chiefly from newspaper sketches, from the romantic literature of picturesque villains, from popular pseudo-scientific treatises, and from the galleries of Madame Tussaud. To register the extinction of this superstitious criminology, and to lay the foundations of a science of the criminal, truly accurate,

21

and unbiassed by prejudice, is the purpose of an investigation, which, as described in a prefatory note,* was inaugurated by the Directors of Convict Prisons in 1902, and was successfully accomplished in 1908. This investigation consisted of a statistical survey of a random sample of 3,000 English male convicts: the immediate purpose of the survey being the acquisition of a mass of data which, collected without partisanship to any particular penal system, or criminological theory, would provide, it was thought, an unique field for the scientific study of the criminal.

For many years, a vast amount of statistical information relating to the personal condition, social estate, and penal histories of convicts, has been accumulating in official records. This information is of immense scientific and practical value; but, scattered as it is, without plan or arrangement, through penal and medical records, police reports and other official documents, it is never available for any coordinated scientific purpose. The data resulting from the survey in question consist of information gathered from these various sources, amplified by physical measurements, by details of family and personal history, and by descriptions of physical and mental qualities revealed through our examination and inquiry. The data of each individual were arranged in a schedule, carefully planned to facilitate the subsequent statistical reduction of the records. The whole series of data, thus arranged, has been published in a separate volume, which contains altogether some 96 statements with regard to each one of 3,000 individuals; and which forms a representative and unprecedented statistical portrait of those of our population who become convicts.

These records have furnished, during the past three years, the raw material for a scientific study of the collective criminal, the object of which has been twofold : —

(i) To clear from the ground the remains of the old criminology, based upon conjecture, prejudice, and questionable observation ;

(ii) to found a new knowledge of the criminal, upon facts scientifically acquired, and upon inferences scientifically verified : such facts and inferences yielding, by virtue of their own established accuracy, unimpeachable conclusions.

The first object, although a negative one, is not on that account unimportant. The recovery of truth is as valuable as its original discovery. But, it may be objected, does the particular truth we are now considering really stand in need of recovery? It has been maintained that the fallacies of criminal anthropology are so self-evident that they do not require to be demonstrated scientifically. We have been told that, to the scientific imagination, Lombroso's system, being dead from its birth, can no more be affected by thrashings than the proverbial horse. This may be so : but, as we have said, that system is not extinct to the public mind; and, in many influential quarters, it is dormant only, and ever ready to be revivified under official

---

* See preface to the first edition of this work.

22

patronage. During the past year, three books of scientific pretensions have been published*; one dedicated to Lombroso himself; all three devoted to the propagation of his discoveries and
creed. The reformatory of Elmira in America stands to-day as
an example of the fruitfulness of Lombroso's teaching. It must,
however, be remembered that, in this inquiry, our first object is
not to disprove the Lombrosian doctrine, nor is it to prove the
falsity of the conclusions of criminal anthropology, upon which
this doctrine is based. Our attack, in so far as it is an attack
at all, is directed not against *conclusions*, but against the *methods*
by which they were reached. We cannot presuppose, at the
outset, the invalidity of these dogmas, nor make any judgment
upon the extent of their falsity or their truth : we can only assert
that, since they were arrived at by unscientific means, they must
not be accepted without further investigation.

In addition to an inquiry into the existence or non-existence
of criminal characteristics, the scientific study of the criminal
must also concern itself with a wide range of problems. Even
though the first effort of our investigation should result only in
proving a negative, as critics have anticipated, our data has still
to deal with very positive matters. Having failed to trace a
criminal type, the object of our search must still be to find the
types of people,who become criminal—which is a very different
thing. What are the nature and origin of the criminal? How
and why, if at all, does a criminal differ physically and mentally,
in health and disease, from law-abiding persons? What do we
know of his antecedents? What are the constitutional determinants, and environmental conditions, which lead to his lapse
into crime.?

Now, the inquiry, whose two principal objects we have just
described, can only, in our opinion, be pursued satisfactorily by
the statistical method, *i.e.*, by the mathematical analysis of
large series of carefully collected data. That opinion will not
pass unchallenged. We shall be told that the knowledge, ultimately acquired by the analysis of these statistics, could have
been equally well obtained by ordinary observational experience
of individual criminals. There is contained in this criticism the
implication of an essential difference in character between the
statistical and other methods of scientific inquiry. We do not
admit the distinction. Statistical inquiry, all scientific inquiry,
is observational in character: that is to say, it is based upon the
observation of individual facts. But these facts, in themselves,
do not constitute knowledge. Knowledge consists in the discovery of relationships revealed by the systematic study, and by
the legitimatised weighing, of facts. No series of biological or
social data, obtained by the observation of criminals—whether the
observations be recorded as statistics, or whether they be stored
as impressions in the memory—no such series does, in itself, constitute *knowledge* of the criminal. That knowledge lies potential
in the facts, but ineffectual for use until their associations with
each other have been accurately weighed. It is this weighing of

---

* "*Les femmes homicides*," by Dr. Pauline Tarnowski; *Criminal Anthropology*,
by Maurice Parmelee ; *Criminal men*, by G. L. Ferrero.

23

observations which demands, for the present inquiry, the employment of statistical methods: such methods being merely a regulated mechanism by which the relation between certain orders of facts can be precisely estimated.

There is not, as is sometimes imagined, any *special* theory or hypothesis involved in conclusions revealed by statistics. The science of statistics provides only for the systematised study and legitimatised interpretation of observed facts: such interpretation consisting mainly in one and the same process—the associating or dissociating of one set of facts with and from another. Before any association can be legitimately postulated, certain conditions must be fulfilled: evidence must be produced to show that the relation, affirmed to exist, is not a chance or accident, but a natural, association; that it is not one resulting from co-incidence, but that it represents an inseparable connection between natural phenomena. In some orders of observation there is no need for a calculating mechanism to trace and prove the existence of association—this lies revealed upon the surface of the facts observed. The relationship between the phenomena of fire and burning by fire is of this order; and so also is much of the clinical experience of the physician: although associations of phenomena with disease are never entirely unquestionable or definitely precise. The precision and validity of so-called clinical experience depends upon the aptitude for memorising the frequency of past relations, and for correctly estimating by a mental statistical process the probabilities of their recurrence. Observations of the clinician being mainly estimates of quality, rather than of degree, the disturbing effects of chance associations can be allowed for mentally and without aid from the elaborate meticulousness of statistical processes. But in social and biological science, and very often in the science of medicine, and sometimes even in physical science, the phenomena under observation are of an entirely different order to those referred to above. The attributes and conditions of living things are so widely variable, are so delicately graduated in different individuals, that their correlation can seldom be legitimately postulated, and can never be precisely estimated, without aid from a correlation calculus: that is to say, social science almost entirely, and biological and medical sciences to a great extent, can only be built up after preliminary mathematical analysis of large series of carefully collected data. And that is why we assert that statistical methods are indispensible for the scientific study of the criminal.

Criminological study, whatever branch of it is being pursued, and by whatever method it may ultimately proceed, should be *based upon*, and originally consist in, the statistical treatment of facts which, in their crude form as revealed to direct observation, are valueless for construction. Were criminality a morbid state, akin to insanity, with physical signs comparable to those that indicate disease, much study of the criminal could be profitably conducted without mathematical aid. There was, for instance, no need for mathematics to trace and measure the relationship between tubular breathing and pneumonia. But there are **no** characters, physical or mental, peculiar to criminals which, *apart*

24

from differences in degree, are not shared by all people.* We
observe the endless variety in shape and size of the heads of
criminals: we observe that the heads of the law-abiding public
are, in the same way, endlessly varied; but the interpretation of
these observations is different and distinct from the art of observing itself; no bird's eye view of criminals, however wide, can
reveal to us the relation between size of head and criminality, or
the extent to which some subtle moulding of the head is associated
with criminal proclivity; a meticulous precision in extracting
data from observation, mathematical accuracy in dissecting the
data, can alone supply that knowledge.

When we come to study the relation of the criminal to sickness
and disease, or the particular association between crime and any
of the recognised forms of abnormality†—as, for instance, when
we are estimating the proportional frequency of these conditions,
or are determining to what extent they originate from, or are
fostered, or are ameliorated by, prison environment, or to what
extent they are special factors in the causation of crime—in all
these problems, we shall be dealing with subtle numerical associations, latent only in those facts visible to observation, but
ripe for discovery by the dissecting process, and significant for
the co-ordinating purpose, of the science of statistics.

The etiological factors in crime, the influence of heredity and
of environment upon the production of criminals, are problems
which, hitherto, observers have attempted to solve by employing
deductive methods in the study of individuals.   Authorities,
quoting their general experience, have often dogmatically
asserted that poverty, intemperance, lack of education, irreligion,
parental neglect, feebleness of physical constitution, age, love
of excitement, laziness, &c., &c., are causes of crime; and all of
these, including also the force of heredity, have in their turn
been appointed a place in the making of criminals.   But the
effect of these factors upon any one individual cannot be traced
with certainty or be accurately estimated.   We cannot be certain
that because poverty, or lack of education, or parental neglect are
found associated with an individual who commits a crime, these
associations are therefore anything more than chance relations;
and, consequently, to quote, as is frequently done, such association as facts in the causation of crime is entirely misleading.
Some instances of crime may find in their attending circumstances
a plausible explanation; other instances may thus be accounted
for on grounds which appear to be beyond cavil or question.   But
we are dealing with influences so subtle, so elaborate, so elusive,
that far-reaching conclusions as to their effect upon separate
individuals can never be more than conjecture.   What we have

* The anomalous characters which it has been alleged stigmatise the criminal
are, as we have already shown, not qualitative in their nature, but only so by
verbal implication.

† The view we have expressed, that there are no abnormal characters peculiar
to criminals, does not preclude the existence of any form of recognised abnormality amongst criminals. The insane, the epileptic, the tubercular, the diseased,
the imbecile, may occur anywhere, and are obviously not excluded by the prison
walls. There may even be atavistic people in prison as well as out of prison.
And if there are " savages who wander into strange environments," it would be
strange if some of them did not wander into jail.

25

to do, all that can be done, is to measure, by the statistical method of *averaging large numbers* the extent to which an increasing tendency to commit anti-social acts is correlated with different degrees or variations of the personal, economic, and social conditions under investigation.

That the scientific study of the criminal should be conducted, primarily and principally, by the statistical method of inquiry—a presupposition which, in the present investigation, led to the preliminary collecting of our statistical data—involves an assumption : we must assume that the criminal is a normal human being; that the criminal thing, whatever its nature may ultimately be shown to be, is not a pathological product, but is a physiological condition of the human mind; that whatever difference there may be underlying the acts of the law-breaker and those of the law-abiding person, the difference is one of degree only, and not of kind. It is important, at the outset, to examine the grounds for this assumption.

Interpreted colloquially, two very different ideas are associated with the term " criminal." There is the criminal who is a definite legal fact; and there is the criminal who is a very vague ethical conception. The former—an offender against the law, convicted and sentenced to imprisonment—is a legal reality : and, as such, is human material appropriate for scientific study. The latter, on the other hand—an incarnation of original sin—does not necessarily correspond to any reality in life; and cannot, therefore, as a product of the imagination, be scientifically studied. When we speak of a scientific study of the criminal, what then is to be the criminal thing under investigation? Do we refer to the study of men who actually commit crimes, or to the study of the kind of men who, whether they have or have not committed crime, we believe to be inherently base, or criminal at heart? It is important to be clear upon this point because, unfortunately, the two ideas associated with the word "criminal" have been inextricably confused.* The idea that a man is technically designated " criminal," because he has committed an offence against the law, has got allied with the idea that all offenders against the law are specifically criminal in constitution. Apart from the common tendency to sin, which he shares equally with all men, the law-breaker is conceived as being stigmatised, by an inward and spiritual quality of sinfulness, by some qualitative flaw in character, which differentiates him from the law-abiding person, who, it is supposed, is entirely without this quality.

Now we do not deny that the law-breaker, by his anti-social acts, is sinful: we might doubt, but would not deny, that offenders, legally designated " criminal," possess a greater average tendency to commit anti-social acts, and, consequently, a greater degree of sinfulness, than the remainder of society:

* Lombroso's application of the tenets of criminal anthropology to the identification of " anthropological " criminals ; his inclusion of Charlotte Corday, and of other historical personages, within the purview of this science ; the notion, frequently expressed, that criminology is an impossible science, because many real criminals are never imprisoned, whereas many prisoners are not really criminals —herein we have illustrations of the confusion referred to above, and of the consequent necessity for a clear definition, at the outset, of the extent and limitations of criminological inquiry.

26

but that the criminal, on the *prima facie* evidence alone that he
has offended against the law, gives proof of some *special* quality
of iniquity in him, unshared in any degree by the whole of law-
abiding humanity, we cannot see any grounds for accepting as
a valid hypothesis.

Nothing can be more important to our purpose than the truth
or the falsity of this presumption as to the moral alienation of
the legal offender. The whole method of studying the criminal
depends upon our answer to the following question: is an infraction of the law in itself *prima facie* evidence of the moral
alienation of the perpetrator? That is to say, does it prove the
existence in him of a *morbid* state, entirely *foreign* to any
psychological development of the law-abiding public, and akin,
for instance, to the delusional state which differentiates the
mental processes of the insane.*

Now, unless we stand by an *a priori* conviction, that, although
elusive to analysis, there must be a specific undefinable quality in
illegal acts, which differentiates them from other forms of anti-
social offences, we are driven to the conclusion that crime,
although relatively rare, must be included in the catalogue of
common possibilities, and the criminal in the category of normal
human beings, amongst whom the righteous and iniquitous are
distinguished by degree only. Nevertheless we must admit there
is a universal instinctive tendency to the opposite belief. It
would be neither appropriate nor possible to suggest here the
innumerable reasons that may have engendered this instinct,
among which figure religious convictions,† social expediencies,

---

* The frame of mind of a person harbouring a delusion—of one who ineradi-
cably believes he is made of glass, for instance—is unthinkably detached from
any comparable mental state of healthy persons. On the other hand, in the will
to commit any crime, however atrocious, there is no element so completely alien
to the normally constituted mind that the perpetration of such crime becomes
similarly unthinkable. Yet the Lombrosian notion of the "criminal né," *i.e.*,
of men and women "born to do evil," presupposing, as it does, a conscious
acceptance by the outcast of a mission of sinfulness, involves the conception of a
moral state which, to any person of natural moral development, is quite as
unthinkably remote from the normal as is the mental state of delusional
insanity.

† We can only speculate upon the origin and evolution of the tendency to
regard the detected and convicted offender as almost a distinct species, separated
from the rest of mankind by an absolute difference in the nature, as opposed to
the degree, of its moral identity. A likely source may be found in the theological and ecclesiastical tradition by which all our ethical ideas have been influenced in the past. It is safe to say that the gradual recognition of the criminal,
as a definite element in society, was coincident with the foundation of the criminal
law, and the developing perception of abstract, as opposed to personal, right and
wrong. Now, the characteristic feature of the law's administration was the
infliction of punishments upon its enemies and offenders; and in the inhuman
quality of these punishments—"death, mutilation, every kind of torture were
the almost inevitable doom of those convicted of the pettiest larceny"—we discover more than the desire for personal retaliation, more than the fulfilment of
the demands of abstract justice: we see in them, rather, a propitiation of the
Divine wrath. The criminal came to be looked upon not only as the enemy of
the individual, the rebel of society, but as a voluntary outcast from the spiritual
world. His offence may have been a trifling one, but with the verdict of the law
upon it, it became symbolic of hidden iniquity. In the spiritual dualism universally preached and accepted, there were Good and Evil, there were Light and
Darkness. The soul of man was either black or it was white; there were no
intermediate shades. Man was either for God or the Devil; and the criminal,
by his act had proved himself to be on the side of the latter.

27

and psychological subtleties of all kinds; but we are convinced that much confusion as to the nature of crime, and the anomalous character of criminals, influencing the mind of the public in general, and of the old criminologists in particular, has been fostered by the continual misuse and ambiguous interpretation of the words " normal " and " abnormal." The proposition that crime is an unusual act, committed by a perfectly normal person, can only be properly intelligible after a precise differentiation between these two terms.

The wide divergence in the physical and mental constitution of all people is a patent biological fact that may be accepted without proof. Thus, we distinguish between tall and short people, between people who are thin and those who are corpulent, between young and old, wise and foolish, good and bad, and so on, with all physical and mental characters and conditions. There is, however, in these verbal distinctions, the suggestion of a *qualitative* element which has no existence in reality. Nature distributes her attributes in a continuous *quantitative* series: and any apparent differences of quality, in a *normal* series of people, will invariably be found, upon analysis, to consist ultimately in a difference of degree only. There is no line of demarcation, for instance, between good temper and bad temper, and no qualitative difference, as the verbal distinction suggests; there is, rather, every degree of temper between an extreme serenity of good temper and an extreme violence of bad temper. And in the, same way, there is no line of demarcation between short people and tall people: short merging into tall, by insensible gradations. A normal character is not a specific physical or mental entity, of one definite degree: it is a character which may exist in any and every degree of relation, in different people. Very extreme degrees of any character are, of course, rare; extreme degrees are unusual; moderate degrees are customary: but no matter what the degree, all degrees have this in common, that they are every one of them *perfectly normal* in the sense that they are all *perfectly natural*.

The point we would emphasise is that the terms " abnormal " and " unusual " are not really interchangeable as, colloquially, they may appear to be. Colloquially, a very tall man is described as " abnormally tall "; a very self-centred man as " abnormally egotistic "; a very dull man as "abnormally unintelligent." Now, between the terms abnormal and unusual there is a real and important difference, upon the recognition of which clarity of thought depends. The failure to recognise this difference is responsible for an immense amount of confusion. The essential idea in what we call " unusual " is *rarity* of existence: and the term implies nothing more than this; on the other hand, connected with the term " abnormal," there is an idea of *unnaturalness* and *morbidity*, which forms an essential part of its connotation. The unusual is always quite natural, and is the outcome of natural laws. Unusually tall people are rare, but their stature is part of natural growth, and is the outcome of the natural laws of growth.* The abnormal, on the other hand, is essentially

---

* Excluding cases of pathological dwarfism or giantism, the rare occurrences of extremes of stature are as essentially part of the law of growth as are the more frequent occurrences of moderate degrees of stature.

28

morbid, and implies a condition of things against nature. Thus, a victim of acromegaly might have hands which, although not unusually large as hands go, would be abnormally large for him. An unusually tall child, suffering from spinal disease, might become thereby abnormally short. To sum up: we may say, generally, that the abnormal is a qualitative variation from the natural; whereas the unusual, no matter what its extent may be, is never anything more than a deviation in degree from the normal average.

Now, every judgment of abnormality presupposes a definition of what is normal. What, then, is the idea of normality, the standardised notion by reference to which the anomalous nature of any human state, character, or condition, can be determined? Criminologists, although they make frequent use of some standard, have consistently evaded its definition.* We would assert, then, that a normal mental or physical character, no matter to what degree it deflects from any ideal standard, is one which is an outcome of the natural physiological and psychological laws of existence; and that any such character only is, or becomes, abnormal, when these laws are interfered with, or are supplanted by some pathological process.

This, then, is our contention: admitting the criminal does possess all the characters that have been attributed to him; admitting, even, that he is marked by a "dome-shaped" head, and by a face like a "bird of prey"; admitting that he is drunken, impulsive, obstinate, dirty, and without control—despite all this, we maintain he is not an abnormal man. He may represent a selected class of normal man; many of his qualities may present extreme degrees from the normal average: yet the fact remains that, in the pattern of his mind and body, in his feelings, thoughts, desires, and recognition of right and wrong, and in his behaviour, however outrageous it may be, he exists by the same nature, and is moved by the same springs of action, that affect the conduct, and constitute the quality, of normal human beings.

The principle we have enunciated, that the criminal, although probably a selected, is a normal, human being, involves no theory as to the kind of normal person, mentally, morally or physically, that he represents. We have maintained that the iniquity of law-breaking is not different in kind from that of any other anti-social act. Some people, accepting this view, might nevertheless contend that indictable sinfulness, although not differing

---

* They describe, for instance, a low forehead, a high palate, asymmetry of head, as "anomalous"; they compare the number of "anomalies" found in criminals with the number found in "normal" people; and Lombroso has maintained that characters, such as projecting cheek-bones, which are "anomalous" in the male, are quite "normal" in the female. But nowhere is it explicitly stated upon what grounds these characters are thus regarded. Sometimes it seems probable that the designation refers to an artistic standard of beauty; at other times the reference appears to be to an ethical standard of perfection. Sometimes the term "abnormal" is used with a pathological suggestion, sometimes, as above, with only a physiological implication. Generally, with these writers, and most consistently, any marked deviation from the mean is regarded as "abnormal": the adopted standard of "normality" then being apparently the statistical *average*.

29

in quality, is greater in degree than is non-indictable sinfulness; that the primitive impulses actuating the will of all men—the impulse, for instance, which tends to make a man relentless in hatred and desire for revenge, selfish in lust, rapacious in gain— are uncontrolled to a greater degree amongst legal, than amongst non-legal offenders: and that, consequently, the former are the more iniquitous. Following this contention, it might be assumed that the criterion upon which the legal designation of " criminal " depends is a man's moral position on a scale of criminality, between extremes of iniquity and righteousness.* But scienti- fically, we can make no such assumption; nor do we see how, without omniscience of the factors and circumstances that control men's destinies, individuals could be so distributed upon any such scale. An elaborate understanding of the foundations of society, and a capacity for keeping, or evading, the Law, are not necessarily coincident with a simple religious instinct for acting upon the verdict of conscience as to what is right and what is wrong. The thief, forger, or incendiary, being more radically inimical to the constitution of society, may be logically regarded as more anti-social than, say, the law-respecting juggler in financial operations; but he is not necessarily more iniquitous, nor is he, as Garofalo would assert him to be, necessarily being guided less in his conduct of life by the passion of pity.

·So far, our criticism of prevalent notions of " criminality " has been entirely destructive. We have still to decide what may be legitimately assumed with regard to the moral identity of the criminal. We have found no *a priori* justification for assuming, even as a provisional hypothesis, the Lombrosian idea of the criminal as the delegate of a spiritual mission of sinfulness; nor for the notion that he represents a morbid type of human being, akin to the type of the insane; nor for the claim that he should be regarded as necessarily corresponding to the iniquitous or to any other particular moral class of normal humanity. Ulti- mately, with scientifically acquired evidence in hand, we may be. compelled to adopt one or the other of these conceptions; but, for the time being, we are not justified in taking our stand by any one of them. What, then, may be our assumption? What notion of the mental and moral constitution of the criminal would it be legitimate to adopt as a provisional working hypo- thesis for our inquiry? The suggestion will be proffered to us, no doubt, that there is no need for any hypothesis at all. It will be said that the scientific investigator, approaching his problem in a spirit of complete detachment, must look upon criminals with dispassionate tranquillity, as upon a collection of men brought together merely by the fortuitous hazard of the Law. For, it will be maintained, all we do definitely know of our subjects at the outset of an inquiry, is that they are individuals, detected of committing breaches of the law sufficiently serious to be dealt with by imprisonment—we know nothing more, nothing less than this. Such is the fact: yet no man, we think, would undertake to pass sentence upon an offender, nor would he pledge

---

* Or, following Garofalo's analysis of the criminal mind, one might be inclined to assume the relative absence of the passion of pity as one's criterion.

30

himself to introduce penal reform, or to construct a policy of administration, without framing some hypothesis as to the nature of the human material with which he was dealing. And the criminal cannot be studied, satisfactorily to science, without similar premising in respect of the same notion. Our ultimate aim is to arrive at an explicit conception of criminality, which will make the phenomenon of crime intelligible. To achieve this end, we must start with some provisional hypothesis as to the nature of the mental and moral identity of the legal offender.

We have traced the starting point of the " criminality " idea to the evolution of the criminal law,* when the criminal was regarded as an outcast from the spiritual world. Innately, all men were mentally and morally equal: by deliberate choice the criminal had enlisted away from the side of the angels. It was against this first notion, and against the severity of the punishments it engendered, that the classical school protested† : all men were mentally and morally equal, but crime very often was the result, not of the criminal's deliberate selection of evil, but of his misdirected choice. Next came the Lombrosian notion. All normal men were mentally and morally equal: therefore the criminal's abnormal choice of evil was a proof of disease. Finally, the latest *a priori* development of the notion of criminality yields the same refrain. All healthy men are mentally and morally equal, and, consequently, the criminal must either be morally insane, or he must be solely and entirely the product of an adverse environment.

We have, in this series of notions of criminality, the logical outcome of deductive reasoning from one fundamental assumption, whose truth has been regarded as incontestable: the assumption that, organically, all normal persons are mentally and morally alike—that there are no differences between them of constitutional or germinal origin. Admitting the truth of this proposition, it follows, logically and inevitably, either (i) that the presence or absence of criminality depends upon the deliberate choice of an individual between good and evil (the classical idea); or (ii) that the criminal is not a normal individual, and that his criminality is a product of disease, (the Lombrosian notion); or (iii) that criminality is a traditional moral acquirement, resulting solely and entirely from misdirected education (the modern deduction).

---

* The relation of the criminal to the criminal law is summed up in the retort of the brigand, who, when threatened by the law is said to have exclaimed : " The law ! I am the law ! "

† Even up to the middle of the last century the punishments for criminal offences were very severe. The c ank, the treadmill, and the silence cells, the insanitary prisons where the labour was so severe that men would voluntarily mangle their limbs to avoid both the work and the merciless penalties inflicted upon those who shirked it—these penal conditions persisted even up to forty years ago. And that the public regard for the criminal is not even now quite free from ferocity is shown by the following suggestion, lately proposed in America, as an alternative to the death penalty. It was suggested that, instead of being hanged, a convicted murderer should be placed in a cell underground, and that this inscription should be written upon the door of his cell :—" Here lies A.B. convicted for the murder of C.D. ; his food is the coarsest bread, his drink is water mingled with his tears, he is dead to the world, this cell is his tomb."

31

We wish to approach the present inquiry from a very definite standpoint regarding the theory of original equality, the exactitude of which hitherto has been regarded as beyond question; and, in so doing, we must assert two things. First, that, in view of the intricate nature of the mind of man, and of the mutability and complexity of environmental influences, it is impossible to state dogmatically, on a priori grounds, whether the criminal is born or made; and to what extent criminality results from a constitutional quality of moral fibre; or to what extent this condition is a purely traditional acquirement. All we can assume, and what we must assume, is the possibility that constitutional, as well as environmental, factors play a part in the production of criminality. And the second assertion defining our standpoint is this: that however much alike all normal persons may be in the *quality* of their mental and moral attributes, there is a vast *quantitative* range of difference between them: that when estimates of moral value are measured no longer by variations in quality which, among normal people, are admittedly non-existent, but by variations in degree, whose existence cannot be gainsaid—the differences amongst normal people become almost infinite in extent. This, then, being our standpoint in regard to the old principle that all men are mentally and morally equal, we arrive at the provisional working hypothesis we are seeking: we are, in fact, forced to an hypothesis of the possible existence of a character in all men which, in the absence of a better term, we will call the *criminal diathesis.**

Using the word "criminal," not necessarily in description of moral defectiveness, but merely to designate, in legal terminology, the fact that an individual has been imprisoned—using "criminal" in this sense, the term "diathesis" implies a hypothetical character of some kind, a constitutional proclivity, either mental, moral or physical, present to a certain degree in all individuals, but so potent in some, as to determine for them, eventually, the fate of imprisonment. Direct evidence of the existence of a criminal diathesis cannot, of course, be given. The criminal diathesis, like the tubercular diathesis, if existent, would not be visible to the senses. Direct experience of the existence of either is impossible. But, just as we are compelled to assume that the existence of a tubercular diathesis is revealed by the phenomenon of tubercular disease, so are we compelled to assume the possible existence of a criminal diathesis from the phenomenon of crime. We make no presumption as to what qualities constitute this diathesis: but unless the committing of crime, and the apprehension and conviction following it, be regarded as a series of absolutely fortuitous catastrophies—unless the criminal in the dock is chosen as much at random as is the juryman in the box—we do not see how the conclusion can be evaded that the criminal diathesis, although present in greater

---

* In every branch of our investigation, we shall be compelled to assume the possible existence of this so called " criminal diathesis "; that is to say, we shall have to pursue our research with a mind open to the possibility that innate or constitutional, as well as environmental factors, play a part in determining the fate of the criminal.

32

average intensity among the lawless, is a certain constitutional fact, common to the whole of humanity. In fine, however criminality may be analysed, or crimes may be classified, however the penal record of the criminal may be accounted for, we must presume that, determining his fate, there may be, within the criminal himself, some quality or combination of qualities, some constitutional tendency of stupidity, perhaps, or of lack of control, or, as the cynic might suggest, of unfortunate *naïveté*, which leads to his being found out, while his more acute fellow scoundrel escapes—something in him, we must presume, there may be, which, as we have stated, is a character common to mankind.

Our object will be to find out how far this criminal diathesis, as measured by criminal records, is associated with environment, training, stock, and with the physical attributes of the criminal.

Descriptions of the various statistical methods employed in the pursuit of this object will be given, as they are referred to, in the course of the text.

The merits of these methods, applied to the study of social and biological problems, are the following:—Firstly, by employing material composed of all the facts, and not merely of such straws of fact as chance may blow before our eyes, the statistical method builds up our knowledge of organic beings upon foundations as solid and reliable as those of physical science. Secondly, the method is so detached from the subject under investigation that it records facts in their original crudity, unaffected by partisanship to any particular system or theory. Thirdly and chiefly, investigations conducted by the statistical method are developed from the outset upon a consciously chosen plan, and proceed logically, and by steps explicitly defined, to inevitable conclusions.

We owe much to the experimental methods of investigating natural phenomena in plants and animals; but, in the future, our debt will be as great to the statistical method, which has already begun to throw light upon the many hitherto obscure phenomena related to the lives and conditions of human beings. From lack of suitable data, and in the absence of experts with sufficient statistical knowledge to handle such data as have been collected, the employment and development of this method of inquiry has been, in the past, exclusively the pursuit of a small body of workers, inspired by the genius of Francis Galton, and of Quetelet, who preceded him. Owing, however, to the stimulating personality, and to the brilliant mathematical researches of one master,* who has recently reduced to order the previous chaos of statistical science, the singular importance of the method is at last being appreciated and applied by other workers in innumerable directions with ever increasing fruitfulness.

---

* Karl Pearson.

121

VIII. *Conclusion.*

To sum up: all English criminals, with the exception of those technically convicted of fraud, are markedly differentiated from the general population in stature and body-weight; in addition, offenders convicted of violence to the person are characterised by an average degree of strength and of constitutional soundness considerably above the average of other criminals, and of the law-abiding community;* finally, thieves and burglars (who constitute, it must be borne in mind, 90 per cent. of all criminals), and also incendiaries, as well as being inferior in stature and weight, are also, relatively to other criminals and the population at large, puny in their general bodily habit. These are the

---

* A stout, strong, healthy, thick set individual, if anything rather below the average stature of his class : this is the typical portrait of a person prone to commit criminal violence.

122

facts: and, according to the results of our statistical inquiry, *they are the sole facts at the basis of criminal anthropology;* they are the only elements of truth out of which have been constructed the elaborate, extravagant, and ludicrously uncritical criminological doctrines of the great protagonist of the " criminal type " theory. The utmost we can concede from our final conclusion, formulated in Part I., is that criminal anthropology is not entirely without basis in fact: but fact perverted by credulity and fanaticism. The danger of the Lombrosian doctrine is not a theoretical one: persistently in the past, and progressively in the future, this doctrine has impeded and will continue to impede—until its interment be officially registered—the rational treatment of criminological problems that call urgently for solution.

269

CONCLUSION.

The ends of Criminological Science, of all Social Science, must be approached across facts, and facts only. The collecting of opinion, the exercising of dialectical ingenuity, the referring to authority, the quoting of illustrative cases—these uncharted ways of the old descriptive sociologists have led only to confusion, dogma, and superstition: they must be abandoned. The discoveries of the explorer cannot be recognised until he produces a verifiable map of his journey; if the goal, professed to have been reached by the sociological pioneer, is to be accepted, he must show that the path he has pursued is one which others may follow.

Now, the road we have attempted to shape, during the past eight years, is paved with statistical facts; each of which, within the limits of our search, we believe to be indestructible by controversy. The credentials of our every statement will be found in the scheduled data, in the tables of analysed data, in the figures resulting from these analysed data; and, by their aid, our path may be re-traced step by step, its bearings tested, and its direction criticised. If we have gone astray anywhere, the fault can be logically demonstrated by the critic pointing the error in our data, or in the analysis of these data, or in their interpretation. But he must not dismiss our results because they may be opposed to his opinion, or to current opinion: he must enforce any condemnation he may make by the production of statistics more representative than ours, and related to a more exhaustive and accurate observation.

Let us resume our results. What is the final point of view we have attained? We need not recapitulate all the qualifying details, and minor issues, explicitly set forth at the close of every chapter. It is sufficient to restate certain broad relations, which appear to underlie the genesis of crime; certain fundamental conclusions, connected with the origin of the criminal: and to contrast these with the current doctrines of criminologists.

In the first place, we were confronted with the notion of a distinct anthropological criminal type: with the idea of the criminal being such in consequence of an hereditary element in his psychic organisation, and of certain physical and mental peculiarities, which stigmatised him as predestined to evil, and which differentiated him from the morally well-conditioned person. In accordance with this notion, every individual criminal is an anomaly among mankind, by inheritance; and can be detected by his physical malformations, and mental eccentricities: the inevitable deduction being that any attempt at his reform must prove vain.

The preliminary conclusion reached by our inquiry is that this anthropological monster has no existence in fact. The physical and mental constitution of both criminal and law-abiding persons, of the same age, stature, class, and intelligence, are identical. There is no such thing as an anthropological criminal type. But, despite this negation, and upon the evidence of our statistics, it appears to be an equally indisputable fact that there is a

270

physical, mental, and moral type of normal person who tends to be convicted of crime: that is to say, our evidence conclusively shows that, on the average, the criminal of English prisons is markedly differentiated by defective physique—as measured by stature and body weight; by defective mental capacity—as measured by general intelligence; and by an increased possession of wilful anti-social proclivities*—as measured, apart from intelligence, by length of sentence to imprisonment.

Reviewing the general trend of our results, it would seem that the appearances, stated by anthropologists of all countries to be peculiar to criminals, are thus described because of a too separate inspection, and narrow view of the facts, by these observers. They cannot see the wood for the trees. Obsessed by preconceived beliefs, small differences of intimate structure have been uncritically accepted by them, and exaggerated to fit fantastic theories. The truths that have been overlooked are that these deviations, described as significant of criminality are inevitable concomitants of inferior stature and defective intelligence: both of which are the differentia of the types of persons who are selected for imprisonment. The thief, who is caught thieving, has a smaller head and a narrower forehead than the man who arrests him: but this is the case, not because he is more criminal, but because, of the two, he is the more markedly inferior in stature. The incendiary is more emotionally unstable, more lacking in control, more refractory in conduct, and more dirty in habits, etc. than the thief; and the thief is more distinguished by the above peculiarities than the forger; and all criminals display these qualities to a more marked extent than does the law-abiding public: not because any one of these classes is more criminal than another, but because of their interdifferentiation in general intelligence. On statistical evidence, one assertion can be dogmatically made: it is, that the criminal is differentiated by inferior stature, by defective intelligence and, to some extent, by his anti-social proclivities; but that, apart from these broad differences, there are no physical, mental, or moral characteristics peculiar to the inmates of English prisons. We need not recapitulate the social, economic, and legal selective processes which, without drawing upon theories of degeneracy or atavism, have seemed to us sufficient simple explanation of the criminal's physical and mental distinctions. The following figure, however, may assist the imagination in realising the nature and proportions of this differentiation. We may take it that only a proportion —let us call it 1 in x—of persons in the general population are convicted at some time of life for indictable offences. If the total adult population were made to file by in groups of x, and, out of each group, one person was selected, who happened to be the smallest there in stature, or the most defective in intelligence, or who possessed volitional anti-social proclivities to a more marked degree than his fellows in the group—the band of individuals resulting from this selection

* We find that it is the most intelligent recidivists who are guilty of the most serious acquisitive offences, (*see* page 207).

271

would, in physical, mental, and moral constitution, approximate more closely to our criminal population than the residue.

The second conclusion resulting from our inquiry defines the relative importance of constitutional and environmental factors in the etiology of crime. The criminal anthropologists assert that the chief source of crime lies in the personal constitution. His physical and mental stigmata, they argue, while showing the anomalous biological origin of the law-breaker, prove also the existence in him of a peculiar constitutional psychic quality: by reason of which he is destined from birth to do evil, and will become criminal, however favourable or unfavourable his circumstances may be. On the other hand, the criminal sociologists say that the source of crime must be sought, not in the constitution of the malefactor, but in his adverse social and economic environment. He is not born, but is made, criminal, it is contended: his physical, mental, and moral characteristics, and the ultimate fate of imprisonment these entail, are products of unfavourable circumstances; in the absence of which, even inborn criminal tendencies will fail to develop.

We have traced and measured the relations of conviction for crime in a variety of constitutional and environmental conditions: and while, with many of the former, high degrees of association have been revealed, with practically none of the latter do we discover any definite degree of relationship. Thus, as already stated, we find close bonds of association with defective physique and intelligence; and, to a less intimate extent, with moral defectiveness, or wilful anti-social proclivities—as demonstrated by the fact that it is the most intelligent recidivists who are guilty of the most serious acquisitive offences. We find, also, that crimes of violence are associated with the finer physique, health, and muscular development, with the more marked degrees of ungovernable temper, obstinacy of purpose, and inebriety, and with the greater amount of insane and suicidal proclivity, of persons convicted of these offences; and that tall persons are relatively immune from conviction for rape; and that fraudulent offenders are relatively free from the constitutional determinants which appear to conduce to other forms of crime. Alcoholism, also, and all diseases associated with alcoholism; venereal diseases, and all conditions associated with venereal diseases; epilepsy, and insanity—appear to be constitutional determinants of crime: although, upon the evidence of our data, it would seem that these conditions, in their relation to conviction, are mainly accidental associations, depending upon the high degree of relationship between defective intelligence and crime. On the other hand, between a variety of environmental conditions examined, such as illiteracy, parental neglect, lack of employment, the stress of poverty, etc., etc., including the states of a healthy, delicate, or morbid constitution *per se*, and even the situation induced by the approach of death*—between these conditions and the committing of crime, we find no evidence of any significant

---

* At all ages of life up to fifty-five the death rates of prisoners are practically identical with the general population rates.

272

relationship. Our second conclusion, then, is this: that, relatively to its origin in the constitution of the malefactor, and especially in his mentally defective constitution, crime is only to a trifling extent (if to any) the product of social inequalities, of adverse environment, or of other manifestations of what may be comprehensively termed the force of circumstances.

Our third conclusion refers to the influence of imprisonment upon the physical and mental well-being of prisoners. We find that imprisonment, on the whole, has no apparent effect upon physique, as measured by body weight, or upon mentality, as measured by intelligence; and that mortality from accidental negligence is pronouncedly diminished, and the prevalency of infectious fevers due to defective sanitation—taking enteric as a type—is lessened, by prison environment; on the other hand, mortality from suicide, and from conditions involving major surgical interference amongst prisoners, greatly exceeds the general population standard; while, with regard to the prevalency of, and mortality from, tuberculosis, in English prisons, criminals may be regarded as a random sample of the general population—one-fourth to one-fifth of all deaths in the general population, as well as amongst prisoners, being due to some form of tubercular disease.* We find, moreover, that long terms of imprisonment militate against the regularity of a convict's employment when he is free from prison, but tend to increase the standard of his scholastic education; and that frequency of incarceration leads to a diminution of the fertility of the convict, owing to the circumstance that, after a certain period of continually interrupted married life, habitual criminals are deserted by their wives, or by the women with whom they have lived.

Our fourth conclusion disposes of the current allegation that "criminals share in the relative sterility of all degenerate stocks." Upon the evidence of our statistics, we find the criminal to be unquestionably a product of the most prolific stocks in the general community; and that his own apparent diminution of fertility is not due to physiological sterility, but to the definite, psychological, human reaction we have just affirmed.

---

* A fact which demonstrates that the current allegations (i) of criminality and tubercular diseases being kindred manifestations of the same form of human decadence, and (ii) that prison conditions foster tubercular disease, are both unsupported by statistical facts.

With regard to sickness generally, the fraction of a year spent, on the average, in hospital, by the inmates of English prisons, is a few hours less than, or practically identical with, the average period during which the members of one of our largest friendly societies receive pay, and are absent from work, on account of sickness.

[12]

Lucia Zedner

Women, Crime, and Penal Responses: A Historical Account

ABSTRACT

In the eighteenth and nineteenth centuries, women were more commonly convicted of crimes than they are today. Their crimes appear to have been determined more by their socioeconomic situation than by any innate sex differences. Contemporaries reacted very differently to female offenders. Male prison regimes emphasized discipline and deterrence; female prisons developed individualized programs of "moral regeneration." In the latter years of the nineteenth century, biological explanations of crime grew increasingly popular. They were found particularly plausible in explaining female crime long after they had been discredited in relation to men. In the early years of the twentieth century the growing influence of psychiatry focused attention on mental inadequacy as a cause of crime. Many female offenders were reassessed as "mad" rather than "bad." For mainly historical reasons, penal policy continues to be dominated by the belief that women prisoners are likely to be mentally disturbed or inadequate.

This essay examines the dimension of gender in perceptions, explanations, and responses to crime during the nineteenth and twentieth centuries. It owes two major intellectual debts. The first is to the recent development of social histories of punishment that have opened up an exciting area of historical research and developed an analytical framework for understanding the development of crime control. The second is to the development of feminist criminology that has highlighted the concentration of criminological studies almost exclusively on men and

Lucia Zedner, lecturer in law, London School of Economics, University of London, and honorary research fellow, Centre for Criminological Research, Oxford, is grateful to Roger Hood for comments on earlier drafts. This essay is based on research carried out as a prize research fellow, Nuffield College, Oxford.

308   Lucia Zedner

has sought to redress this imbalance by focusing both specifically on the study of female criminality and, more generally, on the issue of gender. These developments, in both historical and feminist criminology, have made major contributions to our understanding of crime and its control. In North America they have already resulted in valuable research into the history of the incarceration of women and girls in industrial schools, reformatories, and prisons (Schlossman 1977, 1978; Brenzel 1980; Hahn 1980a, 1980b; Rosen 1980; Freedman 1981; Rafter 1983a, 1983b, 1985a, 1985b). In Britain to date there has been little work of comparable depth and quality (though see Dobash, Dobash, and Gutteridge 1986). There has been no empirical research into the perceptions and explanations of female criminality that shaped the development of penal institutions for women.

In this essay I show that up to the mid-nineteenth century the predominant approach to female criminality was moralistic. Women criminals were judged against a highly artificial notion of the ideal woman—an exemplary moral being. Women's crimes not only broke the criminal law but were viewed as acts of deviance from the "norm" of femininity. Prison regimes focused on individual women's failings of character and sought—through external management, educational provision, or self-discipline—to restore inmates to the ideal of femininity.

Toward the end of the nineteenth century attention focused increasingly on the constitution of the offender and particularly on the internal attributes that, it was believed, made people criminal. Criminality in women became the focus of considerable concern not least because, in their role as mothers, they were identified as the biological source of crime and degeneracy. Victorian notions of women as the "weaker sex" made them particularly susceptible to a process of medicalization that has endured into the twentieth century. Biological, and later psychological, interpretations of female criminality were suffused with a highly moral view of what constituted deviance and what constituted normality in women. The apparent shift from moralizing about crime to scientific investigation was rather less marked, therefore, than many have assumed. By building on Victorian assumptions about women's supposed moral weaknesses and by seeking to endow them with quasi-scientific status, these constitutional explanations found greater and more enduring plausibility in relation to female than to male criminality.

Section 1 of this essay begins by acknowledging the intellectual developments on which it builds—most notably, recent social histories of the prison, the development of historical criminology, and the growth of writings by feminist criminologists. Section II provides, as a benchmark, a brief survey of what is known about the nature and extent of female crime in the eighteenth and nineteenth centuries. For all the well-known weaknesses of official criminal statistics, these provide some basis against which to assess changing views of crime. Section III examines those views, beginning with the development of theories of female criminality in the early nineteenth century. It considers why moralistic approaches to female criminality predominated for much of the nineteenth century and examines to what extent such approaches demanded differential treatment of women in prison. I suggest that this moralizing approach both exacerbated concern about female crime and drew attention to "crimes of morality" committed by women, such as prostitution or public drunkenness. Section IV examines the emergence of biological theories of crime in the late nineteenth century, culminating in the writings of Cesare Lombroso—the most famous proponent of biological positivism. This section looks in detail at the context and the content of such writings. I suggest that they were less novel and certainly less scientific than has generally been thought. Section V traces the emergence of psychological theories that laid stress instead on the incidence of mental defect, again particularly among female offenders. It asks why the growing intervention of psychiatry into the penal sphere focused primarily on female offenders and with what results for those women who were identified as mentally inadequate. Section VI argues that, until relatively recently, the twentieth century has seen remarkably little advance in the understanding of female criminality. Today, penal responses to female crime remain locked within the turn-of-the-century view of criminal women as mentally ill or otherwise inadequate. If anything, this view has spread to encompass not just a group of identifiably deficient women; it suggests that all women who offend are likely to be in some way psychologically disturbed. The continuing prevalence of such a view is explicable only by understanding the extent to which Victorian moral concepts of "normal" and "deviant" women underpin modern psychiatric analysis.

I. Intellectual Acknowledgments

In recent years there has been considerable valuable research into the history of crime in both Europe and America. The major areas of historical interest and controversy have been the development of the police and of custodial institutions: the prison, the reformatory, and the asylum (Foucault 1967, 1977; Rothman 1971, 1980; Ignatieff 1978; Scull 1979, 1981; Bailey 1981; Harding et al. 1985). These writers have looked critically at traditional interpretations that presented the growth of crime control in terms of gradual progress motivated by humanitarian idealism. They have questioned to what extent the aims of late eighteenth and nineteenth century penal reformers were actually achieved; they have looked beyond the rhetoric of reform to examine social, economic, and political forces behind the expansion of crime control and changes in penal policy; and they have focused particularly on the relations between penal institutions and wider mechanisms for maintaining social discipline and asked why the prison emerged as the preeminent punitive solution.

In Europe many of these so-called revisionist writers have worked more or less self-consciously in the shadow of the French philosopher Michel Foucault. His *Discipline and Punish* (1977) developed a schematic vision of the emergence of the "carceral archipelago," in which the prison was only the most extreme of a series of institutions designed to maintain discipline throughout society. Foucault suggested that the conception of power as knowledge formed the basis of this disciplinary order. Penal institutions were primarily observatories in which offenders could be watched, known, and thereby controlled (Foucault 1977, chap. 2). Foucault's thesis suggests an intimate relationship between the history of the prison and the development of criminological knowledge. Only by examining how criminality was perceived and explained can we fully understand the development of institutions designed for its control.

Following Foucault, while explicitly rejecting his more extravagant visions, a generation of writers has sought to delineate the development of the modern apparatus of "penality" (see Cohen and Scull 1983 for a collection of the best of such writings). Writers such as Michael Ignatieff and Patricia O'Brien in England, and David Rothman, Andrew Scull, and Nicole Hahn Rafter in the United States, among others, have produced important works on the history of prisons, reformatories, asylums, and other agencies set up to control deviance (Beattie 1975; Ignatieff 1978, 1983a, 1983b; O'Brien 1978, 1982; Scull 1979, 1981; Bailey 1980; Hay 1980; Rothman 1980; Cohen and Scull 1983; Rafter 1983b; Cohen 1985; Rudé 1985; Radzinowicz and Hood 1986). Penal institutions have been seen as epitomizing a much more generalized encroachment of the state, imposing discipline and controlling more and more aspects of social life. The converging interest of histo-

Women, Crime, and Penal Responses 311

rians, sociologists, and criminologists has thus provided for a fruitful cross-fertilization of ideas and a genuinely critical reappraisal of the development of state control of crime.

This intense concentration of interest in the development of institutions and agencies of crime control has tended to be at the expense of Foucault's parallel interest in the construction of the "power-knowledge spiral" (Foucault 1977, chap. 3). Until recently, relatively little has been written about the accumulation of criminological knowledge over the course of the nineteenth century, about the birth of criminology as a distinct academic discipline around the turn of the century, or about its effect on changing penal policy. In England the vast, pioneering work of Sir Leon Radzinowicz (Radzinowicz 1948, 1956a, 1956b, 1966, 1968), was the only notable attempt to understand changes in conceptions of crime or in the apparatus of punishment. Only in the past few years have criminologists as a group been admonished that "its [their discipline's] history and development have escaped the close and critical scrutiny usually afforded to powerful forms of social knowledge" (Garland 1985a, pp. 109–10). Attempts to redress this oversight have been initiated in the main not by historians but by historically minded criminologists anxious to understand the theoretical framework within which the discipline of criminology emerged (Garland 1985a, 1985b, 1988; Radzinowicz and Hood 1986). Garland described his own work as an "account of the theoretical formation of the criminological program, its internal characteristics and its relationship to its social conditions of emergence" (Garland 1985a, p. 110). In tracing the emergence of criminology in Britain in the latter years of the nineteenth century, he has mapped out the relationship between the formation of criminological understanding and the development of penal ideologies and institutions that it supported. He recognized that the most important of criminology's precursors was the "ecclesiastical law of penance," which focused attention not on the offense but on the sinfulness of the offender. The birth of positivist criminology rested on a fundamental shift of focus so that "the basis of crime no longer lay in sin or in faulty reasoning but in an aberration or abnormality of the individual's constitution" (Garland 1985a, p. 111).

This essay takes up Garland's notion of a general shift in criminological understanding from the "moral" to the "medical." It suggests that, in relation to female offenders, this shift was rather less marked than has been thought. For, in relation to female criminality at least, the questions, methods, and, indeed, findings of the new medical and psychiatric approaches to crime remained bound by the traditional moral framework. I argue later that these new interpretations achieved their greatest currency in relation to female criminality for the very reason that they appeared to provide "scientific" confirmation of existing assumptions about "normal" and "deviant" women. As a result, medicine, particularly psychiatry, has continued to inform responses to female criminality through the twentieth century.

As yet there has been very little interest among historical criminologists in the question of gender (Zedner 1988). Probably the main reason is the feeling, common to members of many academic disciplines, that women are marginal to the big, important questions. Criminal men were, indeed, the primary target of the development of formal policing and the proliferation of prisons—and the histories have reflected this. Yet little attention has been paid to the question of how far gender informed these developments; the degree to which notions of appropriate male behavior colored definitions of male criminality; how far emerging explanations of crime were differentiated according to the sex of the offender; the extent to which penal institutions were identifiably masculine in their culture and orientation. In sum, the history of criminality and its control has been documented with remarkably little regard to the issue of gender (with a few important exceptions: for example, O'Brien 1978, 1982; Freedman 1981; Rafter 1983*a*, 1983*b*, 1985*a*, 1985*b;* Hartman 1985).

Differential perceptions of men's and women's characters, roles, and statuses were far more important in nineteenth-century society than they are today. This essay examines the ways in which gender, particularly as constructed in notions of masculinity and femininity, informed early criminological theories. It suggests that female offenders were perceived and treated very differently from men. In Britain the lack of interest in the history of female criminality is doubly surprising given that women made up a far larger proportion of those coming before the courts and going into prison than they do today. While women comprise only 3 percent of the daily average prison population in England and Wales today, a hundred years ago they made up over 17 percent.

Whether as prison doctors, chaplains, governors, or matrons, many of those who dealt with criminals took an intense interest in the criminality of their wards. As they studied and published their findings, they came to be respected as informed commentators, and some were even recognized as experts on crime. Many of these observers and investigators were deeply interested in female criminality and espe-

Women, Crime, and Penal Responses 313

cially in the inmates of women's prisons; as Dobash, Dobash, and Gutteridge (1986, p. 101) have recognized, "Some developed elaborate theories about the nature of criminal women, and the ideas of a few gained considerable prominence." The leading commentators on crime were commonly concerned about female criminality, writing articles, substantial sections in larger works, and occasionally entire monographs on the subject (for example, Carpenter 1858, 1864*a*, 1864*b*; Crofton 1867, 1873; Morrison 1891; Adam 1914; Thomson 1925; Mayhew 1968). To give just an indication of the scope of other writings that had something to say about female criminality, the authors may usefully be divided up into groups. Many works were written by prison chaplains (Field 1846; Kingsmill 1854; Clay 1861; Horsley 1887, 1898, 1913; Merrick 1891). Men and women who worked with prisoners, for example, as prison directors, police court missionaries, or aftercare specialists also wrote about their experiences (Griffiths 1884, 1894, 1904; Davenport-Hill 1885; Holmes 1900, 1908; Bedford 1910; Gordon 1922). Learned societies such as the Social Science Association attracted a variety of contributors and published reports of their proceedings (Frazer 1863; Jellicoe 1863; Safford 1867; Nugent 1877; Wells 1877; Wilson 1878). More specifically, philanthropic ladies who visited women inmates produced books and pamphlets, often as a means of raising funds for their work (Wrench 1852; Hill 1864; Meredith 1881; Scougal 1889; Steer 1893; Orme 1898; Higgs 1906; see also the fictitious works by "A Prison Matron" 1862, 1864, 1866). Unfortunately, very few women wrote about their own experiences as prisoners; two who did were Americans: Mrs. Maybrick (1905), a Southern belle suspected of poisoning her husband, and Susan Willis Fletcher (1884), an upper-class American lady spiritualist accused of theft by deception. In addition, many lesser figures, including a great many anonymous writers, contributed to the journals and periodicals of the day. Such writers merit closer attention than they have so far received, for they are important to understanding responses to female crime both historically and today.

In large part, the questions posed here arise out of, and build on, a wealth of research by social historians and historical criminologists. However, the agenda of this essay owes a second intellectual debt. In the past decade or so, feminist criminologists in America, and more recently in Europe, have sought to pinpoint and to explain differences in female crime and responses to it. Given the huge growth of such writings, any list of writers is bound to be incomplete (to cite just a selection: Giallombardo 1966; Brodsky 1975; Smart 1976, 1977; Vicinus 1977, 1980; Bowker 1978; Crites 1978; Klein 1978; Smart and Smart 1978; Hutter and Williams 1981; Morris and Gelsthorpe 1981; Leonard 1982; Rafter and Stanko 1982; Heidensohn 1985; Morris 1987; Gelsthorpe and Morris 1988). Feminists have criticized existing criminology for its failure to address female criminality, emphasizing the inadequacy of any account that does not encompass gender. As Gelsthorpe and Morris (1988, p. 233) have insisted, "Theories are weak if they do not apply to half of the potential criminal population . . . whether or not a particular theory helps us to understand women's crime better is of fundamental, not marginal, importance for criminology."

In Britain, Carole Smart's *Women, Crime and Criminology* (1976) is generally regarded as the starting point of feminist criminological studies, setting an agenda that has been explored and expanded by subsequent writers (see Gelsthorpe and Morris [1988] for a critical overview of the development of feminist criminology in Britain since Smart). It is not without significance that Smart began her work with an entire chapter devoted to historical studies of female criminality in an attempt to uncover the roots of current attitudes toward female crime. She was immediately criticized by one leading British sociologist who condemned the inclusion of such a lengthy historical section as "the true work of exhumation. It resembles the activities of the resurrection men, the disinterring of the buried for the purposes of clinical analysis" (Rock 1977, p. 394). And yet, as many subsequent feminist criminologists have concurred, it is only by looking at the past that we can begin to understand the genesis of modern views of criminal women. The primary interest of feminist criminologists has been, therefore, less in history per se than in the extent to which the legacy of historical understanding continues to exert an influence over contemporary thinking. Unfortunately, this interest has not yet encouraged empirical historical research but has led, rather, to a general reliance on received historical wisdom.

Carole Smart set the birth of the criminology of women in 1893 with the publication in Italy of Lombroso and Ferrero's *La Donna Delinquenta*—a massive study of the biological characteristics of criminal women. It quickly appeared in an English version in 1895 as *The Female Offender* and, as I show later on, had an influence on explanations of female crime that endured long after Lombrosian positivism had been discredited in mainstream criminology (i.e., that relating to men).

Women, Crime, and Penal Responses 315

Smart saw *The Female Offender* as a "pioneer" study and thus established a presumption among subsequent feminist criminologists that there had been no interest in the criminality of women before Lombroso (Klein 1978; Pollock and Chesney-Lind 1978). Following Smart, the British sociologist Frances Heidensohn has argued that criminologists concentrate on Lombroso and Ferrero because they "actually wrote about women . . . when their contemporaries were silent" (Heidensohn 1985, pp. 111–12). Similarly, the American writer Eileen B. Leonard (1982) suggests that Lombroso marked the beginning of "scientific" criminology. As the purposes of these works were not primarily historical but looked to the past only insofar as it informed present thinking, it is, no doubt, inappropriate to criticize their historical research. However, in this essay I seek to put forward a rather more historically grounded view based on extensive research into earlier writings on female crime to show that interest in female offenders long predated Lombroso (Zedner 1988). His studies were only part of a longer shift from early moralistic understandings of crime to the rise of secular, scientific, and increasingly exculpatory interpretations and responses to female criminality.

The lack of research into explanations of female crime prior to 1895 has led to a common overstatement of Lombroso's influence on criminological thinking at that time. The very reason why many, especially outside continental Europe, were skeptical of his ideas was because they had already developed sophisticated theories of their own. Perhaps, more important, the lack of research masks the reasons why biological positivism has endured. Dorie Klein (1978, p. 8) is right to note that "the road from Lombroso to the present is surprisingly straight." What is needed now is some explanation of why biological and psychological explanations of female criminality were so readily accepted at the time and why they persist long after constitutional explanations of criminality have lost currency in relation to male crime. Put simply, why has the view endured that the female offender is likely to be sick or inadequate?

Building on this feminist criminological scholarship and extending my account of the historical development of women and crime back beyond Lombroso, I hope to trace the roots of these views of the female offender. I suggest that their enduring influence is not simply attributable to the persuasive powers of Italian positivism but harks back to an older and far wider assumption that all women are morally weak because they are biologically and psychologically inferior to men.

316   Lucia Zedner

II. The Extent and Nature of Female Crime in the
Eighteenth and Nineteenth Centuries

Before the development of criminological knowledge concerning
women can be assessed, it is essential to establish some picture of
women's crime itself. Official criminal statistics can scarcely be said to
provide an accurate picture of "real" crime, so great is the unreported
and unrecorded "dark figure." Even if official figures are used only as a
benchmark rather than as an accurate representation, it is important to
note that changing attitudes, the development of formal policing, and
changes in court administration and sentencing policy can all have a
major effect on the figures recorded. The fact that the statistics give a
better indication of perceptions and responses to crime than of criminal
activity itself may be less of a problem, however, if the primary interest
is in changes in crime control. Bearing these caveats in mind, what
follows is an attempt to draw in broad brush strokes a picture of known
female crimes in England during the eighteenth and nineteenth centuries.

In eighteenth-century England, mobility was highly restricted for
most women: they were confined for much of their time to the home
and to the duties of child care; they spent little time in the public sphere
and had relatively few opportunities to meet with other women. By
comparison, men spent far more time in public, frequented pubs or
bars, and congregated on the streets where they could both devise and
commit crimes. Women living in rural communities were likely to be
particularly limited in their movement and closely observed in public.
Their apparent lack of criminal propensity may well have been due
largely to a simple lack of opportunity. Urban life, conversely, not only
provided fewer effective checks, less security, and more irregular work
but also obvious temptations such as gambling, drinking, and opportunities for prostitution. The Canadian historian J. M. Beattie (1975) has
investigated the amount and type of crime of which women were convicted in eighteenth-century England. By statistical analysis of the extent to which women accounted for recorded crime, he provides an
important benchmark against which to set historical beliefs and, most
important, to measure the gap between widely held assumptions about
female criminality and actual levels of recorded crime committed by
women. Beattie has found that not only was the crime rate for women
living in urban areas far higher than for those remaining in rural Britain, but that city women tended to commit more serious property
offenses than their rural counterparts. While the relative passivity of

country women may be partly explained by reference to the greater strictures and closer surveillance over their lives, it may also be that rural rebels simply migrated to the city.

Broadly speaking, Beattie found that men outnumbered women in nearly all types of criminal convictions but that women were engaged in roughly the same range of crimes as men and followed similar patterns of offending behavior within this range. Beattie did find qualitative differences between the types of crime for which men and women were convicted: for example (perhaps not surprisingly), he found that women who committed assault were generally less violent than men. More significantly, he confounded many common assumptions about the different nature of female crime. He suggested that women did not, as it was assumed, rely on the supposedly feminine attributes of stealth and deception any more than men did; nor did female murderers necessarily favor poisoning as they were believed to do (Beattie 1975, p. 83). Indeed, Beattie concluded that differences between female and male criminality were determined as much by social situation as by gender.

Surveying the extent and nature of crime over the nineteenth century indicates the relatively high rates of participation by women compared with today. The following figures are taken from the official figures or "Judicial Statistics" published annually in Britain (Judicial Statistics 1857–92). For much of the nineteenth century, women made up nearly a fifth of summary convictions and over a quarter of those committed for trial on indictment (a remarkably high proportion as compared to today). As in the eighteenth century, patterns of crime by men and women were broadly similar to one another with the exception of a number of sex-specific offenses, most notably relating to prostitution.

The largest single category of summary convictions for both sexes was for drunkenness. Perhaps surprisingly, drunkenness accounted for an even larger proportion of female convictions than it did of male convictions. It may well be, however, that a drunken woman attracted more opprobrium and was more likely to find herself arrested than was a man found drunk in public. The second largest category of summary offense for which both men and women were convicted was common assault. Surprisingly, this again made up a larger proportion of female than male crime. Anecdotal evidence suggests that assaults committed by women were often drink related, for example, brawls between women outside pubs or assaults by prostitutes resisting arrest, against drunken clients, or seeking to defend their pitch from rival trade (Jones 1982, p. 105). Of course, this is not to suggest that women were necessarily more violent than men. Fights between men may have been ignored by the police as inoffensive "manly" behavior (unless they seriously threatened public order or the lives of those involved), whereas women fighting in the street would quickly attract police attention. Both sexes were convicted of proportionately fewer assaults over the second half of the nineteenth century, perhaps reflecting the increasing stability of late Victorian society.

For women, the next most common summary offense was prostitution. It is interesting that the proportion of female convictions made up by prostitution was not as high as Victorian literary sources would lead us to believe. As a percentage of female summary convictions, prostitution fell from 13 percent in 1857 to barely 7 percent by 1890. It may well be, however, that many of those convicted of drunkenness, disorderly behavior, or theft were, in fact, prostitutes arrested in the course of their business.

Besides these main categories of summary convictions, a mass of petty offenses such as vagrancy, begging, breach of the peace, and offenses against local acts and bylaws brought both men and women before the courts. Convictions for such offenses were common among the poor living both in rural areas and, increasingly, on the streets of the growing towns and cities. One offense for which convictions of women consistently outnumbered those of men was "offenses against the Pawnbroker's Act by persons unlawfully pledging and disposing." Women working in the sweated trades sometimes pawned the raw materials given them by their employers in order to buy food and then found themselves unable to redeem the goods in time to return them as finished garments or goods. The preponderance of women convicted of this offense tells us much both of the role of women in managing and attempting to eke out an inadequate household budget and also of the place of petty crime in the economy of the urban female poor. Beattie's (1975) conclusion that female crime in the eighteenth century was primarily determined by their socioeconomic situation would seem, therefore, to hold good also for the nineteenth century. Women's offenses, like those of men, were determined largely by the habitat, opportunities, and difficulties of life especially in the growing urban slums inhabited by the very poorest sections of the population.

More serious offenses were tried on indictment. Unfortunately, we do not have statistics for convictions broken down by sex and are forced to rely, therefore, on figures for committal to trial. Women formed a large, though declining, proportion of those proceeded against by indictment—falling from 27 percent in 1857 to only 19 percent by the final decade of the century. By far the largest category of trials on indictment was for larceny. For much of the second half of the nineteenth century women made up nearly a quarter of those tried for "simple larceny," well over a third of those tried for "larceny against the person," and nearly a third of those tried for larceny "by servants."

The next largest category for which both men and women were tried on indictment was "offenses against the person." These made up an increasing proportion of trials on indictment of both sexes—8 percent of female and 13 percent of male at midcentury, rising to 13 and 20 percent, respectively, by the end of the century.

It is perhaps significant that for much of the nineteenth century women made up a striking 40 percent of all those tried for murder. Since murder is probably the least likely of all offenses to go undetected, this figure raises interesting questions about the amount of other serious female crime which was perhaps not so readily detected and counted in the crime statistics. In the last decades of the nineteenth century, statistics for murder were grouped by the age of the victim with the result that women fell to less than a quarter of those offenders tried for the murder of victims over one year but made up nearly all of those tried for the murder of infants. Infant murder was distinguished from "concealing the birth of infants," under which many cases of suspected infanticide were tried (Hoffer and Hull 1981). Given the difficulty of establishing whether the baby was born dead, died during delivery, or was deliberately killed, women were often found guilty only of failing to prepare responsibly for the impending birth of their child—obviously a much lesser charge than the capital offense of child murder. Not surprisingly, nearly all those tried for this crime of "concealment" were women.

Women made up much smaller proportions of other categories such as offenses against property with violence, or forgery, or offenses against the currency. The only other offense for which commitments of women consistently outnumbered men was that of "keeping disorderly houses" or brothels, for which women were between 54 and 70 percent of all those tried.

In the main, then, women were tried on indictment for financially motivated crimes. These were often planned, organized, and entailed some degree of skill. Such findings tend to belie the widely held notion of female criminals as sexually motivated or driven by impulse to commit irrational, behavioral offenses.

320   Lucia Zedner

III. Moral Approaches to Female Crime in the
Nineteenth Century

It is important to bear the preceding figures in mind as the writings and responses of nineteenth-century social scientists and early criminological observers are examined. For it quickly becomes apparent that, while all writings about crime can only be understood within the more general framework of Victorian morality, responses to female crime were deeply embedded in an even more complex value structure, at the heart of which was the highly artificial construct of ideal womanhood. Men who committed many of the less serious forms of crime could be seen as displaying attributes not too far removed from Victorian notions of masculinity: entrepreneurial drive, initiative, courage, physical vigor, and agility were all thought to be appropriate male traits. Although male criminals undoubtedly broke the law, they did not necessarily deviate from accepted notions of "manliness." By contrast, the literature surveyed in this section suggests that criminal women were seen to repudiate revered qualities of femininity. In doing so, they offended not only against the law, but against their ascribed social and moral roles.

The Victorian construction of femininity has generated an entire historiography of its own (Klein 1946; Houghton 1957; Cominos 1963; Basch 1974; Christ 1977; Delamount and Duffin 1978; Banks 1981; Gorham 1982; Davidoff 1983; Showalter 1987). This literature has explored the extent to which, well into the nineteenth century, Victorian social thought was heavily influenced by the legacy of the medieval view of woman as virginal, pure, asexual, and an uplifting influence. Yet, at the same time, women were also seen as Eve-like, both corrupt and corrupting. This duality largely explains the many apparent contradictions in nineteenth-century views of women. Women were lauded as honest, restrained, sober, innocent, and yet they were also feared to be deceitful, designing, avaricious, and dangerously susceptible to corruption. This gap between the feminine ideal and the feared potential for female immorality could only be breached by enforcing an elaborate code of prescribed feminine behavior which might suppress the "darker self" beneath.

The female criminal, the prostitute, and the female drunk were held up as the very negation of the feminine ideal, a warning to other women to conform (Gorham 1982; Walkowitz 1982). And the seriousness of female crimes was measured primarily in terms of women's failure to live up to the requirements of the feminine ideal. Note, for example,

Women, Crime, and Penal Responses 321

the description of criminal women by Henry Mayhew (1862, p. 464), a famous English journalist and social investigator: "in them one sees the most hideous picture of all human weakness and depravity—a picture the more striking because exhibiting the coarsest and rudest moral features in connection with a being whom we are apt to regard as the most graceful and gentle form of humanity." For the most part, criminal women were viewed not so much as economically damaging, physically dangerous, or destructive of property but as a moral menace. Mary Carpenter (1864*b*, 1:31–32), an influential philanthropist and penal reformer generally sympathetic to the plight of women in prison, nonetheless argued: "the very susceptibility and tenderness of woman's nature render her more completely diseased in her whole nature when this is perverted to evil; and when a woman has thrown aside the virtuous restraints of society and is enlisted on the side of evil, she is far more dangerous to society than the other sex." Descriptions of crime frequently referred to the female offender's past sexual conduct, marital status, abilities as a wife and mother, lack of regret, or apparent "shamelessness." In sum, discussion of crime by women went far beyond the offense committed to build up a damning portrait of the character of the offender.

The following contribution by one writer in the popular *Cornhill Magazine* perhaps gives a flavor of a common view of the character of criminal women. "The man's nature may be said to be hardened, the woman's destroyed. Women of this stamp are generally so bold and unblushing in crime, so indifferent to right and wrong, so lost to all sense of shame, so destitute of the instincts of womanhood, that they may be more justly compared to wild beasts than to women" (Owen 1866, p. 153).

It can be seen from quotes such as these that, although male criminals were also seen as sinners, women who offended provoked a quite different response—not least an extraordinary sense of moral outrage. The moralizing approach to crime that predominated in the early nineteenth century clearly distinguished, therefore, according to sex. While the male offender was merely immoral, his female counterpart was likely to be seen as utterly depraved irrespective of any actual, objective difference between them.

Just how far such attitudes affected judgments made about women actually on trial, to what extent courts demanded information about female defendants' moral credentials, and how far they passed sentence on the basis of this strictly irrelevant information remains unknown.

How far differential views of male and female offenders affected penal policy regarding women and were translated into institutional practice has been largely overlooked by historians. Most prison histories have ignored the extent to which treatment of offenders was differentiated by sex, and one British study has gone so far as to assert, "Prison was a man's world; made by men, for men. Women in prison were seen as somehow anomalous: not foreseen and therefore not legislated for. They were provided with separate quarters and female staff for reasons of modesty and good order—but not otherwise dealt with all that differently" (Priestley 1985, p. 69). In fact, women prisoners were seen as quite different creatures from men, requiring special treatment appropriate to their sex. The result was that, at both local and national levels, penal policymakers recognized the need to modify regimes for women.

Given that, throughout the early Victorian era, perceptions and explanations of crime were highly moralistic, it is perhaps not surprising that penal policy focused on the central aim of reform. Policymakers in Britain were divided between those who advocated the "silent system" of prisons (in which prisoners were allowed to work communally but not to talk to one another) and those who advocated the "separate system" (in which prisoners were isolated in individual cells and their solitary confinement was to be broken only by visits from the chaplain). These systems gained prominence in England only after the visit of two highly eminent prison inspectors, William Crawford and Whitworth Russell, to America to investigate the rivalry between the silent associated system, evolved at Auburn Penitentiary, New York, and the separate system, which was rather harshly enforced at the Western Penitentiary, Philadelphia. Both regimes isolated inmates from wider society and prevented communication between prisoners with the ultimate aim of securing their moral reform (Forsythe 1987). While strenuous efforts were made to limit contact among all prisoners, the benefits of isolation were held to be even greater in the case of women. As Whitworth Russell insisted, "With Women . . . I would have Silence and Separation strictly observed, for Women contaminate one another even more than Men do" (Russell 1835).

The silent system was widely criticized by those in Britain who felt that it would be impossible to enforce silence on prisoners without continual recourse to punishment. Since women were considered to have lesser powers of self-discipline, imposing silent association on them was seen to be both more difficult and possibly more damaging to their more delicate nervous health. The separate system was much more popular with British policymakers and prison administrators (Henriques 1972). It fitted well with the prevailing view of criminals as sinners incapable of self-control and was seen as a more likely means of achieving spiritual and moral reform (Forsythe 1987). In Britain, although prisoners were isolated in separate cells, they were to be visited regularly by the chaplain, the scripture reader, and warders (Field 1846; Kingsmill 1854; Clay 1861; Mayhew 1862). In this respect, the rigors of separation were mitigated rather more than in the American model.

Many argued that the central aim of securing moral reform by isolating prisoners from one another was even more important in the case of women than of men. For women were believed to be more impressionable than men and, therefore, at the same time, both more easily corrupted and more susceptible to reformatory influences. One county prison chaplain applauded the benefits of separation arguing that women who "under the old system, must have gone out corrupted and ruined by association with the most depraved and basest of their sex, have under that now in operation been discharged from prison impressed with better principles, and possessed of a real desire to retrieve their characters and to become useful members of society" (Chaplain of Stafford County Gaol 1854, p. 42).

In Britain, the mass of offenders were sentenced to short periods of a few weeks or months in one of over a hundred small local prisons scattered across the country. Until 1877, these prisons were under local government, often poorly organized, and commonly overcrowded (Delacy 1986). Women composed just over a fifth of the local prison population but, with the exception of two or three special institutions, were housed in wards or wings within male prisons. Removing women to separate accommodation was all too often regarded as impractical on grounds of expense, so women were fitted in wherever practical, often in conditions far worse than those suffered by men convicted of like offenses. Provision was generally maintained at a minimum so even a small rise in the number of commitments could overburden existing accommodation intolerably. In many local prisons, separation was not even attempted—for example, in 1857, prison inspectors at Carmartheon Jail found fourteen women and two children sharing only five beds in filthy conditions. In the face of such inadequate resources, prison administrators put great emphasis on the role of female prison staff in creating a regime suitable for women. "Successful treatment of female criminals . . . largely depends on the tone and disposition of female prison officers. Harshness and impatience . . . are only calculated to aggravate violence and insubordination. Despair and hopelessness fill the minds of the most criminal women: the antidote to which is the feeling of hope" (Bremner 1874, p. 282).

While petty offenders were sentenced to local prisons, more serious ones were transported to the colonies as "convicts." The increasing reluctance of the colonies to take British convicts in the first half of the nineteenth century generated a period of intense innovation in penal theorizing as policymakers struggled to come up with an alternative form of punishment. The ending of "transportation" in the 1850s thus led to the establishment of a second tier of national or "convict" prisons (many of which are still standing and in use today). These held prisoners for long terms of "penal servitude" set originally at a minimum of five years, though this was later reduced to three. The need to hold prisoners for such long periods meant that regimes, purposes, and priorities of convict prisons were necessarily very different from those in local prisons.

Although the development of penal policy for convicts was primarily male oriented, it was widely accepted that women must be treated differently from men. As the prison inspector Whitworth Russell (1835, p. 124) insisted, women required "a very different System of Penal Discipline . . . I hardly see anything in common between the Case of a Male and a Female Convict." There were, of course, leading and highly influential women in the field of penal reform, such as Elizabeth Fry (1827a, 1827b), Susanna Meredith (Lloyd 1903), and Mary Carpenter (1864a, 1864b, 1872). Yet even they were less than confident about how the prison regime could best be adapted for women, as Carpenter (1864b, 1:31) herself admitted, "It is well known to all persons who have the care of criminals, whether old or young, that the treatment of females is far more perplexing than that of males. It demands, indeed, peculiar consideration and comprehension of the special difficulties to be grappled with."

Women convicts were held initially at three prisons, all in London, at Millbank, Brixton, and Fulham (though other convict prisons were set up over the century at Parkhurst, Woking, Aylesbury, and Holloway). The difficulties of holding women for long periods of penal servitude were seen to be even greater than for men. Not only was it feared that women would "not have the same physical and mental powers which enable them to bear up against the depressing influence of prolonged imprisonment" (Jebb 1855), but for practical reasons "females must of necessity be employed chiefly indoors, and will have neither the varied work, nor the complete change afforded to Male Convicts by removal to the public works" (Jebb 1855). That is, whereas male convicts passed their days outside the prison at hard manual labor on "public works," female convicts were to be held permanently, and monotonously, within the prison itself. As a result, whereas male-convict prisons were primarily concerned with inculcating work discipline, the predominant goal of the female prison was to achieve some degree of "moral regeneration." The emphasis on moral reform in female prisons sprang partly from the belief that female offenders were generally more depraved than male prisoners and had, therefore, greater moral ground to recover. Paradoxically, the very fact that they were considered to be more impressionable also gave greater hope for reform. More pragmatically, it was recognized that, while men could generally get some sort of rough work after release, most respectable work for women, particularly if it were in domestic service, required testimonies as to their character and conduct. The creator and head of the English convict prison system, Major Joshua Jebb (1854, p. 64), recognized that "the difficulties in the way of a woman of the character of the majority of these prisoners returning to respectability are too notorious to require description. They beset her in every direction the moment she is discharged."

Whereas in male-convict prisons regulations were enforced with militaristic precision, the regimented and uniformed convicts marching lockstep to and from their work, in women's prisons, inmates were subject to a more individualized, manipulative regime. The superintendent of Brixton Prison described the discipline in her prison accordingly: "although it is in strict accordance with the rules laid down, yet it varies in some degree according to the disposition and habits of the prisoner. Indeed, without this individual treatment the attempt to reform them would be most superficial" (Surveyor-General 1857–58, p. 50). Though the emphasis was on "treatment" rather than discipline, it would be wrong to assume this necessarily created a more lenient regime. Male prisoners were expected only to work hard and refrain from breaking prison rules; every aspect of women prisoners' appearance, manner, and conduct was required to conform to highly artificial constructions that made up the ideal femininity. As a result, a much higher level of surveillance prevailed in women's prisons, raising tensions, inviting rebellion, and so increasing the punishment rate (Carpenter

1864*b*, 2:426). It might well be instructive to compare this situation with that in modern prisons where the current rate of punishment of women prisoners for rule infractions is proportionately more than twice that of men (Morris 1987, p. 122).

Over the second half of the nineteenth century, faith in the efficacy of moral reform was badly shaken. "Habitual offenders," who defied all reformatory efforts and returned to the prison time and again, forced even the most ardent supporters of reform to admit that this group, at least, was irredeemable. The atmosphere of moral regeneration and religious awakening that had prevailed under the leadership of Joshua Jebb now disappeared under the regime of Sir Edmund Du Cane (director from 1865 to 1898; see Du Cane 1876, 1885), to be replaced by an emphasis on discipline and deterrence. Prisons had become dumping grounds for the socially inadequate, and prison officials were disturbed to find that there was a sizable core of criminal women who appeared almost immune to the pains of imprisonment. Although women formed less than a fifth of all prisoners, they actually outnumbered men in the class of those who had ten or more previous convictions—the so-called hardened habituals. Du Cane (1885) argued that the repeated reappearance of the same core of offenders signified a measure of success in that it indicated that new "recruits" were being deterred from entering the prison system. Indeed, over the second half of the nineteenth century, the number of women committed to penal servitude steadily declined from an annual high of 1,050 in 1860 to a mere ninety-five in 1890 ("Women Convicts" 1887, p. 473; Johnston 1901). The obvious success of deterrence was, however, at the expense of any attempt to reform those who did end up in prison. For the later years of the nineteenth century saw a marked decline in the confidence of those who had once propounded moral reform, particularly in relation to women. For example, in its annual report for 1880, the leading reform agency, the Howard Association, admitted that "it is well known that the least hopeful subjects of moral influence are habitual criminals, and most of all, criminal and debased *women*" (Howard Association 1880, p. 11).

The apparent inability of the prison to reform clearly caused even greater anxiety in the case of female prisoners than of male. This was mainly because women were supposed to act as a potential moralizing force in society. Among the urban poor, especially, women were seen as a means to police those communities least susceptible to more formal controls. In *The Policing of Families* (1979), Jacques Donzelot has traced

Women, Crime, and Penal Responses 327

the genesis in France during the eighteenth and nineteenth centuries of the "social sector." This he defines as the process of identifying social problems and establishing personnel qualified to combat them, of specialist institutions, and of social programs as a means of both preventive and remedial control. In these developments, Donzelot sees the family as the crucial point of intersection between the private and social spheres. The family, with a woman at its heart, was both the focus of state intervention and itself held up as a moralizing agent. Donzelot's thesis can be usefully applied to much of western Europe where the pace of industrialization led to intense pressure on the family to withstand the demoralizing effects of urbanization, to lessen the corrupting effects of overcrowding, and, above all, to police its own members. Women, as wives and mothers, were central figures in this endeavor (Summers 1976; Christ 1977; Roberts 1984). Not surprisingly, if they then repudiated their supposedly moral duty, by failing to act as feminine exemplars of respectability, it caused intense anxiety. Note the following observations, all made during the middle years of the nineteenth century. "Female crime has a much worse effect on the morals of the young, and is therefore of a far more powerfully depraving character than the crimes of men . . . the influence and example of the mother are all powerful: and corruption, if it be there, exists in the source and must taint the stream" (Symons 1849, p. 25). "The conduct of the female sex more deeply affects the well-being of the community. A bad woman inflicts more moral injury on society than a bad man" (Hill 1864, p. 134). "There is domestic purity and moral life in a good home, and individual defilement and moral ruin in a bad one" (Gibb 1875, p. 334). Or, finally, and most dramatically, "Woe to that country in which men are not able to consider women as living lives on the whole more sober, righteous and godly than their own!" (Horsley 1887, p. 62).

It was commonly held that corruption or criminality in mothers was a major source of juvenile delinquency (Carpenter 1858, 1864*b*). Women who led their children into crime were doubly condemned, for they were seen not only to have offended against their maternal instincts but to have repudiated their responsibilities to society in general. Even crime among grown men was traced back to the corrupting influence of a woman—a single prostitute became "the seducer of virtue, not in one, but in hundreds of young men: [she] robs them of their strength, their money, their character" (Kingsmill 1854, p. 64). This biblical notion of the sinful woman leading men astray was pervasive throughout mid-nineteenth-century criminological literature and, perhaps not surprisingly, was even adopted by male criminals anxious to displace blame. One influential prison chaplain interviewed hundreds of male prisoners and recounted the explanations they gave for their crimes: one asserted that "a bad wife was the first cause of all my trouble," another blamed "bad company, particularly female," and another claimed that "one female so persuaded me to adopt her life that, in order to gratify her wishes . . . I was led to steal" (Kingsmill 1854, pp. 285 ff.). The supposed potential for criminal women to lead others into crime thus amplified the costs of female criminality far beyond the offenses committed by women alone. The criminal woman not only disavowed her role as a benign moral influence but, infinitely worse, became a source of "moral contagion."

The moralizing role ascribed to women was instrumental not only in responding to female criminality but also in designating what types of crime were regarded as most serious when committed by women. As the historian David Jones (1982, p. 129) has noted, mid-nineteenth-century Britain witnessed a rising obsession with "crimes of morality": sexual offenses, prostitution, drunkenness, vagrancy, and illegal gambling. To the middle classes, the urban poor seemed to be turning their backs on precepts of respectability, self-restraint, and sobriety (Symons 1849; Mayhew 1861–62; Greenwood 1981). A growing body of wealthy philanthropists decided to sponsor statistical research into the problems of Victorian society with a view to seeking their solution. "Ameliorism," as this movement was known, viewed most social problems as being caused by the combination of two main factors: the strains of difficult social environments and the moral weakness of the individual. The conjunction of social circumstance and individual failure was held up as the cause of all the major social problems of the day (for more detailed discussion of Ameliorism as a movement, see Abrams 1968, pp. 33–52; Radzinowicz and Hood 1986, chap. 3, "The Ameliorative Creed").

While this concern with immorality informed views of crime generally, it became a veritable obsession in defining female criminality. An apparent rise in the proportion of female offenders in the first half of the century was regarded as indicative of the "increasing demoralisation" of the population as a whole (Symons 1849, p. 25). Links were made between female crime and sexual morality, not least because all female sexual activity outside the bounds of marriage was seen as an undesirable and particularly damaging form of deviance. This thinking had the effect, first, of encouraging the Victorians to search for a sexual element in all female crime, even that which had no obvious sexual content and, second, of placing special emphasis on sexual misdemeanors committed by women. The Victorian tendency to compound female sexuality with deviancy in women has attracted a quite distinct historical literature of its own (Cominos 1963; Marcus 1966; Finnegan 1979; Walkowitz 1980; Weeks 1981; Mort 1987).

The prostitute attracted most attention for she epitomized what Peter Cominos (1963, pp. 166–68) has identified as "The Tainted Model." Although prostitution itself was not illegal, it was responded to and policed in much the same way as crime. Throughout much of continental Europe and, to a lesser extent, in Britain (until the repeal of the Contagious Diseases Acts in 1883), prostitutes were subjected to strict regulation. Prostitution was the most commonly recognized and carefully documented area of female deviance, and it is significant in early criminological literature that little distinction was made between female criminality and unchastity. This was partly because observers tended to confound sexual delinquency with crime in women but also because many women who engaged in prostitution supplemented their income by other offenses. For example, in their massive study of London lowlife, the social investigators Henry Mayhew and John Binney declared, "We found it impossible to draw an exact distinction between prostitution and prostitute thieves"; of the lower-class prostitutes, they maintained, "Most of them steal when they can get an opportunity" (Mayhew 1968, 4:355–66). In a subsequent study, Mayhew (1862, p. 462) worked from the assumption that "it will, we believe, be found to be generally true that those countries in which the standard of female propriety is the lowest, or where the number of prostitutes is the greatest, there the criminality of the women is the greatest."

Opportunities for crime were seen to arise in the course of the prostitute's daily activities: petty theft from the person or burglary of their homes, assault or even murder of difficult clients, or the fencing of articles stolen by less honest ones. Prostitution as a motivational cause of crime was explained with unwitting reference to the moral code enforced against women. Since women were believed to need social approbation for their self-respect, once a woman became a prostitute, she was thought to collapse under the burden of shame. She was said to become reckless in her actions and turn to crime in desperation. Significantly, the overriding concern with the moral costs of prostitution meant that even the prostitute whose original motivation was eco-

330   Lucia Zedner

nomic and who used her trade primarily for the purposes of petty theft, was, nevertheless, seen as a sexual deviant without economic rationale. The legacy of such views in the tendency to sexualize female criminality continues today and has been recognized by modern feminist criminologists (Heidensohn 1985; Morris 1987).

Undoubtedly the most important attempt to question these assumptions about prostitution was William Acton's massive 1857 study *Prostitution, considered in its Moral, Social, and Sanitary Aspects*. Acton's work differed from other contemporary studies of prostitution not merely in its size and scope but in its attempt to move beyond the imagery of the "harlot" as the negation of all that was good in woman. Instead, he saw prostitution "as an inevitable attendant upon civilized, and especially closely-packed, population" (Acton 1972, p. 3). His relative restraint from moralizing allowed for far more systematic investigation than had been achieved before. For example, Acton challenged the common assumption that prostitutes necessarily followed a downward path through destitution, drunkenness, and disease to the hospital or the pauper's grave. He maintained instead that most prostitutes returned eventually to ordinary life, to respectable work, or to marriage.

This interpretation of the role of prostitution in the economy of the female poor has been reexamined by several historians (Finnegan 1979; McHugh 1980; Walkowitz 1980, 1982). Following Acton, Walkowitz (1980, p. 25) has suggested that prostitutes were far from cut off from the society of the urban poor and that prostitution represented a means by which young working-class women could retain their independence during periods of hardship. However, that women chose to turn to prostitution does not necessarily support any romanticization of their lives but may merely attest to their lack of power, to the limited opportunities open to them. Historian Frances Finnegan (1979, p. 215), on the basis of an in-depth study of the lives of prostitutes in one nineteenth-century city, has argued, "The criminality and drunkenness of York's prostitutes reveals conclusively that they were brutalized and degraded by the occupation, that they suffered both physically and mentally and that they were regarded both by society and themselves as social outcasts." The contrast between the two views of nineteenth-century prostitution presented by Walkowitz and Finnegan is not easily resolved. Yet what stands out and unites both studies is the gap between the ideals of Victorian middle class morality and the realities of working-class life.

Alongside prostitution, alcoholism was a major preoccupation of

Victorian moralists. Public houses, spirit shops, and dancing saloons, and the drunkenness that accompanied them, were seen as sources of corruption, degradation, and, ultimately, of criminality. Drunkenness originally attracted the attention of social observers primarily as a moral issue. Pubs tempted both men and women out of the home and away from their families. Drink was thought to lessen self-control, to encourage promiscuity, and to lead women into prostitution. Many prostitutes claimed to have been seduced first when drunk, alcohol being used to break down resistance and to excite sexual passion in both men and women. Moreover, drinking halls provided a trading ground for potential clients.

The links made between prostitution and alcoholism are worth observing for they epitomize the moralizing approach to female criminality more generally. For example, Dr. Norman Kerr (1880, p. 9), a leading medical and social reformer, assumed that "by drink, the 'unfortunates' deadened their conscience and stifled stirrings of remorse, thus fortifying themselves to ply their hideous calling." The Reverend G. P. Merrick, Chaplain to Millbank Prison, London, conducted a massive study of 14,100 prostitutes in prison. He ascribed even greater importance to alcoholism in overcoming what he assumed to be women's natural resistance to a "wicked and wretched mode of life," asserting that prostitutes: "loathe it, and their repugnance to it can only be stifled when they are more or less under the influence of intoxicating drinks" (Merrick 1891, p. 29). How far this supposed hatred was genuinely felt, merely professed for the benefit of a pious prison chaplain, or blithely ascribed by observers insensitive to the equal misery of alternative forms of employment is unclear. What is striking is the apparent readiness of observers to see alcohol consumption not as part and parcel of urban working-class life, where supplies of uncontaminated water were scarce and expensive, but as indicative of a more general moral decline.

Alcoholism in women was seen to have particularly serious moral consequences given women's responsibilities for home life and child care (MacLeod 1967). Toward the latter years of the nineteenth century an increasing number of writers concerned themselves with the social and moral consequences of female alcoholism. The prominent campaigner, Dr. Norman Kerr (1880, p. 142), insisted "that the female parent is the more general transmitter of the hereditary alcoholic taint I have little doubt." Female alcoholism was considered to be potentially far more damaging than that in men, for example, if a woman was

drunk during conception, or if she continued to drink during pregnancy. Numerous studies (many of which were published in medical
journals or a specialist periodical, the *British Journal of Inebriety*) were
devoted entirely to investigating the extent and effects of maternal
alcoholism. Debates raged about the effects of alcoholism on fertility
rates and on infant health (Kerr 1880, 1888; Sullivan 1906; Kelynack
1907; Scharlieb 1907). While some suggested that long-term alcoholism
made women sterile, others feared that drunken women were giving
birth to an "ever-increasing multitude of social failures." This literature
was highly moralizing in tone, condemning the inebriate mother for her
irresponsibility or her deliberate defiance of maternal duties. Women
who drank were condemned for failing to clean, feed, clothe, or care for
their infants; for leaving them at home to fend for themselves; and for
spending the household budget on drink (Alford 1877; Kerr 1880, 1888;
Holmes 1903; Westcott 1903; Zanetti 1903; Kelynack 1907). The lack
of sympathy for women who sought to escape the miseries of destitution in drink is all the more marked when one notes the relative lack of
comparable censure of men.

    In these writings the moral implications of women's behavior were
further exacerbated by the costs of their drunkenness for future generations. Yet one must also wonder how far concern ostensibly about the
genetic implications of female alcoholism was fed by the threat to traditional morality such women posed. For example, during the second
half of the nineteenth century, women increasingly went into pubs to
drink (Scharlieb 1907). Their presence there signified a direct violation
of a traditional male bastion and the invasion of an arena which had
previously operated outside and, in many ways, in opposition to the
ideal of domesticity. The extent to which moral fears and genetic concerns fed off each other in the minds of contemporary observers is
illustrated by the following condemnation of the trend toward women
drinking in public: "Women have shown an unforeseen facility for
adopting masculine vices, without the saving grace of masculine self-
respect. When they give way at all they are lost: and the temptation to
which they are thus exposed by the removal of conventional safeguards
is much greater than that which assails men, by reason of the physical
weakness and emotional sensibility peculiar to their sex" (Shadwell
1902, p. 76).

    The combined concerns of medical lobbyists and moral reformers
proved to be a powerful interest group. They were highly influential in
drawing attention to the problem of women alcoholics, to the futility of

Women, Crime, and Penal Responses 333

sending them repeatedly to prison for short terms, and to the need for more appropriate provision. Successive legislation to provide for inebriates in the 1870s and 1880s singularly failed to address the plight of poor, mainly female, inebriates whose repeated reappearance before the courts represented a growing public scandal (one apparently notorious woman, Jane Cakebread, had achieved 278 police court appearances by 1895). A new consensus that compulsory, long-term commitment to publicly funded, specialist institutions was the only hope of reform led to the introduction of a two-tier system of certified and state reformatories under the Inebriates Act of 1898. The act identified two main, though not necessarily discrete, groups: habitual drunkards and those who committed serious offenses while drunk. It was hoped that if placed in a sufficiently propitious environment and subjected to benign moral influences these drunkards could be "cured" of their addiction. Significantly, women were overwhelmingly the subjects of this legislation—by 1904 over 90 percent of those admitted to certified reformatories were women.

Unlike most female prisons, which were generally located in the hearts of the areas from which they recruited their clients, reformatories for alcoholics were built almost exclusively in rural locations (e.g., at Farmfield in Surrey; Aylesbury in Buckinghamshire; Ashford in Middlesex). In their organization, regime, and even in the goals they pursued they were remarkably similar to the reformatories set up to socialize and domesticate wayward women in later nineteenth- and early twentieth-century America (Brenzel 1975; Freedman 1981; Rafter 1983b). Established in rural settings, they were organized around large country houses or groups of cottages designed to maximize the potential for curing and domesticating women in an environment far removed from the potential temptations of modern city life. Both American and British institutions provided "protection" for the women in their care. Their avowed aims were to encourage self-respect and to promote an active interest and competence in feminine pursuits through domestic training. More often, reformatories on both sides of the Atlantic resorted to systems of petty rewards and sanctions in an attempt to rehabilitate their "wayward" charges, effectively infantilizing them in the process.

The form and means adopted by the reformatory endeavor suggested a fulsome rejection of women's increasing invasion of the public sphere, particularly in the growing towns and cities. In establishing reformatories in the countryside where women could be returned to a nostalgic version of rural domestic life, penologists reflected the growing belief that female emancipation necessarily led to increased rates of female crime. Such fears prompted comparative studies of crime rates in different areas that were used to demonstrate that the extent of women's movement into the public sphere correlated directly with the number of crimes they committed (Ellis 1890; Morrison 1891). The emerging "new woman" quickly became a scapegoat, held responsible for the decline of the family, and a forcible argument for resisting further movement of women outside the home. "One thing at least is certain, that crime will never permanently decrease till the material conditions of existence are such that women will not be called upon to fight the battle of life as men are, but will be able to concentrate their influence on the nurture and education of the young" (Morrison 1891, p. 157). Modern-day criminologists will recognize in such dramatic prophesies parallel predictions made with equal force in response to the second wave of the women's movement in the second half of the twentieth century (see, e.g., Adler 1975).

The growing concern about female alcoholism reflects how, in the middle years of the nineteenth century, traditional moralistic explanations of offending behavior were increasingly overlaid with a rising obsession with physiological causes. Views of crime as the product of individual moral choice were gradually replaced by a newer and more disturbing perception of criminals as an almost separate species, distinct from the rest of the population in constitution and appearance. This perception was, in part, the product of large-scale migration to industrial cities that raised fears about the health of the nation's stock and generated theories of hereditary national decline. The historian Gareth Stedman Jones has shown how the Victorian middle classes feared that the vast and ever-increasing urban population would sink further into the so-called residuum or outcast classes with each successive generation (Stedman Jones 1971; Soloway 1982).

The extraordinary growth of writing on crime over the course of the nineteenth century suggests a preoccupation with the failure of prison regimes to deter a substantial core of "habitual offenders." Even in England, where in the second half of the century official returns seemed to suggest that crime was decreasing (Gatrell, Lenman, and Parker 1980; Radzinowicz and Hood 1986, pp. 113–24), social commentators and researchers in the nascent discipline of criminology focused attention on that group of criminals who seemed to be impervious to "civilizing" or reformative influences. Journalists and other social researchers ventured into the slum areas to investigate what were feared to be "criminal areas" of dense, frenetic criminal activity (e.g., Carpenter 1864*b*; Greenwood 1869; Morrison 1891; Mayhew 1968; Mearns 1970). They focused particularly on the costs of overcrowding in unsanitary and demoralizing living conditions that it seemed could only degrade those who suffered them. Women were seen to be especially impressionable and ill-equipped to resist the degradation of their environment. One prison chaplain observed "the indiscriminate herding together of the poor of all sexes and ages in their cramped, comfortless and inconvenient houses has a necessary tendency to sap that instinctive modesty and delicacy of feeling which the Creator intended to be the guardians of virtue, and which are more especially necessary for the defense of the female character" (Rogers 1850, p. 45). As a result, it was feared women were most likely to succumb to promiscuity, to alcoholism, and to crime.

The reformer Mary Carpenter (1864*b*) categorized slum dwellers as falling into two distinct social groups—the "perishing and dangerous classes," that is, those at risk from demoralization and those who had already turned to crime. Women in the latter group caused Carpenter particular concern. "Convict women usually spring from a portion of society quite cut off from intercourse with that in which exists any self-respect, and they are entirely lost to shame or reputation . . . [they] . . . belong to a pariah class, which exists in our state as something fearfully rotten and polluted" (Carpenter 1864*b*, 2:208). This notion of pollution may be seen as arising from an organic view of society as the "Body Politic" (Davidoff 1983)—a body of interdependent parts with the middle-class male as its head, the middle-class female as its heart, and the working classes as its hands. Criminal women, and prostitutes especially, represented various unmentionable and distasteful bodily functions. Consequently two interrelated, if somewhat contradictory, biological images of criminal women arose—one as pathological, rotten, and corrupting; the other as a necessary drain of society's "effluvia" protecting the purity of middle-class wives and daughters at the expense of their own. Whichever view prevailed, the end result was the same—to set criminal and "fallen" women apart as a distinct, debased group within society.

IV. Late Nineteenth-Century Biological Theories of Female Crime

It is clear that, although this period saw traditional moralizing interpretations replaced by newly emergent "scientific" conceptions of human behavior, the very impetus to this new body of research was firmly grounded in Victorian morality. Although the rise of the "scientific" represented an attempt at a higher understanding—a search for the rational, for the clinically testable—such theories were in no sense value free. A growing number of physicians and biologists took an interest in social problems, yet the very way in which they defined these problems and the range of solutions they proposed remained bounded by a value-laden normative framework.

Figures like Auguste Comte and Herbert Spencer were highly influential in arguing that it was possible to derive principles of social organization and action on the basis of biological models (see Conway 1970). They inspired doctors working in the prison service to argue that it was possible to develop laws of criminality parallel to those of natural science. Attention turned to the internal or constitutional attributes believed to make people into criminals. Whatever their true scientific status, new "specialisms" like physiognomy became extremely popular (Sturma 1978). In Britain writers indulged in lengthy discussions about the physiognomy of female offenders, subjecting their facial traits to endless analysis broken only by exclamations of horror. For example, the writer Frederick Robinson observed of one woman, "[A] physiognomist might have guessed much of her character from her countenance—it was so disproportionate and revolting" ("A Prison Matron" 1862, 1:284). It is notable how often supposedly scientific observation of female facial features descended to impassioned comparison with some ideal of feminine beauty—against which many ill-nourished, filthy, or elderly female offenders fared very poorly. While physiognomy was also avidly applied to criminal men, there was no comparable standard of male appearance against which men were judged. This is especially important since facial features were taken to be the outward signs of "moral corruption and weak character."

In these accounts we see the beginnings of what was to become a veritable obsession with the constitutional characteristics of the female offender, the strength of which can only be understood by looking back to earlier Victorian assumptions about female biology. As the historian Roger Smith (1981*b*, p. 143) has pointed out, for the Victorians, "Conceptions of women's social position were integrated with naturalistic descriptions of disease types and deterministic explanatory schemes. It was relatively easy to objectify women as part of physical nature." All women were seen to be closely bound to their biology, and their psyche was thought to be intimately connected with the reproductive cycle, the health or pathology of which directly determined their mental

Women, Crime, and Penal Responses 337

health (see discussions in Skultans 1975, p. 4; Showalter 1987). Pioneering sociologists like Herbert Spencer suggested that the reproductive cycle so taxed women's energies that they had little surplus for other activities (Conway 1970). Even in the normal woman, the round of biological crises—from puberty through menstruation, pregnancy, and labor to menopause was fraught with dangers for her mental health. The influential "alienist" Henry Maudsley catalogued the range of disorders attendant on these biological crises: from the hysterical melancholy of pubescent girls to the recurrent mania liable to be provoked by menstruation (Maudsley 1870). To the extent that a woman could be seen as a prisoner of her biology she could deny her culpability even for serious offenses. Maudsley (1874, p. 163) later affirmed: "cases have occurred in which women, under the influence of derangement of their special bodily functions, have been seized with an impulse, which they have or have not been able to resist, to kill or to set fire to property or to steal."

Deviant behavior could also be explained as the product of a series of mental conditions: delicate nerves, emotional disorder, or mental defect all of which were related back to woman's biology. Havelock Ellis (1904, p. 293), pursuing a strong interest in the nascent discipline of criminal anthropology, argued that women were so much victims of their monthly cycle that "whenever a woman has committed any offense against the law, it is essential that the relation of the act to her monthly cycle should be ascertained as a matter of routine."

A more damaging view was that the criminal woman's constitution was inherently pathological. This suggested a far more dangerous type of criminal woman who lacked the inner resources to overcome the tremendous pull of degeneracy. Seeking to identify the attributes of such a type, scientifically minded observers, such as British prison doctors G. Wilson, J. Bruce Thomson, and David Nicolson, began to investigate and to describe in minute detail the physical characteristics of prison inmates (Prewer 1974; Radzinowicz and Hood 1986, pp. 3–11). Typographies of offenders were developed for both men and women but were all the more extreme and grotesque in the case of women. Havelock Ellis (1890) claimed that women guilty of infanticide were endowed with excessive down on their faces, that female thieves went grey more quickly, were uglier, and exhibited more signs of degeneracy (especially of the sexual organs) than ordinary women. Although Ellis was writing before the publication of *The Female Offender* in 1895, he drew heavily on the research already carried out by Lombroso and Ferrero. He went so far as to proffer an extraordinary explanation of the low levels of female crime based on a crude model of sexual selection. "Masculine, unsexed, ugly, abnormal woman—the woman, that is, most strongly marked with the signs of degeneration, and therefore the tendency to criminality—would be to a large extent passed by in the choice of a mate, and would tend to be eliminated" (Ellis 1890, p. 217).

While Ellis claimed that his conclusions were based on the work of professional criminal anthropologists including Lombroso, it is not difficult to call into question the validity of such findings. The attributes that he supposed were innate are more likely to have been the products of poor environment, meager diet, or inadequate access to light and clean water. Together these would account for the stunted growth, deformities, and sickly physical appearance of the many women who turned to crime not out of "innate depravity" but for the very reason that they were poor. Ellis failed to consider the possibility that poverty and poor environment, rather than innate pathology, had determined the appearance of many criminal women.

It is striking how far the physical characteristics attributed to criminal women, when taken together, represent an uncanny negative to Victorian imagery of feminine beauty and propriety. It is almost as if observers chose to "see" traits in female offenders that represented the antithesis of the feminine ideal. Moreover, the frequency with which the research studies discussed by Ellis noted the "masculine" appearance of criminal women indicates how far the supposedly scientific process of observation was tightly bound by culturally determined expectations of femininity. As Carole Smart perceptively pointed out in 1977: "where gender appropriate behavior is seen as biologically determined, women who adopt 'masculine' forms of behavior become labeled 'masculine' themselves and this has connotations of 'maleness' which are seen to be linked to hormonal or genetic abnormalities" (Smart 1977, p. 93).

Ellis's *The Criminal* (1890), a potboiler of existing criminal anthropology, was hugely popular in Britain. It passed through four editions, the latter two being substantially revised and enlarged. Outside continental Europe, Ellis was one of the few to take up criminal anthropology and was largely responsible for the promotion of Lombrosian positivism in the English-speaking world. Recent feminist commentators have not recognized the extent to which Lombroso was preceded by Ellis's proselytizing endeavors. Yet if it had not been for Ellis's fascination with

Women, Crime, and Penal Responses 339

the subject it seems unlikely that Lombroso and Ferrero's *The Female Offender* would have received much attention beyond the Continent.

In *The Female Offender*, Lombroso elaborated on the established conception of female criminality as biologically determined. He endorsed the view of criminal woman as atavistic. According to him she was even more biologically primitive than criminal man (Lombroso and Ferrero 1895, p. 107). And yet when Lombroso tried to investigate the physical characteristics of women criminals, he found it extremely difficult to confirm his hypothesis (Lombroso and Ferrero 1895, pp. 54 ff.). Instead of abandoning his theory as unfounded, Lombroso invoked the generally held belief, described above, that all women were biologically inferior to men. If all women were, to a degree, atavistic, he argued, it would obviously be more difficult to discern atavism in criminal women because the distinguishing signs would be relatively less marked. Following Lombroso's own logic through, Frances Heidensohn (1985, p. 112) has pointed out that this assertion of women's biological inferiority ought to mean that "a much higher crime rate would be predicted for women than for men." Given that this was evidently not the case, the only explanation of this apparent illogicality is that Lombroso did not differentiate between crime and sexual delinquency in women. Seeing prostitution as the most "natural" outcome of female degeneracy, it could legitimately be included in any assessment of overall levels of female delinquency. This would then push the female level up to match rates of male crime (Heidensohn 1985, p. 114). This interpretation seems to be born out by Lombroso's having "found" the prostitute to be the epitome of primitive woman. He claimed that she was abundantly endowed with atavistic traits masked only by the plumpness of her youth and her elaborate makeup.

Closer investigation of the traits Lombroso claimed to have observed reveals how far his supposedly scientific objectivity was colored by culturally determined conceptions of what constituted normality and deviance in women. Moreover, he evidently found it impossible to confine his explanation to the supposedly inherent or pathological qualities of his subjects and referred constantly to their social background, sexual history, and marital status. The claims of Lombroso's research to impartiality were further marred by his patent desire to seek confirmation in biology of his social judgment of woman, namely that she was in all respects inferior to man, as can be seen in the following quotation: "The normal woman is deficient in moral sense, and possessed of slight criminal tendencies, such as vindictiveness, jealousy, envy, malignity, which are usually neutralized by less sensibility and less intensity of passion. Let a woman, normal in all else, be slightly more excitable than usual, or let a perfectly normal woman be exposed to grave provocations, and these criminal tendencies will take the upper hand" (Lombroso and Ferrero 1895, p. 263). In this and in other descriptions of criminal women as "masculine," even "virile" in appearance, coarse voiced, and unusually strong, his sense of distaste was barely concealed (Lombroso and Ferrero 1895, pp. 93–99).

In this scarcely dispassionate frame of mind, Lombroso conducted his famous anthropometric measurements. He was severely hampered by the difficulty of testing those of criminal women against any "control" or "normal" women—"it not being too easy to find subjects who will submit to the experiment" (Lombroso and Ferrero 1895, p. 56). This was hardly surprising since most women, inculcated with a deep sense of modesty, not unreasonably objected to Lombroso's requests to take his measuring instruments to their necks, thighs, and legs. In the end he was obliged to confine his sample of "normal women" to only fourteen—a tiny number that rather belies the weight often attributed to his lengthy and detailed findings. Undaunted, Lombroso presented his catalog of supposedly anomalous characteristics as certain proof of atavism in the criminal woman. For example, he claimed that, whereas normal women had markedly different skulls than men, the skulls of criminal women "approximate more to males, both criminal and normal, than to normal women" (Lombroso and Ferrero 1895, p. 28) and most closely resembled those of ancient man. Thus, argued Lombroso, criminal woman was proved to be a throwback to an earlier, less civilized, age.

In line with the then current vogue for classification, Lombroso subdivided criminal women into various supposedly distinct groups: the "occasional," the "hysterical," the "lunatic," the perpetrator of "crimes of passion," and the "born female criminal." Only the relatively small class of born female criminals, "whose criminal propensities [were] more intense and more perverse than those of the male prototypes," clearly fitted Lombroso's conception of degeneracy (Lombroso and Ferrero 1895, p. 147). The born female criminal was the very antithesis of femininity, "excessively erotic, weak in maternal feeling, inclined to dissipation, astute and audacious" (Lombroso and Ferrero 1895, p. 187). She was even endowed with masculine characteristics, such as her love of violence and vice and "added to these virile characteristics [were] often the worst qualities of woman: namely, an excessive desire for

Women, Crime, and Penal Responses   341

revenge, cunning, cruelty, love of dress, and untruthfulness" (Lombroso and Ferrero 1895, p. 187). Lombroso condemned the born female criminal as "completely and intensely depraved," as "more terrible than any man."

That his condemnation derived from an ideology which demanded higher qualities of women than of men is only too evident from Lombroso's (Lombroso and Ferrero 1895, p. 152) most damning exclamation: "As a double exception, the criminal woman is consequently a monster." As was true of writings half a century earlier, responses to the female offender were determined by the fact that she was seen not only to have flouted the criminal law but, more heinously still, the norms of femininity. It would seem, then, that Lombroso's writings were in many ways far less novel than subsequent commentators have suggested. While vigorously expounding his anthropometric theories, Lombroso remained squarely within the moral framework of his day.

Of course, Lombroso's wilder theories about criminal women did not have to wait until the emergence of feminist criminology in the late twentieth century to face criticism. Even at the height of his influence in Italy and Germany, Lombroso's brand of criminal anthropology met with considerable skepticism in France and particularly in English-speaking countries. In the United States one of the first people to put Lombroso's findings systematically to the test was the sociologist Frances Kellor (1901). Her work is discussed in detail in the context of emerging American criminology in Estelle Freedman's *Their Sisters' Keepers* (Freedman 1981, pp. 111–15). Kellor replicated Lombroso's work on a much larger scale using as her sample fifty-five white female students and ninety black and sixty white female criminals, applying his anthropometric measures to every aspect of these women's bodies. In addition she introduced psychological tests of faculties, senses, memory, and color and collected detailed sociological data including family background, occupation, religion, education, "amusements," "conjugal conditions," and environment. Unable to confirm Lombroso's findings, she severely criticized the conclusions that he had derived from such tests and refuted his interpretation of female criminality as biologically determined. Kellor (1901, quoted in Freedman 1981, p. 113) criticized Lombroso for ignoring the "tremendous force of social and economic environment" and pointed out that Lombroso's methods would tend to confuse ethnic and national traits with criminal ones. The extent to which Lombroso operated within the prevailing double standard was also recognized by Kellor (1901, quoted in Freedman 1981, p. 115). "We say that a woman is worse, but we judge her so by comparison with the *ideal* of woman, not with a common ideal."

A decade later in England, Hargrave Adam, the author of a major monograph, *Women and Crime* (1914), launched probably the most scathing attack on *The Female Offender*. Lombroso's thesis was, he said, "an utter fallacy" with no foundation in fact and counter to common sense. "What nonsense it all is. As if we do not know that prostitutes are of all sizes and shapes, from the very thin to the very fat. . . . The mystery is how such a fallacy ever came to be taken seriously" (Adam 1914, p. 23).

Lombroso's influence in Britain and America was certainly limited by such criticism. However, in the case of female criminality it proved obstinately enduring. Women's primary role as mothers remained at the heart of concern about female crime and ensured a continuing preoccupation with the physiology of female offenders. This, together with the enduring belief that women were biologically inferior to men, ensured that the constitution of the female offender remained central to criminological explanation long after biological positivism had been derided and discarded in explanations of male crime. The continuing effect of biological positivism lay primarily in its influence on the development of psychological approaches to female criminality.

V. Early Twentieth-Century Views of Female Crime as the Product of Innate Defect

The general rejection of Continental biological positivism was by no means wholesale for it was mitigated in large part by the development of the "eugenics" movement (Searle 1976; Freeden 1979, 1986; Soloway 1982). This movement sought to draw attention to the dangers to society of hereditarily transmitted defects and to promote means of controlling the mental and physical qualities of future generations. "Negative eugenics," as it was called, focused particularly on the need to prevent the criminal, the weak, and the defective from reproducing. These groups were reproducing at a faster rate than the middle classes. If not curtailed they would, it was argued, eventually swamp society with increasing numbers of enfeebled offspring.

The growth of this concern about degeneracy can only be understood with reference to its wider historical context. For example, in Britain, by the close of the nineteenth century, Victorian optimism had been badly shaken by economic crisis and the rise of foreign competition—both commercial and military. Eugenic theories of hereditary

Women, Crime, and Penal Responses 343

degeneration provided ready explanations for the relative decline of Britain's international status. The Edwardians, disillusioned with the preoccupation with biological positivism in continental Europe, focused instead on mental defect as the root of a whole range of pathological conditions. This trend toward psychiatric interpretation grew in large part out of the continuing vogue for "objective" scientific observation of the peculiarities of prison inmates. It was also heavily influenced by studies such as *The English Convict*, a massive work by Charles Goring (1913) in which he studied nearly 4,000 male convicts. Goring resoundingly denied the existence of a physically distinctive criminal type along the lines described by Lombroso. Although the proper interpretation of Goring's findings was a matter of considerable controversy, they did seem to point to a greater incidence of defective intelligence among convicts. Many eugenicists were quick to pick up on Goring's work as a basis for substantiating their claim that mental degeneracy could be observed in a significant proportion of the casual poor, slum dwellers, and the prison population. The origins, and particularly the political implications, of this rising concern with mental degeneracy has attracted considerable historical interest (Stedman Jones 1971; Searle 1976; Nye 1984; Bynum, Porter, and Shepherd 1985; Garland 1985*b*; Freeden 1986; Radzinowicz and Hood 1986; Harris 1989).

Eugenicism inevitably focused on women, for it was feared that the "degenerate women" of the slum-dwelling "dangerous classes" were innately promiscuous and, despite their weak constitutions, highly fertile. If allowed to continue to breed unchecked, the so-called unfit would increasingly outnumber the "fit" (Rentoul 1906; Tredgold 1909). If women were alcoholic, sexually promiscuous, or mentally or otherwise deficient, it was believed that their failings would be multiplied in the next generation. Social observers like Hargrave Adam began to explore the extent to which female alcoholism, prostitution, and crime were products of mental defect. He called for investigation into "the intimate connection which exists between nervous disorders and crime" (Adam 1914, p. 34). Interest in mentality was widespread: analyses of body type and skull dimension were largely replaced by studies of psychological characteristics and the investigation of mental deficiencies in both men and women (in Britain, Tredgold 1908, 1909, and 1910; Meredith 1909; Devon 1912). However, just as physical explanations of criminality had once been found particularly plausible in relation to women, new interest in the weaknesses and abnormalities of the criminal mind gained most credibility as a means of explaining female criminality. For these theories fitted only too well with the long-standing belief that criminal women not merely broke the law but tended to exhibit fundamental flaws of character. Note the observation by Hargrave Adam (1914, pp. 3–4) that some criminal women were "almost entirely devoid of any gentle or redeeming trait; some . . . indeed, are, in baseness, cunning, callousness, cruelty, and persistent criminality far worse than the worst male offender known to law."

The search for hard "scientific" evidence for the causes of crime was strongly influenced by the methods of the psychiatric profession. Increasingly prestigious, it provided criminology with a quasi-medical status. In its early years British criminology borrowed heavily from psychiatry the vocabulary, theories, categories, and strategies of what was then commonly known as the medical speciality of "alienism" (Walker 1968; Walker and McCabe 1973). Criminological interest in psychiatric interpretation was reflected in the growing numbers of medical men within the penal system who entered into debates in "mental science" journals (Guy 1863, 1869; Thomson 1870*a*, 1870*b*; Nicolson 1873). It was largely from this discourse that new diagnoses of offenders as mentally deficient were to be drawn.

The relationship between criminology and psychiatry was by no means one way. By informing and directing the development of criminology, psychiatry sought to expand its influence into the judicial and penal arena. Both David Garland and Roger Smith ask to what extent psychiatric intervention should be seen as empire building by a group of specialist professionals anxious to assert their status (Smith 1981*a*; Garland 1985*b*). Psychiatrists certainly did not see themselves in that way but rather as impartial observers, elevating criminological understanding with their techniques of observation and classification. Rothman (1980, p. 133) suggests that in America intervention by psychiatrists into the penal sphere was quite popular with prison officials. The early twenties saw an influx of psychiatric professionals into American prisons so that, by 1926, sixty-seven institutions employed psychiatrists and forty-five employed psychologists. How to interpret the growth of psychiatric intervention in deviance control remains the subject of much historiographical controversy (Skultans 1975; Mc-Candless 1978; Rothman 1980; Smith 1981*a*, 1981*b*; Garland 1985*a*, 1985*b*). Should one see turn-of-the-century psychiatrists merely as unscrupulous entrepreneurs? As innovative scientists? As guardians of the

Women, Crime, and Penal Responses 345

moral order? Or, as Vieda Skultans (1975) suggests, as agents of social control?

Given prevailing beliefs in the physiological inferiority of women, and given the assumption that women's mental health was more closely tied to their biology than men's, it was perhaps not surprising that psychologically informed views of female deviance became popular (Thomson 1870*a*, 1870*b*; Nicholson 1873). Manifestations of mental disorder or even insanity were not merely unsurprising but almost to be expected in a constitution innately predisposed to upheaval and crisis. Nor was this view of female psychology tied only to her reproductive functions, it found even greater currency in relation to traditional concerns about wayward sexuality. Middle-class norms of propriety set the female sexual appetite at zero and established complete passivity, bordering on indifference, as the healthy sexual state for women. Any deviation from this condition of sexual apathy could be seen, therefore, as indicative of a disordered mind. Almost any expression of sexual desire by a woman could be interpreted as pathological and clinically described as nymphomania. Henry Maudsley (1870, p. 82) characterized nymphomania as "the irritation of the ovaries or uterus . . . a disease by which the most chaste and modest woman is transformed into a raging fury of lust." Premarital sex, infidelity, or even open expressions of sexual desire, might also be seen as symptoms of this dangerous sexual mania and so justify drastic psychiatric or even surgical intervention.

With the ascendancy of "scientific" discourse around the end of the century, outraged vilifications of the sexually active woman were increasingly replaced by apparently clinical discussion of her sexual exploits as symptomatic of cerebral disorder. Yet the technical language of these discussions barely conceals the extent to which conventional morality continued to infuse supposedly scientific thinking and underpin arguments about what constituted "normality" in women.

The extent to which new psychiatric concepts were built onto traditional moral concerns is illustrated by the work of Hargrave Adam (1914) who investigated the "the sex question" (prostitution) in relation to mental defect. Denying the traditional assumption that prostitutes were victims of male lust or perverted by modern life, he argued that the majority were quite simply nymphomaniacs. And this notion of deviant women as driven by sexual mania was carried over to explain more serious female crimes. Poisoners, murderesses, and vitriol throw-ers were, according to Adam (1914, p. 34), primarily sexually motivated. "Sexual mania" was, he suggested, a widespread cause of female deviance. That sexual desire in women thus came to be identified as a disease depended on a moral code that insisted that women were without such impulses.

Psychiatric discourse was employed not only to explain the clearly criminal but also to establish standards of mental normality. It was particularly influential in defining the margins between acceptable behavior and that which, by contravening accepted norms of propriety, could be classed as abnormal (Tredgold 1908, 1909, 1910; Meredith 1909; Melland 1911; Devon 1912). The prevailing belief that women were mentally as well as physically weak ensured that they were more readily and enduringly integrated into the psychiatric model. Categorizations of women as abnormal, mentally weak, "feebleminded," or insane were then as much a product of contemporary values as were earlier explicitly moral and social interpretations.

While eugenicists sought to draw attention to the general problem of mental deficiency among prisoners, their investigations led to the identification of a group who were classified as "feebleminded." These were that portion of the prison and reformatory population who were apparently incapable of submitting to discipline and impervious to all attempts to appeal to their moral sense. Seen cynically, the "discovery" of feeblemindedness provided a means of explaining the failure of prisons and reformatories to reform. It is, indeed, debatable whether feeblemindedness represented some actual, identifiable medical condition, or whether it was merely a label for a section of society. Significantly, it had no precise medical definition but was used as a generic term to encompass all those who were unable to make "correct" moral judgments. The feebleminded were that dangerous subsection of the mentally deficient who were not so impaired as to show external signs of deficiency but who seemed, nonetheless, to be incapable of surviving in normal society. Outside the prison they lived on the margins, often destitute and homeless, relying on charity or petty theft to survive.

That, in Britain, women were the majority of those labeled and confined as feebleminded has so far been largely overlooked (with a few notable exceptions, e.g., Simmons 1978; Radzinowicz and Hood 1986). The predominant concern with feeblemindedness in women raises a number of questions that have yet to be studied in depth by historians or criminologists. Were women prisoners actually more commonly mentally deficient than men or were they simply more likely to be diagnosed as such? What were the social costs of allowing feebleminded women to live outside custody? Why did contemporaries fear such women enough to demand their long-term or even permanent segregation (Meredith 1909)?

It is, perhaps, significant that feeblemindedness in women was defined as much by reference to moral as mental considerations. Assessments of a woman's moral conduct, her apparent degree of self-control, or lack of it, were taken as evidence of her mental state. By far the largest single group of feebleminded women were assumed to have become prostitutes, not because they were thought to be sinful, but because "many of these women, sometimes even mere girls, are possessed of such erotic tendencies that nothing short of lock and key will keep them off the streets" (Rentoul 1903; Tredgold 1910, p. 270). This tendency to confound mental deficiency with sexual immorality in women greatly exacerbated fears about its potential results.

Many articles in early twentieth-century editions of *The Eugenics Review* and the *British Medical Journal* focused on the supposed fertility of feebleminded women. Ostensibly scientific analyses of relative fertility rates were used to substantiate highly dramatic visions of hoards of feebleminded women producing multitudes of defective children (Potts 1905; Tredgold 1910). Moreover, it was asserted that "when illegitimate children are borne by such young women, the chances are enormously in favor of their turning out to be either imbeciles, or degenerates, or criminals" (Royal Commission on the Care and Control of the Feeble-minded 1904–8, p. 120). Significantly, this commentator apparently did not feel it necessary to clarify why he thought that the "illegitimate" offspring of the feebleminded would be more susceptible to their mother's mental condition than those born within marriage. The questionable logic of these views did not prevent their having a significant effect on the ensuing legislation. Under the 1913 Mental Deficiency Act, a woman receiving poor relief (state aid) when pregnant with, or at the time of giving birth to, an illegitimate child could be labeled "feebleminded," even if there was no medical evidence of any mental deficiency. As a result, she could be incarcerated in a mental hospital indefinitely simply because she acted outside the conventions of marriage and had the misfortune to get pregnant without a male provider for her child.

Often feebleminded women charged with neglect or cruelty to their children were subsequently found to be "mentally incapable of taking care of them" (Devon 1912, pp. 56–58). Some women thus charged were, on assessment, judged to be so defective as to be certifiable; far more were simply deemed feebleminded.

There was much concern, even sympathy, for the plight of the women themselves. Their lives were portrayed as often wretched, existing in poverty and filth on the margins of society. They were seen as easy prey, incapable of escaping the attentions of men who sought to exploit their weak will. Much of the evidence given to the Royal Commission on the Care and Control of the Feeble-Minded (1904–8) emphasized the need to extend control over feebleminded women in order to save them from sexual violation. The dangers of attack, of prostitution, of disease and the need, therefore, to protect such women were invoked to justify incarceration (Royal Commission on the Care and Control of the Feeble-Minded 1904–8). In a debate in the House of Commons in 1912, one M.P., Dr. Chapple, argued: "To obtain control early of such a woman is humanitarian, and it is the bounden duty of the State to mitigate the sufferings of such women by getting them early under proper control. They are not in prison when under control."

Dr. Chapple's reference to prison was highly pertinent since the presence of feebleminded women within the penal system was one of the main motivating factors behind calls for legislation. Feebleminded women committed to prison tended to receive lighter sentences in recognition of their condition. While in prison they were less able to comply with the structures of the regime and inevitably undermined any attempt to impose uniform discipline. Held for only a few weeks or months, they were released unimproved and unaided into a world whose demands they could not meet. All too often they fell to the margins of society, resorting to prostitution or petty theft to survive. Returned to the prison on a new charge after the shortest of intervals, they were liable to enter into a round of repeated short-term sentences from which they were unlikely ever to escape. The immediate costs of their recidivism were amplified by the fact that this continual round of imprisonment and temporary release created stresses that aggravated existing mental inadequacies.

It is not surprising that prison governesses, visitors, and administrators all called for the removal of the feebleminded from the prison to specialist institutions. The English prison commissioners, in their report for 1909, declared that feebleminded women "constitute one of the saddest and most unprofitable features of prison administration" (Prison Commissioners 1909, p. 158). To a degree, these demands for the removal of the feebleminded from the prison system, by rejecting the penal in favor of the medical sphere, constituted a tacit decriminalization of those women who could be judged mentally deficient.

After several years of heated debate, both inside and outside Parliament, the Mental Deficiency Act was passed in 1913. It included provision for the removal of the feebleminded from prisons, workhouses, and reformatories to be held instead in special institutions. Women who could be judged in any way defective were liable to be removed from prison, and those who were deemed violent were sent to new institutions where any pretension to reform or rehabilitation was replaced by long-term containment, ostensibly "not to punish but to protect" (Board of Control 1916, p. 40). Removed from the penal sphere, diagnosed as sick rather than sinful, even these most dangerous women were effectively decriminalized.

VI. The Legacy in the Twentieth Century

Over the first half of the twentieth century, the numbers of women sent to prison in Britain decreased remarkably. In 1913, the year of the Mental Deficiency Act, 33,000 women were committed to prison. Within eight years of the act, the number had fallen to 11,000 and by 1960, it had declined to less than 2,000. These figures are, in part, attributable to the growing view that many women who committed crimes were mentally or socially inadequate and so were not deserving of punishment. Many female offenders were sufficiently inadequate to require protection and treatment in suitable nonpenal institutions. However, there remained large numbers who were not certifiable under the 1913 Mental Deficiency Act (or under the subsequent Mental Deficiency Act of 1927). These women occupied the "borderland" of sanity, incapable of surviving unprotected in wider society yet entirely inappropriate for imprisonment. Repeatedly sentenced to prison for petty offending or public disorder, their continued presence there was a constant cause of disruption and a source of anxiety to prison commissioners throughout the interwar years (Smith 1962, pp. 230–36).

The concern that the prison was a wholly unsuitable environment for many women inmates led eventually to the Mental Health Act (1959) which, in repealing the 1913 act, sought to expedite the further removal of mentally deficient women from prisons. Significantly, the preoccupations motivating this reform seem to have changed little from those that had prompted the original legislation half a century earlier. Note, for example, the observations of one commentator writing just after the

350   Lucia Zedner

1959 act was passed: "Social inadequacy and social inefficiency which
are typical of mental defect often influence women to commit the types
of crime to which their sex is particularly prone. . . . The majority of
such women are quite unable to take advantage of any training offered
in prison. They disrupt the routine, and hamper the progressive
schemes for work and education. Even borderline cases who can profit
by some form of training require care and protection, not imprisonment" (Smith 1962, p. 231).

In the second half of the twentieth century, the view that much
female crime is the product of mental inadequacy has become commonplace, infiltrating the mainstream prison system itself. Significantly,
the most important of the prisons for women in Britain today, the new
Holloway prison in north London, was designed on the assumption
that "most women and girls in custody require some form of medical,
psychiatric or remedial treatment . . . [Holloway] will be basically a
secure hospital to act as the hub of the female system. Its medical and
psychiatric facilities will be its central feature and normal custodial
facilities will comprise a relatively small part of the establishment"
(James Callaghan, then British home secretary, speaking in 1968,
quoted in Morris 1987, p. 109). As Carole Smart observed in 1977:
"The assumption underlying this policy is that to deviate in a criminal
way is 'proof' of some kind of mental imbalance in women" (Smart
1977, p. 96). The new Holloway was intended to replace punishment
with psychiatric treatment related to the perceived psychological
"needs" of each woman. It has been argued that the supposedly sym-
biotic relation between mental inadequacy and criminality in women
sets up psychological disturbance as an "alternative" to crime for
women. While the rather simplistic conclusion that mental illness in
women is equivalent to male criminality begs more questions than it
answers, there can be little doubt that assumptions about the propensity of women to mental illness have had a profound effect on the
organization and regimen of female prisons.

While Holloway has remained more punitive than was perhaps originally intended, its special facilities for mentally disturbed prisoners are
testament to continuing psychiatric interpretations of female criminality. What began as a view that a proportion of criminal women were
inadequate now extends to envelop views of the female prison population as a whole. Today psychotropic drugs are dispensed in far larger
quantities in female prisons than in those for males (Heidensohn 1985,
pp. 73–75), ostensibly in response to women prisoners' greater mental

problems. The tendency to self-mutilate has at times become almost endemic in female prisons but there seems to be no self-destructive equivalent among male prisoners. That women in British prisons have a punishment rate for disciplinary violations roughly double that of men is also cited as evidence of their greater psychiatric disturbance. The expectation that women in prison are likely to be in some way inadequate is now accepted among many penal policymakers. The possibility that women, for a host of social rather than psychiatric reasons (not least the fact that many are mothers forced to leave their children outside), simply find prisons harder to take has yet to be fully explored.

Until the relatively recent developments in feminist criminology, theories of female crime have altered remarkably little. If one considers the huge and rapidly changing array of theories concerning male criminality, the lack of advance becomes all the more striking (see discussions in Heidensohn 1981; Leonard 1982; Morris 1987). The birth of feminist criminology contains the promise of new gender-based theories that may radically alter our understanding of both male and female criminality (e.g., see Gelsthorpe and Morris 1988). For the moment, however, our criminal justice programs and penal systems rest on understandings of female criminality that continue to be dominated by theories preeminent around the turn of the century. The resolute persistence of these ideas is explicable only if we appreciate the extent to which psychological responses to female crime are founded on earlier, deeply moralistic theories about what constitutes normality and what deviance in women. If the mass of women in prison are seen as "sick" and prison regimes are organized around therapy and treatment, this then presupposes some notion of the "healthy," the "natural," the "good" woman. We must ask where, or, indeed, when, such notions derive?

VII. Conclusion

Victorian perceptions, assessments, and explanations of female crime are explicable only in relation to their wider moral and social context. The finding that these views about criminal women related directly to prevailing notions of femininity raises important questions about the extent to which male behavior was also assessed in relation to parallel constructs of masculinity. Whereas male criminals often acted out supposedly manly traits, criminal women not only broke the law but also contravened various prescriptions about femininity deemed essential to the moral order of Victorian society. The extent to which female crime was seen to repudiate feminine moral duties partly explains the high level of anxiety it seems to have provoked. Anxiety about female crime sprang directly from the preoccupations of the day: urban filth and overcrowding, disease and degeneration, and the threat posed by urbanization to community and family. These were major concerns that partly explained, but also exacerbated, the costs of female crime. By studying attempts to control crime historically, this essay has shown how concern about crime is a mirror for the wider problems that preoccupy society at any given time. As such it has important implications for present-day criminology.

Around the turn of the century, links drawn between criminality, alcoholism, and insanity crystallized long-standing eugenic fears about deviance in women. Female crime came to be seen less as the deliberate contravention of social norms or laws but instead as the manifestation of innate pathology. For those women who could be seen as sick or mad, rather than bad, punitive responses came to be seen as less appropriate than specialized treatment outside the penal sphere. Although the intervention of medicine, particularly psychiatry, tended to decriminalize female deviancy, paradoxically, in stressing its hereditary aspects psychiatrists also amplified its perceived costs. The new reformatories for alcoholics and asylums for the so-called feebleminded catered overwhelmingly to women. Whether women were really so much more mentally deficient than men is questionable, for assessments of normality and abnormality in women were measured against a continuing notion of the feminine ideal. Whatever the case, it does seem likely that the smaller scale of female imprisonment allowed for experimentation not possible in the much larger male system.

This essay has traced a path, albeit uneven and patchy, from moralizing attitudes and responses to female criminality that prevailed until the mid-nineteenth century to the development of medicalized interpretations and endeavors around the opening of the twentieth century. The aim was to remove inadequate or "incorrigible" women from the penal sphere altogether to new specialist institutions. In these, moral reform gave way to medicalized "treatment" and the indefinite segregation of those who could not be "cured."

The nineteenth-century view that criminal women were distinct creatures requiring differentiated treatment appropriate to their sex has endured into the twentieth century. "Sex" not only "remained the basis for the difference in institutional response for most of the 19th century" as historian Patricia O'Brien has argued (1978, p. 516) but has con-

Women, Crime, and Penal Responses 353

tinued to do so in the twentieth. Therapeutic approaches to female criminality have become commonplace. But the extent to which these ostensibly scientific, medicalized responses were erected on the foundation of older, culturally derived assumptions about women's character and behavior has been largely overlooked. Only by historical research can we expose how far this model of femininity determined what was later to be seen as natural and what unnatural, dangerous, or deviant in women. By looking to the past in this way, we can begin to recognize how far, and in what guises, Victorian assumptions about women continue to inform penal policy today.

REFERENCES

Abrams, Philip. 1968. *The Origins of British Sociology: 1834–1914*. Chicago: University of Chicago Press.

Acton, William. 1972. *Prostitution: Considered in Its Moral, Social, and Sanitary Aspects in London and Other Large Cities and Garrison Towns*. London: Frank Cass. (Originally published 1857. London: John Churchill & Sons.)

Adam, Hargrave. 1914. *Woman and Crime*. London: T. Werner Laurie.

Adler, Freda. 1975. *Sisters in Crime*. New York: McGraw-Hill.

Alford, Stephen S. 1877. "The Necessity of Legislation for the Control and Cure of Habitual Drunkards." In *Transactions of the National Association for the Promotion of Social Science 1876*. London: Longmans.

Bailey, Victor. 1980. "Crime, Criminal Justice and Authority in England." *Society for the Study of Labour History Bulletin* 40:36–46.

———. 1981. *Policing and Punishment in Nineteenth Century Britain*. London: Croom Helm.

Banks, O. 1981. *Faces of Feminism*. Oxford: Martin Robertson.

Basch, F. 1974. *Relative Creatures*. London: Allen Lane.

Beattie, J. M. 1975. "The Criminality of Women in Eighteenth Century England." *Journal of Social History* 8:80–116.

Bedford, Adeline M. 1910. "Fifteen Years' Work in a Female Convict Prison." *Nineteenth Century and After* 68(404):615–31.

Board of Control. 1916. *Report of the Board of Control*. Parliamentary Papers. London: H.M. Stationery Office.

Bowker, Lee H., ed. 1978. *Women, Crime and the Criminal Justice System*. Toronto: Lexington.

Bremner, John A. 1874. "What Improvements are Required in the System of Discipline in County and Borough Prisons?" In *Transactions of the National Association for the Promotion of Social Science 1873*. London: Longmans.

Brenzel, Barbara. 1980. "Domestication as Reform: A Study of the Socializa-

354   Lucia Zedner

tion of Wayward Girls, 1856–1905." *Harvard Educational Review* 50:196–213.

Brodsky, Annette M. 1975. *The Female Offender*. Beverly Hills, Calif.: Sage.

Bynum, W. F., R. Porter, and M. Shepherd, eds. 1985. *The Anatomy of Madness: Essays in the History of Psychiatry*. Vols. 1–2. London: Tavistock.

Carpenter, Mary. 1858. "Reformatories for Convicted Girls." In *Transactions of the National Association for the Promotion of Social Science 1857*. London: Longmans.

———. 1864a. "On the Treatment of Female Convicts." In *Transactions of the National Association for the Promotion of Social Science 1863*. London: Longmans.

———. 1864b. *Our Convicts*. 2 vols. London: Longmans.

Chaplain of Stafford County Gaol. 1854. "Nineteenth Report of the Prison Inspectors." *Parliamentary Papers*. Vol. 34. London: H.M. Stationery Office.

Christ, Carol. 1977. "Victorian Masculinity and the Angel in the House." In *A Widening Sphere*, edited by Martha Vicinus. Bloomington: Indiana University Press.

Clay, W. L. 1861. *The Prison Chaplain: A Memoir of the late Revd John Clay*. London: Macmillan.

Cohen, Stanley. 1985. *Visions of Social Control: Crime, Punishment and Classification*. Cambridge: Polity.

Cohen, Stanley, and Andrew Scull, eds. 1983. *Social Control and the State: Historical and Comparative Essays*. Oxford: Martin Robertson.

Cominos, Peter. 1963. "Late Victorian Sexual Respectability and the Social System." *International Review of Social History* 8:18–48, 216–50.

Conway, Jill. 1970. "Stereotypes of Femininity in a Theory of Sexual Evolution." *Victorian Studies* 14(1):47–62.

Crites, Laura. 1978. *The Female Offender*. Lexington, Mass.: Lexington.

Crofton, Walter. 1867. "Female Convicts, and Our Efforts to Amend Them." In *Transactions of the National Association for the Promotion of Social Science 1866*. London: Longmans.

———. 1873. "Female Criminals—Their Children's Fate." *Good Words for 1873*. London: W. Isbister & Co.

Davenport-Hill, Florence. 1885. "Art. II. Women Prison Visitors." *Englishwoman's Review* 16(152):536–46.

Davidoff, Leonore. 1983. "Class and Gender in Victorian England." In *Sex and Class*, edited by Judith Newton. London: Routledge & Kegan Paul.

Delacy, Margaret E. 1986. *Prison Reform in Lancashire, 1700–1850: A Study in Local Administration*. Manchester: Manchester University Press.

Delamount, Sara, and Lorna Duffin, eds. 1978. *The Nineteenth Century Woman: Her Cultural and Physical World*. London: Croom Helm.

Devon, James. 1912. *The Criminal and the Community*. New York: John Lane.

Dobash, Russell P., R. Emerson Dobash, and Sue Gutteridge. 1986. *The Imprisonment of Women*. Oxford: Basil Blackwell.

Donzelot, Jacques. 1979. *The Policing of Families: Welfare versus the State*. Translated by Robert Hurley. London: Hutchinson.

Women, Crime, and Penal Responses   355

Du Cane, E. F. 1876. "Address on the Repression of Crime." In *Transactions of the National Association for the Promotion of Social Science 1875*. London: Longmans.

———. 1885. *The Punishment and Prevention of Crime*. London: Macmillan.

Ellis, Havelock. 1890. *The Criminal*. London: Walter Scott.

———. 1904. *Man and Woman: A Study of Human Secondary Sexual Characters*. 4th ed. London: Walter Scott.

Field, J. 1846. *Prison Discipline*. London: Longmans.

Finnegan, Frances. 1979. *Poverty and Prostitution: A Study of Victorian Prostitutes in York*. Cambridge: Cambridge University Press.

Fletcher, Susan Willis. 1884. *Twelve Months in an English Prison*. Boston: Lee & Shepard.

Forsythe, William James. 1987. *The Reform of Prisoners, 1830–1900*. London: Croom Helm.

Foucault, Michel. 1967. *Madness and Civilisation: A History of Insanity in the Age of Reason*. Translated by Richard Howard. London: Tavistock.

———. 1977. *Discipline and Punish: The Birth of the Prison*. Translated by Alan Sheridan. London: Penguin.

Frazer, Catherine. 1863. "The Origin and Progress of the British Ladies' Society for Promoting the Reformation of Female Prisoners, Established by Mrs. Fry in 1821." In *Transactions of the National Association for the Promotion of Social Science 1862*. London: Longmans.

Freeden, Michael. 1979. "Eugenics and Progressive Thought: A Study in Ideological Affinity." *Historical Journal* 22(3):645–71.

———. 1986. *The New Liberalism—an Ideology of Social Reform*. Oxford: Oxford University Press.

Freedman, Estelle B. 1981. *Their Sisters' Keepers: Women's Prison Reform in America, 1830–1930*. Ann Arbor: University of Michigan Press.

Fry, Elizabeth. 1827a. *Observations on the Visiting, Superintending, and Government of Female Prisoners*. 2d ed. London: John & Arthur Arch.

———. 1827b. *Sketch of the Origins and Results of Ladies' Prison Associations, with Hints for the Formation of Local Associations*. London: John & Arthur Arch.

Garland, David. 1985a. "The Criminal and His Science: A Critical Account of the Formation of Criminology at the end of the Nineteenth Century." *British Journal of Criminology* 25(2):109–37.

———. 1985b. *Punishment and Welfare—a History of Penal Strategies*. Aldershot: Gower.

———. 1988. "British Criminology before 1935." *British Journal of Criminology* 28(2):131–47.

Gatrell, V. A. C., Bruce Lenman, and Geoffrey Parker, eds. 1980. *Crime and the Law: The Social History of Crime in Western Europe since 1500*. London: Europa.

Gelsthorpe, Loraine, and Allison Morris. 1988. "Feminism and Criminology in Britain." *British Journal of Criminology* 28(2):223–40.

Giallombardo, Rose. 1966. *Society of Women: A Study of a Women's Prison*. New York: Wiley.

356   Lucia Zedner

Gibb, David. 1875. "The Relative Increase of Wages, of Drunkenness, and of Crime." In *Transactions of the National Association for the Promotion of Social Science 1874*. London: Longmans.

Gordon, Mary. 1922. *Penal Discipline*. London: Routledge & Kegan Paul.

Gorham, Deborah. 1982. *The Victorian Girl and the Feminine Ideal*. London: Croom Helm.

Goring, Charles. 1913. *The English Convict*. Report. London: H.M. Stationery Office.

Greenwood, James. 1981. *The Seven Curses of London—Scenes from the Victorian Underworld*. Oxford: Basil Blackwell. (Originally published 1869. London: Stanley Rivers & Co.)

Griffiths, Arthur. 1884. *Memorials of Millbank and Chapters in Prison History*. London: Chapman & Hall.

———. 1894. *Secrets of the Prison-house or Gaol Studies and Sketches*. 2 vols. London: Chapman & Hall.

———. 1904. *Fifty Years of Public Service*. London: Cassell.

Guy, W. A. 1863. "On Some Results of a Recent Census of the Population of the Convict Prisons in England; and Especially on the Rate of Mortality at Present Prevailing among Convicts." In *Transactions of the National Association for the Promotion of Social Science 1862*. London: Longmans.

———. 1869. "On Insanity and Crime; and on the Plea of Insanity in Criminal Cases." *Journal of the Statistical Society* 32:159–91.

Hahn, N. F. 1980*a*. "Female State Prisoners in Tennessee, 1831–1979." *Tennessee Historical Quarterly* 39(4):485–97.

———. 1980*b*. "Matrons and Molls—the Study of Women's Prison History." In *History and Crime*, edited by James Inciardi and Charles E. Faupel. Beverly Hills, Calif.: Sage.

Harding, Christopher, Bill Hines, Richard Ireland, and Philip Rawlings. 1985. *Imprisonment in England and Wales: A Concise History*. London: Croom Helm.

Harris, Ruth. 1989. *Murders and Madness—Medicine, Law, Society in the Fin de Siècle*. Oxford: Clarendon.

Hartman, Mary S. 1985. *Victorian Murderesses: A True History of Thirteen Respectable French and English Women Accused of Unspeakable Crimes*. London: Robson.

Hay, Douglas. 1980. "Crime and Justice in Eighteenth- and Nineteenth-Century England." In *Crime and Justice: An Annual Review of Research*, vol. 2, edited by Norval Morris and Michael Tonry. Chicago: University of Chicago Press.

Heidensohn, Frances. 1981. "Women and the Penal System." In *Women and Crime*, edited by Allison Morris and Loraine Gelsthorpe. Cropwood Conference Series no. 13. Cambridge: Cambridge University, Institute of Criminology.

———. 1985. *Women and Crime*. Basingstoke: Macmillan.

Henriques, Ursula. 1972. "The Rise and Decline of the Separate System of Prison Discipline." *Past and Present*, no. 54, pp. 61–93.

Higgs, Mary. 1906. *Glimpses into the Abyss*. London: King.

Hill, Rosamond. 1864. "XXII.—A Plea for Female Convicts." *English Woman's Journal* 13(74):130–34.

Women, Crime, and Penal Responses 357

Hoffer, Peter C., and N. E. H. Hull. 1981. *Murdering Mothers: Infanticide in England and New England, 1558–1803*. New York: New York University Press.

Holmes, Thomas. 1900. *Pictures and Problems from the London Police Courts*. London: Nelson.

——. 1903. "The Criminal Inebriate Female." *British Journal of Inebriety* 1(2):69–72.

——. 1908. *Known to the Police*. London: Edward Arnold.

Horsley, Canon J. W. 1887. *Jottings from Jail: Notes and Papers on Prison Matters*. London: Unwin.

——. 1898. *Prisons and Prisoners*. London: Pearson.

——. 1913. *How Criminals are Made and Prevented: A Retrospect of Forty Years*. London: Unwin.

Houghton, Walter E. 1957. *The Victorian Frame of Mind, 1830–1870*. New Haven, Conn.: Yale University Press.

Howard Association. 1880. *Annual Report*. London: Howard Association.

Hutter, Bridget, and Gillian Williams, eds. 1981. *Controlling Women: The Normal and the Deviant*. London: Croom Helm.

Ignatieff, Michael. 1978. *A Just Measure of Pain: The Penitentiary in the Industrial Revolution, 1750–1850*. London: Macmillan.

——. 1983*a*. "State, Civil Society and Total Institutions: A Critique of Recent Social Histories of Punishment." In *Social Control and the State*, edited by Stanley Cohen and Andrew Scull. Oxford: Basil Blackwell.

——. 1983*b*. "Total Institutions and Working Classes: A Review Essay." *History Workshop* 15:167–73.

Jebb, Joshua. 1854. "Report of the Surveyor-General for the Year 1853." *Parliamentary Papers*. Vol. 33. London: H.M. Stationery Office.

——. 1855. "Letters to Henry Waddington." Unpublished papers held at the University of London, London School of Economics.

Jellicoe, Anne. 1863. "A Visit to the Female Convict Prison at Mountjoy, Dublin." In *Transactions of the National Association for the Promotion of Social Science 1862*. London: Longmans.

Johnston, M. F. 1901. "The Life of a Woman Convict." *Fortnightly Review* 75:559–67.

Jones, David. 1982. *Crime, Protest, Community and Police in Nineteenth Century Britain*. London: Routledge & Kegan Paul.

"Judicial Statistics." 1857–92. Parliamentary Papers. Vols. 37–72. London: H.M. Stationery Office.

Kellor, Frances. 1901. *Experimental Sociology: Descriptive and Analytical*. New York: Macmillan.

Kelynack, T. N., ed. 1907. *The Drink Problem: In Its Medico-sociological Aspects*. London: Methuen.

Kerr, Norman. 1880. *Female Intemperance*. London: National Temperance Union.

——. 1888. *Inebriety: Its Etiology, Pathology, Treatment and Jurisprudence*. London: Lewis.

Kingsmill, Joseph. 1854. *Chapters on Prisons and Prisoners and the Prevention of Crime*. London: Longmans.

358   Lucia Zedner

Klein, Dorie. 1978. "The Etiology of Female Crime: A Review of the Litera-
   ture." In *The Female Offender*, edited by Laura Crites. Lexington, Mass.:
   Lexington.
Klein, Viola. 1946. *The Feminine Character—History of an Ideology*. London:
   Routledge & Kegan Paul.
Leonard, Eileen. 1982. *Women, Crime and Society*. London: Longmans.
Lloyd, M. A. 1903. *Susanna Meredith: A Record of a Vigorous Life*. London:
   Hodder & Stoughton.
Lombroso, Cesare, and William Ferrero. 1895. *The Female Offender*. London:
   Unwin.
McCandless, Peter. 1978. "Liberty and Lunacy: The Victorians and Wrongful
   Confinement." *Journal of Social History* 11(3):366–86.
McHugh, Paul. 1980. *Prostitution and Victorian Social Reform*. London: Croom
   Helm.
MacLeod, Roy M. 1967. "The Edge of Hope: Social Policy and Chronic Al-
   coholism, 1870–1900." *Journal of the History of Medicine* 22(3):215–44.
Marcus, Steven. 1966. *The Other Victorians: A Study of Sexuality and Pornography
   in Mid-Nineteenth Century England*. London: Weidenfeld & Nicolson.
Maudsley, Henry. 1870. *Body and Mind: An Inquiry into Their Connection and
   Mental Influence*. London: Macmillan.
———. 1874. *Responsibility in Mental Disease*. London: P.S. King & Son.
Maybrick, Florence Elizabeth. 1905. *My Fifteen Lost Years*. New York: Funk &
   Wagnalls.
Mayhew, Henry. 1862. *The Criminal Prisons of London and Scenes of Prison Life*.
   London: Griffin & Bohn.
———. 1968. *Those That Will Not Work*. Vol. 4 of *London Labour and London
   Poor*. London: Dover. (Originally published 1861–62. London: Griffin &
   Bohn.)
Mearns, Andrew. 1970. *The Bitter Cry of Outcast London: An Inquiry into the
   Condition of the Abject Poor*. London: Frank Cass. (Originally published 1883.
   London: London Congregational Union.)
Melland, Charles H. 1911. "The Feeble-minded in Prisons." *Report of the Na-
   tional Conference on the Prevention of Destitution*. London: P. S. King & Son.
Meredith, M. 1909. "Women and the Nation—the Outcasts II: The Feeble-
   minded." *Englishwoman* 2(4):406–22.
Meredith, Susanna. 1881. *A Book about Criminals*. London: James Nisbet.
Merrick, G. P. 1891. *Work among the Fallen as Seen in the Prison Cell*. London:
   Ward & Lock.
Morris, Allison. 1987. *Women, Crime and Criminal Justice*. Oxford: Basil Black-
   well.
Morris, Allison, and Loraine Gelsthorpe. 1981. *Women and Crime*. Cambridge:
   Cambridge University, Institute of Criminology.
Morrison, W. D. 1891. *Crime and Its Causes*. London: Swan Sonnenschein.
Mort, Frank. 1987. *Dangerous Sexualities: Medico-moral Politics in England since
   1830*. London: Routledge & Kegan Paul.
Nicolson, David. 1873. "The Morbid Psychology of Criminals." *Journal of
   Mental Science* 19(86):222–32, 398–409.

Nugent, James. 1877. "Incorrigible Women: What are We to Do with Them?" In *Transactions of the National Association for the Promotion of Social Science 1876*. London: Longmans.

Nye, Robert A. 1984. *Crime, Madness and Politics in Modern France: The Medical Concept of National Decline*. Princeton, N.J.: Princeton University Press.

O'Brien, Patricia. 1978. "Crime and Punishment as a Historical Problem." *Journal of Social History* 11(4):508–20.

―――. 1982. *The Promise of Punishment—Prisons in Nineteenth Century France*. Princeton, N.J.: Princeton University Press.

Orme, Eliza. 1898. "Our Female Criminals." *Fortnightly Review* 69:790–96.

Owen, M. E. 1866. "Criminal Women." *Cornhill Magazine* 14:153.

Pollock, Joy, and Meda Chesney-Lind. 1978. "Early Theories of Female Criminality." In *Women, Crime, and the Criminal Justice System*, edited by Lee H. Bowker. Toronto: Lexington.

Potts, W. A. 1905. "Causation of Mental Defect in Children." *British Medical Journal* 2:946–48.

Prewer, R. R. 1974. "The Contribution of Prison Medicine." In *Progress in Penal Reform*, edited by Louis Blom-Cooper. Oxford: Oxford University Press.

Priestly, Philip. 1985. *Victorian Prison Lives: English Prison Biography, 1830–1914*. London: Methuen.

Prison Commissioners. 1909. *Report of the Prison Commissioners for 1909*. Parliamentary Papers. Vol. 45. London: H.M. Stationery Office.

"A Prison Matron" (pseudonym, attributed to Frederick William Robinson). 1862. *Female Life in Prison*. 2 vols. London: Hurst & Blackett.

―――. 1864. *Memoirs of Jane Cameron*. 2 vols. London: Hurst & Blackett.

―――. 1866. *Prison Characters Drawn from Life with Suggestions for Prison Government*. 2 vols. London: Hurst & Blackett.

Radzinowicz, Leon. 1966. *Ideology and Crime: A Study of Crime in Its Social and Historical Context*. London: Heinemann.

―――. 1948, 1956a, 1956b, and 1968. *A History of English Criminal Law and Its Administration from 1750*. 4 vols. London: Stevens & Son.

Radzinowicz, Leon, and Roger Hood. 1986. *The Emergence of Penal Policy*. Vol. 5 of *A History of English Criminal Law and Its Administration from 1750*. London: Stevens & Son.

Rafter, Nicole Hahn. 1983a. "Chastizing the Unchaste: Social Control Functions of a Women's Reformatory, 1894–1931." In *Social Control and the State*, edited by Stanley Cohen and Andrew Scull. Oxford: Basil Blackwell.

―――. 1983b. "Prisons for Women, 1790–1980." In *Crime and Justice: An Annual Review of Research*, vol. 5, edited by Michael Tonry and Norval Morris. Chicago: University of Chicago Press.

―――. 1985a. "Gender, Prisons, and Prison History." *Social Science History* 9(3):233–47.

―――. 1985b. *Partial Justice*. Boston: Northeastern University Press.

Rafter, Nicole Hahn, and Elizabeth Anne Stanko. 1982. *Judge, Lawyer, Victim, Thief: Women, Gender Roles, and Criminal Justice*. Boston: Northeastern University Press.

360   Lucia Zedner

Rentoul, Robert Reid. 1903. *Proposed Sterilisation of Certain Mental and Physical Degenerates*. London: Walter Scott.

———. 1906. *Race Culture; or, Race Suicide? (A Plea for the Unborn)*. London: Walter Scott.

Roberts, Elizabeth. 1984. *A Woman's Place: An Oral History of Working Class Women, 1890–1940*. Oxford: Basil Blackwell.

Rock, Paul. 1977. "Review Symposium." *British Journal of Criminology* 17:390–95.

Rogers, Foster. 1850. "Reports of the Governors and Chaplains of Middlesex Prisons." Unpublished manuscripts. London: Greater London Record Office.

Rosen, Ruth. 1980. *The Lost Sisterhood: Prostitution in America, 1900–1918*. Baltimore: John Hopkins University Press.

Rothman, David. 1971. *The Discovery of the Asylum—Social Order and Disorder in the New Republic*. Boston: Little, Brown.

———. 1980. *Conscience and Convenience—the Asylum and Its Alternatives in Progressive America*. Boston: Little, Brown.

Royal Commission on the Care and Control of the Feeble-minded. 1904–8. *Parlimentary Papers*. Vols. 35–39. London: H.M. Stationery Office.

Rudé, George. 1985. *Criminal and Victims: Crime and Society in Early Nineteenth Century England*. Oxford: Clarendon.

Russell, W. 1835. "Select Committee of the House of Lords on Gaols and Houses of Correction, Minutes of Evidence." *Parliamentary Papers*. Vol. 11. London: H.M. Stationery Office.

Safford, A. Herbert. 1867. "What are the best means of preventing Infanticide?" In *Transactions of the National Association for the Promotion of Social Science 1866*. London: Longmans.

Scharlieb, Mary. 1907. "Alcoholism in Relation to Women and Children." In *The Drink Problem*, edited by T. N. Kelynack. London: Methuen.

Schlossman, Steven L. 1977. *Love and the American Delinquent: The Theory and Practice of "Progressive" Juvenile Justice, 1825–1920*. Chicago: University of Chicago Press.

———. 1978. "The Crime of Precocious Sexuality: Female Juvenile Delinquency in the Progressive Era." *Harvard Educational Review* 48:65–94.

Scougal, Francis (pseudonym for Felicia Mary Francis Skene). 1889. *Scenes from a Silent World or Prisons and Their Inmates*. London: William Blackwood.

Scull, Andrew. 1979. *Museums of Madness: The Social Organisation of Insanity in Nineteenth-Century England*. London: Allen Lane.

———, ed. 1981. *Madhouses, Mad-Doctors and Madmen: The Social History of Psychiatry in the Victorian Era*. London: Athlone.

Searle, G. R. 1976. *Eugenics and Politics in Britain, 1900–1914*. Leyden: Noordoff International.

Shadwell, Arthur. 1902. *Drink, Temperance and Legislation*. London: Longmans, Green.

Showalter, Elaine. 1987. *The Female Malady: Women, Madness, and English Culture, 1830–1980*. London: Virago.

Simmons, Harvey G. 1978. "Explaining Social Policy: The English Mental Deficiency Act of 1913." *Journal of Social History* 11(3):387–483.

Women, Crime, and Penal Responses 361

Skultans, Vieda. 1975. *Madness and Morals: Ideas on Insanity in the Nineteenth Century*. London: Routledge & Kegan Paul.

Smart, Carole. 1976. *Women, Crime and Criminology: A Feminist Critique*. London: Routledge & Kegan Paul.

———. 1977. "Criminological Theory: Its Ideology and Implications concerning Women." *British Journal of Sociology* 28(1):89–100.

Smart, Carole, and Barry Smart, eds. 1978. *Women, Sexuality and Social Control*. London: Routledge & Kegan Paul.

Smith, Ann. 1962. *Women in Prison*. London: Stevens & Son.

Smith, Roger. 1981*a*. "The Boundary between Insanity and Criminal Responsibility in Nineteenth Century England." In *Madhouses, Mad-Doctors and Madmen*, edited by Andrew Scull. London: Athlone.

———. 1981*b*. *Trial by Medicine: Insanity and Responsibility in Victorian Trials*. Edinburgh: Edinburgh University Press.

Soloway, Richard. 1982. "Counting the Degenerates: The Statistics of Race Deterioration in Edwardian England." *Journal of Contemporary History* 17(1):137–64.

Stedman Jones, Gareth. 1971. *Outcast London—a Study in the Relationship between Classes in Victorian Society*. Oxford: Clarendon.

Steer, Mary H. 1893. "Rescue Work by Women among Women." In *Woman's Mission*, edited by Baroness Burdett-Coutts. London: Sampson, Low & Marston.

Sturma, Michael. 1978. "Eye of the Beholder: The Stereotype of Women Convicts, 1788–1852." *Labour History* 34:3–10.

Sullivan, W. C. 1906. *Alcoholism: A Chapter in Social Pathology*. London: James Nisbet.

Summers, Anne. 1976. *Damned Whores and God's Police: The Colonisation of Women in Australia*. Victoria, Australia: Penguin.

Surveyor-General. 1857–58. "Report of the Surveyor General for 1856–57." *Parliamentary Papers*. Vol. 29. London: H.M. Stationery Office.

Symons, Jelinger C. 1849. *Tactics for the Times: As Regards the Condition and Treatment of the Dangerous Classes*. London: John Olivier.

Thomson, Basil. 1925. *The Criminal*. London: Hodder & Stoughton.

Thomson, J. B. 1870*a*. "The Hereditary Nature of Crime." *Journal of Mental Science* 15(72):487–98.

———. 1870*b*. "The Psychology of Criminals." *Journal of Mental Science* 17(75):321–50.

Tredgold, A. F. 1908. *Mental Deficiency*. London: Baillere, Tindall & Cox.

———. 1909. "The Feeble-minded—a Social Danger." *Eugenics Review* 1(2):96–104.

———. 1910. "The Feeble-minded." *Contemporary Review* 97(534):717–27.

Vicinus, Martha. 1977. *A Widening Sphere—Changing Roles of Victorian Women*. Bloomington: Indiana University Press.

———, ed. 1980. *Suffer and Be Still: Women in the Victorian Age*. London: Methuen.

Walker, Nigel, ed. 1968. *The Historical Perspective*. Vol. 1 of *Crime and Insanity in England*. Edinburgh: Edinburgh University Press.

Walker, Nigel, and Sarah McCabe, eds. 1973. *New Solutions and New Problems*.

362   Lucia Zedner

Vol. 2 of *Crime and Insanity in England*. Edinburgh: Edinburgh University Press.

Walkowitz, Judith. 1980. *Prostitution and Victorian Society: Women, Class and the State*. Cambridge: Cambridge University Press.

———. 1982. "Male Vice and Feminist Virtue: Feminism and the Politics of Prostitution in Nineteenth Century Britain." *History Workshop* 13:77–93.

Weeks, Jeffrey. 1981. *Sex, Politics and Society: The Regulation of Sexuality since 1800*. London: Longmans.

Wells, Ashton. 1877. "Crime in Women; Its Sources and Treatment." In *Transactions of the National Association for the Promotion of Social Science 1876*. London: Longmans.

Westcott, W. M. Wynn. 1903. "Inebriety in Women and the Overlaying of Infants." *British Journal of Inebriety* 1(2):65–68.

Wilson, John Dove. 1878. "Can any Better Measures be Devised for the Prevention and Punishment of Infanticide?" In *Transactions of the National Association for the Promotion of Social Science 1877*. London: Longmans.

"Women Convicts." 1887. *Englishwoman's Review* 18(173):473–74.

Wrench, Matilda, ed. 1852. *Visits to Female Prisoners at Home and Abroad*. London: Wertheim & Macintosh.

Zanetti, Frances. 1903. "Inebriety in Women and Its Influence on Child-Life." *British Journal of Inebriety* 1(2):47–57.

Zedner, Lucia. 1988. "The Criminality of Women and Its Control in England, 1850–1914." Ph.D. dissertation, University of Oxford.

[13]

THE BRITISH JOURNAL

OF

CRIMINOLOGY

| Vol. 25 | April 1985 | No. 2 |

THE CRIMINAL AND HIS SCIENCE

A Critical Account of the Formation of Criminology at the End of the Nineteenth Century

DAVID GARLAND *(Edinburgh)**

THE last decades of the nineteenth century witnessed the formation of a new form of knowledge which has become familiar to us as the "science of criminology". Within a remarkably brief period, perhaps no more than 20 years after the appearance of Lombroso's *L'Uomo Delinquente* in 1876, this knowledge developed from the idiosyncratic concerns of a few individuals into a programme of investigation and social action which attracted support throughout the whole of Europe and North America. This explosion of interest in the criminological enterprise led to the publication of hundreds of texts, the formation of dozens of national and international congresses, conferences and associations, and the assembly of an international social movement which pressed the claims of criminology upon the legislatures and penal institutions of virtually every western nation.

The widespread success of that movement in establishing criminology as an accredited discipline in the institutions of government, penology and education means that a detailed description of that programme might today appear to be unnecessary. The character and concerns of this knowledge are well known. Its premises and implications have been frequently discussed, either with approval or, more recently, with some dismay. Its concepts and recommended practices, for better or for worse, underpin many of the penal sanctions and institutions of nations throughout the modern world.

But for all that it is a familiar and established discipline in today's world, it would seem that its history and development have escaped the close and

* University of Edinburgh; currently a Davis Fellow, Princeton University, United States.

DAVID GARLAND

critical scrutiny usually afforded to powerful forms of social knowledge. There has yet to be produced an intensive history of the discipline, either in terms of its internal development or else its social effects, despite the beginnings made in this direction by Jeffrey (1960), Radzinowicz (1966). Cohen (1974) and Matza (1964). This failure of criminologists to reflect critically upon their own practice has meant that our knowledge of criminology's development is sparse and inadequate. We are left with, on the one hand, hagiographies of the "founding fathers" and their "scientific mission" (see Mannheim, 1960) and, on the other, wholesale dismissals of the "reactionary purpose" and legacy of "positivism" with all the simplifications and over-statements which these entail (see Taylor *et al.*. 1973). What is missing is any detailed account of the theoretical formation of the criminological programme, its internal characteristics and its relationship to its social conditions of emergence. The following account does not claim to make good this absence. But it does attempt to take these issues seriously and to deal with the evidence of concrete texts, statements and events. In particular, it examines the *theoretical framework* of criminology, asking how this structure of problems, propositions and concepts came to be assembled, and how it related to the events and institutions of the social world. It is hoped that such an account can begin to explain the peculiar lines of development subsequently taken by the discipline, as well as indicating the basis of its affinity to the institutions of power which were later to embrace it in their practices and ideologies.

I have termed this a "critical" account—as opposed, perhaps, to an "impartial" one—and I should say at the outset what is meant by this and what its limitations are. In the pages that follow there is little space given to the progressive features of positivist criminology. These features are well enough known since they are inscribed in the prefaces and pages of virtually every positivist text, but, lest they be lost sight of, let me repeat them here. The new criminology of the late nineteenth and early twentieth century promised an exact and scientific method for the study of crime, a technical means of resolving a serious social problem, and a genuinely humane hope of preventing the harm of crime and improving the character of offenders. The present paper does not seek to deny these progressive elements, nor to question the motivation of the individuals who took up criminology and promoted its demands. But it does seek to question the notions of science, of crime and of rehabilitation which underpinned this movement, and it suggests that in the detailed formulation of its arguments criminology colluded in a definite set of political assumptions and policies. The paper's critical stance derives from a recognition of the unstated and unjustified nature of this collusion and from the view of the author that its consequence was more often the continued repression of disadvantaged sectors of the population than the liberation of society from the problem of crime.

Conditions of Existence

The emergence of this new form of knowledge, with its concepts, objects

110

THE CRIMINAL AND HIS SCIENCE

and methods of study, required for its possibility much more than the ecstatic discoveries of an Italian doctor in the prisons and asylums of Pavia.[1] Similarly its ability to attract the attentions and support of so many powerful individuals and organisations rested upon a certain resonance between the concerns of this new discipline and the preoccupations and affairs of men of science and public office in this period. The following section will give a brief outline of some of the conceptual, institutional and political conditions which made possible the emergence of this new criminological movement, its discoveries and its desires.

No new form of knowledge is ever without a line of precursors and a hazy ancestry of analogous practices and objectives. And if we consider particular features of this knowledge, for example the commitment of the criminological programme to a practice of correctionalism, reform and rehabilitation, then certain lines of descent become obvious. Thus the ecclesiastical law of penance prefigured the new criminology in focusing not upon the individual's act but rather the personal state (of sin or of grace) from which the act arose. This state of the soul was to be the target of ecclesiastical intervention and transformation just as punishment was to be directed towards the correction of character within the new criminological programme.[2] A more immediate precursor of this correctionalism was the reformative objectives of men such as Howard and Bentham, whose notions of reform, in either evangelical or utilitarian form, had been a constituent objective of penal institutions for more than a century, at least in the rhetoric of officials and reformers. But although this line of precursors provided historical echoes and precedents which gained support and authority for the new movement, the parallels involved were far from exact. As I shall discuss shortly, the conception and methods of correction involved differed markedly between the old and the new. The basis of crime no longer lay in sin or in faulty reasoning but in an aberration or abnormality of the individual's constitution. Similarly the process of reform no longer attended upon the visitation of God's Grace or the return of true Reason but instead mobilised its own positive techniques of intervention and transformation.

Again if one considers its project of tracing patterns of behaviour and action back to a source in the physical constitution of the criminal, then we find a further historical precursor in the work of F. J. Gall and J. C. Spurzheim. These two writers were the leading exponents of "phrenology", a form of knowledge which conceived mental faculties as localised brain functions, thereby allowing the analysis of personality to take place by

[1] Lombroso (1911, p. xiv) describes his "discoveries" thus: "In 1870 I was carrying on for several months researches in the prisons and asylums of Pavia upon cadavers and living persons in order to determine upon substantial differences between the insane and criminals, without succeeding very well. At last I found in the skull of a brigand a very long series of atavistic anomalies, above all an enormous middle occipatal fossa and a hypertrophy of the vermis analogous to those that are found in inferior vertebrates. At the sight . . . of these strange anomalies the problem of the nature and of the origin of the criminal seemed to me resolved. This was not merely an idea, but a flash of inspiration. At the sight of that skull, I seemed to see all of a sudden, lighted up as a vast plain under a flaming sky, the problem of the nature of the criminal."

[2] Cf. Saleilles (1913, p. 203): "In Ecclesiastical law . . . the conception of 'castigatio' was allied to that of 'discipline' and 'remedium'."

DAVID GARLAND

examining the shape and contours of the individual's cranium (*cf.* Smith, 1981; Gould, 1984). Quite clearly the work of Lombroso, Boies, Ellis and Goring, as well as many other criminological writers, gained support from this earlier form of "physicalism" and from what De Quiros (1911, p. 2) terms "the old longing to discover in man the relations beween body and soul, the correspondence between spirit and matter".

But between the early physicalism of the phrenologists and the opening up of the criminological field lay one very important attempt to answer this ancient question. The search for scientific explanations of human and social life, for the discovery of the laws of movement of "man" himself, was in the nineteenth century expressed in the methods and concerns of "scientism" in general and "positivism" in particular. And although the criminologists of the 1880s and 1890s sought to distance themselves from the particular philosophy and historicism which characterised this positivist movement in its Comtean form, there can be no doubt that the *project* of positivism (in a more modest version) and its corresponding *methods* formed the broad intellectual basis for the criminological programme. As we shall see later, observation, classification and procedures of induction, quantitative methods, "naturalism" and the formulation of causal laws, were all aspects of this positivist inheritance which fundamentally shaped the configuration of this new knowledge.

In addition to these historical continuities, and the intellectual heritage and social support derived from these traditions, there were a number of more proximate and immediate conditions which allowed the emergence of criminology. Above all, the criminological genesis was tied to three main conditions: (1) the development of statistical data, produced by surveys, institutions, government and private research; (2) the advances made in the realm of psychiatry and the growth of that knowledge in intellectual and social standing; and (3), of greatest importance, the existence of the prison as an institutional surface of emergence for the concerns, techniques and data of the new discipline.

To take these in turn, the development of statistical information and method was obviously an important precondition for a discipline which sought to classify and differentiate a population on quantitative and scientific basis. Of course the formulation of precise techniques and conceptual means (*e.g.* the techniques of regression, correlation and factor analysis, and the non-parametric methods, etc.) had to await the work of Karl Pearson, Charles Spearman and R. A. Fisher in the early years of the twentieth century, but the production of statistical data preceded its scientific interpretation. In fact the collection and collation of data—on births, deaths, marriages, crimes, migration, incomes, etc.—developed correlatively with the growth of the modern centralised State and its increasing desire to regulate its subject population.[3] By the 1830s and 1840s this state science had become more ordered and regular, producing

---

[3] On the development of statistical technique, see McKenzie (1981). On the history of statistical information in general, see Cullen (1975), especially the Prelude "Social Statistics in Britain, 1660–1830". For criminal statistics in particular, see Wiles (1971) and Gatrell and Hadden (1972).

census materials, governmental inquiries and reports and the annual statistical reports of the various official agencies (including prisons, police, asylums, judiciary, poorhouses, etc.). These resources were employed not just by governments and their institutions but also by private individuals and associations who grasped these figures as evidence for particular programmes of social regulation or reform. Thus in France the "moral statisticians", Quetelet and Guerry, established patterns of regularity in the levels of crime, pauperism, marriage, etc. and proposed appropriate calculations on the part of government, while in Britain a Statistical Society was formed to expand the production of social data and thereby further the campaigns of its membership for social hygiene and institutional reform. By the 1890s this movement had been augmented by the detailed social surveys of the likes of Mayhew, Booth and the Charity Organisation Society and by the increasing generation of data provided by the expanding State sector.[4] These resources, which allowed quantitative comparisons to be drawn between the characteristics of particular categories (say prisoners, or the asylum population) and the population at large, were to be the basic raw material upon which criminology worked. That there was an absence of rigorous methods of interpretation which could specify the real significance of this material was not perceived as a major limitation to the claims of the criminologists. For this absence of rigour was overshadowed by the prestige accorded to the "facts" of statistical data—and the technical limitations of their mode of production, the crude manner in which they were interpreted and the massive speculations involved in the processes of induction, were perceived as no more than minor considerations which barely detracted from the achievements of this new "positive" science.

The second major basis for the development of criminology lay in the claims and concepts of psychiatrists and psychiatry. From its inception to the present day, criminology has relied upon the data and the prestige of the psychiatric movement to support its own propositions and concerns, to provide "hard", "scientific" evidence or, more often, to derive a certain social power from the quasi-medical image of that discipline. In a sense, criminology has ridden upon the back of the psychiatric institution, using it as an ally and support for its own more eclectic and social policy-oriented concerns. As with the philosophy of "positivism", there was never a complete identification between criminology and its psychiatric support

[4] See Guerry (1833) and Quetelet (1835). The work of these "moral statisticians" has sometimes been referred to as the first phase of criminological science, in so far as they applied "scientific" techniques to criminological data (see, for instance, Bonger, 1916). Whether or not this compliment is granted, the "science" of these writers differs significantly from the "science of criminology" with which we are concerned, and is perhaps more properly viewed as an early sociology of deviance. Guerry and Quetelet were concerned to show that crime is a social fact, with the regularities and social basis of all such phenomena. In so far as they have a conception of individual criminal behaviour, this appears to have been neo-classical in form, assuming choice within social constraints. See Morris (1957, pp. 48 *et seq.*). On Mayhew and other 19th century writers who investigated and documented the "ecology" of English crime and criminals, see Lindesmith and Levin (1971) and Morris (1957). It is significant that the untheorised but persistently *sociological* approach of writers such as Mayhew, Rawson, Fletcher and others was marginalised or else reformulated by the appearance of the new positivist criminology. On this marginalisation, see Morris (1957) and Garland (1985).

DAVID GARLAND

but, particularly in the early years, a considerable borrowing of concepts, proposals and social standing took place.

Between about 1845 and 1880 the new medical specialism of "alienism" or "psychological medicine" succeeded in establishing itself as an independent and institutionalised discipline known as "psychiatry". The national network of lunatic asylums formed after the 1845 Acts, together with the professional organisations formed by alienists in the same period, provided an institutional enclosure and an organisational basis for the development of this area as a career specialism (*cf.* Smith, 1981; Scull, 1979). Moreover the development of physiological investigation into the field of brain functions appeared to give a scientific basis to psychiatry's theories and correspondingly advanced its social standing.

The early criminologists leaned heavily upon this newly established science and its propositions. Not only was the concern with observation, classification and positive data endorsed and emulated, but specific theories and categories were taken over and employed in criminological discourse. Thus the application of determinist principles to human behaviour and the consequent rejection of free-will doctrines were presented by early criminologists such as Ferri and Garafalo as conclusive and indisputable findings provided by the psychiatric sciences. Similarly, categories such as "the moral imbecile", "moral insanity", "degeneracy" and "feeble-mindedness" were taken over wholesale from the work of Maudsley, Pritchard, Morel and Nordau and used as a basis for criminological argument.[5]

However, this systematic borrowing was not without its advantages for the psychiatrists, whose favourite terms were thus repeated and reproduced. The psychiatric movement, in the late nineteenth century, saw its major line of expansion as lying in the judicial domain—not just in dealing with criminal lunatics and the insane residents of Broadmoor, but in pronouncing upon the psychiatric state of *all* accused persons before the courts, the petty as well as the monstrous. In this it found an important ally in the criminological movement which pressed these claims for psychiatric intrusion as part of its more general programme of penal reform. Thus while psychiatry provided conceptual conditions for the emergence of criminology, the latter promised in exchange to promote psychiatric knowledge and expertise in the judicial field.

Finally, there is an important sense in which the emergence of criminology owes its possibility not to an intellectual movement or a theoretical discovery but to a particular *institution*—namely the prison. Just as the clinic formed the real basis for the development of medicine, and the barracks, the monastery and the schoolroom supported the foundation of a disciplinary knowledge and practice (*cf.* Foucault, 1977), so the prison acted as an institutional surface of emergence for criminology and its

---

[5] See Smith (1981) and Walker (1968). De Quiros (1911) states the following texts as the most influential in criminology's development: Clapham and Clarke's *The Criminal Outline of the Insane and the Criminal* (1846); Winslow's *Lettsonian Lectures on Insanity* (1854); Thompson's *Psychology of Criminals* (1870) and "The Hereditary Nature of Crime" in *The Journal of Mental Science* (1870); and Maudsley's *Mental Responsibility* (1873).

THE CRIMINAL AND HIS SCIENCE

particular concerns. The prison provided a kind of experimental laboratory, a controlled enclosure in which the new knowledge could develop. It provided the possibility for the long-term observation of criminals who could be examined, measured, photographed and catalogued in an organised and rigorous manner. It produced statistical data on conviction rates, recidivism patterns and criminal careers which were invaluable criminological materials unavailable elsewhere. It even allowed a degree of experimentation in so far as various regimes of labour, diet, discipline and so on could be compared with one another to assess the effects of each upon the prison population and the causes of crime.

There was a natural link between the prison as an institution which sought to deter and reform offenders and a knowledge which posed the question of what an offender *is*. As Ruggles-Brise (1925; p. 10) clearly saw, *"la science penitentiare* develops gradually into the science of the discovery of the causes of crime—the science of criminology". Hence the *international* emergence of this new knowledge (prisons being established throughout the Western world) and hence the abiding criminological concern with prison populations and the data drawn from them.

But there is one more linkage between the prison and its criminological offspring, a linkage which goes straight to the heart of the criminological enterprise and ties it firmly to a particular project and a definite politics. The linkage concerns the dual concepts of *individualisation* and *differentiation*, two terms which establish the very basis of the criminological project and shape the methods, concepts and techniques which are most characteristic of this knowledge. I will be discussing the significance of these terms later, so my purpose here is merely to locate their institutional origin and to indicate how these theoretical terms were promoted by their institutional context. To take "individualisation" first, it is clearly a fundamental architectural feature of the prison that it has as its primary unit, its basic term, the individual cell containing the individual prisoner. This cellular structure has a number of obvious practical purposes such as isolation, prevention of communication and contamination, and ease of surveillance and control, which no doubt account for its widespread use. But, once established, this practical organisation affects the way in which offenders are viewed. The Victorian prison promotes a way of seeing its inmates which is quite different from older goals which did not seek to isolate and individuate their inmates. It is also different from other nineteenth-century punishments such as the fine, corporal punishment or transportation in which this individualising element is neither so pronounced nor so prolonged. This new way of seeing the offender as an isolated individual, separately observed and separately dealt with, was taken up and reproduced by criminology. When criminological investigation was brought to bear upon the prison population, it found the individual criminal already "there", made visible for observation and made "obvious" for analysis. But this fixing of the individual as penal and criminological object is not without its social and political conditions and connotations. All the premises of bourgeois individualism—of private

DAVID GARLAND

responsibility for action and crime, of free-will and liberty in the face of social forces, of the individual source of criminality—are in this way reproduced in the prison and in criminological theory. The politics and the ideologies of liberalism are thus inscribed into the physical and conceptual architecture of the institutions and discourses which deal with crime, though this inscription occurs without question or acknowledgement. And although, as we shall see, criminology would drastically revise the liberal notions of responsibility and action, at no point did it question this fixing of the individual as the source of crime and the proper object of study and correction.

As for "differentiation", there is a clear sense in which this theoretical project also exists ready-made in the context of the prison. In the nineteenth century, when incarceration was the primary sanction employed by the criminal law, the clearest and simplest demarcation between the criminal and non-criminal populations was provided by the prison walls. Those who were placed behind these walls were, by this fact alone, members of a distinctive criminal class. Consequently, as was noted above, the characteristics of the criminal could most easily be ascertained by observing the prison population, while the control groups of the non-criminal would be drawn from the free population outside—from army recruits, undergraduates, boys' club members or whatever. This convenient demarcation and basis of comparison was used extensively by the early criminologists, as indeed it continues to be used today, albeit in a more closely controlled manner. But the direction of this research and the special characteristics which were hypothesised (and duly found) involved the covert introduction of a definite premise into the argument; for it was assumed that the difference in legal status and social placing which marked off the prison population from the population "at large" corresponded to a constitutional difference between the individuals who composed the two groups. In other words, the prison demarcation became a natural demarcation which criminology first presupposed and then "discovered".[6]

To explain this process we need to show more than its practical convenience and possibility; we need to show that its direction and assumptions were likely or probable in these circumstances. And to do this we need look no further than the strategy of social politics which prevailed

---

[6] Garafalo (1914) argues explicitly that criminology's proper object of study is "the natural delinquent". Goring (1913) is more circumspect than Ferri or Lombroso, stating this as an *hypothesis* rather than an *a priori* assumption: ". . . we are forced to the hypothesis of the possible existence of a character in all men which we call the 'criminal diathesis' " Goring (1913, p. 26), or again: "Assuming that conviction and reconviction for crime are not purely circumstantial occurrences, and constitutional factors play some part in this eventuality . . ." Goring (1913, p. 123).

The development of IQ theories in psychology demonstrates precisely the same, unjustified leap of faith—a process that Gould (1984, p. 24) describes as *reification:* "The argument begins with one of the fallacies—*reification,* or our tendency to convert abstract concepts into entities. We recognize the importance of mentality in our lives and we wish to characterize it, in part so that we can make the divisions and distinctions among people that our cultural and political systems dictate. We therefore give the word 'intelligence' to this wondrously complex and multifaceted set of human capabilities, this shorthand symbol is then reified and intelligence achieves its dubious status as a unitary thing. Once intelligence becomes an entity, standard procedures of science virtually dictate that a location and physical substrate be sought for it. Since the brain is the seat of mentality, intelligence must reside there."

THE CRIMINAL AND HIS SCIENCE

in Britain and elsewhere in Europe in the late nineteenth century. The desire to differentiate and individualise the criminal (which establishes not only the methods and concepts of criminology but also its purposes and politics) is in this sense the intellectual expression of the political strategy of differentiation which was embodied in the practices of the Poor Law, of charity, and of criminal justice in this period.[7] It is a strategy which sought to divide and demarcate the masses against themselves, to specify and enforce divisions (rough/respectable, deserving/mendicant, law-abiding/ delinquent, etc.) the better to control a general population. Without this "desire" and its institutional and strategic surface of emergence, there is no basis for the criminological enterprise. Why should it be supposed that criminals are constitutionally abnormal or "different" when common sense and previous philosophies suggest the opposite? Why should there be a science of the individual criminal and his differentiation when there is no science which differentiates the rich or the poor or the law-abiding or the masterful? Why? Simply because a configuration of social, institutional and intellectual conditions made it at once possible and manifestly desirable.

The Critique of Classicism and the Status Quo

One other obvious condition which facilitated the rise to prominence of this criminological programme was the social and penal crisis of the 1890s. The failure of the existing strategy to deal effectively with crime was used as a tactical point of entry for the new programme which offered a radical critique of the current strategy, its institutions and particularly its classical jurisprudence. Thus Enrico Ferri (1917, p. xli): "It is our experience (noted every day, in every country, on both sides of the ocean) that the penal laws inspired as they still are by the traditional doctrines, are powerless to preserve civil society from the scourge of criminality." And Baron Garafalo (1914, p. xxvi): "It is useless to protest against verdicts of acquittal or the leniency of judges. What we see is, after all, the triumph of judicial logic, but a triumph which is at the expense of social security and morality."

This political failure was referenced again and again in the work of the new criminologists, and its source was each time traced to the philosophical framework of classicism and the procedures and practices which it implied. In fact, if we are to describe the elements of this new programme and the themes and concerns which its exponents shared, then there is no better place to begin than with the critique of classicism. The assault upon this jurisprudence was pursued by virtually every text in the field, as much to establish the practical advantages of a penal system based on positive criminology as to demarcate the differences between the two forms of discourse. And one should emphasise that this was indeed an *assault*. In its early stages the new programme sought no accommodation with classicism, no revision or reform or theoretical compromise. Instead it attacked

---

[7] On the character and detail of this political strategy, see Jones (1971), Williams (1981) and Garland (1985).

DAVID GARLAND

the very heart of classical philosophy, and established its own discursive
space and right to exist *against* the traditional principles.

    . . . *Against the doctrines of free-will and responsibility*, which formed the basis
of the whole legal edifice, there were counterposed the conclusions of
science. Thus Ferri (1917, p. 38): "Positive psychology has demonstrated
that the pretended free-will is a purely subjective illusion." No need for
argument or contestation here; science has had its say. But of course the
practical consequences were the real issue at stake: if free-will was illusory
then "responsibility" and "guilt" were equally suspect and need no longer
limit the exercise of penal control. Thus Emile Faguet of the French
Academy (quoted in Smithers, 1911–12): "It is not at the point of
culpability that one must place oneself. That is too obscure and
metaphysical. . . . It is not necessary to consider criminals as responsibles,
semi-responsibles, irresponsibles—that concerns only the philosophers. It
is necessary to consider them as very dangerous, dangerous, semi-
dangerous and not dangerous. Only that, and nothing else should be
considered." "Free-will", "responsibility", "guilt" and "punishment"—
not just fictions out of favour with science but metaphysical concepts which
posed a danger to society's security, leaving society practically defenceless
against the most dangerous criminals. Saleilles put it best when he
counterposed the exchange logic of retribution to the utilitarian design of
social defence. Seen in this light, the classical way with penalties is: "the
most dangerous theory for society . . . because, though it attempts to make
criminals pay for their debts, it does not succeed in preventing them from
contracting new and equally irresponsible ones." (Saleilles, 1913, p. 61)

    . . . *Against*, therefore, *"penal proportion" and its attendant "metaphysics"*. To
reject free-willed responsibility is to relieve the penal system of the task of
measuring justice in these "impossible" terms. And once freed of these
burdens it can concentrate upon its proper defensive tasks: thus Enrico
Ferri (1917, xl): ". . . penal justice instead of having a mission of measuring
the 'moral fault' of the delinquent (a measure which is unalterably
impossible), and of measuring a 'proportionate punishment' (a proportion
which is impossible, because, for instance, science and practice can have no
absolute criteria by which to determine whether the proportionate
punishment for murder should be death, life imprisonment, or imprisonment for a certain number of years), instead of this mission, penal justice
can only be a tactical defence against the danger and injury represented by
crime." The abuse of this "metaphysics" was a favourite tactic, used by
psychiatrists like Maudsley and Robertson as much as their criminological
allies. In place of this speculative contemplation of its "straight lines,
regularities and fictions" (Saleilles, 1913, p. 73), the criminologists insisted
upon "the positive study of the facts" (Ferri, 1917, p. 14). The new
programme aimed: "to substitute the realities of experience for purely
judicial abstractions; to give fact a place above law, the spirit of
observation a place above the legal spirit." (Saleilles, 1913, p. 72). And if
the rejection of these metaphysics implied that the doctrine of individual
rights should also be abandoned then this was hardly a calamity, since

THE CRIMINAL AND HIS SCIENCE

according to philosophers like F. H. Bradley (1893–9, p. 272): "The old metaphysical doctrines of individual's rights became obsolete early in this [nineteenth] century [and] can hardly today be considered a rational principle."

... *Against uniformity of punishment*, its assumptions and effects. Up until now, the prevailing system of criminal justice had been premised upon these mistaken principles—penal proportion, individual rights, equality of treatment. The consequence was the "uniformity" of punishment, now seen not as an achievement but rather as a lack of refinement or discernment—"the promiscuous consignment to the common form of imprisonment" (Prison Commission Report, 1901–02, p. 8)—the "antiquated blunderbuss of punishment" (Ellis, 1910, p. xxv). Not only was there a lack of diversity in the available sanctions, but within prison itself there was no adequate classification or differentiation. Penal classification was "just as legal, abstract and final as the sentence itself" (I.P.P.F., 1951, p. 54). The new criminologists protested against this "uniformity" and its egalitarian assumptions. The findings of "anthropology" were summarily asserted to disprove this well-intentioned fiction[8] while its egalitarian effect was stood on its head: "It has been said that in prison all men are equal; but their natural inequalities are not removed by putting men in custody; they are only ignored; and prison treatment, being uniform, is therefore unequal treatment of individuals." (Devon, 1908)

But the consequence was more than a uniform inequality: it involved a failure of prison to reform or even to incapacitate society's most dangerous elements. The prison was presented as a breeding ground for delinquents, a regime in which *le bon detenu* was also *le mauvais sujet*, where "the ideal of a 'good prisoner' is the recidivist, the veteran, the habitual criminal, whose prison experience and the docility he has acquired are guarantees of his orderly conduct" (Lombroso, 1911, p. 333). The assertion of "science" against "metaphysics" thus had a practical pay-off—for the new criminology could show that behind the practical failure of the prison, the rising recidivism rates[9] and the various malfunctions of criminal justice lay the glaring inadequacies of the system's classicist foundations.

[8] *Cf.* Ferri (1917, p. 37): "Anthropology shows by the facts that the delinquent is not a normal man; that on the contrary he represents a special class, a variation of the human race through organic and physical abnormalities, either hereditary or acquired."
In one sense, of course, the arguments of anthropology and of human differentiation are beside the point. Classicism and liberal philosophy did not assert that "all men are equal" but only that all men should be treated as equal, despite natural or social differences. When faced with this argument criminology could only reply that such political equality was "inexpedient", which is perhaps why the political argument was so consistently evaded.
[9] As early as the Gladstone Report in 1895, the increasing number of habitual recidivists was registered as a problem, particularly in local prisons and in regard to offences against property. As the Report pointed out, the re-committal rate for simple larceny was as high as 78 per cent. (79 per cent. for larceny against the person) and more than half of all those convicted at Assizes or Quarter Sessions had undergone a previous conviction. By 1896 the Scottish Commissioners could report that over 500 of those committed in that year to Scottish prisons had been there more than 50 times before (Report of the Prison Commissioners for Scotland 1896, p. 7). Some indication of the alarm and concern caused by this problem in the early 1900s is given by J. F. Sutherland in the preface to his 1908 text on *Recidivism:* "Perhaps at no time within living memory has there been such activity and anxiety as is at present manifested by Ministers of State concerned with Home Affairs, by the executives responsible to them, by judges and magistrates, by social reformers, by the Salvation Army, by Churches, by philanthropic agencies, by publicists and by the press, to check recidivism." (Sutherland, 1908, p. v).

DAVID GARLAND

Finally, there was one more aspect of the status quo from which the new programme wished to assert its distance. It proclaimed itself wholeheartedly *against the compromises of "neo-classicism"* and its recommended practices. The neo-classical school (Joly, Rossi, etc.), with its revision of the classical doctrines, had some success in establishing itself within the judicial systems of Europe in the late nineteenth century (*cf.* Taylor *et al.*, 1973). Concepts such as "diminished responsibility" and "extenuating circumstances" appeared to prefigure the new programme and to represent one way in which its demands might be met. Against this the new criminologists resolutely set their face. While Ferri (1917, p. 372) contemptuously dismissed this "compromise with reason" Garafalo addressed himself to the practical logic of the neo-classicists and its potential results. As far as he was concerned neo-classicism had modified the rules of classicism in a manner which actually weakened their capacity for social defence. Notions of "partial responsibility" and of "extenuating circumstances" remained firmly in the jurisprudential paradigm (of responsibility, guilt and punishment) while simultaneously *reducing* the degree to which offenders would be sanctioned. In terms of logic and practice this compromise had less in common with the new criminology than did classicism itself, as Garafalo (1914, p. xxv) indicates in the following *reductio ad absurdum*: "Now there are but few cases in which the offender is without some 'extenuating circumstances'. In fact there is no crime in which it is not easy to discover them. It requires but a slight investigation and they swarm on all sides. In short, the only criminals who appear to us to be without excuse, and those for whom we have not taken the trouble to find it." And the practical effect of this infinite regress into the realms of good excuse would, for Garafalo, seem to be: ". . . the acquittal of the most ferocious type of murderer [for] once establish his extreme natural brutality or the irresistability of his criminal impulses, and no shred of moral responsibility remains. The outcome of every case would be the proportionate diminution of punishment, according as the causes of the evil inclinations become better known."

In terms of its conceptual logic and in its practical implications for sanctioning, the neo-classical compromise was seen as an *impediment* to the new programme rather than an early form of its implementation. As such it was criticised and ridiculed along with the other elements of the judicial status quo. However, there was one very important (if unacknowledged) sense in which neo-classicist concepts and procedures did prepare the ground for the new programme, acting as an intermediary between classical jurisprudence and the scientism of criminology. This concerned the question of *knowledge*.

If there had to be a single term which was to stand for the difference between the old system of criminal jurisprudence and the new criminology, this would be, above all, the element of "knowledge" in regard to the offender. For classicism it was an article of faith that each individual (excepting the mad and the infant) possessed the faculties of will, responsibility and reason. These qualities were deemed to be known in

THE CRIMINAL AND HIS SCIENCE

advance, a universal *a priori* without need of positive proof. This *a priorism* obviated the need for a personal investigation of the accused who, in the absence of any glaring evidence of irresponsibility, could simply be presumed a full legal subject. As far as the new criminologists were concerned, this judicial attitude was merely a prejudiced ignorance with regard to the criminal—an *absence* of knowledge masquerading as intuitive truth. No wonder classicism had failed in the war against crime—it preferred to indulge its prejudices rather than recognise its foe: ". . . to fight with any hope of success we must know our enemy. The enemy which we are called upon to face is unknown to the followers of the judicial school. Knowledge of him comes only from long-continued observation in prisons, penitentiaries and penal colonies." (Garafalo, 1914, p. xxxiii).

Criminology's mission was to supply this precious knowledge; to extend the inquiries of penal science "into regions where our fathers could see nothing at all . . ." (Whiteway, 1898, p. 25). Albert Wilson (1908, p. 204) put it nicely when he said: "When a criminal is caught . . . his case should be sifted from before the time when he saw daylight. The questions to settle are: Who are you? How are you? Why are you? What are you?"

This inquiry, and the "vast field of re-examination" which it opened up, was to be the proper domain of criminological science. Indeed criminology *was* just this knowledge, in the same way that classicism was the framework of judicial premises which were now in question. And the point to be made about the neo-classical revision was that it formed a kind of bridge between these two forms of discourse and procedure. Of course it retained the premises of classicism while modifying their practical application—and it was this reformist retention which was so heavily criticised. But the fact was that this modification introduced, in a routine and systematic way, *questions of knowledge* in regard to offenders: questions regarding their degree of responsibility (and consequently their mental state, their personality, etc.); questions regarding their circumstances (and so their history, their finances, their families). And though the basis and terms of inquiry proposed by criminology were quite other than those of this compromise position, there can be no doubt that neo-classicism supplied a definite opening through which criminology would later approach the judicial establishment.

Theoretical Resources—Arguments, Concepts and Evidence in the Criminological Programme

Until now I have characterised the new criminology negatively (against classical jurisprudence) and historically (emerging from a number of conditions of existence). In this section I will begin to describe the positive content of this new programme by reference to its theoretical resources and principles, setting out the characteristics which give this new discourse its specifically criminological character.

If one reads through the vast range of criminological literature which had appeared at the turn of the century, the most notable feature which emerges is the remarkable unity which characterises those texts. Despite

DAVID GARLAND

their international origins and the differences of detail, they express a
remarkable unity of purpose and of principle. This unity goes beyond a
common commitment to positivist methods and eclectic procedures to
include many other shared positions, arguments and recommendations
which are not entailed by their "scientific" orientation. This common
theoretical structure emerged from a general commitment to a number of
positions which could be listed as *differentiation* and *individualisation, pathology*
and *correctionalism,* and finally *interventionism* and *statism.*

These general positions did not appear as such in the texts themselves.
Rather they were implicit in the premises of arguments, the selected objects
and objectives of research, or else the particular choice of recommendations
which followed. Consequently, if we wish to present evidence of these
shared positions, we must do so at the level of the explicit textual
arguments which were presented, showing what these arguments were, and
how they entailed the general positions which have been listed. Before
doing so, however, we might simply note that these shared positions were
supported by more than the theoretical logic of individual texts. The
criminological enterprise was a self-conscious social movement, geared to a
very definite practical programme and supported by a number of
motivated organisations and institutions. The uniformity and repetitive-
ness of criminological discourse owed as much to this movement and its
scientific crusade as to its own internal logic.

I have already referred to criminology as the field of inquiry and
knowledge which follows from the question "what in fact *is* the criminal?"
This question, which forms the basis of criminology, already presupposes a
number of operations which allow such a problem to be meaningfully
posed. Thus, as we have seen, it assumes a position of *individualisation* which
fixes the individual as the proper object and unit of analysis,[10] and a
differentiation which hypothesises a qualitative and substantiated difference
between the criminal individual and his law-abiding counterpart.

The first of these two positions—individualisation—is not difficult to
comprehend. As we saw, it was written into the established system of law
and of criminal justice and was a position shared by the classical
jurisprudential framework. "Differentiation", however, is a position quite
at odds with that jurisprudence and its specified system of law, even if, as
we saw, it was promoted by the prison and by contemporary political
strategies. In classical jurisprudence the only difference between criminal
and non-criminal is a contingent event: one has chosen, on occasion, to
behave in a criminal fashion while the other has not. This difference of
conduct reveals nothing beyond itself. The individual in each case is
assumed to be similarly constituted—as a free, rational, human subject.

Criminology founds itself in a re-interpretation of this logic. Having
rejected the "metaphysics" of free-will and chosen action, the difference
beween criminal and non-criminal takes on an entirely new significance.
The law of universal determinism abolishes the realm of contingency and

[10] *Cf.* Healy (1915, p. 22): "The dynamic center of the whole problem of delinquency and crime will
ever be the individual offender."

THE CRIMINAL AND HIS SCIENCE

freedom and demands that phenomena—even human phenomena—be viewed in terms of cause and effect. As Spinoza put it, "consciousness of our liberty is but ignorance of the causes which make us act". Consequently the difference between an individual who offends and one who does not is no longer a contingent or formal matter. It is a difference of substance and necessity. A criminal offends because he is caused to do so in a way which a non-criminal is not; "crime is a detected sign, symptom and result of a human personal condition" (Boies, 1901, p. 35). In a single operation "freedom" is replaced by determinism, the criminal is differentiated in a qualitative fashion, and the search for the causes of crime begins.

If we follow this operation through its various stages we can clearly see how the criminological enterprise is discursively established. First of all, the critique of human "freedom", based, as we have seen, upon the method of positivism and the data of psychiatry: "Free-will is a delusion. Human movements, the actions of men, like the other movements of the world, obey natural laws . . . the first of these laws is that nothing is created out of nothing. All things are engendered." (De Fleury, 1901, p. 57).

Following from this, a move from a *philosophy* of freedom to a *psychology* of human behaviour and its determinants. This move entails a radical re-ordering of the elements of human action. It rejects the spritual notion of the Ego as sovereign, "the absolute monarch of Consciousness and of Will" (De Fleury, 1901, p. 35). It rejects the idea of an intangible and unknowable point of creativity and choice—the human soul. In place of this spiritual essence is fixed an entity which has definite conditions and is amenable to investigation and perhaps even change—the *personality* or *character* of the individual. This personality "is not one and independent" but is rather complex and "constituted" (De Fleury, 1901, p. 32). Thus Garafalo (1914, p. 274): "We know that the Ego cannot create itself, and that the character has already been formed by a series of anterior facts." and Claye Shaw (1902–04): "It is personal character that is the ultimate cause of volition. . . . Instead of will being free, it is, in fact, a determined process." This "personality" or "character" depends for its construction upon "hereditary, physiological and social circumstances" (Hollander, 1908. p. 2), and forms the basis and proximate source of individual conduct.

The implications of this philosophy-to-psychology shift are complex and wide-ranging. To begin with, it promotes the possibility of a *positive* knowledge of human subjects. As Saleilles (1913, p. 184) put it, "In the newer view the personality . . . becomes amenable to a precise psychological analysis"; and it is upon this knowledge that criminology stakes its claim to be a superior form of discourse regarding the criminal. Secondly, it provided a new object to be assessed and administered in the courts of law: "The terms of free will and responsibility must be reconsidered in the light of fresh knowledge. We are but machines of varying potential, endurance and capacity, and according to the quality of the mechanism so we should be judged." (Wilson, 1908, p. 236). Finally it opens up the possibility of techniques which can *transform* this object and its determinants. As De

DAVID GARLAND

Fleury (1901, p. 21) vividly put it, ". . . the soul is there, under our scalpel".

The next stage in this operation is a simple question of logical differentiation. If personality or character is the basis of individual behaviour, then different forms of behaviour signify different forms of character. The criminal act now signifies more than itself, being a sign of the criminal character from which it sprang. As Boies (1901, p. 38) phrased it, "Criminal moral depravity is an actual condition of individual character, not a transitory passion or disposition". And for criminologists at least, this logic was amply confirmed by experience: as Marro (quoted in Garafalo, 1914, p. 67) put it, "all who deal with the physical study of the criminal are forced to the conclusion that he is a being apart", to which Garafalo adds, "Few who have ever visited a prison or penitentiary will maintain the contrary."

Thus by a process of differentiation and classification, tracing effects back to causes, criminology arrives at the distinctive "criminal character". It is at this point we see the introduction of the "pathological principle". According to the logic of the operation so far, we have the identification of a character-object and its classification according to the type of behaviour it promotes. As yet, there is no hierarchy of character-types. The introduction of the notion of *pathology* fixes a definite norm of social and individual "health" and places the criminal character below that norm. It becomes a "theorem" of criminology:

> "that criminality is a diseased condition of human character." (Boies, 1901, p. 35).

> "the delinquent is not a normal man; . . . on the contrary he represents a special class, a variation on the human race through organic or physical abnormalities, either hereditary or acquired." (Ferri, 1917, p. 38).

> ". . . crime is *always* the effect of an anomaly or of a pathological condition. . . ." (Ferri, 1917, p. xl).

We should note that the uncontentious entry of this principle marks another point at which social and political criteria are directly inscribed into the categories of criminological discourse. Criminal behaviour ceases to be a violation of conventional norms and becomes instead a deviation from "the normal". And in treating social deviance as personal pathology, the implication must be that the laws of the land correspond to the minimal standards of behavioural health and normality. Criminology is this fixed in its place as a correctionalist discipline, fundamentally uncritical of existing legal and social relations.

We have, then, the notion of criminal behaviour as a product and expression of a distinctive pathological entity, "the criminal character". Or rather, since the personality is deemed to be complex and not singular, we have "criminality" as a pathological element of individual character. In this concept of criminality, criminology finds both its *raison d'être* and its *practicable object*. For if criminality is the source of criminal behaviour, then

124

THE CRIMINAL AND HIS SCIENCE

a systematic knowledge of it—a criminology—is obviously necessary. And once known and identified, this object should clearly become the target for—the practicable object of—investigation, observation and finally transformation.

But we should pause here long enough to note that the evidence for this entity—for the crucial phenomenon of criminality—is entirely external and inferential. Criminality has not been discovered, traced or identified in any direct sense which would allow us to see it, touch it, isolate it, or identify its mechanisms and mode of operation. Instead it is an entity which is speculatively inferred from a diverse variety of behavioural conducts, unified only by their common violation of something called the "criminal law". And this speculation is "confirmed", not by the positive proof of direct observation (which one is entitled to expect from positivist science) but instead by a rag-bag amalgam of differences and stigmata which investigators claim to have discovered in the bodies and features of the criminal (most of them socially conditioned or within the spectrum of normal variation in human characteristics). "Criminality" then is no less a metaphysical construct than the classical "free-will" and "reason" which it seeks to replace, though its claimed status and forms of argumentation suggest just the opposite.

In claiming to have discovered criminality in the bodies or the brains or the "milieux" of criminals, criminology claimed a social and scientific space for itself. In the century that has passed since that discovery that space has been expanded and extensively worked over, and the position and character of criminality has been repeatedly reviewed and relocated. It has been seen as an entity which completely characterises an individual as "the criminal type" or, more recently, as a more limited characteristic which can affect individuals, families and even neighbourhoods. Nevertheless, criminologists have remained committed to this hypostatised object for the simple reason that without its existence there can be no grounding for criminology as an independent discourse or discipline. The discovery of criminality, then, is the discovery of criminology itself. Henceforth its mission would be, in its theoretical phase, to *investigate* criminality, and in its practical phase (*qua* penology) to *eliminate* criminality from the individual and from society itself.

(a) *The investigation of criminality*

If the discovery of criminality founds a science of its further investigation, it also sets in place the need for further investigative procedures, apparatuses and qualified personnel. Consequently it was a constant demand of the criminological programme that the legal system should open itself up to a staff of non-legal experts. The precise nature of the required expertise varied according to the predelictions of the criminologist in question—thus B. Hollander (himself an M.D.) maintained that "crime calls for intelligent and scientific treatment which lies with the future learning of the medical profession" (Hollander, 1908, p. 13) while Albert

DAVID GARLAND

Wilson (1908, p. 236) insisted that criminals "require careful examination ... not by the police, the lawyer or even the judge but by the expert psychologist", and Lydston (1904, p. 599) recommends "the direction of wise and experienced men of broad information and a thorough knowledge of the physical aspect of crime and of the principles of sociology". Other demands were less specific, calling for "medico-psychologic examinations by psychologic physicians" or merely "highly and specially trained persons", but the consistent thrust of the programme was for the introduction of an expert staff of a non-legal character.

Indeed the desire of the criminological argument was to shift the very object of forensic investigation away from "the criminal fact" and towards "the criminality of the agent as revealed by the fact" (Garafalo, 1914, p. 408). And if lawyers, judges and judicial procedures had been adequate to the investigation of "acts" and "facts", the investigation of criminality required quite other means. Hence the demand for assessment centres, "mental and physical observatories", "court clinics" and a revised criminal procedure which accorded these apparatuses their due authority (cf. Elliot, 1929). Hence the call for: "The development of machinery adequate to the requirements of the psychiatric point of view in criminal trials and hearings including court clinics and psychiatrists and ultimately a routine compulsory psychiatric examination of all offenders with latitude and authority in the recommendations made to the court as to the disposition and treatment of the prisoner." (Elliot, 1929, p. 36–37) If, as Ferri (1917, p. vi) claimed, "the great truth of the present and the future for criminal science" lay in "the individualisation of penal treatment—for that man, and for the cause of that man's crime", then this individualisation implied a very definite process or procedure. It implied firstly *observation* and, on that basis, the *production of information and knowledge* concerning the individual and his criminality. From this springs the demand for an investigative apparatus which would provide the materials for criminology as a positive scientific knowledge *and* for penology as the application of that knowledge in the practical sphere. It then implied a system of *assessment, classification* and *differentiation,* which entailed the demand for trained "diagnostic" personnel, and the endless production of classificatory schemes and typologies. Finally, as we shall see, it implied a wide and differentiated array of sanctions, dispositions and treatments which would be adequate to the different categories, forms and types of individual criminality.

(b) *The elimination of criminality*

I have emphasised throughout this discussion of the criminological programme that criminology was no innocent academic pursuit but in fact an applied, disciplinary discourse which aimed to establish itself in the institutions and practices of power. I also noted that the object which formed the focus of scientific investigation—namely criminality—was at the same time a *practicable object,* the focus of policy demands and practices.

126

THE CRIMINAL AND HIS SCIENCE

Criminality was to be an object of disinterested research but also the target for penal practices and forms of regulation. It was a scientific problem but also a social problem to be addressed, atacked and transformed. In view of this crucial unity of theory and practice it comes as no surprise to find that the criminological programme was heavily committed to a definite *penology,* and that, moreover, the common theoretical and discursive positions identified above were tied to a shared programme of practical demands and recommendations.

Having identified criminality as the real source of criminal behaviour, the practical programme of the criminologists addressed itself solely to this object and its elimination (it was not until later that "containment" came to be seen as a more realistic objective). Whereas the old system had punished the criminal for having "chosen" crime and then had set him free to make the same choice again, the new criminology aimed to remove his criminality once and for all. Given the existence of criminality, three separate modes of elimination were available. First of all, criminality might be *reformed.* The individual criminal might be transformed in some way which brought about his social adaptation or re-attachment—his character might be transformed and his criminality cured.[11] Secondly, where such reform was impossible or impractical, criminality might simply be *extinguished.* Thus the incorrigible criminal could be executed, transported, or else permanently segregated in such a way as to remove his criminality from the social body. Finally, for the future, criminality might be *prevented.* If the determinants and causes of criminality could themselves be altered or eliminated, then new generations could be immunised against the condition and its gradual extinction could be achieved.

In fact, all three of these modes or objectives were concurrently proposed by nearly all of the criminological texts and manifestoes. Thus Henry Boies: "The unintermitted, continual restraint of the incorrigible criminal, the reformation of the curable, and the wholesome rearing of every child constitute the triplicate solution by Science of the social problem of Criminality." (Boies, 1901, p. 447). And again: "The problem is resolved into three elementary phases, those of prevention, of reformation, and of extinction—the last the most important of all." (Boies, 1893, p. 292). Or the 1906 Turin Congress: "To instruct ignorant criminals, to reform the corrigible, to prevent the incurable from offending, are the duties which the State must fulfil with loyalty and zeal." (Congress resolution, quoted in De Quiros, 1911, p. 96). Finally Enrico Ferri: "In sociological medicine, the great classes of hygienic measures (preventive means), therapeutic remedies (reparative and repressive means) and surgical operations (eliminative means) form the arsenal which enables society to face the permanent means of its own preservation." (Ferri, 1917, p. 420)

Criminality was thus to be eliminated, either by prevention, reformation or extinction. This triple strategy required not only procedures of

[11] This was variously described as "correctionalism" or "penal tutelage" (De Quiros, 1911) or even "moral orthopaedics" (Hall, 1917, p. 409) as well as simply "reformation". It implied positive techniques of transformation, not just the provision of space or time for the individual to will his own improvement.

DAVID GARLAND

assessment and classification which could identify offenders as corrigible or incorrigible, but also a *diversity of dispositions, sanctions and techniques* to implement these objectives. Thus we find that a major demand of the criminologists was for an extended repertoire of penal sanctions and institutions,[12] including juvenile reformatories, preventive detention institutions, institutions for inebriates, for the feeble-minded, a variety of prison regimes, forms of supervision, conditional liberation, indeterminate sentences and "pre-delinquent interventions". And although there was a degree of variation between different criminologists in their lists of recommended sanctions—particularly in regard to more controversial innovations such as sterilisation or execution—by and large most of these sanctions were given general endorsement.[13]

There was thus a remarkable consistency in the positions, arguments and recommendations proposed by the various proponents of the new criminological programme. Indeed, if we were to take this further and identify the specific topics which were most discussed by criminologists we would discover that it was the same few issues and problem-categories which are discussed over and over again in the literature. Nor was this choice arbitrary or coincidental: the favoured items of discussion— juveniles, habituals, the feeble-minded, the inebriate—were precisely those items on which either "science" or social policy had most to say. The most "easily explained" categories (the undeveloped juvenile, the disturbed defective) or else the most dangerous (the habitual, the professional thief) were those used to provide exemplary models of criminality which could then be extended to apply to offenders who were neither dangerous nor, in any conventional sense, defective.

What was the basis of this consistency? How could this new discourse establish such stability and uniformity in such a small space of time and over such a large, international terrain? The answer to such a question can only be tentative and, to a certain degree, speculative. Nonetheless, I would suggest that the consistency of this early criminological discourse does not lie in scientific truth, frequently discovered, but is a product of (1) the simple repetition or paraphrasing of earlier work, and (2) the theoretical implications of the ideological ("social problem") basis of the discourse. If one reads closely the texts of the criminological programme in this period, there is a surprising shortage of any actual research of positive data underlying their statements. To a considerable extent these texts are simply commentaries, compilations or glosses upon other, earlier texts often adding little in the way of new or substantial information. Despite its claims to be a positive science, criminology in this early period more nearly resembles a new theology with its dogmas, glosses and evangelists. Hence

[12] *Cf.* The resolution of the 1906 Turin Congress: ". . . the Judge must be given the power to choose, with unlimited freedom and according to the exigencies of the individual case, from a series of measures . . .." Quoted in De Quiros (1911, p. 98). See also Ellis (1910, p. xxv).
[13] For typical lists of these recommended sanctions, see Boies (1901) and the resolutions of the Congress of Cincinatti (1870), quoted in Ruggles-Brise (1925). As will later be argued, it is significant that most of the major sanctions and techniques recommended by the criminology programme actually pre-dated it. Thus for example the Cincinatti resolutions of 1870 are in most respects identical with the criminological recommendations of 40 years later.

ffff

THE CRIMINAL AND HIS SCIENCE

the remarkable degree of repetition and the static nature of the discipline through time.

As for its theoretical foundations, criminology had tied itself to a search for the antecedent, observable causes of criminal behaviour. Its commitment to a positivist methodology of observation, correlation and induction meant that it was fundamentally *eclectic* in character, prepared to encompass any number of factors in its explanations. Consequently, different causal explanations, involving different "factors" and determinants, were not always seen as competing or contradictory accounts. For instance, after the initial period of debate between proponents of biological and of social factors, most explanations took on an eclectic multi-factorial approach which simply listed a multitude of factors in a bid for comprehensiveness rather than coherence. This *additive, eclectic* character is well illustrated by Ferri's text *Criminal Sociology* which was 160 pages long when it first appeared in 1884, but by the fifth, 1900 edition, had reached 1,000 pages through the accumulation of other "relevant factors" derived from the growing literature on crime. This massive eclecticism was in turn possible because, as we have seen, criminology's object and direction of inquiry were dictated not by scientific discovery but by practical social policy concerns. "Criminality" was a social problem demanding a "scientific" solution and its investigators were committed more to that solution than to any single or coherent theory of human behaviour.

This social problem orientation brings me to my final point in this section. Underlying the concern to provide new principles and procedures for penal regulation there is the constant figure of the State as the presumed subject of this enterprise. Just as classical jurisprudence had organised itself around a liberal conception of the State/individual relation, criminology too assumed that the State and the individual were the proper subject and object of this process—though the nature of these terms and their relationships were fundamentally revised, moving from a liberal mode to a more authoritarian, interventionist one. In particular, criminology's arguments were explicitly directed towards an increased interventionism on the part of the State, and to a new conception of the individual and the means employed against him. But this assumption that the central State is indeed the proper subject of this process (and not private organisations, or more localised administrations), and the political arguments and ideologies which might justify such a position, are so entrenched in this programme that they go mostly unspoken. At one point we see Saleilles object strongly to the private nature of Brockway's experiments in the United States, insisting that only the State can be entrusted with the penal function, and occasionally Conference resolutions are explicit about "State establishment and control," but more often the issue is passed over in the silence of self-evidence.[14] However, in his statement of the "Principles of Scientific Penology" Boies supplies us with an expression of this basic principle and

[14] See Ruggles-Brise (1925, p. 93) where this issue is discussed and Saleilles' objections quoted and endorsed. Also the Report on the Proceedings of the Seventh International Penitentiary Congress (1906, p. 26).

DAVID GARLAND

demonstrates that not only the politics but also the practical ambitions of criminology necessitate the State as their subject: "Scientific Penology is impossible, all social penal effort is futile, or worse than futile, unless it is initiated, directed and controlled by the State, so that it shall include every unit of the population within its constant scope and care." (Boies, 1901, p. 446).

Criminology's Social Implications

Having described at length the criminological programme, its conditions, structure and elements, the last few sections of this essay will briefly indicate the kind of social implications this movement entailed. I began by emphasising the pertinence of the new criminology to the political strategies of the 1890s. This pertinence lay in the *regulatory* and *ideological* possibilities offered by the new programme, possibilities which allowed the extension of effective disciplinary control while doing so in a manner which had strong claims to legitimacy. As we have seen, criminology allowed a *differentiation* to be produced which would mark off the field and population of criminality in stark contrast to the universalism of classical jurisprudence. The classical insistence that all men are equal, free and rational (derived from Christianity and humanism as well as from liberal theory) put definite limits upon the operation and presentation of regulatory forms. All subjects in law had to be seen to be treated equally, impartially and without differentiation. Only by their acts could they be judged and on that basis alone the law was empowered to intervene in their affairs.[15] As a form of discipline, then, the traditional criminal law is severely limited. It functions through the specification and prohibition of definite acts and is thereby limited to the policing of these acts rather than the general inspection and control of individuals themselves. Moreover, the criminal law is inextricably bound up with the question of legitimacy. Its prohibitions are a public declaration of the limits of individual freedom and require to be justified as such. Its intersection with the discourse of political obligation precludes it from functioning with the requisite discretion, flexibility or penetration. The advantages of criminology lay in its rejection of this formal liberal egalitarianism. It insisted upon a qualitative differentiation which would trace out the dangerous classes and the real contours of criminality. But where this strategy differed from previous attempts to do this in the realm of charity or the Poor Law was in its terms and justifications. It abjured the blatant moralism and class bias of distinctions such as "deserving/undeserving" or "respectable/rough", which had anyway become politically intolerable by this time. Instead it phrased its distinctions in the terms of a "scientific" discourse which excluded any reference to politics or morality. The unspoken advantage of criminological discourse in this troubled period was its capacity to

---

[15] This is not to suggest that the law was actually practised in line with these ideals. But whenever it *was* partial, and took account of class or "character", it always risked scandal by this failure to conform to its public principles.

THE CRIMINAL AND HIS SCIENCE

differentiate in terms of "abnormality", "pathology" and the unquestioned norms of physical and mental "health".

At the end of the nineteenth century, an expanding franchise, mass unionisation of the unskilled, and the growing political force of the lower classes, made it less and less prudent to adopt openly repressive policies towards the poor. In this context, the obvious harshness and class bias which characterised criminal justice (as well as the Poor Law and "scientific charity") was an embarrassment which failed to disguise the grave social and economic inequalities which the law reproduced. The new criminology went some way towards relieving this legitimatory deficit. For one thing it offered a scientific and reformatory approach which promised to further the welfare of the State *and* the individual. For another, it characterised the problem of crime in a new way which radically divorced it from social and political processes. Crime was no longer an option resorted to by hard-pressed people whose conditions of life would explain their "choice". Instead it was an inevitable outcome of a particular kind of character or constitution.

The existence of a class which was constantly criminalised—indeed the very existence of an impoverished sector of the population—could now be explained by reference to the natural, constitutional propensities of these individuals, thereby excluding all reference to the character of the law, of politics or of social relations.

So differentiation was possible within more acceptable ideological terms. But this discursive shift also allowed a new and extended basis for disciplinary intervention and regulation. Firstly, because the range of the "abnormal" can exceed the "criminal", criminology allowed a wider scope for control than did the criminal law. Its proponents argued that the law was not an absolute measure of normality nor even the best one available. Individuals could behave within the terms of the law and yet be abnormal, dangerous and in need of control. In contrast, the terms of criminology permitted—indeed demanded—the firm regulation of all those groups such as inebriates, the feeble-minded, vagrants, epileptics and habituals which were previously "within the law" and hence "beyond control".[16] It even allowed the extension of this logic of pathology and normalising regulation to include the whole class of "paupers" and the destitute poor, as writers such as Henry Boies (1893) and the eugenists made perfectly clear.[17]

Secondly, criminology's purported ability to identify "criminality" in the bodies of criminals (and not merely in their acts) opened up the possibility of an *anticipatory* form of regulation. It produced the categories of the "pre-delinquent", the "near-criminal" or the "presumptive criminal" and

[16] See, for example, the Howard Association (1882, 1907, 1908, 1909 and 1910) which argue for such "provision" to be made for inebriates, epileptics and vagrants. As Thomas Holmes, Secretary of the Association, said in his letters to *The Times* and the *Daily Telegraph* of September 17, 1907: "The cry of the inebriate is heard all through the land, but unless the wretched victims succeed in getting into the hands of the police at least four times in one year the law does not heed the cry." See also Quinton (1910, p. 119) who would extend powers of detention to all of the "socially inefficient".

[17] See Darwin (1914–15 and 1926) and Rentoul (1903 and 1906). For a discussion of the mutual influences of the eugenic and criminological movements, see Garland (1985).

131

DAVID GARLAND

accompanied them with arguments for pre-emptive intervention: "It is evident, then, that the supreme function of the Science of Penology is the discovery of the infected members of society *before* their disease has become an actual offence." (Boies, 1901, p. 66).[18]

Finally, the shift of focus from the offender's act to the offender himself implied a new and more penetrating form of intervention. Sanctions were to be aimed not at meeting degrees of guilt but at transforming aspects of character. Questions of the duration, nature and seriousness of the sanction were not to be limited by considerations of desert or proportionality. Moreover, sanctions should be *personalised* or *individualised*, seeking to address the very fabric of the offender's person in a manner which need not be embarrassed by liberal considerations of individual freedom and privacy.

"The act", "guilt", "desert", "proportion", all of these were dismissed as the marks of an outdated and metaphysical system: "The new penology is no longer activated by vengeance and does not look at the moral gravity of the offence. . . . 'Judge not' is its maxim." (Hall, 1917, p. 393). In place of these judicial notions, criminology proposed standards of health, doctrines of utility, and measures of social defence. In this new logic the measure of an offence was not its intrinsic moral seriousness, but its capacity for repetition, its potential for generalisation, its symptomatic value (*cf.* Foucault, 1977, pp. 92–93). "Punishment is measured by the perversity of the criminal" and not his crime, and accordingly attempt is no different from action and proclivity no less dangerous than actual practice.[19]

But if the framework of judicial reasoning was to be abandoned, along with the limitations and restraints of legality, what stood between the penal system and a completely arbitrary power? In fact this vital question was all but absent from the discussions of the criminologists, being explicitly framed only by Raymond Saleilles (1913, pp. 51 and 97) who warned against replacing the "objectivism" of the classical regime with a "subjectivism" which would allow complete and arbitrary discretion.[20] But Saleilles' solution to this problem, and the solution which most criminologists assumed without the necessity of argument, was an objective code of scientific norms and standards which prescribed the proper ideals of moral,

[18] *Cf.* Castel (1975, p. 252): ". . . mental medicine was trying to erect a new apparatus . . . an intervention which would not always be bound to come too late, for it would be based on a knowledge capable of *anticipating the possibility* of criminal behaviour before the act was put into execution." De Quiros (1911, p. 127) provides the term "near criminals". Boies (1901, p. 60) argues that the identification of "Presumptive Criminals" is "a sufficient substitute for judicial decision" and it is within this context that we must understand his demand that the Bertillon system of identification be used to record the details of every individual over ten years old in the population.

[19] *Cf.* Garafalo (1914, p. 312): "Once punishment is measured by the perversity of the criminal, the question of attempt by insufficient means completely disappears. If the attempt, quite as much as the executed crime, suffices to reveal the criminality of the agent, there can be no difference between the two."

[20] Jeffrey (1960, p. 388) mentions the Spanish criminologist Pedro Dorado Montrero as worthy of interest because he "placed emphasis on the protection of individual rights and the limitation of the power of the State". In fact as Lopez-Rey (1960, pp. 320–21) argues, Montrero believed that the interests of the "Individual and Society" become identical in the process of correction: "In the application of penal treatment, the individual rights should be considered as subordinated to the effectiveness of such treatment aimed at the moral correction of the offender."

THE CRIMINAL AND HIS SCIENCE

mental and physical health. It is an important testimony to the nature of this movement that these norms and ideals—the actual values and standards which were presupposed whenever pathologies or differentiations or rehabilitation were discussed—were never explicitly identified or adequately described. Usually these norms were simply assumed, unstated, on the basis that reasonable men from a similar social situation were talking one to the other, sharing a framework of values and ideologies which could go unsaid. Bradley (1893–94, p. 270) illustrates this assumption well when, in his argument for "social surgery" and the "unrestricted right" of the community in this regard, he begins: "We may leave welfare undefined, and for present purposes need not distinguish the community from the State." It was thus left to the wisdom of science and the mutual understandings of reasonable men to indentify and act upon "objective" standards of social health. Law was to be replaced by "normalisation"; punishments by the improvement of characters, the identification and repair of behavioural abnormalities; but no one saw any need to debate or even describe the actual norms to be imposed through these procedures.

The major implication of the criminological programme was perhaps this social engineering capability which it claimed to offer. Criminology would replace the ineffectual niceties of legal punishment by practical technologies involving diagnostic, preventative and curative instruments and institutions. Criminality was now a knowable positive entity which, with the aid of scientific investigation and appropriate practical techniques could be removed from the social body. But if we examine these claims carefully we find that the programme repeatedly offered *arguments* and *legitimations* for intervention, but actually offered few effective *means* of carrying this out. In fact, if we consider the techniques and apparatuses proposed at this time, it becomes evident that the powerful claims of criminology in this regard were somewhat lacking in technological substance.

Perhaps the most repetitive aspect of what is generally a rather repetitive literature is the section in each text devoted to penological techniques. One finds that again and again the same items appear on the pages— "reformative" prisons, indeterminate sentences, supervisory orders, preventive detention of one form or another, partial or complete "elimination" through deportation, sterilisation or even execution. And while these recommended sanctions may differ from those displayed by the classical system, they hardly amount to a technical repertoire of prevention and rehabilitation. Certainly the demand for reformatories, indeterminate sentences, supervision and so on, provided a *space* for characters to be transformed, but the point is that very little discussion addressed the question of exactly how this transformation was to be achieved. Criminology, despite its claims, provided few techniques of its own to support its social engineering ambitions.

There were of course grand-sounding schemes involving "neuro-electricity in the service of penitentiary work", technical inventions like the

133

DAVID GARLAND

"plethysmograph",[21] or else special regimes of physical exercise for the training of adolescents, but these were invoked by way of impressive illustration and were never discussed in any detail. Instead rehabilitation had to rely upon the unspecified effects of "personal influence" and "the power of a normal or healthy personality" to overcome criminal tendencies (Pepler, 1915, pp. 4–5). Prison training should involve physical, intellectual and moral aspects—but then it always had done, with little notable success.

In fact the only area in which any real technical advance took place concerned the development of identification techniques. Anthropometry, finger-printing, the Bertillon system, elaborate systems which marked the bodies of ex-offenders with a sign language of indelible marks, and various other identification techniques, were extensively discussed and developed, not least because they had the full backing and support of police and prison authorities in every country.[22]

The technical armoury provided by the criminological movement thus amounted to a number of elaborate identification techniques, a range of eliminative means such as deportation, labour colonies, preventive detention, etc. which owed little to criminological theory, and a faith that medicine and psychiatry could be relied upon to provide effective rehabilitative techniques, if not now, at least in the near future. In terms of its technological profile, then, the criminology programme offered an effective social defence—through eliminative means and police techniques—but little in the way of prevention[23] or rehabilitation. However much it described itself as a curative programme, what was actually on offer was a technology of segregative control.

A final social implication which may be noted here is the promotion of an extended Statism, which in turn entailed the promotion of certain professions and functionaries at the expense of others.[24] Criminology implied an elevation in the status and power of the likes of prison executives, forensic scientists, psychiatrists and other "penological experts". It widened the fields of medicine, psychiatry and even sociology to cover what has previously been a judicial domain, and sought to effect a shift of power away from the judiciary and towards a non-legal executive staff. In part, then, the theoretical debates between criminology and

[21] Bruck-Faber suggested "neuro-electricity" at the 1906 Turin Congress (quoted in De Quiros. 1911, p. 96). The "plethysmograph"—a device for testing variations in the circulation of the blood. resting for its usefulness upon the way the circulation "responds to what is passing in the mind"—was invented by Mosso and is endorsed by Lombroso (1911, p. 253).

[22] See De Quiros (1911) and especially Gross (1911). *The Report of the Departmental Commission on the Identification of Habitual Criminals* (1894) demonstrates the early official adoption of registry systems. using anthropometric systems such as the Bertillon method, and also the finger-printing method developed by Sir William Herschel and Francis Galton. These systems were soon extended to include most prisoners and convicted offenders—often at the instigation of Chief Constables of Police. See S.P.R.O. HH. 35/4.

[23] Some writers, such as Bonger (1916), Ferri (1917) or Devon (1912) offered ideas for prevention, but these were derived from socialist or social reform programmes and were not theoretically integrated into criminological discourse. This splitting off of an individualistic criminology from the study of social relations was a crucial development with important policy implications. See footnotes 4 and 10.

[24] *Cf.* Boies (1901, p. 438): "The State must provide skilled penologists to superintend the treatment of all convicts."

THE CRIMINAL AND HIS SCIENCE

classicism concealed a competition between professions seeking to advance or defend their positions in the social division of labour. But the significance of this debate was not confined to the level of theory or even to the level of professional competition in the "administration of deviance". The challenge which criminology posed to legalism, and the rival principles and values carried by these contesting professions, had a profound ideological significance which, though rarely acknowledged, was at the very heart of this struggle. As we have seen, the challenge posed by criminological discourse to established concepts such as individual "freedom", "responsibility", "rationality" and "rights" raised major political and ideological issues and offered important possibilities for the wider field of social politics and legitimation. The extent to which criminology has succeeded in its struggle for a place in the institutions of power is, then, a powerful index of the political transformations which have occurred in the last hundred years, and the place of this "human science" within them.

REFERENCES

BOIES, H. M. (1893). *Prisoners and Paupers,* New York: G. P. Putnams.

BOIES, H. M. (1901). *The Science of Penology,* London: Putnams.

BONGER, W. A. (1916), *Criminality and Economic Conditions,* Boston: Little, Brown and Co.

BRADLEY, F. H. (1893–94). "Some Remarks on Punishment", in *The International Journal of Ethics,* No. IV.

CASTEL, R. (1975). "The Doctors and Judges", in Foucault, M. (ed.), *I, Pierre Rivière,* Harmondsworth: Penguin.

CLAYE SHAW (1902–04). "Impulsive Insanity", in *The Transactions of the Medico-Legal Society.*

COHEN, S. (1974). "Criminology and the Sociology of Deviance in Britain", in Rock, P. and McIntosh, M. (eds.), *Deviance and Social Control,* London: Tavistock.

CULLEN, M. J. (1975). *The Statistical Movement in Early Victorian Britain,* Hassocks: Harvester Press.

DARWIN, L. (1914–15). "The Habitual Criminal", in *The Eugenics Review,* No. 6.

DARWIN, L. (1926). *The Need for Eugenic Reform,* London: John Murray.

DE FLEURY, M. (1901). *The Criminal Mind,* London: Downey and Co.

DE QUIROS, B. (1911). *Modern Theories of Criminality,* London: Heinemann.

DEVON, J. (1912). *The Criminal and the Community,* London: John Lane.

ELLIOT, M. A. (1929). "Conflicting Theories of Penology in certain phases of criminal statutory legislation in thirteen states from 1900–1927", Ph.D. Thesis, Northwestern University.

ELLIS, H. (1910). *The Criminal* (1st edition, 1889), London: Contemporary Science Series.

FERRI, E. (1917). *Criminal Sociology,* London: Heinemann.

FOUCAULT, M. (1972). *The Archaeology of Knowledge,* London: Tavistock.

DAVID GARLAND

FOUCAULT, M. (1977). *Discipline and Punish: The Birth of the Prison,* London: Allen Lane.

GARAFALO, R. (1914). *Criminology,* London: Heinemann.

GARLAND, D. (1985 forthcoming). *Punishment and Welfare,* London: Heinemann.

GATRELL, V. and HADDEN, T. (1972). "Criminal Statistics and their Interpretation", in Wrigley, E. (ed.), *Nineteenth Century Society,* Oxford: Oxford University Press.

GORING, C. (1913). *The English Convict,* Prison Commission. London: H.M.S.O.

GOULD, S. J. (1984). *The Mismeasure of Man.* Harmondsworth: Penguin.

GROSS, H. (1911). *Criminal Investigation,* London: Heinemann.

GUERRY, A. M. (1833). *Essai sur la statistique morale de la France,* Paris.

HALL, W. CLARKE (1917). *The State and the Child,* New Commonwealth Books.

HEALY, W. (1915). *The Individual Delinquent,*

HOLLANDER, B. (1908). *Crime and Responsibility,* London: Ethological Society.

HOWARD ASSOCIATION (1907–10). *Crime of the Empire and its Treatment.* Annual Reports of the Howard Association for promoting the most efficient means of penal treatment and crime prevention. (1907, 1908, 1909, 1910), London.

INTERNATIONAL PENAL AND PENITENTIARY FOUNDATION, THE (1951). *Modern Methods of Penal Treatment,* Paris.

JEFFREY, C. R. (1960). "The Historical Development of Criminology", in Mannheim, H., *Pioneers in Criminology,* London: Stevens and Sons.

JONES, G. STEDMAN (1971). *Outcast London: A Study in the Relationship between Classes in Victorian Society,* Oxford: Clarendon Press.

LINDESMITH, L. and LEVIN, Y. (1971). "English Ecology and Criminology of the Past Century", in Carson, W. G. and Wiles, P. (eds.), *Crime and Delinquency in Britain,* Oxford: Martin Robertson.

LOMBROSO, C. (1876). *L'Uomo Delinquente,* Milan: Hoepli (5th edition, Turin: Bocca).

LOMBROSO, C. (1911). *Crime, Its Causes and Its Remedies,* London: Heinemann.

LOPEZ-REY, M. (1960). "Pedro Dorado Montero", in Mannheim, H. (ed.), *Pioneers in Criminology,* London: Stevens and Sons.

LYDSTON, G. FRANK (1904). *The Diseases of Society (the Vice and Crime Problem).* London.

MANNHEIM, H. (1960). *Pioneers in Criminology,* London: Stevens and Sons.

MATZA, D. (1964). *Delinquent and Drift.* New York: Wiley.

MCKENZIE, D. (1981). *Statistics in Britain, 1835–1930,* Edinburgh: Edinburgh University Press.

MORRIS, T. (1957). *The Criminal Area,* London: Routledge and Kegan Paul.

PEPLER, H. D. (1915). *Justice and the Child.* London: Constable and Co.

QUETELET, L. A. J. (1835). *Essai du Physique Sociale.* Bruxelles.

QUINTON, R. F. (1910). *Crime and Criminals.* London: Longmans.

RADZINOWICZ, L. (1966). *Ideology and Crime.* London: Heinemann.

RENTOUL, R. R. (1903). *Proposed Sterilization of Certain Mental and Physical Degenerates: An Appeal to Asylum Managers and Others.* London: Walter Scott Publications.

RENTOUL, R. R. (1906). *Race Culture or Race Suicide.* London: Walter Scott Publications.

THE CRIMINAL AND HIS SCIENCE

REPORT of the Departmental Committee on the Identification of Habitual Criminals (1894) P.P. 1893–94 LXXII.

REPORT of the Departmental Committee on Prisons (1895) (The Gladstone Report). P.P., LVII.

REPORT, The Nineteenth Annual Report of The Prison Commissioners for Scotland (1896) P.P. 1897, XL.

REPORT of the Prison Commissioners (1901–02) P.P. 1902 XLVI.

REPORT to the Secretary of State for the Home Department on the Proceedings of the Seventh International Penitentiary Congress (Buda-pesth) by E. Ruggles-Brise (1906) P.P.1906 LI.

RUGGLES-BRISE, E. (1899). Some Observations on the Treatment of Crime in America, P.P. 1899 XLIII.

RUGGLES-BRISE, E. (1925). *Prison Reform at Home and Abroad.* London: Macmillan.

SALEILLES, R. (1913). *The Individualisation of Punishment.* London: Heinemann.

SCULL, A. (1979). *Museums of Madness: Social Organisation of Insanity in Nineteenth Century England.* Harmondsworth: Penguin.

SMITH, R. (1981). *Trial by Medicine.* Edinburgh: Edinburgh University Press.

SMITHERS, W. W. (1911–12). "The 1910 Meeting of the International Union of Penal Law", in *Journal of the American Institute of Criminal Law and Criminology,* **2,** 381.

SUTHERLAND, J. F. (1908). *Recidivism.* Edinburgh: Wm. Green.

TAYLOR, I., WALTON, P. and YOUNG, J. (1973). *The New Criminology.* London: Routledge and Kegan Paul.

WALKER, N. (1968). *Crime and Insanity in England.* Edinburgh: Edinburgh University Press.

WHITEWAY, A. R. (1898). *Recent Object Lessons in Penal Science.* London: Waterlow Bros.

WILES, P. (1971). "Criminal Statistics and Sociological Explanations of Crime", in Carson, W. G. and Wiles, P. (eds.), *Crime and Delinquency in Britain.* Oxford: Martin Robertson.

WILLIAMS, K. (1981). *From Pauperism to Poverty.* London: Routledge and Kegan Paul.

WILSON, A. (1908). *Education, Personality and Crime.* London: Greening and Co.

Argument: The Persistence
of Shadow Criminology

Argument: The Persistence
of Shadow Criminology

[14]

H. MAYHEW

PICKPOCKETS

IN tracing the pickpocket from the beginning of his career, in most cases we must turn our attention to the little ragged boys living by a felon's hearth, or herding with other young criminals in a low lodging-house, or dwelling in the cold and comfortless home of drunken and improvident parents. The great majority of the pickpockets of the metropolis, with few exceptions, have sprung from the dregs of society—from the hearths and homes of London thieves—so that they have no reason to be proud of their lineage. Fifteen or twenty years ago many of those accomplished pickpockets, dressed in the highest style of fashion, and glittering in gold chains, studs, and rings, who walk around the Bank of England and along Cheapside, and our busy thoroughfares, were poor ragged boys walking barefooted among the dark and dirty slums and alleys of Westminster and the Seven Dials, or loitering among the thieves' dens of the Borough and Whitechapel.

Step by step they have emerged from their rags and squalor to a higher position of physical comfort, and have risen to higher dexterity and accomplishment in their base and ignoble profession.

We say there are a few exceptions to the general rule, that the most of our habitual thieves have sprung from the loins of felon parents. We blush to say that some have joined the ranks of our London thieves, and are living callous in open crime, who were trained in the homes of honest and industrious parents, and were surrounded in early life with all those influences which are fitted to elevate and improve the mind. But here our space forbids us to enlarge.

The chief sources whence our pickpockets spring are from the low lodging-houses—from those dwellings in low neighbourhoods where their parents are thieves, and where improvident and drunken people neglect their children, such as Whitechapel, Shoreditch, Spitalfields, New Cut, Lambeth, the Borough, Clerkenwell, Drury Lane, and other localities. Many of them are the children of Irish parents, costermongers, bricklayers' labourers and others. They often begin to steal at six or seven years of age, sometimes as early as five years, and commit petty sneaking thefts, as well as pick handkerchiefs from gentlemen's pockets. Many of these ragged urchins are taught to steal by their companions, others are taught by trainers of thieves, young men and women, and some middle-aged convicted thieves. They are learned to be expert in this way. A coat is suspended on the wall with a bell attached to it, and the boy attempts to take the handkerchief from the pocket without the bell ringing. Until he is able to do this with proficiency he is not considered well trained. Another way in which they are trained is this:—The trainer—if a man—walks up and down the room with a handkerchief in the tail of his coat, and the ragged boys amuse themselves abstracting it until they learn to do it in an adroit manner. We could point our finger to three of these execrable wretches, who are well known to train schools of juvenile thieves—one of them, a young man at Whitechapel; another, a young woman at Clerkenwell; and a third, a middle-aged man residing about Lambeth Walk. These base wretches buy the stolen handkerchiefs from the boys at a paltry sum. We have also heard of some being taught to pick pockets by means of an effigy; but this is not so well authenticated.

Great numbers of these ragged pickpockets may be seen loitering about our principal streets, ready to steal from a stall or shop-door when they find an opportunity. During the day they generally pick pockets two or three in a little band, but at dusk a single one can sometimes do it with success. They not only steal handkerchiefs of various kinds, but also pocket-books from the tails of gentlemen's coats. We may see them occasionally engaged at this work on Blackfriars Bridge and London Bridge, also along Bishopsgate, Shoreditch, Whitechapel, Drury Lane, and similar localities. They may be seen at any hour of the day, but chiefly from 10 to 2 o'clock. They are generally actively on the look-out on Saturday evening in the shopping streets where the labouring people get their provisions in for the Sunday. At this early stage the boys occasionally pick pockets, and go about cadging and sneaking (begging and committing petty felonies).

The next stage commences—we shall say—about fourteen years of age, when the stripling lays aside his rags, and dresses in a more decent way, though rather shabby. Perhaps in a dark or gray frock-coat, dark or dirty tweed trousers, and a cap with peak, and shoes. At this time many of them go to low neighbourhoods, or to those quieter localities where the labouring people reside, and pick the pockets of the wives and daughters of this class of persons; others steal from gentlemen passing along thoroughfares, while a few adroit lads are employed by men to steal from ladies' pockets in the fashionable streets of the metropolis. These young thieves seldom commit their depredations in the localities where they are known but prowl in different parts of the metropolis. They are of a wandering character, changing from one district to another, and living in different lodging houses—often leaving their parents' houses as early as ten years of age. Sometimes they are driven by drunken, loafing parents to steal, though in most cases they leave their comfortless homes and live in lodging houses.

When they have booty, they generally bring it to some person to dispose of, as suspicion would be aroused if they went to sell or pawn it themselves. In some cases they give it to the trainer of thieves, or they take it to some low receiving house, where wretches encourage them in stealing; sometimes to low coffee-houses, low hairdressers or tailors, who act as middlemen to dispose of the property, generally giving them but a small part of the value.

In the event of their rambling to a distant part of London, they sometimes arrange to get one of their number to convey the stolen goods to these parties. At other times they dispose of them to low wretches connected with the lodging houses, or other persons in disreputable neighbourhoods.

At this time many of them cohabit with girls in low lodging-houses; many of whom are older than themselves, and generally of the felon class.

These lads frequently steal at the "tail" of gentlemen's coats, and learn the other modes of picking pockets.

Stealing the handkerchief from the "tail" of a gentleman's coat in the street is generally effected in this way. Three or four usually go together. They see an old gentleman passing by. One remains behind, while the other two follow up close beside him, but a little behind. The one walking by himself behind is the looker out to see if there are any police or detectives near, or if anyone passing by or hovering around is taking notice of them. One of the two walking close by the gentleman adroitly picks his pocket, and coils the handkerchief up in his hand so as not to be seen, while the other brings his body close to him, so as not to let his arm be seen by any passer by.

If the party feel him taking the handkerchief from his pocket, the thief passes it quickly to his companion, who runs off with it. The looker out walks quietly on as if nothing had occurred, or sometimes walks up to the gentleman and asks him what is the matter, or pretends to tell him in what direction the thief has run, pointing him to a very different direction from the one he has taken.

They not only abstract handkerchiefs but also pocketbooks from the tail of gentlemen's coats, or any other article they can lay their fingers on.

This is the common way in which the coat pocket is picked when the person is proceeding along the street. Sometimes it happens that one thief will work by himself, but this is very seldom. In the case of a person standing, the coat tail pocket is picked much in the same manner.

These boys in most cases confine themselves to stealing from the coat pocket on the streets, but in the event of a crowd on any occasion, they are so bold as to steal watches from the vest-pocket. This is done in a different style, and generally in the company of two or three in this manner:—One of them folds his arms across his breast in such a way that his right hand is covered with his left arm. This enables him to use his hand in an unobserved way, so that he is thereby able to abstract the watch from the vest pocket of the gentleman standing by his side.

A police-officer informed us that when at Cremorne, about a fortnight ago, a large concourse of people was assembled to see the female acrobat, termed the "Female Blondin," cross the Thames on a rope suspended over the river, he observed two young men of about twenty-four years of age, and about the middle height, respectably dressed, whom he suspected to be pickpockets. They went up to a smart gentlemanly man standing at the riverside looking eagerly at the Female Blondin, then walking the rope over the middle of the river. As his attention was thus absorbed, the detective saw these two men go up to him. One of them placed himself close on the right hand side of him, and putting his right arm under his left, thus covered his right hand, and took the watch gently from the pocket of the gentleman's vest. The thief made two attempts to break the ring attached to the watch, termed the "bowl" or swivel, with his finger and thumb.

After two ineffective endeavours he bent it completely round and yet it would not break. He then left the watch hanging down in front of the vest, the gentleman meanwhile being unaware of the attempted felony. The detective officer took both the thieves into custody. They were brought before the Westminster police court and sentenced each to three months' imprisonment for an attempt to steal from the person.

The same officer informed us that about a month or six weeks ago, in the same place, on a similar occasion, he observed three persons, a man, a boy, and a woman, whom he suspected to be picking pockets. The man was about twenty-eight years of age, rather under the middle size. The woman hovered by his side. She was very good looking, about twenty-four years of age, dressed in a green coloured gown, Paisley shawl, and straw bonnet trimmed with red velvet and red flowers. The man was dressed in a black frock coat, brown trousers, and black hat. The boy, who happened to be his brother, was about fourteen years old, dressed in a brown shooting coat, corduroy trousers, and black cap with peak. The boy had an engaging countenance, with sharp features and smart manner. The officer observed the man touch the boy on the shoulder and point him towards an old lady. The boy placed himself on her right side, and the man and woman kept behind. The former put his left hand into the pocket of the lady's gown and drew nothing from it, then left her and went about two yards farther; there he placed himself by two other ladies, tried both their pockets and left them again. He followed another lady and succeeded in picking her pocket of a small sum of money and a handkerchief. The officer took them all to the police station with the assistance of another detective officer, when they were committed for trial at Clerkenwell sessions. The man was sentenced to ten years' penal servitude, the boy to two months' hard labour, and three months in a reformatory, and the woman was sentenced to two years' imprisonment, with hard labour, in the House of Correction at Westminster.

It appeared, in the course of the evidence at the trial, that this man had previously been four years in penal servitude, and since his return had decoyed his little brother from a situation he held, for the purpose of training him to pick pockets, having induced him to rob his employer before leaving service.

The *scarf pin* is generally taken from the breast in this way. The thief generally has a handkerchief in his hand, pretending to wipe his nose, as he walks along the street. He then places his right hand across the breast of the person he intends to rob, bringing his left hand stealthily under his arm. This conceals his movements from the eyes of the person. With the latter hand he snatches out the pin from the scarf. It is sometimes done with the right hand, at other times with the left, according to the position of the person, and is generally done in the company of one or more. The person robbed is rarely aware of the theft. Should he be aware, or should anyone passing by have observed the movement, the pin got from the scarf is suddenly passed into the hands of the other parties, when all of them suddenly make off in different directions, soon to meet again in some neighbouring locality.

At other times the thief drives the person with a push, in the street, bringing his hands to his breast as if he had stumbled against him, at the same time adroitly laying hold of the pin. This is done in such a way that the person is seldom aware of the robbery until he afterwards finds out the loss of the article.

The *trousers pocket* is seldom picked on the public street, as this is an operation of considerable difficulty and danger. It is not easy to slip the hand into the trousers pocket without being felt by the person attempted to be robbed.This is generally done in crowds where people are squeezed together, when they contrive to do it in this way:—They cut up the trousers with a knife or other sharp instrument, lay open the pocket, and adroitly rifle the money from it; or they insert the fingers or hand into it in a push, often without being observed, while the person's attention is distracted, possibly by some of the accomplices or stalls. They often occasion a disturbance in crowds, and create a quarrel with people near them, or have sham fights with each other, or set violently on the person they intend to rob. Many rough expedients are occasionally had recourse to, to effect this object.

Sometimes the pocket is picked in a crowd by means of laying hold of the party by the middle as if they had jostled against him, or by pressing on his back from behind, while the fingers or hand are inserted into the pocket of his trousers to snatch any valuables, money or otherwise, contained therein.

This mode of stealing is sometimes done by one person, at other times by the aid of accomplices. It is most commonly done in the manner now described.

By dint of long experience and natural skill, some attain great perfection in this difficult job, and accomplish their object in the most clever and effective manner. They are so nimble and accomplished that they will accost a gentleman in the street, and while speaking to him, and looking him in the face, will quietly insert their hand into his vest pocket and steal his watch.

In a crowd, the pin is sometimes stolen with dexterity by a person from behind inserting his hand over the shoulder. Sometimes the watch is stolen by a sudden snatch at the guard, when the thief runs off with his booty. This is not so often done in the thoroughfares, as it is attended with great danger of arrest. It is oftener done in quiet by-streets, or by-places, where there are many adjacent courts and alleys intersecting each other, through which the thief has an opportunity of escaping.

These are various modes by which gentlemen's pockets are generally picked.

A lady's pocket is commonly picked by persons walking by her side, who insert their hand gently into the pocket of her gown. This is often effected by walking alongside of the lady, or by stopping her in the street, asking the way to a particular place, or inquiring if she is acquainted with such and such a person. When the thief is accomplished, he can abstract the purse from her pocket in a very short space of time: but if he is not so adroit, he will detain her some time longer, asking further questions till he has completed his object. This is often done by a man and a woman in company.

A lady generally carries her gold or silver watch in a small pocket in front of her dress, possibly under one of the large flounces. It is often stolen from her by one or two, or even three persons, one of the thieves accosting her in the street in the manner described. They seldom steal the guard, but in most cases contrive to break the ring or swivel by which it is attached. Let us suppose that two pickpockets, a man and a woman, were to see a lady with a watch in the public street; they are possibly walking arm in arm; they make up to her, inquire the way to a particular place, and stand in front of her. One of them would ask the way while the other would meantime be busy picking her pocket. If they succeed, they walk off arm in arm as they came.

Sometimes two or three men will go up to a lady and deliberately snatch a parcel or reticule bag from her hand or arm, and run off with it.

At other times a very accomplished pickpocket may pick ladies' pockets without any accomplice, or with none to cover his movements.

Walking along Cheapside one day, toward the afternoon, we observed a well-dressed, good-looking man of about thirty years

of age, having the appearance of a smart man of business, standing by the side of an elderly looking, respectably dressed lady
at a jeweller's window. The lady appeared to belong to the
country, from her dress and manner, and was absorbed looking
into the window at the gold watches, gold chains, lockets, pins,
and other trinkets glittering within. Meantime the gentleman
also appeared to be engrossed looking at these articles beside her,
while crowds of people were passing to and fro in the street, and
the carts, cabs, omnibuses, and other vehicles were rumbling
by, deadening the footsteps of the passers-by. Our eye accidentally
caught sight of his left hand dropping by his side in the direction
of the lady's pocket. We observed it glide softly in the direction
of her pocket beneath the edge of her shawl with all the fascination of a serpent's movement. While the hand lay drooping, the
fingers sought their way to the pocket. From the movement we
observed that the fingers had found the pocket, and were seeking
their way farther into the interior. The person was about to
plunge his hand to abstract the contents when we instinctively
hooked his wrist with the curve of our walking stick and prevented
the robbery. With great address and tact he withdrew his hand
from the lady's pocket, and his wrist from our grasp, and walked
quietly away. Meantime a group of people had gathered round
about us, and a gentleman asked if we had observed a pocket
picked. We said nothing, but whispered to the lady, who stood
at the window unaware of the attempted felony, that we had
prevented her pocket being picked, and had just scared a thief
with his hand in her pocket, then walked over to the other side
of the street and passed on.

The more accomplished pickpockets are very adroit in their
movements. A young lady may be standing by a window in
Cheapside, Fleet Street, Oxford Street, or the Strand, admiring
some beautiful engraving. Meantime a handsomely dressed young
man, with gold chain and moustache, also takes his station at
the window beside her, apparently admiring the same engraving.
The young lady stands gazing on the beautiful picture, with her
countenance glowing with sentiment, which may be enhanced by
the sympathetic presence of the nice looking young man by her
side, and while her bosom is thus throbbing with romantic
emotion, her purse, meanwhile, is being quietly transferred to the
pocket of this elegantly attired young man, whom she might find
in the evening dressed as a rough costermonger, mingling among

the low ruffians at the Seven Dials or Whitechapel, or possibly lounging in some low beershop in the Borough.

There are various ranks of pickpockets, from the little ragged boy, stealing the handkerchief from a gentleman's coat pocket, to the fashionable thief, promenading around the Bank, or strolling, arm in arm, with his gentlemanly looking companion along Cheapside.

The swell mob are to be seen all over London, in crowded thoroughfares, at railway stations, in omnibuses and steamboats. You find them pursuing their base traffic in the Strand, Fleet Street, Holborn, Parliament Street, and at Whitehall, over the whole of the metropolis, and they are to be seen on all public occasions looking out for plunder.

Some commence their work at 8 and 9 in the morning, others do not rise till 11 or 12. They are generally seen about 11 or 12 o'clock—sometimes till dusk. Some work in the evening, and not during the day, while others are out during the day, and do nothing in the evening. In times of great public excitement, when crowds are assembled, such as at the late fire at London Bridge, when those great warehouses were burnt down—they are in motion from the lowest to the highest. They are generally as busy in summer time as in the winter. When the gentry and nobility have retired to their country seats in the provinces, crowds of strangers and tourists are pouring into the metropolis every day.

They often travel into the country to attend races such as Ascot, the Derby at Epsom, and others in the surrounding towns. They go to the Crystal Palace, where the cleverest of them may be frequently seen, also to Cremorne, the Zoological Gardens, Regent's Park, the theatres, operas, ball-rooms, casinos and other fashionable places of amusement—sometimes to the great crowds that usually assemble at Mr. Spurgeon's new Tabernacle.

They also occasionally make tours in different parts of the United Kingdom and to Paris, and along the railways in all directions.

The most accomplished pickpockets reside at Islington, Hoxton, Kingsland Road, St. Luke's, the Borough, Camberwell, and Lambeth, in quiet, respectable streets, and occasionally change their lodging if watched by the police.

They have in most cases been thieves from their cradle; others

are tradesmen's sons and young men from the provinces, who have
gone into dissipated life and adopted this infamous course. These
fast men are sometimes useful as stalls, though they rarely acquire
the dexterity of the native born, trained London pickpocket.

There are a few foreign pickpockets, French and others. Some
of them are bullies about the Haymarket. There are also some
German pickpockets, but the foreigners are principally French.
As a general rule, more of the latter are engaged in swindling
than in picking pockets. Some of the French are considered in
adroitness equal to the best of the English. There are also a few
Scotch, but the great mass are Irish cockneys, which a penetrating eye could trace by their look and manner. Many of them
have a restless look, as if always in dread of being taken, and
generally keep a sharp look out with the side of their eye as they
walk along.

They differ a good deal in appearance. The better class dress
very fashionably; others in the lower class do not dress so well.
The more dexterous they are, they generally dress in higher
style, to get among the more respectable and fashionable people.
Some of the female pickpockets also dress splendidly and have
been heard to boast of frequently stealing from £20 to £30 a day
in working on ladies' pockets. They are sometimes as adroit as
the men in stealing ladies' purses, and are less noticed lingering
beside them on the streets, by the shop windows, and in places of
public resort.

Yet, though well dressed, there is a peculiarity about the look
of most of the male and female pickpockets. The countenance
of many of them is suspicious to a penetrating eye. Many of
them have considerable mental ability, and appear to be highly
intelligent.

The most dexterous pickpockets generally average from twenty
to thirty-five years of age, when many of them become depressed
in spirit, and "have the steel taken out of them" with the anxiety
of the life and the punishments inflicted on them in the course
of their criminal career. The restlessness and suspense of their life
have the effect of dissipation upon a good many of them, so that,
though generally comparatively temperate in the use of intoxicating liquors, they may be said to lead a fast life.

Some of them take a keen bold look, full into your countenance; others have a sneaking, suspicious, downcast appearance,
showing that all is not right within.

They dress in various styles; sometimes in the finest of super-fine black cloth; at other times in fashionable suits, like the first gentlemen in the land, spangled with jewellery. Some of them would pass for gentlemen—they are so polite in their address. Others appear like a mock-swell, vulgar in their manner—which is transparent through their fine dress, and are debased in their conversation, which is at once observed when they begin to speak.

The female pickpockets dress in fashionable attire; sometimes in black satin dresses and jewellery. Some of them are very lady-like, though they have sprung originally from the lowest class. You may see very beautiful women among them, though vulgar in their conversation. The females are often superior in intellect to the men, and more orderly in their habits. They are seldom married, but cohabit with pickpockets, burglars, resetters, and other infamous characters. Their paramour is frequently taken from them, and they readily go with another man in the same illicit manner.

They are passionately fond of their fancy man in most cases; yet very capricious—so much so that they not infrequently leave the man they cohabit with for another sweetheart, and afterwards go back to their old lover again, who is so easy in his principles that he often welcomes her, especially if she is a good worker—that is, an expert pickpocket.

The greater part of these women have sprung from the class of Irish cockneys; others have been domestic servants and the daughters of labourers, low tradesmen, and others. This gives us a key to many of these house robberies, done with the collusion of servants—a kind of felony very common over the metropolis. These are not the more respectable genteel class of servants, but the humbler order, such as nursery girls and females in tradesmen's families. Many of them have come from the country, or from labouring people's families over the working neighbourhoods of the metropolis. They are soon taught to steal by the men they cohabit with, but seldom acquire the dexterity of the thief who has been younger trained. They seldom have the acuteness, tact, and dexterity of the latter.

They live very expensively on the best of poultry, butcher meat, pastry, and wines, and some of them keep their pony and trap; most of them are very improvident, and spend their money foolishly on eating and drinking—though few of them drink to excess—on dress, amusements, and gambling.

They do not go out every day to steal, but probably remain in the house till their money is nearly spent, when they commence anew their system of robbery to fill their purse.

The female pickpockets often live with the burglars. They have their different professions which they pursue. When the one is not successful in the one mode of plunder, they often get it in the other, or the women will resort to shoplifting. They must have money in either of these ways. The women do not resort to prostitution, though they may be of easy virtue with those they fancy. Some of them live with cracksmen in high style, and have generally an abundance of cash.

Female pickpockets are often the companions of skittle-sharps, and pursue their mode of livelihood as in the case of cohabiting with burglars. Their age averages from sixteen to forty-five.

The generality of the pickpockets confine themselves to their own class of robberies. Others betake themselves to card-sharping and skittle-sharping, while a few of the more daring eventually become dexterous burglars.

In their leisure hours they frequently call at certain beershops and public-houses, kept possibly by some old "pals" or connexions of the felon class, at King's Cross, near Shoreditch Church, Whitechapel, the Elephant and Castle, and Westminster, and are to be seen dangling about these localities.

Some of the swell-mobsmen have been well-educated men, and at one time held good situations; some have been clerks; others are connected with respectable families, led away by bad companions, until they have become the dregs of society, and after having been turned out of their own social circle, have become thieves. They are not generally so adroit as the young trained thief, though they may be useful to their gangs in acting as stalls.

Many of them are intelligent men, and have a fund of general information which enables them to act their part tolerably well when in society.

Argument about Argument:
The Persistence of Shadow Criminology

[15]

ENGLISH ECOLOGY AND CRIMINOLOGY OF THE PAST CENTURY

YALE LEVIN[1] and ALFRED LINDESMITH[1a]

The emphasis that has been placed in recent years upon what is known as the "ecological approach" to the study of crime makes it appropriate to pay attention to a period in English history when ecological studies of this subject appear to have been as much in fashion as they are today. Roughly between the years 1830 and 1860, a considerable interest in territorial or regional studies of crime was manifested in England. Over a period of several decades there were accumulated a mass of data and a body of knowledge which were never really discredited or displaced by work of superior scientific merit along the same lines, but were simply relegated to the background in favor of the psychiatric, biological and other types of theories of the later 19th century, and eventually forgotten or disregarded. Although present day criminologists who adopt the ecological approach do not refer to their English predecessors for guidance and corroboration, it is surprising to find that the emphasis which is being placed upon social factors in the causation of crime is closely paralleled in these earlier studies of what might be called the Pre-Lombrosian era. The recent revival of some of these old points of view and techniques suggests the comparison of the older studies with contemporary ones in order to evaluate more precisely the progress criminology has made in the last hundred years. The enthusiasm of social scientists often leads them to attribute greater originality to contemporary studies and less value to the old than is actually warranted by the facts in the case. In the descriptions of some of these older studies which follow, we have attempted to keep in mind contemporary work along the same lines so as to facilitate comparison. Limitations of space prevent more than passing reference to many maps, tables, or discussion which deserve far more extended treatment than we shall attempt in the present article.

Before analyzing the statistical data in these earlier studies, it should be noticed that numerous general observations regarding

---

[1] University of Chicago.
[1a] Indiana University.

the concentration of crime in 'low' neighborhoods were made by
writers and officials dealing with criminals. Thus, on the basis of
his observations, and not with the aid of statistics, Walter Buchanan,
one of Her Majesty's Justices of the Peace for the County of Middlesex, writing in 1846, noted that

"The great recesses of juvenile crime in the metropolitan districts to
the north of the Thames are Spitalfields, Bethnal-Green, Shoreditch,
Hoxton, Wapping, Ratcliffe, White Chapel, Shaffron-Hill, Almonry, Tot-
hill Fields, Gray's Inn Lane, St. Giles, Seven Dials, Drury Lane, Field
Lane, and Lisson Grove; and although in some parts of Maryle-Bone,
St. Pancras, Chelsea, Islington, Clerkenwell, Limehouse, Paddington,
Kensington and elsewhere in and about the metropolis, young thieves
resort, they are not to be compared in number to those who are to be
found issuing from the above named places. In the densely crowded
lanes and alleys of these areas, wretched tenements are found, containing in every cellar and on every floor, men and women, children both
male and female, all huddled together, sometimes with strangers, and too
frequently standing in very doubtful consanguinity to each other. In
these abodes decency and shame have fled; depravity reigns in all its
horrors."[2]

That juvenile delinquents and adult criminals were concentrated in the deteriorated areas of the large towns and cities was
a matter of common observation. Not only those whose work
brought them in direct contact with criminals and youthful delinquents, but others, notably writers on social and political economy,
observed the effects of deteriorated housing conditions. Allison
observes that

"If any person will walk thru St. Giles, the crowded alleys of Dublin,
or the poorer quarters of Glasgow at night, he will no longer worry at
the disorderly habits and profligate enjoyments of the lower order; his
astonishment will be, that there is so little crime in the world. . . . The
great cause of human corruption in these crowded situations is the contagious nature of bad example. . . . A family is compelled by circumstances or induced by interest to leave the country. The extravagant
price of lodgings compels them to take refuge in one of the crowded
districts of the town, in the midst of thousands in similar necessitous
circumstances with themselves. Under the same roof they probably find
a nest of prostitutes, in the next door a den of thieves. In the room
which they occupy they hear incessantly the revel of intoxication or are
compelled to witness the riot of licentiousness."[3]

The author relates of this family that one of the sons becomes

---

[2] Buchanan, Walter, *Remarks on the Causes and State of Juvenile Crime in
the Metropolis With Hints for Preventing Its Increase* (1846) pp. 6-7.
[3] Allison, A., *Principles of Population* (1840) p. 76.

ENGLISH ECOLOGY 803

a member of one of the numerous bands of thieves, commits a housebreaking, and is sentenced to be transported. The daughters become prostitutes and the children of a once happy and virtuous family are thrown upon the streets to pick up a precarious subsistence. He concludes that this unhappy history of a family proceeds not from any extraordinary depravity in their character, but from the almost irresistible nature of the temptations to which the poor are exposed.

Contemporary observers of what we now call the Industrial Revolution carefully noted the growth of large towns, which was one of the marked features of the transformation of England from an agricultural country to an industrial one. In the early decades of the nineteenth century, students of political economy began to assess the growth of the factory towns, a growth which was apparent to every one. In a volume published in 1843, a writer discusses the growth of manufacturing in England and its attendant good effects on the population, such as the growth of large and princely fortunes, the encouragement given to the arts, the enterprise and energy created by the establishment of factories. At the same time he declares that

"Among the numerous causes which appear inseparable from manufactories, producing crime and immorality, the following deserve particular notice. The crowding together of the working classes in narrow streets, filthy lanes, alleys and yards, is a serious evil and one which has hitherto increased in all manufacturing towns. The poor are not resident in these places from choice, but from necessity. Families are not huddled together into dark ill-ventilated rooms from any peculiar pleasure it affords. They may indeed have become insensible of the inconvenience and wretchedness of such situations, but slender and uncertain means do not enable them to command more comfortable abodes. They are fixed there by circumstances."[4]

In his evidence before a Select Committee of Crime in 1830, the Governor of Coldbath Prison stated that:

"In my opinion the crowning cause of crime in the metropolis is to be found in the shocking state of the habitations of the poor, their confined and fetid localities, the consequent necessity for consigning children to the streets for requisite air and exercise. These causes combine to product a state of frightful demoralization. The absence of cleanliness, of decency, and of all decorum; the disregard of any heedful separation

---

[4] Holland, G. C., *Vital Statistics of Sheffield* (1843) p. 138.

between the sexes; the polluting language; and the scenes of profligacy, hourly occurring, all tend to foster idleness and vicious abandonment."[5]

When the reformatories were established in the 1850 decade, the Chief Inspector, Sydney Turner, noted in his annual report for 1856 that the juvenile delinquents committed from the deteriorated districts of London presented a special problem because of their association in gangs. He advocated that these delinquents be committed to various reformatories instead of being permitted to concentrate in any one reformatory.[6]

The following quotation from M. D. Hill, Recorder of Birmingham, will serve to illustrate how the effects of city life upon personal conduct were analyzed in the middle of the nineteenth century:

"A century and a half ago, as far as I have been able to ascertain, there was scarcely a large town in the island except London. When I use the term 'large town' I mean where an inhabitant of the humbler classes is unknown to the majority of the inhabitants of that town. By a small town, I mean a town where, 'a converso' every inhabitant is more or less known to the mass of people of that town. I think it will not require any long train of reflection to show that in small towns there must be a sort of natural police, of a very wholesome kind, operating upon the conduct of every individual, who lives, as it were, under the public eye. But in a large town, he lives, as it were, in absolute obscurity; and we know that large towns are sought by way of refuge, because of that obscurity, which, to a certain extent, gives impunity. Again, there is another cause which I have never seen much noticed, but which, having observed its operation for many years, I am disposed to consider it very important, and that is the gradual separation of classes which takes place in towns by a custom which has gradually grown up, that every person who can afford it lives out of town, and at a spot distant from his place of business. Now this was not formerly so; it is a habit which has, practically speaking, grown up within the last half century. The result of the old habit was that rich and poor lived in proximity; and the

---

[5] Quoted in "The Causes of Crime in the Metropolis," *Taits Edinburgh Magazine,* Vol. 17 (1830) p. 332.

[6] On the formation and habits of juvenile gangs and the prevention of juvenile delinquency, see *Report of the Select Committee on Criminal and Destitute Juveniles* (1852); "The Garrett, The Cabin, and the Goal," *Irish Quarterly Review,* Vol. 3 (1853) pp. 229-381; "Reformatory Schools in France and England," *ibid.* Vol. 4 (1854) pp. 691-792; "Our Juvenile Criminals—The Schoolmaster or the Gaoler," *ibid.* Vol. 4 (1854) pp. 1-71; "Juvenile Delinquents and Their Management," *ibid.* Vol. 5 (1855) pp. 773-822. *Report of the Special Committee Appointed by the National Assembly of France to Consider the Treatment of Juvenile Offenders,* Dec. 14th, 1849. (Trans. 1850.) Mary Carpenter, *Juvenile Delinquents: Their Condition and Treatment* (1853); "Juvenile Criminals," *North British Review,* Vol. 10 (1848) pp. 1-38. *First Report of the Commissioners Appointed to Inquire as to the Best Means of Establishing an Efficient Constabulary Force in the Counties of England and Wales* (1839).

superior classes exercised that species of silent but very efficient control over their neighbors, to which I have already referred. They are now gone, and the consequence is, that large masses of the population are gathered together without those wholesome influences which operated upon them when their congregation was more mixed, when they were divided, so to speak, by having persons of a different class of life, better educated, amongst them. These two causes, namely, the magnitude of towns and the separation of classes, have acted so concurrently, and the effect has been that we find in very large towns, which I am acquainted with, that in some quarters there is a public opinion and a public standard of morals very different from what we should desire to see. Then the children who are born amongst these masses grow up under that opinion, and make that standard of morals their very own; and with them the best lad, or the best man, is he who can obtain subsistence, or satisfy the wants of life, with the least labour, by begging or by stealing, and who shows the greatest dexterity in accomplishing his object, and the greatest wariness in escaping the penalties of the law; and lastly the greatest power of endurance and defiance, when he comes under the lash of the law."[7]

II

We have selected for examination the works of two authors, Henry Mayhew[8] and Joseph Fletcher, who utilized official statistics

[7] Evidence before Select Committee on Criminal and Destitute Juveniles, *op. cit.*, p. 33. Nearly a century later, another student of urban life observed: "The mobility of the city has broken down the isolation of the local community, admitting divergent elements of experience, divergent standards and values, divergent definitions of social situations. At the same time it has resulted in a rate of movement that makes strangers of neighbors. A large part of the city's population lives much as do people in a great hotel, meeting but not knowing one another. The result is a dissolution of social solidarity and public opinion. Face to face and intimate relationships in local areas are replaced by casual, transitory, disinterested contacts. There arises an extreme individuation of personal behavior that makes of the local area within the city something vastly different from the town or village community. There is no common body of experience and tradition, no unanimity of interest, sentiment and attitude which can serve as a basis of collective action." See H. W. Zorbaugh, *The Gold Coast and the Slum* (1929) pp. 250-251.

[8] The careers of Henry Mayhew (1812-1887) and two of six brothers, Horace and Augustus, are separately recorded in the *Dictionary of National Biography*. All three brothers devoted themselves to literature, drama and journalism, at early ages. Abandoning the study of law, Henry Mayhew's first venture was the publication, with Gilbert a Beckett of 'Figaro in London,' a weekly periodical 1831-1839; later he wrote several dramas. He is best known, however, as one of the originators, and for a short time, one of the editors of 'Punch,' and as the first one to mark out a new path in philanthropic journalism which takes the poor of London as its theme. His principal work, in which he was assisted by John Binny and others, was *London Labour and the London Poor*, a series of articles, anecdotic and statistical, on the petty trades of London, originally appearing in the 'Morning Chronicle.' Two volumes were published in 1851; but their circulation was interrupted by litigation in Chancery. In 1856 a continuation of it appeared in monthly parts as the "The Great World of London" which was ultimately completed and published as the *Criminal Prisons of London and Scenes*

in investigating the problems of crime in their wider aspects. Mayhew's volume, *The Criminal Prisons of London*, in addition to containing a detailed description of the prisons of London, as the title indicates, includes also a wealth of statistics and illuminating observations on such subjects as: juvenile delinquency, the evolution of the juvenile offender into the habitual criminal, recidivism, female crime, the concentration of various types of crime in certain localities within London and in certain counties of England and Wales, classifications of crime and criminals, the evaluation of police statistics, the history of the 'delinquency areas' of London, methods of prison administration and prison discipline, and the role of early family and community conditions in producing criminals. Many of the statistical tables cover all of England and Wales by counties; some give data by police districts within London, other tables compare cities and other territorial divisions. It is interesting in connection with the general problem of the relation of crime to the soical life of the period that Mayhew introduces his study with a general topographical description of London and London streets, giving population and other general descriptive data for the city as a whole. He has a section entitled "Some Idea of the Size and Population of London" and a "Table Showing the Area, Number of Houses, and proportion of Houses to Each Acre in London, 1851" by districts—36 of them. In a similar manner he notes the "Distribution and Density of the Population of London in 1851" in terms of the same 36 districts and, on the page facing this table, represents the same data on a shaded ecological map of the city. He does the same for the average income tax assessments and poor rate assessments per house in these districts, and gives us an idea of "mobility" by listing the number of vehicles passing through each of the principal London streets in 24 hours.

Perhaps of even greater interest in this volume is the ecological study of the residences of the members of the various branches of

---

of *Prison Life* (1862). A portion of this volume was written by John Binny. Mayhew's *London Labour and the London Poor* (4 vols.) appeared in its final form in 1864 and again in 1865. The title page of each volume is as follows: *London Labour and the London Poor: a cyclopedia of the Condition and Earnings of Those That Will Work, Those That Cannot Work, and Those That Will Not Work*. The fourth volume acknowledging the assistance of John Binny and other contributors, is devoted to thieves. swindlers. beggars, and prostitutes. In his preface of *London Labour and the London Poor*, Mayhew writes that his volume is "The first attempt to publish the history of a people, from the lips of the people themselves—giving a literal description of their labour, their earnings, and their sufferings, in their own 'unvarnished' language. It is the first commssion of inquiry into the state of the people undertaken by a private individual and the first 'blue book' ever published in twopenny numbers."

the legal profession in London, in which Mayhew shows the concentration in what he calls the "legal capital," Chancery Lane, which he describes in detail. He traces the ramifications radiating out from this legal capital and describes the legal "suburbs" of the city, listing more than a hundred "legal localities." In order to place this material in its proper setting, he precedes it with the statistics showing the proportion of the population included in the professional classes of each of the counties of England and Wales and in London.

The other volume, "Those Who Will Not Work," is remarkable in revealing the full extent and detailed character of Mayhew's ecological description of London crime. In it he classifies London "beggars, thieves, prostitutes, cheats and swindlers" into a total of more than one hundred specific groups. He and his collaborators discuss and describe the habitat and mode of making a living of each of these groups and specify quite exactly the districts in which they commit their depredations as well as the streets and localities where they live. This volume abounds in graphic descriptions of the various crime areas and in personal testimony obtained by interviews with persons in the walks of life and areas under consideration, in the manner of the "participant observer" of contemporary sociology. There are recorded in this volume more than a dozen narratives of professional criminals, written in the first person in the criminal's own words, telling his life history, describing the natural evolution of the professional from the juvenile criminal, and giving vivid descriptions of the modus operandi in the various "rackets," as we would call them.[9]

---

[9] The importance of a direct personal study of criminals outside of institutions in order to gain understanding of their attitudes and motives and techniques was emphasized by many writers in addition to Mayhew and Binny. A revewer, commenting on a book by Mary Carpenter, stated: "Miss Carpenter has at last supplied us with the material needed to qualify us so to understand the conditions of a life altogether unlike our own, as to enable us to perceive what sort of minds we have to deal with. . . . The main object of Miss Carpenter's book is to establish the principles on which our treatment of criminals should proceed. . . . She has perhaps rendered a greater service in disclosing to us the entire natural history of the lawless classes. She supplies us with the material essentially necessary as the basis of action on any theory of judgment and punishment of offenders. . . . But the first requisite to action under any of these views is to understand the peculiar character of criminal life, in its origin and progress." *Edinburgh Review*, Vol. 122 (1865) p. 337-371. In an article on "Professional Thieves" another writer remarked, "Thieving, considered as an art, is only just beginning to be understood in this country; it is scarcely thirty years since honest men turned their attention to the subject with a determination to master it. . . . But obviously, crime will never be cured until its origin and career are thoroughly understood. . . . Would that the professional thieves would be induced to come forward and candidly tell us all about it. We will never fully understand them until they explain themselves. Police, prison discipline, fence masters, penal servitude, on each of these subjects a conference of old thieves, earnest and out-

In the appendix of Mayhew's "Those Who Will not Work" there is a series of fifteen maps with accompanying tables showing the distribution (by rates whenever appropriate) of the following, in each of the counties of England and Wales:

    Map No. 1—Density of Population
            2—Intensity of Criminality
            3—Intensity of Ignorance
            4—Number of Illegitimate Children
            5—Number of Early Marriages
            6—Number of Females
            7—Committals for Rape
            8—Committals for Carnally Abusing Girls
            9—Committals for Disorderly Houses
           10—Concealment of Births
           11—Attempts at Miscarriage
           12—Assaults with Intent
           13—Committals for Bigamy
           14—Committals for Abduction
           15—Criminality of Females

The tables usually cover a ten year period (1841-1850). In arriving at correlations without the use of the coefficient, which was not know at that time, Mayhew lists the counties above and below the average according to their respective deviations from the average, and then juxtaposes two such series and analyzes their differences and similarities.[10]

Perhaps one of the major points made in recent ecological studies of crime, and one that has received a great deal of attention

---

spoken, would speedily teach the public more than they can ever learn from associations for the promotion of social science, parliamentary committees, government commissioners, prison inspectors and police reports. Believing that we cannot understand people of any class or character unless we go among them, see them in their open hours of unreserved communication, and hear what they have to say for themselves. I have for some time past made the most of every opportunity of becoming, as a clergyman, acquainted with the origin, character, acts and habits of professional thieves." *Cornhill Magazine*, Vol. 6 (1862) p. 640-653.

[10] Mayhew points out that the official system of classification of crimes fails to divide criminals into two main types, habitual and casual. "It is impossible to arrive at any accurate knowledge of the subject of crime and criminals generally, without first making this analysis of the several species of offenses according to their causes; or, in other words, without arranging them into distinct groups or classes, according as they arise, either from an habitual indisposition to labour on the part of some of the offenders, or from the temporary pressure of circumstances upon others. The official returns on this subject are as unphilosophic as the generality of such documents, and consist of a crude mass of incongruous facts, being a statistical illustration of the *"rudis indigestaque moles"* in connection with a criminal chaos, and where a murderer is classed in the same category with the bigamist, a sheep-stealer with the embezzler, and the Irish rebel or traitor grouped with the keeper of a disorderly house, and he, again, with the poacher and perjurer." *The Criminal Prisons of London* (1862) p. 87.

and been heralded as a landmark in the scientific study of crime, is that crime rates, juvenile and adult, vary from one community to another within cities; and that crime is concentrated in certain areas and not distributed uniformly. This fact was well known to Mayhew, who, in addition to working out rates by counties and cities, also computed rates for police districts within London, and went a step farther in specifying what particular kinds of crimes were to be found in particular areas within the city. He calls attention to the fact that London's "rookeries" of crime have long histories, some of which extend back more than five hundred years. He made personal investigations of these areas, which have been "nests of London's beggars, prostitutes and thieves" continuously for centuries. His masterly descriptions of such districts as St. Giles, Spitalfields, Westminster, and the Borough are precise delimitations of characteristic areas of London vice and crime. The following excerpt is typical:

"There is no quarter of the Metropolis impressed with such strongly-marked features as the episcopal city of Westminster. We do not speak of that vague and straggling electoral Westminster, which stretches as far as Kensington and Chelsea to the west, and even Temple Bar to the east; but of that Westminster proper— that triangular snip of the Metropolis which is bounded by the Vauxhall Road on one side, St. James Park on another, and by the Thames on the third—that Westminster which can boast of some of the noblest and some of the meanest buildings to be found throughout London (the grand and picturesque old Abbey, and the filthy and squalid Duck Lane—the brand new and orate Houses of Parliament, and the half-dilapidated and dingy old Almonry) which is the seat at once of the great mass of law makers and law-breakers—where there are more almshouses, and more prisons and more schools—more old noblemen's mansions and more costermonger's hovels—more narrow lanes, and courts, and more broad unfinished highways— whose Hall is frequented by more lawyers, and whose purlieus are infested by more thieves—whose public houses are resorted to by more paviors—whose streets are thronged by more soldiers—on whose doorsteps sit more bare-headed wantons—and whose dry arches shelter more vagabond urchins than are to be noted in any other part of the Metropolis—ay, and perhaps in any other part of the world."[11]

In his analysis of juvenile crime Mayhew compares rates in the various counties and notes that the rates of juvenile delinquency are highest in those counties which have large cities in them. He takes note of the difference in age distribution from one locality to

---

[11] *The Criminal Prisons of London*, p. 353.

another when he makes these comparisons.[12] In the county containing London he shows that 41% of the juvenile offenders came from one of the seven police districts and 24% from another. The other districts contributed an average of between 5% and 8% and the country only 5½% of the total. He further splits up the rural returns to show that most of the rural offenders came from one district—Hammersmith. He lists areas and streets of London which particularly abound in gangs of juvenile delinquents. The following excerpts taken from *'Those Who Will Not Work"* show clearly an amazing ecological knowledge of London crime of that day:

"In order to find these houses it is necessary to journey eastwards, and leave the artificial glitter of the West-end, where vice is pampered and caressed. Whitechapel, Wapping, Ratcliff Highway, and analogous districts are prolific in the production of these infamies. St. Georges in-the-east abounds with them." . . . "Whitechapel has always been looked upon as a suspicious unhealthy locality. To begin with, its population is a strange amalgamation of Jews, English, French, Germans and other antagonistic elements." . . . "Ship alley is full of foreign lodging houses." . . . "Tiger Bay like Frederick Street is full of brothels and thieves lodging houses." . . . "The most of those engaged in this kind of robbery in Oxford Street come from the neighborhood of St. Giles and Lisson Grove." . . . "The most accomplished pickpockets reside at Islington, Hoxton, Kingsland Road, St. Lukes, The Borough, Camberwell and Lambeth in quiet respectable streets, and occasionally change their lodging if watched by the police." . . . "Some Londoners are in the habit of stealing horses. These often frequent the Old Kent Road, and are dressed as grooms or stablemen." . . . "Dog stealing is very prevalent, particularly in the West-end of the Metropolis, and is a rather profitable class of felony. These thieves reside at the Seven Dials, the neighborhood of Belgravia, Chelsea, Knightsbridge, and low neighborhoods, some of them men of mature age." . . . "There are great numbers of expert cracksmen known to the police in the different parts of the Metropolis. Many of these reside on the Surrey side, about Waterloo Road and Kent Road, the Borough, Hackney and Kingsland Road and other localities."

It is no doubt true that many of the facts having to do with the concentration of crime in particular areas were noted long before the time of Mayhew, inasmuch as London's crime areas had acquired histories of several centuries when he wrote. What is particularly noteworthy about Mayhew, as well as the other students of his day was that they used these facts definitely and consciously for the purposes of what was known as "moral" or "social science." Thus Mayhew remarks:

[12] See also Neison, F. G. P., "Statistics of Crime in England and Wales for the Years 1842, 1843, 1844." *Journal of the Statistical Society* vol. 9 (1846) p. 223-276.

ENGLISH ECOLOGY 811

"Surely even the weakest-minded must see that our theories of crime, to be other than mere visionary hypotheses, must explain roguery and vagabondage *all over the world,* and not merely be framed with reference to that little clique among human society which we happen to call our State."[13]

Students of today who are in the habit of considering Lombroso the first scientific student of crime will be surprised to find Mayhew anticipating in the middle of the 19th century the criticisms of the early Lombrosian viewpoint which were advanced near the end of the 19th and in the first part of the 20th century. He states:

"But crime, we repeat, is an effect with which the shape of the head and the form of the features appear to have no connection whatever. . . . Again we say that the great mass of crime in this country is committed by those who have been bred and born to the business, and who make a regular trade of it, living as systematically by robbery or cheating as others do by commerce or the exercise of intellectual or manual labour."[14]

He thus definitely rejects the view of the criminal as a distinct physical type in favor of what might be called an environmental or sociological view. In fact, if we were to select the main theme of his books we should say that it was the point that habitual crime is the result of a natural evolution of juvenile crime in response to the impact of social factors. He even calculates the number of juvenile offenders who each year must have graduated to the ranks of the adult convicts to have maintained this latter group at a constant figure.[15]

---

[13] Mayhew, H., *The Criminal Prisons of London,* p. 383.

[14] ibid., p. 413.

[15] His own estimate, compiled from the criminal returns of England, is that about one-third of the gross number of the young criminal population of the country (15,000 to 20,000) are removed from the ranks, through the influences of reformatories, farm schools, and industrial institutions; also that some 2,000 criminals, at least, are required to be added every year to the general stock "in order to maintain that steady ratio of offenders to the population, which has continued in this country for nearly the whole of the present century." Mayhew, *op. cit.,* pp. 394-396. He further states, "Indeed, the only rational conclusion to be arrived at—and it is one to which we have come after testing statistically, we repeat, almost every theory on the subject that has been propounded—is, that the great mass of crime is a trade and a profession among us, and that those forms of dishonesty which make up nearly four-fifths of the delinquency of the country are practiced as a means of living by certain classes, as regularly as honesty is pursued for the same purpose by others" . . . Also, "Crime, in its habitual form, seems to us as radically incurable as lock-jaw. . . . The only hope is to *prevent* juvenile delinquency." Mayhew, H., *op. cit.,* p. 452.

III

In 1847 and 1849 Joseph Fletcher read three papers before the British Association for the Advancement of Science and the Statistical Society of London, which he later incorporated in a book, *Summary of Moral Statistics in England and Wales,* which might, in many respects, be taken as a model ecological work of the period.[16] It is not as encyclopedic as Mayhew's work but it is more minute and specialized. The entire book is centered around a series of 12 ecological maps in the appendix of the volume and an ecological map in the frontispiece colored to represent what we might call "natural areas" in England and Wales. These areas were determined on the basis of the prevailing economic organization, whether agricultural, mining, manufacturing, et cetera, in the various counties, grouping like ones together. He proceeds by means of a complex series of tables, coordinated with these maps to analyze what he calls "indices to moral influences" and "indices to moral results" in the various regions specified, listing 36 conclusions as a result of this analysis. Some 80 pages are then devoted to a more detailed tabular presentation of the data on which the conclusions are based, and this is followed by the series of 12 maps and accompanying tables giving the distribution of the above mentioned "indices of moral influences and results" by counties and by districts in England and Wales. The maps are shaded in seven tints and those relating to crime are in terms of rates adjusted to the ages of the population. The following "indices" are graphically represented on these maps:

1. Dispersion of the population

[16] The only life of Joseph Fletcher (1813-1852) is that in the *Dictionary of National Biography.* "Fletcher was educated as a barrister; from the age of nineteen he was engaged upon works and reports in connection with health, occupations, and well-being of the people. He was secretary to the Hand-loom inquiry Commission, and afterwards to the Children's Employment Commission. His valuable reports of these Commissions formed the basis of useful legislation. In 1844 Fletcher was appointed one of Her Majesty's Inspectors of Schools, and his voluminous reports were among the most serviceable contributions to British educational statistics. For many years Fletcher was one of the honorary Secretaries of the Statistical Society of London, and was also during the same period Editor of the Statistical Journal and responsible for the collection and arrangement of the vast collection of documents published in that Journal. In 1850 he published his *Summary of the Moral Statistics of England and Wales,* and in the following year a work on *Education: National, Voluntary and Free.* He paid great attention to foreign educational systems and issued (1851-52) two treatises on *The Farm School of the Continent and Its Applicability to the Present Reformatory Education of Pauper and Criminal Children in England and Wales.* He was an ideal statistician, having in a singular degree the power of grasping facts and realizing their relative significance."

2. Real property in proportion to the population
3. Persons of independent means in proportion to the population
4. Ignorance, as measured by the percentage of signatures by marks in the marriage registers
5. Crime as indicated by criminal commitments of males (allowance made for the ages of the population)
6. Commitments for the more serious offenses against the person and malicious offences against property (allowance made for age distribution)
7. Commitments for all offences against property, excepting the malicious (allowance made for age distribution)
8. Commitments for assaults and miscellaneous offences for males in proportion to the total male population
9. Improvident marriages, or those entered into by males less than 21 years old
10. Bastardy as indicated by the registers of births
11. Pauperism
12. Deposits in savings banks in proportion to the population.

Commenting on his method, Fletcher remarks:

"Rather than rush to one generalization upon aggregate results, it is better to retain the facts in manageable groups, by means of which to compare one class with another, one district with another, and one period with another; and by the alternate use of analytical and synthetical methods, to bring the several elements into every possible combination, and detect the laws of their coincidence and relationship, or obtain new views as to the direction which should be given to more refined observation. . . . In framing the accompanying tables I have throughout adhered to one general division of the Kingdom into distinct industrial provinces, drawn with as much accuracy as was permitted by the large and varying size of the counties; the civil divisions which are the integral ones for nearly all my data. These provinces are portrayed in the accompanying map which will serve as a key to the whole of the following tables. A glance down the vertical columns of these tables will convey all that could be pictured forth by an expensive series of shaded maps showing the relative intensity of each element; at the same time that their horizontal lines will convey the collective results in a manner far more compendious than could be obtained by any pictorial means."[17]

His attempt to obtain an index to the crime of the various counties and districts of England and Wales which would not be affected by the migration of the "depraved" is interesting. He tries to make allowances for the "influence of the denser populations rather to *assemble* the demoralized than to *breed* an excess of demoralization." He is led by his reasoning along these lines to accept the rate of "more serious offences against the person and

[17] Fletcher, J., *Summary of Moral Statistics of England and Wales* (1850) p. 3.

malicious offences against property" as a truer index of the moral
state of a community less affected by mere migrations, than other
forms. He finds this form of crime to be highly correlated with
ignorance, speaking of "its universal excess wherever ignorance is
in excess." His principal concern is with the importance of education. Mayhew, however, refuted this view by contending that all
education did was to increase the proportion of educated criminals
without reducing the total number of them at all; but he, unlike
Fletcher, regarded the habitual offences or professional crime, as
constituting the heart of the problem.[18]

IV

In conclusion, we wish to call attention again to the fact that the
scientific study of crime is usually said to have begun in the last
quarter of the nineteenth century with the founding of the "Italian
School" by Lombroso. Thus, George W. Kirchwey remarks, "It
is incredible, but it is a fact, that, prior to the publication of
Lombroso's *L'uomo delinquente* (The Criminal) which was given
to the world in 1876, there had never been offered a serious,
scientific approach to the study of the criminal."[19] Of Lombroso,
Harry Elmer Barnes stated: "By taking the discussion of crime out
of the realm of theology and metaphysics, and putting it on the
positivistic basis of a consideration of the characteristics of the
criminal, he may be said to have founded modern criminology."[20]
All of the English studies to which we have referred were published
at least a decade before the appearance of *L'uomo delinquente*.
Although this early regional and sociological approach suffered an
eclipse in the later decades of the nineteenth century (particularly
in England), due perhaps to the philosophic pre-occupations of
sociologists under the influence of Spencer and Comte, it has been
resumed by American sociologists in the past two decades. In the

[18] See also Rawson. R. W.. "An Inquiry Into the Statistics of Crime in England
and Wales" *Journal of the Statistical Society*, vol. 2 (1839) p. 316-344. Rawson, R.
W., "Police of the Metropolis in 1836-37" *Ibid.* vol. 1 (1839) pp. 96-103. Redgrave, S.
"Abstract of Criminal Tables for England and Wales With Remarks Thereupon,"
Ibid. Vol. 1 (1838) p. 231-245. Rev. Whitworth Russell, "Abstract of the Statistics
of Crime in England and Wales from 1839 to 1843," *Ibid.* Vol. 10 (1847) p. 38-61.
[19] *Encyclopedia Brittanica*, 14th ed., article on Criminology.
[20] *Encyclopedia of the Social Sciences*, Vol. 4, article on Criminology. Some
European students have taken a different view. Thus, J. Lottin in his volume
A. Quetelet: Statisticien et Sociologue (1912) speaks of Guerry and Quetelet as
the founders of the scientific sociological study of crime and refers to several
other European students who held similar views. See also W. Bonger *Criminality
and Economic Conditions* for references to the early English and Continental
writers on crime.

evolution of criminological theory, it would appear that the work of Lombroso was in the nature of an interlude and interruption.

Contrary to widely circulated assertions which speak of the "ecological approach" to the study of crime as a twentieth century development, we believe that it has been amply demonstrated that this approach was systematically employed in the early part of the nineteenth century by scholars in different countries who were aware of each other's work. The first systematic work in this field was apparently done in France by A. M. Guerry and in Belgium by A. Quetelet in the 1830's. The English writers to whom we have referred were influenced by both of these men and frequent references to their publications are found in their works. The work of Comte[21] did not directly affect this movement at all. It was, in fact, too philosophical to have interested these students who were concerned with empirical research and were not interested in the broad speculative problems with which the Comtean tradition dealt. Mayhew, for example, heaped scorn upon the classical political economists of his day, speaking of them as a "sect of social philosophers" who "sat beside a snug sea-coal fire and tried to think out the several matters affecting the working classes, or else they have retired to some obscure corner, and there remained, like big-bottomed spiders, spinning their cobweb theories among heaps of rubbish."[22]

The "moral statistics" of the eighteenth century were too defective to have made possible any such significant widespread development as occurred in the nineteenth century. When accurate governmental statistics became available, English and French students (and those in other countries) zealously employed these statistics in making regional studies of crime, suicide, insanity, illegitimacy, vagrancy, pauperism, and other social problems which interest the sociologist today.[23] Individualistic theories which sought

---

[21] His *Cours de Philosophie Positive*, 6 vols., appeared from 1830 to 1842, and his *Systeme de Philosophie Positive*, 4 vols., from 1851 to 1854.

[22] Mayhew, H., *Low Wages: Their Causes, Consequences and Remedies*, London, (1851) p. 126. "That the assumptions of Political Economy, however, *should* be true is beyond the bounds of probability, for it is well known that Adam Smith, the founder of the *pseudo* science, when about to develop the laws of capital and labour, retired to an obscure Scotch village, and there sat dreaming in his arm-chair for fifteen years about the circumstances affecting production and the pro-ducers. As well might we suppose a person capable of excogitating in a back parlour the laws of chemistry, or natural history, or any other of those systematic aggregation of facts which we term science." *Ibid*, p. 126.

[23] According to Joseph Lottin in his volume *A. Quetelet: Statisticien et Sociologue* (1912) p. 128-139, shaded ecological maps to represent crime rates were

causal explanations of crime in terms of the characteristics of the criminal had not yet come into vogue, and in the works of these earlier writers there were elaborated many viewpoints which attributed primary causal significance to external environmental or social factors in much the same manner as do present day sociological theories.

first used in 1829 by A. M. Guerry and Balbi in a work on education and crime. Others who employed shaded maps on crime and related subjects, in the 1830's are W. R. Greg, *Social Statistics of the Netherlands* (1835) in which there are five such maps; Comte A. D'Angeville, *Essai Sur la Statistique de la Population Francaise* (1836) wherein will be found sixteen ecological maps of the condition of the people. Similar maps will be found in Parent-Duchatelet *La Prostitution dans la Ville de Paris* (1837); A. M. Guerry *Essai Sur la Statistique Moral de la France* (1833) and in his *Statistique Moral de l'Angleterre Comparee Avec la Statistique Moral de la France* (1860). Quetelet is also reported to have employed them at an early date. See *Westminster Review* vol. 18 (1833) p. 353, wherein it is stated "A peculiarity in recent works of this kind is the addition of pictorial illustrations. Maps showing the distribution of crime and education have been used by the author, by his coadjutor Balbi, by Quetelet, Dupin, and others."

Part IV
The Fourth Phase: Criminology as an Academic Pursuit

Argument: The Big Ideas

The Medico-Psychological Model

[16]

M. HAMBLIN-SMITH

PREFACE

THIS book is based upon twenty-three years'
experience in local and convict prisons, and
more particularly upon the work which I have
done, during the past three years, with offenders from
Courts in Birmingham and the adjacent districts.

My main object has been to demonstrate how important is the thorough examination of the individual
offender, especially in regard to his mentality. It is
only by a great extension of this line of investigation
that we can hope to solve the problems which criminality
presents.

THE PROBLEM STATED 17

Practically all recidivists commence their delinquent career in early life. The late Dr. C. Goring,[1] in his monumental study, showed, what was already well known to all workers who had investigated the life-histories of offenders, that the majority of recidivists commence their delinquent career between the ages of fifteen and twenty years. And it must be remembered that a first conviction does not, by any means, necessarily imply a first offence. Even in cases which are placed on Probation it very frequently happens that the first appearance in Court only follows on a long series of

[1] " The English Convict."

18 THE PSYCHOLOGY OF THE CRIMINAL

offences which have been undetected or undealt with. And it follows that the determining factors of a delinquent life are to be found among the conditions of the offender's early years. (In Chapters III and IV we shall see how this fits in with the theory and the practical findings of psycho-analysis.) Consequently, if these determining factors are to be estimated rightly they must be studied, as far as may be, when they are most active. And they are far clearer in youth than they are in later years. When recidivism has become established various other conditions come into play; alcoholism, long periods of social disfavour, the establishment of an anti-social grudge, and the ill results of repeated imprisonments. All these conditions render the correct estimation of the fundamental factors in any case much more difficult.

Many of the personal and environmental conditions which tend towards delinquency commence to operate in early life. Knowledge of these conditions is of vast moment, and this knowledge is more easily obtained when the conditions are of recent origin. Let the reader reflect how little he really knows of the early influences which have made him what he is (whatever that may be) and he will partly realize the difficulties of our task.

Once again, youth is the time to investigate offenders, for as years go on there is development of reticence, and of the anti-social feeling, and these render the finding of fundamental conditions to be harder. Psychoanalysis shows us that it is easier to obtain a knowledge of mental conflicts (and these are of vast importance) at a time when the subject has not to probe too deeply for these conflicts, and when succeeding experiences have not buried the complex resulting from the conflict so completely.

Yet once more, all those who take a part in any schemes for the reformation of offenders feel rightly

THE PROBLEM STATED   19

that the case is far more hopeful when taken in hand young.   To see the truth of this we have only to compare our feelings when dealing with young prisoners and with old convicts.

But although we have laid much stress on the predominant need for the careful study of commencing delinquency, we must not depreciate the importance of work with the older offenders.   The intensive examination of the younger cases tends to a fuller comprehension of the needs of the older cases.   Knowledge of the causative factors which are, as just explained, most easily ascertained among the young, will lead to better diagnosis and treatment of offenders of every age, however long may have been their delinquent careers. When considering an older offender we must try, as far as may be, to ascertain what were the factors which operated at the start of his delinquent course.   Thus, careful study of these factors will help us with every class of offender.   We may often be unable to ascertain all the factors in a given case.   But the investigation is always useful, always should be made, so long as we remember that it is necessary to avoid any hasty diagnosis, any rapid attempt to classify our case.   Study of cases will not always ensure success in the definite assignment of the important factor or factors of causation.   We shall generally find that diagnosis implies the careful weighing and estimation of a number of factors.

There is one marked difference between the recidivist and the man who has committed a single offence (always keeping in mind the warning that a first conviction does not necessarily imply a first offence).   The man who has committed a single, non-repeated offence has found some reason for the non-repetition.   Penologists are entitled to make what they can of the argument that the punishment awarded is the reason for this non-repetition.   Doubtless it is so in some cases.   Or the particular circumstances which produced the

20 THE PSYCHOLOGY OF THE CRIMINAL

offence may not recur.   An offence may be committed in some sudden access of passion, and the occasion of this may have been unique.   A mental conflict may result on one occasion in an offence, and may not issue into action in this way again.

There are delinquents who do not come within the purview of the Courts at all.   This is, of course, no new knowledge to any person of experience.   But the author has had most interesting confirmation of this fact in his work.   A certain amount of newspaper publicity naturally accrues to Court work.   And he has found himself consulted, sometimes personally, sometimes by letter, by people who have difficult cases on their hands.   Such cases are usually those of young boys or girls, though sometimes of older persons, who are a trouble to their relatives on account of their repeated offences.   Sometimes these offences are those of dishonesty, of stealing from their affectionate relations who have to deal with the matter without the aid of the law, sometimes of stealing from others who have been placated or recompensed by the relations, and so have not brought the matter before the Courts.   In other cases the delinquency has taken other forms. The author has been unable, from lack of time and other reasons, to deal with these cases otherwise than by general advice.   But he has sometimes been able to suggest that the advice and treatment of a fellow-worker should be obtained, and, in certain instances, the results have been excellent.   These cases are by no means infrequent, and they may be appallingly sad.   There is a great opening for work in this direction.   And as the science of psycho-analysis grows, it may be hoped that there will be an increase in the number of persons with skill, experience, and discretion, who will be ready to undertake the treatment of such cases, and so to diminish the amount of sadness in the world.

Throughout this book the author has avoided

THE PROBLEM STATED   21

the use of the words " sin " and " vice ". Without
entering into highly controversial matters, it must
be clear that the use of these words implies the adoption
of some more or less arbitrary standard.   We have
only to read old books on penology to see the confusion
which resulted from regarding offenders as " sinners ".
This view is not so much in vogue now.   But, in any
case, we must not introduce it into a scientific investigation.   We have " no need of that hypothesis ".   Apart
from the fact that many " sins " which are not punished
by the criminal law may have results far more dire
and far-reaching than certain offences which are so
punished, there is this other consideration.   The great
question is not so much what a man has done, but what
he is.   We shall lay down the fundamental position
that conduct is the direct result of mental life, that mis-
conduct, like all other forms of conduct, results from
mental causes.   The particular act with which a man is
charged in Court is only a symptom produced by these
mental causes.   Groszman [1] puts it well, when he says—
" For every symptom we must train ourselves to look
for a cause.   Proper observation implies a careful
distinction between facts observed and the interpretation we may give them.   It is a common error to substitute our interpretation of a fact for the fact itself ".
And he illustrates the principle in this way—" To say
that to-day the child was naughty means nothing.
Such a statement implies a foregone conclusion, a judg
ment, not a record of fact, unless of the fact that the
child's conduct affected the recorder in a certain
manner ".   It follows that the real question is not so
much what should be done to an offender in the way of
punishment, but what can be done for him in the way
of treatment.

The first great advance in the study of the offender
was made by Lombroso and his disciples.   He was the

[1] " The Exceptional Child."

22 THE PSYCHOLOGY OF THE CRIMINAL

founder of what may be called the " anatomical "
school of criminology. His conception of the offender
was based upon generalizations (perhaps unwise)
which were derived from premisses far too small. Many
of his conclusions are now considered to be erroneous.
There is much in his theory of the offender as being an
" atavistic " survival, which is confirmed by the
researches of psycho-analysis. But his theory of the
relation between epilepsy and delinquency is now
generally abandoned, and was only tenable by giving
a very extended meaning to the term epilepsy. The
fact, however, that his theories have had to be revised,
in no way detracts from the value of the service which
he rendered to science, and so to the world. For in
Lombroso's work, one great principle transcends all
the details which he gathered. His great glory lies in
his insistence on the fact, practically overlooked before
his time, that the offender is to be studied in himself,
as an individual, and apart from any particular offence
with which he might happen to be charged. Like
Columbus, Lombroso did not rightly recognize the
country which he had discovered. His followers, perhaps, find no feature in his maps which can stand uncor-
rected. His undying fame rests on the fact that he
did lead us to a new country, and opened out a new field
for our explorations.

We do not now talk of a " criminal type " of cranium
or ear. We recognize the " stigmata of degeneration ",
as they are called. We know them to be common among
offenders. But it is now understood that they have no
special relation to the offender as such, in no way differentiate him from the non-offender, and are common
among our delinquents, simply because many delinquents are defective or subnormal mentally. All
facts are, of course, worthy of study. And we do
well to measure heads and ears, so long as we recognize
that such abnormalities are not in themselves causes

THE PROBLEM STATED   **23**

of delinquency, any more than are an offender's nationality or his religious faith.

From whence then, comes the light upon the stony road which we have to travel? The answer is, From Psychology. This, the youngest of the sciences, was engaged for many years in the study of academic problems, and was not much concerned with matters of ordinary life. Psychology was reproached with its aloofness from the affairs of the world. But the seclusion of this science was well. For in this seclusion it was studying its methods and perfecting its technique. We must not say learning its limitations. For in its own sphere it has no limitations. Human psychology may, from one point of view, be regarded as the science which investigates human conduct. No nobler study can be conceived. Conduct is the direct result of mental life. None of the causes of delinquency just enumerated can have any effect in this direction except in so far as they affect mental life. Psychology studies human conduct, and the mental elements which produce human conduct, the motives of human conduct in the individual and in the mass. It studies these in the " normal ", the " average " individual, and then proceeds to the study of them in the pathological, the diseased. This leads directly to the view that the offender must be studied as an individual, and that he must be regarded, not as a constant, but as the most variable element in the problem.

Psychology has now emerged from the gloom, and stands ready, with the other sciences, to assist mankind in its struggles. The value of the study of the " conscious " mind has long been known. Various methods of mental testing, to be described in some detail in the next chapter, have proved to be of the greatest service

24 THE PSYCHOLOGY OF THE CRIMINAL

in the unravelling of some problems in delinquency. But we should still have been groping in the dark had it not been for the latest achievement of psychology, the hypothesis of the " unconscious mind ", and the methods of its investigation. This, the greatest achievement of modern times, perhaps of all times, will be dealt with, after an elementary fashion, in Chapters III and IV.

The dependence of conduct upon mental life has, of course, long been recognized in certain practical bearings, although its basis is only just beginning to be investigated. The demagogic politician, the popular newspaper, the religious leader, the advertising agent, have long made use of this dependence. We now claim that the science of psychology indicates the road which we must follow in our study of delinquents, the only road which we can follow with the hope of attaining ultimate peace, because the only road which leads us to the study of what the delinquent really is.

If we consider for a moment the immediate antecedents of any example of delinquency, we see at once how intimately related are conduct and mental life. One man kills another, and the action was the result of the emotion of anger produced by what the victim had said or done. Or, again, in a burglary the action was the result of a deliberately formed mental plan. Or, yet again, a man has yielded to some sudden impulse which prompted him to the gratification of some desire. So it is abundantly clear that the one way to investigate the causes of an offence is to ascertain, as far as may be done, the mental processes which have produced the delinquent action. To overlook this mental factor, is a sure way to the formation of erroneous conclusions. It is thus that the general causation theories have led to so much misapprehension. This is why the easy " explanation " of assigning some external cause for delinquency has led so often to mistaken conclusions.

THE PROBLEM STATED   **25**

The subject may be an alcoholic, yet the real cause of his delinquency may be congenital mental defect. The subject's environment or his family-history may have been hopelessly bad, but the true cause of his delinquency was some buried mental conflict. Here we see the true solution of the problem often put to us, Why is it that of a number of persons in a given environment, or with a particular family-history, or of similar habits, one or more become delinquent, while the rest do not so become ? We have but to consider this, to reject, once and for all, the " general " theories of crime. These easy " explanations " have drawn us from our true goal, the study of the individual. It has been well said " savages explain, science investigates ".

And so, although we must deeply respect the work of Lombroso and his followers, who first grasped the necessity of the study of the delinquent as an individual, we see why it was that their work led to such inadequate results. They failed to see that it is needful to investigate the mind of the offender, and to ascertain what are the immediate mental mechanisms which produced his delinquency. The social and biological causes which assist in the production of delinquency are of great importance, and we must not underrate them. They are worthy of deep study, and they should, if possible, be amended. But they are of quite secondary importance, as compared with the study of the mental mechanisms of the individual. We can only arrive at a correct diagnosis by means of this study of mental mechanisms, and this study is also the surest line to devising correct methods of treatment.

[17]

THE
YOUNG DELINQUENT

BY

SIR CYRIL BURT

A crime is not a detached or separable fact, self-contained and self-subsisting. It is only a symptom. It is a mental symptom with a mental origin. And there is now a definite body of ascertained knowledge, tracing mental symptoms to their causes, just

PROBLEMS AND METHODS   5

as medical knowledge tracks down the sources of bodily disorders, and so can prescribe for each its proper treatment or appropriate cure. The study of the criminal thus becomes a distinct department of this new science —a branch of individual psychology ; and the handling of the juvenile offender is, or should be, a practical application of known psychological principles. To whip a boy, to fine him, to shut him up in a penal institution, because he has infringed the law, is like sending a patient, on the first appearance of fever, out under the open sky to cool his skin and save others from the infection. It is as blind and unintelligent as the primitive treatment of malaria, in the days when the parasite was unlooked for and the mosquito ignored. With moral disorders as with physical, we must find and fight not symptoms but causes. Not before causes have been discovered can cures be advised.

The Method of the Psychologist.—The psychologist, therefore, in approaching the young delinquent takes a path very different from that of the policeman or detective. It is not on the investigation of the offence, but on the investigation of the offender, that his efforts are primarily focussed. To discover the culprit, to prove the charge, to bring the transgression under its proper legal category, these are but the first and the easiest steps in the treatment of a criminal of seven. With the misdeeds of immature boys and girls, the main issue to be answered is not—by whom was this crime committed ? but, why did this particular child commit any crime at all ? And throughout it becomes the concern of the psychological adviser, in every case and on every occasion, to study, first and foremost, the delinquent as an individual.

What, then, is the special method which the scientific investigator adopts in searching for the causes of any particular misdeed ? It is nothing less than the taking of a complete case-history. He institutes an intensive inquiry into the whole psychological situation, with a survey, as detailed and as comprehensive as he can make it, of the past, the present and the future.

6   THE YOUNG DELINQUENT

(A) THE OFFENDER'S PRESENT SITUATION

1. *His Offence.*—In most cases, the convenient starting-point will be the nature and apparent motive of the last offence. It is, however, upon the inward character of the act, not upon its outward, formal classification, that the psychologist chiefly concentrates. He inquires, of course, what precisely it is that the parent or officer complains of; but he seeks to view the child's transgression from the standpoint of the child himself. As a preliminary, he may reconstruct, with all the minuteness possible, the actual conditions of the incident, what the child was probably feeling, thinking of, or wishing for, at the moment of the deed.[1]

---

[1] I do not, of course, mean that the first question put to the child should be—'What made you commit this offence?' I am speaking rather of the first question the psychologist puts to himself.

Into the technique of interrogating young delinquents, I have no space to enter at length. The order of the headings, as given in the text, is by no means the invariable order of advance. Personally, I prefer a circuitous enveloping approach, a series of outflanking movements, with resources first accumulated and then kept ambushed in reserve, rather than a blunt frontal attack. Official reports from the school and the home-visitor should be procured, if possible, beforehand. Then the parent is interviewed, but never, of course, in the presence of the child. With the child himself I usually commence, not with any stern or direct cross-examination, but with simple tests of mental ability—tests, to begin with, of a fairly mechanical kind, such as reading, spelling, or arithmetic, passing to harder tests, as the child's initial apprehensions are calmed and overcome, and working through most of the intellectual tests before the child's fears or tears are re-excited by any allusion to the actual trouble. The analysis of character and conduct is rendered infinitely easier when a knowledge of the child's intelligence and general calibre has thus been gained at the outset. With older children a vocational inquiry, or sometimes an inquiry into health, is more likely to disarm suspicion and establish friendly relations. But in every case where the child's guilt is still problematic, the investigator should be equipped in advance with all the available facts.

PROBLEMS AND METHODS   7

2. *The Offender's Personality.*—Having gained a provisional picture of the true nature of the offence, the
psychologist begins with a routine examination of the
child himself. He notes the health, the strength, the
general condition of the young delinquent's body ;
and then tests and reviews in turn the various capacities
of his mind—his level of intelligence, his traits of
character, his daily habits, interests, and emotions—all
the while considering whether some specific defect,
physical or psychical, of temperament, intellect, or will,
may have contributed to the final outbreak. Here, in
this early part of the main investigation, the analysis is
greatly aided by the use of psychological tests. The
new device of mental testing, and particularly the
measurement of intelligence, have entirely revolutionized
the old methods of studying the criminal ; incidentally,
too, they have swept away much of the value of earlier
observations and conclusions, based as these were on
mere personal impression and vague inference.

3. *The Offender's Environment.*—Having learnt all he
can of the child's general nature, the psychologist proceeds next to influences that surround him. With a
clear knowledge of the offence and the offender, he now
knows what are the crucial points to determine. In
most instances, he must survey the child's whole social
setting, both moral and material—the home in which
he is living, the companions with whom he plays, the
opportunities and temptations that beset him, the
efficiency of the restraint that should hold him back,
the success or failure of the superintendence that his
parents are able to bestow.

8 THE YOUNG DELINQUENT

(B) The Offender's Past History

But to take, as it were, a cross-section of the child's position at a given minute of his life, though suggestive and essential, is still far from enough. One cut across the trunk tells little of the weight or rottenness of the timber as a whole. No human action is a sudden, isolated birth of will, the mushroom upstart of an hour. It has its gradual genesis—a seed, a root, a growth, a fructification. The delinquent's character and conduct, what he now is and what he has just done, these are the fruit of a long and complicated process of development ; and his present predicament, with all its problems and temptations, must be viewed, not as the mere sum of its contemporary constituents, but as the product of converging forces operating cumulatively throughout his life.

We come, therefore, to the second main stage in the inquiry, often the longest stage of all: our survey of the present must be supplemented by a history of the past. A preliminary outline may already have been constructed. From the teachers' reports, from the Court and Care Committee records, from the points noted at successive medical inspections, the salient facts may already have been gleaned. The gaps can be filled in from the replies of the parents. And having thus obtained a thorough insight into the general background of the case, the psychologist at last comes back to the offender and his offence. Then, and not till then, will he seek to elicit the boy's own story.

PROBLEMS AND METHODS   9

We have, then, in each investigation, to dig back
and uncover the underground foundations. We must
explore all the antecedent influences that have been
making, moulding, perhaps marring the young offender,
day by day and year after year, from the first instant
when he was still a single cell within his mother's womb.
And here, in this second portion of the whole inquiry,
another new device of technical procedure brings aid
to the psychologist. What the method of mental
testing does for the study of intellectual capacity, that
the method of so-called psychoanalysis performs for the
study of the growing character. By this and other
expedients, by a scrutiny of all available records and
reports, by renewed interviews with the child and his
parents and his teachers, the investigator should at last
be able to retrace, in fullest detail, the whole biography
of the offending individual ; and so gradually to discover
what forces in the past have brought the child to where
he now stands.

(C) THE OFFENDER'S FUTURE PROGRESS

Thirdly, the psychological adviser must look forward
to the future. To predict what will make a bad boy
good, is of even greater consequence than to learn what

10   THE YOUNG DELINQUENT

has made a good boy bad. To discover the possible
means of ultimate reform is as urgent and essential as
to ascertain the probable causes of previous mis-
demeanours. No psychologist, therefore (unless, as too
often happens, he is compelled) should decide a case
after a single hearing. A few provisional recommendations he may put forward—a word to the mother upon
discipline, a note to the school upon health and intelligence, a suggestion to the care committee for a regular
visitation to the home, and perhaps a grave talk with
the child himself ; but these are to be regarded, not as
final remedies, far less as expiations that wipe the slate
clean, but rather as the beginning of a fresh and specific
experiment in individual psychology.

A man is not a planet ; his further movements cannot
be deduced merely from a record of past tendencies and
present situation, however exhaustive that record may
be. He must be tried and treated first by one method
and then by another. The psychologist, with the aid
of his colleagues, watches the working of some provisional plan ; modifies it tentatively from time to
time ; and corrects his expectations by the verified
results. Indeed, it is this further following-up, with
the child all the while under expert eyes, that often
proves the most instructive source of information.

In its broadest outlines, then, every psychological

PROBLEMS AND METHODS

examination should pursue these three directions—conspective, retrospective, and prospective in turn. It should comprise, first, a systematic survey of the whole situation as it is at present ; secondly, a genetic study of the history of the offender throughout his past ; and, thirdly, a trial scheme of recommendations regarding treatment for the future, all checked and supplemented, as time goes on, by an after-study of the effects secured. In every case, no matter what the crime or who the delinquent, the psychologist begins anew with each child as he finds him, coming to him individually, and regarding him throughout as a unique human being, with a special constitution, a special life-story, a special place and problem of his own.

This seems, at first sight, an overwhelming programme. It is as though each little criminal were to be made the central subject of a protracted and methodical research. That, in a measure, is unquestionably true. Yet the undertaking is less formidable than it sounds. There are certain facts, certain wide generalizations of modern psychology, which greatly simplify the vastness of the problem. The investigator, after studying a long succession of cases, finds himself beginning to recognize a series of recurrent types. In different individuals, and in varying combinations, the same causes, the same motives, the same accessory factors, come before his notice again and again. It is not, indeed, that a given offence has always an identical origin, as, in medical diagnosis, a given group of symptoms is often assignable to some specific germ. Rather, certain outer situations, reacting internally upon certain mental tendencies, seem peculiarly liable to provoke a criminal outburst—whether of theft, truancy, or personal assault—much as the mingling of two composite chemical substances may result in an explosion. By mere superficial observation —from the loudness of the noise, or the colour of the flame—it may not be possible to deduce precisely what perilous reagents have been present ; yet the probable conjunctions are limited in number, and the expert quickly learns for what ingredients he must look.

Anomie Theory

[18]

SOCIAL STRUCTURE AND ANOMIE

ROBERT K. MERTON
Harvard University

THERE persists a notable tendency in sociological theory to attribute the malfunctioning of social structure primarily to those of man's imperious biological drives which are not adequately restrained by social control. In this view, the social order is solely a device for "impulse management" and the "social processing" of tensions. These impulses which break through social control, be it noted, are held to be biologically derived. Nonconformity is assumed to be rooted in original nature.[1] Conformity is by implication the result of an utilitarian calculus or unreasoned conditioning. This point of view, whatever its other deficiences, clearly begs one question. It provides no basis for determining the nonbiological conditions which induce deviations from prescribed patterns of conduct. In this paper, it will be suggested that certain phases of social structure generate the circumstances in which infringement of social codes constitutes a "normal" response.[2]

The conceptual scheme to be outlined is designed to provide a coherent, systematic approach to the study of socio-cultural sources of deviate behavior. Our primary aim lies in discovering how some social structures *exert a definite pressure* upon certain persons in the society to engage in nonconformist rather than conformist conduct. The many ramifications of the scheme cannot all be discussed; the problems mentioned outnumber those explicitly treated.

Among the elements of social and cultural structure, two are important for our purposes. These are analytically separable although they merge imperceptibly in concrete situations. The first consists of culturally defined goals, purposes, and interests. It comprises a frame of aspirational reference. These goals are more or less integrated and involve varying degrees of prestige and sentiment. They constitute a basic, but not the exclusive, component of what Linton aptly has called "designs for group living." Some of these cultural aspirations are related to the original drives of man, but they are not determined by them. The second phase of the social

---

[1] E.g., Ernest Jones, *Social Aspects of Psychoanalysis*, 28, London, 1924. If the Freudian notion is a variety of the "original sin" dogma, then the interpretation advanced in this paper may be called the doctrine of "socially derived sin."

[2] "Normal" in the sense of a culturally oriented, if not approved, response. This statement does not deny the relevance of biological and personality differences which may be significantly involved in the *incidence* of deviate conduct. Our focus of interest is the social and cultural matrix; hence we abstract from other factors. It is in this sense, I take it, that James S. Plant speaks of the "normal reaction of normal people to abnormal conditions." See his *Personality and the Cultural Pattern*, 248, New York, 1937.

SOCIAL STRUCTURE AND ANOMIE   673

structure defines, regulates, and controls the acceptable modes of achieving these goals. Every social group invariably couples its scale of desired ends with moral or institutional regulation of permissible and required procedures for attaining these ends. These regulatory norms and moral imperatives do not necessarily coincide with technical or efficiency norms. Many procedures which from the standpoint of *particular individuals* would be most efficient in securing desired values, e.g., illicit oil-stock schemes, theft, fraud, are ruled out of the institutional area of permitted conduct. The choice of expedients is limited by the institutional norms.

To say that these two elements, culture goals and institutional norms, operate jointly is not to say that the ranges of alternative behaviors and aims bear some constant relation to one another. The emphasis upon certain goals may vary independently of the degree of emphasis upon institutional means. There may develop a disproportionate, at times, a virtually exclusive, stress upon the value of specific goals, involving relatively slight concern with the institutionally appropriate modes of attaining these goals. The limiting case in this direction is reached when the range of alternative procedures is limited only by technical rather than institutional considerations. Any and all devices which promise attainment of the all important goal would be permitted in this hypothetical polar case.[3] This constitutes one type of cultural malintegration. A second polar type is found in groups where activities originally conceived as instrumental are transmuted into ends in themselves. The original purposes are forgotten and ritualistic adherence to institutionally prescribed conduct becomes virtually obsessive.[4] Stability is largely ensured while change is flouted. The range of alternative behaviors is severely limited. There develops a tradition-bound, sacred society characterized by neophobia. The occupational psychosis of the bureaucrat may be cited as a case in point. Finally, there are the intermediate types of groups where a balance between culture goals and institu-

---

[3] Contemporary American culture has been said to tend in this direction. See André Siegfried, *America Comes of Age*, 26–37, New York, 1927. The alleged extreme(?) emphasis on the goals of monetary success and material prosperity leads to dominant concern with technological and social instruments designed to produce the desired result, inasmuch as institutional controls become of secondary importance. In such a situation, innovation flourishes as the *range of means* employed is broadened. In a sense, then, there occurs the paradoxical emergence of "materialists" from an "idealistic" orientation. Cf. Durkheim's analysis of the cultural conditions which predispose toward crime and innovation, both of which are aimed toward efficiency, not moral norms. Durkheim was one of the first to see that "contrairement aux idées courantes le criminel n'apparait plus comme un être radicalement insociable, comme une sorte d'elément parasitaire, de corps étranger et inassimilable, introduit au sein de la société; c'est un agent régulier de la vie sociale." See *Les Règles de la Méthode Sociologique*, 86–89, Paris, 1927.

[4] Such ritualism may be associated with a mythology which rationalizes these actions so that they appear to retain their status as means, but the dominant pressure is in the direction of strict ritualistic conformity, irrespective of such rationalizations. In this sense, ritual has proceeded farthest when such rationalizations are not even called forth.

tional means is maintained. These are the significantly integrated and relatively stable, though changing, groups.

An effective equilibrium between the two phases of the social structure is maintained as long as satisfactions accrue to individuals who conform to both constraints, viz., satisfactions from the achievement of the goals and satisfactions emerging directly from the institutionally canalized modes of striving to attain these ends. Success, in such equilibrated cases, is twofold. Success is reckoned in terms of the product and in terms of the process, in terms of the outcome and in terms of activities. Continuing satisfactions must derive from sheer *participation* in a competitive order as well as from eclipsing one's competitors if the order itself is to be sustained. The occasional sacrifices involved in institutionalized conduct must be compensated by socialized rewards. The distribution of statuses and roles through competition must be so organized that positive incentives for conformity to roles and adherence to status obligations are provided *for every position* within the distributive order. Aberrant conduct, therefore, may be viewed as a symptom of dissociation between culturally defined aspirations and socially structured means.

Of the types of groups which result from the independent variation of the two phases of the social structure, we shall be primarily concerned with the first, namely, that involving a disproportionate accent on goals. This statement must be recast in a proper perspective. In no group is there an absence of regulatory codes governing conduct, yet groups do vary in the degree to which these folkways, mores, and institutional controls are effectively integrated with the more diffuse goals which are part of the culture matrix. Emotional convictions may cluster about the complex of socially acclaimed ends, meanwhile shifting their support from the culturally defined implementation of these ends. As we shall see, certain aspects of the social structure may generate countermores and antisocial behavior precisely because of differential emphases on goals and regulations. In the extreme case, the latter may be so vitiated by the goal-emphasis that the range of behavior is limited only by considerations of technical expediency. The sole significant question then becomes, which available means is most efficient in netting the socially approved value?[5] The technically most feasible procedure, whether legitimate or not, is preferred to the institutionally prescribed conduct. As this process continues, the integration of the society becomes tenuous and anomie ensues.

---

[5] In this connection, one may see the relevance of Elton Mayo's paraphrase of the title of Tawney's well known book. "Actually the problem *is not that of the sickness of an acquisitive society; it is that of the acquisitiveness of a sick society." Human Problems of an Industrial Civilization*, 153, New York, 1933. Mayo deals with the process through which wealth comes to be a symbol of social achievement. He sees this as arising from a state of anomie. We are considering the unintegrated monetary-success goal as an element in producing anomie. A complete analysis would involve both phases of this system of interdependent variables.

SOCIAL STRUCTURE AND ANOMIE 675

Thus, in competitive athletics, when the aim of victory is shorn of its institutional trappings and success in contests becomes construed as "winning the game" rather than "winning through circumscribed modes of activity," a premium is implicitly set upon the use of illegitimate but technically efficient means. The star of the opposing football team is surreptitiously slugged; the wrestler furtively incapacitates his opponent through ingenious but illicit techniques; university alumni covertly subsidize "students" whose talents are largely confined to the athletic field. The emphasis on the goal has so attenuated the satisfactions deriving from sheer participation in the competitive activity that these satisfactions are virtually confined to a successful outcome. Through the same process, tension generated by the desire to win in a poker game is relieved by successfully dealing oneself four aces, or, when the cult of success has become completely dominant, by sagaciously shuffling the cards in a game of solitaire. The faint twinge of uneasiness in the last instance and the surreptious nature of public delicts indicate clearly that the institutional rules of the game *are known* to those who evade them, but that the emotional supports of these rules are largely vitiated by cultural exaggeration of the success-goal.[6] They are microcosmic images of the social macrocosm.

Of course, this process is not restricted to the realm of sport. The process whereby exaltation of the end generates a *literal demoralization*, i.e., a deinstitutionalization, of the means is one which characterizes many[7] groups in which the two phases of the social structure are not highly integrated. The extreme emphasis upon the accumulation of wealth as a symbol of success[8] in our own society militates against the completely effective control of institutionally regulated modes of acquiring a fortune.[9] Fraud, corruption, vice, crime, in short, the entire catalogue of proscribed

---

[6] It is unlikely that interiorized norms are completely eliminated. Whatever residuum persists will induce personality tensions and conflict. The process involves a certain degree of ambivalence. A manifest rejection of the institutional norms is coupled with some latent retention of their emotional correlates. "Guilt feelings," "sense of sin," "pangs of conscience" are obvious manifestations of this unrelieved tension; symbolic adherence to the nominally repudiated values or rationalizations constitute a more subtle variety of tensional release.

[7] "Many," and not all, unintegrated groups, for the reason already mentioned. In groups where the primary emphasis shifts to institutional means, i.e., when the range of alternatives is very limited, the outcome is a type of ritualism rather than anomie.

[8] Money has several peculiarities which render it particularly apt to become a symbol of prestige divorced from institutional controls. As Simmel emphasized, money is highly abstract and impersonal. However acquired, through fraud or institutionally, it can be used to purchase the same goods and services. The anonymity of metropolitan culture, in conjunction with this peculiarity of money, permits wealth, the sources of which may be unknown to the community in which the plutocrat lives, to serve as a symbol of status.

[9] The emphasis upon wealth as a success-symbol is possibly reflected in the use of the term "fortune" to refer to a stock of accumulated wealth. This meaning becomes common in the late sixteenth century (Spenser and Shakespeare). A similar usage of the Latin *fortuna* comes into prominence during the first century B.C. Both these periods were marked by the rise to prestige and power of the "bourgeoisie."

676 AMERICAN SOCIOLOGICAL REVIEW

behavior, becomes increasingly common when the emphasis on the *cultur-ally induced* success-goal becomes divorced from a coordinated institutional emphasis. This observation is of crucial theoretical importance in examining the doctrine that antisocial behavior most frequently derives from bio-logical drives breaking through the restraints imposed by society. The difference is one between a strictly utilitarian interpretation which con-ceives man's ends as random and an analysis which finds these ends deriv-ing from the basic values of the culture.[10]

Our analysis can scarcely stop at this juncture. We must turn to other aspects of the social structure if we are to deal with the social genesis of the varying rates and types of deviate behavior characteristic of different so-cieties. Thus far, we have sketched three ideal types of social orders con-stituted by distinctive patterns of relations between culture ends and means. Turning from these types of *culture patterning*, we find five logically possible, alternative modes of adjustment or adaptation *by individuals* within the culture-bearing society or group.[11] These are schematically presented in the following table, where (+) signifies "acceptance," (−) signifies "elimination" and (±) signifies "rejection and substitution of new goals and standards."

	Culture Goals	Institutionalized Means
I. Conformity	+	+
II. Innovation	+	−
III. Ritualism	−	+
IV. Retreatism	−	−
V. Rebellion[12]	±	±

Our discussion of the relation between these alternative responses and other phases of the social structure must be prefaced by the observation that persons may shift from one alternative to another as they engage in different social activities. These categories refer to role adjustments in specific situations, not to personality *in toto*. To treat the development of this process in various spheres of conduct would introduce a complexity unmanageable within the confines of this paper. For this reason, we shall be concerned primarily with economic activity in the broad sense, "the

[10] See Kingsley Davis, "Mental Hygiene and the Class Structure," *Psychiatry*, 1928, I, esp. 62–63; Talcott Parsons, *The Structure of Social Action*, 59–60, New York, 1937.

[11] This is a level intermediate between the two planes distinguished by Edward Sapir; namely, culture patterns and personal habit systems. See his "Contribution of Psychiatry to an Understanding of Behavior in Society," *Amer. J. Sociol.*, 1937, 42:862–70.

[12] This fifth alternative is on a plane clearly different from that of the others. It represents a *transitional* response which seeks to *institutionalize* new procedures oriented toward revamped cultural goals shared by the members of the society. It thus involves efforts to *change* the existing structure rather than to perform accommodative actions *within* this structure, and introduces additional problems with which we are not at the moment concerned.

SOCIAL STRUCTURE AND ANOMIE

production, exchange, distribution and consumption of goods and services" in our competitive society, wherein wealth has taken on a highly symbolic cast. Our task is to search out some of the factors which exert pressure upon individuals to engage in certain of these logically possible alternative responses. This choice, as we shall see, is far from random.

In every society, Adaptation I (conformity to both culture goals and means) is the most common and widely diffused. Were this not so, the stability and continuity of the society could not be maintained. The mesh of expectancies which constitutes every social order is sustained by the modal behavior of its members falling within the first category. Conventional role behavior oriented toward the basic values of the group is the rule rather than the exception. It is this fact alone which permits us to speak of a human aggregate as comprising a group or society.

Conversely, Adaptation IV (rejection of goals and means) is the least common. Persons who "adjust" (or maladjust) in this fashion are, strictly speaking, *in* the society but not *of* it. Sociologically, these constitute the true "aliens." Not sharing the common frame of orientation, they can be included within the societal population merely in a fictional sense. In this category are *some* of the activities of psychotics, psychoneurotics, chronic autists, pariahs, outcasts, vagrants, vagabonds, tramps, chronic drunkards and drug addicts.[13] These have relinquished, in certain spheres of activity, the culturally defined goals, involving complete aim-inhibition in the polar case, and their adjustments are not in accord with institutional norms. This is not to say that in some cases the source of their behavioral adjustments is not in part the very social structure which they have in effect repudiated nor that their very existence within a social area does not constitute a problem for the socialized population.

This mode of "adjustment" occurs, as far as structural sources are concerned, when both the culture goals and institutionalized procedures have been assimilated thoroughly by the individual and imbued with affect and high positive value, but where those institutionalized procedures which promise a measure of successful attainment of the goals are not available to the individual. In such instances, there results a twofold mental conflict insofar as the moral obligation for adopting institutional means conflicts with the pressure to resort to illegitimate means (which may attain the goal) and inasmuch as the individual is shut off from means which are both legitimate *and* effective. The competitive order is maintained, but the frustrated and handicapped individual who cannot cope with this order drops out.

---

[13] Obviously, this is an elliptical statement. These individuals may maintain some orientation to the values of their particular differentiated groupings within the larger society or, in part, of the conventional society itself. Insofar as they do so, their conduct cannot be classified in the "passive rejection" category (IV). Nels Anderson's description of the behavior and attitudes of the bum, for example, can readily be recast in terms of our analytical scheme. See *The Hobo*, 93–98, *et passim*, Chicago, 1923.

Defeatism, quietism and resignation are manifested in escape mechanisms which ultimately lead the individual to "escape" from the requirements of the society. It is an expedient which arises from continued failure to attain the goal by legitimate measures and from an inability to adopt the illegitimate route because of internalized prohibitions and institutionalized compulsives, *during which process the supreme value of the success-goal has as yet not been renounced.* The conflict is resolved by eliminating *both* precipitating elements, the goals and means. The escape is complete, the conflict is eliminated and the individual is a socialized.

Be it noted that where frustration derives from the inaccessibility of effective institutional means for attaining economic or any other type of highly valued "success," that Adaptations II, III and V (innovation, ritualism and rebellion) are also possible. The result will be determined by the particular personality, and thus, the *particular* cultural background, involved. Inadequate socialization will result in the innovation response whereby the conflict and frustration are eliminated by relinquishing the institutional means and retaining the success-aspiration; an extreme assimilation of institutional demands will lead to ritualism wherein the goal is dropped as beyond one's reach but conformity to the mores persists; and rebellion occurs when emancipation from the reigning standards, due to frustration or to marginalist perspectives, leads to the attempt to introduce a "new social order."

Our major concern is with the illegitimacy adjustment. This involves the use of conventionally proscribed but frequently effective means of attaining at least the simulacrum of culturally defined success,—wealth, power, and the like. As we have seen, this adjustment occurs when the individual has assimilated the cultural emphasis on success without equally internalizing the morally prescribed norms governing means for its attainment. The question arises, Which phases of our social structure predispose toward this mode of adjustment? We may examine a concrete instance, effectively analyzed by Lohman,[14] which provides a clue to the answer. Lohman has shown that specialized areas of vice in the near north side of Chicago constitute a "normal" response to a situation where the cultural emphasis upon pecuniary success has been absorbed, but where there is little access to conventional and legitimate means for attaining such success. The conventional occupational opportunities of persons in this area are almost completely limited to manual labor. Given our cultural stigmatization of manual labor, and its correlate, the prestige of white collar work, it is clear that the result is a strain toward innovational practices. The limitation of opportunity to unskilled labor and the resultant low income

---

[14] Joseph D. Lohman, "The Participant Observer in Community Studies," *Amer. Sociol. Rev.*, 1937, 2:890–98.

SOCIAL STRUCTURE AND ANOMIE   679

can not compete *in terms of conventional standards of achievement* with the high income from organized vice.

For our purposes, this situation involves two important features. First, such antisocial behavior is in a sense "called forth" by certain conventional values of the culture *and* by the class structure involving differential access to the approved opportunities for legitimate, prestige-bearing pursuit of the culture goals. The lack of high integration between the means-and-end elements of the cultural pattern and the particular class structure combine to favor a heightened frequency of antisocial conduct in such groups. The second consideration is of equal significance. Recourse to the first of the alternative responses, legitimate effort, is limited by the fact that actual advance toward desired success-symbols through conventional channels is, despite our persisting open-class ideology,[15] relatively rare and difficult for those handicapped by little formal education and few economic resources. The dominant pressure of group standards of success is, therefore, on the gradual attenuation of legitimate, but by and large ineffective, strivings and the increasing use of illegitimate, but more or less effective, expedients of vice and crime. The cultural demands made on persons in this situation are incompatible. On the one hand, they are asked to orient their conduct toward the prospect of accumulating wealth and on the other, they are largely denied effective opportunities to do so institutionally. The consequences of such structural inconsistency are psychopathological personality, and/or antisocial conduct, and/or revolutionary activities. The equilibrium between culturally designated means and ends becomes highly unstable with the progressive emphasis on attaining the prestige-laden ends by any means whatsoever. Within this context, Capone represents the triumph of amoral intelligence over morally prescribed "failure," when the channels of vertical mobility are closed or narrowed[16]

---

[15] The shifting historical role of this ideology is a profitable subject for exploration. The "office-boy-to-president" stereotype was once in approximate accord with the facts. Such vertical mobility was probably more common then than now, when the class structure is more rigid. (See the following note.) The ideology largely persists, however, possibly because it still performs a useful function for maintaining the *status quo*. For insofar as it is accepted by the "masses," it constitutes a useful sop for those who might rebel against the entire structure, were this consoling hope removed. This ideology now serves to lessen the probability of Adaptation V. In short, the role of this notion has changed from that of an approximately valid empirical theorem to that of an ideology, in Mannheim's sense.

[16] There is a growing body of evidence, though none of it is clearly conclusive, to the effect that our class structure is becoming rigidified and that vertical mobility is declining. Taussig and Joslyn found that American business leaders are being *increasingly* recruited from the upper ranks of our society. The Lynds have also found a "diminished chance to get ahead" for the working classes in Middletown. Manifestly, these objective changes are not alone significant; the individual's subjective evaluation of the situation is a major determinant of the response. The extent to which this change in opportunity for social mobility has been recognized by the least advantaged classes is still conjectural, although the Lynds present some suggestive materials. The writer suggests that a case in point is the increasing frequency of cartoons which observe in a tragi-comic vein that "my old man says everybody can't be Presi-

680   AMERICAN SOCIOLOGICAL REVIEW

in a society which places a high premium on economic affluence and social ascent for all *its members.*[17]

This last qualification is of primary importance. It suggests that other phases of the social structure besides the extreme emphasis on pecuniary success, must be considered if we are to understand the social sources of antisocial behavior. A high frequency of deviate behavior is not generated simply by "lack of opportunity" or by this exaggerated pecuniary emphasis. A comparatively rigidified class structure, a feudalistic or caste order, may limit such opportunities far beyond the point which obtains in our society today. It is only when a system of cultural values extols, virtually above all else, certain *common* symbols of success *for the population at large* while its social structure rigorously restricts or completely eliminates access to approved modes of acquiring these symbols *for a considerable part of the same population*, that antisocial behavior ensues on a considerable scale. In other words, our egalitarian ideology denies by implication the existence of noncompeting groups and individuals in the pursuit of pecuniary success. The same body of success-symbols is held to be desirable for all. These goals are held to *transcend class lines*, not to be bounded by them, yet the actual social organization is such that there exist class differentials in the accessibility of these *common* success-symbols. Frustration and thwarted aspiration lead to the search for avenues of escape from a culturally induced intolerable situation; or unrelieved ambition may eventuate in illicit attempts to acquire the dominant values.[18] The American stress on pecuniary success and ambitiousness for all thus invites exaggerated anxieties, hostilities, neuroses and antisocial behavior.

This theoretical analysis may go far toward explaining the varying correlations between crime and poverty.[19] Poverty is not an isolated variable.

dent. He says if ya can get three days a week steady on W.P.A. work ya ain't doin' so bad either." See F. W. Taussig and C. S. Joslyn, *American Business Leaders*, New York, 1932; R. S. and H. M. Lynd, *Middletown in Transition*, 67 ff., chap. 12, New York, 1937.

[17] The role of the Negro in this respect is of considerable theoretical interest. Certain elements of the Negro population have assimilated the dominant caste's values of pecuniary success and social advancement, but they also recognize that social ascent is at present restricted to their own caste almost exclusively. The pressures upon the Negro which would otherwise derive from the structural inconsistencies we have noticed are hence not identical with those upon lower class whites. See Kingsley Davis, *op. cit.*, 63; John Dollard, *Caste and Class in a Southern Town*, 66 ff., New Haven, 1936; Donald Young, *American Minority Peoples*, 581, New York, 1932.

[18] The psychical coordinates of these processes have been partly established by the experimental evidence concerning *Anspruchsniveaus* and levels of performance. See Kurt Lewin, *Vorsatz, Wille und Bedurfnis*, Berlin, 1926; N. F. Hoppe, "Erfolg und Misserfolg," *Psychol. Forschung*, 1930, 14:1–63; Jerome D. Frank, "Individual Differences in Certain Aspects of the Level of Aspiration," *Amer. J. Psychol.*, 1935, 47:119–28.

[19] Standard criminology texts summarize the data in this field. Our scheme of analysis may serve to resolve some of the theoretical contradictions which P. A. Sorokin indicates. For example, "not everywhere nor always do the poor show a greater proportion of crime . . . many poorer countries have had less crime than the richer countries . . . The [economic] improve-

SOCIAL STRUCTURE AND ANOMIE   681

It is one in a complex of interdependent social and cultural variables. When viewed in such a context, it represents quite different states of affairs. Poverty as such, and consequent limitation of opportunity, are not sufficient to induce a conspicuously high rate of criminal behavior. Even the often mentioned "poverty in the midst of plenty" will not necessarily lead to this result. Only insofar as poverty and associated disadvantages in competition for the culture values approved for *all* members of the society is linked with the assimilation of a cultural emphasis on monetary accumulation as a symbol of success is antisocial conduct a "normal" outcome. Thus, poverty is less highly correlated with crime in southeastern Europe than in the United States. The possibilities of vertical mobility in these European areas would seem to be fewer than in this country, so that neither poverty *per se* nor its association with limited opportunity is sufficient to account for the varying correlations. It is only when the full configuration is considered, poverty, limited opportunity and a commonly shared system of success symbols, that we can explain the higher association between poverty and crime in our society than in others where rigidified class structure is coupled with *differential class symbols of achievement*.

In societies such as our own, then, the pressure of prestige-bearing success tends to eliminate the effective social constraint over means employed to this end. "The-end-justifies-the-means" doctrine becomes a guiding tenet for action when the cultural structure unduly exalts the end and the social organization unduly limits possible recourse to approved means. Otherwise put, this notion and associated behavior reflect a lack of cultural coordination. In international relations, the effects of this lack of integration are notoriously apparent. An emphasis upon national power is not readily coordinated with an inept organization of legitimate, i.e., internationally defined and accepted, means for attaining this goal. The result is a tendency toward the abrogation of international law, treaties become scraps of paper, "undeclared warefare" serves as a technical evasion, the bombing of civilian populations is rationalized,[20] just as the same societal situation induces the same sway of illegitimacy among individuals.

The social order we have described necessarily produces this "strain toward dissolution." The pressure of such an order is upon outdoing one's competitors. The choice of means within the ambit of institutional control will persist as long as the sentiments supporting a competitive system, i.e., deriving from the possibility of outranking competitors and hence en-

---

ment in the second half of the nineteenth century, and the beginning of the twentieth, has not been followed by a decrease of crime." See his *Contemporary Sociological Theories*, 560–61, New York, 1928. The crucial point is, however, that poverty has varying social significance in different social structures, as we shall see. Hence, one would not expect a linear correlation betweem crime and poverty.

[20] See M. W. Royse, *Aerial Bombardment and the International Regulation of War*, New York, 1928.

joying the favorable response of others, are distributed throughout the entire system of activities and are not confined merely to the final result. A stable social structure demands a balanced distribution of affect among its various segments. When there occurs a shift of emphasis from the satisfactions deriving from competition itself to almost exclusive concern with successful competition, the resultant stress leads to the breakdown of the regulatory structure.[21] With the resulting attenuation of the institutional imperatives, there occurs an approximation of the situation erroneously held by utilitarians to be typical of society generally wherein calculations of advantage and fear of punishment are the sole regulating agencies. In such situations, as Hobbes observed, force and fraud come to constitute the sole virtues in view of their relative efficiency in attaining goals,— which were for him, of course, not culturally derived.

It should be apparent that the foregoing discussion is not pitched on a moralistic plane. Whatever the sentiments of the writer or reader concerning the ethical desirability of coordinating the means-and-goals phases of the social structure, one must agree that lack of such coordination leads to anomie. Insofar as one of the most general functions of social organization is to provide a basis for calculability and regularity of behavior, it is increasingly limited in effectiveness as these elements of the structure become dissociated. At the extreme, predictability virtually disappears and what may be properly termed cultural chaos or anomie intervenes.

This statement, being brief, is also incomplete. It has not included an exhaustive treatment of the various structural elements which predispose toward one rather than another of the alternative responses open to individuals; it has neglected, but not denied the relevance of, the factors determining the specific incidence of these responses; it has not enumerated the various concrete responses which are constituted by combinations of specific values of the analytical variables; it has omitted, or included only by implication, any consideration of the social functions performed by illicit responses; it has not tested the full explanatory power of the analytical scheme by examining a large number of group variations in the frequency of deviate and conformist behavior; it has not adequately dealt with rebellious conduct which seeks to refashion the social framework radically; it has not examined the relevance of cultural conflict for an analysis of culture-goal and institutional-means malintegration. It is suggested that these and related problems may be profitably analyzed by this scheme.

---

[21] Since our primary concern is with the socio-cultural aspects of this problem, the psychological correlates have been only implicitly considered. See Karen Horney, *The Neurotic Personality of Our Time*, New York, 1937, for a psychological discussion of this process.

Social Ecology

[19]

CLIFFORD R. SHAW *and* HENRY D. McKAY

CHAPTER I

INTRODUCTION

D URING the past century many studies have been made which indicate that the incidence of officially recorded delinquency and crime varies from one locality to another. One such study, *Delinquency Areas*, was published in 1929 by the authors and their colleagues.[1] This monograph reported a study of the distribution of the home addresses of approximately 60,000 male individuals in Chicago who had been dealt with by the school authorities, the police, and the courts as actual or alleged truants, delinquents, or criminals. It was clearly demonstrated in this report that the rates of all three groups varied widely among the local communities in the city. The low-income communities near the centers of commerce and heavy industry had the highest rates, while those in outlying residential communities of higher economic status were more or less uniformly low.

The present volume brings the delinquency data for Chicago up to date, provides comparative data for several other large American cities, and includes much new material on the differential characteristics of local communities with varying rates of delinquents. Specifically, in this volume an attempt is made further to explore the following questions in regard to the ecology of delinquency and crime in American cities:

1. To what extent do the rates of delinquents and criminals show similar variations among the local communities in different types of American cities?

2. Does recidivism among delinquents vary from community to community in accordance with rates of delinquents?

3. To what extent do variations in rates of delinquents correspond to demonstrable differences in the economic, social, and

---

[1] Clifford R. Shaw, Frederick Zorbaugh, Henry D. McKay, and Leonard S. Cottrell, *Delinquency Areas* (Chicago: University of Chicago Press, 1929).

3

4 JUVENILE DELINQUENCY AND URBAN AREAS

cultural characteristics of local communities in different types of cities?

4. How are the rates of delinquents in particular areas affected over a period of time by successive changes in the nativity and nationality composition of the population?

5. To what extent are the observed differences in the rates of delinquents between children of foreign and native parentage due to a differential geographic distribution of these two groups in the city?

6. Under what economic and social conditions does crime develop as a social tradition and become embodied in a system of criminal values?

7. What do the rates of delinquents, when computed by local areas for successive periods of time, reveal with respect to the effectiveness of traditional methods of treatment and prevention?

8. What are the implications, for treatment and prevention, of wide variations in rates of delinquents in different types of communities?

It is not assumed that this study will provide an answer to all of these questions. Certain facts are presented, however, which are useful in analyzing the nature of the problem of delinquency in urban communities and which have definite implications for the development of control techniques. Although it long has been recognized that the social conditions in low-income areas are such as to give rise to delinquency among a disproportionately large number of boys and young men, this fact has not been given the attention which its importance warrants in the development of therapeutic and preventive programs. It is hoped that the data in this volume will help to serve this purpose by focusing attention upon the need for broad programs of social reconstruction and community organization. It would appear from the findings of this study that successful treatment of the problem of delinquency in large cities will entail the development of programs which seek to effect changes in the conditions of life in specific local communities and in whole sections of the city. Diagnosis and supervision of individual offenders probably will not be sufficient to achieve this end. As Plant suggests:

INTRODUCTION 5

The effects of social institutions upon the personality—those ways in which the cultural pattern in one or another way affects the working out of the individual's problem—are of only academic importance unless we can in one way or another alter the environment to meet the needs that appear.[2]

REGIONAL AND COMMUNITY VARIATIONS IN RATES
OF DELINQUENCY AND CRIME

As previously indicated, many studies of variation in the incidence of delinquency and crime in relation to different social and cultural backgrounds have been published during the past century. In the earliest of these studies, attention was focused primarily upon differences in rates of delinquency and crime among cities or large districts within a given country. These were followed by studies showing that such differences obtained also among local areas, communities, or neighborhoods within the corporate limits of large cities.

Among the very early ecological studies of crime were those made by Guerry in France and reported in his *Essai sur la statistique morale de la France* in 1833. In this study Guerry computed crime rates for the 86 departments of France.[3] These rates were based upon the number of persons accused of crime during the period 1825–30, inclusive. The variations in rates were marked. The number of persons accused of crime against the person varied from 1 out of 2,199 inhabitants in Corse, to 1 out of 37,014 in Creuse, with an average for all 86 departments of 1 out of 17,085 inhabitants. The number of persons accused of crimes against property varied from 1 out of 1,368 inhabitants in Seine, to 1 out of 20,235 inhabitants in Creuse, with an average of 1 out of 6,031 for all departments.[4]

---

[2] James S. Plant, M.D., *Personality and the Cultural Pattern* (New York: Commonwealth Fund, 1937), p. 234.

[3] André Michel Guerry, *Essai sur la statistique morale de la France* (Paris, 1833).

[4] The maps and tables prepared by Guerry were reproduced and discussed by Henry Lytton Bulwer in his work on *France, Social, Literary, and Political* (3d ed.; London: Richard Bentley, 1836), I, 169–210.

Other pertinent studies made in France include H. Joly, *La France criminelle* (Paris, 1891), and Gabriel Tarde, *Penal Philosophy*, trans. Rapelje Howell (Boston, 1912).

6   JUVENILE DELINQUENCY AND URBAN AREAS

During the early part of the past century numerous statistical and government reports were published which indicated that the number of known criminals in relation to the population varied widely among the counties of England and Wales. As early as 1839 Rawson reported that the relative number of criminals was five times greater in certain counties than in others.[5] Twenty-three years later Mayhew published a rather exhaustive study of delinquency and crime in England.[6] Among other things this study included a series of maps showing the incidence of criminality and various types of crime by counties. In certain counties the incidence of criminality was almost four times as great as in other counties. The number of crimes per 10,000 inhabitants in the total population ranged from 26.1 to 7.1 in the 41 counties of England and Wales.

In addition to the numerous studies showing the variations in the incidence of criminality by towns and counties in England and Wales, similar comparisons were made between districts within particular counties. In 1856 John Glyde published a study showing the relative number of criminals in the 17 poor law unions in Suffolk County, England. The ratio between the number of criminals and the population ranged from 1 in 1,344 to 1 in 464 inhabitants for the 17 districts. Wide variations in the incidence of delinquency were also noted between the urban and rural dis-

---

[5] W. Rawson, "An Inquiry into the Statistics of Crime in England and Wales," *Journal of the Statistical Society of London*, II (1839), 334–44.

[6] Henry Mayhew, *London Labor and the London Poor* (London, 1862), IV, 455.

For similar studies reported during this early period see S. Redgrave, "Abstract of Criminal Tables for England and Wales," *Journal of the Statistical Society of London*, I (1838), 231–45; F. G. P. Neison, "Statistics of Crime in England and Wales for the Years 1834–1844," *ibid.*, XI (1848), 140–65; Joseph Fletcher, "Moral and Educational Statistics of England and Wales," *ibid.*, pp. 344–66, and *ibid.*, XII (1849), 189–336; W. M. Tartt, "Report on Criminal Returns," *ibid.*, XX (1857), 365–77; Mary Carpenter, "Importance of Statistics to the Reformatory Movement, with Returns from Female Reformatories," *ibid.*, pp. 33–40; J. Thackray Bunce, "On the Statistics of Crime in Birmingham, as Compared with Other Large Towns," *ibid.*, XXVIII (1865), 518–26; James T. Hammick, "On the Judicial Statistics of England and Wales, with Special Reference to the Recent Returns Relating to Crime," *ibid.*, XXX (1867), 375–426; and Leone Levi, "A Survey of Indictable and Summary Jurisdiction Offenses in England and Wales, 1857–1876," esp. IX, "Locality of Crime," *ibid.*, LXIII (1880), 423–56.

)

INTRODUCTION 7

tricts and between different cities in the same county. Glyde concluded his report by stating that "as tables of crime for all England include counties of various degrees of criminality, so does the average for the county of Suffolk include districts, towns, and villages of opposite moral tendencies as developed by their criminal aspects."[7]

Lombroso and Niceforo, to mention only two of the early Italian students, found that both the number of criminals per unit of population and the incidence of certain types of crimes varied widely from one city to another and from one province to another. Niceforo, in a study of criminality in the island of Sardinia, found that the ratio between the number of cases of robbery and extortion and the total population ranged widely among the districts of the island.[8] With reference to the incidence of criminality in various parts of Italy, Lombroso stated:

> In every part of Italy, almost in every province, there exists some village renowned for having furnished an unbroken series of special delinquents. Thus, in Liguria, Lerice is proverbial for swindlers, Campofreddo and Masson for homicides, Pozzolo for highway robberies. In the province of Lucca, Capannori is noted for its assassinations, and Carde in Piedmont for its field thefts. In southern Italy, Soro, Melfi, and St. Fele have always had their bandits since 1860, and the same is true of Partinico and Monreale in Sicily. . . . . But the most famous of all is the village of Artena in the province of Rome. . . . . It is to be noted that in Sicily brigandage is almost exclusively confined to that famous valley of the Conca d'Oro.[9]

Similar data are presented for Austria and Germany by Aschaffenburg. In summarizing the data for Germany he states:

> While in the whole of Germany there were 1104 convicted persons to every 100,000 persons of punishable age, the number of such convicts in the government districts was: Oppeln 1860, Bromberg 1842, Gumbinnen 1746, Bremen 1732, The Palatinate 1657, Danzig 1541, Upper Bavaria 1528, Königsberg 1526, Marienwerd 1522, Lower Bavaria 1484, Posen 1424, and Mannheim 1211. On the other hand, Schaumburg-Lippe had only 419, and Waldeck 439 convictions. Waldeck offers an excellent opportunity for com-

[7] "Locality of Crime in Suffolk," *Journal of the Statistical Society of London*, XIX (1856), 102.

[8] Alfredo Niceforo, *La Delinquenza in Sardegna* (Palermo, 1897).

[9] Cesare Lombroso, *Crime: Its Causes and Remedies* (New York: Little, Brown & Co., 1911), pp. 23–24.

8   JUVENILE DELINQUENCY AND URBAN AREAS

parison with a section containing approximately the same number of inhabitants. In 1890 Waldeck had a population of 38,986, Pirmasens 38,327.
In Waldeck there were annually 172 convictions, while in Pirmasens there
were 885![10]

Systematic studies of the relative incidence of delinquency in
local districts within cities are, for the most part, of more recent
development than the more general studies referred to in the previous pages, although the close association between conditions
prevailing in particular districts within the city and the incidence
of delinquency was emphasized in the very earliest investigations
of the problem of delinquency. Throughout the early official reports and investigations of crime in London frequent reference is
made to the so-called "low neighborhoods" in which delinquents
and criminals were found in disproportionately large numbers. As
early as 1840 Allison, in his *Principles of Population*, stated:

If any person will walk through St. Giles', the crowded alleys of Dublin,
or the poorer quarters of Glasgow by night, he will meet with ample proof of
these observations; he will no longer wonder at the disorderly habits and
profligate enjoyments of the lower orders; his astonishment will be, not that
there is so much, but that there is so little crime in the world. The great
cause of human corruption in these crowded situations is the contagious nature of bad example and the extreme difficulty of avoiding the seductions of
vice when they are brought into close and daily proximity with the younger
part of the people. Whatever we may think of the strength of virtue, experience proves that the higher orders are indebted for their exemption from
atrocious crime or disorderly habits chiefly to their fortunate removal from
the scene of temptation; and that where they are exposed to the seductions
which assail their inferiors, they are noways behind them in yielding to their
influence. It is the peculiar misfortune of the poor in great cities that they
cannot fly from these irresistible temptations, but that, turn where they will,
they are met by the alluring forms of vice, or the seductions of guilty enjoyment. It is the experienced impossibility of concealing the attractions of vice
from the younger part of the poor in great cities which exposes them to so
many causes of demoralization. All this proceeds not from any unwonted or
extraordinary depravity in the character of these victims of licentiousness,
but from the almost irresistible nature of the temptations to which the poor
are exposed. The rich, who censure their conduct, would in all probability
yield as rapidly as they have done to the influence of similar causes. There

[10] Gustav Aschaffenburg, *Crime and Its Repression* (New York: Little, Brown
& Co., 1913), p. 43.

INTRODUCTION 9

is a certain degree of misery, a certain proximity to sin, which virtue is rarely able to withstand, and which the young, in particular, are generally unable to resist. The progress of vice in such circumstances is almost as certain and often nearly as rapid as that of physical contagion.[11]

Emphasis upon the influences of "low neighborhoods" was again indicated in the writings of Henry Mayhew in 1862. He states:

There are thousands of neglected children loitering about the low neighborhoods of the metropolis, and prowling about the streets, begging and stealing for their daily bread. They are to be found in Westminster, Whitechapel, Shoreditch, St. Giles', New Cut, Lambeth, the Borough, and other localities. Hundreds of them may be seen leaving their parents' homes and low lodging-houses every morning, sallying forth in search of food and plunder. They are fluttering in rags and in the most motley attire. Some are orphans and have no one to care for them; others have left their homes and live in lodging-houses in the most improvident manner, never thinking of to-morrow; others are sent out by their unprincipled parents to beg and steal for a livelihood; others are the children of poor but honest and industrious people, who have been led to steal through the bad companionship of juvenile thieves. Many of them have never been at a day-school nor attended a Sunday school, and have had no moral or religious instruction. On the contrary, they have been surrounded by the most baneful and degrading influences, and have been set a bad example by their parents and others with whom they came in contact, and are shunned by the honest and industrious classes of society. . . . .

These juvenile thieves are chiefly to be found in Lucretia Street, Lambeth; Union Street, Borough Road; Gunn Street, and Friars Street, Blackfriars Road; also at Whitechapel, St. Giles's, Drury Lane, Somers Town, Anderson Grove, and other localities. . . . .

The chief sources whence our pickpockets spring are from the low lodging-houses—from those dwellings in low neighborhoods, where their parents are thieves, and where improvident and drunken people neglect their children, such as Whitechapel, Shoreditch, Spitalfields, New Cut, Lambeth, the Borough, Clerkenwell, Drury Lane, and other localities. . . . .[12]

These early observations received statistical confirmation in Burt's study of juvenile delinquency in London in 1925.[13] In this

[11] Archibald Allison, *The Principles of Population and the Connection with Human Happiness* (Edinburgh: Wm. Blackwood & Son, 1840), II, 76–78.

[12] Mayhew, *op. cit.*, IV, 273, 278, 304.

[13] Cyril Burt, *The Young Delinquent* (London: D. Appleton & Co., 1925), pp. 67–90.

10 JUVENILE DELINQUENCY AND URBAN AREAS

study Burt secured the address of each boy and girl reported as
an industrial school case during the years 1922 and 1923, and
calculated the ratio between the number of cases in each electoral
area in London and the total number of children on the rolls of
the council's schools. The ratio for the several areas ranges from
0.42 to 0.0, while the average for the city as a whole is 0.14. The
map for the entire city indicates that the areas having the highest
rates (0.25 and upward) are located adjacent to the central district of London, while those having the lowest rates (0.05 and less)
are located in the outlying sections near the periphery of the city.
It is interesting to observe, also, that the "low neighborhoods,"
which were regarded by the early students as the chief source of
delinquency, fall within the areas having the highest rates of delinquency. Furthermore, these areas of delinquency correspond
rather closely to the poverty areas revealed in the earlier study
by Charles Booth.[14]

After the turn of the century many students became interested
in the ecological study of delinquency in American cities. In 1912
Breckinridge and Abbott published a study showing the geographic distribution of cases of juvenile delinquency in the city of Chicago. They utilized for this purpose the cases of boys and girls
brought before the Juvenile Court of Cook County on petitions
alleging delinquency during the years 1899–1909. Among other
things they prepared a map showing the location of the homes of
these children. This map indicated that a disproportionately large
number of the cases were concentrated in certain districts of the
city. In this connection they state:

> A study of this map makes possible several conclusions with regard to
> "delinquent neighborhoods." It becomes clear, in the first place, that the
> region from which the children of the court chiefly come is the densely popu-
> lated West Side, and that the most conspicuous centers of delinquency in
> this section have been the congested wards which lie along the river and
> the canals. . . . .
> . . . . The West Side furnished the largest quota of delinquency across
> the river. These are chiefly the Italian quarter of the Twenty-Second Ward
> on the North Side; the First and Second Wards, which together include the

---

[14] *Life and Labor in London* (London, 1891), Vol. II, Appen., "Showing Map
of London Poverty by Districts."

INTRODUCTION

district of segregated vice and a portion of the so-called "black belt" of the South Side; and such distinct industrial communities as the districts near the steel mills of South Chicago and near the stockyards.[15]

It should be noted that this study did not relate the number of delinquents to the population in the various districts of the city. While the distribution map served to localize the problem of delinquency and to show the absolute number of cases in the various districts, rates by geographic units were not computed. Hence, it was not possible to conclude from this study that the observed concentration of cases was due to anything other than a greater density of population in these areas. Since the publication of the findings of Breckinridge and Abbott, studies have been carried on in which the rate of delinquents (ratio between the number of delinquents and the appropriate population group) has been used as a basis for comparisons among unit areas within the city.

In 1915 Ernest W. Burgess, under the direction of Professor F. W. Blackmar, conducted a survey of social conditions in Lawrence, Kansas. This survey included a study of the geographic distribution of alleged delinquent children for the city as a whole, the absolute number of delinquents in the various districts, and the rates of delinquents for the several areas. Both the number of cases and the rates of delinquents show wide variations among the several areas. The ratio between the number of alleged delinquent children and the total population aged 5–16 years varied from 8.36 to 0.82 for the 6 wards of the city. In this connection Burgess states:

The significant fact to be gathered from the records of the children of Lawrence is the large proportion of juvenile delinquents in the entire child population in the fourth ward. One child out of every twelve children five and over, but under seventeen years old, appeared in the juvenile court in the two-year period studied. If this proportion were maintained for a twelve-year period, comprising the age groups between five and seventeen, the presumption is that at least one-half of the children in the fourth ward would have appeared before the juvenile judge before reaching seventeen years. Since the proportion of juvenile delinquency in the fourth ward is three times as large as that in any other ward, the conclusion naturally follows that certain factors are at work here which are absent elsewhere in Lawrence. . . . .

[15] Sophonisba P. Breckinridge and Edith Abbott, *The Delinquent Child and the Home* (New York: Russell Sage Foundation, 1912), pp. 150–53.

12 JUVENILE DELINQUENCY AND URBAN AREAS

The low percentages of delinquency in wards 5 and 6, in North Lawrence, is to be accounted for by the semi-rural character of the community, with its opportunities for play, and by the distance from the industrial and business part of the community. . . . .[16]

Two years after the publication of the Lawrence survey R. D. McKenzie conducted a general study of Columbus, Ohio. In addition to showing the actual geographic distribution of the homes of delinquent children, this study also included rates of delinquents by wards, along with certain indexes of neighborhood situations and an intensive study of a local community. The rate of delinquency, which in this study represented the ratio between the number of delinquents and the number of registered voters, ranged from 1.66 to 0.35 for the 16 wards of the city.[17]

During recent years additional studies of the ecology of delinquency and crime have been made in a number of American cities.[18] All of these revealed rather wide variations in the rates

[16] F. W. Blackmar and E. W. Burgess, *Lawrence Social Survey* (Lawrence: University of Kansas, 1917), pp. 71–72.

[17] *The Neighborhood: A Study of Local Life in the City of Columbus, Ohio* (Chicago: University of Chicago Press, 1923).

[18] The following is a partial list of these studies: (a) Irwin W. Halpern, John N. Stanislaus, and Bernard Botein, *A Statistical Study of the Distribution of Adult and Juvenile Delinquents in the Boroughs of Manhattan and Brooklyn* (New York: Polygraphic Co. of America, 1934); Norman S. Hayner, "Delinquency Areas in the Puget Sound Region," *American Journal of Sociology*, Vol. XXXIX; Calvin F. Schmid, *Social Saga of Two Cities* (Minneapolis: Minneapolis Council of Social Agencies, 1937); R. Clyde White, "The Relation of Felonies to Environmental Factors in Indianapolis," *Social Forces*, Vol. X; J. B. Lottier, "Distribution of Criminal Offenses in Metropolitan Regions," *Journal of Criminal Law and Criminology*, Vol. XXIX; Herman Adler, Frances Cahn, and Johannes Stuart, *The Incidence of Delinquency in Berkeley, 1928–32* (Berkeley: University of California Press, 1934); Donald Trauger, L. Kral, and W. Rauscher, *Social Analysis of Des Moines* (Des Moines: Iowa State Planning Board, 1935); Vernon E. Keye, "Survey of Juvenile Delinquency in Evanston, Illinois" (Work Projects Administration Report, 1940); Emil Frankel, "New Brunswick Delinquency Areas Study" (Work Projects Administration Report, 1936); Donald R. Taft, "Testing the Selective Influence of Areas of Delinquency," *American Journal of Sociology*, XXXVIII, 1933; M. C. Elmer, "Maladjustment of Youth in Relation to Density of Population," *Proceedings of the American Sociological Society*, Vol. XXII; Howard Whipple Green, *Population Characteristics by Census Tracts, Cleveland, Ohio* (Cleveland: Plain Dealer Pub. Co., 1931); Sophia M. Robison, *Can Delinquency Be Measured?* (New York:

INTRODUCTION 13

of delinquency by local areas. In some instances attention was focused almost exclusively upon variations in rates among areas while in others the rates were correlated with indexes of varying community backgrounds. In general, these studies support the findings reported in the authors' earlier publication, *Delinquency Areas*.[19] Brief reports of a few of these studies are included in this volume.

It may be observed that some of the studies presented are not of recent date. This fact does not detract from their theoretical value, since the primary interest is in the study of the relationship between the community and delinquency. A study completed ten years ago may serve this purpose as adequately as a current one. Whenever possible, data representing different periods of time have been utilized as a means of studying long-time trends in the relationship between volume of delinquency and local community characteristics.

In this attempt to analyze the variations in rates of delinquents by geographic areas in American cities a variety of statistical data are utilized for the purpose of determining the extent to which differences in the economic and social characteristics of local areas parallel variations in rates of delinquents. The methods employed include spot maps, statistical tables showing the rates of delinquents and economic and social variables computed for large zones

---

Columbia University Press, 1936); H. D. Shelden, "Problems in the Statistical Study of Juvenile Delinquency," *Metron*, XII, 1934; E. Franklin Frazier, *The Negro Family in Chicago* (Chicago: University of Chicago Press, 1933), pp. 204-19; William J. Ellis, *Delinquency Areas in Essex County Municipalities* (New Jersey Department of Institutions and Agencies, Trenton, 1938); Clarence W. Schroeder, *Delinquency in Peoria* (Peoria, Illinois: Bradley Polytechnic Institute, 1939); Edwin H. Sutherland, "Ecological Survey of Crime and Delinquency in Bloomington, Indiana," Indiana University, 1937; J. B. Maller, *Maladjusted Youth* (Report of the Children's Court Jurisdiction and Juvenile Delinquency Committee [Legislative Document No. 75 (1939), 201 pages]); J. B. Maller, *Juvenile Delinquency in the State of New York* (Report of the Children's Court Jurisdiction and Juvenile Delinquency Committee [Legislative Document No. 62 (1940), 115 pages]); Kimball Young, John L. Gillin, Calvert L. Dedrick, *The Madison Community* ("University of Wisconsin Studies," No. 62 [Madison: University of Wisconsin, 1934]); and W. Wallace Weaver, *West Philadelphia: A Study of Natural Social Areas* (Ph.D. thesis, University of Pennsylvania, 1930).

[19] *Op. cit.*

14 JUVENILE DELINQUENCY AND URBAN AREAS

and classes of areas, zero-order correlations, and, in a few instances, higher-order correlations. While these maps and statistical data are useful in locating different types of areas, in differentiating the areas where the rates of delinquency are high from areas where the rates are low, and in predicting or forecasting expected rates, they do not furnish an explanation of delinquent conduct. This explanation, it is assumed, must be sought, in the first place, in the field of the more subtle human relationships and social values which comprise the social world of the child in the family and community. These more distinctively human situations, which seem to be directly related to delinquent conduct, are, in turn, products of larger economic and social processes characterizing the history and growth of the city and of the local communities which comprise it.

In this study the Chicago delinquency data are dealt with in a much more detailed manner than in the other cities for which data are presented. All of chapters ii–vii (Part II) are concerned with Chicago. These give a description of the growth and configuration of the city; the geographic distribution of delinquents and criminals, rates of infant mortality, tuberculosis, and insanity; and indexes of the variations in the economic, social, and cultural characteristics of local areas for which rates of delinquency have been computed.

Chapters viii through xii (Part III) comprise studies prepared by the authors on the distribution of delinquency in five cities or metropolitan areas which include a total of 24 separate municipalities. Although a few series of delinquent girls are included in certain of these studies, the primary emphasis has been placed upon ecological aspects of delinquency among males. Chapter xiii (Part IV) includes a summary of the findings, an interpretation in terms of a general theory, and a brief discussion of some of the implications of these studies for treatment and prevention. Chapters xiv through xvi (Part V) were prepared especially for this edition. They update data on delinquents and commitments in Chicago and bring to bear new data on Chicago suburbs.

Subcultural Theory

[20]

A Delinquent Solution

Albert K. Cohen

WHAT THE DELINQUENT SUBCULTURE HAS TO OFFER

THE DELINQUENT subculture, we suggest, is a way of dealing with the problems of adjustment we have described. These problems are chiefly status problems: certain children are denied status in the respectable society because they cannot meet the criteria of the respectable status system. The delinquent subculture deals with these problems by providing criteria of status which these children *can* meet.

This statement is highly elliptical and is based upon a number of assumptions whose truth is by no means self-evident. It is not, for example, self-evident that people whose status positions are low must necessarily feel deprived, injured or ego-involved in that low status. Whether they will or not depends upon several considerations.

                                    Our ego-involvement in a
given comparison with others depends upon our "status
universe." "Whom do we measure ourselves against?" is
the crucial question. In some other societies virtue may
consist in willing acceptance of the role of peasant, low-
born commoner or member of an inferior caste and in
conformity to the expectations of that role. If others are
richer, more nobly-born or more able than oneself, it is
by the will of an inscrutable Providence and not to be imputed to one's own moral defect. The sting of status inferiority is thereby removed or mitigated; one measures himself only against those of like social position. We have suggested, however, that an important feature of American
"democracy," perhaps of the Western European tradition
in general, is the tendency to measure oneself against "all
comers." This means that, for children as for adults, one's
sense of personal worth is at stake in status comparisons
with all other persons, at least of one's own age and sex,
whatever their family background or material circumstances. It means that, in the lower levels of our status
hierarchies, whether adult or juvenile, there is a chronic
fund of motivation, conscious or repressed, to elevate one's
status position, either by striving to climb within the established status system or by redefining the criteria of status
so that one's present attributes become status-giving assets.
It has been suggested, for example, that such typically
working-class forms of Protestantism as the Holiness sects
owe their appeal to the fact that they reverse the respectable status system; it is the humble, the simple and the
dispossessed who sit at the right hand of God, whereas

A Delinquent Solution [123]

worldly goods, power and knowledge are as nothing in His eyes. In like manner, we offer the view that the delinquent subculture is one solution to a kindred problem on the juvenile level.

Another consideration affecting the degree of privation experienced in a given status position is the "status source." A person's status, after all, is how he stands in somebody's eyes. Status, then, is not a fixed property of the person but varies with the point of view of whoever is doing the judging. I may be revered by some and despised by others. A crucial question then becomes: "Whose respect or admiration do I value?" That *you* think well or ill of me may or may not *matter* to me.

It may be argued that the working-class boy does not *care* what middle-class people think of him, that he is ego-involved only in the opinions of his family, his friends, his working-class neighbors. A definitive answer to this argument can come only from research designed to get at the facts. This research, in our opinion, is yet to be done. There is, however, reason to believe that most children are sensitive *to some degree* about the attitudes of *any persons* with whom they are thrown into more than the most superficial kind of contact. The contempt or indifference of others, particularly of those like schoolmates and teachers, with whom we are constrained to associate for long hours every day, is difficult, we suggest, to shrug off. It poses a problem with which one may conceivably attempt to cope in a variety of ways. One may make an active effort to change himself in conformity with the expectations of others; one may attempt to justify or explain away his inferiority in terms which will exculpate him; one may tell oneself that he really doesn't care what these people think; one may react with anger and aggression. But the least probable response is simple, uncomplicated, honest indifference. If we grant the probable truth of the claim that most American working-class children are most sensitive to status sources on their own level, it does not follow that they take lightly rejection, disparagement and censure from other status sources.

Even on their "own" social level, the situation is far from simple. The "working class," we have repeatedly emphasized, is not culturally homogeneous. Not only is there much diversity in the cultural standards applied by one's own working-class neighbors and kin so that it is difficult to find a "working-class" milieu in which "middle-class" standards are not important. In addition, the "working-class" culture we have described is, after all, an ideal type; most working-class *people* are culturally ambivalent. Due to lack of capacity, of the requisite "character structure" or of "luck," they may be working-class in terms of job and income; they may have accepted this status with resignation and rationalized it to their satisfaction; and by example, by class-linked techniques of child training and by failure to support the middle-class agencies of socialization they may have produced children deficient in the attributes that make for status in middle-class terms. Nevertheless, all their lives, through all the major media of mass indoctrination—the schools, the movies, the radio, the newspapers and the magazines—the middle-class powers-that-be that manipulate these media have been trying to "sell" them on middle-class values and the middle-class standard of living. Then there is the "propaganda of the deed," the fact that they have seen with their own eyes working-class contemporaries "get ahead" and "make the grade" in a middle-class world. In consequence of all this, we suspect that few working-class parents unequivocally repudiate as intrinsically worthless middle-class objectives. There is good reason to believe that the modesty of working-class aspirations is partly a matter of trimming one's sails to the available opportunities and resources and partly a matter of unwillingness to accept the discipline which upward striving entails.

However complete and successful one's accommodation to an humble status, the vitality of middle-class goals, of the "American dream," is nonetheless likely to manifest itself in his aspirations for his children. His expectations may not be grandiose, but he will want his children to be "better off" than he. Whatever his own work history and social reputation may be, he will want his children to be "steady" and "respectable." He may exert few positive pressures to "succeed" and the experiences he provides his children may even incapacitate them for success; he may be puzzled at the way they "turn out." But whatever the measure of his own responsibility in accounting for the product, he is not likely to judge that product by unadulterated "corner-boy" standards. Even "corner-boy" parents, although they may value in their children such corner-boy virtues as generosity to friends, personal loyalty and physical prowess, are likely also to be gratified by recognition by middle-class representatives and by the kinds of

achievement for which the college-boy way of life is a
prerequisite. Even in the working-class milieu from which
he acquired his incapacity for middle-class achievement,
the working-class corner-boy may find himself at a status
disadvantage as against his more upwardly mobile peers.

Lastly, of course, is that most ubiquitous and inescapable of status sources, oneself. Technically, we do not call
the person's attitudes towards himself "status" but rather
"self-esteem," or, when the quality of the self-attitude is
specifically moral, "conscience" or "superego." The important question for us is this: To what extent, if at all, do
boys who are typically "working-class" and "corner-boy"
in their overt behavior evaluate themselves by "middle-
class," "college-boy" standards? For our overt behavior,
however closely it conforms to one set of norms, need not
argue against the existence or effectiveness of alternative
and conflicting norms. The failure of our own behavior to
conform to our own expectations is an elementary and
commonplace fact which gives rise to the tremendously
important consequences of guilt, self-recrimination, anxiety
and self-hatred. The reasons for the failure of self-expecta-
tions and overt conduct to agree are complex. One reason
is that we often internalize more than one set of norms,
each of which would dictate a different course of action
in a given life-situation; since we can only *do* one thing
at a time, however, we are forced to choose between them
or somehow to compromise. In either case, we fall short
of the full realization of our own expectations and must
somehow cope with the residual discrepancy between
those expectations and our overt behavior.

A Delinquent Solution [127]

Corner-boy children (like their working-class parents) internalize middle-class standards to a sufficient degree to create a fundamental ambivalence towards their own corner-boy behavior. Again, we are on somewhat speculative ground where fundamental research remains to be done. The coexistence within the same personality of a corner-boy and a college-boy morality may appear more plausible, however, if we recognize that they are not simple antitheses of one another and that parents and others may in all sincerity attempt to indoctrinate both. For example, the goals upon which the college-boy places such great value, such as intellectual and occupational achievement, and the college-boy virtues of ambitiousness and pride in self-sufficiency are not as such disparaged by the corner-boy culture. The meritoriousness of standing by one's friends and the desire to have a good time here and now do not by definition preclude the desire to help oneself and to provide for the future. It is no doubt the rule, rather than the exception, that most children, college-boy and corner-boy alike, would like to enjoy the best of both worlds. *In practice,* however, the substance that is consumed in the pursuit of one set of values is not available for the pursuit of the other. The sharpness of the dilemma and the degree of the residual discontent depend upon a number of things, notably, the intensity with which both sets of norms have been internalized, the extent to which the life-situations which one encounters compel a choice between them, and the abundance and appropriateness of the skills and resources at one's disposal. The child of superior intelligence, for example, may find it easier than

his less gifted peers to meet the demands of the college-
boy standards without failing his obligations to his corner-
boy associates.

It is a plausible assumption, then, that the working-
class boy whose status is low in middle-class terms *cares*
about that status, that this status confronts him with a genuine problem of adjustment. To this problem of adjustment there are a variety of conceivable responses, of which
participation in the creation and the maintenance of the
delinquent subculture is one. Each mode of response entails costs and yields gratifications of its own. The circumstances which tip the balance in favor of the one or the
other are obscure. One mode of response is to desert the
corner-boy for the college-boy way of life. To the reader
of Whyte's *Street Corner Society* the costs are manifest.
It is hard, at best, to be a college-boy and to run with the
corner-boys. It entails great effort and sacrifice to the
degree that one has been indoctrinated in what we have
described as the working-class socialization process; its
rewards are frequently long-deferred; and for many working-class boys it makes demands which they are, in consequence of their inferior linguistic, academic and "social"
skills, not likely ever to meet. Nevertheless, a certain proportion of working-class boys accept the challenge of the
middle-class status system and play the status game by
the middle-class rules.

Another response, perhaps the most common, is what
we may call the "stable corner-boy response." It represents
an acceptance of the corner-boy way of life and an effort
to make the best of a situation. If our reasoning is correct,

A Delinquent Solution [129]

it does not resolve the dilemmas we have described as inherent in the corner-boy position in a largely middle-class world, although these dilemmas may be mitigated by an effort to disengage oneself from dependence upon middle-class status-sources and by withdrawing, as far as possible, into a sheltering community of like-minded working-class children. Unlike the delinquent response, it avoids the radical rupture of good relations with even working-class adults and does not represent as irretrievable a renunciation of upward mobility. It does not incur the active hostility of middle-class persons and therefore leaves the way open to the pursuit of some values, such as jobs, which these people control. It represents a preference for the familiar, with its known satisfactions and its known imperfections, over the risks and the uncertainties as well as the moral costs of the college-boy response, on the one hand, and the delinquent response on the other.

What does the delinquent response have to offer? Let us be clear, first, about what this response is and how it differs from the stable corner-boy response. The hallmark of the delinquent subculture is the explicit and wholesale repudiation of middle-class standards and the adoption of their very antithesis. *The corner-boy culture is not specifically delinquent.* Where it leads to behavior which may be defined as delinquent, *e.g.,* truancy, it does so not because nonconformity to middle-class norms *defines* conformity to corner-boy norms but because conformity to middle-class norms *interferes with* conformity to corner-boy norms. The corner-boy plays truant because he does not like school, because he wishes to escape from a dull and unrewarding and perhaps humiliating situation. But truancy is not defined as intrinsically valuable and status-giving. The member of the delinquent subculture plays truant because "good" middle-class (and working-class) children do not play truant. Corner-boy resistance to being herded and marshalled by middle-class figures is not the same as the delinquent's flouting and jeering of those middle-class figures and active ridicule of those who submit. The corner-boy's ethic of reciprocity, his quasi-communal attitude toward the property of in-group members, is shared by the delinquent. But this ethic of reciprocity does not sanction the deliberate and "malicious" violation of the property rights of persons outside the in-group. We have observed that the differences between the corner-boy and the college-boy or middle-class culture are profound but that in many ways they are profound differences in emphasis. We have remarked that the corner-boy culture does not so much repudiate the value of many middle-class achievements as it emphasizes certain other values which make such achievements improbable. In short, the corner-boy culture temporizes with middle-class morality; the full-fledged delinquent subculture does not.

It is precisely here, we suggest, in the refusal to temporize, that the appeal of the delinquent subculture lies. Let us recall that it is characteristically American, not specifically working-class or middle-class, to measure oneself against the widest possible status universe, to seek status against "all comers," to be "as good as" or "better than" anybody—anybody, that is, within one's own age and sex category. As long as the working-class corner-boy clings

A Delinquent Solution [131]

to a version, however attenuated and adulterated, of the middle-class culture, he must recognize his inferiority to working-class and middle-class college-boys. The delinquent subculture, on the other hand, permits no ambiguity of the status of the delinquent relative to that of anybody else. In terms of the norms of the delinquent subculture, defined by its negative polarity to the respectable status system, the delinquent's very nonconformity to middle-class standards sets him above the most exemplary college boy.

Another important function of the delinquent subculture is the legitimation of aggression. We surmise that a certain amount of hostility is generated among working-class children against middle-class persons, with their airs of superiority, disdain or condescension and against middle-class norms, which are, in a sense, the cause of their status-frustration. To infer inclinations to aggression from the existence of frustration is hazardous; we know that aggression is not an inevitable and not the only consequence of frustration. So here too we must feel our way with caution. Ideally, we should like to see systematic research, probably employing "depth interview" and "projective" techniques, to get at the relationship between status position and aggressive dispositions toward the rules which determine status and toward persons variously distributed in the status hierarchy. Nevertheless, despite our imperfect knowledge of these things, we would be blind if we failed to recognize that bitterness, hostility and jealousy and all sorts of retributive fantasies are among the most common and typically human responses to public humiliation. However, for the child who temporizes with middle-class morality, overt aggression and even the conscious recognition of his own hostile impulses are inhibited, for he acknowledges the *legitimacy* of the rules in terms of which he is stigmatized. For the child who breaks clean with middle-class morality, on the other hand, there are no moral inhibitions on the free expression of aggression against the sources of his frustration. Moreover, the connection we suggest between status-frustration and the aggressiveness of the delinquent subculture seems to us more plausible than many frustration-aggression hypotheses because it involves no assumptions about obscure and dubious "displacement" of aggression against "substitute" targets. The target in this case is the manifest cause of the status problem.

It seems to us that the mechanism of "reaction-formation" should also play a part here. We have made much of the corner-boy's basic ambivalence, his uneasy acknowledgement, while he lives by the standards of his corner-boy culture, of the legitimacy of college-boy standards. May we assume that when the delinquent seeks to obtain unequivocal status by repudiating, once and for all, the norms of the college-boy culture, these norms really undergo total extinction? Or do they, perhaps, linger on, underground, as it were, repressed, unacknowledged but an ever-present threat to the adjustment which has been achieved at no small cost? There is much evidence from clinical psychology that moral norms, once effectively internalized, are not lightly thrust aside or extinguished. If a new moral order is evolved which offers a more satisfactory solution

A Delinquent Solution [133]

to one's life problems, the old order usually continues to press for recognition, but if this recognition is granted, the applecart is upset. The symptom of this obscurely felt, ever-present threat is clinically known as "anxiety," and the literature of psychiatry is rich with devices for combatting this anxiety, this threat to a hard-won victory. One such device is reaction-formation. Its hallmark is an "exaggerated," "disproportionate," "abnormal" intensity of response, "inappropriate" to the stimulus which seems to elicit it. The unintelligibility of the response, the "over-reaction," becomes intelligible when we see that it has the function of reassuring the actor against an *inner* threat to his defenses as well as the function of meeting an external situation on its own terms. Thus we have the mother who "compulsively" showers "inordinate" affection upon a child to reassure herself against her latent hostility and we have the male adolescent whose awkward and immoderate masculinity reflects a basic insecurity about his own sex-role. In like manner, we would expect the delinquent boy who, after all, has been socialized in a society dominated by a middle-class morality and who can never quite escape the blandishments of middle-class society, to seek to maintain his safeguards against seduction. Reaction-formation, in his case, should take the form of an "irrational," "malicious," "unaccountable" hostility to the enemy within the gates as well as without: the norms of the respectable middle-class society.[1]

If our reasoning is correct, it should throw some light upon the peculiar quality of "property delinquency" in the delinquent subculture. We have already seen how the

rewardingness of a college-boy and middle-class way of life
depends, to a great extent, upon general respect for property rights. In an urban society, in particular, the possession and display of property are the most ready and public
badges of reputable social class status and are, for that
reason, extraordinarily ego-involved. That property actually is a reward for middle-class morality is in part only a
plausible fiction, but in general there is certainly a relationship between the practice of that morality and the
possession of property. The middle-classes have, then, a
strong interest in scrupulous regard for property rights,
not only because property is "intrinsically" valuable but
because the full enjoyment of their status requires that
that status be readily recognizable and therefore that property adhere to those who earn it. The cavalier misappro-
priation or destruction of property, therefore, is not only
a diversion or diminution of wealth; it is an attack on the
middle-class where their egos are most vulnerable. Group
stealing, institutionalized in the delinquent subculture, is
not just a way of *getting* something. It is a means that is
the antithesis of sober and diligent "labour in a calling."
It expresses contempt for a way of life by making its opposite a criterion of status. Money and other valuables are
not, as such, despised by the delinquent. For the delinquent and the non-delinquent alike, money is a most
glamorous and efficient means to a variety of ends and one
cannot have too much of it. But, in the delinquent subculture, the stolen dollar has an odor of sanctity that does not
attach to the dollar saved or the dollar earned.

This delinquent system of values and way of life does

its job of problem-solving most effectively when it is adopted as a group solution. We have stressed in our chapter on the general theory of subcultures that the efficacy of a given change in values as a solution and therefore the motivation to such a change depends heavily upon the availability of "reference groups" within which the "deviant values" are already institutionalized, or whose members would stand to profit from such a system of deviant values if each were assured of the support and concurrence of the others. So it is with delinquency. We do not suggest that joining in the creation or perpetuation of a delinquent subculture is the only road to delinquency. We do believe, however, that for most delinquents delinquency would not be available as a response were it not socially legitimized and given a kind of respectability, albeit by a restricted community of fellow-adventurers. In this respect, the adoption of delinquency is like the adoption of the practice of appearing at the office in open-collar and shirt sleeves. Is it much more comfortable, is it more sensible than the full regalia? Is it neat? Is it dignified? The arguments in the affirmative will appear much more forceful if the practice is already established in one's milieu or if one senses that others are prepared to go along if someone makes the first tentative gestures. Indeed, to many of those who sweat and chafe in ties and jackets, the possibility of an alternative may not even occur until they discover that it has been adopted by their colleagues.

This way of looking at delinquency suggests an answer to a certain paradox. Countless mothers have protested that their "Johnny" was a good boy until he fell in with a

certain bunch. But the mothers of each of Johnny's companions hold the same view with respect to their own offspring. It is conceivable and even probable that some of
these mothers are naive, that one or more of these youngsters are "rotten apples" who infected the others. We suggest, however, that all of the mothers may be right, that
there is a certain chemistry in the group situation itself
which engenders that which was not there before, that
group interaction is a sort of catalyst which releases poten-
tialities not otherwise visible. This is especially true when
we are dealing with a problem of status-frustration. Status,
by definition, is a grant of respect from others. A new system of norms, which measures status by criteria which
one can meet, is of no value unless others are prepared to
apply those criteria, and others are not likely to do so unless
one is prepared to reciprocate.[2]

We have referred to a lingering ambivalence in the delinquent's own value system, an ambivalence which threat-
ens the adjustment he has achieved and which is met
through the mechanism of reaction-formation. The delinquent may have to contend with another ambivalence, in
the area of his status sources. The delinquent subculture
offers him status *as against* other children of whatever social
level, but it offers him this status *in the eyes of* his fellow
delinquents only. To the extent that there remains a desire
for recognition from groups whose respect has been forfeited by commitment to a new subculture, his satisfaction in his solution is imperfect and adulterated. He can
perfect his solution only by rejecting as status sources
those who reject him. This too may require a certain mea-

sure of reaction-formation, going beyond indifference to active hostility and contempt for all those who do not share his subculture. He becomes all the more dependent upon his delinquent gang. Outside that gang his status position is now weaker than ever. The gang itself tends toward a kind of sectarian solidarity, because the benefits of membership can only be realized in active face-to-face relationships with group members.

This interpretation of the delinquent subculture has important implications for the "sociology of social problems." People are prone to assume that those things which we define as evil and those which we define as good have their origins in separate and distinct features of our society. Evil flows from poisoned wells; good flows from pure and crystal fountains. The same source cannot feed both. Our view is different. It holds that those values which are at the core of "the American way of life," which help to motivate the behavior which we most esteem as "typically American," are among the major determinants of that which we stigmatize as "pathological." More specifically, it holds that the problems of adjustment to which the delinquent subculture is a response are determined, in part, by those very values which respectable society holds most sacred. The same value system, impinging upon children differently equipped to meet it, is instrumental in generating both delinquency and respectability.

Argument: Some of the Big Ideas Applied

[21]

THE CRIMINAL AREA

A Study in
Social Ecology

by
TERENCE MORRIS

THE DESIGN OF THE RESEARCH

Broadly speaking, the aim of the inquiry was to survey the crime position in Croydon and to discover whether there was any significant relationship between the crime pattern and the ecological characteristics of the town. Thus far it was an attempt to test out some of the hypotheses of Shaw and McKay in an

---

[1] cf., Benny, M. and Geiss, H. "social class in one or other of its protean manifestations is the chief determinant of political behaviour", 'Social Class and Politics in Greenwich', *British Journal of Sociology*, Vol. 1, No. 4, 1950, p. 326.

Delinquency Areas in Croydon

urban community markedly different from those studied in the
United States and reported in *Juvenile Delinquency and Urban Areas*.
Further than this it was hoped to investigate the statement that
Croydons' delinquents were not "slum" children but those of the
middle classes, and the provisions made for the prevention and
treatment of delinquency and crime.

The difficulties inherent in the single handed study of crime in
a town of a quarter of a million inhabitants need scarcely to be
elaborated. The major problem of research design was to define
those few avenues of inquiry which could be pursued in some
detail and which were likely to provide meaningful data. It was
decided at the outset to concentrate on a single year, 1952, during
which the Craig and Bentley affair took place. In many ways a
synchronic study would have been more fruitful in that it might
have shown important trends in the distribution of both crime
and criminals, but the task of handling the statistics for three
years, let alone five or ten, would have proved well-nigh insu-
perable in the two years available for the research. In addition to
the statistical material it was decided to collect a number of
individual case studies in view of the fact that case studies play
a valuable complementary role to statistics in understanding the
dynamics of individual delinquencies. The data were collected
therefore under three main headings:

Series I: A complete list of all indictable offences, and certain
    non-indictable offences of a "criminal" character, known to
    the police and committed in the Borough during 1952, classi-
    fied by type and geographical location.

Series II: A list of all persons aged 8 years and over, charged in
    1952 with offences committed in the Borough and classified by
    offence, age, sex and residence.

Series III: The Case Histories of all Juvenile offenders placed
    on Probation, under Supervision, or committed to Approved
    Schools in the period January 1st - December 31st, 1952, by
    the Borough Juvenile Court, or (in the case of certain Proba-
    tioners) dealt with by other Courts which immediately trans-
    ferred the order to the offender's home town.

Series I: THE DISTRIBUTION OF OFFENCES

The majority of offences in this Series were indictable, that is
to say crimes of a fairly grave nature as far as the community is

119

The Criminal Area

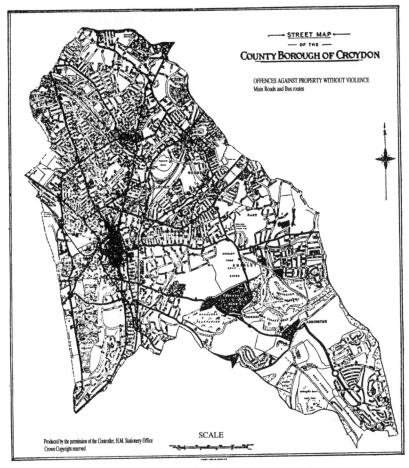

Croydon: Offences against Property without violence.
Each spot represents one offence.

concerned. Certain types of non-indictable offence had nevertheless to be included on the grounds that they are actions which
are strongly deprecated by the community, such as dangerous and
drunken driving, unlawful possession, being found upon enclos-
ed premises, indecent exposure, and immoral soliciting by males,
and are closely akin in character to many indictable offences.

The figures of "Crimes cleared up" is to some degree an index
of police efficiency, and it was fortunate that in 1952 at least the
percentage of crimes cleared up was actually higher in the "Z"

Delinquency Areas in Croydon

Division than it was for the Metropolitan Police District as a whole, being 35.41 % compared with 31.9 %.[1] The efficiency of the police determines in no small degree the reliability of the data in Series I, and also that of Series II in that the more efficient the police, the less likely are offenders to slip through the net and not be charged with their crimes.

It is difficult to make valid comparisons between Croydon and other towns on the basis of Crimes Known to the Police because there are few towns of the same approximate size and even fewer of the same size with similar ecological characteristics.

TABLE 12

COMPARATIVE INCIDENCE OF INDICTABLE URBAN CRIME

Source: *Home Office*. Supplementary Criminal Statistics for 1952.

	Pop. Nearest '000	Variation in size by '000	Indictable crimes per 10,000 pop.	% Crimes cleared up
Portsmouth	243	—7	130	48
Cardiff	245	—5	138	43
Croydon	250	—	82(86†)	35†
Coventry	261	+11	158	48
Stoke-on-Trent	272	+22	73	66
Leicester	286	+36	102	54
Bradford	288	+38	115	44
Newcastle	290	+40	153	55
Kingston-upon-Hull	298	+48	133	50
England and Wales	43,940*	—	117	48

* Based on an estimate of the Registrar-General before the availability of the 1951 Census material.
† Based upon Series I and therefore inclusive of certain non-indictable offences akin to indictable crime.
‡ Based on figure for "Z" Division which is not co-extensive with the County Borough.

In terms of size Croydon compares very favourably with Cardiff and Portsmouth which is perhaps hardly surprising since docks and a transitory seafaring population are likely to increase the crime rate. Coventry, on the other hand, which is similar in size has a rate over 70% higher, while Stoke-on-Trent which is both larger and more industrialised has a rate which is appreciably lower.

[1] Report of the Commissioner of Police for the Metropolis for 1952. Cmd. 8944, H.M.S.O., 1953. 'Z' Division covers the whole of Croydon and parts of the surrounding area.

The Criminal Area

TABLE 13
TYPES OF OFFENCE: CROYDON C.B. 1952
Source: Series I

	No.		% of total	
a. Offences against the person (excluding sex offences)	15 ⎫		0.70 ⎫	
	⎬ 123		⎬ 5.70	
b. Sex offences	108 ⎭		5.00 ⎭	
c. Larcenies without violence (excluding receiving)	1456 ⎫		67.72 ⎫	
	⎬ 1847		⎬ 85.92	
d. Breakings including attempted breakings, burglary and unlawful entry	391 ⎭		18.20 ⎭	
e. Receiving, unlawful possession, frauds and miscellaneous offences	179		8.38	8.38
TOTAL	2,149		100.00	

From this broad analysis of the types of crime committed it can be seen that there is nothing particularly unusual in the pattern of offences, crimes against property, (c) and (d), accounting for nearly 86% of all crime. The gravity of these offences varied considerably, but for the most part the bulk were petty crimes. Simple larcenies, for example, were 800 in number, larcenies from unattended motor vehicles 200, and the larceny of pedal cycles 172.

Offences, against the person, if one excludes sex offences, form a very small percentage of the total. Of the 15 crimes in question only 5, two murders and three felonious woundings were very grave offences. Although sex offences constituted 5% of all those in Series I, again, relatively few were really serious. For one case of rape and 11 indecent assaults, there were 63 cases of indecent exposure and 20 cases of male solicitation. With the exception of 2 cases of defilement of girls under 16 years of age, and one homosexual assault on a boy, all the rest were cases of homosexuality between consenting adults. As far as it was possible to discover, no female prostitutes had been prosecuted in the town since the war, and it is in fact virtually impossible to find a real prostitute in Croydon since the West End of London is so near, both for the local girls who wish to follow this occupation and the men who require their services.

Ward Distribution of Crime. Central Ward, comprising the central business district was the major blackspot, most of the total being made up of a very large number of larcenies of all

122

Delinquency Areas in Croydon

Croydon: Areas of Delinquent Residence

kinds. The average number of crimes for each of the remaining
15 wards was 109.14, or about 1/5th of the total.

After Central Ward the satellite shopping districts of London
Road (Norbury), High Street (Thornton Heath), High Street
and Portland Road (South Norwood), and Westow Street (Upper
Norwood) had the greatest concentrations of larceny. In addi-
tion the building sites at the new power station in Waddon Ward
(MC District) and on the New Addington housing estate (SG
District) reflected the opportunities afforded for crime.

Just as crimes against property were concentrated in those

The Criminal Area

areas providing the greatest opportunity, so too were sex offences located where opportunities for their commission were
greatest. Thus although there was a wide scatter of such offences,
streets which were poorly lit, shaded by trees or with few passers-
by, especially to the east of the central business district, were
commonly the scene of indecent exposures and assaults.

Series II: THE DISTRIBUTION OF OFFENDERS

The basic data for this Series were derived from en analysis of
the charge books in the police stations in the "Z" Division. The
choice of charge books as a source was made mainly because they
represented a more systematic record than those of the Court.
Records of Summonses were ignored on the grounds that they
would relate mainly to petty offences of a non-indictable kind,
mostly to do with the Road Traffic Acts. Broadly speaking, a
"charge" means something fairly serious, except perhaps in the
case of drunkenness or a minor disturbance of the peace. Nevertheless, if the object of a rate constructed from such a source is to
identify those areas of a town which produce the bulk of what
might be described as its "social problem group" then the inclusion of such charges is relevant. From a sociological point of
view one might expect the brawlers, hooligans and drunks to
originate from much the same ecological areas as many delinquents and criminals.

Information was assembled on some 997 persons, all of whom
had been charged with at least one offence committed in Croydon during 1952. Of these, 758 were Croydon residents, and 139
either lived outside the Borough or had no fixed address. On the
basis of the 758 Croydonians a set of *rates of delinquent residence*
were calculated. It may be argued that such rates are subject to
error on account of the unknown numbers of "expatriate" offenders; but on the other hand, it may be to some extent assumed
that the error is evenly distributed over the 16 Wards.

Ward Distribution. The greatest concentrations of both adult
and juvenile offenders occur in the same areas which may be
approximately ranked as follows:

(1) The deteriorating area which lies along the north east side
of Mitcham Road, mainly in Broad Green and partly in
West Thornton,

124

Delinquency Areas in Croydon

(2) The inter-war council estate situated south of the Mitcham Road, in Broad Green Ward,

(3) The deteriorating slum area of Whitehorse Manor, known as "Bang 'Ole",

(4) The Waddon Council estate, especially in its south west corner,

(5) The old area of Central Ward, with its small Council estate known as "Old Town",

(6) The old and declining area in Thornton Heath, north of the High Street,

(7) The Ashburton Council estate in East Ward.

Because ward boundaries do not exactly coincide with "natural areas" the ward statistics do not always reflect the criminogenic character of certain areas. Nevertheless, the total of crimes or the rate of delinquents in any ward is usually determined by their concentration in a natural area which happens to fall within its boundaries. Thus when Waddon Ward has a high rate of delinquent residence it is due almost entirely to a high rate on the Council estate; in the case of East Ward which has a low rate, the rate would be lower still but for the Ashburton estate.

The average number of offenders per ward was 47.39. Those wards which exceeded this, Thornton Heath, Whitehorse Manor, Broad Green, Central and Waddon were those which contain either extensive tracts of deteriorating housing or large Council estates.

TABLE 14

CROYDON RESIDENTS CHARGED WITH OFFENCES IN CROYDON BY WARD AND AGE

	8 & under 14	14 & under 17	17 & under 21	21 & under 30	30 & under 40	40 & under 50	50 & under 60	60 & over		TOTAL
Upper Norwood	8	—	2	7	5	2	2	5	—	31
Norbury	1	4	3	8	1	2	3	1	—	23
West Thornton	2	4	9	7	10	2	3	2	—	39
Bensham Manor	3	17	—	1	4	5	2	—	—	32
Thornton Heath	18	11	5	12	10	9	5	6	+	76
South Norwood	1	9	2	8	6	4	7	—	—	37
Woodside	4	10	6	9	5	4	2	1	—	41
East	7	2	1	8	5	—	1	4	—	28

125

The Criminal Area

(Continued)	8 & under 14	14 & under 17	17 & under 21	21 & under 30	30 & under 40	40 & under 50	50 & under 60	60 & over		TOTAL
Addiscombe	12	5	4	7	5	6	3	2	—	44
Addington	6	2	1	21	5	5	3	—	—	43
Shirley	1	2	3	—	5	2	—	1	—	14
Whitehorse Manor	3	10	16	14	12	11	8	—	+	74
Broad Green	20	16	11	22	15	7	7	5	+	103
Central	4	4	11	22	15	11	3	—	—	72
Waddon	21	21	13	12	12	6	—	1	+	67
South	2	2	3	7	8	6	1	2	—	34
Croydon CB.	113	113	90	165	123	82	50	30		758

+ indicates above Average
— ,, below ,,

In area (6) most of the juvenile offenders lived in a fairly homogeneous area and attended two particular schools. Over half of them were under 14 and most of their offences were highly localised larcenies. Supplementary information suggested that there was a loosely knit delinquent sub-culture, but one which excluded adults. This is an area which has in local parlance "gone down" very much in the last fifteen years and has experienced probably as much social and economic change as any in the town. The rather prosperous generation of artisans many of whom were the original tenants are fast disappearing; the once flourishing shopping districts of Beulah Road and High Street have junk shops where there were once furniture dealers, a dairy has become basket works, a garage a breakers yards, and so on.

Whereas Thornton Heath has become known for its delinquents since the war, the old area of Whitehorse Manor (3) has had a "delinquent reputation" for many years, and if it had not been for the devastation caused by the bombing and a consequent reduction in population density, its delinquents would probably have been as numerous as those of the adjacent Broad Green Ward with which it has many features in common. 'Bang 'Ole" is the home of a great many stallholders in the Surrey Street market and of many of the market workers. While by no means all of them are serious lawbreakers—indeed the majority are law abiding citizens, this area, with others is the home of not a few of the groups of young rowdies who disturb the bright light district of North End.

The Broad Green area (1) has perhaps fewer people associated with the market and rather more who make a living from the junk trade or the second-hand car business. Alongside them live

Delinquency Areas in Croydon

the unskilled labourers from whom they differ virtually only in income and politics. The Mitcham Road (or Broad Green) Council estate (2) which adjoins, although not physically dilapidated has a population with similar characteristics. Both districts are depressing in that industry dominates both the skyline and the atmosphere with a rain of grit and smoke.

The Waddon Council estate (4) produced in 1952 about as many offenders as the Mitcham Road estate. They were, however, concentrated in one part of the estate, which may be due to the fact that in contrast to Mitcham Road, the Waddon estate is much less socially homogeneous. What is perhaps interesting here is that there are large open spaces to the north and south, indicating that at least where juveniles are concerned the provision of play space is less relevant to delinquency than is sometimes supposed.

The Ashburton estate in East Ward (7) is much smaller than those at Waddon or Broad Green, but in terms of residential or social status is similar to Waddon. It lies partly in East Ward and partly in Woodside forming a working class enclave in a predominantly middle class area.

Old Town (5) is a mixed area of Central Ward containing both old cottage properties and a small Council estate in what was once an Italian immigrant quarter. Ecologically the area extends up the hill into what is politically Waddon Ward. If anything, adult offenders were more numerous than juveniles in this area, but they were individuals who began street quarrels or who unlawfully received stolen goods rather than "professional" criminals.

The gross distribution of offenders is, however, only a general indication of where delinquents live, and to translate the data into more meaningful terms a series of rates of delinquent residence were calculated. These rates are subject to a further error than that previously mentioned, insofar as the denominators of each fraction (of which they are expressions in percentages) were derived from the 1% Sample Data of the 1951 Census. The "blown up" size of the various age categories was therefore subject to a measurable sampling error. In order to minimise this, the age categories used in the preceding table were combined to form three new categories namely,

1   Juveniles (under 17)
2   Young Adults (17-39)
3   Older Adults (40 and over).

127

The Criminal Area

The rates for each ward were then classified as "high" or "low" in relation to the Borough rate for each category.

TABLE 15

RATES OF DELINQUENT RESIDENCE

i.e. Distribution of Offenders expressed as a percentage of Population at Risk

	Under 17	Rank Order	17-30	Rank Order	40+	Rank Order	All ages ward rate	Rank Order
Upper Norwood	−0.19	12	−0.23	14	0.14	7	−0.18	12
Norbury	−0.20	11	−0.25	13	−0.08	12	−0.15	15
West Thornton	−0.12	15	−0.28	12	−0.12	9	−0.25	9
Bensham Manor	+0.42	7	−0.08	16	−0.99	11	−0.17	13
Thornton Heath	+0.97	4	+0.53	6	+0.26	3	+0.48	4
South Norwood	−0.36	8	−0.32	10	−0.13	8	−0.23	10
Woodside	−0.33	9	−0.45	7	−0.10	10	−0.26	8
East	−0.24	10	−0.30	11	−0.06	13	−0.16	14
Addiscombe	+0.43	6	−0.34	9	+0.15	6	−0.27	7
Addington	−0.14	13	+0.59	5	+0.20	5	0.30	5
Shirley	−0.06	16	−0.17	15	−0.06	13	−0.09	16
Whitehorse Manor	+0.68	5	+1.24	1	+0.28	2	+0.61	3
Broad Green	+1.57	1	+0.87	3	+0.32	1	+0.75	1
Central	+1.00	3	+1.17	2	+0.24	4	+0.66	2
Waddon	+1.10	2	+0.60	4	−0.09	11	+0.33	5
South	−0.13	14	−0.42	8	0.14	7	−0.21	11
Croydon C.B.	0.39		0.48		0.14		0.30	

+ indicates above Borough Rate
—   ,,   below   ,,   ,,

The four wards with the highest rates for all age groups, (all of which are well above the Borough rate) Broad Green, Central, Whitehorse Manor and Thornton Heath are those with the largest tracts of property in decline, and where the worst housing is situated. The four with the lowest rates, Shirley, Norbury, East and Bensham Manor are by no means as similar, East and Shirley being highly prosperous middle class areas of relatively recent development, Norbury being a rather less prosperous area, and Bensham Manor a much older and socially more heterogeneous district. The four high rate wards also have high rates in each of the separate age categories, confirming the view that high juvenile and high adult rates tend to occur together. The low rate wards conversely had rates which were uniformly low,

Delinquence Areas in Croydon

with a few noticeable exceptions. Bensham Manor, Addiscombe and Addington each had one category in which the rate was high in contrast to the others, and Waddon one category, that of 40 and over, for which the rate was surprisingly low in comparison with the Ward rate.

The high Ward rate of Waddon is in effect the high rates for juveniles and young adults on the Waddon estate, just as the high adult rate of Addington is in reality the high adult rate of the New Addington estate. To some extent variations of rates within a ward may be explained in terms of the age structure; at New Addington, for example, there are many more children under the age of criminal responsibility than there are between say 8 and 17 years of age. Much of the difficulty of explaining such ano-malous rates springs from the fact that they are calculated upon the basis of political and administrative boundaries rather than natural areas.

Bensham Manor and Addiscombe are interesting in that they are highly diversified in both land use and social class. The former tends to be middle class in its J. Index 0.5 above the Borough Index, and the latter working class with a J. Index 3.4 below it. The offenders in Bensham Manor were widely scattered but came almost invariably from those streets or parts of streets which were predominantly working class. The picture in Addis-combe was remarkably similar with the special feature that many of the adult offenders came from the area which was once an upper-middle class residential district in which the large old houses are being or have been converted into flats. West Thorn-ton, South Norwood and Woodside, althoug having consistently low rates, must also be considered in this context. In West Thornton, for example, CE and CC districts are an extension of the natural area of Broad Green. If these districts were abstracted, the West Thornton Ward rate would be appreciably lower.

Croydon has not developed radially as so many American cities appear to have done and there are as a result no well defined zones to which variations in the rates can be meaningfully related, nevertheless, the three highest ward rates occur in those wards which make up and immediately surround the central business district. It is unlikely, however, that this is either relevant or indeed exactly true. Considering the precise areas of delinquent residence one finds them to be spatially separate from the central area and highly varied in their ecological characteris-

9 THE CRIMINAL AREA   129

The Criminal Area

tics. The suggestion implicit in so much of the work of Clifford Shaw and his collaborators is that the physical deterioration of a neighbourhood is somehow vitally related to the problem of delinquency and crime. The evidence, at least from Croydon, suggests that the physical characteristics of the area are of little relevance save as an indirect determinant of the social status of an area. Low status and low rentals are normally found together in urban areas and physical deterioration, where it helps to depress both status and rentals, can be said to be a feature likely to attract those individuals who may be loosely described as the core of the "social problem group". But where the provision of housing is not solely within the province of the market, and the local authority has stepped in to provide housing as a social amenity for a not inconsiderable proportion of the population, then the natural ecological processes of selection manifesting themselves in the cycle of "invasion-dominance-succession" are likely to be severely modified by social policy with strikingly different results. The ecological process may be modified yet there is still crime and delinquency, though this is not to suggest that the concept of a criminal or delinquent sub-culture resulting from the interplay of ecological influences is necessarily invalidated; far from it. It does suggest, however, that there must be a shift of interest from the natural area which has grown up of its own accord to the "planned" area which has resulted from conscious social and political deliberation. In particular, emphasis must be laid upon the individual cultural unit, the family, which remains essentially unaltered as a social institution for the transmission of cultural values and as an agency of social control. By analogy, plants are plants whether on the mountainside or in the window box, and the relationships they have to one another and to their habitat, though differing in character are no less real. So too the interaction of individuals resulting in the establishment of some kind of social order, however artificially defined, are its territorial limits or its social and demographic characteristics. It is the individual delinquent and his family whom we must now go on to consider.

[22]

DAVID M. DOWNES

8

SUMMARY AND CONCLUSIONS

I SUMMARY

The use of the concept of the delinquent subculture by Cohen and—adapted—by Cloward and Ohlin is not wholly satisfactory since 'subculture' is too readily applied as a blanket term to any set of sub-group norms, values and beliefs that deviate from an 'ideal-type' dominant middle-class normative system. The distinction by Yinger between 'subculture' and 'contraculture' is thought to clarify the issue, though Yinger's assumption that 'contraculture' subsumes delinquent subculture is in advance of empirical validation. (Confusion re 'subculture' simply reflects the traditional confusion over—and multiple definitions of— 'culture'). Yet neither subculture nor contraculture necessarily apply only to the value-systems of gang delinquents, nor is the gang framework a sufficient proof of a contracultural value-system: this point is illustrated by reference to two empirical studies which embody this issue.

The two major approaches to delinquent subcultural theorisation—those by Cohen (and Short) and by Cloward and Ohlin— have tended to be regarded as either mutually exclusive (as by Cloward and Ohlin themselves) or as essentially homogeneous (as by some empirical investigators, notably Clark and Wenninger.) Examination of their hypotheses in detail suggests that the points of difference which emerge in the exposition of their theories are due more to differential concentration on certain aspects of the 'five classes of questions' inherent in this theorisation, rather than to substantive differences. Moreover, after the differences due to differential exposition have been eliminated, the apparently

255

Summary and Conclusions

substantive differences remaining are seen to flow from Cloward
and Ohlin's over-simplification of the Cohen-Short position on
two variables: first, middle-class orientation; and second, the
'parent subculture'. These differences can feasibly be reconciled
by the introduction of community-type and age-level variables,
as utilised in part by Clark and Wenninger and Reiss and Rhodes,
and despite the discarding of the latter by Cloward and Ohlin.
These innovations would possibly accommodate also their
disagreements over types of subcultural *process*.

The welter of critiques on the above subcultural theorisation
can be classified into four main types: 'limiting', 'extensive',
'applied' and 'basic'. With the exception of one 'applied' study
of values in gang delinquency, all critiques so far can be shown
either to have internal inconsistencies, to have been anticipated
by subcultural theorisation, to be compatible with the major
hypotheses, or to enrich them. Despite this, subcultural theorisation is far from validation, and can likely survive only at the
expense of considerable modification. Herein lies its promise,
but the danger is that it will be applied recklessly to disparate
phenomena. What is needed is a firm sense of the limitations of
subcultural theorisation on delinquency.   Such an
example of recklessness might be the attempt to apply subcultural theorisation to the English scene, where delinquency in
general is hardly a major social problem, where gang delinquency
on the American model is non-existent, and where lack of
research makes for difficulties not experienced by American
investigators. What data exist, however, suggest the reality of
subculture, if not contraculture, in large urban and metropolitan
areas. The real research question emerges as being whether or
not, or to what degree, the male working-class 'failure' is faced
with a 'problem of adjustment' at all.

Statistical data on crime commission and delinquent residence
(ages 8–25) in two East London boroughs, Stepney and Poplar,
were used to test two limited propositions inferred from the
theorisation of Cohen and of Cloward and Ohlin, on age-level
differences and on between-area differences. A fairly distinct
offence structure broadly characterised three age-levels: pre- to
mid-adolescence, mid- to late-adolescence, early adulthood. Only
the early adult offences differed between the boroughs; through
adolescence, the regularities of delinquent behaviour appeared

Summary and Conclusions

more striking than the between-borough differences, though a more distinct semi-'conflict' pattern emerged in Poplar than in Stepney. The data support Cohen's emphasis on age-level differences, and his concept of the 'parent male' subculture seems most relevant to the illegal behaviour involved. But the character of the West Stepney 'criminal' area makes comparative judgment difficult about the proposition inferred from Cloward and Ohlin. More generally, the data confirmed the absence of gang delinquency, although the group factor—declining in importance with age—is still important in late adolescence; also, accomplice rates varied very much by offence. Recidivism rates for all ages were shown to be heavier for the two boroughs than for the MPD generally. Lack of convergence between the delinquency rates for different age-levels by 'natural' area led to the conclusion that either age-specific delinquency and adult crime derived from distinct aetiologies, or the nature of habitual adult crime in the East End acted more as a repellent than a stimulus to young offenders. It was hypothesised that working-class adolescents associated adult criminality with downward mobility, rather than the reverse. Also (while about one-eighth of delinquents not in school had been unemployed for more than three months) the full-employment situation, in London and the South-East, probably crucially influences the mode of delinquent response. Hence, the pattern of delinquency is of a very different order to that emphasised by American sources. This pattern of offences peculiar to mid- to late-adolescents did not seem to be much affected by the presence in Stepney—but not in Poplar— of what the police term a 'criminal class'.

This picture was confirmed by informal observation in the boroughs, in particular with one group in Poplar, whose offences fitted the pattern shown by the crime data: petty break-ins, take-and-drive-away, minor rowdyism, various larceny offences. While their expressed norms, values and beliefs hardly differed markedly from those of the adult lower working-class, which are essentially conservative, their differential concentration on these norms, etc. in a specifically 'leisured' context warrants the use of the subculture concept, though not that of contraculture. Their illegal behaviour seemed to be due not to 'alienation' or 'status frustration', but to a process of dissociation from middle-class dominated contexts of school, work and recreation. This

257

Summary and Conclusions

disenchantment provoked an over-emphasis on purely 'leisure' goals—sedulously fostered by commercial 'teenage' culture—rather than on other non-work areas. In a situation where he both needs to attain such goals, and cannot readily do so legitimately, the working-class boy is especially prone to illegal behaviour as a means of 'manufacturing' their ethos. Yet the working-class boy who has undergone this process, who has been hampered in school by his attachment to working-class values, reacts to 'failure' not by frustration, reaction-formation etc., but by the re-affirmation of the working-class value-system. Its social constraints still broadly apply, and the normative early marriage—with its family responsibilities, need for a steady job, need to 'get by' if not 'get on'—rob the leisure context of its attraction: alternative solutions have been provided. The need for 'exploit' is killed. This pattern of delinquency is to be distinguished from adolescent offences which characterise offenders of all age-levels generally, whose recent increases have been due, hypothetically, to an increasingly emphasised 'mild economic anomie'. It is also to distinguish it from delinquency springing from gross personal pathologies. It is thought that the pattern outlined above accounts for a serious proportion of group juvenile delinquency, and any general increase in 'dissociation' from the realms of school and work, and exacerbation of leisure goals as a consequence, will result in more delinquency of an 'exploit' variety. There is clearly room along this leisure dimension for goal-restriction severe enough and visible enough to generate contracultural, as distinct from subcultural, modes of adaptation. This may have already occurred in areas less traditionally working-class than the areas studied.

We are now in a better position to answer the question does the English 'corner boy', accounted a failure in school and work by middle-class standards, typically encounter any 'problem of adjustment' at all? From the evidence presented it appears that he may do, but not of the kind depicted by Cohen as facing his American counterpart. The English 'corner boy' successfully traverses the humiliations of school and job allocation by his re-affirmation of traditional working-class values. This is much what Cohen meant by saying that he 'revises his aspirations downwards'. But in one sphere, that of leisure proper, the old values have lost their potency, and it is to this sphere that

Summary and Conclusions

the 'corner boy' displaces his search for achievement from the areas of school and work, and from other non-work areas. Beer and skittles, the darts match, the working men's club and the union have little significance for him. In leisure, therefore, the old solutions no longer apply; for the 'corner boy' with 'time on his hands' and 'nothing to lose', the palliated delinquent sub-culture is an attractive and functional solution to a most intensely-felt problem. This is not to say that non-delinquent working-class and middle-class youth face no 'problems of adjustment' in leisure: however, to echo Cohen's emphasis on the different distribution of problems throughout the social class structure, the working-class 'corner boy' is the only one to depend exclusively on leisure as the framework for 'exploit'.

II CONCLUSIONS

On the working basis that dissociation—not alienation—is the normative response of working-class male adolescents to semi- and unskilled work (and to no work at all), and that this is the primary source of much of the delinquency *peculiar* to male adolescents—the analysis should take into account possible preventive measures in three areas: work, school and leisure. Research should also be directed at the efficacy of various 'intervening variables' which operate to keep the delinquency-prone youth from delinquency, assuming that all working-class boys whose 'life chances' push them inexorably towards semi- and unskilled work are in a delinquency-promoting life situation. This is to reverse the conventional procedure, which is to assume that all adolescents are in a conformity-promoting life-situation, and which directs research towards 'intervening variables' which operate to make a boy delinquency-prone. The vast bulk of research in criminology has been directed along these lines in the search for factors which divert the boy from conformity to deviance: 'broken homes', maternal/paternal deprivation, family fragmentation, character-structure: even much sociological theory has implied that it is only when a crime-oriented 'lower class culture' wins out against the conformist conventional culture that a boy adopts deviant behaviour-patterns. However, if it is assumed that the working-class boy *starts out* in a delinquency-prone life-situation, these variables are seen as *aggravating*

Summary and Conclusions

rather than as intervening factors, and the researcher is freed to look for variables which keep the working-class boy *from* delinquency: 'college-boy' performance at school; stable middle-class-orientated or 'respectable' stable working-class family back-ground; promise of skilled employment; political activity; com-munity activity; home-centredness; stable courtship; legitimate leisure opportunities, etc. It is obvious that this approach involves research no less difficult than the usual approach: but at least its frame of reference appears more realistic. Instead of regarding the working-class delinquent as a deviant in a conformity-promoting society, it is possible to regard the working-class boy as born into a pre-ordained delinquency-promoting situation. Our task can only then be to change that situation, so that the bulk of working-class youth is freed from pressures to deviancy and heavy personal costs.

Of the three areas mentioned as in need of re-organisation, leisure is the most amenable and the most attractive proposition, but it is here argued that—as indicated in the previous chapter —the 'leisure' problem is at root a work and education problem. Were it not for our educational system's failure to engage the interests and energies of the average and below-average working-class boy, with its subsequent corollaries of dissociation from areas of work and school, his leisure problem would be far less acute. It is instructive here to contrast the dissociation-alienation reaction polarities between British and American youth, taking as a reference point a start made by Turner's distinction between *modes* of ascent through education.[1] Turner maintains that in any industrial society, the *mode* of upward mobility via education is just as crucially important as the *extent* of upward mobility. In Britain, elite status is *given* by existing elites on the basis of ability-linked qualities; in America, elite status is *won* by ability-linked achievement: the first Turner terms 'sponsored', the second 'contest' mobility. Here, one strand of Turner's argument stands out: that in the 'sponsored' system, final selection decisions are made as early as possible in the educational cycle, so that the process of acculturation can get under way; in the 'contest' system, final selection decisions are delayed as long as possible

---

[1] R. H. Turner, 'Modes of Ascent Through Education: "Sponsored" and "Contest" Mobility'. Ch. 12 in Floud, Halsey and Anderson, *Education, Economy and Society* (1961).

Summary and Conclusions

so that equality of opportunity is ensured. The central problem for the British system is thus refinement of the criteria for *selection*; for the American system, the development of incentives for *motivation*. In both, a core issue is the 'drop-out' (America) or the 'early leaver' (Britain), but here there are crucial differences in definition: the American 'drop-out' is any boy who refuses to finish high school and so qualify for college entrance; the British 'early leaver' is a boy who has already been pre-selected for higher education in the grammar school, but fails or refuses to stay the course. The point at issue here is that for the British boy, the educational contest is over by the age of 11 or, inferentially, by the age of 7–8 when 'streaming' begins;[2] for the American boy, the contest is technically open until the age of 17. Either way, the costs of failure are severe, but they differ in the reactions they evoke. For the British boy, dissociation is engendered and strengthened by the earliness at which selection (and rejection) takes place: the result is a certain fatalism towards the roles in school and work to which he has been allocated,[3] and an overt stress on fulfilment through leisure comes early. For the American boy, alienation is engendered and strengthened by the lateness with which final decisions are made, but rejection or inability to conform to ultimate criteria is anticipated, and an overt stress on protest comes early. Moreover, the American system lends itself more readily to the entertainment of unrealistic ambitions late into adolescence, so that rejection (in effect) comes all the more cruelly: the British adolescent has had no time and no incentives to nurture such ambitions. It is no surprise to find that the ambitions of British secondary modern pupils are not only firmly geared to their actual life-chances (Veness),[4] but are also much less prone to 'fantasy' aspirations than their American counterparts (M. D. Wilson).

[2] A point confirmed in J. W. B. Douglas, *The Home and the School* (1964).

[3] So much so that, in anticipation of rejection at 11 +, the bulk of working-class boys in turn reject the 11 + ethic, *preferring* the secondary modern to the grammar school and opting out of the academic rat-race prior to selection procedures. This is truly subversive of meritocracy, and represents a refusal to be motivated to strive . . . etc. Unfortunately, this involves not only immense wastage of ability, but a premature cynicism about the role of education in their personal and social development which limits their scope for, and awareness of, *choice* in every sphere of life, not simply the occupational.

[4] T. Veness, *The School-leavers* (1962); Mary D. Wilson, The Vocational Preferences of Secondary Modern School-children,' *Brit. J. Educ. Psych.*, Vol. 23, 1953, pp. 97–113.

Summary and Conclusions

Hence, the working-class male adolescent's leisure problems originate in the school- and work-situations to which he is destined by socioeconomic role allocation. These connections are concealed, since his reactions to work-school are not in general of an alienation–status–frustration variety, but the relatively toned-down response of dissociation. Moreover, this propensity for dissociation from the semi- and unskilled job will feasibly worsen as the prospects for semi- and unskilled labour deteriorate. The process is well under way already, and automation will further erode the market- and work-situation of these levels of occupation, at the same time as it increases the visibility of the occupational rewards for skill and educational/technical qualifications.[5] If the situation of the semi- and unskilled young worker is not to deteriorate much further, radical re-organisation of the areas of school and work are basic, and must go further than 'revolutions' we have failed to at worst initiate and at best fulfil in the past.

[5] At present, union strength and collective bargaining have gained some equivalence between much manual and white collar work in terms of income, if not in terms of status, security, 'fringe' benefits, etc., but see R. M. Titmuss, *Income Distribution and Social Change* (1962).

Part V
The Fifth Phase:
The Institutionalization of Criminology

Argument: Some More Big Ideas
and the Young Turks

Social Reaction, Phenomenology and Symbolic Interactionism

[23]

Social Pathology

E. Lemert

A GENERAL STATEMENT OF OUR THEORY

Stated in the most general way, our theory is one of social differentiation, deviation, and individuation. For a summary description we may turn to an excerpt from a paper by the present writer:[22]

We may pertinently ask at this juncture whether the time has not come to break abruptly with the traditions of older social pathologists and abandon once and for all the archaic and medicinal idea that human beings can be divided into normal and pathological, or, at least, if such a division must be made, to divest the term "pathological" of its moralistic unscientific overtones. As a step in this direction, the writer suggests that the concepts of social differentiation and individuation be rescued from the limbo of older textbooks on sociology, dusted off, and given scientific airing, perhaps being supplemented and given statistical meaning with the perfectly usable concept of deviation. There seems to be no cogent reason why the bulk of the data discussed in textbooks and courses on social pathology cannot be treated as a special phase of social and cultural differentiation and thus conveniently integrated with general sociological theory as taught in courses in introductory sociology. . . .

Because some method must be found to distinguish that portion of differentiation which can be designated as appropriately falling within the field of social pathology, the second necessary postulate is that there is a space-time limited societal awareness and reaction to deviation, ranging from strong ap-

[22] Lemert, Edwin M., "Some Aspects of a General Theory of Sociopathic Behavior," *Proceedings of the Pacific Sociological Society*, 1948, Research Studies, State College of Washington, 16, No. 1, pp. 24f.

proval through indifference to strong disapproval. Thus, by further definition, sociopathic phenomena simply become differentiated behavior which at a given time and place is socially disapproved even though the same behavior may be socially approved at other times and in other places.

To recapitulate, then, we start with the idea that persons and groups are differentiated in various ways, some of which result in social penalties, rejection, and segregation. These penalties and segregative reactions of society or the community are dynamic factors which increase, decrease, and condition the form which the initial differentiation or deviation takes. This process of deviation and societal reaction, together with its structural or substantive products, can be studied both from its collective and its distributive aspects. In the first instance, we are concerned with sociopathic differentiation; and, in the second, our concern is with sociopathic individuation.

THE POSTULATES WITH WHICH WE START

In order to give further precision to the above statement, it can be resolved into a series of postulates. These postulates are simple statements of fact for which the writer feels no obligation to supply proof. They differ from axioms, upon which mathematical and symbolic systems are constructed, in that they contain empirical elements. They are the building blocks for the theory of this treatise and *ipso facto* they must be accepted as points of departure for the analysis which follows. The question as to whether these postulates are the relevant ones or whether they are too few must await answer until after the theory has been tested. The postulates are as follows: [23]

1. There are modalities in human behavior and clusters of deviations from these modalities which can be identified and described for situations specified in time and space.

[23] While in general we found the social problems and the social disorganization viewpoints lacking in theoretical fulfillment, it is not our intention here to insist that all recent treatments of social pathology are without value and that "ours is the only theory." Several books on social pathology have presented fairly defensible theoretical positions. L. Guy Brown's *Social Pathology* is distinguished in the main for its internal consistency and interrelated framework of ideas, and for the integrity with which its central scheme is made the basis for each successive discussion of problem behavior. *Social Pathology*, by Stuart Queen and Jeannette Gruener, merits favorable comment for the simplicity and economy of its conceptual presentation, features which, as we have shown, are desirable in all theory. Whether their attempt to study social pathology exclusively in terms of social participation is an oversimplification remains to be seen. Certainly it is a necessary concept, as we shall try to show; but alone, at least as it has been used by others, it remains an incomplete formulation. Another position which deserves comment here because of its obvious bearing upon certain phases of our theory is the value-conflict conception of social problems. In this conception,

INTRODUCTION 23

2. Behavioral deviations are a function of culture conflict which is expressed through social organization.

3. There are societal reactions to deviations ranging from strong approval through indifference to strong disapproval.

4. Sociopathic behavior is deviation which is *effectively* disapproved.

5. The deviant person is one whose role, status, function, and self-definition are importantly shaped by how much deviation he engages in, by the degree of its social visibility, by the *particular* exposure he has to the societal reaction, and by the nature and strength of the societal reaction.

6. There are patterns of restriction and freedom in the social participation of deviants which are related directly to their status, role, and self-definitions. The biological strictures upon social participation of deviants are directly significant in comparatively few cases.

7. Deviants are individuated with respect to their vulnerability to the societal reaction because: *(a)* the person is a dynamic agent, *(b)* there is a structuring to each personality which acts as a set of limits within which the societal reaction operates.

THE PLACE OF THIS THEORY IN GENERAL SOCIOLOGICAL THEORY

In keeping with our high scientific resolve the various terms employed in stating our postulates are intended to be amoral and nonevaluational, having obvious statistical implications and derivations. There is no intimation that concepts like "restricted participation," "sociopathic behavior," or "deviation" connote either goodness or badness. The objective of this work is to study a limited part of deviation in human behavior and a certain range of societal reactions, together with their interactional products, and by the methods of science to arrive at generalizations about the uniformities in these events. The aim is to study sociopathic behavior in the same light as normal behavior and, by implication, with extensions or derivations of general sociological theory. By the same token, we hold

---

chief emphasis is placed upon the clash of ideals, opinions, judgments, and meanings as the source of social problems. In our estimation this is a special variety of culture-conflict theory, and we freely recognize its importance in studying deviation. However, the value-conflict theory remains a highly generalized statement which fails to make a sharp delimitation of the field. For example, it does not tell us how much or what kind of conflict is necessary in order to have a social problem. No distinction is struck between effective value-conflicts and those which are purely spurious and have little or no effect upon the organization and interaction of groups and participating individuals. Furthermore, it makes no allowance for cultural inconsistencies or contradictory value systems within the same culture which are reciprocals or necessary derivatives of each other. For statements of the value-conflict view see Waller, W., "Social Problems and the Mores," *American Sociological Review,* 1, December, 1936, pp. 922–933; Fuller, R., and R. Myers, "Some Aspects of a Theory of Social Problems," *ibid.,* 6, February, 1941, pp. 24–32; Cuber, J., and R. Harper, *Problems of American Society,* 1948.

24   *THEORY*

that, with certain modifications in our frame of reference, variations from
social norms in desirable and enviable directions should be explored as
profitably as the more frequently studied sociopathic variations. The behavior of the genius, the motion-picture star, the exceptionally beautiful
woman, and the renowned athlete [24] should lend itself to the same systematic analysis as that which is applied to the criminal, the pauper, or the
sex delinquent. [25]

A question for parenthetical consideration is whether or not it is possible
to apply our theory with logical extensions to the analysis of behavior
systems and persons which are differentiated but which do not excite
polarized reactions of social approbation or disapproval. In data like these
the chief conditioning factors appear to be the special qualities of the
societal reaction. Thus, for example, the primary influences in forming the
occupational personality of a locomotive engineer are such things as time,
mobility, and income. The small amount of dislike for the railroad man
sometimes found in small towns has little to do with the formation of his
role and self-conception. [26] Whatever may be the answer to our question,
we can readily recognize the gains to be made by integrating the growing
body of research on behavior systems of occupational and functional
groups and the sort of trend in sociological analysis this book represents.
Such an integration would broaden the possible scope of this kind of
research and generalization to encompass such monographic studies as
those of the railroader, the waitress, and the musician, as well as those of
the professional thief, the hobo, or the beggar. [27]

---

[24] We lack a good concept to designate this kind of deviation. We think of such
terms as "honorific behavior" or "emulative behavior" without being very satisfied
with them.

[25] We have raised the question in graduate seminars as to whether our theory is applicable to the study of minority or ethnic groups. Generally this question has to be
left unanswered. While ethnic groups are often comparable to the type of deviant
groups in which we are interested, it is also true that in some cases their large size and
occasional positions of considerable power in local areas mean that they differ
significantly from the deviant groups we shall be studying.

[26] See Cottrell, W. F., *The Railroader*, 1940.

[27] It is only fitting to acknowledge the contribution which has been made by E. H.
Sutherland in his criminological research by bringing before American sociologists the
importance of behavior systems as research areas. See also Hollingshead, A. B., "Behavior Systems as a Field of Research," *American Sociological Review*, 4, December,
1939, pp. 816–822.

[24]

Howard S. Becker

1 Outsiders

ALL social groups make rules and at-
tempt, at some times and under some circumstances, to enforce
them. Social rules define situations and the kinds of behavior
appropriate to them, specifying some actions as "right" and
forbidding others as "wrong." When a rule is enforced, the
person who is supposed to have broken it may be seen as a
special kind of person, one who cannot be trusted to live by
the rules agreed on by the group. He is regarded as an *outsider*.

But the person who is thus labeled an outsider may have
a different view of the matter. He may not accept the rule by
which he is being judged and may not regard those who judge

him as either competent or legitimately entitled to do so. Hence, a second meaning of the term emerges: the rule-breaker may feel his judges are *outsiders*.

In what follows, I will try to clarify the situation and process pointed to by this double-barrelled term: the situations of rule-breaking and rule-enforcement and the processes by which some people come to break rules and others to enforce them.

Some preliminary distinctions are in order. Rules may be of a great many kinds. They may be formally enacted into law, and in this case the police power of the state may be used in enforcing them. In other cases, they represent informal agreements, newly arrived at or encrusted with the sanction of age and tradition; rules of this kind are enforced by informal sanctions of various kinds.

Similarly, whether a rule has the force of law or tradition or is simply the result of consensus, it may be the task of some specialized body, such as the police or the committee on ethics of a professional association, to enforce it; enforcement, on the other hand, may be everyone's job or, at least, the job of everyone in the group to which the rule is meant to apply.

Many rules are not enforced and are not, in any except the most formal sense, the kind of rules with which I am concerned. Blue laws, which remain on the statute books though they have not been enforced for a hundred years, are examples. (It is important to remember, however, that an unenforced law may be reactivated for various reasons and regain all its original force, as recently occurred with respect to the laws governing the opening of commercial establishments on Sunday in Missouri.) Informal rules may similarly die from lack of enforcement. I shall mainly be concerned with what we can call the actual operating rules of groups, those kept alive through attempts at enforcement.

2

Finally, just how far "outside" one is, in either of the senses I have mentioned, varies from case to case. We think of the person who commits a traffic violation or gets a little too drunk at a party as being, after all, not very different from the rest of us and treat his infraction tolerantly. We regard the thief as less like us and punish him severely. Crimes such as murder, rape, or treason lead us to view the violator as a true outsider.

In the same way, some rule-breakers do not think they have been unjustly judged. The traffic violator usually subscribes to the very rules he has broken. Alcoholics are often ambivalent, sometimes feeling that those who judge them do not understand them and at other times agreeing that compulsive drinking is a bad thing. At the extreme, some deviants (homosexuals and drug addicts are good examples) develop full-blown ideologies explaining why they are right and why those who disapprove of and punish them are wrong.

Definitions of Deviance

The outsider—the deviant from group rules—has been the subject of much speculation, theorizing, and scientific study. What laymen want to know about deviants is: why do they do it? How can we account for their rule-breaking? What is there about them that leads them to do forbidden things? Scientific research has tried to find answers to these questions. In doing so it has accepted the common-sense premise that there is something inherently deviant (qualitatively distinct) about acts that break (or seem to break) social rules. It has also accepted the common-sense assumption that the deviant act occurs because some characteristic of the person who commits it makes it necessary or inevitable that he should. Scientists do not ordinarily question the label "deviant"

3

when it is applied to particular acts or people but rather take it as given. In so doing, they accept the values of the group making the judgment.

It is easily observable that different groups judge different things to be deviant. This should alert us to the possibility that the person making the judgment of deviance, the process by which that judgment is arrived at, and the situation in which it is made may all be intimately involved in the phenomenon of deviance. To the degree that the common-sense view of deviance and the scientific theories that begin with its premises assume that acts that break rules are inherently deviant and thus take for granted the situations and processes of judgment, they may leave out an important variable. If scientists ignore the variable character of the process of judgment, they may by that omission limit the kinds of theories that can be developed and the kind of understanding that can be achieved.[1]

Our first problem, then, is to construct a definition of deviance. Before doing this, let us consider some of the definitions scientists now use, seeing what is left out if we take them as a point of departure for the study of outsiders.

The simplest view of deviance is essentially statistical, defining as deviant anything that varies too widely from the average. When a statistician analyzes the results of an agricultural experiment, he describes the stalk of corn that is exceptionally tall and the stalk that is exceptionally short as deviations from the mean or average. Similarly, one can describe anything that differs from what is most common as a deviation. In this view, to be left-handed or redheaded is deviant, because most people are right-handed and brunette.

So stated, the statistical view seems simple-minded, even

1. Cf. Donald R. Cressey, "Criminological Research and the Definition of Crimes," *American Journal of Sociology*, LVI (May, 1951), 546–551.

4

trivial. Yet it simplifies the problem by doing away with many questions of value that ordinarily arise in discussions of the nature of deviance. In assessing any particular case, all one need do is calculate the distance of the behavior involved from the average. But it is too simple a solution. Hunting with such a definition, we return with a mixed bag—people who are excessively fat or thin, murderers, redheads, homosexuals, and traffic violators. The mixture contains some ordinarily thought of as deviants and others who have broken no rule at all. The statistical definition of deviance, in short, is too far removed from the concern with rule-breaking which prompts scientific study of outsiders.

A less simple but much more common view of deviance identifies it as something essentially pathological, revealing the presence of a "disease." This view rests, obviously, on a medical analogy. The human organism, when it is working efficiently and experiencing no discomfort, is said to be "healthy." When it does not work efficiently, a disease is present. The organ or function that has become deranged is said to be pathological. Of course, there is little disagreement about what constitutes a healthy state of the organism. But there is much less agreement when one uses the notion of pathology analogically, to describe kinds of behavior that are regarded as deviant. For people do not agree on what constitutes healthy behavior. It is difficult to find a definition that will satisfy even such a select and limited group as psychiatrists; it is impossible to find one that people generally accept as they accept criteria of health for the organism.[2]

Sometimes people mean the analogy more strictly, because they think of deviance as the product of mental disease. The

2. See the discussion in C. Wright Mills, "The Professional Ideology of Social Pathologists," *American Journal of Sociology*, XLIX (September, 1942), 165–180.

5

behavior of a homosexual or drug addict is regarded as the
symptom of a mental disease just as the diabetic's difficulty
in getting bruises to heal is regarded as a symptom of his
disease. But mental disease resembles physical disease only
in metaphor:

> Starting with such things as syphilis, tuberculosis, typhoid
> fever, and carcinomas and fractures, we have created the class
> "illness." At first, this class was composed of only a few items,
> all of which shared the common feature of reference to a state of
> disordered structure or function of the human body as a physio-
> chemical machine. As time went on, additional items were added
> to this class. They were not added, however, because they were
> newly discovered bodily disorders. The physician's attention had
> been deflected from this criterion and had become focused in-
> stead on disability and suffering as new criteria for selection.
> Thus, at first slowly, such things as hysteria, hypochondriasis,
> obsessive-complusive neurosis, and depression were added to the
> category of illness. Then, with increasing zeal, physicians and
> especially psychiatrists began to call "illness" (that is, of course,
> "mental illness") anything and everything in which they could
> detect any sign of malfunctioning, based on no matter what norm.
> Hence, agoraphobia is illness because one should not be afraid of
> open spaces. Homosexuality is illness because heterosexuality is
> the social norm. Divorce is illness because it signals failure of
> marriage. Crime, art, undesired political leadership, participation
> in social affairs, or withdrawal from such participation—all these
> and many more have been said to be signs of mental illness.[3]

The medical metaphor limits what we can see much as the
statistical view does. It accepts the lay judgment of something
as deviant and, by use of analogy, locates its source within
the individual, thus preventing us from seeing the judgment
itself as a crucial part of the phenomenon.

3. Thomas Szasz, *The Myth of Mental Illness* (New York: Paul B. Hoe-
ber, Inc., 1961), pp. 44–45; see also Erving Goffman, "The Medical Model
and Mental Hospitalization," in *Asylums: Essays on the Social Situation of
Mental Patients and Other Inmates* (Garden City: Anchor Books, 1961),
pp. 321–386.

6

Some sociologists also use a model of deviance based essentially on the medical notions of health and disease. They look at a society, or some part of a society, and ask whether there are any processes going on in it that tend to reduce its stability, thus lessening its chance of survival. They label such processes deviant or identify them as symptoms of social disorganization. They discriminate between those features of society which promote stability (and thus are "functional") and those which disrupt stability (and thus are "dysfunctional"). Such a view has the great virtue of pointing to areas of possible trouble in a society of which people may not be aware.[4]

But it is harder in practice than it appears to be in theory to specify what is functional and what dysfunctional for a society or social group. The question of what the purpose or goal (function) of a group is and, consequently, what things will help or hinder the achievement of that purpose, is very often a political question. Factions within the group disagree and maneuver to have their own definition of the group's function accepted. The function of the group or organization, then, is decided in political conflict, not given in the nature of the organization. If this is true, then it is likewise true that the questions of what rules are to be enforced, what behavior regarded as deviant, and which people labeled as outsiders must also be regarded as political.[5] The functional view of deviance, by ignoring the political aspect of the phenomenon, limits our understanding.

Another sociological view is more relativistic. It identifies

4. See Robert K. Merton, "Social Problems and Sociological Theory," in Robert K. Merton and Robert A. Nisbet, editors, *Contemporary Social Problems* (New York: Harcourt, Brace and World, Inc., 1961), pp. 697–737; and Talcott Parsons, *The Social System* (New York: The Free Press of Glencoe, 1951), pp. 249–325.

5. Howard Brotz similarly identifies the question of what phenomena are "functional" or "dysfunctional" as a political one in "Functionalism and Dynamic Analysis." *European Journal of Sociology*, II (1961), 170–179.

deviance as the failure to obey group rules. Once we have described the rules a group enforces on its members, we can
say with some precision whether or not a person has violated
them and is thus, on this view, deviant.

This view is closest to my own, but it fails to give sufficient
weight to the ambiguities that arise in deciding which rules
are to be taken as the yardstick against which behavior is
measured and judged deviant. A society has many groups,
each with its own set of rules, and people belong to many
groups simultaneously. A person may break the rules of one
group by the very act of abiding by the rules of another
group. Is he, then, deviant? Proponents of this definition may
object that while ambiguity may arise with respect to the
rules peculiar to one or another group in society, there are
some rules that are very generally agreed to by everyone, in
which case the difficulty does not arise. This, of course, is a
question of fact, to be settled by empirical research. I doubt
there are many such areas of consensus and think it wiser to
use a definition that allows us to deal with both ambiguous
and unambiguous situations.

Deviance and the Responses of Others

The sociological view I have just discussed defines deviance
as the infraction of some agreed-upon rule. It then goes on
to ask who breaks rules, and to search for the factors in their
personalities and life situations that might account for the
infractions. This assumes that those who have broken a rule
constitute a homogeneous category, because they have committed the same deviant act.

Such an assumption seems to me to ignore the central fact
about deviance: it is created by society. I do not mean this in

8

the way it is ordinarily understood, in which the causes of deviance are located in the social situation of the deviant or in "social factors" which prompt his action. I mean, rather, that *social groups create deviance by making the rules whose infraction constitutes deviance*, and by applying those rules to particular people and labeling them as outsiders. From this point of view, deviance is *not* a quality of the act the person commits, but rather a consequence of the application by others of rules and sanctions to an "offender." The deviant is one to whom that label has successfully been applied; deviant behavior is behavior that people so label.[6]

Since deviance is, among other things, a consequence of the responses of others to a person's act, students of deviance cannot assume that they are dealing with a homogeneous category when they study people who have been labeled deviant. That is, they cannot assume that these people have actually committed a deviant act or broken some rule, because the process of labeling may not be infallible; some people may be labeled deviant who in fact have not broken a rule. Furthermore, they cannot assume that the category of those labeled deviant will contain all those who actually have broken a rule, for many offenders may escape apprehension and thus fail to be included in the population of "deviants" they study. Insofar as the category lacks homogeneity and fails to include all the cases that belong in it, one cannot reasonably expect to find common factors of personality or life situation that will account for the supposed deviance.

What, then, do people who have been labeled deviant have

6. The most important earlier statements of this view can be found in Frank Tannenbaum, *Crime and the Community* (New York: McGraw-Hill Book Co., Inc., 1951), and E. M. Lemert, *Social Pathology* (New York: McGraw-Hill Book Co., Inc., 1951). A recent article stating a position very similar to mine is John Kitsuse, "Societal Reaction to Deviance: Problems of Theory and Method," *Social Problems*, 9 (Winter, 1962), 247–256.

in common? At the least, they share the label and the experience of being labeled as outsiders. I will begin my analysis
with this basic similarity and view deviance as the product of
a transaction that takes place between some social group and
one who is viewed by that group as a rule-breaker. I will be
less concerned with the personal and social characteristics of
deviants than with the process by which they come to be
thought of as outsiders and their reactions to that judgment.

Malinowski discovered the usefulness of this view for
understanding the nature of deviance many years ago, in his
study of the Trobriand Islands:

> One day an outbreak of wailing and a great commotion told
> me that a death had occurred somewhere in the neighborhood. I
> was informed that Kima'i, a young lad of my acquaintance, of
> sixteen or so, had fallen from a coco-nut palm and killed himself.
> . . . I found that another youth had been severely wounded by
> some mysterious coincidence. And at the funeral there was ob-
> viously a general feeling of hostility between the village where
> the boy died and that into which his body was carried for burial.
>
> Only much later was I able to discover the real meaning of
> these events. The boy had committed suicide. The truth was that
> he had broken the rules of exogamy, the partner in his crime be-
> ing his maternal cousin, the daughter of his mother's sister. This
> had been known and generally disapproved of but nothing was
> done until the girl's discarded lover, who had wanted to marry
> her and who felt personally injured, took the initiative. This rival
> threatened first to use black magic against the guilty youth, but
> this had not much effect. Then one evening he insulted the cul-
> prit in public—accusing him in the hearing of the whole com-
> munity of incest and hurling at him certain expressions intoler-
> able to a native.
>
> For this there was only one remedy; only one means of escape
> remained to the unfortunate youth. Next morning he put on
> festive attire and ornamentation, climbed a coco-nut palm and
> addressed the community, speaking from among the palm leaves
> and bidding them farewell. He explained the reasons for his

10

desperate deed and also launched forth a veiled accusation against the man who had driven him to his death, upon which it became the duty of his clansmen to avenge him. Then he wailed aloud, as is the custom, jumped from a palm some sixty feet high and was killed on the spot. There followed a fight within the village in which the rival was wounded; and the quarrel was repeated during the funeral. . . .

If you were to inquire into the matter among the Trobrianders, you would find . . . that the natives show horror at the idea of violating the rules of exogamy and that they believe that sores, disease and even death might follow clan incest. This is the ideal of native law, and in moral matters it is easy and pleasant strictly to adhere to the ideal—when judging the conduct of others or expressing an opinion about conduct in general.

When it comes to the application of morality and ideals to real life, however, things take on a different complexion. In the case described it was obvious that the facts would not tally with the ideal of conduct. Public opinion was neither outraged by the knowledge of the crime to any extent, nor did it react directly— it had to be mobilized by a public statement of the crime and by insults being hurled at the culprit by an interested party. Even then he had to carry out the punishment himself. . . . Probing further into the matter and collecting concrete information, I found that the breach of exogamy—as regards intercourse and not marriage—is by no means a rare occurrence, and public opinion is lenient, though decidedly hypocritical. If the affair is carried on *sub rosa* with a certain amount of decorum, and if no one in particular stirs up trouble—"public opinion" will gossip, but not demand any harsh punishment. If, on the contrary, scandal breaks out—everyone turns against the guilty pair and by ostracism and insults one or the other may be driven to suicide.[7]

Whether an act is deviant, then, depends on how other people react to it. You can commit clan incest and suffer from no more than gossip as long as no one makes a public accusa-

7. Bronislaw Malinowski, *Crime and Custom in Savage Society* (New York: Humanities Press, 1926), pp. 77–80. Reprinted by permission of Humanities Press and Routledge & Kegan Paul, Ltd.

tion; but you will be driven to your death if the accusation is made. The point is that the response of other people has to be regarded as problematic. Just because one has committed an infraction of a rule does not mean that others will respond as though this had happened. (Conversely, just because one has not violated a rule does not mean that he may not be treated, in some circumstances, as though he had.)

The degree to which other people will respond to a given act as deviant varies greatly. Several kinds of variation seem worth noting. First of all, there is variation over time. A person believed to have committed a given "deviant" act may at one time be responded to much more leniently than he would be at some other time. The occurrence of "drives" against various kinds of deviance illustrates this clearly. At various times, enforcement officials may decide to make an all-out attack on some particular kind of deviance, such as gambling, drug addiction, or homosexuality. It is obviously much more dangerous to engage in one of these activities when a drive is on than at any other time. (In a very interesting study of crime news in Colorado newspapers, Davis found that the amount of crime reported in Colorado newspapers showed very little association with actual changes in the amount of crime taking place in Colorado. And, further, that peoples' estimate of how much increase there had been in crime in Colorado was associated with the increase in the amount of crime news but not with any increase in the amount of crime.) [8]

The degree to which an act will be treated as deviant depends also on who commits the act and who feels he has been harmed by it. Rules tend to be applied more to some persons than others. Studies of juvenile delinquency make the point clearly. Boys from middle-class areas do not get as far in the

8. F. James Davis, "Crime News in Colorado Newspapers," *American Journal of Sociology*, LVII (January, 1952), 325–330.

12

legal process when they are apprehended as do boys from slum areas. The middle-class boy is less likely, when picked up by the police, to be taken to the station; less likely when taken to the station to be booked; and it is extremely unlikely that he will be convicted and sentenced.[9] This variation occurs even though the original infraction of the rule is the same in the two cases. Similarly, the law is differentially applied to Negroes and whites. It is well known that a Negro believed to have attacked a white woman is much more likely to be punished than a white man who commits the same offense; it is only slightly less well known that a Negro who murders another Negro is much less likely to be punished than a white man who commits murder.[10] This, of course, is one of the main points of Sutherland's analysis of white-collar crime: crimes committed by corporations are almost always prosecuted as civil cases, but the same crime committed by an individual is ordinarily treated as a criminal offense.[11]

Some rules are enforced only when they result in certain consequences. The unmarried mother furnishes a clear example. Vincent [12] points out that illicit sexual relations seldom result in severe punishment or social censure for the offenders. If, however, a girl becomes pregnant as a result of such activities the reaction of others is likely to be severe. (The illicit pregnancy is also an interesting example of the differential enforcement of rules on different categories of people. Vincent notes that unmarried fathers escape the severe censure visited on the mother.)

9. See Albert K. Cohen and James F. Short, Jr., "Juvenile Delinquency," in Merton and Nisbet, *op. cit.*, p. 87.
10. See Harold Garfinkel, "Research Notes on Inter- and Intra-Racial Homicides," *Social Forces*, 27 (May, 1949), 369–381.
11. Edwin H. Sutherland, "White Collar Criminality," *American Sociological Review*, V (February, 1940), 1–12.
12. Clark Vincent, *Unmarried Mothers* (New York: The Free Press of Glencoe, 1961), pp. 3–5.

Why repeat these commonplace observations? Because, taken together, they support the proposition that deviance is not a simple quality, present in some kinds of behavior and absent in others. Rather, it is the product of a process which involves responses of other people to the behavior. The same behavior may be an infraction of the rules at one time and not at another; may be an infraction when committed by one person, but not when committed by another; some rules are broken with impunity, others are not. In short, whether a given act is deviant or not depends in part on the nature of the act (that is, whether or not it violates some rule) and in part on what other people do about it.

Some people may object that this is merely a terminological quibble, that one can, after all, define terms any way he wants to and that if some people want to speak of rule-breaking behavior as deviant without reference to the reactions of others they are free to do so. This, of course, is true. Yet it might be worthwhile to refer to such behavior as *rule-breaking behavior* and reserve the term *deviant* for those labeled as deviant by some segment of society. I do not insist that this usage be followed. But it should be clear that insofar as a scientist uses "deviant" to refer to any rule-breaking behavior and takes as his subject of study only those who have been *labeled* deviant, he will be hampered by the disparities between the two categories.

If we take as the object of our attention behavior which comes to be labeled as deviant, we must recognize that we cannot know whether a given act will be categorized as deviant until the response of others has occurred. Deviance is not a quality that lies in behavior itself, but in the interaction between the person who commits an act and those who respond to it.

14

Whose Rules?

I have been using the term "outsiders" to refer to those people who are judged by others to be deviant and thus to stand outside the circle of "normal" members of the group. But the term contains a second meaning, whose analysis leads to another important set of sociological problems: "outsiders," from the point of view of the person who is labeled deviant, may be the people who make the rules he had been found guilty of breaking.

Social rules are the creation of specific social groups. Modern societies are not simple organizations in which everyone agrees on what the rules are and how they are to be applied in specific situations. They are, instead, highly differentiated along social class lines, ethnic lines, occupational lines, and cultural lines. These groups need not and, in fact, often do not share the same rules. The problems they face in dealing with their environment, the history and traditions they carry with them, all lead to the evolution of different sets of rules. Insofar as the rules of various groups conflict and contradict one another, there will be disagreement about the kind of behavior that is proper in any given situation.

Italian immigrants who went on making wine for themselves and their friends during Prohibition were acting properly by Italian immigrant standards, but were breaking the law of their new country (as, of course, were many of their Old American neighbors). Medical patients who shop around for a doctor may, from the perspective of their own group, be doing what is necessary to protect their health by making sure they get what seems to them the best possible doctor; but, from the perspective of the physician, what they do is wrong

15

because it breaks down the trust the patient ought to put in his physician. The lower-class delinquent who fights for his "turf" is only doing what he considers necessary and right, but teachers, social workers, and police see it differently.

While it may be argued that many or most rules are generally agreed to by all members of a society, empirical research on a given rule generally reveals variation in people's attitudes. Formal rules, enforced by some specially constituted group, may differ from those actually thought appropriate by most people.[13] Factions in a group may disagree on what I have called actual operating rules. Most important for the study of behavior ordinarily labeled deviant, the perspectives of the people who engage in the behavior are likely to be quite different from those of the people who condemn it. In this latter situation, a person may feel that he is being judged according to rules he has had no hand in making and does not accept, rules forced on him by outsiders.

To what extent and under what circumstances do people attempt to force their rules on others who do not subscribe to them? Let us distinguish two cases. In the first, only those who are actually members of the group have any interest in making and enforcing certain rules. If an orthodox Jew disobeys the laws of kashruth only other orthodox Jews will regard this as a transgression; Christians or nonorthodox Jews will not consider this deviance and would have no interest in interfering. In the second case, members of a group consider it important to their welfare that members of certain other groups obey certain rules. Thus, people consider it extremely important that those who practice the healing arts abide by certain rules; this is the reason the state licenses physicians,

13. Arnold M. Rose and Arthur E. Prell, "Does the Punishment Fit the Crime?—A Study in Social Valuation," *American Journal of Sociology,* LXI (November, 1955), 247–259.

16

nurses, and others, and forbids anyone who is not licensed to engage in healing activities.

To the extent that a group tries to impose its rules on other groups in the society, we are presented with a second question: Who can, in fact, force others to accept their rules and what are the causes of their success? This is, of course, a question of political and economic power. Later we will consider the political and economic process through which rules are created and enforced. Here it is enough to note that people are in fact always *forcing* their rules on others, applying them more or less against the will and without the consent of those others. By and large, for example, rules are made for young people by their elders. Though the youth of this country exert a powerful influence culturally—the mass media of communication are tailored to their interests, for instance —many important kinds of rules are made for our youth by adults. Rules regarding school attendance and sex behavior are not drawn up with regard to the problems of adolescence. Rather, adolescents find themselves surrounded by rules about these matters which have been made by older and more settled people. It is considered legitimate to do this, for youngsters are considered neither wise enough nor responsible enough to make proper rules for themselves.

In the same way, it is true in many respects that men make the rules for women in our society (though in America this is changing rapidly). Negroes find themselves subject to rules made for them by whites. The foreign-born and those otherwise ethnically peculiar often have their rules made for them by the Protestant Anglo-Saxon minority. The middle class makes rules the lower class must obey—in the schools, the courts, and elsewhere.

Differences in the ability to make rules and apply them to other people are essentially power differentials (either legal

17

or extralegal). Those groups whose social position gives them weapons and power are best able to enforce their rules. Distinctions of age, sex, ethnicity, and class are all related to differences in power, which accounts for differences in the degree to which groups so distinguished can make rules for others.

In addition to recognizing that deviance is created by the responses of people to particular kinds of behavior, by the labeling of that behavior as deviant, we must also keep in mind that the rules created and maintained by such labeling are not universally agreed to. Instead, they are the object of conflict and disagreement, part of the political process of society.

18

[25]

Observing Deviance

Jack D. Douglas

Until recently, sociologists have relied almost exclusively on official information on deviance to develop and test their theories of deviance. They have done so both because of the prevailing structural perspective on deviance and because they have found it personally difficult, or even distressing, to attempt to get information on deviance in any other way. Sociologists have only two obvious alternatives to making use of official information or to studying those subjects provided by officials. They are: (1) sociologists can claim omniscience, then take the common-sense stance and impose those meanings on deviance that they find most useful for the practical purpose at hand (which until recent times was to denounce sin and to help officials to "control" it, but which lately has been to "show sympathy for the underdog"); or (2) sociologists can take a firsthand look at deviance, certainly commonsensical and long the standard practice of journalists. Sociologists have always been quite aware of both possibilities, but when committing themselves to an alternative to official information, they have almost always chosen to assume sociological omniscience.

There are some practical reasons why sociologists have chosen commitment to official information and armchair omniscience over learning through participation. Participation is very time-consuming and arduous, especially when one must keep the offbeat hours of many deviants, as is evident from John Irwin's study of criminals. It is far quicker and easier to use previously constructed official information. Indeed, it is easier still to *impose* meanings on deviance rather than to have to beg, wheedle, inveigle, browbeat, threaten, or buy the information from individuals so "ignorant" as to distrust the intentions of the social scientist.

3

4   JACK D. DOUGLAS

It is also safer, since it protects the sociologist from both deviants and law enforcement agents. And, finally, it is more respectable than keeping strange hours with odd people, which seems to be the crux of the matter.

As Ned Polsky has said, ". . . most sociologists find it too difficult or distasteful to get near adult criminals except in jails or other official settings, such as the courts and probation and parole systems." Most of the "practical" reasons given for what we shall see is the very impractical surrender of the one reliable form of information on deviance have probably been rationalizations for what Polsky has rightly called the "sociologists' cop-out."

This situation is crucial to contemporary sociology, especially to that part of it concerned with the study of the fundamental aspects of moral meanings and moral actions in society—that is, with the study of deviance. We now know quite clearly that official information is not only an unreliable source for studying deviance but is systematically biased in line with the needs and desires of officials and important segments of the public, so that it provides a systematically distorted picture of deviance. We are equally convinced that we cannot do worthwhile scientific studies of deviance by assuming sociological omniscience, but must, rather, see the social meanings of the actions of members of society as fundamentally problematic to them and to ourselves as sociological observers. In short, *the only alternative is to use almost exclusively some form of participation in order to observe deviance in its natural setting.*

We also know that we must become involved in the everyday lives of the individuals we wish to study so that we can come to share enough of the commonsense meanings of those activities to the individuals doing them to be able to understand what those meanings are. Only through such involvement can we "observe" the all-important social meanings of actions, since human beings are very subtle in controlling the impressions they give off about themselves. This is especially true of those groups considered deviant by important other groups in our society. As we shall see, the necessity to become involved in the everyday lives of those labeled deviant entails some basic problems, including the danger that "hip sociologists" will *go native* and become "sympathetic" spokesmen for *moral interest groups* rather than seek objective knowledge of those groups. But these dangers simply must be met and overcome.

OBSERVING DEVIANCE 5

The tradition of field research developed by the Chicago sociologists, which is the only highly developed tradition of field research in sociology, generally involves the assumption that secret methods are both ineffective and immoral. Effectiveness is really the primary issue, since one must first decide that secrecy is somehow effective before he cares whether it is moral. Invalid information, whether morally or immorally obtained, is worthless.

Gouldner has rightly argued that a fundamental aspect of the whole problem of objectivity is the moral one: there is a very real question of honesty involved here.   When an individual becomes committed to the interests of a specific group, he is especially apt to approach understanding of and, even more, public reporting of that group as political activities—that is, he is likely to *want* to present the group favorably, so he will think about it and report on it primarily in terms of his understanding of what he wants the audience to think about "his group." Individuals undoubtedly sometimes do this very cynically, especially when they feel they are doing politics, advertising, or public relations. But it is normally more subtle than this.

[26]

STANLEY COHEN

Criminology and the sociology of deviance in Britain

A recent history and a current report

A danger that faces the sociologist who indulges in the current vogue for 'sociologies of sociology' or 'self-reflexive sociology' is that he will end up playing what Goffman (1959: 149) describes as the 'discrepant role' of go-between or mediator. In this role, he 'learns the secrets of each side and gives each side the true impression that he will keep its secrets; but he tends to give each side the false impression that he is more loyal to it than to the other.' The sociologist, as a member of many more than two teams, is continually doing this sort of thing: telling society all the sordid secrets of his discipline, its inconsistencies, dishonesties, evasiveness, and then telling his colleagues how unreasonable, reactionary, irrational this society is. He goes continually backwards and forwards to employers, students, the profession, making sincere noises about responsibility, truth, relevance, or whatever the appropriate demand is.

Such manœuvres can be exciting; but we live dangerously when we publish or give conference papers, because then we are always and inevitably in the simultaneous presence of all our teams. Goffman suggests what may then happen: 'When a go-between operates in the actual presence of the two teams of which he is a member, we then obtain a wonderful display, not unlike a man desperately trying to play tenis with himself.' Papers of the 'current report' type are particularly prone to such displays, especially if the writer is, however insignificantly, part of what he is supposed to be reporting on.

I have tried where possible to avoid these problems, but it would be disingenuous to claim that the paper is a detached report from a spectator with no team loyalties. Let me indicate three further but

2   *Stanley Cohen*

more mundane limitations of this paper, which arise primarily from the brief that was given to me:

(1) I have concentrated on the *recent* history of criminology and the sociology of deviance; this implies for criminology going back not much further than the immediate pre-war years and for sociology the post-war expansion of the subject in its academic settings. This does not mean that a proper chronology (which could be a rewarding sociological exercise) would not have to go much further back, at least, for example, to Booth, Rowntree, Mayhew, and others.[1]

(2) A full scale treatment of the subject would have to deal first with the ideas involved in all the disciplines under review, secondly with the institutional contexts in which they arose and were diffused, and thirdly with the wider ideological and structural contexts in which they manifested themselves. This three level distinction corresponds more or less to the one made by Horowitz (1968) between 'the inner life of sociology', 'the academic life of sociology' and 'the political life of sociology'. This paper deals more fully, if still selectively, with the second of these levels, about which Horowitz's remarks apply even more forcibly if one substitutes 'criminology' for 'sociology':

'Without an appreciation for the institutional setting for sociology – the place after all where most sociologists make their living and legitimize their careers – the analysis of theory appears a formalistic exercise in the passage of novel ideas from great man to great man ... sociological history is embodied in the educational agencies and research bureaucracies from which sociologists issue forth their proclamations and projections.' (Horowitz 1969: Preface)

Only at a few points do I try to make explicit the wider political contexts in which such education and research must be located.

(3) I have chosen to deal with a number of aspects of the subject superficially, rather than concentrating on a few in any depth. Questions of values and methodology, for example, need a much more sustained treatment than is given here, nor can I pretend to do full justice to the individuals or institutions whose work is reviewed.

The paper is divided into five sections. The first identifies a number of rudimentary signposts pointing to the directions in which the sociology of deviance seems currently to be going. Then a selective review of British criminology is presented which partly uses these

Criminology and the sociology of deviance in Britain 3

signposts as evaluative criteria and partly analyses further related characteristics which acted as an impetus for the 'new' sociology of deviance to develop in this country. A third section deals briefly with the response of British sociology to the substance and theory of studying crime and deviance – again, only in so far as this response stimulated new developments in the sociology of deviance. The origins and impact of the National Deviancy Conference are then sketched and in the final section the traditional criminological institutions and the newer sociology of deviance are polarized and assessed.

IDENTIFYING A SOCIOLOGY OF DEVIANCE

In this brief section, I would like to list four signposts by which most self-styled 'genuine' sociologists of deviance would probably identify the ways they are moving. To repeat, this is not meant to be a sociology-of-knowledge exercise on how this subject has evolved; such an exercise is in any event partly redundant after Matza's analysis of criminological positivism (1964) and his subsequent chronicle and recommendation (1969) of the naturalist perspective on deviance. On a more parochial level and for a general public, I have tried elsewhere (1971) to identify how what I called the 'sceptical' approach to deviance differs from more established positions.

The term 'genuine' is, of course, tendentious and the distinction between 'new' and 'old' is also not particularly satisfactory. To make the polarizations on which the paper depends, I will refer simply to *mainstream criminology* and the *sociology of deviance*. In a somewhat religious vein, I use texts from four influential American contributors – Becker, Lemert, Matza, and Skolnick – to point to my four signposts:

(1) *Continuity with sociology*

It would seem absurd to insist on the self-evident, but one of the characteristic features of the study of crime, delinquency, and social problems has been its non-sociological or even anti-sociological nature. It is therefore the first and minimal criterion of the field that its connexions, if not continuity, with sociology should be recognized. Becker is justified in claiming that whatever 'labelling theory' is (and this claim is not of course peculiar to it) it fulfils this criterion:

4   *Stanley Cohen*

' "Labelling theory" so called, is a way of looking at deviance which actually represents a complete continuity with the rest of sociology. In other words, if a sociologist were going to study any topic, he would probably take such an approach, unless there were reasons not to. But there have been reasons not to approach criminology and the study of crime in the same way we might approach some more neutral topic. In studying most kinds of social organization, we will more likely understand that we have to study the actions of all the people involved in that organization . . . But somehow when sociologists studied crime, they didn't understand the problem that way. Instead they accepted the commonsense notion that there must be something wrong with criminals, otherwise they wouldn't act that way . . . The study of crime lost its connections with the mainstream of sociological development and became a very bizarre deformation of sociology.' (Becker, in Debro, 1970: 165–6)

(2) *The significance of social control*

It is not necessary for a sociologist of deviance to accept all the implications of labelling theory, the societal reaction perspective or its variants. What is necessary is to recognize the problematic nature of social control. Lemert presents one perspective on this problem with typical restraint:

'. . . older sociology tended to rest heavily upon the idea that deviance leads to social control. I have come to believe that the reverse idea, i.e. that social control leads to deviance, is equally tenable and the potentially richer premise for studying deviance in modern society.' (Lemert 1967: v)

There are many levels at which such a proposition can be approached, and sociologists might find any or all of these levels weak. But at least they would concede that the problem of deviance and control is a real one.

(3) *Appreciation*

I take from Matza the crucial contrast between 'correction' and 'appreciation' (Matza 1969: Chapter 2). The correctional stance takes for granted the objective of getting rid of the deviant phenomenon under question – and in so doing it 'systematically interferes with the capacity to empathize and thus comprehend the subject of enquiry'. Mainstream criminology has refused to go beyond the correctional stance: a weak demand from sociologists is to question the applicability of this ideology; a stronger demand would be to accept appreciation and the subjective view as the only defensible one. This acceptance, as Matza indicates, is a 'fateful decision': it entails a commitment to render the phenomenon with fidelity and without violating its integrity. In a more fundamental way:

> 'It delivers the analyst into the arms of the subject who renders the phenomenon, and commits him, though not without regrets or qualifications, to the subject's definition of the situation. This does not mean that the analyst always concurs with the subject's definition of the situation; rather that his aim is to comprehend and to illuminate the subject's view and to interpret the world *as it appears to him.*' (Matza 1969: 24, 25)[2]

(4) *The political implications of studying deviance*

It follows from my second and third criteria and it *should* follow from the first that the very categories of crime and deviance and hence how one studies them, are problematic in specifically political ways. That is, the field has something to do with control, power, legitimacy, ideology. Skolnick points to two cases: 'it's becoming increasingly apparent to a whole generation of criminologists and sociologists, that it is increasingly difficult to distinguish between crime and political and moral dissent' (Skolnick, in Carte 1969: 115). Then, in connexion with drug legislation, if one asks questions such as how the political structure ever allowed laws like this to be passed, '... as a criminologist or sociologist you necessarily come into the field of political science' (117). Leaving aside disciplinary demarcations, the problem is the structural and political *loci* of definitions of deviance, a problem that has been accentuated rather than created by recent convergences between the 'ideological' and the 'criminal'.[3]

I have listed these four signposts as ones that would be recognized by the current generation of adherents to the sociology of deviance 'institution' but have been largely ignored or by-passed by mainstream criminology. I am not setting these up as articles of faith to be demanded by some new orthodoxy, still less as criteria for evaluating research, methodology or theory. They do however, singly or together,

6   *Stanley Cohen*

serve to demarcate significantly one set of collective self-conceptions
from another.

   The drift of my argument in the next section is that the history
and, to a large extent, the current state of British criminology, are
antithetical to the sociology of deviance as conceived above – as well
as containing intrinsic limitations many of which are peculiarly
British. It has not moved out of its paradigm, and even its uncomfortable recognition that 'where it's happening' is elsewhere cannot
change the position much. It tries to graft on new bodies of thought,
concepts, models, leaving the basic structure intact. Because this
structure has an integrity of its own, a certain impressive weight and
an umbrella-like quality which is able to embrace so much, I do not
believe that our task as sociologists should be to reform it. To a large
extent we will have to remain partly parasitic on it while improving
our critique of it. Although the analogy is not exact, the relationship
might be similar to that between the sociology of industry on one
hand, and industrial relations on the other.[4]

MAINSTREAM BRITISH CRIMINOLOGY

In many respects, Charles Goring, author of *The English Convict*
(1913) and perhaps the first recognized major figure in British
criminology, epitomizes the whole tradition which followed him. It is
not just that as an archetypal representative of positivism he survived
in the spirit of criminology long after the substance of his contribution was repudiated (though this is so and what Matza says about
positivist criminology in general is doubly true in Britain). I am not
dealing with the 'inner life' of criminology in this way. My point is
that Goring's contribution can be characterized in further ways that
found themselves mirrored in the history of mainstream British
criminology in the sixty years after his work.[5] I have picked out four
such characteristics, only the last of which relates to Matza's evaluation of positivism: these are (1) *pragmatism*; (2) criminology as *interdisciplinary science, insulated from sociology*; (3) the *correctional and
reformative* positions and (4) the *positivist trap*.

   Goring's approach was totally pragmatic. He belonged to no
criminological school and, starting from his day to day experience as
a prison doctor, simply set out more systematically to test the claims
of Lombroso. (This pragmatism carried with it another quality, a
certain amateur, whimsical spirit which at one stage I thought of

Criminology and the sociology of deviance in Britain 7

tracing in later criminology; the parallels are not always clear though and in the case of, say, the Cambridge Institute of Criminology, hardly apply. Goring did combine an odd mixture of what was at the time a fairly sophisticated control group technique with a rather bizarre notion of where to select his controls. His choice of Scottish, Oxford and Cambridge undergraduates, University of London professors, inmates of a general hospital, British Royal Engineers and German army recruits did, though, enable him to indulge in the following: 'From a knowledge only of an undergraduate's cephalic measurement, a better judgement could be given as to whether he were studying at an English or Scottish University than a prediction could be made as to whether he would eventually become a university professor or a convicted felon.' When this tone appears in later British criminology, one finds it – depending on aesthetic preferences – either disarming or wholly irritating.)

Goring was not just pragmatic, but in his combination of disciplines – some background in philosophy, a training as a doctor, a bit of psychological speculation, a familiarity with statistical techniques – he exhibited one of the most characteristic features of British criminology, its inter-disciplinary approach, which as I will show was more than usually catholic and indiscriminate. And, although the same may be said for most national criminologies excluding the American, this mixture never really allowed for a sociological perspective. As Mannheim correctly states, this applied even more to Goring than Lombroso (Mannheim 1965: 227). Goring wrote: 'Crime is only to a trifling extent (if to any) the product of social inequalities of adverse environment and of other manifestations of . . . the force of circumstances.' And, as a prison doctor, Goring's interests in doing research were fairly clear-cut: one had to find better ways of dealing with convicted criminals, presumably by treating them on the basis of their supposed psychological characteristics.

Finally, Goring seemed caught in the positivist trap in a way which keeps recurring in British criminology. His statistical analysis disproved Lombroso, but instead of stopping at this point, he went on to develop a causal account as predictable and as misleading as Lombroso's and pointing in a specifically clinical direction. I will try to show that later British criminologists, even with an intellectual awareness which Goring could never have had of the paradoxes of this model, fall into the same trap.

I have chosen these four characteristics to organize my review of

8   *Stanley Cohen*

British criminology because they are the ones which provide the main impetus for the new sociology of deviance to take root in the middle 1960s. The main institutions under review are: (1) the Home Office and particularly the Home Office Research Unit, set up in 1957 to carry out a long term research programme, mainly concerned with the treatment of offenders and to act as 'a centre of discussion with universities and other interested organizations'; (2) the Institute for the Study and Treatment of Delinquency (ISTD), set up in 1931, and crucial in that it directly produced the British Society of Criminology (BSC) and the only criminological journal in the country, the *British Journal of Criminology* (*BJC*); (3) the Institute of Criminology at Cambridge, set up under Home Office sponsorship in 1958 and (4) the teaching of criminology in London, particularly the work of Hermann Mannheim. These institutions and individuals by no means represent a monolithic establishment, and there are many cross links, for example, the Cambridge Institute has close links with the Home Office, but not with the *British Journal of Criminology* group.

(1) *Pragmatism*

The pragmatic approach has become an indisputable feature of British criminology. This is not a characterization made in retrospect by current observers (see, for example, Carson and Wiles, 1971: 7) but one that has been proudly proclaimed by the leading representatives of the indigenous British criminological tradition. Thus Radzinowicz (1966) after surveying what he calls the 'liberal' and 'deterministic' theories of crime, ends up by endorsing what he himself terms the 'pragmatic position'. This he sees as a 'new realism': there is no single purpose of punishment, there is no single causal theory of crime, therefore any or all perspectives, from Burt to Merton, have something to recommend themselves and in this 'lies the strength and promise of the pragmatic position' (1966: 128).

The pragmatic frame of reference is the one that shapes the few general textbook-type works produced by British criminologists (e.g. Walker 1965; Jones 1965; Mannheim 1965; West 1967) as well as the organization of research and teaching. One finds an overall distrust for theory or for some master conception into which various subjects can be fitted.

The impediments to a theoretical criminology are easier to find than account for. One major reason has been alluded to at several

Criminology and the sociology of deviance in Britain 9

points by Radzinowicz (1961, 1966): that the fact that the whole idea of 'schools' of criminal law and criminology in the Continental sense is quite alien to the British legal tradition. On the Continent, major schools of criminal law – liberal, classical determinist, positivist, social defence – flourished for decades, partly because of the powerful position of professors of criminal law in the legal system. In England such positions of influence were the prerogative of the judiciary, the makers and interpreters of the law, 'to them the formulation of an all-embracing doctrine and the emergence of a school was something quite alien' (Radzinowicz 1966: 21). Criminology had to take root in this pragmatic legal tradition.

In making the contrast with America, the significant point is that although an autonomous criminology, as in Britain, also developed, it was from the outset located among the social sciences (in the broadest sense). As Radinowicz (1961: 119) among others has suggested, this location was partly due to the American ideology of optimism in which crime could be seen as the product of remediable social forces. There has also been something different about American legal training: quite unlike Britain, lawyers have for a long time been exposed to the social sciences in their undergraduate training. The strong American legal-sociological tradition has been virtually absent in Britain.

There was little opportunity then for either a legally or a sociologically based theoretical criminology to emerge.

In a wider sense, the pragmatic tradition is part of the national culture. I am referring not just to the amateur, muddling-along air which foreigners detect about British life but, for example, to the Fabian type of pragmatism in which disciplines such as criminology with obvious practical implications are located. The attitude behind many enterprises in such fields has been more or less one of finding out the facts, and letting the well-meaning chaps (say, in the Home Office) make the obvious inferences and do the rest. Contrasted to America, the collection of information for policy making is very different; compare say the composition of the National Commission on the Causes and Prevention of Violence, with its impressive range of experts, the professionalism with which it could produce about fifteen massively documented volumes in less than two years, to the typical Royal Commission with its motley collection of peers, bishops, judges, very part-time experts, and 'informed laymen', and its unbelievably slow rate of productivity.[6]

Although I do not accept the drift of much of his argument, all these points need to be put into a broader context such as the one suggested by Anderson (1968). His argument is that there is not just an absence of a tradition of revolutionary thought in Britain, but an absence of major intellectual traditions at all. Thus the weakness of sociology (which he overstates) is diagnosed in terms of its failure to produce any classical tradition and its historical dependence on the charity, social work, and Fabian institutions. Significantly, from the point of this paper, Anderson finds one reason for the absence of a separate intelligentsia in the factor I have already mentioned – the absence of Roman Law in England and the blocking of an intelligentsia based on legal faculties, teaching abstract principles of jurisprudence (Anderson 1968: 15). Another – somewhat less secure – plank of his argument is the influence of European *émigrés* (Popper, Wittgenstein, Berlin, Eysenck, *et al.*). These were '. . . intellectuals with an elective affinity to English modes of thought and political outlook' who found British empiricism and conservatism – the way it shunned theories and systems even in its rejection of them – quite congenial (18–19).

It is (aesthetically at least) appealing to apply much of this analysis to British criminology. To give a specific parallel, the careers of the major founders of contemporary British criminology – Mannheim, Radzinowicz, Grünhut – are not too far removed from those of the *émigrés* Anderson considers. Mannheim, for example, after a distinguished judicial career in Germany, came to London in 1934, where – according to all his biographers and ex-students – his natural empiricism and tendency to relate his teaching to practical work in the courts found an affinity in 'the ideas of English social reformers, the work of the probation service and expedients in the after care of prisoners' (Croft 1965: xvi).[7] To point to this pragmatic frame of mind does not, of course, detract from the contributions, for example in teaching or reform, of figures such as these – indeed, this might be their strength – but it does provide a necessary lens through which to view their work.

(2) *The interdisciplinary conception*

Pragmatism and empiricism are perspectives which often go hand in hand with the interdisciplinary ideology. Criminology cannot, I believe, be other than interdisciplinary in the sense that it has to draw on the findings of what Morris (1966: 62) refers to as the 'strange

Criminology and the sociology of deviance in Britain   11

motley of investigators who have at some time or another borne the
title of criminologist' – doctors, lawyers, statisticians, psychiatrists,
clinical psychologists, and others more bizarre than these. It would be
a waste of time then to labour this point, if not for two additional
turns this feature has taken in British criminology – the first has been
to make a religion out of the necessity of drawing on different disciplines
and the second has been the playing down of the sociological contribution to this pantheon, pushing criminology either in the legalistic
direction or (more frequently and more unfortunately) towards the
clinical/psychological/forensic ideology.

Again, let me start with an assertion from Radzinowicz (1961: 177)
to the effect that progress in criminology can only be made by the
interdisciplinary approach: 'a psychiatrist, a social psychologist, a
penologist, a lawyer, a statistician joining together on a combined
research operation'. In the British context, the fact that a sociologist
is not even mentioned is predictable. By the end of the 1950s the
major figures in teaching and research were Radzinowicz (legal),
Grünhut (legal), Mannheim (legal training and later psychiatric and
especially sociological interest). The major institutions directly or
marginally contributing – the Maudsley Hospital, the Tavistock
Institute, the ISTD, the BSC, and the *BJC* – heavily weighted the
field towards psychology and psychiatry. This weighting remained
despite the later contribution by sociologists such as Mays, Morris,
and later Downes.

This multidisciplinary image was reflected at a number of levels. It
was part of the criminologist's presentation of self to the public.[8] It
could be found in criminological conferences in textbooks and in
lecture courses. Thus in Walker's (1965) text, out of fifty-seven pages
devoted to the topic of explaining crime, seven are given to 'constitutional theories', fifteen to 'mental subnormality and illness', twenty to
psychological theories of 'maladjustment, the normal offender, and
psychopathy' and fifteen to 'environmental theories' (including
'economic theories', 'topographical aspects' and 'the human environment'). Mannheim's work is more difficult to characterize in this way
because, although he clearly sees criminology as multi-disciplinary and
his own training was legal,[9] he made significant sociological contributions in such books as *Social Aspects of Crime in England between
the Wars* and his treatment of most sociological theories (with exceptions such as differential association) is as comprehensive as the rest
of his 1965 text.

12 *Stanley Cohen*

A very clear statement in favour of criminology remaining exceptionally wide in scope was provided by another leading British criminologist, Gibbens, at a recent Council of Europe Criminological Conference:

'... most of the important ideas and research hypotheses in criminology still come from the parent disciplines of law, social science, psychology and psychiatry ... major contributions to criminology continue to come from studies which are not originally designed to come within its scope. Geneticists stumbled upon the significance of the XYY syndrome, the Danish twin study was a by-product of medical study, the English study of a sample of the population born on the same day was originally designed to study midwifery and infant mortality ...' (Gibbens 1970: 5)

Other institutions reveal much the same, with an even more striking weighting towards the legal or clinical disciplines. The twelve research reports published to date by the Home Office Research Unit contain mainly topics of a statistical, social administrative type, together with highly technical psychological research (e.g. on the Hewitt and Jenkins hypothesis, and the use of the Jesness Inventory).

The character of British criminology is seen very distinctively in the ISTD, BSC, *BJC* axis. The Institute for the Scientific Treatment of Delinquency, set up in 1931, was the only one of its kind until the establishment of the Cambridge Institute. Its original objects included 'to initiate and promote scientific research into the causes and prevention of crime', to provide educational and training facilities and 'to establish observation centres or other auxiliary services for the study and treatment of delinquency'.

The essentially clinical nature of its approach was not altogether removed after its 'Psychopathic Clinic' was taken over by the National Health Service in 1948 and the phrase 'Scientific Treatment' was changed to 'Study and Treatment'. Thus in its 1957–8 *Annual Report* the case against handling crime from the penal end of the system and just using outside scientific information was stated and the case made for moving from the outside towards 'extending the principle of treating offences whenever possible as behaviour disorders calling for appropriate psycho-social measures' (p. 4). Clinical positivism was stressed as the scientific ideal; in the following year's *Report* the phrase '... the root problem of delinquency, viz. the condition of "pre-delinquency"' (p. 3) occurred.

Criminology and the sociology of deviance in Britain 13

The possibility of predicting delinquency – an obsession in British criminology – was always stressed and the 1960–1 *Report* complained that there were still resistances to dealing with crime as a 'behaviour problem with characteristic antecedents ... Judging by comparative study of *other* forms of mental disorder, it is in the highest degree probable that in all cases the existence of a "predelinquent" stage can be established ...' (p. 3, emphasis mine).

It is of course true that the ISTD was uniquely dominated by the psychiatrists (Edward Glover and Emmanuel Miller being the most notable) but Mannheim was a leading member from the outset and a scrutiny of the Annual Reports from 1950 onwards shows that virtually every leading British criminologist (with the exception of Radzinowicz) held some office in it. The parent organization had considerable import through its educational activities, but also through its offshoots, the *BJC*, started in July 1950 as the *British Journal of Delinquency*, with Glover, Miller, and Mannheim as its editors[10] (the name was changed in July 1960), and the BSC, which started off life within the ISTD in 1953 as the Scientific Group for the Discussion of Delinquency Problems.

The contents of the *BJC* over its twenty years have fairly accurately reflected the concerns of the discipline. Considerable attention is given to penology, to abnormal psychology, to delinquency and institutions for delinquents, and there is consistent interest in matters of legal and penal reform. A detailed classification of the contents (Wright 1970) contains the following frequencies of articles etc. appearing between 1950 and 1970: penology (including institutions, probation, capital punishment) 205; criminology (including delinquency classification, special types of offences) 379; social work 28; law 33; administration of justice 67; psychology 24; abnormal psychology 80; psychiatry 37; social sciences (including 'social factors', education) 79. This classification does not reveal disciplinary origins (for example, under criminology and penology) very clearly, nor does it convey the characteristic flavour of the journal. The attention given to very practical issues and the reprinting of addresses such as those given by a Commissioner of Police of the Metropolis (April 1968) clearly moves the journal away from a strictly academic format. And despite what to an outsider might look as a fair proportion of space given to clinical material, one of the editors recently complained: 'Where, we may ask, are the brave, resourceful, and imaginative clinical papers of yesterday?' (Glover 1970: 315)

14   *Stanley Cohen*

The BSC reveals a more or less similar pattern. The make-up of its original Organizing Committee in 1961 (the year after it changed its name) included one representative each from the following: biology; criminal law and justice; organic medicine; psychiatry; psychoanalysis; psychology; social work; criminology; statistics; treatment of offenders; education and ethics, and moral philosophy. (Currently the Committee is made up of four representatives each from criminal law and the administration of justice; criminological medicine and psychology; treatment of offenders; criminological treatment of research; 'other persons'.)

One of its first meetings (in November 1953) was addressed by the two physiological psychologists, while its seventieth meeting (in February 1971) was addressed by a forensic psychiatrist on the subject of epileptics in prison. Out of 96 guest speakers at its meetings (some conferences or meetings had more than one speaker), there were 16 sociological criminologists, 16 psychologists (7 from the Home Office Research Unit, 2 from prisons), 12 psychiatrists, 12 lawyers, 5 Home Office administrators, 5 'criminologists', 4 Home Office statisticians, 6 social workers, 6 social administrators, 5 police officers, and a miscellaneous group of 10 including historians, geneticists, prison officers, prison doctors, and prison governors.

This rapid analysis of the disciplinary content and preoccupations in British criminology is not meant to give the impression that sociologists were somehow wilfully excluded due to some conspiracy. The imbalance is there partly because sociological criminology has not demonstrated its practical pay-off, but more simply, in Britain, because there was just so little of it available. As the editors of a recent collection on the sociology of crime and delinquency point out:

'Our reliance upon theories developed in other countries and particularly the United States is sometimes so pronounced in the teaching context, that students gain the impression of an almost complete hiatus in British research. Erroneous as such an impression may be the fact remains that the heavy traffic in ideas about delinquency has tended to flow almost exclusively in one direction.' (Carson and Wiles 1971: 48)

As I will show in the next section, the impression of a hiatus in sociological attention on crime is not all that erroneous. With the notable exceptions of Morris's ecological study and its predecessors (Mays, Sprott, Jephcott, Carter, and Kerr) the Morrises' sociological

Criminology and the sociology of deviance in Britain 15

studies of prison, and some work on sentencing, there was virtually nothing before the post-1965 wave following Downes' book (Hargreaves, Willmott and others). Two of the most frequently cited works of sociological relevance before the 1960s – Sainsbury's study of the ecological patterns of suicide in London and Scott's description of delinquent gangs – were in fact both done by psychiatrists. An index of the paucity of indigenous sociology – and of the fact that one does not have to invoke conspiracy theories – is that the Institute of Criminology has often 'imported' leading American sociological criminologists such as Cressey and Wolfgang.

While it is difficult altogether to blame British sociology for paying so little attention to indigenous sociology, it cannot be exonerated easily from two further charges: a certain *parochialism* which wilfully excluded American sociology of crime and deviance for so long and, then, a clear *misunderstanding* as to what sociology is about. Mannheim is partly guilty on the first charge, with his apparent policy of selecting for his textbook American work only when British or European work could not be found; while the work of West is a clear example on both these counts. Curious notions about sociology being concerned with 'area' or 'environmental' factors appear, sociology is identified with statistics, and concepts such as anomie, subculture, or deprivation are distorted.[11]

In summary, the off-putting features of the interdisciplinary approach are the rigidity with which it is defended, the way it is skewed to exclude sociology and lean in the clinical direction, its parochialism, and its misunderstanding of sociology. These features may be illustrated by the following anecdote: during a visit two years ago David Matza was introduced to a body of British criminologists by a leading British criminologist, who said that although he hadn't actually read any of Professor Matza's work, he'd been told it was very interesting. . .

(3) *Correction, reform, and the problem of values*

British criminology has always been tied to two interests: the first, the administrative interest of making the correctional system more efficient and the second the humanitarian interest in reforming the system. These interests are not, of course, necessarily incompatible especially in their recent appearance under the psychiatric ideology which

16   *Stanley Cohen*

rationalizes the treatment approach as being both more efficient and
more humane.

The problems these interests raise are complex and although it is
easy enough to find instances in British criminology where investigators have compromised themselves by their institutional connexions
or their open espousal of correctional interests, the charge against
criminology is that it has simply not even realized the complexity of
the issue. Correctional aims are apparently taken for granted:

> 'Criminology, in its narrow sense, is concerned with the study of
> the phenomenon of crime and of the factors or circumstances...
> which may have an influence on or be associated with criminal
> behaviour and the state of crime in general. But this does not and
> should not exhaust the whole subject matter of criminology. There
> remains the vitally important problem of combating crime... To
> rob it of this practical function, is to divorce criminology from
> reality and render it sterile.' (Radzinowicz 1961: 168)

Or attempts are made to divorce criminology from such 'practical
functions'. Walker, for example, states that 'Perhaps the hardest impression to eradicate is that the criminologist is a penal reformer' and
concedes that although his findings might form the basis of reform
campaigns such campaigns are humanitarian not scientific in nature:

> 'It is no more his [the criminologist's] function to attack or defend
> the death penalty than it is the function of the political scientist to
> take part in an election campaign. The confusion, however, between
> criminologists and penal reformers has been encouraged by crimino-
> logists themselves, many of whom have also been penal reformers.
> Strictly speaking, penal reform is a spare time occupation for
> criminologists just as canvassing for votes would be for political
> scientists. The difference is that the criminologists' spare time occu-
> pation is more likely to take this form, and when it does so it is
> more likely to interfere with what should be purely criminological
> thoughts.' (Walker 1965: preface)

It is to Walker's credit that he states his resolution of the problem
so clearly. In contrast, the major institutions of British criminology
have apparently quite unselfconsciously accepted the goals of social
control taking up, within these, various correctional or reformative
stances. Contributions are made by those (like Goring) who are part
of the system, those who are sponsored by the system (e.g. doing

Criminology and the sociology of deviance in Britain 17

research financed by the Home Office) or by the numerous institutions part of whose policy is to encourage cooperation between so-called 'scientific' and so called 'practical' objectives. These styles appear in various guises in the ISTD, the *BJC*, the BSC, and the Cambridge Institute. Thus, for example, when the BSC held a conference four years ago on 'The Role of the Prison Officer' the speakers were the Secretary of the Prison Officers Association, a Chief Prison Officer, the Principal of the Officers Training School, a prison psychiatrist, and the Assistant Secretary of State in the Home Office Prison Department. When such styles appear in the work of bodies as the Cambridge Institute, they are more sophisticated and it would be insulting to suggest that the individuals involved in such research or communication are unaware of potential tensions and conflicts of interests. But I would repeat that if any such self awareness is there, it has not – with few exceptions – been manifested in any public way.

Now, while Walker's solution is clear, it is both over-simplified and untenable. One cannot believe that what has been problematic to social scientists for generations – for Weber, Myrdal, and Mills no less than in the special deviancy context for Becker, Polsky, Gouldner, and others – can be resolved by asserting that there are such things as 'purely criminological thoughts'. The constraints that operate in the very selection of certain subjects as worthy of research, the methods one chooses, the way one is funded and sponsored, how one's results will be used... these and numerous other problems cannot be brushed under the carpet. Unless and until the private doubts that most criminologists express – what to do, for example, if the Home Office refuses to let one's research assistant look at records because he is a security risk – are made public, these criminologists should not complain that the outsider believes that they do not have these doubts.

This is not, of course, a problem peculiar to criminology. There are many parallels, for example, in contemporary research on race relations, where there is the continual conflict between accepting official goals, taking a reformist position, siding with particular interest groups, or showing an allegiance to some professional ethic. In studying crime and deviance, where what Becker (1967) terms the hierarchies of credibility and morality are so much taken for granted, the problems are heightened. It is not enough for the Social Science Research Council to comment as follows on its policy in regard to criminological research:

18   *Stanley Cohen*

'the great grant-giving foundations do not appear to have any place
in the present quasi-official arrangements between the Home Office,
the Cambridge Institute and the Advisory Council on the Treatment of Offenders and this again might well be a matter for consideration by the SSRC which could well accept responsibility for
co-ordination in the allocation of funds and maintain a balance
between the interests involved.' (SSRC 1968)

It must be made clear just whose 'interests' are being 'balanced'.

(4) *The positivist trap*

The heavy dominance of clinical positivism within the interdisciplinary
rubric of British criminology is one of many indices that support my
contention that the basic model which shaped Goring's thought has
not really been transcended. It should be made clear that this is not
an objection to explanations at the psychological level *per se* (unlike
most of my sociological colleagues, I believe that such objections are
theoretically indefensible) but to demonistic psychology of the Eysenck
type. As this is not the level of analysis the paper is primarily concerned with, let me just give two brief examples of the trap.

The first surrounds the concept of determinism, which has been so
controversial an issue in legal, psychiatric and recently sociological
discussions of crime. Jones (1965: 70), a sociological criminologist,
in discussing the implications of the treatment model in imputing
criminal responsibility, cites a distinction made by a philosopher between the kleptomaniac and the thief: the former is not responsible
for his behaviour while the latter is to be treated as a rational person.
'But', Jones comments, 'current psychological and sociological research
gives us reason to question the validity of such a distinction.' Good,
one thinks, even if he is not referring to the general problem about
responsibility as Matza does, he is going to make the specific point
that Cressey makes in his well-known paper (1954, revised 1962)
that so-called compulsive crimes such as kleptomania in fact lack the
characteristics imputed to them by psychiatrists, and if re-examined
in terms of sociological theories of motivation, identification, role-
playing etc. are similar to other motivated, rational behaviour. But no,
Jones is making *exactly the opposite* point, the trap has been well laid:

'The ability to resist temptation, for example, depends upon a person's character structure and this in turn arises out of personal

Criminology and the sociology of deviance in Britain 19

relationships within the family during earliest years of life – experience over which the individual has no control.'

My other example is less specific and will serve to epitomize – as much as Goring did – all the characteristics of mainstream British criminology I have highlighted in this review. It is a recent book by West (1969), the first Report (after seven years work) of the Cambridge Study in Delinquent Development. It is one of the largest single pieces of criminological research ever carried out in this country, financed by the Home Office (£70,000 to March 1968, now under annual review, the project still having some years to go) and with an eminent Consultative and Advisory Committee (including only two out of eleven with more or less sociological backgrounds). In his preface to this report, Radzinowicz hails the research as being '... in the great tradition of explorations of the springs of delinquency. Although on a smaller scale it will ultimately claim a place alongside such classics as the work of Robins, the Gluecks and the McCords. All too little of this sort has been attempted in England' (p. vii).

This assertion is correct: in methodology and conception this research goes no further than the extraordinary jumble of eclectic positivism that rendered the work of the Gluecks such an anachronism. Sociologists cannot be expected to be very impressed with a study which states that although it is more concerned with individual characteristics, it is also interested in the 'demonstration' of the extent to which troublesome boys and other family problems are concentrated among the very poorest: 'It may be that the next stage of the inquiry will go some way to answering the question of whether these problems spring from poverty or whether poverty itself merely reflects an underlying individual inadequacy' [*sic*] (p. vii).

The design involves an eight-year follow-up of some 400 boys selected at the age of eight or nine. Did some overall conception inform the selection of dimensions to be studied? West answers: 'The aim was to collect information on a large number of items, all of them said to have relevance to the development of juvenile delinquency and to see in the event which items or which combination of items would prove to be the clearest determinants of future delinquency' (p. 2). Social factors such as television were excluded because these were too 'universal' and of course – as the Gluecks also argued – neighbourhood influences could be excluded because these were constant. Besides such indices as teachers' ratings and psychological dimensions of the family, items used includes ones such as height, weight, body-type and various tests of psychomotor habits.[12]

The preliminary findings suggest that the social level of the family was the most important single factor in discriminating poorly behaved boys from the rest. From an actuarial point of view, the most efficient prediction might be based on a few easily registered and objective social facts. The index 'family income inadequate' was 'remarkably effective' in identifying the 'problem prone minority'. If this is so (and of course such a finding was the basis of Toby's devastating critique of the Gluecks six years ago) then what is the point of a study like this? Why use the opportunities provided by a long scale longitudinal design in such a way? Leaving aside any theoretical pay-off (which the researchers might want to say does not concern them) the practical advantages of such individualistic prediction studies – as numerous critics have shown – are highly dubious.

If this is the sort of research which is to command prestige and credibility in the future, then British criminology cannot be said to have advanced a great deal and, more particularly, it cannot be expected to command much positive sociological interest.

Let me conclude this review with three important footnotes, without which the point of the exercise could be misunderstood:

(1) These four distinguishing features were chosen not only because they were in some ways characteristic, but because they were ones which were reacted against by the new sociology of deviance. In only the last of these can the reaction be said to be a partial resolution. Pragmatism – if not in the form it takes in British criminology – is partially unavoidable and in some instances can be recommended. Then, it is difficult to see criminology not being inter-disciplinary – although again the particular form it has taken (the advocacy of 'teamwork' for example) is intellectually facile and when it has no theoretical edifice to support it, it is extraordinarily vulnerable to attack from faddishness, not to say charlatanism. The advances of the XYY 'explanation',[13] Eysenck's excursions into criminology, and the onslaught which is just gathering momentum, the ethology kick, do not give one much faith in the subject's integrity. Finally, while sociologists have seemed more aware – at times perhaps obsessed – by the value problem, they can hardly have said to have solved it. Self-images stressing styles such as appreciating, muckraking, cynically commenting, reflecting, might all have their aesthetic appeals, but they do not constitute solutions to doing research, say, on prisons. Such

research cannot but resemble that by orthodox criminologists in being reformist, in laying itself open to be used for other ends, in having to compromise itself at various points.

(2) Talking about 'mainstream' criminology has meant leaving out those few attempts which cannot be characterized by at least all of these features. In sociological criminology the work, say, of Morris and Downes has already been mentioned and the same applies in psychology to that of Trasler: although his 'explanation of criminality' has severe limitations, it at least constitutes a theory. The work of Tony Parker, too often disparaged as being 'just a few good stories', must also be singled out.

(3) There are a number of current developments in the sociology of law, which already has one base in the contributions by Radzinowicz (in his history of the English criminal law) and Walker (in his histories of the use of psychiatric concepts in the legal system). This field has received recent theoretical interest and empirical contributions such as those from the Legal Research Unit at Bedford College, recent studies of the legal profession and allied subjects (by Abel-Smith, Zander, and others), and the current development of a Legal Advice Research Unit (financed by Nuffield) could vitalize the whole field, relating it, for example, to wider sociological interests in social control and the legal order. A second development has been research in the sociology of the police. There have already been a few isolated projects in this field over the last few years and attempts are currently being made – although one has some misgivings about the directions some of these might go – by Banton and others (again with Nuffield Foundation assistance) to 'evaluate recent research and define future priorities'. Finally, an interest in deviance has been shown by students of mass media and mass culture; these are shown in different ways in Stuart Hall's paper to this conference and in the work of the Centre for Mass Communication Research at Leicester (see Halloran, *et al.*, 1970).

THE RESPONSE FROM SOCIOLOGY

That the study of deviant behaviour, crime, and social problems has become insulated from sociology is, I think, self-evident and I have tried to show the form this insulation took in Britain. What, though, was the response from the 'other side', from the mainstream of sociology? No one has considered this problem, although Morris, in his review of Mannheim's text, points out that even if British criminology has not moved in a neo-Lombrosian direction away from the concerns of such Victorian amateurs as Mayhew, it '... would still not have been able to gain much from association with the social sciences in British Universities' (Morris 1966: 61). Without pioneers such as Mannheim, he suggests, criminology would still be where it was in the thirties. But what have sociologists been doing all this time? The answer to this question is important, because there is little doubt that at an intellectual level the new deviance theories are responses to the insulation from sociology and at a personal level, as I will suggest, their adherents see themselves as stigmatized outsiders trying to get back into the respectable, i.e. sociological, community. (Although, as I will also suggest, this is a partially serious passing rather than repentant attempt at full re-socialization.)

One index of the insulation has been the relative lack of interest admitted by sociologists in the pre-occupations of criminology. Few would show a comparable unfamiliarity with other sub-fields – say, educational or industrial sociology. For the most part this indifference is justified, but even potentially important issues in sociological criminology (e.g. white collar crime) have been ignored. On the surface, this state of affairs is all the more surprising as the study of deviance was rooted in the central concerns of sociological theory. As Becker, among others, has pointed out, to theorists like Durkheim 'problems of deviance were problems of general sociology' (Becker 1964: 1). This is no more true for the obvious case of *Suicide* than it is for *Rules* and *Division of Labour*, both works having produced themes explicitly taken up later, for example, by Erikson in the sceptical sociology of deviance.

The reasons for severing these connexions are complex and beyond my scope in this paper. On the side of sociology, they include a sophisticated version of the sort of philistine distrust which greets, say, Durkheim's *Suicide* and the whole work of Freud. How can looking at suicide explain how societies work 'normally'? How can the interpsychic conflicts of a few middle class Viennese Jews explain how the 'normal' mind works? Studying deviance is seen as an esoteric and marginal occupation. Crucial too, has been the development of consensual theories in sociology, in the more mechanistic versions of which crime and deviance are simply the results of the machine going wrong. It is precisely this sort of conception that recent theorists of deviance have reacted against.

Criminology and the sociology of deviance in Britain 23

The major barriers, though, have been created on the other side: the moralistic, non-abstract ways in which deviance has been studied and the early identification of this field with social work, reformative or correctional concerns.[14] As Polsky has noted, criminology has been the least successful of all subfields of sociology in freeing itself from these concerns. He comments on Merton's condemnation of the 'slum encouraged provincialism of thinking that the primary subject matter of sociology was centred on such peripheral problems of social life as divorce and delinquency' that:

> 'Given the perspectives within which delinquency and crime are always studied it is obvious why Merton might regard them as peripheral problems of social life rather than fundamental processes of central concern to sociology.' (Polsky 1967: 142)

Polsky is guilty here of caricaturing criminology and is certainly wrong if the old Chicago School studies of crime and deviance are considered. But clearly the development of criminology has little to recommend itself to sociology.

Returning to the institutional level, would one not expect the reverse in Britain, that the pragmatic Fabian stream in sociology would find criminology and related fields highly congruent with its self-image? To some extent, this *has* been true, but this stream is running dry. On the one hand, sociology is developing scientific, academic, or professional self-images into which certain topics are not respectable enough to be fitted and on the other, soft, liberal attitudes are becoming anathema to the hard radicals of sociology who don't consider deviants as 'really' political. Both these developments, but particularly the first which is the more dominant, lead to those common room sniggerings about 'girls who want to do sociology because they like people'.

Elsewhere (Cohen 1971) in trying to describe the sort of attitudes that were prevalent in the profession, I wrote:

> 'In terms of having congenial people to discuss our work with, we found some of our sociological colleagues equally unhelpful. They were either mandarins who were hostile towards a committed sociology and found subjects such as delinquency nasty, distasteful or simply boring, or else they were self-proclaimed radicals, whose political interests went only as far as their own definition of "political" and were happy to consign deviants to social welfare or

psychiatry. For different reasons, both groups found our subject matter too messy and devoid of significance. They shared with official criminology a depersonalized, dehumanized picture of the deviant: he was simply part of the waste products of the system, the reject from the conveyor belt.'

In an earlier draft I hadn't included 'some of' before 'our sociological colleagues'; the alteration was partly in response to a sociological colleague who had written 'who are these nasties?' next to this passage. I took his point that not all sociologists were like this caricature, but I remain convinced that the mandarin attitude exists.

This attitude is buttressed by the erroneous conception that sociology is being swamped by hordes of deviance researchers while the really important subjects, such as education, industry, and stratification are being neglected. In fact, even a superficial examination of the market will show that this is not the case. A comparison of the three major British sociological journals with, say, the *American Sociological Review* and the *American Journal of Sociology* shows a low proportion of articles even remotely connected with criminology or deviance. Whole substantive areas such as sexual deviance, drug taking, mental illness, are virtually completely missing, and there are no journals like *Social Problems* to cover these areas. In the one – admittedly inadequate – survey of research from the early 1950s to the 1960s (Krausz 1969) nothing much emerges from the five pages on deviance, aside from a few studies of penal institutions and the ecological-subcultural traditions from Mays, Morris, Downes, and Willmott (this, incidentally, being most misleadingly summarized).

More substantial information can be found from the 1966 survey of British sociologists undertaken by the Social Science Research Council in collaboration with the British Sociological Association.[15] In the context of the 'sociological explosion' in Britain (one university chair before the war and over forty in 1967) sociological attention given to crime and deviance is insignificant. The replies from the 416 BSA members whose questionnaires were 'usable' (this included about three-quarters of teachers of the subject) indicated that crime ranked low on each of the separate criteria of 'main interests', 'other special interests', 'research completed 1945–1960', 'research completed 1961–1966', and 'current research'. In terms of 'main interests' for example (excluding 'basic theory', 'methodology', and 'methods') criminology (30) ranked well behind sociology of education (102),

Criminology and the sociology of deviance in Britain   25

industrial sociology/sociology of work (96), social stratification (66), and community studies (46). Out of the 340 projects listed under 'current research', industrial sociology maintains the lead it had in earlier periods with 74, sociology of education next with 51 and, after a big drop to community studies (34), criminology only registered 10. (One might add to this a few of the 25 classified under 'sociology of social services/policy/problems.)

Using these indices at least, it would not appear that British sociology has nurtured much of an interest in crime and deviance. Although the mandarin characterization may be an overstatement I believe there has been and is likely to remain a basic divide between those who, to use Horowitz's terms (1969: 92–3), think that sociology should be *impeccable* and those who think it should be *important*: 'The aesthetic vision of the impeccable sociologist ... preserves him from the worst infections of "helping people".' The gap is more than a matter of aesthetic styles, though '... it demands a specific decision on the part of scholars and researchers as to where they will place their intellectual bets: on scientific autonomy or on social relevance' (1969: 99).[16]

Leaving aside for the moment the complication that much conflict exists *within* the sociology of deviance between impeccability and importance, the obvious political question remains as to what is 'socially relevant' and, more to the point, relevant to whom? This leads me to the stream of political radicalism within and on the margins of sociology that is indifferent, if not hostile, to the field of deviance. The Left have simply followed the liberal rhetoric and consigned deviants to the welfare category while orthodox Marxists (whose sole contribution to the field was that of the Dutch criminologist Bonger some fifty years ago) have written criminals off as the *Lumpen*, or the 'rabble' who, as Marx described to Engels, gathered to jeer at him when he was evicted from his Soho flat. The only stream of radical political thought which is sympathetic is anarchism and it is no accident (!) that five out of the seven founder members of the National Deviancy Conference (although not all anarchists themselves) have published articles about deviance at one time or another in the British journal, *Anarchy*.

The various sources of insulation that I have sketched are, I believe, becoming less potent. Much of the above analysis would not apply to the current younger cohort of British sociologists and, even among the others, an ideology which rejects deviance as a topic of interest is hardly dominant. The present potential of research and theory on deviance is on balance more likely to convince mainstream sociology of its centrality rather than its marginality. But the relationship between deviance and the rest of sociology must always remain strained: the interests of its students, the peculiar institutional constraints it has to operate in, the umbrella-like nature of areas like criminology, are features which cannot be glossed over in the name of some professional consensus. I will refer to more of these strains in the next section.

THE EVOLUTION OF THE NATIONAL DEVIANCY CONFERENCE

At this point in the paper I experience my discrepant role of mediator most acutely, having to describe in a supposedly detached way a development I have been closely concerned with. The greatest danger lies in exaggerating the importance of this development and I would like to stress that I do not consider it (or the sociology of deviance as a whole) worthy of extensive self-reflection. The development is also not unique and has some parallels with the emergence in America of the Society For the Study of Social Problems (in 1951!) although the Society is more closely tied to bodies such as the ASA and is undoubtedly more professional.

I have indicated implicitly throughout the paper the constellation of intellectual reasons which created the 'need' for such a development. By the middle 1960s there were a number of young sociologists attracted to the wholly American field of the sociology of deviance. (I suspect they were turned on first by *Outsiders* and then *Delinquency and Drift.*) These ideas seemed to relate to what they were either teaching or doing research on (subjects including drugs, homosexuality, approved schools, vandalism, youth culture, mental illness, etc.). For reasons I have indicated, official criminology was regarded with attitudes ranging from ideological condemnation to a certain boredom (and I suspect that the latter was more dominant than many would admit). One had to get away from that scene, but being a sociologist wasn't enough, one had to find a separate subculture within the sociological world. The sheer physical isolation of many of us in small departments, teaching a subject with no colleagues in the field and few graduate students, was another contributory pressure.

So, ostensibly for these reasons (although this account sounds suspiciously like colour supplement history), seven of us met in July

Criminology and the sociology of deviance in Britain 27

1968, fittingly enough in Cambridge in the middle of the Third National Conference of Teaching and Research on Criminology, organized by the Institute and opened by the Home Secretary. We decided to form a group to provide some sort of intellectual support for each other and to cope with collective problems of identity, not to mention the problems of reaction formation and the absence of a legitimate opportunity structure. Friends and colleagues were to be sounded out, ideas about circulating reading lists and research plans were discussed and it was proposed to arrange a symposium. Before taking up the subsequent progress of the group, let me speculate on some further reasons for its formation and subsequent rapid growth: it would be dishonest as well as sociologically naïve to suggest that the ostensible intellectual reasons I have given were the only ones.

The first is that we all sensed something in the sceptical, labelling, and societal reaction perspectives, the anti-psychiatry school and similar currents, which struck a responsive political chord. The stress on labelling, injustice, scapegoating, stigmatizing, the implicit underdog sympathy, the whole 'central irony' (as Matza calls it) of the neo-Chicago School and its recognition of Leviathan, the implications of Laing's work – these were all sympathetic ideas. It is precisely the limitations of this sympathy (which I don't believe was ever expressed that simply anyway) which has provoked indiscriminate attacks (such as those by Gouldner 1968) as well as the more discerning remarks such as those of Lemert in the course of his re-examination of the secondary deviance concept: ' "Secondary deviance" may be a convenient vehicle for civil libertarians or young men of sociology to voice angry critiques of social institutions' (Lemert 1967: 59).

Both such interests were present in the original group and these ideas were found appealing for reasons strongly related to the personal background of the group's members. Without exception they had all been involved in orthodox political movements with degrees of commitment ranging through Anarchists, CND, Young Communists and International Socialists. In common with many of their contemporaries they were going through various degrees of disillusionment with such activities. They had all been through the generational experience which only a few commentators such as Jeff Nuttall (1968) have tried to comprehend. Talking or doing something about deviance seemed to offer – however misguided this might now look to an outsider – a form of commitment, a way of staying in, without on the one hand selling out or on the other playing the drab game of orthodox politics, whose simplicities were becoming increasingly irritating.

Such commitment was easier because the historical period was one of growing and visible militancy of deviant groups working outside the political structure. The hope for real social change (or any event, where the action was) seemed to be with the hippies, druggies, squatters and, above all, everything that was happening in the American campuses and ghettoes. These identifications were facilitated by personal involvement in some of these marginal groups. Some of the original members and even more of the later members of the Deviancy Conference were on the fringes of what Jock Young has nicely called 'the Middle Underground'. Involved as participants, they couldn't resist the lure to be observers and make a decent living from it. The romantic, voyeur-like appeal of the subject matter was thus important; one doubts whether a similar group could have sprung up around, say, industrial sociology, educational sociology, or community studies.

I have speculated at some length on this sort of reason because it would seem implausible to suggest that some sort of disinterested quest for knowledge was drawing people to the field. These reasons are complex to unravel and have meant more or less to different people at different stages of their involvement: the organization has become all things to all members. Such a background contains intrinsic tensions, which I will comment on later, but despite such tensions – or because of them? – the sheer numerical strength of the group has increased dramatically, although it has possibly reached some sort of plateau now. The original group of seven increased at the first Conference at York in November 1968 to about twenty (most of them friends) and this number rose to 130 by the seventh Conference in October 1970 (about twenty more having to be turned away for lack of accommodation). The paid-up membership of the organization is now 230.

At a minimal level, the fact that the group has kept going and attracted so many new people shows that it is filling some obvious need. It has tried, not altogether successfully, to involve groups other than sociologists, the largest of these being social workers. Other 'lay' activists or commentators on the scene have also been drawn in as speakers: a crime reporter, the leader of a squatters' group, a detached youth worker. A forum and some support have also been given to groups such as tenants' associations, claimants' unions, Case Con (the

Criminology and the sociology of deviance in Britain 29

militant social work organization), and RAP (Radical Alternatives to Prison). Plans are in hand to formalize contacts with these groups and perhaps in the long run provide them with some sort of umbrella organization. It is possible that a journal might be published and there are plans to publish policy oriented pamphlets on such subjects as aversion therapy of homosexuals, restrictions on prison visiting, invasions of privacy, and drug legislation. Another achievement is presumably to have played the major role in organizing and manning this BSA Conference.

Papers at the seven York conferences have been mainly in the four categories: ethnographies of deviant types, studies of social control, theories of deviance, and critiques; plus attempts to connect with institutions such as social work, psychiatry, and the mass media. There is no shortage of topics, but a semi-conscious colonialism seems to be operating in which whole new territories (for example education and the mass media) are taken over and planted with a sociology-of-deviance flag. Interests listed in the research register range from homosexual prostitutes, crime in the USSR, physical handicap as deviance, to tenants' associations, false consciousness(!), and the sociology of soccer.

As the group has expanded, so its conception of itself has changed and clearly new tensions are introduced in simply coping with the range of interests and involvements. The original circular of invitation to the first Conference simply said '... A group of social scientists who are currently concerned with problems of crime and deviancy have decided to hold a one day symposium related to these areas.' The subjects were described as being a 'mixed bag' but, continued the circular, 'the aim of the symposium is not to create an artificial academic consensus, but rather to bring together a group of people who appear to share certain common perspectives.' A year later, in August 1969, one member of the committee 'at the risk of accusations of Leninism' as he put it, circulated a letter to his fellow members which included the following:

'The most important worry is perhaps over the total nature of the project we're involved in. At the moment, it does seem that we are on the way towards being a "left wing" value committed "social problems" sociology, reinforcing each other periodically in our institutional isolation, revivifying our lecture courses with ideas

30   *Stanley Cohen*

culled from the symposium – but never really moving outside our
chosen . . . occupational roles. Perhaps we might also be helping to
create a new (rather ill-defined, libertarian) sociological culture
among our students and friends. But there are other activities we
should be involved in.'

The 'other activities' he suggested included being a pressure group,
acting as a corrective to official definitions of deviance and social
problems, and the setting up of a kind of anti-sociology. It has become transparent subsequently – and was so all along to anyone aware
of the group's diversity – that there are different and partially
irreconcilable ways ahead. Let me end this section by just listing
some differences which have become manifest so far:

(1) Should the group just drift along, amplifying and if need be
changing, or should some attempt be made at tightening up?

(2) Should one tighten up in the direction of demanding greater
commitment to social action?

(3) Should one tighten up in the direction of demanding greater
theoretical sophistication, making everything more impeccable? As a
corollary, does this mean excluding or limiting the numbers of non-
sociologists?

(4) To what extent should the perceived limitations of the theories
which originally looked so attractive lead to an immersion in 'harder'
and ostensibly more political theories?

My personal inclination, because of an aversion to the apocalyptic,
is to avoid a tightening up in any of these directions; this does not
mean that the tensions which result from these differing conceptions
can always be coped with. One other tension is worth noting, the one
with sociology. I have made much of the desire to get the subject
back into sociology, but my impression is that the commitment to
sociology among many in the Conference is somewhat weak. Mainstream sociologists are not wholly unjustified in seeing the group as
marginals, with loyalties elsewhere, who would prefer, for example,
to teach a group of social workers than a group of honours sociology
students and whose avowed interests in making theoretical links with
the sociological tradition are not always very convincing. Again,
although this might be an important issue to some, I do not personally
see it as a priority.

SOME CURRENT COMPARISONS

In this last, highly speculative, section, I would like to make some assessment of the current position, particularly by comparing main-stream criminology and the sociology of deviance with each other and the world outside. I have used the three criteria of *impact, relevance,* and *commitment.*

(1) *Impact*

There is little question that the institutional position of mainstream criminology is powerful and fairly concentrated. The Institute of Criminology at Cambridge, with its close links to the Home Office, commands prestige and support and in the public eye virtually *is* criminology. Its educational impact has been made through its highly successful diploma course (as well as other short courses) and is strong in a number of law faculties. It has certain high level connexions with bodies such as the Advisory Council on the Treatment of Offenders. The BSC – ISTD – *BJC* axis is perhaps less powerful and its direct influence is more on middle range professionals (probation officers, clinicians) or through the institutional positions of its non-academic members. In terms of access to the mass media, potential influences on policy through official inquiries, reports, commissions etc., these groups are fairly well placed.

In contrast, the sociology of deviance group – although just as inbred as mainstream criminology – has a much more diffuse power base, mainly confined to academic sociology departments. In so far as part of its original aim was to spread to this area, it has been fairly successful. There are about twelve university or polytechnic courses in criminology or deviance run by persons closely associated with the group and perhaps an equal number by those with some ties. Strength with professionals lies more with social workers and others. Many members of the group spend time talking to magistrates, probation officers, prison officers, and others, but I doubt whether this is a very distinctive contribution.

Describing the position in this way does not imply that many members of either group would see themselves as engaging in some sort of power struggle. Also, having prestige or running under-graduate courses hardly means the same as having any impact. Clearly

criminologists do have some impact and are in positions which ensure
that their definitions are given credibility. I suspect though that both
groups, not to mention sociologists as a whole, are given to exaggerating any such influence they may have. Introducing his collection
on *The Impact of Sociology* Douglas (1970: 1) speculates on the
'profound' and 'rapidly accelerating' effects the social sciences are
having on everyday lives. 'While it may still be too prophetic to be
accorded much credibility, I believe that many of us will live to see
the social sciences become the primary means by which we seek to
determine social policies which will rationally order our everyday
lives.'

One doubts it. Matza's passing remarks about functionalism are
relevant here '... the functionalist perspective has had little public
consequence. It has neither bolstered the social order nor subverted it.
Except among a few thousand sociologists it has passed unnoticed'
(Matza 1969: 58). This argument can be used against some of Matza's
own theories: some research and much impressionistic evidence indicates that – in this country at any rate – control agents have simply
not been won over to the positivist ideology and in their day to day
work and reflections about delinquency use a much more common
sense model, which is hardly deterministic at all. In the same light,
one might note Radzinowicz's conclusion that there has not been
much of a connexion between criminological research and penal
reform:

> 'Treatment by probation, the borstal system, the juvenile courts
> and several other innovations were not devised on the strength of
> fresh and precise criminological knowledge. They can be shown to
> have evolved on the whole under the influence of growing social
> consciousness, of religious movements and philanthropic stimulus,
> from some temporary measure, or just from straightforward com-
> mon sense, supported by experience.' (Radzinowicz 1961: 178–9)

Research is needed on just how much, and in what form, the
criminological belief system percolates through to policy makers and
becomes part of the common sense rhetoric.

Finally, in terms of mutual impact, clearly the sociology of deviance
is too mistrustful of British criminology to admit to being influenced
in other than a negative direction. In fact though, as I have suggested,
it will remain somewhat parasitic on criminological knowledge,
partially dependent on the same resources and subject to some of the

Criminology and the sociology of deviance in Britain 33

same pressures. It is beginning to look more on the legal – as opposed to the psychiatric side – of the discipline. One might speculate that the sociology of deviance as a whole, and the way it has appeared in this country, is having some impact on criminology. A number of the York group have taught on the Cambridge post-graduate course and gave papers at the Fourth National Conference on Teaching and Research in Criminology. The more cynical talk about power politics, being lured by the Establishment and so on. I do not agree that such contacts should be avoided, although I do think that the 'Establishment' sees the newer perspective as being simply a fashion which will eventually pass over or (more mistakenly) simply consisting of a few interesting ideas which can be swallowed up without changing the existing paradigm at all.

A more plausible reception to some of the criticism levelled by sociologists can be seen at some points of a recent text by Hood and Sparks (1970), both Assistant Directors of Research at the Institute of Criminology. Not only does their book contain a pronounced sociological content – subcultural delinquency and the sociology of the prison are included among the 'key issues in criminology' – and a nearly complete exclusion of clinical interests, but 'traditional' interests are raised in such a way that their relationship to sociology is made fairly explicit. Thus, attention on self-report studies and hidden delinquency – which in Britain has seemed to be related to a desire to root out all those recalcitrant contributors to the 'dark figure' who refuse to become detected – is justified in terms of the light it may shed on problems of discretion, control, and labelling.

The book is still somewhat pragmatic: as the authors admit, no single theme or theory underlines the subject and the justification for singling out the eight 'key issues' is that a lot of research has been done on them in recent years, in most of them some progress has been made and important questions remain. There are other subjects, they state, '... in particular so called labelling or transactional theory in which too little empirical research has been done. Work in this area ... seems likely to develop rapidly in the future.' As far as policy matters go, Hood and Sparks submit that while most of the subjects they have chosen have implications for penal policy, this is not the reason for their inclusion. They disagree that criminology is the study of the ways of preventing crime and is professionally interested in reforming offenders. Criminology is not a kind of social work and

34   *Stanley Cohen*

there is scope for 'disinterested and purely scientific research' on such matters as the operation of the penal system:

> 'This is not, of course, to say that criminology cannot make any contribution to penal policy. What it cannot do is decide what the *aims* of penal policy should be. But by discovering how much crime is committed and by showing how and why it was committed, criminology can help to show what policy goals are reasonable; and if given certain aims, they can try to discover by research the best means of accomplishing them. It is unfortunately true, however, that at the present time much too little is known ... to permit us to draw definite practical conclusions concerning questions of penal policy.' (1970: 9)

The uncharitable might call such a line defensive, and its model of finding out the facts in a 'disinterested' way, drawing the 'definite practical conclusions' and showing what policy goals are 'reasonable', while attractive, does not confront the fact-value-interest problems that have bedevilled sociology. But at least it is a form of self-consciousness which criminology has not shown very conspicuously in the past.

(2) *Relevance*

Criminology has often chosen to deal with areas which society – or its elected representatives or mass media – have defined as most relevant. This is a theoretically indefensible basis of choice, but it does give criminology its strength: it is *seen* to be relevant.

In contrast, sociologists of deviance, while making a lot of pious noises about 'other' criteria of relevance, have often opted for the esoteric, the catchy, the hip – precisely those areas which seem less relevant. This is due partly to personal preference, but more importantly due to the fact that the interactionist type of approach seems better able to cope with forms of deviance such as homosexuality, drugtaking, certain kinds of behaviour defined as mental illness, which are ambiguous, marginal and already subject to widespread normative dissensus. Until attention is focused on what to the public seem more relevant areas such as violence *or* a coherent case is made for choosing these other areas, this type of sociology will always be at a disadvantage.

(3) *Commitment*

I have probably said more than enough on the problem of values and a whole session in this Conference was devoted to the 'political and ethical implications of deviance theory'. Let me repeat that mainstream criminology has compromised itself too far and too much because of its close connexions with the institutions and ideology of the correctional system. It has complacently thought that there are no problems of competing values and interests. At worst, this has led to an unquestioning acceptance of official goals and policies; at best it has led to sustained and well informed criticism of these policies if not the goals.

The sociology of deviance has been complacent in another way, though, by sometimes giving the impression that it has solved these problems. At worst this has led to a self-indulgent romanticism, at best it has been simply good sociology.

I started off this paper by noting one danger in self-reflective social science; let me end with another: the danger of tilting at windmills. This is not to say that the divisions I have indicated are not real; students who had accused me of exaggerating have come back from occasions such as Institute of Criminology conferences reproaching me for *underplaying* such divisions. The point is that the impact (of the theories at least – as opposed to that of powerful groups) is not as massive and monolithic as some attacks on it credit it with being. This is the same point that Bottomore (1971) makes against Gouldner's *The Coming Crisis of Western Sociology*: why the excessive attention to functionalism when it is very doubtful that it enjoyed the preeminence attached to it? This would all be unimportant if not for the further argument that Bottomore levels against reflexive sociology in general and Gouldner in particular:

> 'In the end, it achieves the opposite of what Wright Mills advocated at the beginning of the radical revival: instead of turning personal troubles into public issues, it turns public issues into personal troubles, by exhorting the sociologist to give his attention narcissistically to the problem of the relationship "between being a sociologist and being a person" and to worry about his relation to his work. I do not believe that such pre-occupations have ever in-

36   *Stanley Cohen*

spired a critical analysis of society or ever will. They are a symptom of an intellectual malaise, not a remedy.'

They can be both symptom and partial remedy though, in areas and contexts where they have hardly ever appeared. It is in these terms that papers of this sort can be justified – if only very slightly.

Notes

1 See the Introduction and Readings in Section A 'The Development of a Sociological Perspective on Crime in Britain' in Carson and Wiles (1971). For an evaluation of nineteenth-century ecological studies see Chapter 3 of Morris (1957) and for a particularly interesting perspective on Mayhew, see Yeo and Thompson (1971).

2 For parallel defences of an appreciation see 'The Defence of Meaning' (Cohen, 1971: Introduction) and Young (1969). For comments on the subjective viewpoint in the context of the Becker-Gouldner debate, see Taylor and Walton (1970).

3 For an important general argument about these convergences, see Horowitz and Liebowitz (1968) and a specific application to the study of violence, Cohen (1969 and 1971).

4 Thus, our criticisms of criminology might be something like those of industrial sociologists writing about a specific institution such as the Human Relations school – see, for example, Brown (1967).

5 The accounts of Goring's work I am mainly relying upon are those by Mannheim (1965: 227-8) and Driver (1960).

6 This is not to say that such bodies ultimately get different treatment from the political structure. Compare President Nixon's reaction to the Report of the Commission on Obscenity and Pornography with the Home Office's reaction to the 'Wootton Report' on cannabis when both came up with the 'wrong' results.

7 For fuller accounts of Mannheim's work see Chorley (1970), Grygier *et al.* (1965) and Morris (1966).

8 See, for example, the collections of papers published in connexion with the centenary of the Howard League for Penal Reform (Klare 1966; Klare and Haxby 1967).

9 Some indication of his approach to the subject is given in his note in the Twentieth Anniversary Number of the *BJC*. See Mannheim (1970).

10 When it added a group of assistant editors, one was a clinical psychologist, one a psychiatrist, one a lawyer and one a sociologist.

11 See Wootton (1959: 69) for a misuse of the concept of anomie.

Criminology and the sociology of deviance in Britain 37

12 Such as the Gibson Maze Test; the Body Sway Test (most of the boys apparently hardly swayed at all, while others found this test unpleasant and anxiety provoking); and the Tapping Test (tapping a pencil on a blank piece of paper for 10 seconds; this apparently reveals extra-punitive personality types and it could be expected that 'boys with delinquent personalities would tend to scatter their dots more widely'. Sceptics will note that the scores did reveal a slight but significant positive correlation with bad conduct as rated by teachers: $r = 0.17$).

13 For a convincing treatment of this explanation as a form of demonism, see Sarbin and Miller (1970).

14 The classic documentation is still to be found in C. Wright Mills (1945).

15 I am relying on three versions of the report of this survey: one is circulated by its author, M. P. Carter, to members of the BSA in 1967, a longer version reproduced by the SSRC at about the same time and a re-draft of this a year later. Another version is in preparation. See also Carter (1968).

16 I would strongly recommend Horowitz's whole essay 'The Sociology of Social Problems: A Study in the Americanization of Ideas' (Horowitz 1969: 80–100), particularly the section entitled 'The metaphysical predispositions of sociologists of social problems'. This is not a simple argument in favour of 'importance'; he points to the considerable dangers of applied sociology and the central contradictions involved in the 'God-like' role of sociologists as therapist. I need hardly add that much deviance research is quite unimportant anyway, compared to, say, the sociology of development.

References

ANDERSON, P. 1968. Components of the National Culture. *New Left Review* 50: 3–57.

BECKER, H. S. (ed.) 1964. *The Other Side: Perspectives on Deviance.* New York: Crowell Collier Macmillan.

—— 1967. Whose Side Are We On? *Social Problems* 14: 239–47.

BOTTOMORE, T. 1971. Has Sociology a Future? *New York Review of Books* 16 (4): 37–40.

BROWN, R. K. 1967. Research and Consultancy in Industrial Enterprises: A Review of the Contribution of the Tavistock Institute of Human Relations to the Development of Industrial Sociology. *Sociology* 1: 33–60.

CARSON, W. G. & WILES, P. (eds.) 1971. *Crime and Delinquency in Britain: Sociological Readings.* London: Robinson.

38 *Stanley Cohen*

CARTE, G. E. 1969. Dialogue with Jerome H. Skolnick. *Issues in Criminology* 4: 109–22.

CARTER, M. P. 1968. Report on a Survey of Sociological Research in Britain. *Sociological Review* 16: 5–40.

CHORLEY, Rt Hon. Lord. 1970. Hermann Mannheim: A Biographical Appreciation. *British Journal of Criminology* 10: 324–47.

COHEN, S. 1969. Ideological and Criminal Violence: Convergences in Labels or Behaviour? Paper given at British Sociological Association Conference (Teachers' Section).

—— (ed.) 1971. *Images of Deviance*. Harmondsworth: Penguin.

—— 1971. Directions for Research on Adolescent Group Violence and Vandalism. *British Journal of Criminology*: 319–40.

CRESSEY, D. R. 1954. The Differential Association Theory and Compulsive Crimes. *Journal of Criminal Law, Criminology and Police Science* 45: 29–40.

—— 1962. Role Theory, Differential Association and Compulsive Crimes. In A. Rose (ed.) *Human Behaviour and Social Processes: An Interactionist Approach*. London: Routledge and Kegan Paul.

CROFT, J. 1965. Hermann Mannheim – A Biographical Note. In T. Grygier *et al.* (eds.) *Criminology in Transition: Essays in Honour of Hermann Mannheim*. London: Tavistock Publications.

DEBRO, J. 1970. Dialogue with Howard S. Becker. *Issues in Criminology* 5: 159–79.

DOUGLAS, J. D. (ed.) 1970. *The Impact of Sociology: Readings in the Social Sciences*. New York: Appleton Century Crofts.

DRIVER, E. D. 1960. Charles B. Goring. In H. Mannheim (ed.) *Pioneers in Criminology*. London: Stevens.

GIBBENS, T. C. N. 1970. *Identification of Key Problems of Criminological Research*. Strasbourg: Council of Europe.

GLOVER, E. 1970. 1950–1970 – Retrospects and Reflections. *British Journal of Criminology* 10: 313–16.

GOFFMAN, E. 1959. *The Presentation of Self in Everyday Life*. New York: Doubleday Anchor.

GOULDNER, A. 1968. The Sociologist as Partisan: Sociology and the Welfare States. *American Sociologist* 3: 103–16.

GORING, C. 1913. *The English Convict*. London: HMSO.

GRYGIER, T. J. H., JONES, H. & SPENCER, J. C. (eds.) 1965. *Criminology in Transition: Essays in Honour of Hermann Mannheim*. London: Tavistock Publications.

HALLORAN, J. D. *et al.* 1970. *Television and Delinquency*. Leicester: Leicester University Press.

HOME OFFICE RESEARCH UNIT AND STATISTICAL DIVISION. 1969. Summary of Research and of Research Supported by Grants.

Criminology and the sociology of deviance in Britain 39

HOOD, R. & SPARKS, R. 1970. *Key Issues in Criminology*. London: Weidenfeld & Nicolson.

HOROWITZ, I. L. 1969. *Professing Sociology: Studies in the Life Cycle of Social Science*. Chicago: Aldine.

HOROWITZ, I. L. & LIEBOWITZ, M. 1968. Social Deviance and Political Marginality: Toward a Redefinition of the Relationship Between Sociology and Politics. *Social Problems* **15**: 280–96.

JONES, H. 1965. *Crime and the Penal System*. London: University Tutorial Press.

KLARE, H. J. (ed.) 1966. *Changing Concepts of Crime and Its Treatment*. Oxford: Pergamon.

KLARE, H. J. & HAXBY, D. (eds.) 1967. *Frontiers of Criminology*. Oxford: Pergamon.

KRAUSZ, E. 1969. *Sociology in Britain: A Survey of Research*. London: Batsford.

LEMERT, E. M. 1967. *Human Deviance, Social Problems and Social Control*. Englewood Cliffs, N.J.: Prentice Hall.

MANNHEIM, H. 1965. *Comparative Criminology*. London: Routledge and Kegan Paul.

—— 1970. 1950–1970: Retrospects and Reflections. *British Journal of Criminology* **10**: 317–20.

MATZA, D. 1964. *Delinquency and Drift*. New York: Wiley.

—— 1969. *Becoming Deviant*. Englewood Cliffs, N.J.: Prentice Hall.

MILLS, C. WRIGHT 1945. The Professional Ideology of Social Pathologists. *American Journal of Sociology* **49**: 165–80.

MORRIS, T. P. 1957. *The Criminal Area: A Study in Social Ecology*. London: Routledge & Kegan Paul.

—— 1965. The Sociology of the Prison. In T. Grygier *et al.* (eds.) *Criminology in Transition*. London: Tavistock Publications.

—— 1966. Comparative Criminology: A Text Book. *Howard Journal* **XII**: 61–4.

NUTTAL, J. 1968. *Bomb Culture*. London: MacGibbon and Kee.

POLSKY, N. 1967. Research Method, Morality and Criminology. In *Hustlers, Beats and Others*. Chicago: Aldine.

RADZINOWICZ, L. 1962. *In Search of Criminology*. London: Heinemann.

—— 1966. *Ideology and Crime: A Study of Crime in its Social and Historical Context*. London: Heinemann.

SARBIN, T. R. & MILLER, J. E. 1970. Demonism Revisited: The XYY Chromosomal Anomaly. *Issues in Criminology* **5**: 195–207.

SOCIAL SCIENCE RESEARCH COUNCIL. 1968. Review of Research in Sociology. Unpublished.

TAYLOR, I. & WALTON, P. 1970. Values in Deviancy Theory and Society. *British Journal of Sociology* **21**: 362–74.

40   *Stanley Cohen*

WALKER, N. 1965. *Crime and Punishment in Britain.* Edinburgh: Edinburgh University Press.

WEST, D. J. 1967. *The Young Offender.* Harmondsworth: Penguin.

—— 1969. *Present Conduct and Future Delinquency.* London: Heinemann.

WOOTTON, B. 1959. *Social Science and Social Pathology.* London: Allen and Unwin.

WRIGHT, M. 1970. Twenty Years of the British Journal of Delinquency/ Criminology. *British Journal of Criminology* 10: 372–82.

YEO, E. & THOMPSON, E. P. 1971. *The Unknown Mayhew.* London: Merlin Press.

YOUNG, J. 1969. The Zookeepers of Deviancy. *Anarchy* 98: 101–8.

Feminism

[27]

Frances Heidensohn*

The deviance of women: a critique and an enquiry

The purpose of this paper is quite simple: it is to focus on an obscure and largely ignored area of human behaviour, namely deviance in women. It is suggested.

(a) that the problems associated with this neglect may, in themselves, be interesting from a sociological point of view.
(b) that the topic has both intrinsic interest for the sociologist today and that it has wider relevance to, for example, aspects of social structure.
(c) that, in so far as it is an example of possibly curious counter-tendencies to certain widespread trends in deviance, it may be of especial interest.

The deviance of women is one of the areas of human behaviour most notably ignored in sociological literature. This apparent lack of interest is remarkable for a number of reasons:

(a) deviance in general (i.e. in practice either male and female deviance together or simply male deviance alone) has long aroused considerable interest. Since Durkheim argued[1] that 'deviant' or 'pathological' behaviour has social as well as individual aspects, the sociology of deviance has been an important and developing field of sociological theorizing and enquiry. Therefore the general unconcern with the potential deviance of approximately half the members of any human society is surprising.
(b) Interest in the changing position of women as it has affected marriage, the family and the division of roles within it has been considerable and has been productive of a vast range of studies, from, moreover, almost every known 'type' of sociologist: from American functionalist theoreticians to the more empirically-minded British.[2]
(c) As will be indicated below, differences between the patterns and manifestations of male and of female deviance were long ago

* Frances Heidensohn B.A.(SOC.) Assistant Lecturer in Sociology, London School of Economics

The deviance of women: a critique and an enquiry

observed;[3] they were observed, moreover, to differ with that kind of regularity and uniformity which normally attract the attention of the social scientist.[4]

Nevertheless the focus of research has been very much away from this particular area, so that a wide-ranging selection of readings on the sociology of crime and delinquency, published in 1962, did not contain one extract on female criminality.[5] Despite this gap, this has remained an often crucial, although unacknowledged dimension of deviance.

Of course, one can advance simple, straightforward reasons for this gap in sociological literature. Women appear to have low rates of participation in deviant activities as measured by such indices as official criminal statistics,[6] the range and number of their socially disapproved sexual outlets,[7] suicide rates,[8] involvement in activities labelled as vagrant,[9] and, although with certain provisos,[10] when defined as mentally ill.

(Perhaps it should be made clear at this point that the activities here selected are not put forward in any sense as integrated components of a comprehensive definition of deviant behaviour; they simply represent a range of categories, commonly thought of as deviant.[11] They thus correspond to the concept defined by Howard S. Becker:[12]

> deviance is not a quality of the act the person commits, but rather a consequence of the application by others of rules and sanctions to an 'offender'. The deviant is one to whom that label has successfully been applied; deviant behaviour is behaviour that people so label.[13]

These modes of behaviour also correspond to Lemert's secondary deviance in that they largely receive institutional reinforcement as deviating behaviour and may become deviant careers[14] for individuals resorting to them.)

Not only do woman *appear* to be remarkably conformist,[15] they seem to have consistently lower rates of deviance than men, with a fairly constant ratio which remains despite fluctuations in rates over time. (There is some suggestion of a diminution of this ratio in recent years, but data for the U.K. do not, on the whole, support this view.) It is perhaps therefore inevitable that male delinquents and deviants should be studied in preference to females: there are more of them and they thus have greater social visibility, are more accessible because more widespread, and are much more likely to appear —and be defined as—a pressing social problem. The last mentioned factor will ultimately affect the research funds available for a particular type of project.[16]

Frances Heidensohn

These reasons to some extent explain the concentration on male deviance, but not the almost total *exclusion* of studies of females from serious literature. One might argue that there is a strong element of pragmatism in this (as in so many other) areas of sociological research. Current focal concerns of society and especially of its rulers and policy-makers have a way of becoming the consuming interests of sociologists.[17] (Note the number of sociologists in the U.K. listed in a recent survey as working on the sociology of education and compare this with involvement of successive governments in educational research and reform.) Certainly students of the sociology of deviance have been often closely (often inevitably, for purposes of data collection) involved with the operators of the social control system. At the very least most workers in this field tend to approach their subject with the dual purposes of investigating then eradicating what they term social 'disorganization' or 'pathology'.[18]

Given this orientation amongst social pathologists, it is interesting to observe, as Professor Mays[19] did recently in a critical review, that concern over a subject—and notably that of juvenile delinquency—is in almost directly inverse relationship to the efficacy of policy. It may well be that the very formulation of a mode of behaviour as a 'problem area' for study may draw public and press attention to it and hence, through greater likelihood of reporting, stepped up police vigilance etc., immensely increase its dimensions; it has been suggested[20] that in the case of the 'Teddy boys' of the nineteen-fifties the 'menace' existed in the public mind long before any activities of the teenagers concerned warranted it.[21] One need not go as far as to argue that high rates of sociological interest in a problem area produce appropriately high 'problem situation' responses; but one might well be forgiven for wondering whether the deviance of women is a non-problem both to the social scientist and to society in general, because so little effort has been devoted to studying it. On one of the very few occasions in recent years that the deviant behaviour of women became a matter for public concern, the reaction of the committee set up to investigate it was to suggest that the social visibility of the activities should be so reduced that the public concern could largely cease,[22] although the deviant behaviour would continue.[23]

As was suggested earlier, when certain factors are taken into account, the picture of deviance amongst women, certainly in the U.K. since the early years of this century, has been an increasingly calm and conforming one. Of course, this statement must be heavily qualified, not least by the view that deviant women may have benefited far more than their male counterparts by the extension of the concept of the sick role and its more widespread application, in that women who might once have been adjudged 'delinquent' may now be defined as 'sick' and are hence excluded from the population of

162

The deviance of women: a critique and an enquiry

'deviants'. Nevertheless, whatever the caveats it is broadly true to say that, for example, the number of women convicted for offences of drunkenness has declined very markedly since 1900, and *much more* rapidly than has the equivalent rate for men.[24] Similarly, it seems to be widely agreed that the numbers and proportion of women involved in prostitution has declined. Undoubtedly the legislation introduced after the Wolfenden Committee reported was aimed at minimizing the social visibility (and hence society's awareness) of prostitution, but this decline seems to be a common international trend.[25] Where indictable offences are concerned, the picture is more complex, but it appears that the numbers of women convicted for, for example, violent offences against the person tended to decline between the wars and began to rise again only after 1945. Rates of convictions of women for indictable offences have increased since the war, but for most categories of offences the proportionate rise has kept pace with the parallel rise in rates of males convicted although rarely has it been as high. This suggests several interpretations, among them that increased willingness to report offences, greater police efficiency in certain directions and a decrease in tolerance of crime amongst the public have affected female offenders only as much but no more than males; again what may either be a general increase in the opportunities for certain types of crime[26] or simply an overall rise in criminal activity has involved women to no greater extent than men.

The most curious feature of this analysis is that one would expect a *more than proportionate* rise in the conviction rates for women over this period; as Barbara Wootton has pointed out,[27] given that the participation of women in social, business and industrial life has been increasing steadily, one might expect a commensurate development in their criminal activities. That this does not appear to be the case reflects significantly upon the deviant behaviour of women and, perhaps more importantly, upon the societal reaction to it.

In this context of societal reaction to female deviance the legislation based upon the recommendations of the Wolfenden Committee[28] was very curious. Basically it rationalized and strengthened statutes against open soliciting, by abolishing the requirement of proven 'annoyance' as a basis for prosecution; yet it retained the term 'common prostitute', thereby preserving a process of damning the accused before conviction, let alone sentence which is, to say the least, unusual in English Law.[29] Thus, contrary to most modern trends in the growth of devices for labelling deviants and the increase in the number of categories available,[30] although the old style term was retained, its potential use was much reduced. For there seems to be widespread agreement that an effect of the 1959 Act was by 'driving' prostitution off the streets (and indeed, any public place) to make it more difficult to observe and check trends and also to 'catch'

Frances Heidensohn

prostitutes and reform them. This was *anticipated* in the Report, as it was that middlemen, taxi-drivers, hotel porters, café proprietors, would enter the 'game' and make matters more complex and difficult to control.[31] That a society is prepared, while keeping its formal, deviant-defining structure to reduce the toll of those so defined and, indirectly, to lose some possibility of controlling them, is surely remarkable.

Many more notable features in the trends of delinquency reported amongst women can be observed—for instance, the sharp rises during the two world wars. Other forms of deviance, while more difficult to study from this point of view, seem to display also certain interesting and often unexpected characteristics: thus it has been suggested that the rising rates of illegitimacy are especially amongst middle class girls[32] and this may in part represent a deviant phenomenon of some dimensions—in terms, for example, of its rejection both of the accepted sexual mores of the group and its 'rational' ethic in regard to birth control.

But the most remarkable common feature of all the varied data on female deviance is the way in which it largely lacks consideration in the appropriate literature. Yet by any standards there would appear to be sufficient grounds for such study, either the pragmatic ones of concern for social problems, or the simple natural-historical one of wishing to observe, measure, categorize and discuss. The answer to this mystery seems to lie not so much in the reasons listed above but in the fact that most theories of crime or deviance within a sociological framework have to make passing reference to female behaviour. Most studies at least begin with the framework imposed by the legal system, which imposes exact definitions of categories of behaviour, and these are often treated as discrete and meaningful groupings.[33] Except for certain specific instances, such as rape, most legal provisions are considered as applying with equal force to both sexes.[34] Behaviourial categories *not* dealt with by law usually follow parallel forms in referring both to male and female deviance from them *as deviant*, (although perhaps not always treating the mis-behaviour of the two sexes as equally heinous). Any hypotheses put forward, any theories offered as explanation or for understanding deviant forms of behaviour are thus bound to take account of both male and female behaviour. Given the ubiquitous nature of the sex differential in crime and in deviance in general, any generalizing theory must point to factors which operate with very different effects upon men and upon women or, alternatively, that their like deviance is dealt with in very different manners by facets of the social system.[35] Indeed whether a particular theory explains feminine delinquency as well as masculine and offers within its framework an explanation for the apparent difference in rates is often a useful touchstone of its

164

The deviance of women: a critique and an enquiry

validity. Most sociologists working in this field are aware, with perhaps some discomfort, of the sex based variation in modes of, and participation in, deviance and do try to allow for it, however awkwardly.

The very stability and ubiquity of the sex differential in crime rates and other forms of deviance already instanced have meant that sociologists involved in the study of deviance have had to put forward explanatory theories based on the male and on masculine forms of acting out behaviour in a social frame—whether the behaviour was genetically determined, culturally framed or an adaptation based on responses to dysfunctional features of industrial/capitalist society. The female side, since it loomed much less significantly, was fitted in as an aspect of such explanations. Early theorists of crime and typologists of criminal behaviour, such as Lombroso, tended to suggest modes of behaviour not formally recognized as crime, notably prostitution, as available to women, but not men, hence their lower participation rates in 'normal' crime. More recent approaches have, like Lombroso, seen deviant behaviour as a single meaningful category of action, but have insisted that in practice the sexes choose different responses or 'outlets' for deviance because of socially prescribed focal concerns and structural characteristics of the social framework. The following brief outline of a few of these approaches will indicate some of their weaker points and suggest that their inadequacies stem from a fundamentally awkward and misconceived approach to the subject.

One major grouping (although it includes Pollak, a more recent writer) may be labelled the 'female iceberg' theorists, since they deny our current perception of the deviant situation and suggest that women are only too deviant but in a different, or a more successfully concealed, manner.[36] Lombroso and Ferrero argued that women criminals are essentially occasional rather than habitual, although they, like their masculine counterparts, had certain allegedly atavistic features, notably unfeminine features and build and dark masculine hair (sic). Lombroso also argued[37] that women would appear to be as criminal as men were their prostitutive activities included in the criminal statistics. In other words, prostitution is the female functional equivalent of crime. This view may be challenged on many counts: first and simply that prostitution appears to be in secular decline, while 'male' crime manifestly is not. Secondly, if female behaviour as in prostitution is not characterized as crime (although being, as it were, an ethical equivalent) *why is* this so? Surely a topic of considerable interest in itself. Thirdly female delinquency, as defined by Lombroso, consists of acts by definition involving men, in fact many more men than women.[38] Fourthly, as Davis (op. cit.) shows, prostitution flourishes when family ties are strong and the status of

Frances Heidensohn

women, especially wives, is low. Hence the decline of prostitution in modern society—with the emancipation of women and rise in status —to be replaced by 'free, mutually pleasurable intercourse'. Can this also be defined as deviant? Finally, of course, there is the question of how the facts of female deviance, particularly the predominance of property offences, notably larceny, fit into this view.

Otto Pollak[39] saw the problem of 'explaining' female deviance in terms of feminine deviousness. Like Lombroso, he argues that much female deviance goes unrecorded, but unlike Lombroso he claims that women commit the same types of offences as men—and indeed have certain special opportunities for theft and murder—but that they are both equipped biologically to dissemble and socialized into so doing. They thus deviate as much as males but take advantage of their talents of dissembling and concealment and their positions in home and family to avoid discovery, and hence social awareness, of the deviant behaviour. This interpretation, although ingenious, begs far too many questions; to select a few of the more obvious: is there any evidence that hidden female crime is much greater than hidden male crime (such as embezzlement, white collar crime, 'knocking-off' in factories, docks, etc., motoring offences). These are likely to be *as least* as frequent, or, alternatively, quite as immeasurable. Pollak does not explain why some female deviance does surface and is 'processed'. Nor does he, any more than Lombroso, answer the query as to what functional needs of society are fulfilled by tacitly permitting women to engage in deviance such as murdering their families, seducing children and stealing from employers and clients.

Modern neofunctionalist theory[40] has made serious attempts to include female deviance in its scheme. The functionalist approach, stressing as it does the impact of social structural features on individuals and groups and also the structuring of situations which lead to opportunities for deviance, has had enormous influence on modern studies of deviance, notably on studies of juvenile delinquency, but also on aspects of mental health and illness, and, rather less directly, on studies of institutions. The concern of this approach has been especially with the effect of certain societal goals (and the structural means, or lack of them, for attaining them) and their impact on specific social groups found, or forced, to be inadequate in these terms, such as lower socio-economic groups, ethnic minorities of low status. The reaction, it is argued,[41] will be into forms of deviance, criminal or retreatist perhaps, depending on the availability of such subcultural opportunities. In these discussions it is assumed that growing adolescent males accept as the focal point of their lives the occupational/financial syndrome and that their actions can be interpreted in this light. It is argued (e.g by Parsons and by Cohen) of girls, whose 'focal concerns' are said to be sexual and marital, that

166

The deviance of women: a critique and an enquiry

female delinquency follows different lines. Women are not required in our society to perform the same instrumental functions in the labour market or in support and protection of their families; their role, on the contrary, is to act through men, through whom they acquire status and are related to the economic system. As a result, sex, and their ability to bargain with it becomes their major interest. As Kingsley Davis puts it: 'Women must depend on sex for their social position much more than men do.' Hence women are more likely to be involved in violating sexual mores than in delinquent activities. The fullest statement of this view appears in G. H. Grosser, *Juvenile Delinquency and Contemporary American Sex Roles* (unpublished Ph.D. thesis, Harvard, 1951), where male and female delinquents are equally fully considered. It is apparent that a number of subsequent writers have delved into Grosser's theoretical formulations and relied on his empirical data—Cohen for one acknowledges such a debt. Yet another curious footnote to this whole discussion might be to wonder why this seminal work has remained unpublished.

These theoretical approaches which have been briefly stated and it is hoped, with a minimum of distortion, pose several initial and straightforward problems. First they ignore, or cannot subsume, substantive knowledge about deviance: their assumptions that young girls find 'role expression' through sexual delinquency rather than other forms of deviance are not borne out by the data, for example, in the U.K. where property offences remain the single largest category of offences—and where, for example, over the age of seventeen, female shoplifters exceed males. The reasons for the lower observed rates of deviant participation are nowhere fully articulated. Are they the result perhaps of sexual success being comparatively easier to obtain than occupational achievement—success criteria in the former context being rapidly fulfilled by marriage, which once achieved is a fairly plateau-like position, there being no promotion available? If this is so, then 'wayward' behaviour in girls may be seen as parallel to delinquency in boys; except that it can hardly be regarded in Grosser's terms as the moral equivalent of stealing, since theft accepts legitimate ends—the acquisition of goods, enhancement of life style, etc.—but rejects the legitimate means of attaining them. Promiscuous behaviour is then much more akin to the negativistic, anti-utilitarian theft-and-vandalism syndrome described by Cohen[42] which rejects both legitimate means and ends. Now this exegesis of one aspect of female deviance is surely overcomplex. Difficulties arise because the masculine and feminine poles of deviance have to be forced on to a single axis. Yet it is quite clear that this leads to the denial of certain characteristics of female deviance and of the nature and meaning of the modes of activity which comprise it. Thus Grosser, who, with

167

Frances Heidensohn

his concept of sex-role-expressive behaviour, perhaps comes nearest to success in explanatory hypotheses concerning female deviance, still adds to a central confusion about sexuality and the female role. He talks, for example, of a continuum of female sex offences from *prostitutive* to *impulsive;* but these points represent surely essentially different types of behaviour in terms of its meaning to the actor. A single shot attack on received values (both bourgeois and respectable working-class) with regard to sexual behaviour—chastity, monogamy, sex should be linked to (responsible) procreation, etc.—can hardly be equated, either in its subjectively perceived aspects, or its societal effects, with any form of prostitution, whether 'casual' or fully professional, where an economic gain is one of the major concerns. This failure to see that prostitution is a deviant career structure, with its own economic organization and even apprenticeships and fee-splitting,[43] leads to it being equated with hysterical gestures of sexual deviance and actual sexual inversion. Yet basically, all they have in common in terms of situational definitions, is that women are, in both instances, being deviant in what Grosser calls a role-expressive way. This is merely tautological and has little analytical value as regards the problems of female deviance.

Possibly the most fruitful source of interpretation and analysis of female deviance in recent thinking could have been that of what Jack P. Gibbs has called the 'new perspective' of the study of societal reactions to deviance.[44] Examples of this approach suggest (in summary) that in contrast to what Gibbs calls the 'biological' approach and 'analytic' approach of previous studies attention should focus on the process of definitions of deviance and the labelling of deviants by means of a complex of feedbacks and reinforcements through societal reaction.

Gibbs chooses for analysis and critique statements from Kitsuse, Erikson and Becker, but the present writer would suggest that much of the work done by, for instance, Lemert[45] could also be included, while the contribution of Wilkins[46] is important too and the recent book by Scheff probably represents this approach carried to its ultimate conclusion.[47]

Such a view would seem to have considerable potential in examining some of the problems posed by female deviance: clearly the fact that this approach focuses on the societal reaction to deviance should make it illuminate an area apparently much influenced by social definitions and attitudes. It is rather remarkable, then, that very little work in this field appears to have been done. One of the few exceptions to this is Lemert's chapter on prostitution in his *Social Pathology.* Although his stated aim in this study is to examine the way in which primary deviance becomes reinforced and redefined into secondary deviance through societal reactions and personal

168

The deviance of women: a critique and an enquiry

definitions, in fact, when dealing with prostitution he concentrates on structural aspects of prostitution: the socio-economic background of prostitutes, occupations associated with prostitution, ecological factors and red light districts. While he indicates the type of women likely to drift into prostitution (e.g. unskilled migrants to urban areas) and suggests that there may be a process of self-definition involved, his actual analysis does not differ markedly from the structural functionalist form taken by Davis.[48]

In a sense, Lemert exemplifies, through his own implicit attitudes which emerge in this article, the importance of societal reaction to, and attitudes towards, deviance, and the process of defining deviance and the deviant. For instance, he begins by regarding prostitution as an example of *sexual deviation*.[49] Now, while the activities of a prostitute clearly deviate from the mores laid down for sexual relations—that is monogamy and fidelity, affection and desire, rather than cash, as the basis for intercourse—nevertheless from her own point of view, they are a 'normal' (within the subculture) instrumental means of earning a living. Bryan,[50] for instance, has shown how a rudimentary apprenticeship system exists in prostitution as a recognized means for girls to learn the ways of the 'game'. Autobiographical accounts of the careers of prostitutes also lay stress on the professional aspects of prostitution: the narrator of *Streetwalker* describes her annoyance at being expected to respond to a leer 'out of business hours' and her account of her discussions and gossip with another young prostitute and her landlady (who has retired from the streets) bear all the marks of occupational 'intalk'. Wayland Young[51] has instanced the learning and association patterns connected with prostitution, the passing on of skills, tricks and techniques. Again, Jackman *et al.*,[52] in their small-scale study of the prostitute's self-image demonstrate the existence of various 'strategies' for managing a career in prostitution despite the status denigration of the occupation; these appear to consist of taking an essentially instrumental view of the prostitute's role and its relation to her existence.[53]

The foregoing somewhat limited account of a number of approaches to female deviance should serve to demonstrate their common inadequacy and inappropriateness for the topic. This is not, of course, to deny that considerable illumination has emerged through many of these works. The point at issue is rather that much more meaningful insight and understanding might be obtained by other approaches, and that distortion of the inherent characteristics of the material is often a consequence of trying to force it into an inappropriate schematic or conceptual framework. Major common flaws appear to be grounded in the laudable scholarly aim of intellectual economy. Thus the sex differential in reported deviance (and the cultural perception of women as generally more conformist in

Frances Heidensohn

social behaviour) was so ubiquitously observed that all theories of deviance have had to take some cognizance of it; however, they have tended to do so by constructing single, homogeneous hypotheses which account for both male and female deviance and their apparent differences. Thus Lombroso saw atavistic hysterical females taking prostitution as an alternative to 'normal' crime; Pollak, concentrating on opportunity structures, argues that women commit at least as much crime as men but conceal it better; the neofunctionalists (Grosser, Cohen, Cloward and Ohlin) claim that the focal concerns of the male in modern society are occupational and financial, for the female they are primarily sexual, hence the difference in deviance and patterns of deviance. All these views acknowledge differences in the social-structural components of sex roles even if only implicitly; they tend to ignore on the one hand the empirical realities of the deviance of women—e.g. the recorded figures on crime which demonstrate that the most (statistically) typical offence for females is theft as it is for males and that so-called sex offences by females tend to be a result of concern over protection of adolescent girls on the one hand or behaviour by prostitutes on the other, of which the latter can just conceivably be so defined, but is probably more helpfully perceived as occupational deviance.

Thus a much more meaningful approach would take female deviance as an aspect of the female sex role and its relationship with social structure, rather than trying to make it conform to patterns apparently observed in the male role and its particular articulation with social structure. It would analyse components of the role, alternative role sets, opportunities for role playing in society, supportive agencies available for aid in role playing, and would view the deviance of women as related to and within this perspective.[54]

Lest this should seem as fruitless a task as some of the attempts mentioned above, it is perhaps useful here to point to two very important contributions to the study of deviant women which have appeared in the last two years and both of which consider social structure in institutions for women.[55] Both these illuminating studies take as their starting point the roles of women in society and the consequent adaptation necessary within a total institution. Their findings not only throw light on institutional life for women—in showing, for instance, that feminine adaptation and structuring of social relations within prison tends to be in terms of homosexual roles (Ward and Kassebaum) or in familial/homosexual clusters (Giallombardo) rather than in occupational or criminal/political terms as in men's prisons[56]—they also throw considerable doubt on many assumptions and assertions about the impact of total institutions and the structuring of inmate society.[57]

Any survey of the literature indicates that at present we barely

170

The deviance of women: a critique and an enquiry

possess the basic components for an initial analysis of the deviance of women. These are lonely, uncharted seas of human behaviour. We lack, for this area, the rich resources of past documentation and research that one can call upon in studying male juvenile delinquency or alcoholism, we have no equivalent of *The Jackroller, The Professional Thief,* still less is there a *Delinquent Girls.* We start very much from scratch, although a recent book by a journalistic writer using a penetrating case-study technique[58] illustrates the kind of initial data required and which, apart from a few studies of prostitutes, by themselves and others, scarcely exist.

Despite the considerable groundwork which has to be put in, there can be little doubt that this will be rewarded by an interesting and valuable outcome. As was suggested in the introduction to this paper, this area qualifies for study both in its own right as being characterized by certain unusual features such as lower levels of deviance participation, differential perception and definition of this deviance by the community, and countertrends to contemporary patterns of deviance. But further as we have seen, neglect of this area and misapprehension about it make it peculiarly interesting to the sociologist of sociology and could perhaps make one wonder about the 'ideology' of social pathologists on this point.[59]

Greater knowledge of the sociology of female deviance would enhance our knowledge of feminine behaviour, of sex roles—their characteristics, norms and socializing processes associated with them; it would broaden our view of deviance in general and especially would it make more meaningful the study of male deviance by freeing it from an embarrassing need to include problems of female deviance.[60]

To summarize, what seems to be needed in the study of female deviance is a crash programme of research which telescopes decades of comparable studies of males. First of all we do not even begin to have a 'natural history' of female deviance, our knowledge of its parameters,[61] its structure and substructures, the types and nature of activities which make it up, are all exceedingly limited. Even those few sources which exist, such as the autobiographical accounts of prostitutes, have nowhere been systematically analysed and studied. Then, as Mannheim has admirably put it, we need to[62] 'avoid the frequent mistake of studying the subject solely under . . . comparative aspects . . . An objective and scientific approach should try to treat female crime as a topic in its own right. Nor, should [we] try to understand female criminality exclusively from the sexual angle.' But it seems at the same time desirable and likely to prove fruitful to continue some aspects of modern approaches, to take, for example, descriptions of the structures of modern societies and analyse how these provide a framework within which certain roles are acted out, such as those of the adolescent girl or the adult woman and how

Frances Heidensohn

deviance occurs, is reinforced (or not) and deviant career patterns and roles for women emerge. Eventually, no doubt, it will be possible to reintegrate the study of male and female deviance, not simply for reasons of intellectual economy, but because a sociology of deviance can only be fully developed if it takes as its field *all* deviant phenomena. But first, of course, these phenomena must have been properly studied within their own context. Where the deviance of women is concerned, there may be a syndrome of 'modification' of female deviance within the social system, rather than the 'amplification' of deviance amongst adolescent males,[63] due perhaps to certain factors of the female role in society and social perceptions of its importance. At present such a suggestion must await further developments in the study of the deviance of women before we have sufficient material to begin to formulate it into fully fledged hypotheses. I hope that in this brief critical enquiry I have indicated some of the features that this research should not have, a few which it could possess and above all, the grounds for deeming it both a proper, necessary and potentially most interesting field for sociological enquiry.

Notes

1. *The Rules of Sociological Method*, Chicago, University of Chicago, 1938 (English translation), ch. III.

2. T. Parsons and R. F. Bales, *Family Socialization and Interaction Processes*, London, Routledge & Kegan Paul, 1955. W. J. Goode, *After Divorce*, New York, Free Press, 1956, as contrasted with the works of the Institute of Community Studies on women and family life, e.g. M. Young and P. Willmott, *Family and Kinship in East London*, London, Routledge & Kegan Paul, 1957, or the book by H. Gavron, *The Captive Wife*, London, Routledge & Kegan Paul, 1966.

3. By, e.g., Quetelet, *Recherches sur le penchant au crime*, 1838, and by Durkheim, *Suicide*, bk. 3, ch. II.

4. See L. Radzinowicz, 'Variability of the Sex Ratio of Criminality, *Soc. Rev.*, vol. 29 (1937).

5. M. E. Wolfgang, L. Savitz and N. Johnston, *The Sociology of Crime and Delinquency*, London, John Wiley, 1962.

6. Radzinowicz, op. cit.; H. Mann-heim, *Comparative Criminology*, London, Routledge & Kegan Paul, 1965, vol. II, ch. 26.

7. A. Kinsey *et al., Sexual Behaviour in the Human Female*, London, Saunders, 1953; M. Schofield, *The Sexual Behaviour of Young People*, London, Longmans, 1965.

8. Durkheim, op. cit.

9. See, e.g., Philip O'Connor, *Britain in the Sixties: Vagrancy*, London, Penguin Books, 1961.

10. But see A. N. Little 'An "Expectancy" Estimate of Hospitalization Rates for Mental Illness in England and Wales'. *Brit. J. Sociol.*, vol. 16, no. 3 (Sept. 1965).

11. The very fact that they have all been the subject of study within a 'social pathological' framework should support this assertion, plus, of course, evidence of popular reaction to such behaviour as evinced by the mass media, and, in some of the cases, the formal sanctions imposed by the legal system and other normative frameworks.

12. H. S. Becker, *Outsiders*, London, Collier-Macmillan, 1963, ch. 1.

172

The deviance of women: a critique and an enquiry

13. Becker acknowledges here the earlier statements of this view by F. Tannenbaum, *Crime and the Community*, New York, McGraw Hill, 1951, and E. M. Lemert, *Social Pathology*, New York, McGraw Hill, 1951: his formulation is used because of its comparative simplicity and conciseness.

14. E. M. Lemert, op. cit., and *Human Deviance, Social Problems and Social Control*, London, Prentice-Hall, 1967, ch. III.

15. This of course also is true of, among other things, their political behaviour (S. M. Lipset, *Political Man*, London, Heinemann, 1960, ch. V) and their conformity to social mores as measured through responses to psychological tests (D. Krech, R. S. Crutchfield and E. L. Ballachey, *Individual in Society*, London, McGraw Hill, 1962, ch. 14).

16. Perhaps also relevant here is the sex ratio among graduate students and researchers in the social sciences! This appears to be an inverse of that obtaining among undergraduates (H. Glennester *et al.*, *Graduate School: a study of Graduate Work at the London School of Economics*, London, Oliver & Boyd, 1967). While from one scientific point of view it may be desirable that students confine themselves to subjects where their empathetic powers are likely to flourish, it may not be helpful for the total development of a subject.

17. Since sociology is essentially a value-relative discipline, whose practitioners are bound by the constraints and limits of their own society this is inevitable and hardly a cause for regret. Concern, however, may be felt when the frontiers of knowledge fail to be extended because of pragmatic considerations or when retrospective interest is baulked by the lack of previous research.

18. In *Soc. Rev.*, vol. 14, no. 3 (Nov. 1966).

19. C. Wright Mills, 'The Professional Ideology of Social Pathologists', *Amer. J. Sociol.*, vol. 44 (Sept. 1942).

20. By S. Cohen and P. E. Rock, 'The Teddy Boy, the Evolution of a Social Type' in V. Bogdanor and R. Skidelsky (eds.), *Britain in the Fifties* (forthcoming).

21. S. Cohen, in an earlier article, ('Mods, Rockers and the Rest', *Howard Journal*, March 1967) has pointed out the effect of mass media in stimulating artificial 'happenings' amongst young people and the syndrome of deviance 'amplification' which results. L. Yablonsky in *The Violent Gang*, London, Collier-Macmillan, 1962, illustrates the way in which the press can influence and distort community conception of delinquent acts.

22. *Report of the Departmental Committee on Homosexual Offences and Prostitution*, Command No. 274: 1956 (the 'Wolfenden Report').

23. It is notable that the work of the Wolfenden Committee produced little response from social scientists on the topic of prostitution, although a good deal was published on the social and moral aspects of male homosexuality. One which did appear *before* the Committee had completed its work was Rosalind Wilkinson, *Women of the Streets*, ed. C. H. Rolph, London, 1955. But the anonymous *Streetwalker*, 1959, was already out of date and of largely historical interest by the time it appeared.

24. In 1908, for instance, some 32,439 females were convicted of either 'simple' drunkenness or 'drunkenness with aggravations'. By 1938 the figure (including a further category of drunkenness at the same time as another offence) had fallen to 7,686, although the female population was of course larger. By 1962 the figure was 4,793 and the rate per 10,000 of population had fallen from 4·50 to 2·54 as compared with a *rise* for males from 30·51 to 45·95 between 1938 and 1962.

25. Most European countries, for example, have abolished their various forms of licensed prostitution since the war.

26. L. T. Wilkins has shown that the rise in the number convicted of taking and driving away vehicles is directly

Frances Heidensohn

related to the increase in motor vehicle registrations issued: *Social Deviance*, London, Tavistock, 1964.

27. Baroness Wootton of Abinger, *Crime and the Criminal Law: Reflections of a Magistrate and Social Scientist* (15th Hamlyn Lectures).

28. Street Offences Act, 1959.

29. For a full discussion of the implications of this term, and of its retention, see J. E. Hall Williams, *Law and Contemporary Problems*, vol. 25 (Spring 1960)—issue on sex offences.

30. Through the sheer growth in the number and range of offences and the development of more elaborate and sophisticated policing, detecting, and processing and judicial apparatus, the likelihood that actors will be observed in acts of primary delinquency and reported is much greater. Further the spread of professional crime and the development of certain new features of the social structure (e.g. the subworld of the hippies and the 'Underground') may well ensure a pattern of increased reinforcement in secondary deviance.

31. Revelations made after the Profumo scandal, indicate how complex indirect arrangements for private catering for sexual wants can become.

32. See, e.g., Clark E. Vincent, *Unmarried Mothers*, New York, Free Press, 1961, and Robert W. Roberts (ed.), *The Unwed Mother*, London, Harper & Row, 1966.

33. This is not to imply that these cannot be meaningful typologies and bases for sociological enquiry—as in Lemert's studies of cheque forging or Cressey's of embezzlers.

34. Under English Law one of the rare exceptions to this rule is the crime of infanticide, a sub-category of homicide which takes cognizance of the postpartum mental state of a mother who kills her own child.

35. Most sociological theorizing about crime and deviance falls, following the still-strong Lombrosian position, into the first category. For a discussion of the implications (and the flaws) of determinism, see David Matza,

Delinquency and Drift, New York, John Wiley, 1964.

36. Lombroso and G. Ferrero, *La Donna Delinquente*, Torino, Roux, 1893.

37. Lombroso, *Crime, its Causes and Remedies*, Boston, 1911.

38. Of course Kingsley Davis has pointed out that society castigates the prostitute, but not her clients, as deviant, but he suggests that this is for practical not other reasons (K. Davis, 'The Sociology of Prostitution' in R. Merton and R. Nisbet (eds.), *Contemporary Social Problems*, London, Hart-Davis, 1963).

39. Otto Pollak, *The Criminality of Women*, Philadelphia, 1950.

40. As e.g., in Talcott Parsons, *Essays in Sociological Theory*, rev. edn., 1954; A. K. Cohen, *Delinquent Boys*, London, Routledge & Kegan Paul, 1955; R. A. Cloward and L. Ohlin, *Delinquency and Opportunity*, London, Routledge & Kegan Paul, 1960.

41. E.g. by A. K. Cohen in *Delinquent Boys* as a 'reaction formation' but also by R. Cloward and L. Ohlin in *Delinquency and Opportunity* as a straightforward reaction to a situation where the desired high-financial goal is only attainable through non-legitimate means.

42. A. K. Cohen, op. cit.

43. On this point see especially, James A. Bryan, 'Apprenticeships in Prostitution', *Social Problems* (Winter 1965) and also the anonymous *Streetwalker*, Bodley Head, 1959, and Wayland Young, *Eros Denied*, New York, Grove Press, 1964.

44. Jack P. Gibbs, 'Conceptions of Deviant Behaviour: the Old and the New', *Pacific Sociol. Rev.* (Spring 1966).

45. In, e.g., his *Social Pathology*, or more recently as expounded in *Human Deviance, Social Problems and Social Control*, New York, Prentice Hall, 1967. Lemert largely antedates the other writers, and is responsible for introducing the concept of secondary deviance into the debate. But see also Frank Tannenbaum, op. cit., above.

174

The deviance of women: a critique and an enquiry

46. L. T. Wilkins, *Social Deviance,* op. cit.

47. Thomas J. Scheff, *Being Mentally Ill,* London, Weidenfeld and Nicholson, 1966.

48. K. Davis, op. cit.

49. He argues, in fact, that he could also have chosen homosexuality as his subject.

50. J. P. Bryan, op. cit.

51. Wayland Young, op. cit.

52. Norman R. Jackman, Richard O'Toole and Gilbert Grieg, 'The Self Image of the Prostitute', *Sociol. Quart.,* vol. 4, no. 2 (April 1963).

53. In such statements as 'I hope that my husband can find a job and gets to working steadily again so I can be an ordinary housewife', 'I figgered [sic] it was easy money . . . prostitution . . .'

54. For some recent studies of sex roles see, e.g., Biddle and Thomas, *Role Theory,* London, John Wiley, 1966, and E. Dahlström, *The Changing Roles of Men and Women,* London, Gerald Duckworth, 1967.

55. David A. Ward and Gene G. Kassebaum, *Women's Prison: Sex and Social Structure,* London, Weidenfeld and Nicholson, 1966; Rose Giallombardo, *Society of Women,* London, John Wiley, 1966.

56. Contrast with the 'tobacco barons' in an English prison, T. Morris and P. Morris, *Pentonville: the Sociology of an English Prison,* London, Routledge and Kegan Paul, 1963.

57. As stated in, e.g., Gresham Sykes, *Society of Captives,* Princeton, 1958.

58. Tony Parker, *Five Women,* London, Hutchinson, 1955.

59. Cf. C. Wright Mills, 'The Professional Ideology of Social Pathologists', *Amer. J. Sociol.,* vol. 49 (Sept. 1942).

60. It may well be, of course, that further study of female deviance in depth may involve some challenging of underlying assumptions about male deviance as instanced in the case of prison studies mentioned above.

61. As this article was being prepared for publication the Home Office Research Unit published a monograph on *Studies of Female Offenders,* A Home Office Research Unit Report, London, H.M.S.O., 1967, which collates and somewhat extends our knowledge in this area.

62. Mannheim, *Comparative Criminology,* London, Routledge & Kegan Paul, 1965, vol. I.

63. As discussed by S. Cohen and S. Cohen and P. E. Rock.

Radical Theory

[28]

Alvin W. Gouldner

DEVIANCE AND ANOMIE

Another similarity between Platonism and Functionalism is to be found in their *explanation* of deviant behavior, which both often approach in fundamentally the same manner. Having the advantage of some two thousand years, Functionalists have, of course, developed the theory importantly, but the basic structure of the explanation of deviance frequently remains the same in both Platonism and Functionalism. To both, deviant behavior often involves a "falling away" from something, a departure from or

426   The Coming Crisis of Western Sociology

lack of something, particularly of certain kinds of moral norms—
that is, in Durkheim's revealing term, a *"poverty* of morality."

Central to the Functionalist's explanation of deviance has always
been the concept of anomie, which, of course, comes from the
Greek concept of *anomos*, meaning without law, lacking in restraint, devoid of temperance, form, or pattern. It is to be *without*
morality. This approach to deviant behavior is fundamentally different, in its most basic model, from, say, the Freudian or the
Marxian, in which tensions are not necessarily seen as due to the
lack of something, but may, indeed, derive from conformity *with*
certain moral values or may be due to a conflict between opposing
forces, all of which are simultaneously present.

One of the merits of Robert Merton's theory of anomie is that,
tacitly basing itself on certain Marxian domain assumptions—
especially those concerning the "internal contradictions" of a
system—it pointed to the manner in which a commitment to
certain culturally transmitted values may, when unrealizable, induce anomie. But here too the pathological terminus, anomie itself,
entails an ultimate renunciation of or disbelief in the socially
shared values. Yet it is not only the unrealizability of such values
that may sometimes warp a man, but all the things that he *can*
and *must* do to realize them successfully; there is the sickness of
the successful. And correspondingly, one might add (but usually
does not) that when a man pursues goals he has been taught to
prize, and then finds them unrealizable, it is quite sensible for him
to renounce these goals; there is, then, a rationality in deviance.

The central civic pathology with which Plato concerned himself
was "injustice," and he saw this as entailing a lack of restraint
such as arises when men fail to mind their own business, when
they violate the Socratic rule, "One Man, One Task," and when
they do not limit themselves to performing their own role obligations. To the contemporary Functionalist, "system disequilibrium"
is similarly held to arise when men fail to perform their role
obligations; when they do not confine themselves to those things
which their culture sanctions and therefore violate the expectations
of those who do.

Neither Platonism nor Functionalism seems to recognize that
when men limit themselves to what their culturally standardized
roles presently sanction, they may be prevented from acting in
ways that might remedy problems that have arisen only after the
earlier crystallization of social roles. They do not recognize that, at
some point, the world simply cannot be kept livable, unless some
men are courageous enough to *shirk* the duty that respectable or
powerful men around them define as theirs. (What, after all,
entitled Socrates—the son of a midwife and a stonecutter—to

become the philosophical gadfly of Athens? Certainly it was not anyone else's conception of his role that required this of him. It was only his own interpretation of the Oracle of Delphi; it was, in short, his own charisma.) Undoubtedly a man gets into trouble and runs risks when he behaves this way, as Socrates' life plainly testifies. But the original question was not, What is a safe way for men to live? It was, Do men and societies always benefit when men mind their own business and limit themselves to the prerogatives and duties of their incumbent roles? Neither Platonism nor Functionalism seems to understand that there are times when men must be intemperate and risk living *without limits*, for both theories are spellbound by a sculptural Apollonian ideal of man as firmly bounded and contained, as temperate and restrained.

It is thus characteristic of Functionalist analysis of deviance that it centers around the *acceptance* and the *nonacceptance* of culturally prescribed means and ends. But there is, at least, a third choice that men have: to fight. Men's "nonacceptance" of social values is not the same as active struggle against those values with which they disagree or on behalf of those in which they believe. Conforming "ritualistically" without belief is not the same as submitting under bitter *protest*. Struggle, conflict, protest seem to find no firm and distinctive place in the Functionalist inventory of men's responses to society, where they remain blurred and ghostly concepts. These are clearly not forms of conformity. And it is not enough to describe them as *non*conformity, for that results in the drug addict and the civil rights protester, those who organize criminal syndicates and those who organize the poor to wage their own war on poverty, those who march for peace and those who engage in delinquent "rumbles," being somehow all placed under the same conceptual umbrella. In focusing on their common character as "deviants," Functionalism sees no significant differences in the nature of their active resistance to society. Only a marginal reality is assigned to those who *oppose* social establishments actively and who struggle to change its rules and membership requirements.

Implicit in this Functionalist perspective is an image of the *good* man, the man who fits into the Functionalist image of the good society. He does his duty in the role in which he finds himself; he may even do it "creatively," yet somehow he manages to remain agreeable. No belligerent troublemaker, he is, rather, a man who usually conforms with a will to the expectations of others. He supports authority in its efforts to bring deviants under control and is docile even when he himself is admonished. He drinks the hemlock when the jailer brings it.

In Functionalism's implicit image of the *good* man, there has been a fatal confusion between the sociable and the social. When the Functionalist says that men's humanness derives from their social experience, this tends to slide softly into the implication that a man's humanness derives from cooperative sociability. Yet what makes a man human is not only the limits that others set upon him and to which he is sensitive, but also that he resents and resists these limits when they chafe. If men cannot become human apart from society, neither can they become persons except in the course of some conflict with it. A man develops his human self as much by his resistance to the requirements of his social roles, as much by struggling against them and other persons, as by conformity and cooperation. He is every bit as human when he bares his teeth as when he bares his heart. While human beings are no more devil than they are angel, they are, after all, an evolved animal species that was long and hard in the coming.

A man who never knew conflict would not be an individual person but some kind of an appendage. Yet both Functionalism and Platonism have been much and deeply discomfited by human individuality, because each senses this as entailing a variation dangerous to consensus among men and inimical to order in society. From wives or property in common, to setting the city distant from the sea, there is scarcely a social remedy that Plato ever proposed that does not aim at a de-individuating consensus. Functionalism has cautioned against that variability in men which is at the core of individuality, not so much in open challenge to it but in affirmation of what it takes to be higher values, social order and the need of society for consensus. When Talcott Parsons comes to the heart of his conception of how equilibrium may be maintained in the relations among men, he sees it as derived from the willingness of each to do as the other expects, which ultimately requires both to share the same value system.

[29]

THE SOCIOLOGIST AS PARTISAN: SOCIOLOGY AND THE WELFARE STATE

ALVIN W. GOULDNER

Washington University

Sociology begins by disenchanting the world, and it proceeds by disenchanting itself. Having insisted upon the non-rationality of those whom it studies, sociology comes, at length, to confess its own captivity. But voluntary confessions should always be suspect. We should try to notice, when men complain about the bonds that enchain them, whether their tone is one of disappointed resentment or of comfortable accommodation.

In 1961, in an address to a learned society, I attacked what I took to be dominant professional ideology of sociologists: that favoring the value-free doctrine of social science. Today, only six years later, I find myself in the uncomfortable position of drawing back from some who found my argument against the value-free myth so persuasive. I now find myself caught between two contradictory impulses: I do not wish to seem ungrateful toward those who sympathized with my position, yet the issue is a serious one and I also do not want to encumber discussions of it with considerations of personal tact or professional courtesy.

In a nutshell: I fear that the myth of a value-free social science is about to be supplanted by still another myth, and that the once glib acceptance of the value-free doctrine is about to be superseded by a new but no less glib rejection of it. My uneasiness concerning this came to a head upon reading Howard S. Becker's paper which boldly raises the problem, "Whose Side Are We on?" Rather than presenting the storybook picture of the sociologist as a value-free scientist, Becker begins by stating that it is impossible for a social scientist to do research "uncontaminated by personal and political sympathies." We are told that, no matter what perspective a sociologist takes, his work must be written either from the standpoint of subordinates or superiors. Apparently one cannot do equal justice to both.

The most telling indication of just how large a change sociology has recently undergone, may be seen not so much from the position that Becker takes but from the way his position is presented. There is nothing defensive in the manner that Becker rejects the older, non-partisan conception of the sociologist's role. Instead, Becker presents his rejection of this position as if it needed no explanation; as if it were completely obvious to everyone; and as if there were nothing to argue about. His posture is not that of the cocky challenger but of a blasé referee announcing the outcome of a finished fight, and whose verdict must be obvious. More than anything else, this suggests that there has been a substantial change in the occupational culture of sociologists in the last decade or so.

Becker's conception of the partisan sociologist would be unimportant were it simply an expression of his own idiosyncratic individuality. The fact is, however, that there is every reason to believe that he is voicing the sentiments of a substantial and probably growing number of sociologists, and, in particular, those whose interests focus upon the study of social problems, or the sociology of "deviant behavior." It is notable that the article in which Becker asks, "Whose Side Are We on?, was delivered originally as his

Presidential Address to the Society for the Study of Social Problems. This implies that Becker's constituency was at least large enough to have elected him to this modestly notable position in the structure of American social science. In short, Becker does not speak for himself alone.

That Becker's is a representative voice is further indicated by his own writings on deviant behavior, especially his books *The Outsiders* and *Social Problems*, which are presently one of the two dominant standpoints in American sociology concerning the analysis of social problems. Becker, then, is a leading spokesman of a viable coterie of sociologists specializing in the study of social deviance, whose members include such able men as Howard Brotz, Donald Cressey, John Kitsuse, Raymond Mack, David Matza, Sheldon Messinger, Ned Polsky, and Albert J. Reiss; and this coterie in turn overlaps with a larger network that essentially comprises the "Chicago School" of sociology. Becker's plea for for a partisan sociology may be regarded as a weather-vane signaling that new winds are beginning to blow. Yet the direction from which they come is not altogether clear.

Since Becker forcefully entitles his discussion, "Whose Side Are We on?", we might reasonably expect that he will, at some point, give a straightforward answer to his own straightforward question. Yet one reads it through and puts it down, only suddenly to notice that Becker gives no direct answer at all to his own question. Indeed, we pick it up

> "... the myth of a value-free social science is about to be supplanted by still another myth, and ... the once glib acceptance of the value-free doctrine is about to be superseded by a new but no less glib rejection of it."

once again to make sure that our first impression is correct and discover that this is indeed the case. If, in an effort to puzzle this through, we turn to Becker's earlier work, *The Outsiders*, we find that he does essentially the same thing there. In the culminating pages of that volume, he also asks: "Whose viewpoint shall we present?" And once again we find that no straightforward answer is given. If there is a difference between this volume and Becker's Presidential Address, it is that, in the earlier volume, he states explicitly that there is no basis in terms of which an answer to the question can be formulated. That is, he holds that neither strategic considerations, nor temperamental and moral considerations can tell us "to which viewpoint we should subscribe."

It seems equally clear, however, that, although Becker refuses explicitly to answer his explicit question, he does have an answer to it. If instead of looking at the explicit formulations advanced by Becker or other members of his group, we look, rather, at the specific researches that they have undertaken, we find that they unmistakably do adopt a specific standpoint, a kind of *underdog* identification. As I have said elsewhere, theirs is a school of thought that finds itself at home in the world of hip, drug addicts, jazz musicians, cab drivers, prostitutes, night people, drifters, grifters, and skidders: the "cool world." Their identifications are with deviant rather than respectable society. "For them, orientation to the underworld has become the equivalent of the proletarian identifications felt by some intellectuals during the 1930's. For not only do they study it, but in a way they speak on its behalf, affirming the authenticity of its style of life." Their specific researches plainly betray, for example, that they are concerned with and resent the legal straitjacket in which the drug addict is confined in the United States, or the degrading impact of the mental hospital on its inmates. In one part, this school of thought represents a metaphysics of the underdog and of the underworld: a metaphysics in which conventional society is viewed from the standpoint of a group outside of its own respectable social structures. At any rate, this is how it began; but it is not how it remains.

When Becker tells us that the world is divided into subordinates and superordinates, and that sociologists must look at the world from one side or the other, his implication seems to be that they should look at it from the standpoint of the deviant, of the subordinate, of the underdog. For these people, Becker says in his Presidential Address, are "more sinned against than sinning." The question arises as to why it is that, although Becker's leanings are clear enough, he chooses not to express them explicitly. Why is it that Becker does not declare openly for the standpoint of the underdog, since he clearly feels this way? If partisanship is inevitable, why doesn't Becker clearly state whose side he is on, rather than simply goading others to take a stand? There are probably both intellectual and practical reasons for Becker's failure to give a definitive answer to his own question—whose side are we on? First, I want to explore briefly some of the intellectual and practical factors that lead to Becker's reticence.

The Theory and Practice of Cool

In *The Outsiders*, Becker makes it plain that his own theoretical contribution leads to a focus, not merely on the rule breakers or deviants, but also to a study of those who make and enforce the rules, and most especially the latter. Although much of Becker's concrete research has been on deviants, his own theory, which came later, has largely focused on rule-makers and rule-enforcers. A crucial stage, in what Becker calls "the deviant career," occurs when someone declares that someone else's behavior has violated the rules of their game. The deviant, in short, is made by society in two senses: first, that society makes the rules which he has broken and, secondly, that society "enforces" them and makes a public declaration announcing that the rules have been broken. The making of the deviant, then, entails a process of social interaction. That being the case, the deviant-making process cannot be understood unless rule-making and rule-enforcing procedures or persons are studied.

The question then arises as to *whose* standpoint shall be adopted when rule-*makers* or rule-*enforcers* are themselves studied. Shall we describe their behavior from their own "overdog" standpoint or from that of the "underdog" deviants? One answer is given by Becker's more general theoretical position, the tradition of George Herbert Mead, which requires that men—even if they are "overdogs"—be studied from the standpoint of their *own* conceptions of reality.

The point here, of course, is that men's definition of their situation shapes their behavior; hence to understand and predict their behavior we must see it as they do. Becker's own specific theory of deviance, then, constrains him to look at the behavior of rule-*enforcers*, while his Meadian tradition requires him to look at it from *their* standpoint, rather than that of the deviant rule-breakers.

But this, by itself, would still create no difficulties. For, if Becker were entirely comfortable with this position, he would simply recommend that studies be conducted from the standpoint of *whoever* is being studied, be they rule-enforcers, rule-makers, or deviant rule-breakers. If he were to be consistent, then, Becker would answer the question, whose side are we on?, simply by stating that we are on the side of whomever we are studying at a given time. In other words, he would advocate the devotional promiscuity of sacred prostitution.

The reason that Becker cannot adopt this fairly obvious conclusion, and why he cannot give any answer to his question, is a simple one: his *sentiments* are at variance with his theories. Becker is sentimentally disposed to view the entire ambience of deviance from the standpoint of the deviant persons themselves. It is this that makes him sit on a fence of his own construction. Caught in the divergence between his theories and his sentiments, he is unable to answer his own question, whose side are we on? His sentimental disposition to see the world of deviance from the standpoint of the deviant conflicts with his theoretical disposition to take the standpoint of whichever group he happens to be studying. Becker "solves" this problem by raising the question, whose side are we on?, with such blunt force that makes the very question seem like an answer; and he evidences his own sentiments so plainly that need not assert them and, therefore, need never take responsibility for them.

In suggesting that Becker has refused to answer his own question because of this conflict between his theories and his sentiments, I do not mean that this is the only reason for his reticence. For there are other, more practical, costs

> "... theirs is a school of thought that finds itself at home in the world of hip, drug addicts, jazz musicians, cab drivers, prostitutes, night people, drifters, grifters, and skidders: the 'cool world.' Their identifications are with deviant rather than respectable society."

that would have to be paid were Becker (or anyone else) to announce such a position in a direct manner. A straightforward affirmation of sympathy with the underdog would, for one thing, create practical difficulties for Becker as a researcher. For he might one day wish access to information held by rule-enforcers and rule-makers who, in turn, might be dismayed to hear that Becker was disposed to view them from the standpoint of those whom they feel to be threats to society. Again, a straightforward affirmation of sympathy with the underdog or deviant might create a certain uneasiness among those who, either directly or indirectly, provide the resources which Becker, like any other research entrepreneur, requires. An outright expression of concern for or sympathy with the underdog thus conflicts with the sociologist's practical and professional interests. In other words: even genuine attachments to the underdog must be compromised with a tacit but no less genuine attachment to self-interest. We are, in short, also on our own side.

There is, I believe, still another reason why Becker fails to say whose side he is on. It has to do with the fact that he is not only on his own side and that, for all its underdog sympathies, his work is also on the side of one of the currently conflicting elites in the welfare establishment. But I must hold this for development at a later point. Becker's reticence about answering his own question, then, derives in part from a conflict between his sentiments and his interests, in part from a conflict between his theories and his sentiments, and, in part also, from a conflict within his sentiments.

There is still another way that Becker copes with the conflict between his sympathetic concern for the underdog and his equally human concern for more practical interests. We can see this if we notice the implicit irony in Becker's position, an irony that contributes importantly to the persuasiveness of his argument. Becker's central thesis is the impossibility of being value-free and the necessity of taking sides. In other words, he argues that real detachment is impossible. Yet one of the very things that makes Becker convincing is that he somehow manages to convey a sense of dispassionate detachment. This is largely accomplished through his *style*. Written in a non-polemical and flaccid style, Becker's rhetoric conveys an image of himself as coolly detached, despite his own explicit argument that partisanship and involvement are inevitable. The limp sobriety of his style projects an image of him as someone who has no axe to grind. It is through his style, then, that Becker invites us to believe that it is possible for a work to be biased without paying intellectual costs.

In effect, Becker appears to hold that emotional blandness is somehow an effective antidote to partisanship. Indeed, at various points, one suspects that Becker believes that blandness is also an effective substitute for analytic probing and hard thought. As I shall later develop, Becker believes that the real enemy of good social science is not a one-sided value commitment, but, rather, something that he calls "sentimentality."

Thus, while Becker invites partisanship, he rejects passionate or erect partisanship. In the very process of opposing the conventional myth of the value-free social scientist, Becker thereby creates a new myth, the myth of the *sentiment*-free social scientist. He begins to formulate a new myth that tacitly claims there is such a thing as a purely cerebral partisanship, which is devoid of emotional commitment and "sentimentality." Underlying this is Becker's tacit assumption that these entail intellectual costs, and costs *alone*. It seems equally reasonable to believe, however, that passion and sentimentality serve not only to produce costs and intellectual blindness, but may just as likely serve to enlighten, and to sensitize us to certain aspects of the social world. Indeed, it may be suspected that it is precisely, in some part, because there are certain intellectual gains derived from emotionally tinged commitments that it is possible for social scientists to sustain such commitments. In short, sentimentality does not seem to be the heartless villain that Becker makes it out to be. It is Becker who is being "sentimental" when he fosters a myth that holds it possible to have a sentiment-free commitment.

To recommend that sociological researches be undertaken from the standpoint of subordinates or underdogs creates as many problems as it resolves. While such a standpoint expresses a sympathy that I share, I still feel obligated to ask: How do we know an underdog when we see one? Who and what are underdogs? What marks someone as an under-

dog? And we have to ask an even more difficult question: Why *should* we undertake our studies from the standpoint of the subordinate, underdog?

Becker may recognize the intellectual bind in which he has placed himself by inviting research from the standpoint of the underdog. But he has only begun to glimpse it. Although acknowledging that a superior may be a subordinate to someone else, he fails to recognize that this works both ways: everyone who is a subordinate, *vis-a-vis* his superior, is also a superior in relation to some third party. If we regard every man as both superior and subordinate, overdog and underdog, how then do we know and on what basis do we select the underdogs whose standpoint we shall take? Clearly, Becker presents no logical solution to this quandary; he can intend it to be resolved only by the impulses of the very sentimentality that he deplores. It is also likely that Becker never confronts this problem—with *which* underdog shall be sympathize?—because he tacitly assumes that good liberals will instinctively know, and always agree, who the true underdogs are.

Let me acknowledge, once for all, that I share Becker's underdog sympathies. Yet I also believe that sociological study from an underdog standpoint will be intellectually impaired without clarifying the *grounds* for the commitment. A commitment made on the basis of an unexamined ideology may allow us to feel a manly righteousness, but it leaves us blind.

Sociology and Suffering

The question then is: Are there any *good* reasons to conduct research from an underdog standpoint? One such reason may be that a feelingful commitment to the underdog's plight enables us to do a better job as *sociologists*. Specifically, when we study a social world from an underdog standpoint, we elevate into public view certain underprivileged aspects of reality. These are aspects of social reality that tend to be comparatively unknown or publicly neglected because they are dissonant with conceptions of reality held by the powerful and respectable. To take the standpoint of the underdog in our researches, then, does two things. First, it gives us new information concerning social worlds about which many members of our society, including ourselves, know little or nothing. Secondly, it may give us new perspectives on worlds that we had thought familiar and presumed that we already knew. To that extent, then, taking the underdog's standpoint does indeed contribute to the successful fulfillment of the intellectual obligations that we have as sociologists. It helps us do the distinctive job we have.

I have acknowledged a sympathy with the underdog and with impulses to conduct researches from his standpoint. Yet in searching for the justification of my sentiments I must also candidly confess that I see no special virtue in those who are lacking in power or authority, just as I see no special virtue that inheres in those who possess power and authority. It seems to me that neither weakness nor power as such are values that deserve to be prized.

The essential point about the underdog is that he suffers, and that his suffering is naked and visible. It is this that makes and should make a compelling demand upon us. What makes his standpoint deserving of special consideration, what makes him particularly worthy of sympathy, is that he suffers. Once we see this, however, the nature of our relationship to the underdog changes; correspondingly, the nature of the obligation that we experience as *sociologists* may also change.

First, we can recognize that there may be forms of human suffering that are unavoidable, that cannot be remedied in some particular society or at some particular time. Correspondingly, however, there are also forms of suffering that are needless at particular times and places. I think that it is the sociologist's job to give special attention to the latter, while recognizing that it is no easy task to distinguish between avoidable and unavoidable suffering, and while fearing that some will all to easily categorize certain kinds of suffering as unavoidable so that they may disregard them with comfort.

Moreover, I would also insist that even when men experience needless suffering, a suffering which is unavoidable, tragic, and truly a part of the eternal human condition, that they still deserve sympathy and loving consideration. It is vital for sociologists also to portray this unyielding part of the world. For this reason, I cannot imagine a humane sociology that would be callous to the suffering of "superiors." A sociology that ignored this would, so far as I am concerned, neither manifest a respect for truth nor a sense of common humanity.

But if all men suffer and to some extent unavoidably, is there any reason at all to feel a special sympathy for underdogs? Is there any reason to make a special effort to conduct research from their standpoint? I think that there is.

For one thing, the suffering of some is still simply and literally unknown to many in society. This is a special and important part of reality which, I think, is one of our important responsibilities to understand and communicate. The problem is not simply that there exists what Becker calls a "hierarchy of credibility"—in which men in power are presumably granted the right to declare what is real and true in the world around them. It is rather that these dominant conceptions of reality, sustained and fostered by the managers of society, have one common defect: they fail to grasp a very special type of reality, specifically the reality of the suffering of those beneath them. In failing to see

> "Becker is sentimentally disposed to view the entire ambience of deviance from the standpoint of the deviant persons themselves. It is this that makes him sit on a fence of his own construction."

this, what they must also fail to see is that those beneath them are indeed very much like themselves, in their suffering as in other ways.

This, in turn, implies that a sociology truly concerned with representing the standpoint of the underdog would most especially seek to communicate the character of his suffering, its peculiar sources and special intensity, the ways and degrees in which it is avoidable, the forces that contribute to it, and his struggle against it. The underdog's standpoint therefore deserves to be heard in sociology not because he has any special virtue and not because he alone lives in a world of suffering. A sociology of the underdog is justified because, and to the extent, that his suffering is less likely to be known and because—by the very reason of his being underdog—the extent and character of his suffering are likely to contain much that is avoidable.

Although Becker leans toward a sympathy and special consideration for the underdog's standpoint, and although the underdog's suffering is particularly visible, it is still one further paradox in Becker's discussion that we find him dis-

playing no such concern for suffering. Rather, what we do find is a fear of such a concern, a fear that this concern will make us lose our cool. I would guess that it is in some part because of this fear that Becker makes such a point of rejecting "sentimentality."

Yet if it is not the suffering of the subordinate or the deviant that involves Becker—and others of his school—with the underdog, then what is it? It is my impression, from many years of reading their researches and of talking with them, that their pull to the underdog is sometimes part of a titillated attraction to the underdog's exotic difference and easily takes the form of "essays on quaintness." The danger is, then, that such an identification with the underdog becomes the urban sociologist's equivalent of the anthropologists's (onetime) romantic appreciation of the noble savage.

The Becker School's view embodies an implicit critique of lower middle class ethnocentrism, of small town respectability, of the paradoxical superiority that one ethnic can feel

> "Thus, while Becker invites partisanship, he rejects passionate or erect partisanship."

toward another. Indeed, one might say that theirs is most especially a critique of the uneducated middle classes. Now this is no mean thing, for the piety of these strata is certainly pervasive in the United States. Becker's rejection of their smug narrowness is wholesome and valuable.

At the same time, however, Becker's school of deviance is redolent of Romanticism. It expresses the satisfaction of the Great White Hunter who has bravely risked the perils of the urban jungle to bring back an exotic specimen. It expresses the Romanticism of the zoo curator who preeningly displays his rare specimens. And like the zookeeper, he wishes to protect his collection; he does not want spectators to throw rocks at the animals behind the bars. But neither is he eager to tear down the bars and let the animals go. The attitude of these zookeepers of deviance is to create a comfortable and humane Indian Reservation, a protected social space, within which these colorful specimens may be exhibited, unmolested and unchanged. The very empirical sensitivity to fine detail, characterizing this school, is both born of and limited by the connoisseur's fascination with the rare object: its empirical richness is inspired by a collector's aesthetic.

It is in part for this reason that, despite its challenging conception of a partisan sociology and its sympathy with the underdog, Becker's discussion is paradoxically suffused with a suprising air of complacency. Indeed, what it expresses is something quite different from the older, traditional sympathy with the plight of the underdog. Basically, it conceives of the underdog as a *victim*. In some part, this is inherent in the very conception of the processes by means of which deviance is conceived of as being generated. For the emphasis in Becker's theory is on the deviant as the product of society rather than as the rebel against it. If this is a liberal conception of deviance that wins sympathy and tolerance for the deviant, it has the paradoxical consequence of inviting us to view the deviant as a passive nonentity who is responsible neither for his suffering nor its alleviation—who is more "sinned against than sinning." Consistent with this view of the underdog as victim, is the more modern conception of him as someone who has to be managed, and should be managed better, by a bureaucratic apparatus of official caretakers. In short, it conceives of the underdog as someone maltreated by a bureaucratic establishment whose remedial efforts are ineffectual, whose custodial efforts are brutal, and whose rule enforcement techniques are self-interested. While it sees deviance as generated by a process of social interaction, as emerging out of the matrix of an unanalyzed society, it does not see deviance as deriving from specified master institutions of this larger society, or as expressing an active opposition to them.

The underdog is largely seen from the standpoint of the difficulties that are encountered when the society's caretakers attempt to cope with the deviance that has been produced in him by the society. Becker's school of deviance thus views the underdog as someone who is being mismanaged, not as someone who suffers or fights back. Here the deviant is sly but not defiant; he is tricky but not courageous; he sneers but does not accuse; he "makes out" without making a scene. Insofar as this school of theory has a critical edge to it, this is directed at the caretaking institutions who do the mopping-up job, rather than at the master institutions that produce the deviant's suffering.

It is in some part for this reason that the kinds of researches that are undertaken from this standpoint tend to exclude a concern with *political* deviance, in which men do actively fight back on behalf of their values and interests. We thus find relatively few studies of people involved in the civil rights struggle or in the peace movement. For however much these deviant groups are made to suffer, no one could easily conceive of them as mere victims well under the control of bureaucratic officialdom. It is not man-fighting-back that wins Becker's sympathy, but rather, man-on-his-back that piques his curiosity.

What we have here, then, is essentially a rejection of unenlightened middle class bigotry. And in its place is a sympathetic view of the underdog seen increasingly from the standpoint of the relatively benign, the well educated, and the *highly* placed bureaucratic officialdom: of the American administrative class. What seems to be a rejection of the standpoint of the superior is, I shall argue, actually only a rejection of the *middle-level* superior.

We may see this more clearly if we return to the problem that gives Becker his greatest uneasiness, the observation that every superior has his own superior, and, correspondingly, Becker's failure to observe that every subordinate has his own subordinate. (Lower than the prostitute is the pimp; lower than the pimp is the errand boy; and lower than the errand boy is the kid on the fringe of the gang who would like his job.) Now, since everyone may have someone or something above or below him, this does not make it more but less possible to know *which* subordinate's standpoint we should adopt. But this does not deter Becker for a moment. As he gayly says, "I do not propose to hold my breath until this problem is solved."

I, for my part, however, continue to be perplexed about the manner in which a specific stratum of underdogs comes to be chosen as the focus for an orienting standpoint. There is a hidden anomaly in any recommendation to look upon the world from the standpoint of underdogs. The anomaly is this: to a surprising degree, underdogs see *themselves* from the standpoint of respectable society; Negroes, in fact, often call one another "niggers." Thus, if we did study underdogs from "their own" standpoint we would, inevitably, be adopting the standpoint of the dominant culture. It is precisely insofar as the deviant and subordinate do accept a role as passive victims rather than as rebels against circumstances, that they do view themselves from the standpoint of the dominant culture.

In the very act of viewing deviants and subordinates from *their own* standpoint, we are bound to see them from the standpoint of respectable society and its dominant institutions. We will also see deviants in terms of conventional categories not only when we look upon them as passive victims, but, also, to the extent that they are looked upon from the standpoint of the bureaucratic caretakers who are publicly chartered either to put them into custody or to correct their behavior. Paradoxically, then, although Becker invites us to adopt the standpoint of the subordinate, and thereby presumably braves giving offense to respectable values, I believe that he himself is still using some version of the outlook of respectable society.

OMBUDSMAN Sociology: Critique of the Middle Man

Becker seems to be adopting the position of the outcast. In point of fact, I believe that he is also embracing the position of "enlightened" but no less respectable liberalism toward the outcast. Becker appears to be taking up arms against society on behalf of the underdog. Actually, he is taking up arms against the ineffectuality, callousness, or capriciousness of the caretakers that society has appointed to administer the mess it has created. Becker's argument is essentially a critique of the caretaking organizations, and in particular of the *low level* officialdom that manages them. It is not a critique of the social institutions that engender suffering or of the high level officialdom that shapes the character of caretaking establishments.

Much of deviant study today has become a component of the new style of social reform which is now engineered through caretaking public bureaucracies. The ideological standpoint implicit in Becker's School embodies a critique of the *conventionl* welfare apparatus and of the *old* style welfare state, before it extricated itself from social movement reform. It is, as such, a critique of the ethnocentrism and the ineffectuality with which deviance is regarded and treated by certain of the local caretakers immediately responsible for it today. Becker's theoretical school is indeed taking sides; it is a party to the struggle between the old and the new elites in the caretaking establishments; between the welfare institutions inherited from the 1930's and those now promoted today; and between the "locals" working in the municipalities and the "cosmopolitans" operating from Washington, D.C. His ideology is, in each case, injurious to the former and supportive of the latter. If this is seen, it can be better understood how certain of the other difficulties in Becker's discussion are to be resolved. We therefore need a temporary detour to obtain a view of these difficulties.

Becker makes a distinction between the conduct of research in two settings: in political and non-political situations. He is moved to make this distinction because he wants to hold that accusations of bias against sociologists, and reactions to them, differ, depending upon whether the situation studied is political or not.

Becker holds that in *non*-political situations sociologists are more likely to accuse one another of bias when their studies adopt underdog perspectives, than when they look at things from the standpoint of superiors. The reason for this, he says, is that in these non-political situations there exists an accepted "hierarchy of credibility" which credits superiors with the right to define social reality in their spheres; since most sociologists, like others, tend to accept the established hierarchies of credibility, they therefore tend to view studies conducted from underdog perspectives as biased.

Now this is very curious. For what Becker is arguing is

that most sociologists, who he says are liberal, will, despite this ideology, nonetheless identify with the overdog in their studies of non-political situations. In short, while most sociologists will presumably give free rein to their liberal ideologies when studying political situations, they will turn their backs on these same liberal ideologies, and act as if they were non-liberal, when studying non-political situations. If this is true, surely one must ask: How is this switch effected? What brings it about? Indeed, is it really a switch? We must consider the other side of the equation; that is, if we ask how some liberal sociologists come to identify with the underdog, we must also ask, how does it happen that others failed to do so?

Becker recognizes that *some* explanation is called for to account for sociologists' adoption of overdog viewpoints in their researches. He says that (in non-political situations) most sociologists tend to accept the dominant hierarchy of credibility. In other words, in these situations, most sociologists conduct their studies from the standpoint of responsible officials, says Becker, because they accept the standpoint of responsible officials. Becker's invocation of this tautology at least acknowledges that an explanation is in order. Yet when it comes to explaining why a minority of sociologists adopt an *underdog* standpoint in the same non-political situations, Becker does not even see that this, too, is a problem that needs explaining.

Bleak Hypotheses

What, indeed, are the sources of these sociologists' identification with underdogs? Clearly we cannot simply hold that such an identification with the underdog stems predominantly from the sociologists' liberal ideology. For Becker is quite right in stating that most sociologists are politically liberal. It is clear therefore that many, if not most, who adopt the overdog standpoint must share this liberal ideology. Thus, while the liberal ideology may be a necessary condition for adopting an underdog standpoint, it cannot be a sufficient condition for doing so. The question here, the most important question we ever confront in understanding how moralities and ideologies work in the world, is: By what specific mechanisms are men kept honest? In other words, how is it that they are made to conform to their ideologies or values?

It may be surprising, but there are actually many things that keep men—including sociologists—honest. First, remember, as Becker acknowledges, that an underdog standpoint is adopted by only a minority of sociologists. Being infrequent, a minority perspective is more likely to be visible in the larger professional community from whom sociologists seek recognition. Of course, such notice may take the form of hostile criticism. But while an underdog standpoint thus has its risks, it may also bring higher and quicker returns than the adoption of an overdog standpoint which, being common, tends to glut the market and to depress the price paid per individual contribution.

An underdog perspective may, then, be thought of as a career strategy more appealing to high variance betters who, in turn, are more likely to be found among the ambitious young. Bear in mind, however, that the larger professional audience to whom their work is addressed will for the most part conceive themselves as "liberals"—and on whose sympathy an underdog standpoint has some claim. Those adopting an underdog standpoint are, therefore, probably not engaged in as risky an undertaking as their minority position might imply. We are, in summary, suggesting a bleak hypothesis: sociologists with liberal ideologies will more likely adopt underdog perspectives when they experience these as compatible with the pursuit of their own career interests.

Implicit in this bleak hypothesis is the assumption that there is probably some positive relationship between the youth and low professional status, on the one hand, and the

> "If this is a liberal conception of deviance that wins sympathy and tolerance for the deviant, it has the paradoxical consequence of inviting us to view the deviant as a passive nonentity who is responsible neither for his suffering nor its alleviation—who is more 'sinned against than sinning.' "

adoption of an underdog perspective, on the other. In brief, I would expect that younger intellectuals would, other things constant, be readier to adopt this high variance bet than older intellectuals. It may also be that older intellectuals who feel that they have been bypassed, or whose rewards have somehow not been appropriate, would also be more likely to adopt an underdog standpoint.

Correspondingly, I would also expect that as sociologists get older, as they become increasingly successful, more likely to live next door to or associate with those who are also successful, or themselves become involved in the practical management of public (including university) affairs, they too will come increasingly to adopt overdog standpoints despite their continued public professions of liberalism. Moreover, as sociologists become better established, recognized, and successful, they are—as they begin to move toward the zenith of their careers—risking more should they make a high variance wager on underdogs. The additional net advantage still possible to them is in this way diminished. In short, for the rising sociologist, identification with the underdog may mean greater risk than it does for the younger or less successful sociologists.

I would, however, suggest one important qualification concerning this disposition of older men toward increasing overdog standpoints. As they achieve (rather than merely approach) the zenith of their careers, the rewards that older sociologists are given for conformity to conventional overdog positions, are especially subject to a diminishing marginal utility; in the result some of them may be less subject to professional controls that dispose them to the conventional standpoints of their contemporaries. Thus some senior sociologists, beginning to think about the judgment of "posterity" rather than the views of their contemporaries, may return to the underdog standpoints of their youth. Moreover, as their own age group thins out through death, they may receive more encouragement from the young with whom they are not in competition, than from the middle aged; and they may begin to feel that the future of their reputations will be more enduringly affected by the judgment of the relatively young. These, at any rate, are some of the ways in which the career and personal interests of some older sociologists may dispose them to defy the established hierarchy of credibility and to opt for the underdog. We might call it the "Bertrand Russell Syndrome."

But men are prompted to heed the voice of conscience and to abide by high principle by still other considerations. We can see some of these if we ask, how is it that the young, high variance betters are not brought under control by their elders in the course of their education, apprenticeship, and common research undertakings, and are in this way constrained to adopt the respectable overdog standpoints more congenial to the older? Here, again, things are not simple. In some part, the young men's underdog impulses will be protected by the academic ideology of collegiality, which nominally governs relationships. Thus even when working under the supervision of older men, the young men can lay claim for the protection of their underdog standpoints.

Once more, however, we must call attention to the role of bleak factors in keeping men honest. These essentially have to do with the ramifying and powerful role of the new funding structures in social science today which, in turn, are linked to the growth of the new welfare state and its new conceptions of social reform.

Nothing is more obvious than that these are plush times for American social scientists, and there is never any reason to underestimate the power of the obvious. So far as the older and better known men are concerned, they are often so fully funded that they may have little time to supervise their researches personally, to administer them with the continuing closeness that could effectively imprint their overdog identifications on the research. Sometimes the older men are so loosely connected with the researches they have funded that even basic research decisions are made by younger men from their different standpoints. Older men today are often constrained to surrender wide discretionary power to their juniors, if they are to keep them in today's seller's market in social research. The irony of the matter, then, is that the more successful the older man is in funding his research, the less successful he may be in having it conducted according to his lights: the research is less likely to be "his."

With the new funding situation and the greater ease of access to research money, it is now also much simpler for younger men to procure funds for themselves, for their own researches, and at an earlier age. Being their own masters, they can now more readily express their own underdog standpoint, insofar as they have one.

But it would seem that there should be a fly in this ointment. For the question that now arises is whether the new funding situation may simply mean that the younger men have only exchanged one master for another; for even if they are no longer subjected to the direct pressure of senior professors, they may now be subjected to the direct pressure of the funding agencies. In my opinion, this is exactly what has happened.

With growing ease of funding, younger men gain independent access to research resources at a time when their liberal underdog ideologies are still relatively strong and can shape their research. At the same time, however, the career gratifications of these funding opportunities, as well as the personal gratifications of being close to men of power, become vested interests that constrain to a dependency on the new sources of funding. Thus the younger man's more salient, underdog identifications now need to be accommodated to his new-found "appreciation" of overdogs. This is in part accomplished by submerging this "appreciation" in a subsidiary awareness that is maintained by a collegial reciprocity: each tactfully agrees not to look the other's "gift horse in the mouth." (There are, alas, "deviant" cases: e.g., those who make a career of denouncing Project Camelot and then themselves apply for a half-million dollar grant from the State Department.)

This accommodation of underdog identification to overdog dependencies is, quite apart from skillful rationalizing, not too difficult today. For the new funding agencies now desperately need information about underdogs; and these

> "Here the deviant is sly but not defiant; he is tricky but not courageous; he sneers but does not accuse; he 'makes out' without making a scene."

are not unreceptive even to researches conducted from the latter's standpoint, for much the same reason that colonial governments supported similar researches in anthropology. Overdogs in the welfare state—in Washington bureaucracies and New York foundations—are buyers of underdog research for much the same political reasons that the Johnson regime initiated the "war on poverty." To explore a few of the implications of this, I must revert to some of the larger institutional changes that come to a head in the welfare state.

Perhaps the crux here is the manner in which social reform in the United States has changed in character. What is new is not the "plight of the cities," however increasing their deterioration, but rather that this becomes an object of a measured "concern" rather than of "shame." What is new, in a somewhat larger historical perspective, is that the locus of reform initiatives and resources is increasingly found on the level of national politics and foundations, rather than in the political vitality, the economic resources, or the zealous initiatives of elites with local roots.

The reform of American cities was once a process that involved small businessmen, muckraking journalists, and local political machines, all of whom had some vital involvement and interest in their local communities. Today, however, with the changing structure, character, and ecology of the middle classes, many who might give leadership to urban reform live neither in the city itself nor in the still politically powerful rural areas, but live rather in suburbia and exurbia. The educated, bureaucratically employed, and highly mobile middle classes have a dwindling localistic attachment and a narrowing base of power on the *local* levels, which could provide them with the economic and political leverage to effectuate urban reform. They must, in consequence, seek a remedy not on the local but the national level.

As the locus of reform efforts moves upward from the local to the national level, the conception and meaning of social reform changes. The urban reforms being sought by this new middle class are now aimed at the reform of a community to which they are less tied by complex interests, urbane pleasures, or by a round of familiarizing daily activities. It is not "their" community that they now wish to reform—for their suburbs are decent enough as they view them. When they concern themselves with the plight of Negroes, it is not even "their" Negroes whom they seek to help, but Negroes viewed abstractly and impersonally.

Social reform now becomes an effort largely motivated by bland political appraisal, removed economic calculus, prudent forecasting, or a sense of pity and sympathy that becomes increasingly remote as it loses rooting in daily experience and encounter. The community to be reformed becomes an object, something apart from and outside the reformer. The nature of the reform becomes less a matter of moral zeal or even of immediate personal interest and more of a concern prompted by a long range appraisal and prudence. Social reform now becomes a kind of engineering job, a technological task to be subject to bland "cost-benefit" or "system-analysis." The rise of the welfare state then means the rise of the uninvolved reformer: It means the rise of re-form-at-a-distance. Reform today is no longer primarily the part-time avocation of dedicated amateurs but is increasingly the full-time career of paid bureaucrats.

Today civil rights reforms and the war against poverty are pursued by many in a Bismarckian mood. Reform is no longer prompted by the twinge of conscience or the bite of immediate personal interest but, rather, by "reasons of state," and on behalf of the "national interest." Personal liberal-ism becomes state liberalism. Liberalism changes in charac-ter from a matter of conscience, which had a penetrating claim upon private and daily decision, to electoral loyalty to the Democratic Party and to marginal differentiations in career strategies. The operational meaning of liberalism for the sociologist now tends to become calibrated in terms of the government agency for which he will work, or whose money he will take. From some current standpoints, for example, a truly "liberal sociologist" is one who will reject money from the Defense Department but will seek and ac-cept it from the State Department!

The funding agencies of social science today, whether government agencies or massive private foundations, are essentially the welfare state's purchasing agents for market research: they are the instrumentalities of this new reform movement. They express the "detached concern" of educated but bureaucratically dependent middle classes who no longer have effective bases in localities; whose cosmopolitan sym-pathies are not personally and deeply engaged by a daily encounter with urban suffering; and whose fears are not deeply aroused by a close dependence upon the deteriorating urban community. Prodded partly by mild discomforts, vague forbodings, prudent extrapolations, partly by concern to maintain a decent image of themselves, and, not least, by the growing rise of the militant politics of public demonstrations, they approach the task of modern urban reform with a thin-lipped, businesslike rationality. This is the social context in which we can better understand some of the ramifying meanings of Becker's bland program for an underdog sociol-ogy. It is the larger context which makes it possible for some sociologists today to stay honest: that is, to implement their liberal ideologies with an effort at underdog identifica-tion.

The superiors whose dominant "hierarchies of credibility" are resisted by this underdog sociology are essentially those whose powers remain rooted in, and hence limited by, the local level. The sociology of the underdog is a sociology that rejects the standpoint of only the *local* officials: the head of the medical school, the warden of the prison, the city director of the housing agency. In short, the respectables who are be-ing resisted, and whose hierarchy of credibility is disputed, are those local officials who, for the most part, do not con-trol access to large supplies of research funds.

Toward a New Establishment Sociology

The new underdog sociology propounded by Becker is, then, a standpoint that possesses a remarkably convenient combination of properties: it enables the sociologist to be-friend the very small underdogs in local settings, to reject the standpoint of the "middle dog" respectables and notables who manage local caretaking establishments, while, at the same time, to make and remain friends with the really top dogs in Washington agencies or New York foundations. While Becker adopts a posture as the intrepid preacher of a

new underdog sociology, he has really given birth to some-thing rather different: to the first version of new Establish-ment sociology, to a sociology compatible with the new character of social reform in the United States today. It is a sociology of and for the new welfare state. It is the sociol-ogy of young men with friends in Washington. It is a sociology that succeeds in solving the oldest problem in personal politics: how to maintain one's integrity without sacrificing one's career, or how to remain a liberal although well-heeled.

The social utility of this new ideology is furthered by the fact that, for some while now, there has been a growing tension between the entrenched local welfare establishments and the newer and powerfully supported federally based agencies and programs of the "Great Society." These new federal agencies, headed by personnel with substantially greater education than the local elites, are presently at-tempting to implement their new programs against the resistance of the local notables. It is the ultimate function of the federally based programs to win or maintain the at-tachment of urban lower and working classes to the political symbols and machinery of the American state in general, and of the Democratic Party in particular. While the local caretaking elites usually share these political aims, they also feel that their own local prerogatives and position are threatened by the growth of programs over which they have less control, since they derive from national resources and initiatives. Becker's new underdog sociology functions to line up sectors of sociology against the "backward" resist-ance the officialdom on the municipal level, and in favor of the most powerful "enlightened" sectors on the national level.

Essentially Becker's type of research does this because, in adopting the standpoint of the underdogs, it simultaneously shows how ignorant local caretakers are of this standpoint and how badly local caretaking officials manage their estab-lishments. It must not be thought for a moment that Becker's work performs this ideological function through any inten-tion to further the ambitions of the upper officialdom or by any intention to conduct his research in any narrowly con-ceived applied manner. It achieves its ideological conse-

> "There is a hidden anomaly in any recommendation to look upon the world from the standpoint of underdogs. The anomaly is this: to a surprising degree, underdogs see *themselves* from the standpoint of respectable society; Negroes, in fact, often call one another 'niggers.' "

quences primarily by taking and revealing the standpoint of those for whom local caretaking officials are responsible and by "unmaking" the ignorance of these officials. This is not an incidental or trivial byproduct; rather, this is exactly what carries the political payload. For it is this discrediting of local officials that legitimates the claims of the higher ad-ministrative classes in Washington and gives them an enter-ing wedge on the local level.

Becker's readiness to sacrifice the middle dogs to the top dogs can be gleaned when he states that there is no point in attempting to adopt the standpoint of middle level official-dom. Looking at the situation from the standpoint of middle level officials—in other words, from the standpoint of the prison warden, the school principal, the hospital administrator—simply leads to an infinite regression, says Becker.

This has a seeming persuasiveness, but it is too glib by far. First, it is by no means certain that an "infinite regress" problem is involved. Is it really true that every superior has a superior who, in turn, limits and prevents him from doing as he really would like? Isn't there some point at which the buck-passing ends? This would seem to be part of what C. Wright Mills had in mind when he spoke of the "power elite." We can, of course, maintain that even the highest officers of state in turn always require the consent of the governed. But this brings us back full circle; and we would then have to acknowledge that the very underdogs, who Becker says are more sinned against than sinning, are at least in part responsible for the sins against them; and why, then, should sociologists conduct their studies primarily from their standpoint?

It would seem that there is one way out of this impasse for Becker. He could say that it is not a matter of superiors and subordinates as such, but, rather, of the *institutions* governing their relationship. He might maintain that the need is not to study social situations from the standpoint of subordinates as an end in itself, but of conducting studies with a view to understanding how some are crushed by certain institutions, and how all alike are subjected to institutions that do not permit them to live as they wish. As I say, this position would be one way for Becker. But he neither sees it nor takes it. For this undercuts his "infinite regress" gambit and leads research inevitably to the doorstep of power; it would force the research focus upward, fastening it on the national levels.

Parenthetically, but not irrelevantly, I think that *radical* sociologists differ from liberals in that, while they take the standpoint of the underdog, they apply it to the study of overdogs. Radical sociologists want to study "power elites," the leaders, or masters, of men; liberal sociologists focus their efforts upon underdogs and victims and their immediate bureaucratic caretakers.

For all its difficulties, Becker's position does provide a vantage point for a criticism of local managers of the Caretaking Establishment, of the vested interests and archaic methods of these middle dogs. This is all to the good. But this vantage point has been bought at a very high price. The price is an uncritical accommodation to the national elite and to the society's master institutions; and this is all to the bad.

There is, I think, one other way in which Becker's position is too glib. It is premised upon a conviction (or sentiment) to the effect that, as he says in *The Outsiders*, while it may be possible to see a situation from "both sides," this "cannot be done simultaneously." This means, explains Becker, that "we cannot construct a description . . . that in some way fuses perceptions and interpretations made by both parties involved in a process of deviance. . . . We cannot describe a 'higher reality' that makes sense of both sets of views." I assume this means that although the sociologist can, at some point, present the views of one group and then, at another point, present the views of a different group, that nonetheless, the sociologist's own standpoint—when he speaks in an omniscient voice—tends inevitably to favor one of these sides more than the other, to present one side more attractively than the other. This frank confession of human fallibility is so appealing that it seems almost churlish to question it. But I do.

One reason that Becker sees no way out of this impasse

is because he is committed to a kind of interpersonal social psychology which, with all its humanistic merits, fails to see that men—superiors as well as subordinates—may be powerfully constrained by institutions, by history, and indeed by biology. Becker's position is largely that of the undefeated, pragmatic, historyless and still optimistic American to whom "everything is possible" in man-to-man, and manly encounter. If, however, we acknowledge that superiors no less than subordinates live within these limits—which may not be impossible to penetrate, but only costly to do so—we do not, I think, degrade their humanity but rather sensitize ourselves to it. We may then see that the issue not only entails a conflict between superiors and subordinates but a larger kind of human struggle. Such a perspective does not require us to restrain our sympathy for the underdog or ignore his special plight, but gives us a broader comprehension of it. To have a sense of man's common humanity does not demand a superhuman capacity to transcend partisanship. But a partisanship that is set within the framework of a larger humanistic understanding is quite different from one devoid of it. This is one difference between the merely political partisanship of daily involvements, and the more

> "Older men today are often constrained to surrender wide discretionary power to their juniors, if they are to keep them in today's seller's market in social research. The irony of the matter, then, is that the more successful the older man is in funding his research, the less successful he may be in having it conducted according to his lights: the research is less likely to be 'his.' "

reflective and tempered partisanship which may well be such objectivity of which we are capable.

There are works of art that manifest this objective partisanship. The dramas of the great classical tragedians are magnificent case in point. What makes them great is their objectivity; and what makes them objective is their capacity to understand even the nobility of their Persian enemies, even the dignity of their "barbarian" slaves, even the bumbling of their own wise men. They do indeed express a viewpoint which in some sense does take the standpoint of both sides, and does so simultaneously. If great art can do this, why should this be forbidden to great social science? That it is not common is precisely what makes its accomplishment an expression of greatness.

Despite the inevitability of bias and the unavoidability of partisanship, the fact remains that two researchers may have the same bias but, nonetheless, may *not* be equally objective. How is this possible? Becker notes "that our unavoidable sympathies do not render our results invalid" and that, despite them, research must meet "the standards of good scientific work." This does not clarify the issue as much as we might wish, for there never was any suggestion that partisanship impaired the "validity" of research. There is also no doubt that partisanship does not necessarily impair the "reliability" of a research. The validity and reliability of researches are matters quite apart from their *objectivity*.

And it is primarily this last concern which is engaged when the problem of partisanship is raised. The question here is only whether partisanship necessarily vitiates objectivity, and, this in turn requires that at some point we clarify our conception of objectivity and of how it may be attained.

Once Again: The Problem of Objectivity

How, then, does Becker seek to enhance the objectivity of even partisan research? His views concerning this are sketchy in the extreme. Although he speaks of a need to maintain scientific standards, he quickly recognizes that there is no way in which we can be sure that sociologists will *apply* these standards "impartially across the board." He also expresses the qualified hope that, over the years, the accumulation of "one-sided" studies will gradually produce a more balanced picture of a social situation; but he also recognizes that this does not help the individual researcher in the here and now.

The remedies in which Becker apparently reposes greater confidence consist rather of two other things. First, he recommends that we honestly confess the partisan position we have adopted, openly acknowledging that we have studied the problem from the standpoint of only certain of the actors involved and not of all. Considering that Becker has himself refused openly to acknowledge his own underdog standpoint, this solution to the problem of objectivity is not entirely confidence inspiring. Secondly, Becker also recommends—and it is this that he seems to feel most strongly about—the avoidance of "sentimentality," whatever that may mean.

For my part, it seems to me that other things might be done.

For one, I would encourage a condemnation of complacency rather than of sentimentality. For it is complacency which allows us to think, *á la* Myrdal, that we have solved the problem of objectivity by good-naturedly confessing that, yes, we do indeed have a standpoint and by openly specifying what it is. Confession may be good for the soul, but it is no tonic to the mind. While the "heart may have reasons of its own," when it simply chooses to assert these without critical inspection, then reason must condemn this as complacency. Of course, it is a good thing for sociologists to know what they are doing; and it is a good thing for them to know and to say whose side they are on. But a bland confession of partisanship merely betrays smugness and naiveté. It is smug because it assumes that the values that we have are good enough; it is naive because it assumes that we know the values we have. Once we recognize that complacency is the mind's embalming fluid and once we move to overcome it, we are then forced to ask, what is it that is now making us so complacent?

The complacency of Becker and of his school of deviance derives in large measure from its own unexamined, comfortable commitment to political liberalism. It has wrapped

"... the new funding situation may simply mean that the younger men have only exchanged one master for another: for even if they are no longer subjected to the direct pressure of senior professors, they may now be subjected to the direct pressure of the funding agencies."

itself in the protective covering of the liberal Establishment which dominates American sociology today, as well as American academic life in general. Becker blandly acknowledges, without making the least effort to explore its appre-

ciable consequences, that "it is no secret that most sociologists are politically liberal . . ." But it is complacency to allow ourselves to be appeased by a confession of the commonplace. To confess that most sociologists are politically liberal is like "confessing" that men are conceived in sexual intercourse. The question is whether Becker sees any *consequences* in the thing confessed. Without considering these, confession becomes a meaningless ritual of frankness.

The important problem is the exploration of the ways in which the political liberalism of many sociologists today affects the worth, the scope, the bite, and the objectivity of their sociology. The very blandness of his confession implies that Becker fails to grasp that liberalism today is not simply the conscientious and liberating faith of isolated individuals. Political liberalism today instead verges on being an official ideology of wide sectors of the American university community as well as broader strata of American life. For many American academicians, liberalism has now become a token of respectability, a symbol of genteel open-mindedness, the fee for membership in the faculty club; in point of fact, liberalism is also an operating code that links academic life to the political machinery of the Democratic Party.

Far from being the conscientious code of isolated individuals, much of liberalism today is the well-financed ideology of a loosely organized but coherent Establishment. It is the dominant ideology of a powerful group that sprawls across the academic community; that is integrated with American politics; that has its opinion leaders in various publications; that has its heroes whose myths are recited. Liberalism, then, is the mythos of one of the dominating American establishments; it is not simply the hard-won faith of a happy few. As the ideology of an establishment, such official liberalism has things to protect. It has reasons to lie. It has all the social mechanisms available to any establishment by which it can reward those who tell the right lies, and punish and suppress those who tell the wrong truths. In its meaner moments, it is an intellectual Mafia. It is not only, therefore, as Becker says, that "officials must lie because things are seldom as they ought to be." Like any other member of an establishment, the sociologist who is a political liberal is expected to lie along with his fellow members of the Establishment, to feel the rightness of their cause and a responsibility for its success.

The bias of the sociologist, then, does not derive simply from the fact that it is inherent in the human condition or in sociological research. The sociologist also lies because he is a political person. It would seem, however, that sociologists have no right to be complacent about anything that they, more than others, should have good reason to know makes liars of them. They thus have no right to be complacent about the intellectual consequences of their own liberalism.

The complacency that oozes from Becker's discussion, the vapid frankness of its confessional style, rests upon a simple sociological condition: upon the fact that it is allied with official liberalism, is embedded in the liberal Establishment, and is supported comfortably by the welfare state.

This still leaves the question as to whether there is any road toward objectivity, and what direction it might take. In my view, the objectivity of sociologists is enhanced to the extent that they critically examine all conventional "hierarchies of credibility," including their own liberal "hierarchy of credibility," which is today as respectable, conventional, and conformist as any. Becker acknowledges that it is sometimes possible to "take the point of view of some third party not directly implicated in the hierarchy we are investigating." This would, indeed, he agrees, make us neutral to the contending groups in the situation under study. But, he adds, this "would only mean we would enlarge the scope of the political conflict to include a party not ordinarily brought in whose view the sociologist has taken." But isn't this precisely one possible meaning of an avenue toward objectivity?

Isn't it good for a sociologist to take the standpoint of someone outside of those most immediately engaged in a specific conflict, or outside of the group being investigated? Isn't it precisely this outside standpoint, or our ability to

---

"Overdogs in the welfare state—in Washington bureaucracies and New York foundations— are buyers of underdog research for much the same political reasons that the Johnson regime initiated the 'war on poverty.'"

---

adopt it, which is one source and one possible meaning of sociological objectivity? Granted, all standpoints are partisan; and, granted, no one escapes a partisan standpoint. But aren't some forms of partisanship more liberating than others? Isn't it the sociologists' job to look at human situations in ways enabling them to say things that are not ordinarily seen by the participants in them? This does not mean that the sociologist should ignore or be insensitive to the full force of the actors' standpoints. But it does mean that he himself must have a standpoint on their standpoint. Objectivity is indeed threatened when the actors' standpoints and the sociologists' fuse indistinguishably into one. The adoption of an "outside" standpoint, far from leading us to ignore the participants' standpoint, is probably the only way in which we can even recognize and identify the participants' standpoint. It is only when we have a standpoint somewhat different from the participants that it becomes possible to do justice to their standpoints.

There are, it seems to me, at least three other possible conceptions of sociological objectivity. One of these can be characterized as "personal authenticity" or "awareness," another can be termed "normative objectification," and the third may be called "transpersonal replicability."

To consider "normative objectification" first: when we talk about the bias or impartiality of a sociologist we are, in effect, talking about the sociologist as if he were a "judge." * Now, rendering a judgment premises the existence of conflicting or contending parties; but it does not imply an intention to *mediate* the difficulties between them. The function of a judge is not to bring parties together but is, quite simply, to do justice. Doing justice does not mean, as does mediation or arbitration, that both the parties must each be given or denied a bit of what they sought. Justice does not mean logrolling or "splitting the difference." For the doing of justice may, indeed, give all the benefits to one party and impose all the costs upon another.

What makes a judgment possessed of justice is not the fact that it distributes costs and benefits equally between the parties but, rather, that the allocation of benefits and costs is made in conformity with some stated normative standard. Justice, in short, is that which is justified in terms of some

* The next paragraph or so is indebted to the excellent discussion by Rostein Eckhoff, "The Mediator, the Judge and the Administrator in Conflict-Resolution," *Acta Sociologica*, Vol. 10, pp. 148–172.

value. The "impartiality" or objectivity of the judge is an imputation made when it is believed that he had made his decision primarily or solely in terms of some moral value. In one part, then, the objectivity of the judge requires his explication of the moral value in terms of which his judgment has been rendered. One reason why Becker's analysis founders on the problem of objectivity is precisely because it regards the sociologists' value commitment merely as an inescapable fact of nature, rather than viewing it as a necessary condition of his objectivity.

Insofar as the problem is seen as one of choosing up sides, rather than a working one's way through to a value commitment, I cannot see how it is ever possible for men to recognize that the side to which they are attached can be wrong. But men do not and need not always say, "my country right or wrong." Insofar as they are capable of distinguishing the side to which they are attached, from the *grounds* on which they are attached to it, they are, to that extent, capable of a significant objectivity.

It should again be clear, then, that I do not regard partisanship as incompatible with objectivity. The physician, after all, is not necessarily less objective because he has made a partisan commitment to his patient and against the germ. The physician's objectivity is in some measure vouchsafed because he has committed himself to a specific value: health. It is this commitment that constrains him to see and to say

---

"It is a sociology that succeeds in solving the oldest problem in personal politics: how to maintain one's integrity without sacrificing one's career, or how to remain a liberal although well-heeled."

---

things about the patient's condition that neither may want to know.

But in saying that the explication of the sociologist's value commitment is a necessary condition for his objectivity, we are saying little unless we recognize at the same time the grinding difficulties involved in this. For one, it is no easy thing to know what our own value commitments are. In an effort to seem frank and open, we all too easily pawn off a merely glib statement about our values without making any effort to be sure that these are the values to which we are actually committed. This is much of what happens when scientists conventionally assert that they believe only in "the truth." Secondly, a mere assertion of a value commitment is vainly ritualistic to the extent that the sociologist has no awareness of the way in which one of his commitments may conflict with or exclude another. For example, there is commonly some tension between a commitment to truth and a commitment to welfare. Third, we also have to recognize that the values in terms of which we may make our judgments may not necessarily be shared by the participants in the situations we have studied. Our objectivity, however, does not require us to share values with those we study, but only to apply the values that we claim are our own, however unpopular these may be. In other words, this form of objectivity requires that we be on guard against our own hypocrisy and our need to be loved. This creates a problem because the values we may actually hold may differ from those we feel that we must display in order to gain or maintain access to research sites.

To come to another meaning of sociological objectivity,

"personal authenticity." If the previous conception of objectivity, "normative objectification," emphasizes that the sociologist must not deceive *others* concerning the value basis of his judgment, then personal authenticity stresses that the sociologist must not deceive *himself* concerning the basis of his judgment. By personal authenticity or awareness, I mean to call attention to the relationship between the sociologist's beliefs about the actual state of the social world, on the one hand, and his own personal wishes, hopes, and values for this social world, on the other hand. Personal authenticity or awareness exists when the sociologist is

"Confession may be good for the soul, but is no tonic to the mind."

capable of admitting the factuality even of things that violate his own hopes and values. People do differ in this regard, some having a greater capacity and need for self-deception and others possessing less talent to attain the comforts born of such self-deception. Not all conservatives are equally blind to the fragility of the *status quo*; not all radicals are equally blind to its stability.

In this sense, then, one form of sociological objectivity involves the capacity to acknowledge "hostile information" —information that is discrepant with our purposes, hopes, wishes, or values. It is not the state of the world, then, that makes information hostile, but only the state of the world in relation to a man's wants and values. Here, then, objectivity consists in the capacity to know and to use—to seek out, or at least to accept it when it is otherwise provided—information inimical to our own desires and values, and to overcome our own fear of such information.

Both forms of objectivity imply a paradoxical condition: namely, that one cannot be objective about the world outside without, to some extent, being knowledgeable about (and in control of) ourselves. In normative objectification, one of the central problems is to *know* our values, and to see that such knowledge is problematic. In personal authenticity there is a need for a similar knowledge of the self, but for a knowledge that goes beyond values into the question of our brute impulses and of other desires or wants that we may not at all feel to be valuable. In both forms of objectivity, also, it would be foolhardy to expect that the requisite knowledge is acquirable through a simple process of frictionless "retrieval." Rather, we must expect that either form of objectivity entails some measure of *struggle* in and with the sociologist's self and, with this, a need for courage. It now should be clear why I have taken up the cudgels against complacency, for it is the very antithesis of the kind of moral struggle required for objectivity.

Professionalism and Objectivity

Insofar as the pursuit of objectivity rests upon what I must reluctantly call "moral character," we can also see another source from which sociological objectivity is deeply undermined today. It is undermined, from one direction, by a compulsive and exclusive cultivation of purely technical standards of research and of education, so that there is neither a regard nor a locus of responsibility for the cultivation of those very moral qualities on which objectivity rests. The truth is that to the extent that sociology and sociological education remain obsessed with a purely technical focus they have abdicated a concern with objectivity; it is

merely hypocritical for those with such a standpoint to enter occasional accusations about other's lack of objectivity.

A second basic inner locus for our default with respect to the problem of objectivity is the growing transformation of sociology into a profession. This may seem paradoxical again, for surely professions profess value commitments, at least to client, if not public, welfare. Professions, however, do not tend to see value commitments as questions of personal commitment but tend, instead, simply to treat the values they transmit as non-problematic givens. Most civic professions tend to take the larger culture and institutions in their society as given. But it is precisely the peculiar nature of the sociologist's task to be able to take them as problematic. The development of professionalization among sociologists deserves to be opposed because it undermines the sociologist's capacity for *objectivity* in any serious sense. In effect, the growth of professionalization means the substitution of a routine and banal code of ethics for a concern with the serious kind of morality on which alone objectivity might rest.

A third specific conception of objectivity common to many American sociologists—and so common, in fact, that even C. Wright Mills agreed with it—is what has been termed "transpersonal replicability." In this notion, objectivity simply means that a sociologist has described his procedures with such explicitness that others employing them on the same problem will come to the same conclusion. In effect, then, this is a notion of objectivity as technical routinization and rests, at bottom, on the codification and explication of the research procedures that were employed. At most, however, this is an *operational* definition of objectivity which presumably tells us what we must *do* in order to justify an assertion that some particular finding is objective. It does not, however, tell us very much about what objectivity *means* conceptually and connotatively. It says only that those findings which are replicated are to be considered to be objective.

It is quite possible, however, that any limited empirical generalization can, by this standard, be held to be objective,

"Whatever one's conclusions concerning the substantive issues, namely, whether Lee Harvey Oswald was the assassin, and whether or not he alone or in conspiracy with others murdered President Kennedy, one miserable conclusion seems unavoidable: that there was scarcely a civic profession—the military, the medical, the police, the legal, the juridical—that was not involved in suppressing or distorting the truth, and which did not bow obsequiously to power."

however narrow, partial, or biased and prejudiced its net impact is, by reason of its selectivity. Thus, for example, one might conduct research into the occupational-political distribution of Jews and come to the conclusion that a certain proportion of them are bankers and Communists. Given the replicability conception of objectivity, one might then simply claim that this (subsequently verified) finding is "objective," and this claim could be made legitimately even though one never compared the proportions of bankers and Communists among Jews with those among Protestants and Catholics. It might be said that, without such a comparison among the three religions, one would never know whether the proportion of bankers and Communists among Jews was higher or lower than that among Protestants and Catholics. But this objection would simply indicate the technical statistical condition that must be met in order to justify a statement concerning the Jewish *differential*. Insofar as one happens not to be interested in making or justifying a statement about this, the objectivity of the original statement remains defensible in terms of the technical conception of objectivity as replicability. Thus it would seem that the replicability criterion falls far short of what is commonly implied by objectivity.

This technical conception of objectivity is in part, but in part only, reminiscent of the manner in which Max Weber conceived of it. We might say that the current conception is a kind of mindless corruption of Weber's. Weber essentially thought of scientific objectivity as something left over. It was a residual sphere of the purely technical, a realm in which decisions should and could be made without thought of their ultimate value relevancies. Weber's approach to objectivity comes down to a strategy of segregation—the conscientious maintenance of a strict separation between the world of facts and the world of values. Weber's emphasis here, therefore, is not on the manner in which scientific objectivity depends upon value commitments; this tends tacitly to be assumed rather than deliberately insisted upon. Weber's stress is placed, rather, upon the separation and discontinuity of facts and values. As a result, one may come away believing that, to Weber, the objectivity of research need not be colored by the scientist's personal values or the manner in which these are arrived at and held. *En principe*, neither the sanity nor maturity of a scientist need affect his objectivity. The madman and the teenager can be as scientifically objective as anyone else in this view, so long as they adhere to purely technical standards of science, once having committed themselves to some problem. Weber's theory invites a fantasy that objectivity may, at some point, be surrendered entirely to the impersonal machinery of research.

The passionate artfulness with which Weber argues this case endows the world that he conjures in imagination to be mistaken for reality, and we may fail to notice just how *grotesque* this conjured world is. Actually, Weber's entire enterprise here is born of his attempt to overcome his conception of the world as grotesque by formulating a salvational myth of a value-free social science. Through this he strives to still his furious sense of uneasiness that the real world, in which science and morality do cohabit, is a world of mutually destructive incompatibles. Weber fantasies a solution in which facts and values will each be preserved in watertight compartments. The tensions and dangers of the conjunction of facts and values are to be overcome by a segregation of the sequential phases of research, so that: first, the scientist formulates his problem in terms of his value interests and, then, having done this, he puts his values behind him, presumably never again allowing them to intrude into the subsequent stage of technical analysis.

To overcome his experience of the world as grotesque, Weber formulates an incipient utopia in which the impure world is split into two pure worlds, science and morality. He then attempts to bridge the cleavage he has created by pasting these two purified worlds together, so that each is made sovereign in a different but adjacent period of time. The incongruity of the world has not so much been overcome as transcended in myth. The experienced unmanageability of the one world gives way to the promised manageability of the two worlds. The reality gives way to the myth, but the grotesqueness abides.

One central difference between Weber's and the current technical conception of objectivity is that Weber recognized that the technical sphere would have to be brought into some sort of alignment with the value sphere. The modern technical conception of objectivity, however, simply regards the value problem and its relation to the technical as either negligible or dull. It allows it to remain unclarified. The modern technical approach to objectivity also differs from the Weberian in a second way. The former takes it for granted that, somehow, social scientists will do the right thing. It assumes that, in some manner, there will be a mustering of motives sufficient to make social scientists conform with their technical standards and rules.

Commonly, the source of these motives is not explored. Sometimes, however, it is today held that the mutual inspection and the checks and balances of modern *professionalization* will suffice to keep social scientists honest. In short, it is assumed that the machinery of professionalism will make the machinery of science work.

This expectation underestimates the ease with which professionalism is corruptible as well as the power of the corrupting forces. Perhaps the most important example of this in the present generation was the work of the Warren Commission appointed by President Lyndon Johnson to investigate the assassination of President John Kennedy. Whatever one's conclusions concerning the substantive issues, namely, whether Lee Harvey Oswald was the assassin, and whether

> "A blind or unexamined alliance between sociologists and the upper bureaucracy of the welfare state can only produce the market research of liberalism."

or not he alone or in conspiracy with others murdered President Kennedy, one miserable conclusion seems unavoidable: that there was scarcely a civic profession—the military, the medical, the police, the legal, the juridical—that was not involved in suppressing or distorting the truth, and which did not bow obsequiously to power. And I am far from sure that this was always motivated by a concern for the national welfare. The more that the respectable professions are transformed from independent vocations into bureaucratic and federally sponsored dependencies the more corruptible they will be in the future. Those who think that professional associations and universities will immunize the professions from the pressures and temptations of power have simply not understood the revelations about the CIA penetration into these very associations and universities. For these show that they were willing and eager parties to their own corruption in the name of a well-financed patriotic devotion.

For his part, however, Weber never assumed that the technical machinery of science would be self-winding and self-maintaining. For Weber, the maintenance of objectivity at least required a persisting moral effort to prevent one's personal values from intruding into purely technical decisions. The machinery was really never thought of as operating successfully apart from men's characters. Weber premises that, even in the purely technical stages of later research, work will be subject to an ongoing superintendence by the social scientist's moral commitment to "truth." Since the continued force of this personal value is conceived to be compatible with the maintenance of technical standards, its significance is left unexplicated. It is only implicitly, therefore, that Weber indicates that the objectivity of research depends continuingly, and not only in the early problem-formulating stages, upon something more than the technical machinery of research.

The question arises, however, as to the meaning of this extra-technical, "transcendental" commitment to the truth. Does it entail anything more than a commitment to the segregation of facts and values? Either it has some meaning beyond this or it does not. If it does not, then we are still left wondering how and why social scientists may be relied upon to adhere to this very segregation of facts and values: What endows it with binding force? If it does, and if the "truth" that it demands is something more than the mere application of technical standards alone, then it must entail something more than a belief in reliability or validity. If "truth" is not merely a summarizing redundancy for these terms it must be embedded with some conception that embodies or resonates value commitments that call for something more than pure truth alone.

The pursuit of "truth for its own sake" is always a tacit quest for something more than truth, for other values that may have been obscured, denied, and perhaps even forbidden, and some of which are expressed in the quest for "objectivity." Objectivity expresses a lingering attachment to something more than the purely technical goods of science alone and for more than the valid-reliable bits of information it may produce. In this sense, "truth for its own sake" is a crypto-ethic, a concealment of certain other substantive values through a strategy that, leaving them entirely in the open, diverts attention from them to another dramatically accentuated valuable: truth. The old Druidic sacred place is not destroyed; it is merely housed in an imposing new cathedral. In affirming that he only seeks the truth for its own sake, the scientist is therefore not so much lying as pledging allegiance to the flag of truth, while saying nothing about the country for which it stands.

What are the other values that lie obscured in the long shadows cast by the light of pure truth? In Western culture, these often enough have been freedom—the truth will set you free—and power—to know, in order to control. Underlying the conception of truth as objectivity there is, however, still another value, a faint but enduring image of the possibility of *wholeness*. One obvious implication of objectivity has commonly been to tell the "whole" story. The longing here is to fit the partial and broken fragments together; to provide a picture that transcends the nagging sense of incompleteness; to overcome the multiplicity of shifting perspectives. Underlying the quest for objectivity, then, is the hope of dissolving the differences that divide and the distances that separate men by uniting them in a single, peace-bringing vision of the world.

In such a conception of objectivity there is, I suspect, the undertow of an illicit yearning that links science to religion. Perhaps this conclusion is an illusion. Worse still, perhaps it is "sentimental." Yet it will not seem so fanciful if it is remembered that the modern conception of an objective social science was born with early nineteenth century Positivism. This set itself the task of creating both an objective social science and a new religion of humanity, each informing the other and aimed at reuniting society. The objectivity of the new sociology was, from its very beginnings, not an end in itself; it was clearly aimed at the enhancement of human unity and it then had the most intimate connection with an openly religious impulse.

The conception of objectivity has commonly projected an image of the scientist as linked to a higher realm, as possessed of a godlike penetration into things, as serenely above human frailties and distorting passions, or as possessed of a priest-like impartiality. The realm of objectivity is the higher realm of *episteme*, of *wahrheit*, of *raison*, of Truth, which have always been something more than sheer information. In other words, the realm of objectivity is the realm of the *sacred* in social science. But why has the quest for this realm been encrusted under the defensive conception of truth for its own sake?

Essentially the fate of objectivity in sociology is linked with, and its fortunes vary with, the changing hopes for a peace-bringing human unity. Some power-tempted social scientists are simply no longer able to hear this music. Others may withdraw because their hope is so vital that they cannot risk endangering it by an open confrontation. For some, an open admission would be dissonant with their conception of themselves as tough-minded and hard-headed. Still others have a genuine humility and feel that the pursuit of this high value is beyond their powers. There are also some who doubt the very value of peace itself because, oddly enough, they want men to endure and to live, and they suspect that the successful quest for a peace-bringing unity spells death: they ask themselves, after unity and peace. what?

Perhaps what has been most discrediting to the quest for human unity is that, since its classical formulation, its most gifted spokesmen have often made totalitarian proclivities; they came to be viewed as enemies of the "open society," who denied the value and reality of human difference. In short, the plea for human unity has often, and quite justifiably, been interpreted as a demand for a tension-free society that was overseen by a close superintendence of men from nursery to graveyard, and was blanketed with a remorseless demand for conformity and consensus. What has really been discredited, however, was this chilling version of the dream of human unity, although it remains extremely difficult to extricate the larger hope from the nightmare form that it was given.

Whether objectivity is thought possible comes down then to a question of whether some vision of human unity is believed workable and desirable. It comes down to the question, as C. Wright Mills once said, of whether there is still some vision of a larger "public" whose interests and needs transcend those of its component and contending factions. In this sense, one possible meaning of objectivity in social science is the contribution it might make to a human unity of mankind. But to make such a contribution the social sciences cannot and should not be impartial toward human suffering; they must not make their peace with any form of human unity that complacently accommodates itself to or imposes suffering.

At the same time, however, an empty-headed partisanship unable to transcend the immediacies of narrowly conceived political commitment is simply just one more form of market research. A blind or unexamined alliance between sociologists and the upper bureaucracy of the welfare state can only produce the market research of liberalism. It rests upon the tacit, mistaken, but common, liberal assumption that the policies of this bureaucracy equitably embody the diverse interests of the larger public, rather than seeing that the bureaucracy is one other interested and powerful contending faction, and is more closely allied with some of the contenders rather than equally distant from all. It is to values, not to factions, that sociologists must give their most basic commitment.

116

[30]

Editors' introduction

Ian Taylor, Paul Walton and Jock Young

The politicization of social philosophy and the human sciences in general over the last decade, in particular, has been subject to considerable comment – most notably, so far as sociology is concerned, by Professor Alvin Gouldner. Few fields of inquiry have been left untouched. We are even witnessing attempts by radicalized natural scientists to unpack the political assumptions underlying the procedures of 'hard' science itself.

But in the area of criminology and deviancy theory, this process of politicization has arguably proceeded farther than in most other, previously 'non-political' areas. At least two reasons can be identified. On the one hand, there is the experience in the Western world of a vast increase in the range of social behaviours deemed appropriate for control *by law*; and, on the other, this experience has forced a reappraisal of the morality of the law being so extended.

Old laws have been reactivated, and new laws created, in order to contain and control (by threat if not actually by apprehension or symbolic prosecution) certain crucially socially-problematic behaviours. In Britain, new laws have been created (in the shape, most outstandingly, of the Industrial Relations Act) to regulate industrial dissent and the rights of workers to organize (and the first victims of associated picketing regulations have been sentenced to prison). Old laws have been resuscitated to enable the nebulous charge of conspiracy to be used against political dissenters; and, in the attempt to control 'squatting' (the possession of unoccupied housing by homeless families) the Forcible Entry Act, 1429, has proven to be a powerful weapon in the hands of local housing authorities. The Housing Finance Act has also created deviants (if not criminals) out of elected local councillors who have refused to implement central government directives to increase the rents in publically-owned housing. And the proposals of the Criminal Law Revision Committee, if implemented,

1

would substantially increase the legal powers of the police to seize and search citizens in everyday police–public interaction. In short, the extension of law has created new criminals, criminals who are no longer so readily identifiable with the stereotypical 'criminals' or 'delinquents' of orthodox 1950s criminology – the disaffiliated or disorganized urban working-class adolescent. The population at risk of criminalization is much more ambiguous and extensive, including not only the criminologist's own students (and the more 'bohemian' criminologist himself), but also the spokesmen and membership of the oppositional social, political and economic movements at large. So, for example, leaders of minority groups as far apart as the migrant grape workers of California and the tenants' associations in public housing in Britain have been increasingly harassed *by law*, and the attempt has been made to define their activities as criminal rather than as political in content.

This shift in the jurisdiction of law has had profound consequences in the teaching, the application, the legitimacy and the meaning of traditional criminology. It has become increasingly difficult to sustain the notion that criminality is a behavioural quality monopolized by a particular and narrow section of the lower class, a behaviour that is removed extraneously from our own everyday experience. The trend in criminology away from a focus on the juvenile 'in need of care, protection or control' towards social theories of rule-creation and rule-breaking, located in a wider, more complex moral and social dynamic, is well illustrated in the attempts by thinkers like Richard Quinney and William Chambliss to create a 'conflict theory' of crime (and law). Examples of their work are included in this volume as an indication of the ways in which the extension of *legal domination* has forced upon criminologists not only a broader subject-matter (a larger population at risk of apprehension), but also a more telling and immediate set of political dilemmas. The extension of law has charged criminologists with a moral responsibility they could often more easily avoid – the *evaluation* of the legal norms (and underlying morality) of a society that criminalizes activities developing out of the contradiction in its political economy. In Britain, the emergence of a critical criminology, moving beyond the confines of the administrative technology of the Home Office and its outposts, occurred slightly later than in America, possibly because of the existence in this country of a radical tradition and a Labour movement that was thought adequate by many for the resolution of the legal, political and economic contradictions of British society. Geoff Pearson's essay in this volume is an attempt to underline, in an historically informed manner, some of the legal, criminal and (notably) personal questions which that radical tradition now appears unable to confront – or, at least, to recognize as a politics in themselves. Jock Young's paper is an attempt to move beyond the kinds of questions that radical deviancy theory erected in reaction to the

2

'Fabianism' of orthodox, correctional criminology and social work, and to erect the elements of a criminology that was concerned, above all else, to act in defence of working-class interests.

It would be premature to suggest that a new 'critical criminological' paradigm has emerged in the West; and it would be even more absurd to believe that anything of the sort is even quiescent in the Soviet bloc, where (as Connor has so ably shown) the dominant criminologies are only now developing beyond the thesis that crime is a Western 'contamination' (Connor, 1972). The object of this volume, however, is to place on record some of the early attempts that are now being made, by radical thinkers and activists in North America and Europe, to transcend what Tony Platt calls the 'hip concerns' of the sociology of deviance, and to confront the facts of extension of law and the ensuing political dilemmas of the radical criminologist.

The early work in the radical criminological perspective is healthily diverse, and the papers collected here are an attempt at representativeness. Chambliss's paper, in this volume, is a valuable example of the conflict perspective's superiority over the 'functional' paradigms, so dominant in orthodox criminology, in pointing empirically to the criminalization of the lower-class populations of Nigeria and the USA by a corrupt political and economic élite. Quinney's essay, in contrast, is evidence of a logic in his work (and increasingly in that of other radical criminologists) that moves from an existentially-based 'conflict theory' (of the kind that we criticized in *The New Criminology*)[1] to a Marxist model of law-creation and crime. This move to a Marxist economism, in turn, highlights the need to incorporate the aetiological and other insights so derived with the libertarian and civil-rights concerns that inform the Schwendingers' much-quoted (though relatively inaccessible) attempt to formulate the elements of a radical *human-rights* criminology (first published in 1970 in *Issues in Criminology*). Tony Platt's overview of developments in radical criminology in the USA indicates that these concerns, of moving towards a materialist criminology, whilst retaining the diversity of human interests that for so long has been a part of American populist *and* New Left individualism, are at the forefront of the developing 'new' criminology in the USA in much the same way as they are in Britain and in Europe.

However, our intention in reprinting the debate between ourselves and Paul Hirst was to underline the fact that a return to Marx in criminology must inevitably raise the thorny issue of how one engages in the 'reading' of Marx. In an intellectual and political climate where 'Marxism' has so often been equivalent to Stalinism, European deviancy theorists have perhaps been more quizzical about the issues involved in Marxist interpretation than their American counterparts (whose problem has been one of overcoming a monolithic rejection of

3

Marxism in whatever form). One of the dominant tendencies in contemporary European Marxism (and perhaps *the* dominant tendency amongst Marxists concerned with 'cultural work' – on law, education or the media) is the structuralist Marxism of Louis Althusser (cf. Althusser, 1970, 1971). This reading of Marx denies the authenticity, and specifically the scientificity, of any reading other than its own. Concerned above all with the objective of social revolution (and arguing that this objective is attainable scientifically through correct theoretical practice), the Althusserians would find little time for the issue of *socialist diversity* we have raised in these pages. Marx's work on *man* (at the forefront of his earlier works and sustained in his later work on political economy) is relegated to the status of metaphysical speculation. The papers by Hirst are included because they constitute a developed attack on what Althusserians would see as the idealism (that is, the ontological concerns) of radical deviancy theorists, and because potentially they form the framework for a sophisticated 'criminology' that could be erected in the name of social defence – of State socialist societies. Even the new radical criminologists, with their turn to a materialist analysis of law, would recognize that such a criminology of social defence could be used, illegitimately, to justify a variety of repressive initiatives (e.g. psychiatric hospitalization of dissenters) carried through in the name of the 'socialist' State.

Critical criminology is still in its infancy, and unsurprisingly there are distinct tendencies within its ranks (some of which we discuss in chapter 1). We would, however, insist upon two unifying features in this international development. First, we would assert that the adequacy of the various theoretical offerings in critical criminology is to be assessed *in practice* – that is, in terms of their utility in demasking the moral and ideological veneer of an unequal society, and in terms of its ability to enliven the critical debate about the modes of change, and the post-capitalist alternatives, contemplated by those committed to a radical alternative (whether the agencies be intellectuals, workers or prisoners). In this respect, we would separate off our theoretical tendency from that of critical phenomenology – where the logic of investigation separates man from society, leaving the facts of imprisonment, criminalization and, in general, the forcible segregation of men *from* society unavailable for investigation or critique.

Secondly, we would distinguish our conception of critical criminology from the critical postures adopted by a few isolated criminologists at international and national congresses,[2] and in the literature, in recent years. It was undoubtedly correct of Professor Nagel, for example, to question the morality of the decision by the International Society for Criminology to hold its 1970 Congress in Madrid, and to use that platform to raise issues about omissions

4

in the subject-matter of criminology (Nagel, 1971). But instant exercises of this kind are not equivalent to the project of posing fundamental and consistent challenges to the everyday political assumptions, practices and implications of one of the most influential and State-dominated branches of applied social 'science' – the 'science' of criminology. It is to that endeavour that each of the contributors to this book is committed, and it is with this project in view that this volume of critical essays has been planned and produced.

Notes

1 I. Taylor, P. Walton and J. Young (1973). In part, this collection is intended as an extension of the 'immanent' critique of existing theories of crime and deviance developed in that text. (Cf. in this volume, in particular, chapters 1 and 2.)

2 The orthodox organizations of international criminology (which, by and large, are sponsored by governments and their law-enforcement agencies) have now been challenged by the establishment of the European Group for the Study of Deviance and Social Control (the first conference of which was held in Florence in September 1973). The influence and significance of these organizations will be discussed in the Introduction to H. Bianchi, M. Simondi, and I. Taylor, eds. (1975).

The End of Theory or Back to Beginnings

[31]

HELPING VICTIMS OF CRIME

The Home Office and the Rise of Victim Support in England and Wales

PAUL ROCK

Crime Surveys

The counting of crimes has long exercised governments. It has become quite conventional to attach political and social significance to the volume and movement of recorded crime. The very moral health of society has been measured by its crime rates. Yet it has also been recognized that those rates are an uncertain outcome of a chain of complicated decisions about the reporting and recording of ambiguous phenomena. Shifts in public tolerance, classification procedures, police practices, or insurance conditions can produce considerable changes in the official rates of crime.

The problem of uncertainty has been addressed in different ways. Government criminologists and statisticians have likened crime rates to an iceberg whose merest tip surfaces in the public statistics. Barely visible below the tip there is a 'dark figure' of unrecorded crimes which would have to be included in any accurate and scientific audit of criminality. The nearer measurement reaches back to the original uncontaminated incidents of crime, it has been argued, the more accurate will records be. Returning to victims and unveiling the dark figure would allow the 'real' extent, distribution, and trends of crime to be known.

The American National Crime Survey[225] was pioneered in 1966 and consolidated in 1972 in the National Crime Panel, a device by which the US Bureau of the Census surveys 60,000 households twice a year. It was the original survey which became a pattern for all the surveys that were to follow. Victims were to be surveyed in country after country.[226] It was as if a crime survey had become part of the equipment of a properly developed state.[227] The National Crime Survey was certainly

---

[225] See C. Kalish *et al.*, *Crimes and Victims*, Washington, DC, US Dept. of Justice, 1974.

[226] For a brief history of the Canadian victimization survey, see Rock, *A View from the Shadows*, ch. v.

[227] In a similar case, it has certainly been argued that the diffusion of policing had much to do with local and central Governments establishing forces as part of a drive

317

318   *The Home Office and Victims*

the prototype before the eyes of the RPU in the beginning of 1981,[228] when proposals were floated to mount a British crime survey.

Members of the RPU were aware of their counterparts' achievements in America, Canada, Holland, Australia, and elsewhere; they sought, as the phrase had it, 'to improve the criminal justice data base'; and they were persuaded that the future prosperity of the unit lay in the creation of large, well-funded, and continuing programmes of work. What was proposed was a smaller and more detailed version of the National Crime Survey, a 'sweep' of 10,000 households in England and Wales which would disclose the 'real' volume and distribution of crime. The utility of a survey was doubted at first by policy officials and Ministers[229]—just as in Canada, there was no little criticism voiced by members of the statistics department, the producer of the recorded crime statistics.[230] It was said that the survey would be too costly. The survey's objectives were unclear. Enough was known about crime; it was not necessary to learn more. Surveys would amplify the public fear of crime. The police would be hostile to a rival source of data that challenged the reliability of their own statistics.

The RPU's proposals had to be handled with delicacy. They were taken out into the world and subjected to a piece of theatre, the dramatization of a visibly objective judgement which would persuade key doubters inside the Home Office. A

---

to appear as modern and efficient as their neighbours. See E. Monkkonen, *Police in Urban America 1860–1920*, Cambridge, Cambridge Univ. Press, 1981.

[228] The formal invitation to a workshop to 'assess the value of mounting a national crime survey in England and Wales' stated that 'a number of countries have conducted surveys along the lines of the American National Crime Survey, and the possibility of conducting such a survey in this country has been frequently discussed within the Home Office' (letter of 5 Feb. 1981). For the Home Office's own brief history of crime surveys, see P. Mayhew *et al.*, *The 1988 British Crime Survey*, Home Office Research Study 111, London, HMSO, 1989, p. 1.

[229] See 'The Value of a National Crime Survey: A Discussion Paper', in *Crime Survey Workshop 6–8 April 1981*, London, Home Office, 1981.

[230] Involved members of the RPU noted that the 1981 criminal statistics contained a rather defensive passage, in which it was argued that the statistics 'do not, of course, show the total amount of crime committed in England and Wales... The propensity to report offences to the police could change over time and be influenced by changes in legislation.... However, recorded figures for individual offence groups have different and statistically seasonal patterns which have been consistent over a long period of time and this suggests that, in general, changes in recording patterns seem likely to be slow' (*Criminal Statistics England and Wales 1981*, London, HMSO, 1982, p. 28).

workshop of insiders, agencies, experts and sceptics was con-
vened in Cambridge in April 1981. There were criminologists,
specialists in social surveys, police officers, and government
officials. Representatives of victims support schemes, the
NAVSS, rape crisis centres, or women's refuges were *not* invited:
they were not taken to be authorities. The conception of victims
embodied in the planned survey was not theirs.

The authors of the National Crime Surveys and the Canadian
and Dutch surveys spoke. Professor Cherns, playing the role of
a sceptic, spoke. There were group discussions. The outcome,
said Mr Brennan, Deputy Under-Secretary at the Home Office
and one of the chief targets of the workshop, was the 'sense ...
that a survey should go ahead, but that was a decision which
would have to be taken elsewhere'.[231] Officials no longer
doubted, but surveys were still thought to be expensive and
risky, and 1981 was a period of financial restraint. It was an
accident which intervened to catalyse judgement, as is so often
the case in the policy-making process. The actual decision
to proceed with the first survey was taken in the immediate
aftermath of the civil disorders in Brixton, and some believed
it was affected by the need not to appear neglectful of research
on crime at such a difficult time. Officials and Ministers were
required to make a demonstration in a hurry, and they turned
to proposals that were usefully at hand. It had been just so with
the Canadian Urban Victimization Surveys in 1976: *they* were
part of a package to allay public fear about the imminent
abolition of capital punishment.[232]

What should be noted is that the British Crime Survey was
not supposed directly to help victims in 1981. Like its Canadian
counterpart, it began as an exercise in revealing the dark figure:
'the case for a *victimisation* component was [built on the argument that] ... victimisation surveys provided the best available
data for assessing the incidence of crime.'[233] Victims were not
needy supplicants but indices, an 'alternative'[234] measure of
crime, which would remedy the unreliability of police and
conviction statistics. To be sure, to the NAVSS and other
outsiders, counting victims could generate knowledge about

---

[231] *Public Surveys of Crime: Report of a Workshop*, London, Home Office, 1981, pp. 9–10.
[232] See Rock, *A View from the Shadows*, ch. v.
[233] *Public Surveys of Crime*, p. 1.
[234] M. Hough and P. Mayhew, *The British Crime Survey*, London, HMSO, 1983, p. 1.

320   *The Home Office and Victims*

victims,[235] but to the authors of the first crime survey it was nothing to do with the 'victims lobby', but about counting *crimes*.[236]

It was claimed that crime surveys would aid criminological theorizing, and most particularly the analysis of 'victim precipitation', an area once cultivated by victimologists.[237] They would show the circumstances and patterning of crime, differential rates of victimization, and the 'crime-proneness' of certain types of individual. Pat Mayhew, co-author of the first and second surveys, argued:

> The main rationale of victim surveys ... has been to get a better estimate of the number of certain crimes actually occurring than is available from offences recorded by the police. A second important aim has [been] to obtain better information about the nature of crime and who is most at risk.[238]

The survey was laid in the larger frame of concern about public confidence in the criminal justice system. Arguments for policies and proposals usually draw on politics currently favoured, even though they can sometimes appear strained in consequence. From the first, and partly as a counterweight to anxieties about the effects of baring the dark figure of crime,[239] it was said that the British Crime Survey would assuage public fear. A survey would supply a very different portrait of crime from that given by rumour and the mass media. Crime would be revealed as trivial, non-violent, and mundane, really not very threatening at all. It would be 'demystified'.[240] It was supposed that a new

[235] The NAVSS observed: 'we have been struggling to work out how many private victims of crime are known. ... The "dark figure" of crime suggests four times as many victims as were previously known' ('NAVSS contribution to the Study Day on the British Crime Survey, Policy Studies Institute, 28.4.1983', London, NAVSS, 1983).

[236] See P. Mayhew and M. Hough, 'The British Crime Survey: Origins and Impact', in M. Maguire and J. Pointing (eds.), *Victims of Crime: A New Deal?*, Milton Keynes, Open Univ. Press, 1988, p. 157.

[237] See L. Curtiss, 'Victim Precipitation', in S. Halleck *et al.* (eds.), *The Aldine Crime and Justice Annual 1974*, Chicago, Aldine, 1975.

[238] P. Mayhew, 'The Effects of Crime: Victims and the Public', 16th Criminological Research Conference, Strasbourg, Council of Europe, Nov. 1984, p. 2.

[239] There was some trepidation about the reception of the first British Crime Survey. The release was managed. It was arranged for an appropriate anticipatory question to be asked in the House of Commons, and a sympathetic report was published in the *Guardian*.

[240] Mayhew and Hough, 'The British Crime Survey', p. 157.

public awareness of the pettiness of most crime would, in its turn, support the wider drive of policies away from crime control and towards crime prevention.

The first British Crime Survey was conducted at the beginning of 1982, and the report was published a year later. It showed that the dark figure was large indeed. Eleven thousand randomly selected people had been interviewed about their exposure to crime in the previous year. Only 8 per cent of vandalism offences, 29 per cent of thefts from motor vehicles, 48 per cent of burglaries, 8 per cent of thefts from the person, 23 per cent of woundings, and 11 per cent of robberies had been recorded in the criminal statistics: there were four times as many crimes known to victims as there were recorded by the police. But it was also found that most of the unrecorded offences were very slight, and 38 per cent of them were not notified because they were 'too trivial, no loss or damage'.[241] Only 9 per cent of burglaries involved losses of more than £500. It could be claimed that the 'real message of the BCS is that it calls into question assumptions about crime upon which people's concern is founded. It emphasises the petty nature of most law-breaking.'[242] If the victim's lot were to be improved, 'there is scope for the police to improve their services . . .'.

The survey's special methodology produced an appropriate image of the victim. The victims of the British Crime Survey had not been asked about the emotional impact of crime. They had not been asked about victims support schemes. They had not been approached in the immediate aftermath of crime, and their interviews were relatively brief. It was about monetary and material losses that they were questioned by strangers, perhaps at some time after the event. They were not the people who poured out their distress before counsellors or therapists,[243] nor the shaken individuals seen by victims support scheme volunteers. Rather, just as the earlier proposals had anticipated, they had suffered rather trivial crimes[244] whose frequency was in inverse proportion to their gravity:[245] 'only a tiny proportion

---

[241] Hough and Mayhew, *The British Crime Survey*, p. 11.

[242] Ibid. p. 33.

[243] See M. Bard and D. Sangrey, *The Crime Victims Book*, New York, Basic Books, 1979.

[244] See Hough and Mayhew, *The British Crime Survey*, p. 33.

[245] Ibid. 7.

322   *The Home Office and Victims*

were crimes of serious violence and very few were serious property crimes such as burglary or car theft.'[246] To be sure, Hough and Mayhew *did* turn to Shapland and Maguire to acknowledge that 'a burglary can signify the destruction of a carefully constructed sense of order ... and an assault can eradicate all trust in strangers'.[247] But, in the main, victimization was depicted as an experience which was not particularly distressing, an occurrence so minor that many victims could not be bothered to report it. Indeed, far from being innocent and upset, victims themselves were often themselves complicit in crime. One of the authors of the survey concluded:

Crime *in its most typical form* does not usually have serious consequences at least as judged by the more objective indicators of loss or injury. It is usually non-violent, relatively petty in the harm caused, and ... quite likely not to be reported to the police.... Sound evidence of the extent of emotional upset is less available than most of the more emotive pro-victim writings might suggest.... The need for specialised, intensive and largely professional help in coping with the immediate aftermath of victimisation is in danger of being overstated.... I believe that the victims' lobby may with more emotion than judgement have exaggerated victims' needs for further assistance ... insofar as the victim movement has based its case on firm evidence at all, it has relied mainly on studies of serious victims...[248]

The NAVSS had not been consulted about the first Crime Survey. No copy of the first survey was sent to the NAVSS. The NAVSS was not named as one of the organizations or people with whose 'help, support and co-operation' the Survey 'came to fruition'.[249] Indeed, the introduction to the survey talked about 'wide-ranging programmes for victim assistance, particularly in Canada and the United States',[250] but it said nothing of victims support schemes in England and Wales. The 1982 survey was not pointed at the provision of better services for victims in England and Wales. The victim of the 1982 survey did not seem to suffer overmuch. The minutes of the policy advisory committee of the NAVSS commented: 'there was

[246] Ibid. 34.
[247] Ibid. 26.
[248] Mayhew, 'The Effects of Crime'.
[249] Hough and Mayhew, *The British Crime Survey*, p. iv.
[250] Ibid. 3.

much anger expressed at the Home Office's failure to acknowledge work done by Victims Support Schemes.'[251]

In 1982, then, the first Crime Survey constructed an image
of the victim chiefly as an index, as one who was often less
than innocent, a person whose sufferings had been somewhat
distorted by the lobbies. But by 1984 argument was starting to
coalesce so fast within the Home Office that the victims of the
second Crime Survey themselves underwent transformation.
Just as in Canada, the uses of crime surveys shifted rapidly, and
in sympathy with events elsewhere. What had started as a way
of counting crimes became, in part, a means of helping victims.
It had always been planned that the British Crime Surveys
'should have "bolt-on" components about current topics'.
Taking Account of Crime,[252] the main report of the second Survey
of early 1984, included questions framed by Maguire and
Mayhew on the effects of crime and victims support schemes.
Its authors remarked: 'many crime surveys, and especially the
BCS, do not simply count crimes, but collect additional information about crime and victims. . . . At a time when victims are
receiving increasing attention, surveys are proving a valuable
research tool.'[253] Hough and Mayhew recognized that 'a sample
survey, with its structured format, is not necessarily the best
instrument for disentangling reactions which are complex and
often hard to articulate'.[254] Other methods produce results with
'different emphases'.

The second British Crime Survey *did* explore the impact of
crime, and it reported that some 8 per cent of victims of
burglary, robbery, and snatch theft said that they had suffered
from depression and allied emotional problems. Burglary and
robbery victims reported that the worst problems of victimization were emotional. Only 1 per cent of victims had been
given an offer of help by victims support schemes, but nearly a
third said that they had heard of such schemes, and 40 per cent
believed that all victims *should* be contacted. There was 'a high
level of support for the notion of Victims Support Schemes . . .
there seemed strong support for Victims Support Schemes.

[251] Minutes of meeting held on 1 Mar. 1983.
[252] M. Hough and P. Mayhew, *Taking Account of Crime: Key Findings from the 1984
British Crime Survey*, London, HMSO, 1985.
[253] Ibid. 2.
[254] Ibid. 29.

324   *The Home Office and Victims*

Those most inconvenienced and upset by victimization were most likely to say they would have found the services of a scheme helpful.'[255]

Just as in Canada, policies began to merge, meanings changed, and the Crime Surveys were beginning to be portrayed as vehicles for learning about how to assist victims of crime.

[255] Hough and Mayhew, *Taking Account of Crime*, pp. 31, 52.

[32]

Solicitor General Solliciteur général
Canada Canada

Canadä

CANADIAN URBAN VICTIMIZATION SURVEY

Victims of Crime

Bulletin

1

Victims of Crime:

Preliminary Findings of the Canadian Urban Victimization Survey

Until recently, little could be said with confidence about which Canadians were most likely to be victimized by crime or even how many were victimized. Crime statistics such as the Uniform Crime Reports give virtually no information on the victims of crime nor on the incidence of crimes not reported to the police.

Early in 1982, however, the Ministry of the Solicitor General with the assistance of Statistics Canada conducted a victimization survey in seven major urban centres: Greater Vancouver, Edmonton, Winnipeg, Toronto, Montreal, Halifax-Dartmouth, and St. John's. The Canadian Urban Victimization Survey provides the most extensive information yet produced concerning the extent of reported and unreported crime during 1981, the risk of criminal victimization, the impact of crime, public perceptions of crime and the criminal justice system and victims' perceptions of their experiences.

1983

During January and February of 1982, Statistics Canada interviewers conducted telephone interviews with a large sample of residents[1] aged 16 and older in the seven urban centres. People under 16 were not interviewed, nor were their personal victimizations reported by others. To maximize reliability of recall, respondents were asked to report on only those incidents which had occurred between January 1 and December 31, 1981.

Because of the very low incidence of some types of crime (such as sexual assault), very large samples are required to ensure that enough cases are "caught" to be statistically representative of all actual cases in the community under study. Sample sizes ranged from 6,910 in one city to 9,563 in another, with more than 61,000 interviews completed overall. Costs of such a large survey would have been prohibitive if face-to-face interviewing methods had been used. On the basis of these interviews, statistical estimates were made for the general population 16 and over in the seven cities. These statistically derived estimates for the population are used throughout this report.

Victimization surveys can provide information about most, but not all types of crimes which are of major concern to the general public. Crimes such as murder, kidnapping, and "victimless" crimes cannot be captured using survey techniques, and were therefore excluded. Crimes committed against commercial establishments were also excluded from this particular survey.

The eight categories of crimes included in this survey are: sexual assault, robbery, assault, break and entry, motor vehicle theft, theft of household property, theft of personal property and vandalism. These offences are ranked in descending order of seriousness.

Incidents which involved the commission of several different criminal acts

appear in the tables only once, according to the most serious component of the event. Thus for example, if sexual assault, theft of money and vandalism all occurred at the same time, the incident would be classified in these tables as sexual assault. An incident would be classified as vandalism (least serious on the hierarchy) only if no other crime which is higher on the seriousness scale occurred at the same time.

Analyses in this report are based on the general offence categories outlined above. At a later date it will be possible to make more refined distinctions between and within offence categories according to other factors such as: whether the incident was only attempted or completed; amount of damage, injury or financial loss incurred; type of weapon used; response of victims; location and time of offence; number of offenders; number of victims; characteristics of offenders; characteristics of victims.

Uniform Crime Reports and Victimization Surveys

One of the persistent problems faced by law enforcers, policy makers and researchers alike has been the inability to determine accurately the incidence and distribution of crime in the community. Although Uniform Crime Reports now provide national police statistics which are based upon standardized definitions of crimes and standardized counting procedures, a significant gap is still known to exist between the number of crimes recorded in these reports, and the number which actually occur.

We know that there are regional and inter-category variations in victim and witness reporting practices, and in police recording practices, but until now no serious attempt has been undertaken to measure these differences in Canada.

Data obtained from victimization surveys provide an important complement to official police statistics because the issue of the so-called "dark" number of actual crimes is addressed directly. Victims are asked to describe both reported **and** unreported incidents in which they have been victimized, and to give their reasons for non-reporting. Such information allows us to examine variations in reporting rates, allows some measure of how victims define incidents, and generally provides us with a better understanding of the functioning of the criminal justice system from the

perspective of the victim than has previously been possible.

As mentioned earlier, certain crimes such as murder or white collar crime cannot be captured using survey techniques and are therefore ommitted, and the range of victims is similarly restricted. In the present survey, for example, incidents involving victims who live outside the survey area, victims who have no telephones or victims who are under 16 years of age are excluded. Similarly, our data include crimes committed against residents of the seven urban centres wherever these crimes may have occurred, but do not include crimes against non-residents (tourists or commuters) which may have occurred while they were in the city, or crimes which have been committed against businesses or public property.

---

[1] *The survey excluded commercial and institutional telephones. For a detailed discussion of the methodology used, consult the forthcoming report from the Ministry of the Solicitor General, "Measuring Crime and Victimization".*

Table 1

Seven Cities

Incident Rates

Personal Offences

Population aged 16 and older in seven cities = 4.975.900
Males = 2.357.000
Females = 2.618.900

Type of Incident	Estimated Incidents	Rates per 1000 Population 16 and older		
		Total	Males	Females
- All personal incidents	702,200	141	154	129
- All violent incidents	352.300	70	90	53
- Sexual Assaults	17,200	3.5	0.8	5.8
- Robbery	49.400	10	13	7
- Assault	285.700	57	79	39
- Personal Theft	349.900	70	66	74

Household Offences

Total households in seven cities = 2.424.900

Type of Incident	Estimated Incidents	Rate per 1000 Households
All household incidents	898.400	369
Break and Enter	227.400	94
Motor Vehicle Theft	40.600	17
Household Theft	417.300	172
Vandalism	213.100	88

Table 2

Seven Cities

Number of Incidents of Selected Types and Proportion not Reported to Police

Type of Incident	Estimated Incidents	Percent of Estimated Incidents	Percent Unreported	Percent Reported
Sexual Assault	17,200	1	62	38
Robbery	49.300	3	55	45
Assault	285,700	18	66	34
Break & Enter	227.400	14	36	64
Motor Vehicle Theft	40.600	3	30	70
Household Theft	417.300	26	56	44
Personal Theft	349.900	22	71	29
Vandalism	213.100	13	65	35
TOTAL	1.600.500	100	58	42

from the suffering caused by their actual material loss. This invasion of one's home often produces a heightened concern about and fear of crime more generally

Who are the Victims?

When incidents are divided into the two general categories of personal offences and household offences it is possible to calculate rates per thousand population or per thousand households. Table 1 and Figure 1 show that about 70 incidents of personal theft per thousand population aged 16 and older occurred in the seven cities studied, and that the more serious the type of incident, the less likely it was to occur. Sex differences are considerable for each category. Not surprisingly, women are about seven times more likely than men to be victims of sexual assault (including rape, attempted rape, sexual molesting and attempted sexual molesting), but they are also more likely than men to have their personal property stolen (theft of personal property). Men are almost twice as likely as women to be victims of robbery or assault (Figure 2).

Risk of victimization is closely tied to age. Contrary to popular belief, however, elderly people are relatively unlikely to be victimized by crime. Those under 25 had the highest rate of victimization in all categories of personal offences, and these high rates decline rapidly with increasing age after this point (Figures 3 and 4). In fact, the actual sample counts of sexual assault and robbery incidents for those over 60 were so low that estimated numbers and rates are unreliable.

The relationship between income and victimization is more complex. As one might expect, the higher the family income of urban residents the more likely they will experience some form of household victimization or personal theft. Furthermore, there may be differences among income groups in their levels of tolerance for and awareness of some types of incidents. For example, higher income residents may be more sensitive to and angered by incidents of vandalism than are lower income residents. However, lower income individuals are as likely or more likely than others to suffer a personal violent victimization – sexual assault, robbery or assault.

[33]

Introduction

Trevor Jones, Brian MacLean
and Jock Young

In 1985 the London Borough of Islington commissioned the Middlesex Polytechnic Centre for Criminology to undertake a crime survey of the Borough. The Islington Crime Survey (ICS) was the culmination of over a decade of British work in the field and a direct descendant of the pioneering National Crime Surveys begun in the United States during the Kennedy–Johnson administrations.

It is no accident that the notion of the mass victimization study as a guide to public policy was innovated in the 1960s by an American Democratic Party committed, at home if not abroad, to what Alan Phipps has rightly called "a vision, social democratic in all but name, of social justice as a necessary basis for social order" (1986, p101). It is perhaps no coincidence that such a technique, sharpened and refurbished, should be brought into play in the mid-1980s in an inner-city area of London by a council committed to a radical socialist programme. Indeed, when one reads Ramsey Clark, the Attorney-General of the period, lambasting against crime, one detects a sentiment in 1970 which pervades the work of the new radical, realist approach to crime today (see Lea and Young, 1984; Young, forthcoming)

> "While on the average a citizen may be the victim of violent crime only once in 400 years, there are indications that the poor black urban slum dweller faces odds five times greater – one in eighty. Since violent crimes are more frequently unreported in the slums, the chance of being a victim there may be substantially higher. If only one-fourth of the violent crime of the ghetto is reported, which is quite possible, the odds for those living there of being a crime victim within a year are one in twenty.
>
> The white middle class city dweller by contrast is likely to be the victim of violent crime at the rate of once every 2,000 years, while upper middle class income and rich suburbanites have one chance in 10,000 years." (R. Clark, 1970, p50).

If you add to the concern for blacks as victims a concern for the working class, for the poor, for the vulnerable and for women, you have an understanding of the realist approach to crime today.

Victimization studies on a national scale arose in the United States in the context of a criminology which was social democratic. It located the

2   *Introduction*

causes of crime in relative deprivation; it saw the role of the state as intervening in the cause of social justice; and it declared a war on poverty
which also embraced a war on crime. Both offender and victim were located in the same structural context, i.e. the lack of opportunities in a
society with extraordinarily high ideals of achievement yet very limited
social mobility. And for a short while, interest in the causes of crime *and*
victimization coexisted in the same theoretical and political framework
(see J. Young, 1986a). But none of this was to last. The move to the right
in American politics was accompanied by the rise of a new administrative
criminology: a criminology no longer interested in causality but focussing
almost solely on matters of social defence and control.

As is argued in *Realist Criminology* (J. Young, forthcoming), the
reason victimization studies began to proliferate in the United States was
qualitative as well as quantitative. The rapidly emerging paradigm of the
new administrative criminology swept all before it. It absorbed victimization studies quite naturally: they provided a mapping of the problem
areas which it was necessary to administer. The victim surveys were, on
the one hand, just what was needed for the natural growth of administrative criminology but, on the other, they caused no anomalies: they assimilated easily into this new paradigm. To a criminology which was interested solely in the problem of where to administer and where to apply resources in the endless and never-to-be-won war against crime, they were
indispensable yet uncontroversial. At no point did they raise the question
of why the patterns of victimization were such – why the structures of
society *caused* crime to appear in one place rather than another and what
could be done to eliminate such patterns of injustice.

If the new administrative criminology moved into the ascendant in the
1970s – both in the United States and Britain – what of radical criminology, the competing paradigm of the period? David Friedrichs, in his
survey of the relationship between a radical perspective and the emerging
discipline of victimology, noted that it was remarkable that victimology
and radical criminology emerged and flourished at exactly the same time,
but: "the two developments . . . have proceeded quite independently of
each other, with little if any reciprocal influence" (1983, p23). He is quite
right, of course. There was not at first much immediate contact between
the two sub-disciplines as they are conventionally constructed. Radical
criminology, after all, was committed to locating the *causes* of crime
within the wider social structure whereas victimology, as it had developed
within the rubric of the new administrative criminology, was concerned
merely with mapping the field for the purposes of prevention and control.
The two paradigms were not talking the same language. But the influence
of the victim was not absent in radical criminology, for very early in the
period a radical victimology had emerged. Friedrichs' myopia regarding
this is simply an inability to look in the direction from which it was coming. That direction was the women's movement. Studies of domestic viol-

Introduction 3

ence, rape, and sexual harassment have been central to the feminist case since the mid-sixties. Feminist victimology was to create enormous theoretical problems for the radical paradigm in criminology, just as feminism as a whole generated very creative debates for socialist thought in general.

Radical criminology had tended to focus on crimes of the powerful and on the way in which vulnerable groups in society are criminalized. All very worthy stuff, but the traditional concern of criminology – crimes occurring within and between the working class – was a conceptual no-go area (see A. Phipps, 1981). This was part of a general tendency in radical thought to idealize their historical subject (in this case the working class) and to play down intra-group conflict, blemishes and social disorganization (see J. Young, 1986b). But the power of the feminist case resulted in a sort of cognitive schizophrenia amongst radicals: they accepted that there were grave problems for women – for example in the inner city – but remained reluctant to see other sorts of crime (eg burglary and assault) as being of great importance. Indeed, the tendency was to see working class crime as only a minor irritant in urban life when compared to the other myriad problems, and to view much of the fear of crime as a "moral panic" fanned by the mass media.

But once breached by the feminists, the walls of the radical paradigm became increasingly vulnerable to the abrasive intrusions arising from the conventional victimization studies. For if victimology created no anomalies for those theoreticians who sought to administer the system – merely providing them with better maps of the problem areas – it created enormous problems for those who worked to change it. In this fashion, both feminist and conventional victimization studies became a central problematic for radical criminology. Thus the results of the studies which chart the high victimization rates of women in terms of male violence raise immediately the problems of a patriarchial social criss-cross cutting problems of class. The insistent findings from conventional victimology of the intra-class and intra-racial nature of much crime pointed to a degree of disorganization, particularly within the working class, which creates self-inflicted wounds outside of those already generated by the corporations, the police and the courts. It was in this theoretical context that radical realism arose within criminology. At heart, this started from the premise of taking people's fear of crime seriously and arguing that these were more realistic than either radical or conventional criminologists made out (see Kinsey, Lea and Young. 1986). Further, criminology must embrace the totality of the criminal process: it must be true to its *reality*. And this reality must include the offender, the victim, informal social control and the state (eg policing). These are the four dimensions of criminology. Victimization studies fit into this paradigm to the extent that they indeed represent an audit of people's experiences, anxieties and problems of crime. Further, as victimization studies extended themselves

4   *Introduction*

from a study of the victims to that of the police, to public attitudes to penality etc., they began to provide the sort of empirical basis necessary for a realist criminology.

Let us turn now to the development of criminal victimization studies in Britain, noting that here, as in the United States, the predominant paradigm was administrative criminology.

The history of victimization studies in Britain is not a long one, but once started the process has proceeded fairly rapidly. The first major study was the pioneering work of Sparks, Genn and Dobb (1977), the main aim of which was to test methodology and technique. Then in 1982 the first large scale national survey was carried out in England and Wales, *The British Crime Survey* (BCS) (Hough and Mayhew, 1983), and in Scotland (Chambers and Tombs, 1984). The second sweep of the BCS occurred in 1984 (Hough and Mayhew, 1985). But a particular problem of national surveys – however useful – was their lack of detail and their inability to deal with the fundamental fact that crime is both geographically and socially focussed (see Lea and Young, 1984). This was recognized by the Home Office: "As the BCS is a national survey, it cannot provide detailed information about the extent and impact of crime in particular neighbourhoods or communities. However, crime tends to be geographically concentrated and its impact in those places is thus correspondingly more severe" (HORU, 1984, p5). For this reason the British Home Office encouraged local surveys and indeed helped finance two: a study of Nottinghamshire and adjacent counties (Farrington and Dowds, 1985) and Merseyside (Kinsey, 1984). The Nottinghamshire study deals brilliantly with the problem of the lack of relationship between crimes recorded by the police and the actual extent of crime in order to explain why a fairly peaceful county like Nottinghamshire tops the "league table" of crime with rates equal to Merseyside and London. The Merseyside Crime Survey (MCS), jointly funded by Merseyside County Council, was a local crime survey with the more conventional aim of mapping crime in Liverpool and the surrounding areas. This survey involved R. Kinsey from the Centre for Criminology, Edinburgh as director and two members of the Centre at Middlesex as consultants (see R. Kinsey, J. Lea and J. Young, 1986). The Islington Crime Survey followed the MCS a year later – the two questionnaires being developed together and overlapping to a high degree.* Of considerable influence on these questionnaires was the work of the Policy Studies Institute on Londoners' attitudes to and experience of the Metropolitan Police (see D. Smith, 1983a and 1983b).

The MCS and ICS questionnaires are hybrids constructed very largely out of the two British Crime Surveys on crime and the PSI study on policing. As second generation victimization studies, this construction emphasizes their movement away from a predominant interest in victimization to include actual responses to crime by the police and public

Introduction 5

evaluation and expectations of police performance. In addition they include, as did the BCS, questions of penality as a further enlargement of
the scope of the victimization survey. Innovations in the ICS are questions on sub-legal harassment (eg being followed, stared at, shouted at in
the street), a documentation of interracial incidents and questions on
heroin use and on victimization and political affiliations. These two local
studies are not only considerably more focussed than the national studies
but embrace a much greater part of the whole process of criminalization –
namely, the pattern of victimization, the impact of crime, the actual
police response to both victim and offender, the public's requirements as
to an ideal police response and the public's notions of appropriate
penalties for various offences. If the aim of a realist criminology is to encompass the total scope of this process then these new-style surveys go a
long way towards providing the necessary empirical base.

What is unique about ICS is that it is the only study (certainly in Britain
and most probably in the US) *of this width* to focus solely on an inner-city
area. The term "inner city" is, of course, frequently ill-used. Many inner-
city areas – like Kensington and Chelsea in London – are far from deprived and include the most desirable residences of the entire city. But
Islington is undoubtedly an impoverished area. Despite pockets of gen-
trification and enclaves of Georgian grandeur there is a high level of
poverty. At least 18 per cent of the working population is unemployed
and 67 per cent of *households* have annual incomes of less than £8,000 –
compared to 60 per cent for the whole of Greater London. According to
the Department of the Environment, Islington is the seventh most deprived area in England and the fifth worst area where housing is concerned. Between 3,000 and 4,000 households live in overcrowded conditions and approximately 6,000 households share a bath and toilet.
There are 7,000 people on the council house waiting list and 9,000 people
waiting for a transfer to better accommodation. Thirty people register as
homeless every week and this figure excludes single people and childless
couples who are not considered to be in "priority need". In terms of social
care, Islington has a higher percentage of children in residential or foster
homes than the whole of Greater London.

* The main differences between the MCS and ICS questionnaire are that the
latter included questions on police malpractices (derived from the PSI study) and
on interracial incidences, on heroin use and on political affiliation and victimization (the latter three areas being innovations) and knowledge of other people
who had crimes committed against them (from the BCS). Less important items
are that the ICS contained questions on frequency of leaving the home, security
locks, and hypothetical response to overhearing people planning a break-in
which were omitted in the MCS, whereas public estimation of graded police response to various crimes was not included in the ICS. The ICS and MCS surveys,
therefore, overlap to a 90 per cent extent and both are comparable with much of
the BCS and PSI databases.

6   *Introduction*

The ICS is able to focus on such a deprived area, with its high crime rate and break down the incidence of victimization and police–public encounters by subgroup, based on age, gender, income and race.

We have described the theoretical perspective out of which a realist criminology emerged. Let us close this introduction by noting the political context in which a radical council ended up commissioning a crime survey. First of all, it had become increasingly obvious that there was an extraordinary hiatus in Labour Party policy over crime. Despite the fact that socialist administrations control virtually every inner-city high crime area in Britain (as is true, incidentally, of most of Europe), the Labour Party had come to regard law and order as the natural and exclusive realm of Conservatives. The question is how to develop policies which help protect women, ethnic minorities and the working class – those who suffer most from the impact of crime – who are the natural constituents of Labour, whilst refusing to accept the draconian policing policies and penal practice of the Tories. That is, how to develop policies which protect and give succour to the victims of crime, who are all the more affected because of their vulnerable position in the social structure, whilst controlling the urban offender who is himself often a product of the same oppressive circumstances. To do this demands humane policies which accurately reflect people's needs, which are guided by the facts and which can be monitored effectively. All of this is provided by the local crime survey. The second political circumstance was the need to have some objective assessment of police–public relations, a gauge of the efficacy of existing police methods and a measure of public demands as to the sort of service they would ideally want. And this endeavour to construct independently a public audit of police behaviour must be seen in the context of the current debate in Britain about the need for democratically accountable police authorities (see Lea and Young, 1984).

Thus the local survey fits into the upsurge in demand for the democratization of public institutions and the need to fit policy to public demand, particularly in the context of a decentralization of power. As such, the lessons to be learnt from such surveys both about crime and policing have a purchase outside of the context of a particular inner-city London Borough. They are essential in formulating and implementing policy in this vital area and the results can be applied to the urban heartlands of all Western industrial societies.

4

Biosocial Factors and Primary Prevention of Antisocial Behavior

Sarnoff A. Mednick

Methods of Primary Prevention

There are parallels which can be drawn between science's struggles to control disease and its struggles to control crime. The two approaches share failures which stem in part from a similarity of approach. A good point in case is science's triumph in dealing with pneumonia. As Gruenberg (1977) has pointed out, before 1936 individuals who suffered from chronic incurable ailments typically did not die of those ailments. Instead they died of secondary terminal infections, chiefly pneumonia. In 1936 the mortality rate for pneumonia was 65 per 100,000. But in 1936 sulfanilamide was discovered. By 1940 the mortality rate from pneumonia had dropped to 20 per 100,000, and by 1949 to 10 per 100,000. Science had triumphed. But in the days before sulfanilamide, physicians typically called pneumonia "the old man's friend" because it frequently mercifully carried off a sufferer from an incurable chronic illness. Today these sufferers live on so that in effect the advent of sulfanilamide (followed by penicillin, aureomycin, and terramycin) has increased the number of sufferers and the amount of suffering. The wonder drugs did nothing to cure the chronic illnesses that existed or to prevent them in others. Today society is paying a huge and ever-growing bill caring for those survivors who are incurably ill. Of course this care must continue and the effort must continue to further develop the astounding technology which is being mobilized to maintain life in these incurably ill. I would argue that, in addition to this stupendous effort and investment, society's resources should also be channeled into research on the primary prevention of these incurable ailments. The benefits of primary prevention, in terms of suffering, greater productivity of the population, and a lessening of the burden on society, are obvious.

The picture regarding crime is not totally different. We are proud of our new jails, we are proud of our rehabilitation programs, we are proud of our development of mace. It is clearly important that we continue to do research studying the operation of the criminal justice system. But all of these attempts are technological patches. As in the field of medicine, primary prevention of

The research reported in this chapter has been supported by grants from the Center for Studies of Crime and Delinquency, NIMH (MH 19225, 24872, 25311).

45

46   New Paths in Criminology

crime is not eagerly studied. I would urge again, as in the field of medicine, that primary prevention become our critical objective.

How might we best effect primary prevention of crime? One approach suggested by many criminologists is societal manipulation. This is the logical approach of the sociocultural etiological view of criminal behavior. This etiological view has basically maintained that the criminal is a normal individual who has been socialized in a deviant manner. Clearly, if we change the socialization for the better, this normal individual will not commit crimes. This point of view has been the dominant one in the twentieth century.

If there are, however, individual characteristics (such as intelligence or the XYY chromosome anomaly) which increase an individual's chances of behaving antisocially, then societal change may not be the only feasible approach. We may need to consider methods of primary prevention which take into account the individual characteristics of the potential offender. Is there evidence that the criminal has distinctive individual characteristics with etiological implications?

I will relate five sets of facts which persuade me that societal manipulation, alone, will not be enough to prevent manifestations of antisocial behavior.

Fact Number One: Twin Studies

There have been a series of studies of criminality in twins which seem to have demonstrated that genetic factors in criminality can not be ruled out. The studies began with the 1929 report of Johannes Lange which suggested that identical twins evidence far more concordance for criminal behavior than do fraternal twins. Lange's study shared a number of methodological problems with most of the early research in this area. More recently Karl Otto Christiansen (1977a) studied a total population of 7,172 Danish twins; he observed 35 percent concordance for criminality in identical twins, while fraternal twins evidenced only 13 percent pairwise concordance. Christiansen's work is solid and compelling. His results suggest that the possibility of genetic factors in criminality cannot be ruled out.

Fact Number Two: Adoption Studies

In three separate studies of adoptees and their biological and adoptive parents, it has become clear that if a child who was adopted at birth later becomes criminal, it is an extremely good bet that his biological father (whom he has never seen) was also a criminal. This was most recently reported in a study by Hutchings and Mednick (1977) who investigated the outcomes of 1,145 adoptions of male children in Denmark. It seems clear that a genetic factor does exist either for some types of criminality or for some percentage of criminals.

47

I would draw only one conclusion from this fact. Individual biological factors must be in part responsible for some types of crime or for some percentage of criminals.

Fact Number Three: Autonomic Nervous System Deviance in Criminals

In a compelling study, Wadsworth (1976) traced all the males registered for delinquency from a sample of 13,687 births which occurred in England, Wales, and Scotland between March 3 and March 9, 1946 (Douglas and Blomfield, 1958). In 1957 these males had their pulse taken just before a school medical examination (a mildly threatening event). This preexamination pulse rate predicted significantly whether or not a boy would achieve a record of serious delinquency by the age of twenty-one. In a sixteen-year longitudinal study Loeb and Mednick (1977) demonstrated that autonomic nervous system variables predict which of a population of boys would exhibit antisocial behavior. Since Lykken's demonstration in 1957, autonomic nervous system variables have been reliable in differentiating the antisocial individual (see Siddle, 1977).

Fact Number Four: The Chronic Recidivist

The oft-quoted finding of Wolfgang, et al. (1972) that a very small percentage of the males of Philadelphia are responsible for a major proportion of the serious crimes in that city suggests to me that the antisocial behavior of this very small proportion of the male population may be partly explained by individual factors.

Fact Number Five: Biosocial Interactions Relating to Criminal Behavior

Karl Otto Christiansen's twin study (1977a, b) suggests the possibility of a genetic effect in criminality. His work however goes beyond this in demonstrating that this genetic effect interacts in a lawful way with social variables. He showed that in a social context where group resistance to crime is greatest, the genetic effect manifests itself most clearly. Also where the group resistance to crime seems to be relatively smaller, the genetic effect is less manifest. In our own research on physiological factors relating to crime, we have seen an analogous relationship. Where family and group pressures which induce criminal behavior are strongest, the physiological variables are least differentiating. In family situations which seem to protect the individual from crime, physiological variables seem to be more differentiating (Mednick et al., 1977). So, we see not only that the individual biological variables relate to criminality but also that they interact in a lawful way with sociocultural factors.

Implications for Primary Prevention

We have suggested that since individual characteristics as well as sociocultural factors seem to be involved in the etiology of criminal behavior the primary prevention of this behavior might be aided by taking these individual characteristics into account. Perhaps it would be in order to suggest a possible initial research approach to the problem of primary prevention of crime. In view of the fact that individual characteristics seem to be able to predict later criminal behavior (Loeb and Mednick, 1977; Wadsworth, 1976) it seems clear that the early detection of some future offenders may be possible. Once such individuals have been detected in the general population methods of preventing their criminal behavior could be explored. A research design which suggests itself is the intensive assessment of a large population selected at some point before the onset of serious criminal behavior. These individuals should then be followed until this serious criminal behavior has manifested itself. Then it will be possible to identify those who have been seriously criminal and see if there are any combination of items in the original assessment which might be useful in early detection. If such a discriminating assessment battery could be validated and its reliability demonstrated, then it could be applied to a new population and methods of primary prevention could be tested.

**A Biosocial Theory of the Origins of Criminal
Behavior: An Illustration**

There may be some heuristic value in illustrating how biological and social factors could interact to teach or fail to teach a child how to behave in a civilized manner. In this section I will examine the learned bases of obedience to society's sanctions. It assumes that law-abiding behavior must be learned and that this learning requires certain environmental conditions and individual abilities. Lack of *any* of these conditions or abilities would hinder socialization learning and might, conceivably, be partly responsible for some forms of antisocial activities.

How do people learn to be law-abiding? This section describes socialization learning in terms of the interaction of early family training and individual physiological characteristics. If there are lacks in either of these spheres learning to be law-abiding will be incomplete, retarded, or unsuccessful.

Most offenders are convicted of having perpetrated only one, two, or three

49

relatively minor offenses. These offenders are doubtless instigated by socio-economic and situational forces. There is, however, a small group of offenders which may be characterized as extremely recidivistic. In a Copenhagen birth cohort of over 30,000 men (described in Witkin et al., 1977) we found that this minute fraction of the male population accounts for more than half of the offenses committed by the entire cohort. Similar results have been reported for the city of Philadelphia by Wolfgang et al. (1972). It is especially this small active group of recidivists that are hypothesized to have had their socialization learning influenced by deviant social and physiological characteristics. In emphasizing biosocial interactions the approach also seeks to help in the explanation of those cases of antisocial behavior which seem to have no apparent social cause as well as those cases in which an individual seems extraordinarily resistant or invulnerable to powerful criminogenic social forces (criminal family, extreme poverty, broken home background).

Before going further with this exposition, perhaps I should make clear that I define a criminal as an individual who is registered as having been convicted of a violation of the penal code. In no case will this mean that our studies have utilized a prison population. All the individuals studied were functioning in society. We are concerned about the possibility that hidden crime may be governed by a different set of laws of nature from registered crime. We are, however, encouraged to continue working with registered crime by relatively strong evidence that the hidden criminal is the less serious, less recidivistic criminal (Christie et al., 1965).

Law-abidance Learning in Children

Children almost certainly do not come into the world with a set of inborn behaviors which unfold into civilized behavior. An objective consideration might in fact suggest that the behavior of young children is dominated by rather uncivilized immediate needs and passions. Becoming civilized consists in part of learning to inhibit or rechannel some of these passions.

Hare (1970), Trasler (1972), and others have discussed the possibility that the psychopath and criminal have some defect in avoidance learning that interferes with their ability to learn to inhibit asocial responses. Much of this has been inspired by the 1957 study by Lykken indicating the difficulties psychopaths have in learning to avoid an electric shock. These results have found some empirical support. Hare has suggested that the empirically observed and reobserved autonomic hyporeactivity of the psychopath and criminal may be, partially, the basis of this poor avoidance learning. To better understand this, let us consider the avoidance learning situation. In particular, let us follow Trasler (1972), and consider how the law-abiding citizen might learn his admirable self-control. When one considers the modern urban center in terms of the temptations and, in fact, incitements it offers to a variety of forms of asocial

50

New Paths in Criminology

behavior, one is impressed with the restraint and forebearance of the 80-90 percent of the population, who apparently manage to avoid committing repetitive or heinous crimes. Novels such as *The Lord of the Flies* and observations of intersibling familial warfare suggest that there actually *are* some strong instincts and passions that society must channel and inhibit to maintain even the poor semblance of civilization we see around us. The type of learning involved in this civilizing process has been termed passive avoidance; the individual avoids punishment or fear by *not* doing something for which he has been punished before.

Let us consider the way children learn to inhibit aggressive impulses. Frequently, when child A is aggressive to child B, child A is punished by his mother. After a sufficient quantity or quality of punishment, just the thought of the aggression should be enough to produce a bit of anticipatory fear in child A. If this fear response is large enough, the raised arm will drop, and the aggressive response will be successfully inhibited.

What happens in this child after he has successfully inhibited such an asocial response is critical for his learning of civilized behavior. Let us consider the situation again in detail.

1. Child A contemplates aggressive action.
2. Because of previous punishment he suffers fear.
3. He inhibits the aggressive response.
4. His fear begins to dissipate, to be reduced.

We know that fear reduction is the most powerful, naturally occurring reinforcement psychologists have discovered. Thus the reduction of fear (which immediately follows the inhibition of the aggression) can act as a reinforcement for this inhibition and will result in the learning of the inhibition of aggression. The fear-reduction-reinforcement pattern increases the probability that the inhibition of the aggression will occur in the future. After many such experiences, the normal child will learn to inhibit aggressive impulses. Each time such an impulse arises and is inhibited, the inhibition will be strengthened by reinforcement. What does a child need in order to learn effectively to be civilized (in the context of this approach)?

1. A censuring agent (typically the family or peers).
2. An adequate fear response.
3. The ability to learn the fear response in anticipation of an asocial act.
4. Fast dissipation of fear to quickly reinforce the inhibitory response.

The speed and size of reinforcement determines the effectiveness of the fourth point. An effective reinforcement is one that is delivered immediately after the relevant response. In terms of this discussion, the faster the reduction of fear,

51

the faster the delivery of the reinforcement. The fear response is, to a large extent, controlled by the autonomic nervous system (ANS). We can estimate the activity of the ANS by means of peripheral indicants such as heart rate, blood pressure, and skin conductance. The measure of most relevance will peripherally reflect the rate or speed at which the ANS recovers from periods of imbalance.

If child A has an ANS that characteristically recovers very quickly from fear, then he will receive a quick and large reinforcement and learn inhibition quickly. If he has an ANS that recovers very slowly, he will receive a slow, small reinforcement and learn to inhibit the aggression very slowly, if at all. This orientation would predict that (holding constant critical extraindividual variables such as social status, crime training, and poverty level) those who commit asocial acts would be characterized by slow autonomic recovery. The slower the recovery, the more serious and repetitive the asocial behavior predicted. Note that although we have concentrated on electrodermal recovery (EDRec), the theory also requires another ANS characteristic, hyporeactiveness, as a predisposition for delinquency. The combination of hyporesponsiveness and slow EDRec should give the maximum ANS predisposition to delinquency.

Tests of the Theory

In our longitudinal study of some thirteen years duration (Mednick and Schulsinger, 1968), we have been following 311 individuals whom we intensively examined in 1962. This examination included psychophysiology. Since 1962, 36 have had serious disagreements with the law (convictions for violation of the penal code). We checked and noted that, indeed, their EDRec was considerably slower than that of controls. Those 9 who have been clinically diagnosed as psychopaths have even slower recovery.

Siddle et al. (1973) examined the electrodermal responsiveness of 67 inmates of an English borstal. On the basis of ten criteria, these inmates were divided into high, medium, and low asociality. Peter Venables suggested to Siddle et al. that they also measure EDRec in their sample. Speed and rate of EDRec varied inversely as a function of asociality. EDRec on a single trial was surprisingly effective in differentiating the three groups (see Siddle et al., 1977).

Bader-Bartfai and Schalling (1974) reanalyzed skin conductance data from a previous investigation of criminals, finding that criminals who tended to be more "delinquent" on a personality measure tended to have slower EDRec.

In view of the relationships that have been reported between psychophysiological variables and asocial behavior, and in view of our interest in better understanding the apparent genetic predisposition to asocial behavior, we next turned to a study of the heritability of psychophysiological behavior. We (Bell, Mednick, Gottesman, and Sergeant) invited pairs of male twelve-year-old twins

52   New Paths in Criminology

into our laboratory. Interestingly enough, EDRec to orienting stimuli proved to have significant heritability (consistently higher for left hand than for right; see Bell et al., 1977). This finding would suggest that part of the heritability of asocial behavior might be attributed to the heritability of EDRec. Thus a slow EDRec might be a characteristic a criminal father could pass to a biological son, which (given the proper environmental circumstances) could increase the probability of the child failing to learn adequately to inhibit asocial responses. Thus we would predict that criminal fathers would have children with slow EDRec. Table 4-1 presents data on the electrodermal behavior of children with criminal and noncriminal fathers. As can be seen, the prediction regarding EDRec is not disconfirmed. It is interesting that the pattern of responsiveness of these children closely resembles that which we might anticipate seeing in their criminal fathers (Hare, 1970). Results of other studies in our laboratory have replicated these findings.

Hare (1975) has recently tested this ANS recovery theory on a sample of maximum-security prisoners. More psychopathic prisoners show significantly slower EDRec than serious, but less psychopathic, maximum-security prisoners. In one figure Hare plots the EDRec of the prisoners along with that of male college students. The prisoner and student curves are worlds apart! In a ten-year

Table 4-1

Skin Conductance Behavior during Orienting Response Testing in Children with Criminal and Noncriminal Fathers

Skin Conductance Function (Right Hand)	Mean Score		F	df	p
	Noncriminal Father	Criminal Father			
Basal level skin conductance	2.51	2.33	0.09	1,193	n.s.
Amplitude (in micromhos)	0.031	0.016	0.03	1,193	n.s.
Number of responses	2.79	1.55	8.51	1,187	0.01
Response onset latency (in seconds)	2.11	2.18	0.07	1,97	n.s.
Latency to response peak (in seconds)	2.05	2.38	5.32	1,95	0.05
Average half recovery time (in seconds)	3.75	5.43	4.26	1,90	0.05
Minimum half recovery time	2.26	4.33	8.80	1,90	0.01

Source: B. Bell, S.A. Mednick, I.I. Gottlesman, and J. Sargeant, "Electrodermal Parameters in Young, Normal Male Twins," in S.A. Mednick and K.O. Christiansen (eds.), *Biosocial Bases of Criminal Behavior* (New York: Gardner Press), 1977. Reprinted with permission.

Note: During Orienting Response testing, the child was presented 14 times with a tone of 1,000 cycles per second.

53

follow-up study of maximum-security prisoners, Hare reports that EDRec was the only variable in a test battery which predicted recidivism (Hare, personal communication, 1978). Hinton (personal communication, 1975) also finds the EDRec of more asocial prisoners (in an English maximum-security prison) to be slower. In an ongoing study we are finding that criminals reared in a noncriminal milieu have slow EDRec. Children reared in a criminogenic milieu who resist criminality evidence fast EDRec (see Mednick et al., 1977).

In conclusion:

1. There is a theory of social learning of law-abiding behavior that has a unique and key element, the specification of specific autonomic nervous system factors as useful aptitudes for effectively learning to inhibit asocial behavior.
2. Some empirical tests were described that could have disconfirmed this hypothesis. No grounds were found for rejection of the hypothesis in experiments conducted in Denmark, Sweden, England, and Canada under a large variety of situational conditions and criterion group definitions.

Please note that my emphasis of these physiological factors in this chapter should only be understood as an attempt to call attention to this type of approach. The percent of text devoted to the physiological variables does not relate to their perceived importance in the total field of criminology.

Bibliography

Adorno, T.W. Soziologie und empirische Forschung. In T.W. Adorno, R. Dahren-dorf, and H. Pilot (eds.), *Der Positivismusstreit in der deutschen Soziologie.* Neuwied: Luchterhand Verlag, 1969.

Alexander, F., and Staub, H. *The Criminal, the Judge and the Public.* Rev. ed. Springfield, Ill.: Charles C. Thomas, 1956.

Allen, F.A. Criminal justice, legal values, and the rehabilitative ideal. *Journal of Criminal Law, Criminology and Police Science*, 1959, 50:226-230.

Alonso, W. Beyond the interdisciplinary approach to planning. *AIP's Fifty-fourth Annual Conference.* Washington, D.C., October 1971, pp. 24-28, offprint.

Andenaes, J. General prevention revisited: Research and policy implications. *Journal of Criminal Law and Criminology*, 1975, 66:338-365.

Anttila, I. *The Cumulation of Sanctions Following a Crime.* Ius humanum, Studia in honorem Otto Brusiin, Annales Universitatis Turkuensis, series B, Tom 101, Turku 1966.

Anttila, I., and Jaakkola, R. *Unrecorded Criminality in Finland.* Institute of Criminology, publications series A:2, Helsinki, 1966.

Aron, R. Macchiavel et Marx. *Contrepoint*, 1971, 4:9-23.

Aubert, V. *Likhet og rett: Essays om forbrytelse og straff* (Equality and law: Essays on crime and punishment). Oslo: Pax Forlag, 1964.

Bader-Bartfai, A., and Schalling, D. *Recovery Times of Skin Conductance Responses as Related to Some Personality and Physiological Variables.* Stockholm: Psychological Institute, University of Stockholm, 1974.

Baechler, J. De quelques principes généraux du libéralisme. *Contrepoint*, 1975, 17:125-147.

———. *Qu'est-ce que l'idéologie?* Paris: Gallimard, 1976.

Bailey, W.C. Correctional outcome: An evaluation of 100 reports. *Journal of Criminal Law, Criminology and Police Science*, 1966, 57:153-160.

Bainton, M.A. Problèmes fondamentaux de la recherche pénologique. *Orienta-tions actuelles de la recherche criminologique, Etudes relatives à la recher-che criminologique.* Conseil de l'Europe, 1970, pp. 38-51.

Baldassini-Faini, G. Criminalitá della strada? *Abstracts on Criminology and Penology*, 1970, 10:519-520.

Ball, D.W. Self and identity in the context of deviance: The case of criminal abortion. In R.L. Henschel and R.A. Silverman (eds.), *Perception in Crim-inology.* New York: Columbia University Press, 1975.

Balvig, F. Af angst for kriminalitet (For the fear of crime). *Socialrådgiveren*, 1975a, pp. 195-205.

———. Tyveriet af en by. Lov-og-orden tendenser i en Dansk provinsby. Krim-inalistisk Institut, Københavns Universitet, 1975b (stencil).

219

220   New Paths in Criminology

Banks, A. *Cross-polity Time Series Data.* Cambridge: MIT Press, 1971.

Becker, H. *Systematic Sociology on the Basis of the Beziehungslehre and Gebildelehre of Leopold von Wiese.* New York: Wiley, 1932.

_____. (ed.). *The Other Side: Perspectives on Deviance.* London: Free Press of Glencoe, 1964.

Bell, B., Mednick, S.A., Gottesman, I.I., and Sergeant, J. Electrodermal parameters in young, normal male twins. In S.A. Mednick and K.O. Christiansen (eds.), *Biosocial Bases of Criminal Behavior.* New York: Gardner Press, 1977.

Bell, D. *The Coming of Post-Industrial Society. A Venture in Social Forecasting.* New York: Basic Books, 1973.

Berglund, E., and Johansson, K. *Rattfyllerister, Rapport nr. 8* (Drivers under Influence of Alcohol, Report No. 8). Stockholm: Kriminalvårdstyrelsen, 1974.

Biderman, A.D., Johnson, L.A., McIntyre, J., and Weir, A.W. *Report on a Pilot Study in the District of Columbia on Victimization and Attitudes Toward Law Enforcement.* U.S. President's Commission on Law Enforcement and Administration of Justice, Field Survey I. Washington D.C.: U.S. Government Printing Office, 1967.

Black, D.J., and Reiss, A.J. Jr. Police control of juveniles. *American Sociological Review,* 1970, 35:63-77.

Blackburn, R. An empirical classification of psychopathic personality. *British Journal of Psychiatry,* 1975, 127:456-460.

Block, R.L. Fear of crime and fear of the police. *Social Problems, 1971,* 19:91-101.

Blom, R. Contentual differentiation of penalty demands and expectations with regard to justice. University of Tempere, Institute of Sociology, 1968 (mimeographed).

Bondeson, U. Argot knowledge as an indicator of criminal socialization. In N. Christie (ed.), *Scandinavian Studies in Criminology.* Vol. 2. Oslo: Universitetsforlaget, 1968, pp. 73-107.

_____. *Fången i Fånesamhället* (The prisoner in prison society). Malmö: Norstedt, 1974.

_____. Det allmänna rättsmedvetandet (The general sense of justice). Paper presented at the Nordic Conference for Young Researchers in Law, August, 1975a (mimeographed).

_____. Survey research as a means to explore general deterrence. In The National Swedish Council for Crime Prevention (eds.), *General Deterrence—A Conference on Current Research and Standpoints.* Stockholm, 1975b.

Borgström, C.A. Eine serie von kriminellen zwillingen. *Archiv für Rassenbiologie,* 1939.

Börjeson, B. *Om påföljders verkningar.* Uppsala: Almquist & Wiksell, 1966.

Bottomley, A.K., and Coleman, C.A. Criminal statistics: The police role in the discovery and detection of crime. *International Journal of Crime and Penology,* 1976, 4(1):33-58.

Bibliography   221

Brännström, G., and Hansson, M. Inställning till och kunskaper om häleri—en interviewundersökning i Stockholm. C:1 Uppsats, Stockholms Universitet, Sociologiska Institutionen, 1975 (stencil).

Bratholm, A. Bør adgangen til å anvende bøtestraff utvides? *Lov og Rett*, 1974, 24-38.

Bratholm, A., and Hauge, R. Reahtionene mot promillehjørere (Reactions against pro mille drivers). *Lov og Rett*, 1974, 24-38.

Brooks, J. The fear of crime in the United States. *Crime and Delinquency*, 1974, 20:241-244.

Buikhuisen, W. Research on teenage riots. In P. Meadows and E.H. Mizruchi (eds.), *Urbanism, Urbanization and Change: Comparative Perspectives.* Reading, Mass.: Addison-Wesley, 1969.

Buikhuisen, W., and Jongman, R.W. A legalistic classification of juvenile delinquents. *British Journal of Criminology*, 1970a, 10:109-123.

_____. Druggebruik en de relatie leeftijd/kriminaliteit bij studenten. *Nederlands Tijdschrift voor Kriminologie*, 1970b, 12:1-11.

Bursten, B., and D'esopo, R. The obligation to remain sick. In T.J. Scheff (ed.), *Mental Illness and Social Processes.* New York: Harper and Row, 1967, pp. 206-219.

Burt, C. *The Young Delinquent.* London: University of London Press, 1938.

Cameron, M.O. *The Booster and the Snitch.* Glencoe, Ill.: The Free Press, 1964.

Cannel, C.F., and Kahn, R.L. L'interview comme méthode de collecte. In L. Festinger and D. Katz (eds.), *Les méthodes de recherche dans les sciences sociales.* Paris: Presses Universitaires de France, 1959.

Census of population: 1970, General population characteristics, Final Report PC(1)-B1, U.S. Summary. Washington, D.C.: Bureau of the Census, 1972.

Chambliss, W.J., and Seidman, R.B. *Law, Order and Power.* Don Mills, Ontario, Canada, 1971.

Chamboredon, J.C. La délinquance juvénile, essai de construction d'objet. *Revue Francaise de Sociologie*, 1971, 12(3):335-377.

Chang, D.H., and Zastrow, C.H. Inmates' and security guards' perceptions of themselves and of each other: A comparative study. *International Journal of Crime and Penology*, 1976, 4:89-98.

Chapman, D. *Sociology and the Stereotype of the Criminal.* London: Tavistock Publications, 1968.

Christiansen, K.O. *Mandlige landssvigere i Danmark.* Copenhagen: Direktoratet for Faengselsvaesenet, 1950.

_____. Landssvigerkriminaliteten i sociologisk belysning. Dissertation. University of Copenhagen, 1955.

_____. Threshold of tolerance in various population groups illustrated by results from the Danish criminologic twin study. In A.V.S. de Rueck and R. Porter (eds.), *The Mentally Abnormal Offender.* Boston: Little, Brown, 1968.

_____. Identification des problèmes clés de la recherche sociologique dans le domaine de la criminologie. *Orientations actuelles de la recherche*

222   New Paths in Criminology

criminologique, Etudes relatives à la recherche criminologique. Conseil de l'Europe, 1970, pp. 81-101.

———. The genesis of aggressive criminality: Implications of a study of crime in a Danish twin study. In J. Dewit and W.W. Hartup (eds.), *Determinants and Origins of Aggressive Behavior*. The Hague: Mouton, 1974.

———. On general prevention from an empirical viewpoint. In the National Swedish Council for Crime Prevention (eds.), *General Deterrence*. Stockholm, 1975, pp. 60-74.

———. A preliminary study of criminality among twins. In S.A. Mednick and K.O. Christiansen (eds.), *Biosocial Bases of Criminal Behavior*. New York: Gardner Press, 1977a.

———. A review of studies of criminality among twins. In S.A. Mednick and K.O. Christiansen (eds.), *Biosocial Bases of Criminal Behavior*. New York: Gardner Press, 1977b.

Christiansen, K.O., and Nielsen, A. Nulevende straffede maend i Danmark (Punished men in Denmark today). *Nordisk Tidsskrift for Kriminalvidenskab*, 1959, 47:18-28.

Christie, M.J., Andenaes, J., and Skerbaekk, S. A study of self-reported crime. *Scandinavian Studies in Criminology*, 1965, 1:86-116.

Christie, N. *Tvangsarbeid og alkoholbruk*. Oslo: Universitetsforlaget, 1960.

Cicourel, A.V. *The Social Organisation of Juvenile Justice*. New York: Wiley, 1968.

———. Delinquency and the attribution of responsibility. In R.A. Scott and J. Douglas (eds.), *Theoretical Perspectives on Deviance*. New York: Basic Books, 1972.

Clark, J.P., and Wenninger, E.P. The attitude of juveniles toward the legal institution. *Journal of Criminal Law, Criminology and Police Science*, 1964, 55:482-489.

Cleckley, H. *The Mask of Sanity*. St. Louis: C.V. Mosby, 1964.

Clinard, B.M. *Sociology of Deviant Behavior*. New York: Holt, Rinehart & Winston, 1963.

Clinard, B.M., and Quinney, R. *Criminal Behavior Systems: A Typology*. New York: Holt, Rinehart & Winston, 1959.

Cloward, R.A., and Ohlin, L.B. *Delinquency and Opportunity: A Theory of Delinquent Gangs*. Glencoe, Ill.: Free Press, 1960.

Cohen, A. *Delinquent Boys: The Culture of the Gang*. Glencoe, Ill.: Free Press, 1955.

———. *Deviance and Control*. Englewood Cliffs, N.J.: Prentice-Hall, 1966.

Cormier. Quoted from H. Mannheim. *Comparative Criminology*. London: Routledge & Kegan Paul, 1965, p. 689.

Coser, L.A. *Continuities in the Study of Social Conflict*. New York: Free Press, 1967.

———. Presidential address: Two methods in search of a substance. *American Sociological Review*, 1975, 40(6):691-700.

Bibliography   223

Council of Europe. *Crime on the Roads*. Council of Europe's Fourth European Conference of Directors of Criminological Research Institute. November 22-25, 1966, Strasbourg.

Cusson, M. Les theóries de l'échange et al délinquance. Unpublished manuscript, University of Montréal, 1976.

Debuyst, C. Les nouveaux courants dans la criminologie contemporaine—La mise en cause de la psychologie criminelle et de son objet. *Revue de Droit Pénal et de Criminologie*, 1974-1975, pp. 845-870.

De Greef, E. *Introduction à la criminologie*. Bruxelles: Van der Plas, 1946.

Devlin, I. Drug talk makes sixth formers queasy. *Times Educational Supplement*, January 30, 1970.

Dickens, C. *American Notes for General Circulation*. London: Chapman and Hall, 1842. Cited by T. Eriksson, *The Reformers: A Historical Survey of Pioneer Experiments in the Treatment of Criminals*. New York: Elsevier, 1976, p. 70.

Dollard, J., Doob, L.W., Miller, N.E., et al. *Frustration and Aggression*. New Haven: Yale University Press, 1950.

Douglas, J.W.B., and Blomfield, J.M. *Children under Five*. London: Allen & Unwin, 1958.

Downes, D.M. *The Delinquent Solution: A Study in Subcultural Theory*. London: Routledge & Kegan Paul, 1966.

Durkheim, E. *The Rules of Sociological Method*. Chicago: University of Chicago Press, 1938, pp. 67-71.

————. *Suicide*, translated by J.A. Spaulding and G. Simpson. Glencoe, Ill.: Free Press, 1951.

Elmhorn, K. Receiving and receivers. A pilot study in Sweden. UNSDRI: August, 1975.

Empey, T., Lubeck, S.G., and Laporte, R.L. *Explaining Delinquency. Construction, Test and Reformulation of a Sociological Theory*. Lexington, Mass.: Lexington Books, D.C. Heath, 1971.

Erickson, E. The problem of identity. *Journal of the American Psychoanalytical Association*, 1956, 4:56-121.

Erikson, K.T. Notes on the sociology of deviance. *Social Problems*, 1962, 9:308.

Erskine, H. The polls: Fear of violence and crime. *Public Opinion Quarterly*, 1974, 38:131-145.

Eysenck, H.J. *Crime and Personality*. London: Routledge & Kegan Paul, 1964.

————. *The Biological Basis of Personality*. Springfield, Ill.: Charles C. Thomas, 1967.

Faugeron, C., and Poggi, D. Les femmes, les infractions, la justice pénale: Une analyse d'attitudes. *Revue de l'Institut de Sociologie*, Université Libre de Bruxelles, 1975, 3-4:375-384.

Faugeron, C., and Robert, P. Un problème de représentation sociale: Les attitudes de punitivité. *Déviance, Cahiers de l'Institut de Criminologie de Paris*, 1974, 1:23-48.

224   New Paths in Criminology

_____. Les représentations sociales de la justice pénale. *Cahiers Internationaux de Sociologie,* 1976, 61:341-366.

Fabrega, H., Jr., and Manning, P.K. Disease, illness and deviant careers. In R.A. Scott and J. Doug'as (eds.), *Theoretical Perspectives on Deviance.* New York: Basic Books, 1972.

Ferracuti, F., Dinitz, S., and de Brenes, E.A. *Delinquents and nondelinquents in the Puerto Rican Slum Culture.* Columbus: Ohio State University Press, 1975.

Ferrero, G. *Pouvoir, les génies invisibles de la cité.* Plon, 1945.

Filipović, V. *Filozofijski rječnik.* Zagreb: Matica Hrvatska, 1965.

Fishman, G. Can labeling be useful? In P.C. Friday and V.L. Stewart (eds.), *Youth, Crime and Juvenile Justice.* New York: Praeger, 1977.

Fox, J.A. *Forecasting Crime Data.* Lexington, Mass.: Lexington Books, D.C. Heath, 1978.

Fromm, E. *The Anatomy of Human Destructiveness.* New York: Holt, Rinehart & Winston, 1973.

Furstenberg, F.F., Jr. Public reaction to crime in the streets. *The American Scholar,* 1971, 40:601-610.

_____. Fear of crime and its effects on citizen behavior. Presented at the Symposium on Studies of Public Experience, Knowledge and Opinion of Crime and Justice. Bureau of Social Science Research, Washington, D.C., March 1972.

Galtung, J. *Fengselssamfunnet.* Oslo: Universitetsforlaget, 1959.

Garfinkel, H. Conditions of successful degradation ceremonies. *American Journal of Sociology,* 1956, 61:421-422.

Gibbons, D.C., Jones, J.F., and Garabedian, P.G. Gauging public opinion about the crime problem. *Crime and Delinquency,* 1972, 18:134-145.

Gibbs, J.P. Conceptions of deviant behavior: The old and the new. *Pacific Sociological Review,* 1966, 9(Spring):9-14.

_____. Issues in defining deviant behaviour. In R.A. Scott and J.D. Douglas (eds.), *Theoretical Perspectives on Deviance.* New York: Basic Books, 1972.

Gillin, J.L. *Criminology and Penology.* New York: Appleton-Century Company, 1945.

Glueck, S., and Glueck, E. *Unraveling Juvenile Delinquency.* Cambridge: Harvard University Press, 1950.

Goffman, E. *Stigma.* Englewood Cliffs, N.J.: Prentice-Hall, 1963.

Goode, E. On behalf of labeling theory. *Social Problems,* 1975, 22(5).

Gouldner, A.W. *The Coming Crisis of Western Sociology.* New York: Basic Books, 1970.

Gove, W.R. Societal reaction as an explanation of mental illness: An evaluation. *American Sociological Review,* 1970, 35:873-874.

Gray, W.J. The English prison medical service. In Ciba Foundation Symposium 16, *Medical Care of Prisoners and Detainees.* Amsterdam: Elsevier, 1973, p. 133.

Bibliography   225

Greve, V. *Kriminalitet som normalitet*. Copenhagen: Juristforbundets Forlag, 1972.

Gruenberg, E.M. The failures of success. *Health and Society*, 1977(Winter):3-24.

Hare, R.D. *Psychopathy: Theory and Research*. New York: Wiley, 1970.

――――. Talk presented at NATO meeting on Psychopathic Behavior, September 1975.

Hauge, R. Tid eller penger. *Nordisk Tidsskrift for Kriminalvidenskab*, 1968, 56:137-140.

――――. (ed.). Drinking-and-driving in Scandinavia. *Scandinavian Studies in Criminology*. Vol. 6. Oslo: Universitetsforlaget, 1978.

Healey, W. *The Individual Delinquent*. Boston: Little, Brown, 1915.

――――, and Bonner, A. *New Light on Delinquency and its Treatment*. New Haven: Yale University Press, 1936.

Henderson, D. *Psychopathic States*. New York: Norton, 1947.

Henshel, R.L., and Silverman, R.A. (eds.). *Perception in Criminology*. New York: Columbia University Press, 1975.

Hindelang, M.J. The commitment of delinquents to their misdeeds: Do delinquents drift?, *Social Problems*, 1970, 17:502-509.

――――. *Public Opinion regarding Crime, Criminal Justice and Related Topics*. Washington, D.C.: Law Enforcement Assistance Administration, 1975.

Hirschi, T. *Causes of Delinquency*. Berkeley: University of California Press, 1969.

Hjort, P. Statement in the daily newspaper *Politiken*. January 10, 1970, p. 3, and January 11, 1970, p. 3.

Høgh, E., and Wolf, P. Project Metropolitan: A longitudinal study of 12,270 boys from the Metropolitan area of Copenhagen, Denmark 1953-1977. In S.A. Mednick (ed.), *Prospective Longitudinal Research in Europe*. London: Oxford University Press, in press.

Hood, R.G. Research on the effectiveness of punishments and treatments. In Council of Europe, European Committee on Crime Problems (eds.), *Collected Studies in Criminological Research*. Vol. 1. Stroudsburg: Council of Europe, 1967, pp. 74-102.

Hurwitz, St., and Christiansen, K.O. *Kriminologi I* (Criminology I). Copenhagen: Gyldendal, 1968.

Hutchings, B., and Mednick, S.A. Criminality in adoptees and their adoptive and biological parents: A pilot study. In S.A. Mednick and K.O. Christiansen (eds.), *Biosocial Bases of Criminal Behavior*. New York: Gardner Press, 1977.

Jensen, E.P. Feature article in *Berlingske Aftenavis*. August 4, 1956, p. 7.

Jessor, R., Graves, T.D., Hanson, R.C., and Jessor, S.L. *Society, Personality and Deviant Behavior*. New York: Holt, Rinehart & Winston, 1968.

Joutsen, M. *Young offenders in the Criminal Justice System of Finland*. Research Institute of Legal Policy Publications No. 14, Helsinki, 1976.

Kahn, E. *Psychopathic Personalities*. New Haven: Yale University Press, 1931.

Kaiser, G. *Kriminologie* (Criminology). Uni-Taschenbücher 594. Heidelberg-Karlsruhe: C.F. Müller Verlag, 1976.

226   New Paths in Criminology

Kallestrup, L.R. Straffefrekvensen i forskellige sociale grupper (The frequency of punishment in various social groups). *Nordisk Tidsskrift for Kriminalvidenskab*, 1954, 42:30-34.

Kandel, L. Reflexions sur l'usage de l'entretien, notamment non directif, et sur les études d'opinion. *Epistémologie Sociologique*, 1972, 13:25-46.

Klein, G.S., and Schlesinger, H.J. Perceptual attitudes of form boundedness and form-liablity in Rorschach responses. Abstract. *American Psychologist*, 1950, 5:321

Klette, H. Some minimum requirements for legal sanctioning systems with special emphasis on detection. In the National Swedish Council for Crime Prevention (eds.), *General Deterrence*. Stockholm, 1975.

Kolakowski, L. *Alienation of Reason: A History of Positivist Thought*. New York: Doubleday, 1969.

––––––. Le diable peut-il etre sauve? *Contrepoint*, Paris, 1976, 20:151-164.

Korn, R.R., and McCorkel, L.W. *Criminology and Penology*. New York: Holt, Rinehart & Winston, 1959.

Kosik, K. *Dialektika konkretnega*. Translated and edited by F. Jerman. Ljubljana: Cankarjeva založoa, 1967.

Kranz, H. Discordant soziales verhalten eineuger zqillinge. *Monatschrift für Kriminalpsychologie und Strafrechtsreform*, 1935, 26:511-516.

Kriminaalihuoltokomitean mietintö (Report of the Committee on Probation and Parole), Committee Report 1972: A 1 (in Finnish only). Helsinki: Government Printing Centre, 1972.

Kriminalstatistik 1974 og 1975 (Crime statistics 1974 and 1975). Statistiske Meddelelser 1976, 3, and 1977, 5. Copenhagen: Danmarks Statistik, 1976, 1977.

Kutchinsky, B. Law and education: Some aspects of Scandinavian studies on "the general sense of justice." *Acta Sociologica*, 1966, 10:21-41.

––––––. Knowledge and attitudes regarding legal phenomena in Denmark. In N. Christie (ed.), *Scandinavian Studies in Criminology*. Vol. 2. Oslo: Universitetsforlaget, 1968, pp. 125-259.

––––––. Advances in Scandinavian studies on knowledge and opinion about law. In J.M.M. Maeijer et al. (eds.), *Rechtssociologie en jurimetrie*. Deventer, Holland: Kluwer, 1970.

––––––. Towards an explanation of the decrease in registered sex crimes in Copenhagen. *Technical Report of the Commission on Obscenity and Pornography*. Vol. 7. Washington, D.C.: Government Printing Office, 1971, pp. 263-310.

––––––. Sociological aspects of the perception of deviance and criminality. In European Committee in Crime Problems (eds.), *Collected Studies in Criminological Research*. Vol. 9. Strasbourg: Council of Europe, 1972.

LaGache, D. *Psycho-Criminogenese: Tenth General Report*. Paris: 2nd International Congress of Criminology, 1950.

Bibliography   227

Lange, J. *Verbrechen als schiskal*. Leipzig: Georg Thieme, 1929. English ed. London: Unwin Brothers, 1931.

Lascoumes, P., and Moreau-Capdevielle, G. Presse et justice pénale, un cas de diffusion idéologique. *Revue Francaise de Science Politique*, 1976, 16(1):41-68.

Lasner, E., and Montgomery, E. de. En explorativ studie av skolungdomars normuppfattning. (An exploratory study of the norm conceptions of youth of the schools). Stockholm: Kriminalvetenskapliga Institutet vid Stockholms Universitet, Afdelningen för allmän kriminalvetenskap och kriminalpolitik, 1974 (stencil Nr. 36).

Legras, A.M. *Psychese en criminaliteit bij twellingen*. Utrecht: Kemink en Zoon N.V. 1932. A summary in German can be found in Psychosen und kriminalitat bei zwillingen. *Zeitschrift fur die gesamte Neurologie und Psychiatrie*, 1933, 198-228.

Lemert, E.M. *Human Deviance, Social Problems and Social Control*. Englewood Cliffs, N.J.: Prentice-Hall, 1967.

Linden, P.A., and Similä, M. General deterrence and the general sense of justice. In the National Swedish Council for Crime Prevention (eds.), *General Deterrence*. Stockholm, 1975.

Lipton, D., Martinson, R., and Wilks, J. *The Effectiveness of Correctional Treatment: A Survey of Treatment Evaluation Studies*. New York: Praeger, 1975.

Loeb, J., and Mednick, S.A. A prospective study of predictors of criminality: 3. Electrodermal response patterns. In S.A. Mednick and K.O. Christiansen (eds.), *Biosocial Bases of Criminal Behavior*. New York: Gardner Press, 1977.

Lofland, J. *Deviance and Identity*. Englewood Cliffs, N.J.: Prentice-Hall, 1969.

Lombroso, C. *Crime: Its Causes and Remedies*. Boston: Little, Brown, 1912, pp. 34-35.

Lykken, D.T. A study of anxiety in the sociopathic personality. *Journal of Abnormal and Social Psychology*, 1957, 55:6-10.

McFarland, R., and Moseley, A.L. *Human Factor in Highway Transport Safety*. Boston: Harvard School of Public Health, 1954.

Maestro, M. Benjamin Franklin and the penal law. *A Journal of Ideas*, 1975, 36:551-562.

Malow, U. Die einstellung der bevölkerung zum strafvollzug: Ein kritischer vergleich empirischer untersuchungen. Unpublished dissertation, Hamburg, 1974.

Martinson, R. What works?—Questions and answers about prison reform. *Journal of Public Interest*, June 1974, 6:22-54.

Marx, K. Bevölkerung, Verbrechen und Pauperismus. *New York Daily Tribune*, September 16, 1859. In *Marx-Engels Werke* Bd. 13. Institut für Marxismus-Leninismus beim ZK der SED. Berlin: Dietz Verlag, 1961.

Mathiesen, T. *The Defences of the Weak*. London: Tavistock Publications, 1965.

Matza, D. *Delinquency and Drift*. New York: Wiley, 1964.

New Paths in Criminology

Mead, G.H. *Mind, Self and Society from the Standpoint of a Social Behaviorist.* Edited by Charles W. Morris. Chicago: University of Chicago Press, 1934.

Mednick, S.A. *Proceedings of the Second International Symposium: The Biological Model, Part 2.* Sao Paulo, Brasil, 1975.

_____. Kirkegaard-Sorensen, L., Hutchings, B., Knop, J., Rosenberg, R., and Schulsinger, F. An example of bio-social interaction research: The interplay of socioenvironmental and individual factors in the eitology of criminal behavior. In S.A. Mednick and K.O. Christiansen (eds.), *Biosocial Bases of Criminal Behavior.* New York: Gardner Press, 1977.

_____, and Schulsinger, F. Some premorbid characteristics related to breakdown in children with schizophrenic mothers. *Journal of Psychiatric Research,* 1968, 6:267-291.

_____, Schulsinger, F., Higgins, J., and Bell, B. *Genetics, Environment and Psychopathology.* Amsterdam: North-Holland/American Elsevier, 1974.

Merton, R. *Social Theory and Social Structure.* Glencoe, Ill.: Free Press, 1957.

Merton, R.K., Fiske, M., and Kendall, P.L. *The Focused Interview: A Manual of Problems and Procedures.* Glencoe, Ill.: Free Press, 1956.

Michelat, G. Sur l'utilisation de l'entretien non directif en sociologie. *Revue Francaise de Sociologie,* 1975, 16:229-247.

Mike, B. Willem Adriaan Bonger's "Criminality and economic conditions": A critical appraisal. *International Journal of Criminology and Penology,* 1976, 3:211-238.

Miller, W.B. Lower class culture as a generating milieu of gang delinquency. *Journal of Social Issues,* 1958, 14:5-19.

Miller, W.C., and Conger, J.J. *Personality, Social Class and Delinquency.* New York: Wiley, 1966.

Moedikdo, P. Criminology and politicization. In G.W.G. Jasperse, K.A. van Leeuwen-Burow, and L.G. Toornvliet (eds.), *Criminology between the Rule of Law and the Outlaws.* Netherlands: Kluwer and Deventer, 1976, pp. 99-131.

Morris, T. *The Criminal Area. A Study in Social Ecology.* London: Routledge & Kegan Paul, 1957.

Mortensson, G. Psykiatrisk undersøgelse af mandlige landssvigere i Danmark. *Nordisk Tidsskrift for Kriminalvidenskab,* 1953, 41:2.

Mulvihill, D.J., Tumin, M.M., and Curtis, L.A. *Crimes of Violence.* Vol. 2. The staff report submitted to the National Commission on the Causes and Prevention of Violence. Washington, D.C.: U.S. Government Printing Office, 1969.

Nielsen, K. *Resumé af arresthusundersogelsen* (Summary of the study of local prisons in Denmark). Research Report No. 2. Copenhagen: The Research Group of the Directorate of Prisons and Probation, 1974.

Nordisk Råd. *Straffesystemer i Norden* (Penal systems in the Nordic countries: A conference report). NU 1977, 25, Stockholm: Nordisk Råd, 1977.

Nunnally, J. *Popular Conceptions of Mental Health.* New York: Holt, Rinehart & Winston, 1961.

Bibliography 229

Nuorisorikollisuustoimikunnan mietintö (Report of the Commission on Juvenile Delinquency). Committee Report 1966: A 2 (in Finnish only). Helsinki: Government Printing Centre, 1966.

Nuorisorikollisuuskomitean mietintö (Report of the Committee on Juvenile Delinquency). Committee Report 1970: A 9 (in Finnish only). Helsinki. Government Printing Centre, 1970.

Nye, J.E., and Short, J.F. Scaling delinquent behavior. *American Sociological Review*, 1957, 22:326-331.

Nyqvist, O. *Juvenile Justice*. Uppsala: Almqvist & Wiksell, 1960.

Packer, H.L. *The Limits of Criminal Sanction*. Stanford: Stanford University Press, 1968.

Pareto, V. *Mind and Society*. Translated and edited by A. Livingston. New York: Harcourt, Brace, 1935.

Parsons, T. *The Structure of Social Action*. Glencoe, Ill.: Free Press, 1949.

———. *The Social System*, Glencoe, Ill.: Free Press, 1951.

Pečuljić, M. *Metodologija društvenih nauka*. Beograd: Službeni list SFRJ, 1976.

Petrie, A. Collins, W., and Solomon, P. The tolerance of pain and sensory deprivation. *American Journal of Psychology*, 1960, 73(1):80-90.

Phillipson, M. *Sociological Aspects of Crime and Delinquency*. London: Routledge & Kegan Paul, 1971.

Pinatel, J. *Etienne De Greeff*, Paris: Cujas, 1967.

———. Aperçu général de la recherche criminologique en France. *Orientations actuelles de la recherche criminologique: Etudes relatives à la recherche criminologique*. Conseil de l'Europe, 1970, pp. 161-194.

———. *La société criminogène*. Paris: Calmann-Lévy, 1971.

———. *Criminologie*. 3d ed. Paris: Dalloz, 1975.

———. Criminologie et pathologie sociale. *Revue de Science Criminelle*, 1976, pp. 181-189.

Platt, A.M. *The Child Savers: The Invention of Delinquency*. Chicago: University of Chicago Press, 1969.

Pollner, M. Sociological and common-sense models of the labeling process. In R. Turner (ed.), *Ethnomethodology*. Harmonsworth: Penguin Books, 1974.

Popper, K.R. *The Logic of Scientific Discovery*. London: Hutchinson, 1959.

Poveda, T.G. The fear of crime in a small town. *Crime and Delinquency*, 1972, 18:147-153.

Quinney, R. *The Social Reality of Crime*. Boston: Little, Brown, 1970.

———. *Criminal Justice in America: A Critical Understanding*. Boston: Little, Brown, 1974.

Ray, I. *A Treatise on the Medical Jurisprudence of Insanity*. Boston: Little, Brown, 1838.

Raymondis, L.M., and Le Guern, M. *Le langage de la justice pénale*. Paris: Centre National de la Recherche Scientifique, 1977.

Reasons, C.E. Images of crime and the criminal, the dope fiend mythology. *Journal of Research in Crime and Delinquency*, 1976, 13(2):133-144.

230   New Paths in Criminology

Reckless, W.C. *American Criminology: New Directions*. New York: Appleton-Century-Crofts, 1973.

Reiss, A.J., Jr. The social integration of queers and peers. *Social Problems*, 1961, 9:102-120.

Rikosoikeuskomitean mietintö (Report of the Penal Law Committee). Committee Report 1976:72 (in Finnish with a Swedish summary). Helsinki: Government Printing Centre, 1977.

Robert, P. La recherche opérationnelle dans le système de justice criminelle. In European Committee on Crime Problems (eds.), *Etudes relatives à la recherche criminologique*. Strasbourg: Conseil de l'Europe, 1971, 8:55.

———. La sociologie entre une criminologie du passage à l'acte et une criminologie de la réaction sociale. *Année Sociologique*, 1973, 24:441-504.

———. Recherches en criminologie de la reaction sociale. In *Neue Perspektiven in der Kriminologie*. Zurich: Verlag der Fachvereine an den Schweizerischem Hochschulen und Techniken, 1975, pp. 55-83.

———. Les statistiques criminelles et la recherche: Réflexions conceptuelles. *Déviance et Societe*, 1977, 1(1):3-28.

———, and Faugeron, C. Analyse d'une représentation sociale, les images de la justice pénale. *Revue de l'Institut de Sociologie*, Université Libre de Bruxelles, 1973a, 1:31-85.

———. L'image de la justice criminelle dans la société. *Revue de Droit Pénal et de Criminologie*, 1973b, 53(7):665-719.

———. Représentation du système de justice criminelle, essai de typologie. *Acta Criminologica*, 1973c, 6:13-65.

———, Faugeron, C., and Kellens, G. Les attitudes des juges à propos des prises de décision. *Annales de la Faculté de Droit de Liège*, 1975, 20:23-152.

———, P., and Laffargue, B. *L'image de la justice dans la société: Le système pénal vu par ses clients*. Paris: Service d'Etudes Penales et Criminologiques, 1977.

———, P., Lambert, T., and Faugeron, C. *Image du viol collectif et reconstruction d'objet*. Geneva, Paris, Médecine and Hygiène: Masson, 1976.

———, P., and Moreau, G. La presse française et la justice pénale. *Sociologia del Diritto*, 1975, 2(2):359-395.

Rosanoff, A.J., Handy, L.M., and Rosanoff, F.A. Criminality and delinquency in twins. *Journal of Criminal Law and Criminology*, 1934, 24:923-934.

Rothman, D. *The Discovery of the Asylum: Social Order and Disorder in the New Republic*. Boston: Little, Brown, 1971.

Rubington, E., and Weinberg, M.S. *Deviance: The Interactionist Perspective*. New York: Macmillan, 1968.

Sagarin, E. *Deviants and Deviance*. New York: Praeger, 1975.

Schachter, S., and Latane, B. Crime, cognition and the autonomic nervous system. *Nebraska Symposium on Motivation*, 1964, 12:221-275.

Scheff, T. *Being Mentally Ill*. Chicago: Aldine, 1966.

———. (ed.). *Mental Illness and Social Processes*. New York: Harper and Row, 1967.

Bibliography   231

_____ . Negotiating reality: Notes on power in the assessment of responsibility. *Social Problems*, 1968, 16:3-17.

Schneider, K. *Die psychopatischen persönlichkeiten*. 4th ed. Vienna: Franz Deuticke, 1940.

Schulsinger, F. Psychopathy: Heredity and environment. *International Journal of Mental Health*, 1972, 1:199-206.

Schur, E. *Labeling Deviant Behaviour*. New York: Harper and Row, 1971.

_____ . A critical assessment of labeling. In R.L. Henshel and R.A. Silverman (eds.), *Perception in Criminology*. New York: Columbia University Press, 1975.

Schwartz, R.D., and Skolnick, J. Two studies of legal stigma. *Social Problems*, 1962, 10:133-142.

Segerstedt, T., Karlsson, G., and Rundblad, B. A research into the general sense of justice. *Theoria*, 1949, 15:321-338.

Sellin, T. *Culture, Conflict and Crime*. New York: Social Science Research Council, 1938.

_____ , and Wolfgang, M.E. *Delinquency: Selected Studies*. New York: Wiley, 1969.

Separovic, Z. Criminological analysis of the personality of traffic offenders. *Abstracts on Criminology and Penology*, 1972, 12:51.

Shah, S.A., and Roth, L.H. Biological and psychophysiological factors in criminality. In D. Glaser (ed.), *Handbook of Criminology*, Chicago: Rand McNally, 1974.

Shaw, C.R., and McKay, H.B. *Social Factors in Juvenile Delinquency*. Vol. 2. The National Committee on Law Observance and Law Enforcement, Report on the Causes of Crime. Washington, D.C.: U.S. Government Printing Office, 1931.

_____ , *Juvenile Delinquency in Urban Areas*. Chicago: University of Chicago Press, 1942.

Shoham, S.G. *Crime and Social Deviation*. Chicago: Henry Regnery, 1966.

_____ . *The Mark of Cain*. St. Lucia: Queensland University Press, 1970.

_____ . *Social Deviance*. New York: Gardner Press, 1976.

_____ . *Salvation through the Gutters*. Washington: Hemisphere Publications, 1978a, in press.

_____ . *The Myth of Tantalus*. St. Lucia: Queensland University Press, 1978b, in press.

_____ . Weissbrod, L., Markowsky, R., and Stein, J. The differential pressures toward schizophrenia and delinquency. In P. Friday and V.L. Stewart (eds.), *Youth, Crime and Juvenile Justice*. New York: Praeger, 1977.

Siddle, D.A.T. Electrodermal activity and psychopathy. In S.A. Mednick and K.O. Christiansen (eds.), *Biosocial Bases of Criminal Behavior*. New York: Gardner Press, 1977.

_____ , Mednick S.A., Nicol, A.R., and Foggitt, R.H. Skin conductance recovery in anti-social adolescents. In S.A. Mednick and K.O. Christiansen (eds.), *Biosocial Bases of Criminal Behavoir*. New York: Gardner Press, 1977.

232   New Paths in Criminology

_____, Nicol, A.R., and Foggitt, R.H. Habituation and overextinction of the GSR component of the orienting response in anti-social adolescents. *British Journal of Social and Clinical Psychology*, 1973, 12:303-308.

Sigsgård, T. *Psykologisk undersøgelse af mandlige landssvigere i Danmark under besaettelsen.* Copenhagen: Direktoratet for Faengsel-svaesenet, 1954.

Simmons, J.L., and Chambers, H. Public stereotypes of deviants. *Social Problems*, 1965, 13.

Sjöbring, H. Strucktur och utvickling. Personlig information, 1954.

Skinner, B.F. *Par delà la liberté et la dignité* (Beyond freedom and dignity). Paris: HMH-Laffont, 1972.

Sorel, G. *Reflexions sur la violence.* Paris: M. Riviere, 1936.

Sorokin, P.A. *Sociological Theories of Today.* New York: Harper and Row, 1926.

Stang Dahl, T. The emergence of the Norwegian Child Welfare Law. *Scandinavian Studies in Criminology*, 1974, 5, 83-98.

Stangeland, P., and Hauge, R. *Nyanser i grått.* En undersokelse av selvraportert kriminalitet bland norsk ungdom. Oslo: Universitetsforlaget, 1974.

Statistical Yearbook. *Statistisk Årbog.* Danmarks Statistik. Copenhagen: Danmarks Statistik, 1977.

Steer, D.J., and Carr-Hill, A. The motoring offender—Who is he? *The Criminal Law Review*, April 1967, pp. 214-224.

Straffelovrådet. *Straffelovrådets betaenkning om spirituspavirkede motorforere. No. 588* (Report no. 588 of the Permanent Committee on Penal Reform on Drivers under the Influence of Alcohol). Copenhagen: Statens Trykningskontor, 1970.

Struggle for justice. A report on crime and punishment in America, prepared for the American Friends Service Committee. New York: Hill and Wang, 1971.

Stumpfl, F. *Die ursprunge des verbrechens. Dargestellt am lebenslauf von zwillingen.* Leipzig: Georg Thieme, 1936.

Stürup, G.K. *Psykiatrisk journalskrivning.* Copenhagen: Nyt nordisk Forlag, 1948.

_____. *Treating the "Untreatable".* Baltimore: The Johns Hopkins Press, 1968.

_____. Therapeutic attitudes to treatment of behavior-disordered criminals. *San Diego Law Review*, 1978, in press.

Stürup, G.K., and Berntsen, K. Tilbagefaldet i ny kriminalitet hos danske stats-faengselsfanger. *Menneske og Miljø.* Copenhagen, 1948, pp. 1-12.

Stürup, G.K., and Christiansen, K.O. 335 statsfaengselsfanger. Unpublished manuscript, Copenhagen, 1946.

Sutherland, E.H. *Principles of Criminology.* Philadelphia: Lippincott, 1934.

_____, and Cressey, D. *Criminology.* 9th ed. Philadelphia: Lippincott, 1974.

Svalastoga, K. *Prestige, Class and Mobility.* Copenhagen: Gyldendal, 1959.

_____, Differential rates of change and road accidents in Western Europe and North America. *Acta Sociologica*, 1970, 13(2):73-95.

Bibliography   233

Sveri, K. Trafiknykterhetsbrottsklientelet (The offending clientele of intoxicated persons in the traffic). *SOU*, 1970, 61:57-72.

Sykes, G.M. *The Society of Captives: A Study of a Maximum Security Prison.* Princeton: Princeton University Press, 1958.

———, and Matza, D. Techniques of neutralisation: A theory of delinquency. *American Sociological Review*, 1957, 22: 664-670.

Syrén, S., and Tham, H. Brottslighet, normer och sanktioner (Delinquency, norm, and sanctions). Uppsala Universitet, Sociologiska Institutionen, 1968 (stencil).

Szabo, *D. Crimes et villes. Étude statistique comparée de la crimalité urbaine et rurale en France et en Belgique.* Paris: Cujas, 1960.

———. *Criminologie sociologique et modèles en délinquance et inadaptation juvéniles.* Montréal: Centre international de criminologie comparée, 1976.

———, Gagne, D., and Parizeau, A. *L'adolescent et la société* (étude comparative). Bruxelles: Charles Dessart, 1972.

Tarde, G. *La criminalité comparée.* Paris: Feliz Alcan, 1924.

Taylor, I., Walton, P., and Young J. *The New Crimonology: For a Social Theory of Deviance.* London: Routledge & Kegan Paul, 1973.

———. *Critical Criminology.* London: Routledge & Kegan Paul, 1975.

Thomas, C.W., and Cage, R.J. Correlates of public attitudes towards legal sanctions. *International Journal of Criminology and Penology*, 1976, 4(3):239-255.

———, Cage, R.J., and Fosters, S.C. Public opinion on criminal and legal sanctions: An examination of two conceptual models. *The Journal of Criminal Law Criminology*, 1976, 67(1):110-116.

Thomas, W.I. *The Unadjusted Girl.* Boston: Little, Brown, 1923.

———. The relation of the individual to the group. *American Journal of Sociology*, 1927, 33:814.

Tienari, P. *Psychiatric Illness in Identical Twins.* Copenhagen: Munksgaard, 1963.

Tillman, W.A., and Hobbes, G.E. The accident prone automobile driver. *American Journal of Psychiatry*, 1949, 106:321-331.

Törnudd, P. *Deterrence Research and the Needs for Legislative Planning.* The National Swedish Council for Crime Prevention, Report No. 2, Stockholm, 1975.

Trasler, G. Criminal behavior, In H.J. Eysenck (ed.), *Handbook of Abnormal Psychology.* London: Putnam, 1972.

Uniform Crime Reports. Washington, D.C.: Federal Bureau of Investigation, 1975.

Verhaegen, B. *Introduction à l'histoire immédiate: essai de méthodologie qualitative.* Gembloux: Editions J. Duculot, 1974.

Vodopivec, K. O društvenim prilikama koje pogoduju soijalnoj patologiji dece i omladine. In *Socijalna patologija dece i omladine*, Simposium Zlatibor 27-29 Oct. 1971. Beograd: Institut za kriminoloska i kriminalistička istraživanja, 1971.

234   New Paths in Criminology

————. (ed.). *Maladjusted Youth–An Experiment in Rehabilitation*. Westmead: Lexington Books, 1974.

Vold, G.B. *Theoretical Criminology*. New York: Oxford University Press, 1958.

von Hirsch, A. *Doing Justice: The Choice of Punishments*. New York: Hill & Wang, 1976.

Vranicki, P. *Historija marksizma*. Vol. 1. Zagreb: Naprijed, 1971.

Waben, K. *The Danish Criminal Code*. Copenhagen: G.E.C. Gad, 1958.

Wadsworth, M.E.J. Delinquency, pulse rates and early emotional deprivation. *British Journal of Criminology*, 1976, 16(3):245-256.

Waldo, G.P., and Hall, N.E. Delinquency and attitudes toward the criminal justice system. *Social Forces*, 1970, 49:291-298.

Ward, D.A. Evaluations of correctional treatment: Some implications of negative findings. In S.A. Yefsky (ed.), *Law Enforcement, Science and Technology*. Washington, D.C.: Thompson, 1967, pp. 201-208.

Warren, C.A.B., and Johnson, J.M. A critique of labeling theory from the phenomenological perspective. In R.A. Scott and J.D. Douglas (eds.), *Theoretical Perspectives on Deviance*. New York: Basic Books, 1972.

Weinberger, J.C., Jakubowicz, P., and Robert P. Il declino del diritto . . . como strumento du controllo sociale. *Questione Criminale*, 1976, 2(1):73-96.

————. Société et gravité des infractions. *Revue de Science Criminelle et de Droit Pénal Comparé*, 1976, 4:915-930

Werner, B. Den faktiska brottsligheten. *Nordisk Tidsskrift for Kriminalvidenskab*, 1971, 1-2:106-141.

Westheuss, K.W. Class and organisation as paradigms in social science. *The American Sociologist*, 1976, 2(1):38-49.

Whiteside, T. Annals of crime: Dead souls in the computer. *The New Yorker*, August 22, 1977, pp. 35-65; August 29, 1977, pp. 34-64.

Willett, T. *Criminal on the Road: A Study of Serious Motoring Offences and Those Who Commit Them*. London: Tavistock Publications, 1964.

Wilson, J.Q. *Thinking about Crime*. New York: Basic Books, 1975.

Wing, J.K. Institutionalism in mental hospitals. In T.J. Scheff (eds.), *Mental Illness and Social Processes*. New York: Harper & Row, 1967, pp. 219-242.

Witkin, H.A., Dyk, R.B., Faterson, H.F., Goodenough, D.R., and Karp, S.A. *Psychological Differentiation*. New York: Wiley, 1962.

Witkin, H.A., Faterson, H.F., Goodenough, D.R., and Birnbaum, S. Cognitive patterning in mildly retarded boys. *Child Development*, 1966, 37:301-316.

Witkin, H.A., Mednick, S.A., Schulsinger, F., Bakkestrom, E., Christiansen, K.O., Goodenough, D.R., Hirschhorn, K., Lundsteen, C., Owen, D.R., Philip, J., Rubin, D.B., and Stocking, M. Criminality, aggression and intelligence among XYY and XXY men. In S.A. Mednick and K.O. Christiansen (eds.), *Biosocial Bases of Criminal Behavior*. New York: Gardner Press, 1977.

Wolf, P. Crime and social class in Denmark. *The British Journal of Criminology*, 1962, 3:5-17.

Bibliography   235

_____ . Forskningsnote angående myten om den paene faerdselssynder (Research note concerning the myth of the respectable traffic offender). *Sociologiske Meddelelser*, 1964, 9(1):73-77.

_____ . A contribution to the topology of crime in Denmark. In K.O. Christiansen (ed.), *Scandinavian Studies in Criminology*. Vol.1. Oslo: Universitetsforlaget; London: Tavistock Publications, 1965.

_____ . *Kriminalitet i velfaerdssamfundet–20 år efter I* (Crime in a welfare society–20 years after I). Serie M, 29. Metropolitgruppen, Sociologisk Institut, University of Copenhagen, 1976.

_____ . Unpublished victimization study carried out for and financed by the local government of the community of Fredensborg-Humlebaek, Denmark, 1977.

_____ , and Høgh, E. *Kriminalitet i velfaerdassamfundet* (Crime in a welfare society). Copenhagen: Jorgen Paludans Forlag, 1975.

_____ , Kaarsen, J., Høgh, E. Kriminalitetshppighenden i Danmark (The frequency of crime in Denmark). *Nordisk Tidsskrift for Kriminalvidenskab*, 1958, 46:113-119.

Wolfgang, M.E. A preface to violence. *The Annals of the American Academy of Political and Social Science*, 1966, 364:1-3.

_____ . The viable future of criminology. *Criminology in Action*. Montreal: University of Montreal, 1968, pp. 109-134.

_____ , and Ferracuti, F. *The Subculture of Violence: Towards an Integrated Theory in Criminology*. London: Tavistock Publications, 1967.

_____ , Figlio, R.M., and Sellin, T. *Delinquency in a Birth Cohort*. Chicago: University of Chicago Press, 1972.

Yablowski, L. *The Violent Gang*. Baltimore: Penguin, 1970.

Yinger, M. Contractulture and subculture. *American Sociological Review*, 1960, 25:625-636.

Yoshimasu, S. Crime and heredity, studies on criminal twins. *Japanese Journal on Race Hygiene*, 1947.

Young, J. The role of the police as amplifiers of deviancy. In S. Cohen (ed.), *Images of Deviance*. Harmondsworth: Penguin Books, 1971.

BRIT. J. CRIMINOL. Vol. 20 No. 2 APRIL 1980

"SITUATIONAL" CRIME PREVENTION:
THEORY AND PRACTICE

R. V. G. CLARKE (*London*)*

CONVENTIONAL wisdom holds that crime prevention needs to be based on a thorough understanding of the causes of crime. Though it may be conceded that preventive measures (such as humps in the road to stop speeding) can sometimes be found without invoking sophisticated causal theory, " physical " measures which reduce opportunities for crime are often thought to be of limited value. They are said merely to suppress the impulse to offend which will then manifest itself on some other occasion and perhaps in even more harmful form. Much more effective are seen to be " social " measures (such as the revitalisation of communities, the creation of job opportunities for unemployed youth, and the provision of sports and leisure facilities), since these attempt to remove the root motivational causes of offending. These ideas about prevention are not necessarily shared by the man-in-the-street or even by policemen and magistrates, but they have prevailed among academics, administrators and others who contribute to the formulation of criminal policy. They are also consistent with a preoccupation of criminological theory with criminal " dispositions " (*cf.* Ohlin, 1970; Gibbons, 1971; Jeffery, 1971) and the purpose of this paper is to argue that an alternative theoretical emphasis on choices and decisions made by the offender leads to a broader and perhaps more realistic approach to crime prevention.

" Dispositional " Theories and their Preventive Implications

With some exceptions noted below, criminological theories have been little concerned with the situational determinants of crime. Instead, the main object of these theories (whether biological, psychological, or sociological in orientation) has been to show how some people are born with, or come to acquire, a " disposition " to behave in a consistently criminal manner. This " dispositional " bias of theory has been identified as a defining characteristic of " positivist " criminology, but it is also to be found in " interactionist " or deviancy theories of crime developed in response to the perceived inadequacies of positivism. Perhaps the best known tenet of at least the early interactionist theories, which arises out of a concern with the social definition of deviancy and the role of law enforcement agencies, is that people who are " labelled " as criminal are thereby prone to continue in delinquent conduct (see especially Becker, 1962). In fact, as Tizard (1976) and Ross (1977) have pointed out, a dispositional bias is prevalent throughout the social sciences.

*Home Office Research Unit, London.
This paper is an edited version of a lecture given at Sam Houston State University, Texas, in October 1979.
I am grateful for the comments made by Research Unit colleagues on drafts of the paper.

"SITUATIONAL" CRIME PREVENTION: THEORY AND PRACTICE

The more extreme forms of dispositional theory have moulded thought about crime prevention in two unfortunate ways. First, they have paid little attention to the phenomenological differences between crimes of different kinds, which has meant that preventive measures have been insufficiently tailored to different kinds of offence and of offender; secondly they have tended to reinforce the view of crime as being largely the work of a small number of criminally disposed individuals. But many criminologists are now increasingly agreed that a " theory of crime " would be almost as crude as a general " theory of disease". Many now also believe, on the evidence of self-report studies (see Hood and Sparks, 1970), that the bulk of crime—vandalism, auto-crime, shoplifting, theft by employees—is committed by people who would not ordinarily be thought of as criminal at all.

Nevertheless, the dispositional bias remains and renders criminological theory unproductive in terms of the preventive measures which it generates. People are led to propose methods of preventive intervention precisely where it is most difficult to achieve any effects, *i.e.* in relation to the psychological events or the social and economic conditions that are supposed to generate criminal dispositions. As James Q. Wilson (1975) has argued, there seem to be no acceptable ways of modifying temperament and other biological variables, and it is difficult to know what can be done to make parents more inclined to love their children or exercise consistent discipline. Eradicating poverty may be no real solution either, in that crime rates have continued to rise since the war despite great improvements in economic conditions. And even if it were possible to provide people with the kinds of jobs and leisure facilities they might want, there is still no guarantee that crime would drop; few crimes require much time or effort, and work and leisure in themselves provide a whole range of criminal opportunities. As for violent crime, there would have to be a much clearer link between this and media portrayals of violence before those who cater to popular taste would be persuaded to change their material. Finally, given public attitudes to offending which, judging by some opinion surveys, can be quite punitive, there may not be a great deal of additional scope for policies of diversion and decriminalisation which are favoured by those who fear the consequences of " labelling".

These difficulties are primarily practical, but they also reflect the uncertainties and inconsistencies of treating distant psychological events and social processes as the " causes " of crime. Given that each event is in turn caused by others, at what point in the infinitely regressive chain should one stop in the search for effective points of intervention? This is an especially pertinent question in that it is invariably found that the majority of individuals exposed to this or that criminogenic influence do not develop into persistent criminals. Moreover, " dispositions " change so that most " official " delinquents cease to come to the attention of the police in their late 'teens or early twenties (presumably because their lives change in ways incompatible with their earlier pursuits, *cf.* Trasler, 1979). Finally, it is worth pointing out that even the most persistently criminal people are probably law-abiding for most of their potentially available time, and this behaviour, too, must equally have been " caused " by the events and experiences of their past.

R. V. G. CLARKE

Crime as the Outcome of Choice

Some of the above theoretical difficulties could be avoided by conceiving of crime not in dispositional terms, but as being the outcome of immediate choices and decisions made by the offender. This would also have the effect of throwing a different light on preventive options.

An obvious problem is that some impulsive offences and those committed under the influence of alcohol or strong emotion may not easily be seen as the result of choices or decisions. Another difficulty is that the notion of " choice " seems to fit uncomfortably with the fact that criminal behaviour is to some extent predictable from knowledge of a person's history. This difficulty is not properly resolved by the " soft " determinism of Matza (1963) under which people retain some freedom of action albeit within a range of options constrained by their history and environment. A better formulation would seem to be that recently expounded by Glaser (1977): " both free will and determinism are socially derived linguistic representations of reality " brought into play for different explanatory purposes at different levels of analysis and they may usefully co-exist in the scientific enterprise.

Whatever the resolution of these difficulties—and this is not the place to discuss them more fully—commonsense as well as the evidence of ethnographic studies of delinquency (*e.g.* Parker, 1974) strongly suggest that people are usually aware of consciously choosing to commit offences. This does not mean that they are fully aware of all the reasons for their behaviour nor that their own account would necessarily satisfy a criminologically sophisticated observer, who might require information at least about (i) the offender's motives; (ii) his mood; (iii) his moral judgments concerning the act in question and the " techniques of moral neutralisation " open to him (*cf.* Matza, 1963); (iv) the extent of his criminal knowledge and his perception of criminal opportunities; (v) his assessment of the risks of being caught as well as the likely consequences; and finally, as well as of a different order, (vi) whether he has been drinking. These separate components of subjective state and thought processes which play a part in the decision to commit a crime will be influenced by immediate situational variables and by highly specific features of the individual's history and present life circumstances in ways that are so varied and countervailing as to render unproductive the notion of a generalised behavioural disposition to offend. Moreover, as will be argued below, the specificity of the influences upon different criminal behaviours gives much less credence to the " displacement " hypothesis; the idea that reducing opportunities merely results in crime being displaced to some other time or place has been the major argument against situational crime prevention.

In so far as an individual's social and physical environments remain relatively constant and his decisions are much influenced by past experience, this scheme gives ample scope to account not only for occasional offending but also for recidivism; people acquire a repertoire of different responses to meet particular situations and if the circumstances are right they are likely to repeat those responses that have previously been rewarding. The scheme also provides a much richer source of hypotheses than " dispositional " views

"SITUATIONAL" CRIME PREVENTION: THEORY AND PRACTICE

of crime for the sex differences in rates of offending: for example, shoplifting may be a " female " crime simply because women are greater users of shops (Mayhew, 1977). In view of the complexity of the behaviours in question, a further advantage (Atkinson, 1974) is that the scheme gives some accommodation to the variables thought to be important in most existing theories of crime, including those centred on dispositions. It is perhaps closest to a social learning theory of behaviour (Mischel, 1968; Bandura, 1973) though it owes something to the sociological model of crime proposed by the " new criminologists " (Taylor *et al.*, 1973). There are three features, however, which are particularly worth drawing out for the sake of the ensuing discussion about crime prevention: first, explanation is focused more directly on the criminal event; second, the need to develop explanations for separate categories of crime is made explicit; and, third, the individual's current circumstances and the immediate features of the setting are given considerably more explanatory significance than in " dispositional " theories.

Preventive Implications of a " Choice " Model

In fact, just as an understanding of past influences on behaviour may have little preventive pay-off, so too there may be limited benefits in according greater explanatory importance to the individual's current life circumstances. For example, the instrumental attractions of delinquency may always be greater for certain groups of individuals such as young males living in inner-city areas. And nothing can be done about a vast range of misfortunes which continually befall people and which may raise the probability of their behaving criminally while depressed or angry.

Some practicable options for prevention do arise, however, from the greater emphasis upon situational features, especially from the direct and immediate relationship between these and criminal behaviour. By studying the spatial and temporal distribution of specific offences and relating these to measurable aspects of the situation, criminologists have recently begun to concern themselves much more closely with the possibilities of manipulating criminogenic situations in the interests of prevention. To date studies have been undertaken of residential burglary (Scarr, 1973; Reppetto, 1974; Brantingham and Brantingham, 1975; Waller and Okhiro, 1978) shoplifting (Walsh, 1978) and some forms of vandalism (Ley and Cybrinwsky, 1974; Clarke, 1978) and it is easy to foresee an expansion of research along these lines. Since offenders' perceptions of the risks and rewards attaching to different forms of crime cannot safely be inferred from studies of the distribution of offences, there might be additional preventive benefits if research of this kind were more frequently complemented by interviews with offenders (*cf.* Tuck, 1979; Walker, 1979).

The suggestions for prevention arising out of the " situational " research that has been done can be conveniently divided into measures which (i) reduce the physical opportunities for offending or (ii) increase the chances of an offender being caught. These categories are discussed separately below though there is some overlap between them; for example, better locks which take longer to overcome also increase the risks of being

R. V. G. CLARKE

caught. The division also leaves out some other " situational " crime prevention measures such as housing allocation policies which avoid high concentrations of children in certain estates or which place families in accommodation that makes it easier for parents to supervise their children's play and leisure activities. Both these measures make it less likely that children will become involved in vandalism and other offences (*cf.* Wilson, 1978).

Reducing Physical Opportunities for Crime and the Problem of Displacement

Variations in physical opportunities for crime have sometimes been invoked to explain differences in crime rates within particular cities (*e.g.* Boggs, 1965; Baldwin and Bottoms, 1975) or temporal variations in crime; for example, Wilkins (1964) and Gould and his associates (Gould, 1969; Mansfield *et al.*, 1974) have related levels of car theft to variations in the number of vehicles on the road. But these studies have not generally provided practicable preventive ideas—for example, the number of cars on the road cannot be reduced simply to prevent their theft—and it is only recently that there has been a concerted effort on the part of criminologists to find viable ways of blocking the opportunities for particular crimes.

The potential for controlling behaviour by manipulating opportunities is illustrated vividly by a study of suicide in Birmingham (Hassal and Trethowan, 1972). This showed that a marked drop in the rates of suicide between 1962 and 1970 was the result of a reduction in the poisonous content of the gas supplied to householders for cooking and heating, so that it became much more difficult for people to kill themselves by turning on the gas taps. Like many kinds of crime, suicide is generally regarded as being dictated by strong internal motivation and the fact that its incidence was greatly reduced by a simple (though unintentional) reduction in the opportunities to commit it suggests that it may be possible to achieve similar reductions in crime by " physical " means. Though suicide by other methods did not increase in Birmingham, the study also leads to direct consideration of the fundamental theoretical problem of " displacement " which, as Reppetto (1976) has pointed out, can occur in four different ways: time, place, method, and type of offence. In other words, does reducing opportunities or increasing the risks result merely in the offender choosing his moment more carefully or in seeking some other, perhaps more harmful method of gaining his ends? Or, alternatively, will he shift his attention to a similar but unprotected target, for example, another house, car or shop? Or, finally, will he turn instead to some other form of crime?

For those who see crime as the outcome of criminal disposition, the answers to these questions would tend to be in the affirmative (" bad will out ") but under the alternative view of crime represented above matters are less straightforward. Answers would depend on the nature of the crime, the offender's strength of motivation, knowledge of alternatives, willingness to entertain them, and so forth. In the case of opportunistic crimes (*i.e.* ones apparently elicited by their very ease of accomplishment such as some forms of shoplifting or vandalism) it would seem that the probability of offending could be reduced markedly by making it more difficult to act. For crimes

"SITUATIONAL" CRIME PREVENTION: THEORY AND PRACTICE

such as bank robbery, however, which often seem to be the province of those who make a living from crime, reducing opportunities may be less effective. (This may be less true of increasing the risks of being caught except that for many offences the risks may be so low at present that any increase would have to be very marked.) Providing effective protection for a particular bank would almost certainly displace the attention of potential robbers to others, and if all banks were given increased protection many robbers would no doubt consider alternative means of gaining their ends. It is by no means implausible, however, that others—for example, those who do not have the ability to develop more sophisticated methods or who may not be willing to use more violence—may accept their reduced circumstances and may even take legitimate employment.

It is the bulk of offences, however, which are neither "opportunistic" nor "professional" that pose the greatest theoretical dilemmas. These offences include many burglaries and instances of auto-crime where the offender, who may merely supplement his normal income through the proceeds of crime, has gone out with the deliberate intention of committing the offence and has sought out the opportunity to do so. The difficulty posed for measures which reduce opportunity is one of the vast number of potential targets combined with the generally low overall level of security. Within easy reach of every house with a burglar alarm, or car with an anti-theft device, are many others without such protection.

In some cases, however, it may be possible to protect a whole class of property, as the Post Office did when they virtually eliminated theft from telephone kiosks by replacing the vulnerable aluminium coin-boxes with much stronger steel ones (*cf.* Mayhew *et al.*, 1976). A further example is provided by the recent law in this country which requires all motor-cyclists to wear crash helmets. This measure was introduced to save lives, but it has also had the unintended effect of reducing thefts of motor-cycles (Mayhew *et al.*, 1976). This is because people are unlikely to take someone else's motor-bike on the spur of the moment unless they happen to have a crash helmet with them—otherwise they could easily be spotted by the police. But perhaps the best example comes from West Germany where, in 1963, steering column locks were made compulsory on *all* cars, old and new, with a consequent reduction of more than 60 per cent. in levels of taking and driving away (Mayhew *et al.*, 1976). (When steering column locks were introduced in this country in 1971 it was only to new cars and, although these are now at much less risk of being taken, overall levels of car-taking have not yet diminished because the risk to older cars had increased as a result of displacement.)

Instances where criminal opportunities can be reduced for a whole class of property are comparatively few, but this need not always be a fatal difficulty. There must be geographical and temporal limits to displacement so that a town or city may be able to protect itself from some crime without displacing it elsewhere. The less determined the offender, the easier this will be; a simple example is provided by Decker's (1972) evidence that the use of "slugs" in parking-meters in a New York district was greatly reduced by replacing the meters with ones which incorporated a slug-rejector device and in which the last coin inserted was visible in a plastic window. For most drivers there would be little advantage in parking their cars in some other district just because they could continue to use slugs there.

The question of whether, when stopped from committing a particular offence, people would turn instead to some other quite different form of crime is much more difficult to settle empirically, but many of the same points about motivation, knowledge of alternatives and so forth still apply. Common-sense also suggests, for example, that few of those Germans prevented by steering column locks from taking cars to get home at night are likely to have turned instead to hijacking taxis or to mugging passers-by for the money to get home. More likely, they may have decided that next time they would make sure of catching the last bus home or that it was time to save up for their own car.

Increasing the Risks of Being Caught

In practice, increasing the chances of being caught usually means attempting to raise the chances of an offender being seen by someone who is likely to take action. The police are the most obvious group likely to intervene effectively, but studies of the effectiveness of this aspect of their deterrent role are not especially encouraging (Kelling *et al.*, 1974; Manning, 1977; Clarke and Hough, 1980). The reason seems to be that, when set against the vast number of opportunities for offending represented by the activities of a huge population of citizens for the 24 hours of the day, crime is a relatively rare event. The police cannot be everywhere at once and, moreover, much crime takes place in private. Nor is much to be expected from the general public (Mayhew *et al.*, 1979). People in their daily round rarely see crime in progress; if they do they are likely to place some innocent interpretation on what they see; they may be afraid to intervene or they may feel the victims would resent interference; and they may encounter practical difficulties in summoning the police or other help in time. They are much more likely to take effective action to protect their own homes or immediate neighbourhood, but they are often away from these for substantial periods of the day and, moreover, the risks of crime in residential settings, at least in many areas of this country, are not so great as to encourage much vigilance. For instance, assuming that about 50 per cent. of buglaries are reported to the police (*cf.* Home Office, 1979), a house in this country will on average be burgled once every 30 years. Even so, there is evidence (Department of the Environment, 1977; Wilson, 1978) that " defensible space " designs on housing estates confer some protection from vandalism, if not as much as might have been expected from the results of Newman's (1973) research into crime on public housing projects in the United States (*cf.* Clarke, 1979; Mayhew, 1979).

A recent Home Office Research report (Mayhew *et al.*, 1979) has argued, however, that there is probably a good deal of unrealised potential for making more deliberate use of the surveillance role of employees who come into regular and frequent contact with the public in a semi-official capacity. Research in the United States (Newman, 1973; Reppetto, 1974) and Canada (Waller and Okhiro, 1978) has shown that apartment blocks with doormen

" SITUATIONAL " CRIME PREVENTION: THEORY AND PRACTICE

are less vulnerable to burglary, while research in this country has shown that vandalism is much less of a problem on buses with conductors (Mayhew *et al.*, 1976) and on estates with resident caretakers (Department of the Environment, 1977). There is also evidence (in Post Office records) that public telephones in places such as pubs or launderettes, which are given some supervision by staff, suffer almost no vandalism in comparison with those in kiosks; that car parks with attendants in control have lower rates of auto-crime (*Sunday Times*, April 9, 1978); that football hooliganism on trains has been reduced by a variety of measures including permission for club stewards to travel free of charge; and that shoplifting is discouraged by the presence of assistants who are there to serve the customers (Walsh, 1978). Not everybody employed in a service capacity would be suited or willing to take on additional security duties, but much of their deterrent role may result simply from their being around. Employing more of them, for greater parts of the day, may therefore be all that is needed in most cases. In other cases, it may be necessary to employ people more suited to a surveillance role, train them better to carry it out, or even provide them with surveillance aids. Providing the staff at four London Underground stations with closed circuit television has been shown in a recent Home Office Research Unit study (Mayhew *et al.*, 1979) to have substantially reduced theft and robbery offences at those stations.

Some Objections

Apart from the theoretical and practical difficulties of the approach advocated in this paper, it is in apparent conflict with the " nothing works " school of criminological thought as given recent expression by Wolfgang (1977): ". . . the weight of empirical evidence indicates that no current preventative, deterrent, or rehabilitative intervention scheme has the desired effect of reducing crime." But perhaps a panacea is being sought when all it may be possible to achieve is a reduction in particular forms of crime as a result of specific and sometimes localised measures. Examples of such reductions are given above and, while most of these relate to rather commonplace offences of theft and vandalism, there is no reason why similar measures cannot be successfully applied to other quite different forms of crime. It has been argued by many people (Rhodes, 1977, provides a recent example) that reducing the availability of hand-guns through gun-control legislation would reduce crimes of violence in the United States and elsewhere. Speeding and drunken driving could probably be reduced by fitting motor vehicles with devices which are now at an experimental stage (Ekblom, 1979). And there is no doubt (Wilkinson, 1977) that the rigorous passenger and baggage screening measures introduced at airports, particularly in the United States, have greatly reduced the incidence of airline hijackings. There are many crimes, however, when the offender is either so determined or so emotionally aroused that they seem to be beyond the scope of this approach. A further constraint will be costs: many shops, for example, which could reduce shoplifting by giving up self-service methods and employing more assistants or even store detectives, have calculated that this would not be worth the

R. V. G. CLARKE

expense either in direct costs or in a reduction of turnover. Morally dubious as this policy might at first sight appear, these shops may simply have learned a lesson of more general application, *i.e.* a certain level of crime may be the inevitable consequence of practices and institutions which we cherish or find convenient and the " cost " of reducing crime below this level may be unacceptable.

The gradualist approach to crime prevention advocated here might also attract criticism from some social reformers, as well as some deviancy theorists, for being unduly conservative. The former group, imbued with dispositional theory, would see the only effective way of dealing with crime as being to attack its roots through the reduction of inequalities of wealth, class and education—a solution which, as indicated above, has numerous practical and theoretical difficulties. The latter group would criticise the approach, not for its lack of effectiveness but—on the grounds that there is insufficient consensus in society about what behaviour should be treated as crime—for helping to preserve an undesirable status quo. Incremental change, however, may be the most realistic way of achieving consensus as well as a more equitable society. Most criminologists would probably also agree that it would be better for the burden of crime reduction to be gradually shifted away from the criminal justice system, which may be inherently selective and punitive in its operation, to preventive measures whose social costs may be more equitably distributed among all members of society. The danger to be guarded against would be that the attention of offenders might be displaced away from those who can afford to purchase protection to those who cannot. This probably happens already to some extent and perhaps the best way of dealing with the problem would be through codes of security which would be binding on car manufacturers, builders, local transport operators and so forth. Another danger is that those who have purchased protection might become less willing to see additional public expenditure on the law enforcement and criminal justice services—and this is a problem that might only be dealt with through political leadership and public education.

Many members of the general public might also find it objectionable that crime was being stopped, not by punishing wrong-doers, but by inconveniencing the law-abiding. The fact that opportunity-reducing and risk-increasing measures are too readily identified with their more unattractive aspects (barbed wire, heavy padlocks, guard-dogs and private security forces) adds fuel to the fire. And in some of their more sophisticated forms (closed circuit television surveillance and electronic intruder alarms) they provoke fears, on the one hand, of " big brother " forms of state control and, on the other, of a " fortress society " in which citizens in perpetual fear of their fellows scuttle from one fortified environment to another.

Expressing these anxieties has a value in checking potential abuses of power, and questioning the means of dealing with crime can also help to keep the problem of crime in perspective. But it should also be said that the kind of measures discussed above need not always be obtrusive (except where it is important to maximise their deterrent effects) and need not in any material way infringe individual liberties or the quality of life. Steel cash

" SITUATIONAL " CRIME PREVENTION: THEORY AND PRACTICE

compartments in telephone kiosks are indistinguishable from aluminium ones, and vandal-resistant polycarbonate looks just like glass. Steering column locks are automatically brought into operation on removing the ignition key, and many people are quite unaware that their cars are fitted with them. " Defensible space " designs in housing estates have the additional advantage of promoting feelings of neighbourliness and safety, though perhaps too little attention has been paid to some of their less desirable effects such as possible encroachments on privacy as a result of overlooking. And having more bus conductors, housing estate caretakers, swimming bath attendants and shop assistants means that people benefit from improved services—even if they have to pay for them either directly or through the rates.

Finally, the idea that crime might be most effectively prevented by reducing opportunities and increasing the risks is seen by many as, at best, representing an over-simplified mechanistic view of human behaviour and, at worst, a " slur on human nature " (*cf.* Radzinowicz and King, 1977). (When the contents of *Crime as Opportunity* (Mayhew *et al.*, 1976) were reported in the press in advance of publication an irate psychiatrist wrote to the Home Secretary demanding that he should suppress the publication of such manifest nonsense.) As shown above, however, it is entirely compatible with a view of criminal behaviour as predominantly rational and autonomous and as being capable of adjusting and responding to adverse consequences, anticipated or experienced. And as for being a pessimistic view of human behaviour, it might indeed be better if greater compliance with the law could come about simply as a result of people's free moral choice. But apart from being perilously close to the rather unhelpful dispositional view of crime, it is difficult to see this happening. We may therefore be left for the present with the approach advocated in this paper, time-consuming, laborious and limited as it may be.

Summary

It is argued that the " dispositional " bias of most current criminological theory has resulted in " social " crime prevention measures being given undue prominence and " situational " measures being devalued. An alternative theoretical emphasis on decisions and choices made by the offender (which in turns allows more weight to the circumstances of offending) results in more support for a situational approach to prevention. Examples of the effectiveness of such an approach are provided and some of the criticisms that have been made of it on social and ethical grounds are discussed.

REFERENCES

ATKINSON, M. (1974). " Versions of deviance." Extended review in *Sociological Review*, **22**, 616–624.
BALDWIN, J. and BOTTOMS, A. E. (1975). *The Urban Criminal*. London: Tavistock.
BANDURA, A. (1973). *Aggression: A Social Learning Analysis*. London: Prentice Hall.
BECKER, H. S. (1962). *Outsiders: Studies in the Sociology of Deviance*. Glencoe: The Free Press.

R. V. G. CLARKE

BOGGS, S. L. (1965). "Urban crime patterns." *American Sociological Review*, **30**, 899–908.

BRANTINGHAM, P. J. and BRANTINGHAM, P. L. (1975). "The spatial patterning of burglary." *Howard Journal of Penology and Crime Prevention*, **14**, 11–24.

CLARKE, R. V. G. (ed.) (1978). *Tackling Vandalism*. Home Office Research Study No. 47. London: HMSO.

CLARKE, R. V. G. (1979). "Defensible space and vandalism: the lessons from some recent British research." *Stadtebau und Kriminalamt* (*Urban planning and Crime*). Papers of an international symposium, Bundeskriminalamt, Federal Republic of Germany, December, 1978.

CLARKE, R. V. G. and HOUGH, J. M. (Eds.) (1980). *The Effectiveness of Policing*. Farnborough, Hants: Gower.

DECKER, J. F. (1972). "Curbside deterrence: an analysis of the effect of a slug-rejector device, coin view window and warning labels on slug usage in New York City parking meters." *Criminology*, August, 127–142.

DEPARTMENT OF THE ENVIRONMENT (1977). *Housing Management and Design*. (Lambeth Inner Area Study). IAS/IA/18. London: Department of the Environment.

EKBLOM, P. (1979). "A crime-free car?" *Research Bulletin No. 7*. Home Office Research Unit. London: Home Office.

GIBBONS, D. C. (1971). "Observations on the study of crime causation." *American Journal of Sociology*, **77**, 262–278.

GLASER, D. (1977). "The compatibility of free will and determinism in Criminology: comments on an alleged problem." *Journal of Criminal Law and Criminology* **67**, 486–490.

GOULD, L. C. (1969). "The changing structure of property crime in an affluent society." *Social Forces*, **48**, 50–59.

HASSAL, C. and TRETHOWAN, W. H. (1972). "Suicide in Birmingham." *British Medical Journal*, **1**, 717–718.

HOME OFFICE (1979). *Criminal Statistics: England and Wales 1978*. London: HMSO.

HOOD, R. and SPARKS, R. (1970). *Key Issues in Criminology*. London: Weidenfeld and Nicolson.

JEFFERY, C. R. (1971). *Crime Prevention Through Environmental Design*. Beverly Hills: Sage Publications.

KELLING, G. L., PATE, T., DIECKMAN, D. and BROWN, C. E. (1974). *The Kansas City Preventive Patrol Experiment*. Washington: Police Foundation.

LEY, D. and CYBRINWSKY, R. (1974). "The spatial ecology of stripped cars." *Environment and Behaviour*, **6**, 53–67.

MANNING, P. (1977). *Police Work: The Social Organisation of Policing*. London: Massachusetts Institute of Technology Press.

MANSFIELD, R., GOULD, L. C. and NAMENWIRTH, J. Z. (1974). "A socioeconomic model for the prediction of societal rates of property theft." *Social Forces*, **52**, 462–472.

MATZA, D. (1964). *Delinquency and Drift*. New York: John Wiley and Sons.

MAYHEW, P. (1977). "Crime in a man's world." *New Society*, June 16.

MAYHEW, P. (1979). "Defensible space: the current status of a crime prevention theory." *The Howard Journal of Penology and Crime Prevention*, **18**, 150–159.

"SITUATIONAL" CRIME PREVENTION: THEORY AND PRACTICE

MAYHEW, P., CLARKE, R. V. G., STURMAN, A. and HOUGH, J. M. (1976). *Crime as Opportunity*. Home Office Research Study No. 34. London: HMSO.

MAYHEW, P., CLARKE, R. V. G., BURROWS, J. N., HOUGH, J. M. and WINCHESTER, S. W. C. (1979). *Crime in Public View*. Home Office Research Study No. 49. London: HMSO.

MISCHEL, W. (1968). *Personality and Assessment*. New York: John Wiley and Sons.

NEWMAN, O. (1973). *Defensible Space: People and Design in the Violent City*. London: Architectural Press.

OHLIN, L. E. (1970). *A Situational Approach to Delinquency Prevention*. Youth Development and Delinquency Prevention Administration. U.S. Department of Health, Education and Welfare.

PARKER, H. (1974). *View from the Boys*. Newton Abbot: David and Charles.

RADZINOWICZ, L. and KING, J. (1977). *The Growth of Crime*. London: Hamish Hamilton.

REPPETTO, T. A. (1974). *Residential Crime*. Cambridge, Mass: Ballinger.

REPPETTO, T. A. (1976). " Crime prevention and the displacement phenomenon." *Crime and Delinquency*, April, 166–177.

RHODES, R. P. (1977). *The Insoluble Problems of Crime*. New York: John Wiley and Sons.

ROSS, L. (1977). "The intuitive psychologist and his shortcomings: distortions in the attribution process." In: Berkowitz, L. (Ed.) *Advances in Experimental Social Psychology (Vol. 10)*. New York: Academic Press.

SCARR, H. A. (1973). *Patterns of Burglary*. U.S. Department of Justice Washington DC: Government Printing Office.

TAYLOR, I., WALTON, P. and YOUNG, J. (1973). *The New Criminology*. London: Routledge and Kegan Paul.

TIZARD, J. (1976). " Psychology and social policy." *Bulletin of the British Psychological Society*, **29,** 225–233.

TRASLER, G. B. (1979). " Delinquency, recidivism, and desistance." *British Journal of Criminology*, **19,** 314–322.

TUCK, M. (1979). " Consumer behaviour theory and the criminal justice system: towards a new strategy of research." *Journal of the Market Research Society*, **21,** 44–58.

WALKER, N. D. (1979). " The efficacy and morality of deterrents." *Criminal Law Review*, March, 129–144.

WALLER, I. and OKIHIRO, N. (1978). *Burglary: The Victim and the Public*. Toronto: University of Toronto Press.

WALSH, D. P. (1978). *Shoplifting: Controlling a Major Crime*. London: MacMillan.

WILKINS, L. T. (1964). *Social Deviance*. London: Tavistock.

WILKINSON, P. (1977). *Terrorism and the Liberal State*. London: MacMillan.

WILSON, J. Q. (1975). *Thinking About Crime*. New York: Basic Books.

WILSON, S. (1978). " Vandalism and 'defensible space' on London housing estates." In: Clarke, R. V. G. (Ed.). *Tackling Vandalism*. Home Office Research Study No. 47. London: HMSO.

WOLFGANG, M. E. (1977). " Real and perceived changes in crime." In Landau, S. F., and Sebba, L. (Eds.) *Criminology in Perspective*. Lexington, Mass: Lexington Books.

147

Name Index